THE CLASSICS
OF WESTERN
SPIRITUALITY

THE CLASSICS OF WESTERN SPIRITUALITY
A Library of the Great Spiritual Masters

iii

JEREMY TAYLOR

SELECTED WORKS

EDITED WITH AN INTRODUCTION BY
THOMAS K. CARROLL

PREFACE BY
JOHN BOOTY

PAULIST PRESS
NEW YORK • MAHWAH

Cover Art: Born, raised and educated in New York, free-lance designer/illustrator ROBERT MANNING has received numerous commissions for religious theme books. This piece is a wood-cut interpretation from a portrait of Jeremy Taylor that hangs in the Rare Books Reading Room of the Palace Green Library, University of Durham, England.

Library of Congress Cataloging-in-Publication Data

Taylor, Jeremy, 1613–1667.
    [Selections. 1990]
    Selected works / Jeremy Taylor; edited with an introduction by Thomas K.
Carroll; preface by John Booty.
        p. cm.—(Classics of Western spirituality)
    Includes bibliographical references.
    ISBN 0-8091-0438-5
    ISBN 0-8091-3175-7 (pbk.)
    1. Church of England—Doctrines. 2. Church of England—Liturgy. 3. Church of Ireland—Doctrines. 4. Church of Ireland—Liturgy. 5. Spiritual life—Anglican authors. 6. Anglican Communion—Doctrines. 7. Anglican Communion—Liturgy. I. Carroll, Thomas K., 1933–   . II. Title. III. Series.
    BX5130.T39   1990
    283—dc20   90-34614
                                                                                        CIP

Published by Paulist Press
997 Macarthur Boulevard
Mahwah, New Jersey 07430

Printed and bound in the United States of America

Contents

Author of Foreword and
Introduction and Editor of This Volume

THOMAS K. CARROLL is a priest of the diocese of Ardagh and Clonmacnois in Ireland. Ordained in Rome in 1959, he holds doctorates from the Angelicum University and from the Pontifical Liturgical Institute. Present at the Second Vatican Council, he has lectured widely throughout the United States, England and Australia and is the author of *Preaching the Word* (1984) and *Liturgical Practice in the Fathers* (1988). He is at present visiting professor at the College of William and Mary, Williamsburg, Virginia.

Author of the Preface

JOHN BOOTY is professor of Anglican studies at the School of Theology of the University of the South, Sewanee, Tennessee. Having received the Ph.D. from Princeton University in 1960, he then concentrated his studies on religion and culture in sixteenth- and seventeenth-century England. His published works include *John Jewel as Apologist of the Church of England* and *John Donne: Selections from* Divine Poems, *Sermons,* Devotions *and Prayers,* a volume in The Classics of Western Spirituality Series. He has edited *The Book of Common Prayer 1559* and Jewel's *Apology* and is an editor of the Folger Edition of the *Works* of Richard Hooker. An ordained priest, Professor Booty is also Historiographer of the Episcopal Church.

Foreword

The scientific soul of our brave new world began in the early seventeenth century with its new approaches to reality, but its evolution and modern prejudices are distinctively its own. In the age of Milton and Bacon neither the Word of God nor the words of man were in any doubt of their ontological significance, although biblical and scientific reality were beginning to be separate. Today, however, there is a crisis in the concept and understanding of language itself, comparable to the philosophical problem at the turn of this century concerning the foundation of mathematics; now confusion reigns before the completion of our Babel, and tells of our incapacity to express in words humanity's innermost truths, sensory experiences, moral and transcendent intuitions. "Political rhetoric," says one modern critic of our times, "the tidal mendacity of journalism and the mass media, the trivializing cant of public and socially approved modes of discourse, have made of almost everything modern urban men and women say or hear or read an empty jargon, a cancerous loquacity. . . . Language has lost the very capacity for truth, for political or personal honesty. It has marketed and mass-marketed its mysteries of prophetic intuition . . . and operates, self-doubtingly, on the sharp edge of silence. We know now that if the Word 'was in the beginning,' it can also be at the end: that there is a vocabulary and a grammar of the death camps, that thermo-nuclear detonations can be designated as 'Operation Sunshine.' It were as if the quintessential, the identifying attribute of man—the Logos, the organon of language—had broken in our mouths.[1]

Jeremy Taylor, "erudite theologian, renowned preacher and faith-

---

1. G. Steiner, *Real Presences* (Cambridge: Cambridge University Press, 1986), p. 5.

ful pastor,"[2] is relevant to our atheistic and deconstructionist times, not because he lived in a century that resembled ours in its political, religious and philosophical upheavals, but because in that age of *scoffers, walking after their own lusts* (2 Peter 3:3), he lived and moved and had his being (cf. Acts 17:28) in the eternal Word of God, made new by the scriptural zeal of the Reformers, and renewed still more by their zeal for the vernacular:

> By the word of God the heavens were of old, and the earth standing out of the water and in the water: Whereby the world that then was, being overflowed with water, perished: But the heavens and the earth, which are now, by the same word are kept in store, preserved unto fire against the day of judgment and perdition of ungodly man. . . .
>
> But the day of the Lord will come as a thief in the night; in the which the heavens shall pass away with a great noise, and the elements shall melt with fervent heat, the earth also and the works that are therein shall be burned up. . . .
>
> Nevertheless we, according to his promise, look for new heavens and a new earth, wherein dwelleth righteousness (2 Peter 3:5–13).

This biblical view of the world was given this fresh and sonorous expression when the Authorized Version of the scriptures, commonly called The King James Bible, was published in Taylor's native town of Cambridge, some two years before his birth in 1613. Like the Greek Septuagint and the Latin Vulgate this new translation was more *begotten* than *made*, and being the consequence of a rare conjunction of circumstances, renewed biblical faith, Renaissance learning and Elizabethan English, must remain in the English language *the* primary text of God's Word.

Mastery of Hebrew, Greek and Latin, the Renaissance legacy to the schools of England, made this translation traditional in content, not just melodious in cadence, and facilitated that *appeal to tradition* that is

---

2. "*Eruditi theologi, diserti oratoris, fidelis pastoris*"—from Taylor's epitaph in Dromore Cathedral, County Down, Ireland.

more distinctive of Anglicanism than either the *sola scriptura* of the Reformers, or the *fides quaerens intellectum* of the Romans, in their doctrinal formulations at Trent. Nevertheless, scripture, tradition and reason were there and then so combined that there emerged not only a renewal of patristic tradition in the vernacular, but a theology that was distinctively spiritual and pastoral:

> High speculations are as barren as the tops of cedars; but the fundamentals of Christianity are fruitful as the valleys or the creeping vine. For know, that it is no meditation, but it may be an illusion, when you consider mysteries to become more learned, without thoughts of improving piety. . . . It was a saying of Aegidius, "that an old and a simple woman, if she loves Jesus, may be greater than was brother Bonaventure." Want of learning and disability to consider great secrets of theology, do not at all retard our progress to spiritual perfections.[3]

The death of Jeremy Taylor in 1667 more or less concluded this formative period of Anglicanism that began around 1595 with Richard Hooker and was distinguished by such names as Lancelot Andrewes and William Laud in England, Arnold Ussher and John Bramhall in Ireland, and a host of others generally known as the Caroline divines. These Carolines, Catholics in a new culture and language, were theologians in the tradition of John, the Divine; by fitting their words to the Word of God, and molding them for worship and prayer, they gave a new quality to the English language, making it as apt as Hebrew, Greek and Latin had been made through liturgical usage to express the realities of grace and the sanctuary. Like Chrysostom in Greek, and Augustine in Latin, Taylor in English is of the same sacramental tradition in word and symbol, recognizing the real presence of the transcendent in true theological discourse, and the sheer emptiness of mere intellectual debate:

> He that desires to enter furthest into the secrets of this mystery (the Eucharist) and to understand more than others, can

---

3. Reginald Heber and Charles Page Eden, eds. *The Whole Works of the Right Reverend Jeremy Taylor, D.D. with a Life of the Author.* 10 vols. (London: Longman, Green, Longmans, Roberts and Green, 1847–52). Hereafter referred to as *Works*.

better learn by love than by enquiry. . . . If he will . . . pass through the mystery with great devotion and purest simplicity, and converse with the purities of the sacrament frequently and with holy intention, this man shall understand more by his experience than the greatest clerks can by all their subtilties, the commentaries of the doctors and the glosses of inquisitive men. "The love of the Lord," saith the wise man, "passeth all things for illumination."[4]

Here one can sense the symbolic language of the ancients, which the biblical words of the Greek and Latin Fathers made sacramental; deadened by the definitions of the later schoolmen, it was revitalized by the Anglican appeal to tradition, and given fresh expression by the Carolines in their Elizabethan prose. This period, rich in faith and utterance, is of significance today in a world where the Word of God and the words of men are in crisis; it is of particular importance for modern spiritual writers, preachers and theologians, since the Roman Church by its recent acceptance of the vernacular has made English more widespread as a theological and liturgical language. Taylor was of this time of theological renewal in Word and words, but his concept of theology and spirituality is classical and transcends time: "From meditation man rises to devotion, and mental prayer, and intercourse with God; and after that, he rests in the bosom of beatitude and is swallowed up with the comprehensions of love and contemplation."[5]

This growth in Catholic tradition came to bloom as the new world, English-speaking and scientific, began to dawn on each side of the Atlantic Ocean, and blossomed throughout the centuries into a spirituality, scriptural and liturgical, ecclesial and personal, that though now in the autumn of its life, is still a living source for a second spring.

The despair of modern man before the limitations of his own empty words can be heard in the final cry of Schoenberg's *Moses und Aron:* "O Word, O Word, which is lacking to me."[6] Nor indeed can the Christian in this post-Christian age be content with the *mysterium tremendum* of God's substantive absence from a new solitude of man. *Lord, to whom shall we go* (John 6:68), remains the pathetic plea of God's

---

4. *Works* 8:47.
5. *Works* 2:135.
6. Steiner, p. 5.

4

chosen and faithful people, for they still believe, even in this world where words have lost their meaning, that their Lord and he alone *has the words of eternal life* (John 6:68). "Christ," said John XXIII in his opening speech at the Second Vatican Council, "is ever resplendent as the center of history and of life."

This proclamation of faith in Christ, "the Word made Flesh" (John 1:14), is the Church's only hope as she journeys through a secular world and dialogues with her deconstructionist critics, who seek to "ruin the Sacred Truths."[7] Furthermore, this vision of faith confers on the words of scripture and tradition the timeless quality of the Eternal Word: "We have heard the words," said Augustine, "but now let us seek the Word." Taylor's language has this timeless quality, and his words mellifluously flowing from image to image, and "falling faintly . . . faintly falling" from cadence to cadence tell of that Eternal Word, which he heard a) in creation, the first sacrament of the Word; b) in Christ, the Word made flesh; c) in scripture, the Word made text; and d) in man, the flesh made Word. He is at all times a poet and preacher of this Word and its presence in his words *charms ever so wisely* (Psalm 58:5) man's inner ear:

> There is in the things of God to them which practice them a deliciousness that makes us love them, and that love admits us into God's cabinet, and strangely clarifies the understanding by the purification of the heart. For when our reason is raised up by the Spirit of Christ, it is turned quickly into experience; when our faith relies upon the principles of Christ, it is changed into vision. And so long as we know God only in the ways of man, by contentious learning, by arguing and dispute, we see nothing but the shadow of Him, and in that shadow we meet with many dark appearances, little certainty, and much conjecture. But when we know Him with the eyes of holiness, and the intuition of gracious experience, with a quiet spirit and the peace of enjoyment, then we shall hear what we never heard and see what our eyes never saw; then the mysteries of godliness shall be opened unto us, and clear as the windows of the morning.[8]

---

7. H. Bloom, *Ruin the Sacred Truths* (Cambridge, MA: Harvard University Press, 1989).
8. *Works* 8:379.

FOREWORD

These primordial words, like those of a poet, are filled with the soft music of infinity; spoken by Taylor, preacher and priest, such words are sacramental and communicate directly to man's soul a presence that is transcendent and real. Taylor's voluminous writings tell of this presence, which becomes on every page a possession, a pleasure and a prayer. Indeed there is scarcely a writer in the tradition of English spirituality, since Taylor or before him, whose words reveal with so much music and peace the secrets of God's Word alive in man's heart:

> There is a sort of God's dear servants who walk in perfectness; . . . and they have a degree of clarity and divine knowledge more than we can discourse of, and more certain than the demonstration of geometry, brighter than the sun, and indeficient as the light of heaven. . . . This is called by the apostle the *apaugasma tou theou.* Christ is this "brightness of God," manifested in the hearts of His dearest servants. . . .

> But I shall say no more of this at this time, for this is to be felt and not be talked of; and they that never touched it with their finger, may secretly perhaps laugh at it in their heart, and be never the wiser. All that I shall now say of it is, that a good man is united unto God, as a flame touches a flame, and combines into splendour and to glory: so is the spirit of a man united unto Christ by the Spirit of God. These are the friends of God, and they best know God's mind, and they only that are so know how much such men do know. They have a special unction from above so that now you are come to the top of all; this is the highest round of the ladder, and the angels stand upon it: they dwell in love and contemplation, they worship and obey, but dispute not: and our quarrels and impertinent wranglings about religion are nothing else but the want of the measures of this state. Our light is like a candle, every wind of vain doctrine blows it out, or spends the wax, and makes the light tremulous; but the lights of heaven are fixed and bright, and shine for ever.[9]

In October 1968 the late John Fendlow, canon of Winchester Cathedral and director of the Anglican Center in Rome, introduced me

---

9. *Works* 8:379.

6

to the writings of Jeremy Taylor. This Center had been founded for the promotion of Anglican-Roman studies after the visit of His Grace, Michael Ramsey, Archbishop of Canterbury, to His Holiness, Pope Paul VI. Shortly afterward, H. R. McAdoo, foremost of Caroline scholars today, and formerly Church of Ireland Archbishop of Dublin, confirmed me in my choice of doctoral dissertation topic. My thesis on the *Sacramental Theology of Jeremy Taylor* was written under the direction of Sebastian Carlson, an American Dominican, and defended at the Angelicum University in Rome in June 1970. In 1973 I presented another doctoral thesis on *Jeremy Taylor, Liturgist and Ecumenist* to the Anselmianum, the Pontifical Liturgical Institute at Rome. Dom Burkhard Neunheuser, monk of Maria Laach Benedictine Monastery in Germany, was then my mentor and guide; he is now a memory and a blessing. This saintly monk was the colleague and friend of Dom Odo Casel, the patristic scholar and liturgical theologian who inspired the modern liturgical renewal. Neunheusser saw the common ground of sacramental faith and language that Taylor and Casel inherited from the Fathers, and he directed my research accordingly.

These theological and liturgical studies brought to light Taylor's spiritual insights and that wealth of religious expression that give his writings their rightful place among the classics of Western spirituality. No less influential in helping me appreciate the divine truth and beauty in the words of Jeremy Taylor were the friends, many and varied, of those past twenty years, whose words were for me the bread of my life along the way:

> For we are not as many, which corrupt the Word of God: but as of sincerity, but as of God, in the sight of God speak we in Christ (2 Corinthians 2:17).

Preface

Jeremy Taylor (1613–67) lived in tumultuous times. A royalist in the English Civil War, he was imprisoned for a short time; lived in retirement for a while as chaplain to Lord Carbery at Golden Grove, where he wrote his major works; and ended his life, after the Restoration, as a bishop in Ireland, doing battle there with Presbyterians and Roman Catholics. He was charged with heresy and accused of being a pelagian in his own time, and accused of pastorally cruel legalism in our time.[1] Taylor does not conform to the popular understanding of a holy man or saint. And yet he is included in such Anglican calendars as that of the Episcopal Church in the United States, where, on August 13, he is commemorated as "a man of prayer and a pastor" who was "deeply sensible of the shortness and uncertainty of human life" and of necessity, therefore, of allowing the "Holy Spirit" to "lead us in holiness and righteousness all our days."[2]

In large part the basis for this commemoration rests upon two classic works, *The Rule and Exercise of Holy Living* (1650) and *The Rule and Exercise of Holy Dying* (1651). The first opens with an exhortation to obedience: "As every man is wholly God's own portion by the title of creation, so all our labours and care, all our powers and faculties must be fully employed in the service of God." To assist in this, Taylor gives practical advice concerning the use of time, chastity, temperance in food and drink, but also the practice of justice and the practice of the Christian religion. On a yet deeper level he speaks of the practice of the presence of God:

---

1. C. Fitzsimmons Allison, *The Rise of Moralism* (New York: Seabury Press, 1966), pp. 80–81.
2. *The Proper for the Lesser Feasts and Fasts*, 3d cd. (New York: The Church Hymnal Corporation, 1980), pp. 292–93.

God is wholly in every place, included in no place; not bound with cords except those of love, not divided into parts, not changeable into several shapes; filling heaven and earth with His present power, and with His never absent nature: so St. Augustine expresses this article. So that we may imagine God to be as the air and the sea, and we all enclosed in his circle, wrapped up in the lap of His infinite nature; or as infants in the wombs of their pregnant mother: and we can no more be removed from the presence of God than from our own being.[3]

The latter classic, *Holy Dying*, is in the tradition of *momento mori*, abounding in practical advice to the sick and the dying, colored by "consideration of the vanity and shortness of man's life" and the necessity of repentance. In 1655 Taylor published *Unum Necessarium*, a treatise on sin and repentance, called by H. R. McAdoo "the fullest analysis of the doctrine [of repentance] in Anglican divinity."[4] Here repentance is defined in terms of conversion—"leaving our sins" and "doing holy actions." Repentance, Taylor wrote, "is a whole state of the new life, an entire change of the sinner." Indeed, holy living and holy dying are fundamentally concerned with repentance understood in this way. All is aimed at that beatitude described by Taylor when speaking of life everlasting:

God shall wipe away all tears from their eyes; there shall be no fear or sorrow, no mourning or death. . . . There shall be fulness without want, light eternal brighter than the sun . . . difference in degree, and yet all full . . . love without dissimulation, excellency without envy, multitudes without confusion, music without discord.[5]

In *The Golden Grove* (1655) there is further practical advice for the conduct of life in preparation for death. Here there is a sequence of *Credenda, or what is to be believed, Agenda, or things to be done,* and the *Via Pacis, a short method of peace and holiness—With a manual of Daily Prayers fitted to the days of the week.* The *Credenda* is a fulsome exposi-

---

3. These quotations here are taken from Chapter 5 of this book.

4. H. R. McAdoo, *The Structure of Caroline Moral Theology* (London: Longmans, Green and Company, 1949), pp. 127–28.

5. The *Credenda*, as found in Chapter 4 of this book.

tion of the Apostles' Creed. The *Agenda* is a "diary, or a Rule to spend each day religiously," full of detailed directions. The *Via Pacis* consists of seven decades, one for each day of the week, much influenced by Thomas à Kempis, and then prayers against the seven deadly sins, ending with "A Prayer for a Holy and Happy Death."

Modern Christians are likely to find all of this archaic and overbearing, but there are glimpses of wisdom here, not affected by the passage of time, and the piety of a man who practiced the presence of God every day, every hour of his tumultuous life. "A Prayer for a Holy and Happy Death" is profoundly expressive of his piety and compares well with the prayers of Lancelot Andrewes in his *Preces Privatae*. Taylor's prayer begins:

> O eternal and holy Jesus, who by death hast overcome death, and by Thy passion hast taken out its sting, and made it to become one of the gates of heaven, and an entrance to felicity; have mercy upon me now and at the hour of my death; let Thy grace accompany me all the days of my life, that I may, by a holy conversation, and an habitual performance of my duty, wait for the coming of our Lord, and be ready to enter with Thee at whatsoever hour Thou shalt come.[6]

The seriousness and characteristics of Taylor as pastor are found at least in part in his *Ductor Dubitantum* (1658), a manual of moral theology designed to assist clergy in the practice of confession. Taylor the theologian is best seen, to my mind, in *The Liberty of Prophesying* (1647). Here he gives evidence of perceiving the interdependence of theology and spirituality in the manner of Hooker and Andrewes before him. "By reason," he said, "I do not mean a distinct topic, but a transcendent that runs through all topics; for reason, like logic, is instrument of all things else; and when revelation and philosophy, and public experience, and all other grounds of probability or demonstration have supplied us with matter, then reason does but make use of them."[7] Reason is, thus, as Hooker's moral law of reason, the candle of the Lord; and theology is a holy occupation beginning, as the Greek Fathers taught, with the contemplation of God. Of equal importance is the

---

6. *Works* 7:648.
7. *Works* 5:498.

emphasis in *The Liberty of Prophesying* on toleration, founded, as the editor of this volume rightly says, not "upon agreement or concession, but upon a broad basis of practical piety, calling all fanatics back to the human and merciful doctrine of Jesus Christ . . . and to the Church . . . hence, 'the unreasonableness prescribing to other men's faith, and the iniquity of persecuting differing opinions.' "[8]

Finally, there is Taylor's very high estimation of the sacraments, with his awareness in them of divine mystery and sacramental presence. In *The Worthy Communicant* (1660) Taylor wrote:

> Now what Christ does in heaven, He hath commanded us to do on earth, that is, to represent his death, to commemorate this sacrifice, by humble prayer and thankful record; and by faithful manifestation and joyful eucharist to lay it before the eyes of our heavenly Father, so ministering in His priesthood, and doing according to His commandment and His example; the church being the image of heaven, the priest the minister of Christ; the holy table being a copy of the celestial altar, and the eternal sacrifice of the lamb slain from the beginning of the world being always the same; it bleeds no more after the finishing of it in the cross; but it is wonderfully represented in heaven, and graciously represented here.[9]

Taylor's practical piety cannot be fully understood without taking into account his sacramental theology. Grace is from above. And yet Taylor time and again stressed the importance of practical piety and objected to the doctrine of original sin, in part because such doctrine tended to undermine piety and was used as a defense by habitually sinful men.

Archbishop McAdoo regards Taylor's theology as "the natural expression of the wholeness of his Anglicanism" grounded as it is in scripture, tradition and reason, and concludes:

> With all his contradictions and the lavish variety of his subject and the richness of his style, his thought moves outward from a steady centre. His devoutness and practicality, his liturgical feeling and his sense of the continuity of the Church, his

---

8. Introduction to Chapter 1 of this book.
9. Cited from Chapter 2 of this book.

concern for the truth in all things and his desire for a relevant theology, all combine with that theological method which is woven into the substance of all his writings, a three-fold cord not easily broken.[10]

In addition, his concern for practical piety and his emphasis on "growth into personal maturity—every man his own casuist"[11] are characteristics shared with other Anglican writers of his time, and he in turn, by the popularity of some of his writings, helped to encourage the development of such characteristics in Anglican moral theology as it proceeded from the latter part of the seventeenth century into the eighteenth.

Undergirding his practical piety was a strong sense of God's presence and an appreciation of prayer. Bishop Moorman, speaking of Taylor, says:

A person's only hope lay in prayer—regular, concentrated and prolonged. Taylor uses a medieval expression in describing prayer as "nothing but an assent of the mind to God." God must be continuously in the thoughts of all Christians, who will delight in "little overflowings of spiritual joy" and "little beams of heaven" which will guide and fortify them on their way through life.[12]

It is with the necessity of the constant remembrance of God's presence and the necessity of endeavoring sincerely to do God's will in mind, that Taylor prays:

O most gracious God, what greater favour is there than that I may, and what easier employment can there be than to pray Thee, to be admitted into Thy presence, and to represent our needs, and that we have our needs supplied only for asking and desiring passionately and humbly? But we rather quit our

---

10. H. R. McAdoo, *The Spirit of Anglicanism* (London: Adam and Charles Black, 1965), p. 80.

11. H. R. McAdoo, "Anglican Moral Theology in the Seventeenth Century: An Appreciation," *The Anglican Moral Choice,* ed. Paul Elmen (Wilton, CT: Morehouse-Barlow, 1983), p. 40.

12. J. R. H. Moorman, *The Anglican Spiritual Tradition* (London: Darton, Longmans and Todd, 1983), p. 109. Quoting *Holy Living* (30th ed., 1820), pp. 261, 275.

hopes of heaven, than buy it at the cheapest rate of humble prayer. Thus, O God, is the greatest infirmity and infelicity of man, and hath an intolerable cause, and is an unsufferable evil.

He then goes on:

O relieve my spirit with Thy graciousness, take from me all tediousness of spirit, and give me a laboriousness that will not be tired, a hope that shall never fail, a desire of holiness, not to be satisfied till it possesses a charity that will always increase; that I making religion the business of my whole life, may turn all things into religion, doing all to Thy glory, and by the measures of Thy word and of Thy spirit.[13]

The further understanding of Jeremy Taylor in our day is greatly enhanced by this volume. We are indeed indebted to Thomas Carroll for making available in this series substantial selections from Taylor's works and for providing us with helpful, illuminating introductions. Let the reader now turn the page and let the journey into the spirituality of Jeremy Taylor begin.

---

13. *Works* 7:646.

Introduction

Life in seventeenth-century England, at least in its upheavals, is frequently compared with the unrest and disturbance of our own times. Certainly it was an age of new forces contending with old, philosophically, politically and religiously. On the one hand there was a search and passion for truth and freedom, and on the other hand there was a loyalty to tradition and a reverence for authority. Bacon upset the old laws of philosophy and led the revolt in which medieval scholastic metaphysics gave way to the observation of fact, and consequently the birth of the scientific mind. In politics the parliamentarians rebelled against the king and his despotic government; Charles I was beheaded and the divine right of kings was no longer credible. In religion the same reforming or Puritan zeal had earlier martyred William Laud, the archbishop of Canterbury, and expelled his bishops, and a new sort of church came to be.

Jeremy Taylor belonged to this age of tradition and change. He was a pastor, a priest and a preacher, but the forces of change—political, religious and philosophical—made him a pilgrim, a theologian and a poet. Hence, this Introduction considers Taylor's life and times under the following headings: (1) pilgrim and pastor; (2) theologian and priest; (3) poet and preacher. These divisions are no more exclusive of one another than are the forces of change that respectively indicate them; but they are, perhaps, helpful in bringing together the fragments of politics, religion and philosophy that might otherwise remain apart.

PILGRIM AND PASTOR

The records of Holy Trinity Church, Cambridge, show that Jeremy, fourth of six children born to Nathaniel and Mary Taylor, was

15

baptized on 15 August 1613 where his father, like his father before him, was a church warden. His attendance at Perse Grammar School in Cambridge is also recorded, as is his entry on 18 August 1626 to Gonville and Caius College as a *pauper scholaris,* or sizer. Thus Taylor was indebted for both his grammar and his college education to the generosity of a certain Dr. Stephen Perse, who founded a free grammar school in Cambridge and endowed six scholarships and six fellowships at Caius College, "preference being given to fit scholars of the Perse School."[1]

From the time of Henry VIII to that of Charles I there were no fewer than 412 of these free grammar schools founded from funds released on the dissolution of the monasteries and supplemented by private benefactors like Dr. Perse. They arose from the appetite for learning in general, and for classical learning in particular, that was generated by the Renaissance and pursued with the enthusiasm of a new discovery. Indeed, such studies were the inspiration of the Cambridge Colleges, which formed the leaders, political and religious, of the new age of tradition and change:

> The annals of the English Church do not, throughout all its period, present a galaxy more resplendent than the admirable band of men united by close sympathies and common views in matters of faith and practice, who adorned the University of Cambridge at that period. Indeed were a synod of the wise and good to be imagined by the glowing fancy of an ardent visionary, which should unite the widest range of learning with the richest eloquence, and the most comprehensive Christian philanthropy with every holier grace of personal character, could it be better bodied forth than in Taylor, Mede, More, Whichcote, Rust, Worthington and Smith?[2]

Such was the brilliant assembly of rare genius that Cambridge then reared and fostered; yet none of these, save Rust, seems to have touched Taylor's secluded life, immersed, as he was, in the study of the classics, the Fathers, and the Schoolmen. Indeed, apart from this and similar general references of later historians, and the few scanty records of

---

1. C. J. Stranks, *The Life and Writings of Jeremy Taylor* (London: S.P.C.K. 1952), pp. 31ff.
2. W. J. Brown, *Jeremy Taylor* (London: Macmillan 1925), p. 9.

church and schools concerning him, little else is known about the humble origins and academic achievements of this Cambridge youth who was to blossom so early in life that he was ordained a priest of the Church of England in 1633, before he had completed his twenty-first year.

Soon after his ordination a chance opportunity to preach at St. Paul's in London brought Taylor to the attention of William Laud, who became bishop of London in 1628, chancellor of the University of Oxford in 1629, and archbishop of Canterbury in 1633. Nothing is known of Taylor's life after this meeting with his new and powerful patron until his arrival at Oxford in November 1635 as a probationary fellow at All Souls and a protege of the chancellor-archbishop. Caius College, like the spirit of Cambridge in general, was in the Puritan mood of reform and change, while All Souls, Laud's own college, like the Oxford of which he was chancellor, was a bastion of doctrine and tradition: hence, Taylor's transfer was probably arranged by Laud, who saw in him a valuable acquisition for the movement that was now being called Laudian.

There is little to record of Taylor's career at Oxford except his frequent absences and regular excursions to Lambeth, which followed his appointment as chaplain to the archbishop. But his clear-cut views on the divine origin of the episcopacy, the divine right of kings, and the divine power of the sacraments belong to this period at Oxford, when he read widely in the symbolic language of the Greek and Latin Fathers, and in the casuistry of the later Schoolmen. At Oxford, too, he came in contact with two men of great influence: Christopher Davenport, a Franciscan Friar named Francis a Santa Clara, who tried to win Taylor to Rome; and William Chillingworth, who had been won back from Rome by Laud himself. On account of such friendships perhaps, Taylor was accused at this time, as Worley said, of leanings towards Rome:

> Of course he rebutted the accusation, but it must be admitted that, from the Calvinistic and Presbyterian point of view, there was much in his cast of mind—his fondness for casuistry, his profound reverence for antiquity, his natural love of the picturesque and poetical features of religion, its ascetic severity on one hand, its august ceremonial on the other, which he was too honest to conceal in his words and works —that would lay him open to the charge. His intellect was too capacious for the narrow Protestantism of the Puritan school.

17

INTRODUCTION

His omnivorous reading would make him a Catholic in the widest sense of the word, and to his opponents in the heated feeling of the time, scarcely distinguishable from a Papist.[3]

In March 1638 Taylor—on Laud's recommendation—was appointed Rector of Uppingham in the diocese of London, a pretty village with a stone Church, which according to diarist John Evelyn, was "a rarity in that part of England, where most of the rural parishes were but of mud."[4] Thus Taylor began the life of a village pastor near to Lambeth and not too far from Oxford and Canterbury. In the fall of that year, on Guy Fawkes' Day, he returned to St. Mary's, the parish church of Oxford to preach before the assembled university and by appointment of the archbishop his *Sermon on Gunpowder Treason*. This sermon, afterward published and dedicated to his patron, the archbishop of Canterbury, signals the beginning of Taylor's public life and future promise, for he now seemed settled in a rising fame as well as fortune. In the following spring, in the parish church where he was rector, he married Phoebe Langsdale, who was probably the daughter of a London gentleman and certainly the mother of six, if not seven, Taylor children. Otherwise we know nothing of Phoebe Taylor's life until her death in 1651, but we know from his *Apology for Liturgy* that he was one of those "who will be so desirous of their liberty as to preserve that in private, when they have no concernments but their own, for matter of order or scandal."[5] Such faint indications as we possess point to an unruffled domestic felicity.

Parish records are scant about the pastor's activity in Uppingham, but they give a few glimpses of his ministry and personal life there. An organ was installed and sacred vessels, altar cloths and vestments were consecrated and dedicated—concerns dear to the heart of his reforming patron. But the real pastor of Uppingham was heard in the pulpit and the sermons preached there were later polished and published in the *Great Exemplar* (1649) as discourses, meditations and prayers. A deep serenity of spirit pervades these compositions, which flow from his practical and devotional reflections on the divinity and incarnation of

---

3. G. Worley, *Jeremy Taylor* (London: Longmans, Green and Co, 1904), p. 68.
4. Ibid. p. 76.
5. E. Gosse, *Jeremy Taylor* (London: Macmillan, 1904), p. 21.

Jesus Christ and always end in prayer. No fewer than forty of these concluding prayers are found in this single volume:

> Holy and eternal Jesus, whose whole life and doctrine was a perpetual sermon of holy life, a treasure of wisdom, and a repository of divine materials for meditation; give me grace to understand, diligence and attention to consider, care to lay up, and carefulness to reduce to practice all those actions, discourses, and pious lessons, and intimations, by which thou didst expressly teach or tacitly imply, or mysteriously signify, our duty. Let my understanding become as spiritual in its employment and purposes, as it is immaterial in its nature; fill my memory, as a vessel of election, with remembrances and notions highly compunctive, and greatly incentive of all the parts of sanctity. Let thy Holy Spirit dwell in my soul, instructing my knowledge, sanctifying my thoughts, guiding my affections, directing my will in the choice of virtue; that it may be the great employment of my life to meditate in thy law, to study thy preceptive will, to understand even the niceties and circumstantials of my duty; that ignorance may neither occasion a sin, nor become a punishment. Take from me all vanity of spirit, lightness of fancy, curiosity and impertinency of inquiry, illusions of the devil, and fantastic deceptions: let my thoughts be as my religion, plain, honest, pious, simple, prudent, and charitable; of great employment and force to the production of virtues and extermination of vice: but suffering no transportations of sense and vanity, nothing greater than the capacities of my soul, nothing that may minister to any imtemperances of spirit; but let me be wholly inebriated with love; and that love wholly spent in doing such actions, as best please thee, in the conditions of my infirmity and the securities of humility, till thou shalt please to draw the curtain, and reveal thy interior beauties, in the kingdom of thine eternal glories: which grant, for thy mercy's sake, O holy and eternal Jesu. Amen.[6]

---

6. *Works* 2:114.

INTRODUCTION

Such was the early promise of the young pastor of Uppingham, who might have become at another time the ideal pastoral divine. But in the reign of the Stuarts, when religious dissent identified itself with the national protest against misgovernment, politics and religion combined to provide a powerful dynamic for insurrection and revolution. Consequently, adulation and abuse have been heaped upon Charles and Laud, according to the outlook of their chroniclers; for example, Charles's flair for misjudging the temper of Parliament and his people is seldom denied, but Laud is always the *Eminence* that is both gray and black:

> Without imagination or the power of looking forward, ignorant of the mainsprings of human action, led by the desire to do what in his contracted earnestness he deemed to be right, at whatever cost to himself or others, the abyss was already opening before him. But he had little conception of it. He thought that he was conquering all along the line of opposition, warding off Rome on the one hand, crushing Puritan nonconformity on the other.[7]

In December 1640 fifteen thousand citizens of London demanded the abolition of the episcopacy, root and branch; consequently Laud was impeached in February 1641, and on 1 March 1641 he was sent to the Tower. These were fatal dates in the career of Jeremy Taylor: "I am robbed," he wrote, "of that which once did bless me,"[8] and the whole house of his hopes began to crash above his head. In May of the following year his youngest son, William, probably named after Laud, and described in the parish registers as "the son of Jeremy Taylor, Rector, and Phoebe, his wife,"[9] is recorded as buried at Uppingham; and so domestic and national sorrow began to mingle and continued together for many years. Shortly afterward Parliament, having by now abolished the episcopacy, ejected from their homes *all scandalous ministers*, that is, those who supported the Laudian movement in the church, and Charles in the state. Thus politics and religion combined and the pastor of Uppingham became a pilgrim whose wanderings for the next few years are difficult to trace.

The Long Parliament of November 1640 had already rejected the

---

7. Gosse, p. 10.
8. Stranks, p. 55.
9. Brown, p. 20.

20

absolutism of the king and the prerogatives of his government, and so on 22 August 1642 Charles raised his standard at Nottingham; for three years the country was plunged in a bloody conflict that ended with the rout of the royal forces at the battle of Naseby in 1645. The two main interests of this war were the political, in which the Lords were opposed to the Commons, and the religious, in which the bishops were opposed to the Puritans; consequently the king, clergy and aristocracy found themselves for the most part pitted against the great body of the people. Sometimes these interests cut across family ties, so that it can truly be said of that conflict that a man's foes were those of his own household, and civil war the name of that game.[10]

The immediate effect of the civil war on the Church of England was to be seen in (1) the havoc wrought in the cathedral and parish churches; (2) the poverty and ignominy to which the exiled clergy were exposed; (3) the stagnation inflicted on spiritual and theological writing; and (4) the suppression and destruction of the solemn liturgy in which the spiritual life of the church had been celebrated for generations. To follow the fortunes of Jeremy Taylor, now the king's official chaplain, during the period is to trace the adventures of Charles as he conducted his forces to and fro throughout the midland counties, in vague and ineffectual maneuvers. But nothing whatever is known of his family, which had been driven out of doors the previous year; for a short while they may have been housed and supported at Overstone, between Northampton and Wellingborough, by Lord and Lady Northampton, his patrons and spiritual disciples from the early days of peace and promise at Uppingham.

The year 1645 was a sort of alpha and omega in the life of Taylor, the pilgrim and pastor. It began with the execution of Laud, his archbishop, on 10 January and saw the defeat of Charles, his king, at the battle of Naseby; it ended, so to speak, with his own capture and imprisonment after the royal defeat at Cardigan Castle in the South of Wales. He afterwards found sanctuary and a decade of peace and quiet "far from the madding crowd's ignoble strife." These bloody deeds sorely disturbed the complacency of one who believed so deeply in the divine right of kings and in the divine origin of the episcopacy; indeed his first scholarly work, *Episcopacy Asserted* (1642), was courageously

---

10. Gosse, pp. 30ff.

published at the beginning of this storm with a touching reference to his patron in the Tower:

> I am engaged in the defence of a great truth, and I would willingly find a shroud to cover myself from danger and calumny; and although the cause both is and ought to be defended by Kings, yet my person must not go thither to sanctuary unless it be to pay my devotion, and I have now no other left for my defence; I am robbed of that which once did bless me, and indeed still does (but in another manner), and I hope will do more; but those distillations of celestial dews are conveyed in channels not pervious to an eye of sense, and now-a-days we seldom look with other, be the object never so beautious or alluring.[11]

Taylor's biographers find difficulty in reconciling the sequence of events that separated him from the royal household and brought him to Wales for temporary imprisonment at Cardigan Castle and ultimate seclusion at Golden Grove, the estate of Richard Vaughan, Earl of Carbery. Here Taylor was more fortunate than most of the deprived clergy in those days of trouble, for he found a refuge for his wife and family free from the ignominious conditions a high-minded man would hesitate to accept. Lord Carbery, and still more Lord Carbery's young and saintly wife, played parts of great importance in the life of this Caroline divine; the earl gave him protection and peace and a means of living, while in Lady Carbery he found his muse and directing genius. It was for her that he wrote his devotional works, and at her suggestion that he published the sermons she so devoutly heard.

At this time and in this place, as we shall see in other sections of this general Introduction, and more specifically in the pages that introduce the different chapters of this volume, Taylor's best work was done:

> In *Holy Living, Holy Dying*, and *A Yearly Course of Sermons*, he shows the astounding variety of his mind. At last the fruit of his tremendous reading comes pouring out; Greek philosophers, Latin historians and poets, the Church Fathers, all

---

11. Stranks, p. 55.

INTRODUCTION

march across his pages. The most curious and bizarre stories rub shoulders with God-impelled flights of thought and with vivid and sensitive descriptions of external nature.[12]

Those first years at Golden Grove brought Taylor out of his times and their controversies and into the timeless delights of nature; his contemplative and devotional works, like many of his sermons, owe their inspiration to the influence of the place around him:

The odour and colour of flowers, the hum of insects and the song of birds, the raging wind, the forest bending beneath the storm, even the worm crawling across the path and stretching out its elastic length after a shower, are all put under contribution to point his moral or adorn his doctrine.[13]

Indeed, his favorite walk, like Scott's on Salisbury Crags, Addison's path at Magdalen, or the terrace at Wells where Ken composed his evening hymn, is still remembered as the scene of his lonely meditations and sustained similes. Like the *qualis vidi* or the *qualis audivi* with which Virgil so often begins, Taylor too with his *so have I seen* or *so have I known* introduces his simile, which he sustains as a perfect poetic miniature to be enjoyed independently of the context, like an illustration in a book:

So have I known the boisterous north wind pass through the yielding air, which opened its bosom, and appeased its violence, by entertaining it with easy compliance in all the regions of its reception. But when the same breath of heaven hath been checked with the stiffness of a tower, or the united strength of a wood, it grew mighty, and dwelt there, and made the highest branches stoop, and made a smooth path for it on the top of all its glories *(Holy Dying)*.[14]

And again:

So have I seen the rays of the sun or moon dash upon a brazen vessel, whose lips kissed the face of those waters that lodged

12. M. Gest, *The House of Understanding* (Philadelphia: University of Pennsylvania, 1954), p. 15.
13. Worley, p. 117.
14. Ibid. p. 118.

23

within its bosom; but being turned back and sent off with its smooth pretences, or rougher waftings, it wandered about the room, and beat upon the roof, and still doubled its heat and motion *(Holy Dying)*.[15]

Nevertheless, Golden Grove, in spite of its distance and seclusion, was not immune to the mood of the times. Indeed, Taylor's *Holy Living* (1650), which has all the marks of an unconscious autobiography, is throughout a commentary on the troublous years on which its author's life was cast:

I am fallen into the hands of publicans and sequestrators, and they have taken all from me: what now? let me look about me. They have left me the sun and moon, fire and water, a loving wife, and many friends to pity me, and some to relieve me, and I can still discourse; and unless I list they have not taken away my merry countenance, and my cheerful spirit, and a good conscience: they still have left me the providence of God, and all the promises of the Gospel, and my religion, and my hopes of heaven, and my charity to them too; and still I sleep and digest, I eat and drink, I read and meditate, I can walk in my neighbour's pleasant fields, and see the varieties of natural beauties, and delight in all that in which God delights, that is, in virtue and wisdom, in the whole creation, and in God himself. And he that hath so many causes of joy and so great, is very much in love with sorrow and peevishness, who loses all these pleasures, and chooses to sit down upon his little hand-ful of thorns.[16]

Domestic sorrow, too, was felt in that place of peace; in the fall of 1650 Lady Carbery died. The funeral discourse preached on that occasion was a new blending in English spirituality of time and eternity, of this life and another life, as every now and then Taylor turns from his wrapt contemplation of death in itself to the woman of Christian faith who was passing through its shadow:

---

15. Ibid. p. 119.
16. Stranks, p. 107.

24

But so it was that the thought of death dwelt long with her, and grew from the first steps of fancy and fear, to a consent, from thence to a strange credulity and expectation of it; and without the violence of sickness she died, as if she had done it voluntarily, and by design. . . . And in this I cannot but adore the providence and admire the wisdom and infinite mercies of God. For having a tender and a soft, a delicate and fine constitution and breeding, she was tender to pain, and apprehensive of it, as a child's shoulder is of a load and burden. . . . But God that knew her fears and her jealousy concerning herself, fitted her with a death so easy, so harmless, so painless, that it did not put her patience to a severe trial. It was not (in all appearance) of so much trouble as two fits of a common ague; so careful was God to remonstrate to all that stood in that sad attendance that this soul was dear to Him: and that since she had done so much of her duty towards it, He that began would also finish her redemption, by an act of rare providence, and a singular mercy. Blessed be the goodness of God, who does so careful actions of mercy for the ease and security of his servants.[17]

Domestic tragedy continued; in the spring following the death of Lady Carbery, Taylor buried his wife, Phoebe. In the fall of that same year he published *Holy Dying,* his unique contribution to English spirituality, theology and literature. The Victorian biographer Edmund Gosse sees *Holy Dying* as Taylor's mystical reaction to his most painful experience of recent death, while Canon Stranks, his most authoritative biographer, does not agree; the dispute, however, seems academic for at his hour of deepest tragedy Taylor reached divine heights of understanding and expression, new in the English language, and still salutary and consoling. Although *Holy Dying* has more feeling in it than any other of Taylor's works, it is never personal in the subjective sense; his silence on Phoebe's death, as on her life, remains throughout, for he seldom, if ever, introduces his personal losses, no more than his gains, into his writings. But his *Sermon on the Marriage Ring,* pronounced divine by no less a critic than Lord Lytton and preached while Phoebe

17. Stranks, p. 110.

was still alive, tells its own tale of love in the home at a time when Milton was publishing his acrimonious pamphlets on divorce, and the Sectaries were recognizing as legal only those marriages that were civil:

> Nothing can sweeten felicity itself but love. But, when a man dwells in love, then the breasts of his wife are pleasant as the droppings on the hill of Hermon, her eyes are fair as the light of heaven, she is a fountain sealed, and he can quench his thirst and ease his cares, and lay his sorrows down upon her lap, and can retire home to his sanctuary and refectory and his gardens of sweetness and chaste refreshments. No man can tell, but he that loves his children, how many delicious accents make a man's heart dance in the pretty conversation of those dear pledges; their childishness, their stammering, their little angers, their innocence, their imperfections, their necessities, are so many little emanations of joy and comfort to him that delights in their persons and society.
>
> But he that loves not his wife and children feeds a lioness at home, and broods over a nest of sorrows; and blessing itself cannot make him happy; so that all the commandments of God enjoining a man to "love his wife" are nothing but so many necessities and capacities of joy. She that is loved is safe, and he that loves is joyful. Love is an union of all things excellent; it contains in it proportion and satisfaction, and rest and confidence.[18]

A number of circumstances, including Lord Carbery's second marriage, soon drove Taylor from Golden Grove and set him once more on the pilgrim's way. His own second marriage, perhaps around this time, to Joanna Bridges, probably provided a mother and a home for his children at Mandinam, her small country house on an estate some ten or twelve miles from Golden Grove. Again, little is known for certain about Joanna Bridges, and biographers conjecture much. By some she was thought to be the illegitimate daughter of Charles I, when he was Prince of Wales, and under the influence of the licentious Buckingham.

Another tradition has linked Taylor with the king in the Tower

18. Worley, p. 79; *Works* 4:224.

during his last hours, before his execution in 1649, and, according to Edmund Gosse, his Victorian biographer, "receiving in token of his regard, his watch, and a few pearls and rubies, which had ornamented the ebony case in which the King kept his bible."[19]

Such royal associations, true or false, were of little help as new years of affliction and poverty stole painfully by. The year 1654 was evidently one of greater tolerance and laxity on the part of the Puritans. In London Taylor preached publicly, as Evelyn records for 15 April 1654: "I went to London to hear the famous Doctor Jeremy Taylor at St. Greg: on 6 Matt. 48, concerning evangelical perfection."[20] About this time, Taylor became Evelyn's "ghostly Father,"[21] and Evelyn, Taylor's new patron and protector, and their correspondence for the next six years, provide many details of the life and times of Jeremy Taylor; for example, Taylor writes that he is "in some disorder by reason of the death of a little child of mine, a boy that lately made us very glad."[22] Here he is obviously referring to a child of his second marriage, but six months later he writes again that he has buried "two sweet hopeful boys,"[23] children of his first marriage. At another time he writes to Evelyn to console him on the loss of his son, with the comment: "The soul returns to God, and that in no sense is death; the soul desires to be reunited, and that which is dead desires not."[24]

In 1655 Taylor published *The Golden Grove,* an innocuous compilation of prayers, devotions and commentaries with a provocative and inflammatory preface in which he refers to Cromwell, by inference, as "The Son of Zippor . . . sent to curse the people of the Lord that had long prospered under the conduct of Moses and Aaron."[25] He likewise attacked the army of Independents who came to power after the dismissal of Parliament in 1653, and, as a result, was understandably imprisoned in Chepstow Castle. Furthermore, by the publication in the same year of *Unum Necessarium,* the controversial work in which he expressed his heterodox views on original sin, free will, predestination and death-bed repentance, Taylor mortally wounded his own Anglican

---

19. Gosse, p. 63.
20. Brown, p. 26.
21. Gest, p. 19.
22. Ibid.
23. Ibid.
24. Ibid.
25. Gosse, p. 112.

establishment and the few bishops that remained in England. Thus, by 1656, Taylor was the most active and outspoken clergyman in England, but he stood alone and in prison, attacked by friend and foe alike. Released on the intervention of Evelyn, who was one of the few in favor with both political parties, Taylor returned to his home in Mandinam, an outcast and a pauper.

An entry in Evelyn's diary for Christmas Day 1655 records "the funeral sermon of preaching,"[26] for this was the last time a priest of the Church of England was allowed to preach or minister the sacraments. There is also in the early New Year another entry telling of the times: "In a private house in London . . . I was given the Blessed Sacrament— the first time the Church of England was reduced to chamber and conventicle."[27] Indeed, Taylor seems to have been in London and its surrounds during much of this time, but at no settled abode and certainly without any fixed income. Again, there is another interesting entry in Evelyn's diary for 7 March 1658: "To London to Dr. Taylor in a private house on XIII Luke 23–24. After the Sermon followed the Blessed Communion of which I participated. In the afternoon, Dr. Gunning at Excester House expounding part of the creede."[28] Taylor was now ministering to private congregations of people who were loyal to king and church, and in 1658 he published for them his *Collection of Offices* when the *Prayer Book* was proscribed. Unfortunately for him, there was printed on the frontispiece a picture of Christ in an attitude of prayer, and so, once more, he found himself a prisoner in the Tower.

A new and final stage in Taylor's life began with his release from prison and his friendship with Lord and Lady Conway, friends of Evelyn and members of his London congregations. The main strength of this Conway family had always lain in the north-eastern part of Ireland where their vast estates surrounded Portmore, their great manor house. Like Golden Grove in Wales, Portmore in the north of Ireland was a home of Anglican faith and piety, which the young Lord was anxious to foster and develop. His wife was similarly committed and was already a disciple of Taylor and his friend, Henry More, the Cambridge Platonist. So, once again, Taylor was offered sanctuary from the storms of the times and invited to Portmore as chaplain to the Conway

---

26. Gest, p. 21.
27. Gest, p. 21.
28. Ibid.

household with a modest teaching post in the nearby town of Lisburn. Thus Jeremy Taylor, pilgrim and pastor, in his forty-fifth year departed London in June 1658 to begin the last decade of his life as an exile, far from the England where he had buried his first wife and five sons and experienced the loss of his king and archbishop.

At Portmore there was leisure and the opportunity to continue in the undisturbed peace of the place the study of casuistry, or cases of conscience, which he had commenced some twenty years earlier. Little remains today of the Great House, which was demolished in 1761 when the Conway peerage became extinct, but its grandeur and grace can be easily imagined. Edmund Gosse described the site in 1904:

> At present it is difficult to find the remains of Portmore, but as the wanderer plashes about in the marshy flats, he becomes aware of a long line of broken brickwork on the crest of a slight eminence looking westward. This ridge, with what was evidently a bowling-green or garden in front of it, descending to the lake, marks the direction of the great terrace which rose from the plans of Inigo Jones soon after the rebellion of 1641. Portmore was not only a noble residence; it was a fortress garrisoned against the Tories of the west. Where now the eye perceives nothing but a low harsh horizon of grazing land to the north and east, in Lord Conway's time there lay a large deer-park of oak-trees. It is probable that a bridge, all traces of which have disappeared, conducted, in a few minutes from Portmore, across the brown and broad trout-stream, to the church in which Jeremy Taylor habitually officiated. To reach the latter now it is necessary to take a long, circuitous route. One arrives at last quite suddenly at its impressive desolation. It stands high on an artificial island in the marshes, with a shallow moat encircling it, although quite close to the banks of Lough Beg, which are so low that the round lake looks like a brimming cask buried in the soft soil. The fragments of the church are covered heavily with ivy, and a loose hedge of seedling larches and sweet-briar enrings them, while here and there great cypresses, relics, it is possible of the Italian gardens of Portmore, soar impressively in the wild, bright place, where there has long ceased to be heard any other sound than the cries of wildfowl. From up among these ruins, the old fragmentary brickwork of Portmore is better visible than

INTRODUCTION

from any other point, and imagination may here rebuild the
vision of it as Jeremy Taylor saw it when he arrived in 1658,
sumptuous and elaborate, with its upper windows looking
towards the sunset over Lough Beg to the melancholy little
inland ocean of Lough Neagh.[29]

The death of Cromwell in the very year of Taylor's arrival at
Portmore changed the political climate of his new retreat, and the
Presbyterians of Ulster lost no time in taking full advantage of it. By
adopting a double policy of intriguing, on the one hand, for the king's
return, and on the other hand, of standing stoutly for the principles of
the Reformation, they took political advantage of the Puritans and
religious advantage of the Anglicans. These Presbyterians had long
since consolidated their position in Ulster, politically and religiously,
driven there from Scotland in the early years of James I with his policy
of "No bishop, no king," which begot what historians call the Ulster
Plantation in 1609. A further confiscation of Catholic lands followed
the Insurrection of 1641, and by the *Act of Settlement* of 1652, which
regarded the whole of Ireland as forfeited property, the spoils of this
war were divided among Cromwell's Puritan soldiers, while the Catholic landowners were driven from Ulster and the rest of fertile Ireland
into the barren Province of Connaught. Thus, by 1659 Ulster was a
province of political and religious unrest as Puritan and Presbyterian
fought viciously for property and belief, while pockets of Anglican
gentry and Roman Catholic peasants held on doggedly to whatever of
each they possessed.

The Restoration of the monarchy in 1660 set the fires of Puritan
power and Presbyterian zeal ablaze, and Ulster was on the march. At
Ballymena in the County Antrim a synod was held of all the ministers
from the Diocese of Down and Connor, and a deputation was sent to
the new king; "they humbly reminded His Majesty of God's wonderful
dealing with him in his preservation and restoration, on which they
heartily congratulated him, but withal, they humbly petitioned the set-
tling of religion according to the rule of Reformation against Popery,
Prelacy, heresy, etc., according to the covenant."[30]

---

29. Gosse, p. 153.
30. Stranks, p. 221.

INTRODUCTION

Taylor was in London at this very time for the publication of *Ductor Dubitantium,* his magnum opus on casuistry; consequently he was suitably on hand to join in the welcome to Charles, as he entered London triumphantly on May 29. Dedicated to his majesty, *Ductor Dubitantium* kept Taylor in the limelight when the new bishoprics were being handed out after the Restoration; as an outstanding royalist clergyman, Taylor was certainly assured of preferment, and probably was in hope of an English bishopric. However, *Unum Necessarium,* with its smack of pelagianism, and *The Liberty of Prophesying,* with its spirit of toleration, were not forgotten by the ecclesiastical establishment. Consequently, the Presbyterian diocese of Down and Connor, in the north-eastern part of Ireland, which wanted no bishop, became the pilgrim's royal reward and the pastor's divine charge.

The storm of protest that broke among Ulster's Presbyterians after Taylor's nomination to the see of Down and Connor was immediate and violent. On 19 December 1660, some months after his August appointment and shortly before his January consecration, he expressed his reservations and fears in a letter to James Butler, Duke of Ormonde, lord lieutenant of Ireland and chancellor of Trinity College, Dublin:

His sacred Majesty and your Excellence intended to prefer me, in giving me the bishopric of Down. But—besides that I find it very much short of what it was represented to me, and much of the rents litigious and uncertain, of which I will not complain,—I perceive myself thrown into a place of torment. The country would quickly be very well, if the Scotch ministers were away, at least some of the prime incendiaries. All the nobility and gentry, one only (Lord Massereene) excepted, are very right, but the ministers are implacable. They have for these four months past solemnly agreed, and very lately renewed their resolution, of preaching vigorously and constantly against episcopacy and liturgy. . . . They talk of resisting unto blood, and stir up the people to sedition. . . . They have now gone about to asperse me as an Arminian, and a Socinian, and a Papist,—or at least half a Papist, . . . and I am not at all guilty, as having no other religion but that of the Church of England, for which I have suffered the persecution of eighteen years. . . . But yet they have lately bought my books, and appointed a committee of Scotch spiders to see if

31

they can gather or make poison out of them, and have drawn some little thing, I know not what, into a paper, and intend to petition to his Majesty that I may not be their bishop.[31]

While the Presbyterians continued in their opposition, Taylor was busy with the affairs of Trinity College in Dublin, for on Ormonde's recommendation he was appointed vice-chancellor shortly after his nomination as bishop. At Trinity he found all things in a perfect disorder, but by his reforms and revisions he quickly laid the foundations of the work that has ever since distinguished that university, and in a few months he set Trinity College firmly and finally on its feet. On the other hand, he continued to fail in his every effort at reconciliation with the Presbyterians of his diocese, and his letter to Ormonde further confirms his generous overtures and their obstinate response:

> My lord; I have invited them to a friendly conference, desired earnestly to speak with them, went to them, sent some of their own to invite them, offered to satisfy them, in anything that was reasonable; I preach every Sunday amongst them, somewhere or other; I have courted them with most friendly offers, did all things in pursuance of his Majesty's most gracious declaration; but they refused to speak with me; they have newly covenanted to speak with no bishop, and to endure neither their government nor their persons. . . . They threaten to murder me. They use all the arts they can to disgrace me, and to take the people's hearts from me, and to make my life uncomfortable and useless to the service of his Majesty and the Church. . . . It were better for me to be a poor curate in a village church than a bishop over such intolerable persons; and I will petition your Excellence to give me some parsonage in Munster, that I may end my days in peace, rather than abide here, unless I may be enabled with comfort to contest against such violent persons. . . . My charge hath in it more trouble than all the dioceses in his Majesty's dominions put together.[32]

The consecration of Taylor as bishop took place nonetheless; with him nine other bishops and two archbishops had been appointed after

---

31. Gosse, p. 173.
32. Stranks, p. 230; Gosse, p. 174.

the Restoration to the vacant sees, and as several of the pre-Common-wealth Irish bishops were still alive, the new were consecrated by the old in a single ceremony in St. Patrick's Cathedral in Dublin on 27 January 1661. The aged bishop of Derry, John Bramhall, was the new primate of Armagh; he planned the service and presided. Civil and military leaders, ecclesiastical and academic figures, all took part in the grand public procession to the cathedral, while the choir sang music specially composed for the occasion; Jeremy Taylor was accorded the exceptional honor of preaching at his own consecration. His sermon on the *Faithful and Wise Steward* of Luke 12:42 was a defense of episcopacy on the lines of his earlier work, *Episcopacy Asserted,* but he dealt at great length with a bishop's responsibility for the lost sheep of his flock.

The new bishop of Down and Connor entered his diocese, which had neither cathedral nor bishop's residence, in February 1661; he was given accommodation at Hillsborough Castle, the house of Colonel Arthur Hill, Taylor's friend from his first days at nearby Portmore. Again, little is known about Taylor's family life in Ireland, but he began his episcopacy at Lisburn Church by burying on 10 March 1661, Edward, his two-year-old boy, the sixth of his seven sons to die. This church, destined to be Taylor's cathedral, soon became the seat of his troubles, for his Presbyterian clergy refused to assemble, when summoned at the end of March, to reestablish the Episcopalian structure of government and worship. Taylor's response was firm but unexpected; the moment for weakness had passed and the gentle and sensitive clergyman acted as if iron had entered his episcopal heart. He declared vacant the parishes of thirty-six of the Presbyterian ministers who confronted him in open revolt, and he invited clergymen from England, who were episcopally ordained, to fill them. Among the large ecclesiastical colony imported from England was George Rust, fellow of Christ College, Cambridge, who became dean of Connor and, after Taylor, bishop of Dromore.

This was, indeed, the beginning and, in a certain sense, the end of the pastor's episcopate:

> The work of turning out the Presbyterian ministers who struggled to retain their parsonages "till it became physically impossible for them to continue," of installing and protecting the new clergy, of conciliating the congregations, of exhorting and cheering and rebuking his flock in all corners of the diocese, of deciding cases where, as at Killead and Antrim, the

ministers could safely be allowed a six months' grace,—all this occupied Jeremy Taylor through the stormy year 1661.[33]

Consequently, Taylor soon requested a transfer to the diocese of Meath, which bordered that of Dublin, and he wrote accordingly to Ormonde: "Here I am perpetually contending with the worst of the Scotch ministers. I have a most uncomfortable employment, but, I bless God, I have broken their knot, I have overcome the biggest difficulty, and made the charge easy for my successor."[34] Ormonde's refusal was but the first of others that were to follow, and Taylor was left to bishop on and on in his Presbyterian see. However, since this diocese was greater in charge than in revenue, and less in value than it was in promise, he was given additional charge of Dromore, a small adjacent diocese served by a handful of priests, whose cathedral had been burned down during the Insurrection of 1641. Thus he is usually known as the bishop of Down, Connor and Dromore, although he never did become the bishop of Dromore.

In his diocese Taylor, the theologian of tolerance, was soon perceived to be the bishop of tyranny for the Presbyterians who struggled on against bishop, book and bell were given no quarter. Eventually the very institution that he so faithfully served distanced itself from his uncompromising stand, for political outlooks change with the times and frequently in the church. Distance, too, contributed to his growing awareness of isolation and his ultimate loss of friends; at first Evelyn sent him some printed tracts, but no more letters, and he too dropped noiselessly out of the affectionate bishop's life. "Only Henry More," says Stranks, "in the academic calm of Cambridge, had time to keep in touch, sometimes by letter; sometimes by affectionate messages and books enclosed in packages for Lady Conway."[35]

Although Taylor was now firmly established in institutional darkness, he was still the brightest light in the Irish hierarchy and remained indispensable to adorn the great occasions with his sermons. In May 1661, after the Restoration in London, he preached at the opening of the new Parliament in Dublin, a sermon on the duty of obedience, in which his attitude to nonconformity was conditioned by his own bitter

33. Gosse, p. 182.
34. Stranks, p. 245.
35. Ibid. p. 248.

experience: "My eyes are almost grown old with seeing the horrid mischiefs, which come from rebellion and disobedience."[36] Yet one year later, in the most glorious of all his sermons, *Via Intelligentiae*, preached to the scholars of "the little, but excellent" University of Dublin, there are moments of transcendence when the bishop of Down and Connor escapes his "place of torment" and speaks of divine experience and vision: "Divine knowledge more than we can discourse of, and more certain than the demonstrations of geometry, brighter than the sun, and indeficient as the light of heaven . . . to be felt and not to be talked of . . . for a good man is united unto God as a flame touches a flame and combines into splendour and to glory."[37]

The death of Archbishop Bramhall in June 1663 brought Taylor at least to the pulpit, if not afterward to the cathedra or episcopal chair of Armagh. Once again he fuses the human and the divine, the mystery in history, so to speak; the sermon is partly a rhapsody on the sure and certain hope of resurrection, and partly a very skillful and picturesque biography. There are echoes here of Golden Grove as he weaves his way through nature's reflections of the resurrection: "Night and day, the sun returning to the same point of east, every change of species, the eagle renewing her youth, and the snake her skin, the silkworm and the swallows, winter and summer, the fall and spring."[38] But there is also the mortal wound of Down and Connor, and when he turns to the portrait of Bramhall, he insists with indignant zeal upon the primate's "heroic passion for the Church, and upon all that he was called upon to suffer, for he was driven into exile and poverty by that wild storm by which great Strafford and Canterbury fell."[39]

From the historical perspective it is difficult to understand the rejection of Taylor by the king and establishment in Ireland as in England: nevertheless, this great luminary of the Church of Ireland was not considered for the primacy, nor for Dublin, when Archbishop Margetson was transferred to Armagh, nor for any other preference in Ireland or in England. Indeed, there is something pathetic about his final request to Sheldon, a lesser light than Taylor in the days of darkness, but at Canterbury no longer hidden under a bushel:

---

36. Gosse, p. 188.
37. Gest, p. 114.
38. Gosse, p. 198.
39. Ibid. p. 199.

INTRODUCTION

I humbly desire that your grace will not wholly lay me aside, and cast off all thoughts of removing me. For no man shall with a greater diligence, humility and observance endeavour to make up his other disabilities than I shall. The case is so that the country does not agree with my health as it hath done formerly, till the last Michaelmas; and if your grace be not willing I should die immaturely, I shall still hope you will bring me to or near yourself once more. But to God and to your grace I humbly submit the whole affair, humbly desiring a kind return to this letter, and the comfort of a little hope.[40]

Taylor, nevertheless, remained useful to the bishops as a theologian on questions of hierarchial concern. Consequently he prepared and published, at their request, his *Discourse on Confirmation,* in which he argued against Presbyterians the defense of that rite, which was popularly called "the bishoping of children." Similarly, *The Dissuasion from Popery,* his most argumentative and apologetical work, was written at the request of the bishops, although at the time there were very few Roman Catholics in the diocese of Down and Connor intellectually capable of persuasion or dissuasion. For Gosse this is the most

unreadable of Jeremy Taylor's writings. It is deformed by patronising remarks about "the poor deluded Irish," and in particular goes out of its way to attack the use and study of the Irish language, which Taylor thought barbarous and deforming, and wished to prohibit. His entire want of sympathy with the Celtic mind is illustrated by the agony of distress into which he is thrown by certain instances of its "miserable superstition and blindness." In every sentence we are conscious of the chasm which divided him from all sections of his flock, of what Matthew Arnold might call "the profound sense of estrangement" from them, "immense, incurable, fatal."[41]

There is little more to tell of Taylor's life or of the events, political and religious, which determined the journey and disturbed the quiet of

---

40. Ibid. p. 203.
41. Ibid. p. 200.

this pilgrim and pastor. He was around the time of his death engaged in a vexatious lawsuit about revenues with the son of Colonel Hill, which was in itself a sad conclusion to the long and harmonious friendship between Jeremy Taylor and the house of Hillsborough. He was also, and more in keeping with his real self, preparing at this time a discourse on the beatitudes; these feelings went with him and no words remain, for this unfinished manuscript seems never to have been printed in this life. But elsewhere and at another time he had written:

> He that hath passed from his childhood in grace . . . and from thence is become an old disciple, and strong and grown old in religion and the conversion of the Spirit: this man best understands the secret and undiscernible economy; he feels this unintelligible mystery, and sees with his heart what his tongue can never express and his metaphysics can never prove.[42]

The mystery of suffering and sorrow continued in the Taylor household until the final consummation: On 22 August 1667 Charles, his seventh and only surviving son, was buried at St. Margaret's, Westminster, at the age of twenty-four; and on the following day Taylor was taken ill. Earlier the pastor had visited a fever patient and caught the disease; ten days later, on 13 August 1667, the pilgrim went his final way. He was survived by his wife, Joanna, and three daughters for whom there was little of the world's goods to share, for he had spent whatever he had on alms and church building. There is no record of the marriage of his daughter, Phoebe, but Mary married Frances Marsh, who later became archbishop of Dublin, and Joanna married Edward Harrison, who became a member of Parliament for Lisburn.

"Bury me at Dromore" were the last words of Jeremy Taylor, pilgrim and pastor.[43] There, where he was not bishop, he had restored the cathedral and at his own expense rebuilt the chancel; in a sense Dromore was for the bishop of Down and Connor the church beyond his church. "God's secrets," he said, "are to Himself and the sons of His House."[44] Here, George Rust, dean of Connor and later bishop of Dromore, preached the panegyric, which is the main source of this brief

---

42. Gest, p. 115.
43. Gosse, p. 207.
44. Gest, M. p. 115.

biography. No memorial other than the elegant words of Rust was erected to his memory until 1827, when the bishop of Down and Connor placed in Lisburn Cathedral a white marble tablet with an elaborate epitaph. Taylor's own words might, perhaps, have said it better:

> Nor do I desire a stately sepulchre, a beautiful urn, or that my name and actions should be engraven in marble.[45]

THEOLOGIAN AND PRIEST

The religious controversies of the seventeenth century had their origin in the political events surrounding the English Reformation. Henry VIII defended his medieval Catholicism against Luther, and the title *Defender of the Faith* was conferred on him by Rome, shortly before a combination of other troubles made him *the Supreme Head* of the church. This supremacy, or rather the lack of it in the boy king, Edward VI (1547–53) opened the doors of the Church of England for the Continental reformers. Soon the relationship of church and state and the doctrine of the eucharist became the major issues, political and religious, of the English Reformation and were hotly debated by men like Tyndale, Hooper, Cranmer, Ridley and Bradford. Cardinal Pole, during the short reign of Mary (1553–58), after the boy king, caused the bodies of some like Martin Bucer and Paul Fagius in Cambridge to be dug up and burned in the marketplace, while Cranmer and others were made the Smithfield Martyrs, "in whose blood the rubrics of the Book of Common Prayer were writ," and the Catholic queen is remembered in history as *Bloody Mary*.

Such was the mood of England, religious and political, when the new queen journeyed from Hatfield to Westminster in November 1558. Elizabeth's sole desire was "to secure and unite the people of her realm in one uniform order to the glory of God, and to the general tranquility";[46] the Elizabethan Settlement of 1559, which promulgated the *Act of Supremacy* and the *Act of Uniformity,* was her hurried political

---

45. Worley, G. p. 209 (from *Contemplations of the State of Man*, a probable Taylor translation).

46. J. Black, *The Reign of Elizabeth* (Oxford: Clarendon Press, 1936), p. 9.

answer to a question that was only in its theological infancy. Although the *Act of Supremacy* avoided the aggressive title of *Supreme Head,* and was content with an oath to the queen "as the only supreme authority in matters spiritual and temporal,"[47] it was, nevertheless, opposed by every bishop in the House of Lords. The *Act of Uniformity* was similarly opposed but eventually passed by a majority of three; it obliged the laity to attend their parish church and adopted as the official liturgy of the realm Cranmer's *Second Prayer Book* (1552), which, unlike the *First Prayer Book* of 1549, was capable of a Zwinglian or Protestant interpretation of the sacraments in general and of the eucharist in particular.

In theory the two great problems of the English Reformation were now solved, but in practice the religious issues continued to aggravate the political scene; within the church men sought publicly and privately, by propaganda or intrigue, to bring both sovereign and country within the influence of either Rome or Geneva. The Elizabethan Settlement, while establishing Protestantism, did not immediately produce either a developed theology or polity, and so the religious and political issues smoldered on, and nearly one hundred years later, William Laud, the archbishop of uniformity, and some few years later, Charles, the king, "the only supreme authority in matters spiritual and temporal," were both executed.

During those fifty years of Elizabeth's reign the Reformation that began in England as a struggle among Catholics about loyalties to pope or king continued as a religious conflict in the Church of England between Catholic tradition and Protestant reform. The *Thirty-Nine Articles,* passed by Convocation in 1563 and given legal sanction in 1571, upheld the reality of the Catholic tradition of the sacraments "as sure witnesses, and effectual signs of grace and God's good will,"[48] but did not prevent the spread of Zwingli's Protestant reform; for him, the sacraments were bare signs or ceremonies by which a man assures other people rather than himself of his saving faith in Christ's redemption; furthermore, in the eucharistic action, as in baptism, there is neither a presence nor a power, but a vivid remembering of the Lord's passion and death as the moment of one's salvation in the past.[49] This debate was further complicated by John Calvin, the Frenchman from Geneva,

---

47. K. Feiling, *A History of England* (London: Macmillan, 1950), p. 390.

48. W. G. Wilson, and J. H. Templeton, *Anglican Teaching* (Dublin: A.P.C.K., 1962), p. 179.

49. G. Dix, *The Shape of the Liturgy* (London: A & C Black, 1945), pp. 724ff.

whose teaching was also gaining ground. For him, the real eucharistic action was individual and internal, for he did not believe in a divine institution or in an ordained ministry.[50] *Virtualism* and *Receptionism*, however undefined, are the terms commonly used to describe the boundaries of this debate. According to virtualism, which has been connected with Calvin, the faithful communicant receives together with the elements the virtue or power of the body and blood of Christ; Receptionism, on the other hand, means generally that the faithful communicant receives with the elements the true body and blood of Christ and more stress is laid upon the disposition of the communicant than in Virtualism.[51]

These controversies in eucharistic theology, and the subsequent chaos in worship that they occasioned, gave rise toward the end of the century to a group of men who were pre-eminently capable of infusing the Elizabethan compromise with a soul that was both Catholic and Reformed. Of these, the first and foremost was Richard Hooker (1554–1600), the country parson whose vast erudition earned him the appointment of Master of the Temple. There followed poets and preachers like John Donne and Jeremy Taylor, bishops and spiritual writers like Andrewes and Cosin, village parsons like George Herbert (products of the same refined culture), and devout and learned laymen like Sir Thomas Browne, Nicholas Ferrar, Thomas Vaughan and the unforgettable Izaak Walton. They all either set out spontaneously along similar paths or deliberately followed the one opened up by Hooker, and since they flourished in the reign of Charles I, and afterward in the time of his son, Charles II, they are known as the Caroline Divines.[52]

Richard Hooker had already published in 1597 his fifth book of the *Laws of Ecclesiastical Polity* before the arrival of James I (1603–25) from Scotland, after the death of Elizabeth, brought the debates on the eucharist into the political arena. Hooker made the church of the Fathers his touchstone of truth, and consequently he easily justified the retention of Catholic institutions like episcopacy and sacraments; but, on his way to England, James received the humble petition of a thousand ministers, or *Millenary Petition* as history has it, demanding the abolition of these very institutions and the purification of the *Prayer Book* from their

---

50. Ibid.

51. T. Hughes, *The Piety of Jeremy Taylor* (London: Macmillan, 1960), pp. 40ff.

52. L. Bouyer, *A History of Christian Spirituality*, vol. 3 (London: Burns and Dates, 1968), pp. 116ff.

contaminating influence. The king consented to a conference between the representatives of the aggrieved and those responsible for the order of the church, and so there took place the Hampton Court Conference (1604), which will be forever associated with the King James version of the bible.[53]

The famous *No bishop, no king* aphorism of James, and his declaration of having "one doctrine and one discipline, one religion in substance and in ceremony" put a halt, however temporary, to Puritan progress while encouraging the Caroline cause. Furthermore, a post-conference commission reconsidered the teaching of the *Thirty-Nine Articles* on the sacraments in general and published the Hampton Court Catechism, in which the influence of the Carolines was most noticeable on episcopacy, or church government, and on eucharist or worship. Lancelot Andrewes, then dean of Westminster, was the great power at this conference and his famous sermon on the eucharist, preached ten years later when he was bishop of Ely, Taylor's diocese of origin, expresses Caroline eucharistic faith, or the teaching of the high churchmen, as they are also called, in 1613, the very year of Taylor's birth:[54]

Two things Christ there gave us in charge: 1. *ANAMNĒSIS*, "remembering" and 2. *LĒPSIS*, "receiving." The same two St. Paul, but in other terms; 1. *KATAGGELIA*, "showing forth"; 2. *KOINŌNIA*, "communicating." Of which, "remembering" and "showing forth" refer to celebremus; "receiving" and "communicating" to epulemur here (1 Cor. V.8. which was part of his text). The first in remembrance of Him, Christ. What of him? *Mortem Domini*, His death, saith St. Paul, "to show forth the Lord's death." Remember Him? That we will and stay at home, think of Him there. Nay, show Him forth ye must. That we will by a sermon of Him. Nay; it must be *Hoc facite*. It is not mental thinking, or verbal speaking, there must be actually somewhat done to celebrate this memory. That done to the holy symbols that was done to Him, to His body and His blood in the Passover; break the

53. Edward Cardwell, *History of the Conference* (Oxford: University Press, 1849), pp. 184ff.

54. G. W. O. Addleshaw, *The High Church Tradition* (London: Faber and Faber, 1941), p. 30.

one, pour out the other, to represent *KLŌMENON* how His sacred body was "broken" and *EKXYNOMENON* how His precious blood was "shed." And in *Corpus fractum* and *Sanquis fusus* there is *immolatus*. This is it in the Eucharist that answereth to the sacrifice in the Passover, the memorial to the figure. To them it was, *Hoc facie in Mei praefigurationem*, "do this in prefiguration of Me": to us it is, "Do this in commemoration of Me." To them *praenuntiare*; to us *annuntiare*: there is the difference. By the same rules that theirs was, by the same way ours be termed a sacrifice. In rigour of speech, neither of them; for to speak after the exact manner of Divinity, there is but one only sacrifice, *veri nominis*, "properly so-called," that is Christ's death. And that sacrifice but once actually performed at His death, but ever before represented in figure, from the beginning; and ever since repeated in memory to the world's end.... The memory of it is still kept fresh in mind by the commemoration of it in ours.[55]

It would appear, therefore, that Andrewes had a definite opinion of what the church actually meant by the idea of sacrifice as applied to the eucharist; for him, the commemorative sacrifice is a reminder to Christians of Christ's death and work, but it is also a showing forth of that death, a recalling of it before God and man, so that it is operative by its effects upon those who are present at the rite. Secondly, on the question of the "real presence," or the secondary question of the presence of Christ in the sacramental elements as distinct from the primary presence in the eucharistic action, the *Catechism* with its three questions and answers reflects the teaching of Andrewes:

The outward part of the Lord's supper was said to be bread and wine, which the Lord had commanded to be received. In answer to the question: what is the inward part or thing signified? the reply was given—the body and blood of Christ which are verily and indeed, taken and received of the faithful in the Lord's Supper. The benefits whereof we are partakers thereby, were said to be the strengthening and refreshing of

---

55. Lancelot Andrewes, *Sermons*, ed. Library of Anglo-Catholic Theology, vol. 2, p. 300. Hereafter *Sermons*.

our souls by the body and blood of Christ, as our bodies are by the bread and wine.[56]

John Overall (1560–1610), the dean of St. Paul's, who probably penned the first draft of the Catechism in his *Praelectiones seu Disputationes de Patrum et Christi anima et de Antichristo*, wrote:

> In the sacrament of the Eucharist or the Lord's Supper the body and blood of Christ, and therefore the whole Christ, are indeed really present, and are really received by us, and are really united to the sacramental signs, as signs which not only signify but also convey, so that in the right use of the Sacrament, and to those who receive worthily, when the bread is given and received, the body of Christ is given and received; and when the wine is given and received, the blood of Christ is given and received: and, therefore, the Whole Christ is communicated in the communion of the sacrament. Yet this is not in a carnal, gross, earthly way by transubstantiation or consubstantiation or any fictions of human reason, but in a way mystical, heavenly, and spiritual, as is rightly laid down in our Articles.[57]

This statement is typical of the best thought of the high churchmen of the period. It enshrines a deep piety and great reverence for the sacrament, and there is no attempt to define the manner of Christ's presence. Indeed, Andrewes told Robert Bellarmine "we believe no less than you that the presence is real . . . concerning the method of the presence we define nothing rashly and I add, we do not anxiously inquire any more than how the blood of Christ washes us in our baptism; anymore than how the human and divine natures are united in one person in the incarnation of Christ."[58] Nevertheless, Andrewes rejected the doctrine of transubstantiation as unknown to the primitive church and without warrant in scripture. This was, perhaps, the most definite point in the teaching of the high churchmen according to Dugmore and

---

56. C. W. Dugmore, *Eucharistic Doctrine in England from Hooker to Waterland* (London: Macmillan, 1942), p. 39.

57. D. Stone, *A History of the Doctrine of the Holy Eucharist*, vol. 2 (London: Longmans, Green and Co., 1909), p. 264.

58. *Sermons* 2:266.

Stone. Thusfar they were in line with the position adopted by Hooker. Like him, Andrewes insisted that in the eucharist there is a real participation of Christ, a union with him. The sacrament consists of a heavenly and an earthly part: the *res sacramenti* and the *signum sacramenti;* the *signum* and the *signatum,* which are united together without either disappearing or being turned into the other. "Christ in the sacrament is truly present and truly to be adored and yet none of us adore the sacrament."[59] Nevertheless, in accordance with the sentiments he expressed to Bellarmine, Andrewes defined nothing rashly, and least of all the exact nature of Christ's presence in the eucharist. In one place he speaks of it as not only his Godhead, but also his flesh:[60] in another he mentions the Holy Ghost with the reception of the body of Christ,[61] while in a third passage he seems to connect the body of Christ received in the eucharist with the state in which it was on the cross.[62]

Richard Montague (1577–1641), bishop of Norwich, was another who rejected transubstantiation explicitly, but maintained that there was no difference between the Church of England and the Church of Rome on the point of the real presence: the difference according to him was only about the mode or manner. "Change, alteration, transmutation and transelementation are not to be denied, and no man otherwise believeth but that the natural condition of the bread consecrated is otherwise than it was: being disposed and used to that holy use of imparting Christ unto the communicants." Thus he exhorted his Roman Catholic opponents: "Be contented with 'that it is,' and do not seek nor define 'how it is,' and we shall not contest nor contend with you."[63]

James Ussher (1581–1656) is another of those high church theologians whose use of the early Greek and Latin Fathers, and ancient liturgical texts particularly, paved the way for Taylor's sacramental understanding of man and worship. Ussher was among the first students to enter Trinity College, Dublin, in 1594, and in 1625, the year of Charles' succession, he became the Irish primate in Armagh. The Insurrection of 1641 caught him in London, and he was never able to return to his native Ireland. Until his death in 1656 he ministered, like

---

59. Ibid.
60. *Sermons* 1:151.
61. *Sermons* 3:278–79.
62. *Sermons* 2:301–2.
63. Stone 2:275.

Taylor and probably with him, to the private congregations of the Church of England in and around London during the civil war and the later Commonwealth. His sermon before Parliament in St. Margaret's Church, Westminster, in 1620, while he was still a priest, shows the same Caroline understanding of real presence in the eucharistic action, and the high church attempt to explain the elements in the language of the Schoolmen, while avoiding the metaphysical notion of transubstantiation:

> In the Lord's supper the outward thing which we see with our eyes, is bread and wine: the inward thing, which we apprehend by faith is the body and blood of Christ. In the outward part of this mystical action, which reacheth to that which is sacramentum only, we receive this body and blood but sacramentally: in the inward, that containeth *rem*, the thing itself in it, we receive them really. And consequently, the presence of these in the one is relative and symbolical, in the other real and substantial. . . . We acknowledge sacraments to be signs; but bare signs we deny them to be. Seals they are, as well as signs, of the Covenant of Grace . . . even pledges and assurances of the interest which we have in the heavenly things that are represented by them.[64]

He laid great stress on the change effected in the bread and wine by the use to which they are appointed.

> The bread and wine are not changed in substance from being the same with that which is served at ordinary tables. But in respect of the sacred use whereunto they are consecrated, such a change is made that now they differ as much from common bread and wine, as heaven from earth. Neither are they to be accounted barely significative, but truly exhibitive also, of those heavenly things whereto they have relation, as being appointed by God to be a means of conveying the same unto us, and putting us in actual possession thereof. . . . And this is that real and substantial presence, which we affirmed to be in the inward part of this sacred action.[65]

---

64. P. More, and F. Cross, *Anglicanism* (London: S.P.C.K., 1957), p. 488.
65. Ibid. p. 489.

These views on eucharistic worship, called high church, soon spread, as Charles on the throne and Laud in Canterbury gave a new lease of life to the *Acts of Supremacy* and *Uniformity* during the first years of their combined zeal. In his attempt to bring the Church of Scotland into *Uniformity,* Charles outlawed the *Book of Common Order* (1562), an Anglican-Puritan compromise that was not a fixed or absolute formulary, but rather a standard of worship which left much to the minister's discretion. His imposition in its stead of the new Scottish *Book of Common Order* (1637), inspired by the more Catholic *Prayer Book* of 1549 and known as *Laud's Liturgy,* provoked the Scots into open revolt: "The *National Covenant,* a document asserting the religious liberty of the Church, was circulated and signed; and in 1638, at the General Assembly convened in Glasgow Cathedral, the bishops were deposed, Presbyterianism was re-established, the King's *Book of Common Order* repudiated, and the first *Book of Common Order* restored."[66]

On the secondary question of the presence of Christ in the eucharistic elements, Laud rejected transubstantiation, together with consubstantiation, in favor of spiritual reception. Nonetheless, he held that adoration should be done at the sacrament, but not to the sacrament; that the true and real presence of Christ in the Eucharist is to be believed, but that there is no corporal presence in or under the elements.[67] In 1640 he persuaded Convocation to embody this teaching in the canons, drawn up for that year, and recommended that "the communion table be called an altar . . . in that sense in which the primitive Church called it an altar . . . that it be placed in the east end of the chancel and railed in to avoid irreverent behaviour . . . and, furthermore, that everyone should do obeisance both at their coming in and going out."[68] These canons, like Charles's *Book of Common Order,* overshot the national inclination, and their formation was among the charges that led to his impeachment and execution.

Supremacy and *Uniformity* did not die with Charles and Laud. On 12 June 1643 Parliament set up a commission of "godly and learned divines," the *Westminster Assembly,* to report on (1) a confession of

---

66. W. D. Maxwell, *An Outline of Christian Worship* (London: Humphrey Milford, 1936), p. 128.

67. D. Stone, *A History of the Doctrine of the Holy Eucharist,* vol. 2 (London: Longmans, Green, and Co., 1909), pp. 267ff.

68. H. R. Trevor-Roper, *Archbishop Laud* (London: Macmillan and Co, 1940), p. 45.

faith, (2) a form of ecclesiastical government to replace the abolished hierarchy, and (3) a suitable form of worship to replace the forbidden *Book of Common Prayer*. Thus, there was published on 3 January 1645 (1) *the Westminster Confession of Faith*, (2) the *Form of Presbyterian Government*, and (3) the *Westminster Directory for Public Worship*, commonly called the *Directory*. This *Directory*, which contains no specific or set forms of prayers, and which simply gives precise directions concerning the order and content of every service, launched Protestantism on its Puritan way: "Prior to 1645, the Reformed Churches were no less liturgical than the Lutheran or Anglican; they came into the world with fully defined and completely expressed *Orders of Worship*, but this was all changed by their acceptance of the *Westminster Directory*."[69] The chaotic situation that followed and in which, broadly speaking, "every man did that which was right in his own eyes," began two centuries of liturgical decadence, especially in Scotland, where the *Directory* remained in liturgical control:

> Towards the close of the 18th century the public services of the Church of Scotland had become probably the baldest and rudest in Christendom. The parish kirks, owing to the niggardliness of the heritors, were comfortless and coarsely furnished. The music was rough and untrained; only in a few of the town churches was it rendered with any attempt at taste or skill. The Bible was scarcely read. The prayers were reduced in number to two at the most, and were drearily long and uninteresting. The Lord's Prayer (and Creed) were never heard. The sermon was the great feature of the service; and it was too often a "screed of dull doctrine or of cold morality."[70]

In 1646, Jeremy Taylor published a short booklet that was both an attack on this *Directory* and a defense of the *Book of Common Prayer;* in 1649 he reissued this *Discourse on Prayer Ex-tempore*, considerably expanded, and under a new title, *An Apology for Authorized and Set-Forms of Liturgy*, in which he defends, at great and tedious length, from history and reason, scripture and theology, the age-old Catholic tradi-

---

69. J. Barkley, *The Worship of the Reformed Church* (Richmond, VA: John Knox Press, 1967), p. 37.
70. J. Story, *Reformed Rituals in Scotland* (Edinburgh: Oliver and Boyd, 1890), p. 36.

47

INTRODUCTION

tion of organized and formal prayer. He also critically analyzes, at equal length and in the same tedious manner, the Puritan innovations of spontaneity or *extempore* prayer. Something of his high church observance and of Puritan practice can be gathered, perhaps, from the following concatenation of quotations, culled from this laborious and repetitious *Apology* and its *Preface*:

On Puritan Innovation

—To innovate in so high a matter, without a warrant to command us, or a promise to warrant us, is no better than vanity in the thing, and presumption in the person. . . . Indeed, in so grave a matter . . . an unlearned man is not to be trusted; and a wise man dare not trust himself: he that is ignorant cannot; he that is knowing will not.

—This way of prayer is without all manner of precedent in the primitive Church; against the example of all famous Churches in all Christendom in the whole descent of fifteen ages; without all command or warrant of Scripture. . . . It is unreasonable in the nature of the thing, against prudence and the best wisdom of humanity because it is without deliberation. . . . It is innovation in a high degree, without that authority which is truly, and by inherent and ancient right, to command and prescribe to us in external forms of worship.

—A form of prayer made by a private man is also my religion made by a private man.

—Whenever a schism or heresy was commenced, the participants not only forsook to pray with one another, but they also altered their forms of prayer by interposition of new clauses, hymns, collects and new rites and ceremonies.

—To pretend the Spirit in so unreasonable a manner, to so ill purposes, and without reason or promise or probability for doing it, is a very great crime and of dangerous consequence . . . for it dishonours the Holy Ghost to make Him the President of imperfect and illiterate rites, the author of confusion, and indeliberate discourses, and the parent of such productions which a wise person would blush to own; it also entitles him to all those doctrines which either chance or design shall expose to the people in such prayers to which they entitle the Holy Spirit as the author and immediate dictator. So that if they please he must not only own their follies, but their impieties too; and how great disreputation this is to the Spirit of Wisdom, of Counsel, and of holiness I wish they may understand by discourse rather than by experiment:

On Catholic Tradition

—The wisest nations and the most sober persons prepared their verses and prayers in set-forms with as much religion as they dressed their sacrifices and observed the rites of festivals and burials. . . . Among the Romans it belonged to the care of the priests to worship in prescribed and determined words. . . . The Greeks did so too . . . their hymns and prayers were ordained peculiar to every god and were usually pronounced, word for word, after the priest and out of written copies. . . . Likewise, the Persians sang hymns to their gods in a premeditated, solemn and metrical form of prayer, and, according to Seneca, "nihil enim ordinatum est quod praecipitatum et properat."

—Unless the work of the Lord is done well enough, when it is done negligently, or that the sanctuary hath the greatest beauty when it hath the least order, it will concern us highly to think our prayers and religious offices as actions fit only for wise men, and, therefore, to be done as the actions of wise men, i.e. deliberately, prudently and with greatest consideration.

—Labour and hard study and premeditation will soonest purchase the gift of prayer and ascertain us of the assistance of the Spirit . . . therefore, set-forms of prayer, studied and considered, are in a true and proper sense, and without enthusiasm, the fruits of the Spirit.

—Whatsoever this spirit of prayer is, it is to be acquired by human industry, by learning of the Scriptures, by reading, by conference and by whatsoever else faculties are improved and habits enlarged. God's Spirit hath done this work sufficiently this way and He loved not either in nature or grace . . . to multiply miracles where there is no need.

—Thus, St. Paul says, "let a man so account of us, as of the Ministers of Christ and stewards of the mysteries of God." Now the greatest ministry of the Gospel is by way of prayer; therefore, since the Holy Ghost hath made the rulers of the Church "stewards of the mysteries" they are, then, by virtue of their stewardship, presidents of prayer and public offices.

—St. Hilary and St. Ambrose composed hymns for the use of the Church and St. Augustine made a hymn against the schism of the Donatists; which hymns, when they were publicly allowed, were used in public offices, but not until then; for Paulus Samosatenus had brought women into Church to sing vain and trifling songs and also some bishops took to themselves too great and incurious a license and brought hymns into the Church whose gravity and piety was not very remarkable, upon occasion of which, the fathers of the Council of Laodicea ordained *HOTI OU DEI IDIOTIKOUS PSALMOS LEGESTHAI EN EKKLESIA*: Gentiam Harvet renders it "private compositions" and Isidore translates it "psalmos ab idiotis compositos" whereas Dionysius Exiguus calls them "psalmos pleblios."[71]

This *Preface* to the *Apology* also contains Taylor's liturgical and historical defense of the *Book of Common Prayer*, "in that second form and modest beauty it was in the edition of MDLII, and which Gilbertus, a German, approved of as a transcript of the ancient and primitive forms."[72] Cranmer "in his purgation, A.D. 1553, made an offer . . . to prove all that is contained in the Book of Common Prayer to be conformable to that order which Our Blessed Saviour, Christ, did both observe and command to be observed."[73] But Cranmer was contending with the Roman Catholics of the Marian restoration that the *Prayer Book of 1552* was not only scriptural but also "is the same that was used in the Church's fifteen hundred years past."[74] Taylor, on the other hand, and nearly a hundred years later, was defending the same book against those who rejected those fifteen hundred years of liturgical tradition, and sought to restore what they thought to be the pure wor-

---

71. *Works* 5:231ff.
72. T. K. Carroll, *The Caroline Liturgical Renewal—A Puritan Controversy*, (Rome: Anselmianum, 1973), pp. 143–75.
73. Ibid. p. 154.
74. Ibid.

ship of the Bible in accordance with their simplistic understanding of scripture as the sole rule of faith and practice: "Another new light is sprung up, according to which the Church should have no liturgy at all; but the worship of God be left to the managing of chance, and indeliberation, and a petulant fancy."[75] Consequently, there is a deliberate fundamentalism in Taylor's approach as he shows the different elements of liturgical tradition retained in the *Prayer Book;* namely, (1) the psalms, lessons and hymns, (2) the prayer for Christ's Catholic Church, (3) the custom of reading St. Paul's epistle and the holy gospel before the sacrament, (4) the litanies and collects, (5) the practice of celebrating not only the liturgical seasons of Christmas, Annunciation, Easter and Ascension, but also the life and death of the saints, and (6) forms of benediction and absolution—to be nothing other than the fulfillment of the scriptural command. Nevertheless, a spirit of liturgical tradition prevails throughout this scriptural defence of the *Prayer Book* and is frequently invoked; for example, he contrasts the form of the general absolution at the beginning of the morning and evening prayer, "which is declarative and by way of proposition," with the communion form, "which is optative and by way of intercession," and, furthermore, he adds that "in the visitation of the sick ... the Church prescribes a medicinal form by way of delegate authority, that the parts of justification may answer to the parts of good life." But, in his conclusion, Taylor reaches beyond the letters of this ritualistic discussion and reveals the spirit of his sacramental vision:

> The Church of England, in these manners of dispensing the power of the keys, does cut off all disputings and impertinent wranglings, whether the priest's power were judicial or declarative; for possibly it is both, and it is optative too; and something else yet, for it is an emanation from all the parts of his ministry, and he never absolves, but he preaches or prays, or administers a sacrament; for this power of remission is a transcendent, passing through all the parts of the priestly offices; for the keys of the kingdom of heaven are the promises and the threatenings of the scripture, and the prayers of the Church, and the word, and the sacraments, and all these are to be dispensed by the priest, and these keys are committed to his

---

75. Ibid.

ministry,—and by the operation of them all, he opens and shuts heaven's gates ministerially, and, therefore, St. Paul calls it "verbum reconciliationis," and says it is dispensed by ministers, as by "ambassadors" or delegates; and, therefore, it is an excellent temper of the Church, so to prescribe her forms of absolution, as to show them to be results of the whole priestly office, of preaching, of dispensing sacraments, of spiritual cure, and authoritative deprecation.[76]

Roman Catholic theologians like Santa Clara, Taylor's contemporary and friend from his Cambridge days, had been renewed in the metaphysics of the Schoolmen by the Council of Trent (1547–63) and, as a result, were as critical of Anglican sacramental theology as they were of the Continental Reformers and the Commonwealth Puritans. In those circumstances Taylor's sporadic comments on Roman pre-Tridentine attitudes to the *Prayer-Book* are of interest from both perspectives, liturgical and historical:

—They were so convinced by the piety and innocence of the *Common Prayer-Book* that they could accuse it of no deformity . . . and, therefore, for ten or eleven years they came to our Churches, joined in our devotions, and communicated without scruple, till a temporal interest of the Church of Rome rent the schism wider, and made it gape like the jaws of the grave.

—It is transmitted to us by the testimony of persons greater than all exceptions that Paulus Quartus, in his private intercourses and letters to Queen Elizabeth, did offer to confirm the English common prayer-book, if she would acknowledge his primacy and authority, and the reformation derivative from him.

—This lenity was pursued by his successor, Pius Quartus, with an "omnia de nobis tibi polliceare"; he assured her she should have any thing from him, not only things pertaining to her soul, but what might conduce to the establishment and confirmation of her royal dignity; amongst which, that the liturgy, new established by her

---

76. Ibid. pp. 135–42; also *Works* 5:249ff.

authority, should not be rescinded by the Pope's power, was not the least considerable.[77]

As a theologian Taylor was involved in the dominant controversies of his time: (1) the divine institution, apostolic tradition and catholic practice of the hierarchy in *Episcopacy Asserted,* and the ordained ministry in *Clerus Domini,* for the supremacy of the "godly prince" did not in Taylor's opinion diminish the office of the bishop; (2) original sin in *Unum Nessarium,* and *Deus Justificatus;* and (3) religious toleration in the *Liberty of Prophesying.* As a priest he was more intimately and personally involved in (1) the spiritual direction and care of souls in the *Great Exemplar, Holy Living* and *Holy Dying;* (2) the sacramental life of the church in the *Worthy Communicant* and the *Real Presence;* and (3) the prayer life of the church in manuals like a *Collection of Offices,* and the *Psalter of David,* which he prepared for the use of the persecuted church when the *Book of Common Prayer* was proscribed. Thus, Taylor continued in controversy and in ministry to debate and to celebrate *Supremacy* and *Uniformity* in church order and worship.

As a priest, Taylor's world was essentially, and above all else, sacramental; that of the Carolines was no less so, for they too felt intuitively the revelation or presence of God's Christ in the words and symbols of the Church's worship, but their theology was scholastic, and consequently, transubstantiation became their major problem in their non-metaphysical age and place. As a theologian, Taylor was different; in fact he was the first of those high churchmen to get behind the Middle Ages, so to speak, and to discover that patristic theology which first gave new content and significance to the concepts and language of the ancients. Consequently, ancient words like *mystery, sacrament, figure, symbol, similitude, type, representation,* came to new life in his seventeenth-century English, as they did previously in early Christian Greek and in later Christian Latin, for Jeremy Taylor was the father of this renewed way of knowing and mode of expression. Word and world were at one in Taylor, as if his text incarnated a real presence of significant being:

> This real presence, as in an icon, as in the enacted metaphor of
> the sacramental bread and wine, is, finally, irreducible to any

---

77. Carroll, pp. 143–75; also *Works* 5:236ff.

formal articulation, to any analytic deconstruction or paraphrase. It is a singularity in which concept and form constitute
a tautology, coincide point to point, energy to energy, in that
excess of significance over all discrete elements and codes of
meaning which we call the symbol or the agency of trans-
parence.[78]

Taylor's sacramental mode of seeing and saying, or *sacramental
representation,* as he frequently and everywhere calls it, transformed
theologically and liturgically, first, what he saw and said of Christ and
his church, and second, what he saw and said of man and his world. The
former he did for the most part as a theologian and priest; the latter,
again for the most part, as a poet and preacher, as we shall see in the next
section. But just as seeing and saying, from the philosophic perspective
are rooted and grounded in being, so too Taylor's sacramental mode,
from the theological perspective, is no less rooted and grounded in the
new being of the risen Christ and the rising church: "For the meaning
of these mysterious and sacramental expressions, when reduced to easy
and intelligible signification is plainly this; by Christ we live and move
and have our spiritual being in the life of grace and in the hopes
of glory."[79]

In this vision of reality, heaven is wedded to earth, and the life of
the one is made present in the other, as the earthly sacraments of the
church represent the heavenly sacrifice of Christ. On the other hand,
Renaissance theologians, especially those at Trent, who distinguished
between decrees on the *Most Holy Sacrifice of the Mass* and on the *Most
Holy Sacrament of the Eucharist,* fragmented the unity of the ancient
rite, which became as a result either a Protestant commemoration of a
past act or a Catholic repetition or re-enactment without any eschatological expression. Church architecture still tells this story: in the
Roman basilicas great baldacchinos were erected over altars of divine
presence and obstructed medieval apses of expectation and hope, which
were eventually replaced by Renaissance domes, while bare tables appeared in more Protestant places to remind believers of the ancient and
Holy Supper that was. In each tradition the rite was grounded or earth-
bound, and became a commemoration, however differently explained,

---

78. Steiner, p. 19.
79. Carroll p. 231; also *Works* 8:111.

of a redemption that was wholly in the past. In those circumstances Taylor's eucharistic theology opened up from the patristic past a new or renewed way of understanding the Mystery that is ever ancient and ever new. By celebrating the sacrifice of Christ within the sacramental framework he restored to the eucharistic rite the commemorative, demonstrative and prophetic dimensions of the sign, which the ancients felt as a unity in which the past and the future were equally present, but which Taylor's contemporaries and Reforming predecessors, both Catholic and Protestant, had fragmented in time and space:

> Here the Lord appears to us in a feast, which is a time of innocent delight. The glory of God is set forth unto us in that which our senses apprehend for sweetness and pleasure, as I appoint unto you a Kingdom—that you may eat and drink at my table, which is translated from bodily pleasure to spiritual, that in the heaven of blessedness the soul shall feed continually as at a banquet, of which we have now a taste in the kingly provision of Christ's supper. It is a Kingly feast, although imparted in a little pittance of bread and wine; yet it is more costly and precious, in that which it signifies, than Solomon and all his court had for their diet day by day. We are brought to eat at the King's table as Mephibosheth was, like one of the King's sons. For he that broke bread and gave it to the apostles, gives it to us as our High Priest, though he be in heaven. Wherefore the spirit saith write: blessed are they that are called to the marriage-supper of the Lord.[80]

Taylor's fullest treatment of the eucharistic sacrifice is found in the *Worthy Communicant* and is based on the *Epistle to the Hebrews*, "as understood by the ancient and holy doctors of the Church, including St. Ambrose, St. Chrysostom, St. Austin and St. Basil."[81] He argues that Christ has commanded us to do on earth what he does in heaven: "to represent his death, to commemorate the sacrifice, by humble prayer and thankful record; and by faithful manifestations and joyful eucharist, to lay it before the eyes of our heavenly Father, so ministering to his priesthood, and doing according to his commandment and example."[82]

---

80. Carroll, p. 282; also *Works* 8:12ff.
81. Carroll, p. 254.
82. Carroll, p. 255; also *Works* 8:38.

Here, Taylor is expressing the distinction made by Gregory Nazianzen between the external and internal sacrifice: "The earthly ministry being a copy, imitation, or representation of the celestial, real, and archetypal offering perpetually presented at the celestial altar."[83] Thus, in the external ministry "the earthly ministers in that unchangeable priesthood imitate the prototype Melchisedech who brought forth bread and wine, and was the priest of the most high God,"[84] while in the internal ministry they imitate "the antitype or substance, Christ himself, who offered up his body and blood for the atonment of us."[85] In this conception reality and symbol are ontologically one: "The sacrifice of the lamb slain from the beginning of the world is always the same; it bleeds no more after the finishing of it on the cross; but it is wonderfully represented in heaven, and graciously represented here: by Christ's action there, by his commandment here."[86] Indeed, this vision gives new significance and content to everyone and everything that is touched by this invisible presence or divine mystery, for "the Church where the eucharist is celebrated becomes the image of heaven, the priest a minister of Christ, and the holy table a copy of the celestial altar."[87]

In *Clerus Domini* Taylor uses St. Cyprian as his source and sets forth the heavenly and eternal priesthood, the sacrifice and intercessions of Christ, who in the heavenly Jerusalem perpetually presents the sacrifice finished on the cross. Thus, the eucharistic action for Taylor was not just an imitation of what Jesus did at the Last Supper, but rather a representation of Christ's celestial priesthood and intercession; we do sacramentally and humbly on earth what Christ performs in heaven in a high and glorious manner. Indeed, in *Holy Living* he develops further this notion of intercession, for every age on account of its sinfulness needs to be in touch with the one redeeming sacrifice of Christ:

> This sacrifice, because it was perfect, could be but one, and
> that once; but because the needs of the world should last as
> long as the world itself, it was necessary that there should be a
> perpetual ministry established, whereby this one sufficient

---

83. Carroll, p. 255.
84. Ibid.
85. Ibid.
86. Ibid.
87. Ibid.

sacrifice should be made eternally effectual to the several new arising needs of all the world who should desire it, or in any sense be capable of it.[88]

But it is to his *Order for the Holy Sacrament of the Lord's Supper*, contained in the *Collection of Offices* (1558), that one must turn to feel and understand the eucharistic theology of Jeremy Taylor. "Collected out of the devotions of the Greek Church with some mixture of the Mozarabick and Aethiopick and other liturgies and perfected out of the fountains of Scripture . . . it is offered as a substitute for the *Book of Common Prayer*, that was forbidden by law and instead of the straw and stubble which was being weakly raked together in the *Directory* by the Puritans to dress their sacrifices." Here, he reveals not only his wide knowledge of the ancient liturgies but also his thoughts concerning the nature of the eucharistic sacrifice. With this treatise, we pass from his consideration of forms of worship to the real nature of the eucharistic sacrifice, which is the summit and apex of all liturgical life: thus, Taylor, according to the ancient law of liturgy, *lex credendi statuat legem orandi*, prays what he believes and believes what he prays:

> O Heavenly Father, according to thy glorious mercies and promises, send thy Holy Spirit upon our hearts, and let Him also descend upon these gifts, that by his good, his holy, his glorious presence, He may sanctify and enlighten our hearts, and he may bless and sanctify these gifts. That this bread may become the Holy Body of Christ. Amen. And this chalice may become the life-giving Blood of Christ. Amen. That it may become unto us all that partake of it this day, a blessed instrument of union with Christ, of pardon and peace, of health and blessing, of holiness and life eternal, through Jesus Christ, our Lord. Amen.[89]

Taylor continually dwells upon the mystical union between Christ as head and the church as his body in the eucharistic action. The members of Christ's body present themselves to God with Christ,

---

88. T. K. Carroll, *The Sacramental Theology of Jeremy Taylor*, (Rome: Angelicum, 1970), p. 81: the second chapter considers *The Heavenly Banquet and its Liturgical Expression*.
89. Ibid. p. xv; also *Works* 8:624.

whom they have spiritually received. "The offering of their bodies, and souls, and services to God in Him, and by Him, and with Him, who is the father's well-beloved, and in whom he is well pleased, cannot but be accepted to all purposes of blessing, grace and glory."[90] This is an admirable commentary on the prayer of oblation after the communion of the people in the Anglican communion rite, as well as a clear exposition of the Augustinian view of the eucharist as the church's self-offering to God through Christ, the Head. In his *Communion Office* of 1658 Taylor places a prayer of self-offering after the communion of the people, where he also places the *Lord's Prayer* and a *Prayer for the Catholic Church*, for he held that the communicants being joined sacramentally to Christ, the High Priest, are admitted to intercede for others, joining their prayers to his intercession: "Having received Christ's body within us, we are sure to be accepted, and all the good prayers we make to God for ourselves and others are sure to be heard."[91] This is Taylor's understanding or theology of prayer. Liturgical prayer is for him man's participation in the prayer of Christ: "What is done on altars upon solemn days, is done in our closets in our daily offices; that is, God is invoked, and God is appeased, and God is reconciled, and God gives us blessings and the fruits of Christ's passion in the virtue of the sacrificed Lamb."[92]

The problem of *Supremacy* was to a certain degree solved by the restoration of the king and the hierarchy in 1660. But the problem of *Uniformity* was more complicated theologically, and continued after the restoration of the *Prayer-Book* in 1662, in spite of its modifications, to plague the churches as they grew more separate. Eventually the eucharist became the sign of these divisions. However, early in our ecumenical century, Anglicans like F.C.N. Hicks, in his book *Fullness of Sacrifice* (1930), and Roman Catholic theologians like Odo Casel, the Benedictine monk of Maria Laach in Germany, with his theory of the *Mysteriengegenwart* (1926) or *Mystery-presence*, began to see again as the ancients saw and to speak their sacramental language. Franz Hildebrandt in *I Offered Christ* notes in passing that "Jeremy Taylor was the first in Anglicanism to make use of this notion which has gained in prominence in our own century with Dom Odo Casel—representare,

---

90. Carroll, *The Sacramental Theology of Jeremy Taylor*, p. xv; also *Works* 8:37.
91. Carroll, *The Sacramental Theology of Jeremy Taylor*, p. xv.
92. Ibid.

in gegenwartig setzen."[93] But, lest representation be mistaken for repetition, Casel was careful to call it sacramental and not historical, and to distinguish between two realities—a historical reality and a mystic or sacramental reality. The means of this representation, according to Casel, is the action of the church's ritual, and this is the notion Taylor seems to have had in mind some three hundred years earlier when he spoke of sacramental representation through words and actions. Thus Roman and Anglican theologians of today's dialogue could certainly turn with profit to Taylor for his patristic understanding of sacramental reality, or that order of being in which Christ's redeeming act is permanently renewed and partaken of by the church. His order of language is no less sacramental or wanting in being, for in him there is no separation of word and world, especially when the word is that of God and the world is that of the church; then old words come to new life and signify new things and old, like the *new wine* in the *old skins*.

POET AND PREACHER

Few, if any, of Taylor's contemporaries, Anglican and Catholic, or his sixteenth-century predecessors, Roman or Reformed, had his sacramental grasp of patristic reality—the fullness of its *totus Christus* vision and the clarity of its poetic language. This unseen world of the early Christian Fathers, like the more ancient world it enlightened or baptized, remained one of mystery and presences that are still real for those who have eyes to see and ears to hear:

> These are not occult notions. They are of the immensity of the commonplace. They are perfectly pragmatic, experiential, repetitive, each and every time a melody comes to inhabit us, to possess us even unbidden, each and every time a poem, a passage of prose seizes upon our thought and feelings, enters into the sinews of our remembrance and sense of the future, each and every time a painting transmutes the landscapes of our previous perceptions (poplars are on fire after Van Gogh, viaducts walk after Klee). To be "indwellt" by music, art, literature, to be made responsible, answerable to such habita-

---

93. F. Hildebrandt, *I Offered Christ* (Philadelphia: Fortress Press, 1967), p. 73.

tion as a host is to a guest—perhaps unknown, unexpected—
at evening, is to experience the commonplace mystery of a
real presence. Not many of us feel compelled to, have the
expressive means to, register the mastering quality of this
experience—as does Proust when he crystallizes the sense of
the world and of the word in the little yellow spot which is the
real presence of a riverside door in Vermeer's View of Delft,
or as does Thomas Mann when he enacts in word and metaphor the coming over us, the "overcoming of us," in Beetho-
ven's Opus III. No matter. The experience itself is one we are
thoroughly at home with—an informing idiom—each and
every time we live a text, a sonata, a painting.[94]

Taylor had such an experience . . . of Christian faith . . . each and
every time he lived a patristic text, and his texts too, reveal God's
Christ, the light without end of the patristic world and his own.

Seventeenth-century England, for all its upheavals, political, religious, philosophical, remained sensitive to the world of divine mystery
and real presences in words and symbols. Bacon's plea for science was
made in an age that was still dominated by religion, while people like Sir
Thomas Browne, at least in the *Religio Medici,* kept pleading for religion, as science was taking over:

Many different worlds or countries of the mind then lay close
together—the world of scholastic learning, the world of scientific experiment, the worlds of classical mythology and of
biblical history, of fable and of fact, of theology and demon-
ology, of sacred and profane love, of pagan and Christian
morals, of activity and contemplation; and a cultivated man
had the freedom of them all.[95]

In the time of John Donne a thought was an experience: "It modi-
fied," as T. S. Eliot said, "his sensibility";[96] but in the new age of
science, philosophy distinguished between metaphor and fact, fancy and
judgment, and soon the division arose between poetry and science and,

---

94. Steiner, p. 19.
95. B. Willey, *The Seventeenth Century Background,* (London: Chatto and Windas, 1934,
re-issued 1979), p. 45.
96. Ibid. p. 47.

ultimately, between religion and life. "All that is real is material," said Hobbes, the philosopher of the new universe, "and what is not material is not real."[97] Already, Descartes' search for clear and distinct ideas had reduced God and the soul, his first certainties, to intellectual abstractions—"God" having no kinship to the God of genuine religious experience, and "I" being merely the thinking part of man. In this world of mathematical certitudes, like that of Bacon and Hobbes, there was no place either for religion or poetry, and by the end of the century, religion had sunk to deism and poetry to embellishment, and neither had any contact with reality. Consequently, in this most biblical of centuries the scriptures were soon seen as an obstacle to truth, because "they were written for the most idiotical sort of men in the most idiotical way," and poetry was no less so, as it catered for delight and the pleasures of the fancy.[98]

Descartes' insistence upon sound and plain reason, or clear and distinct ideas, and in general the mathematical lucidity of his spirit and writings, was decisive in effecting that break with the past which started the modern world on its way. His thought, like all thought that is purely rational and intellectual, was fundamentally unhistorical; consequently, he had little reverence or respect for antiquity as he set out "to arrive at a knowledge highly useful in life . . . knowing the force and action of fire, water, air, the stars, the heavens, and all other bodies that surround us, as distinctly as we know the wages of our artisans: thus we render ourselves the Lords and possessors of nature.[99] This material world did not prevent Descartes, as it did Hobbes, from reasserting the world of the spirit. But he maintained the distinctive sphere of each, for in his clear and distinct idea of things, neither one could enter or penetrate the other: consequently, the rise in seventeenth-century philosophy of that Cartesian dualism that has divided and disturbed all subsequent generations.

There is little space for the human spirit in a world that distinguishes so clearly between a man's feelings and his thoughts; in the words of Eliot, this "dissociation of sensibility" deprives man of the ability to see beyond and leaves poet and preacher equally speechless.[100] To bridge this Cartesian gap, or to combat on the one hand traditional

---

97. Ibid. p. 89.
98. Ibid. p. 84, quoting John Smith, the Cambridge Platonist.
99. Ibid. p. 86.
100. Ibid. p. 83.

church dogma and, on the other hand, the new materialism of Hobbes, there arose at this time a group of men, saintly and scholarly, at Emmanuel College, whom history calls the Cambridge Platonists. Neoplatonism seemed to them the answer now as it was before:

> Here was a system, essentially religious in spirit, which taught the sole reality of the spiritual world and the immortality of the soul, which pictured life as the soul's striving for heaven and prescribed a regimen for its upward ascent: a system too which was not only venerated on its own account by the cultured, but which in its long and intimate association with Christianity had flowed into its stream and become part of it.[101]

In this light, poet and preacher could *see* once more, and words, lifeless through scientific use and creedal abuse, could be spoken again with real meaning; so people like John Smith hailed the intellect of man as "the candle of the Lord" . . . "the brighter eye of our understanding" . . . "the other eye of the soul,"[102] while Ralph Cudworth and others saw God in man, and maintained man's divinity.[103] These philosophers were deeply religious men; by emphasizing the light of faith they hoped to transcend the clouds of creedal difference, and by recognizing the light of reason to bring word and world together again.

Taylor was well-acquainted with these men, who numbered in their company Henry More, their most distinguished member and certainly Taylor's intellectual companion for many a year. More opposed the separation of spirit and matter, and emphasized the continuity in nature and man, and man and God: "Indeed the highest truth can only be grasped by the divine in man";[104] yet there is no scholarly evidence to indicate in any way the direct influence of More, the philosopher, on Taylor, the theologian. Taylor's theology came from his biblical faith, which the early Fathers of the church, Latin as much as Greek, proclaimed and celebrated in their sacramental way; the philosophical disquisitions of the Cambridge Platonists, however mystical their vision and poetic their language, were not his immediate sources. He was a

---

101. Ibid. p. 124.
102. Ibid. pp. 127–40.
103. Ibid. pp. 140–46.
104. Ibid. pp. 146–54.

man of antiquity and revelation, of Bible and ritual, divine word and natural symbol, intrinsically intertwined and interwoven, to reveal and to present in every age the eternal mystery of history, *Jesus Christ the same yesterday, and today and for ever* (Heb 13:8), reflected in nature, announced in Israel, made flesh in Jesus, and present in the ritual of the church: "There is scarce anything ... that can with confidence of argument pretend to derive from the apostles, except rituals and manners of ministration."[105] This daily celebration in ritual of biblical revelation gives to all time its eternal significance, and to man a vision of faith that takes him, in every age, beyond time, so to speak, as the scriptures take us beyond history into our origin and fall in the *Eden* of *Genesis* (2:8, 3:6), and into our eschaton and restoration in the *new heaven* and *new earth* of Revelation (21:1).

Taylor's understanding of man and his fall is totally biblical, however controversial his interpretation. Ironically, his passion for piety and his desire to perfect man in holiness led him in *Unum Necessarium*, the sixth chapter, to emphasize man's moral responsibilities and capabilities, which friend and foe alike denounced as pelagian in tone and inspiration. Consequently, he was forced into controversy and compelled to publish *A Further Explication of the Doctrine of Original Sin*, which was included as the seventh chapter in subsequent editions of *Unum Necessarium*. But *Unum Necessarium*, or his call to repentance, was primarily the work of a preacher and not a theologian; theories about the origin of sin were not the preacher's concern, but by stressing man's practical experience of sin in the world Taylor obscured, perhaps, the traditional notion of heredity, or Calvin's more contemporary one of depravity. However, once the controversy began, Taylor continued, and in further treatment of the subject in *Deus Justificatus* he appealed for support to the Greek Fathers of tradition, and to the Scotists and Arminians of his own times, who held a less gloomy picture of humanity. Thus, a body of controversial literature crept into being that the preacher began and the theologian developed, taking the broader view wherever there was liberty of choice.

The political and religious circumstances of the times kept Taylor, the preacher, involved in constant controversy, and his *Liberty of Prophesying* was published when belligerent loyalty to a sect was considered a virtue. Indeed, this stirring plea for freedom of conscience and for the

---

105. Gest, p. 13, quoting Taylor, *Works* 8:237.

right of every man to interpret the scriptures was made in the England of 1647, when religious belief was considered a law and not an opinion. Taylor's well-reasoned study of tolerance had been somewhat anticipated by Erasmus on the Continent, who favored a few basic simple beliefs, and the right of broad dissent, while Grotius in Holland wanted peace at all cost without either discussion or dissent. At home, Hooker thought the church could be "tolerantly comprehensive," but John Hall and William Chillingworth saw no place for any sect in a church of plain and honest Christians: "Take away these walls of separation and all will quickly be one . . . this damning of men for not subscribing to the words of men as the words of God."[106] The more radical Taylor, however, promoted the liberty of disagreement among all sects including Papists, Anabaptists and Sacramentaries:

> For if it be evinced that one heaven shall hold men of several opinions, if the unity of faith be not destroyed by that which men call differing religions, and if an unity of charity be the duty of us all . . . then I would fain know to what purpose are all those stirs and great noises in Christendom.[107]

These controversial works of Taylor, known as his wartime controversies, were casually dismissed as thoughtless period pieces by the literati of the last century, who rediscovered "literary gems" in his *Sermons* and *Devotions* and confined themselves accordingly: "His polemical works you may skip altogether, unless you have a taste for the exertions of vigorous reason and subtle distinguishing on interesting topics."[108] Matthew Arnold continued this attitude of Charles Lamb to Taylor's controversial prose, and, like Newman, who described a certain type of English prose as having "the note of sanctity," or "the note of antiquity," concluded that Taylor, like Edmund Burke, had "the note of provinciality."[109] However, a recent study on the mind and temper of Taylor in controversy sees him in another light and presents him as the great master of this rhetorical art:

---

106. Ibid. p. 12, quoting from Chillingworth's, *The Religion of Protestants* (1742), p. 204.

107. Ibid. p. 13, quoting Taylor.

108. F. L. Huntley, *Jeremy Taylor and the Great Rebellion* (University of Michigan Press, 1970), p. 11, quoting Charles Lamb.

109. Ibid. p. 1.

INTRODUCTION

My purpose is not to dispute, but to persuade, not to confront anyone but to instruct those that need: not to make a noise, but to excite devotion . . . and to gather together into a union all those several portions of truth, and differing apprehensions of mysteriousness . . . and seemingly opposed doctrines, by which even good men stand at a distance, and are afraid of each other.[110]

On the other hand, in *The Minister's Duty* he warns the preacher of its dangers:

A controversy is a stone in the mouth of the hearer, who should be fed with bread, and it is a temptation to the preacher, it is a state of temptation; it engages one side in lying, and both in uncertainty and uncharitableness; and after all, it is not food for souls; it is the food of contention, it is a spiritual law-suit, and it can never be ended; every man is right and every man is wrong in these things and no man can tell who is right and who is wrong. For as long as a word can be spoken against a word, and a thing be opposite to a thing; as long as places are hard, and men are ignorant or "knowing in part"; as long as there is money and pride in the world, and for ever till men willingly confess themselves to be fools and deceived, so long will the saw of contention be drawn from side to side.[111]

The sermons and devotional writings of Jeremy Taylor have been criticized for their lack of substance by Coleridge, who referred to him as "a Ghost in marble," and by those other Romantics like Lamb, Hazlitt and De Quincey, who at the same time venerated him as a stylist along with Shakespeare, Bacon and Milton.[112] The quotable censure of Coleridge was believed and has been repeated down the years as uncritically as his most extravagant praise. In our own time, Logan Pearsall Smith has continued this fullsome veneration of style and uncritical condemnation of content that the Romantics began:

---

110. Ibid. p. 6, quoting *Works* 8:9.
111. Ibid. p. 6, quoting *Works* 8:531.
112. L. P. Smith, *The Golden Grove* (Oxford: Clarendon Press, 1930), p. xxvii.

His most fervent admirers have to admit that his mental powers were somewhat limited and commonplace, and that he failed in handling the larger questions of religious thought and had no ideas. . . . Nevertheless we still read and still should read his tremulous pages for the beauty of the world which hung upon his pen, a world full of sun and the shimmer of water, a world delicately tinted, fleeting, evanescent, and yet fixed and made imperishable by the incantation of his words . . . now and then as we read him an imagination, radiant and strange . . . seems to dip his pen in enchanted ink: the words begin to dance and glitter, and a splendour falls upon the illuminated page, and when this happens the effect is so surprising that it seems the result of a spell, an incantation, a kind of magic.[113]

Margaret Gest was the first to explode Smith's acceptance of Coleridge's "Ghost in marble" reference, and in her selections from Taylor's writings entitled *The House of Understanding* showed him to be "a great thinker, brilliant in his exposition of tolerance, in his psychological insight, in his keen understanding of the good and evil forces in society,—a prophet in a period of civil war and bigotry who urged search for truth, for sane living, for tolerance, for God."[114]

The most devastating criticism of Taylor from the perspective of this volume was made by Louis Bouyer, the eminent French scholar in his *History of Christian Spirituality:*

Taylor's pastoral intentions cannot be doubted, however, though his talent as poet and writer went far beyond the substance of his wisdom, which was, when all is said and done, fairly limited: a wisdom drawn from all the ancient sources, but to which the bible and experience brought the richest contribution. For all that, he was characteristic of an average, if not a mediocre, Anglicanism in which a deeply poetic culture gave fullness to the commonplaces which otherwise would have bordered on platitude.[115]

---

113. Ibid. pp. xxvii–xxix.
114. Gest, p. 2.
115. Bouyer, 3:117.

INTRODUCTION

This self-contradictory and somewhat confused criticism can only be answered by a volume of this nature, which presents in Taylor's own words the basic theological synthesis that is the source of his wisdom and the inspiration of his language. This synthesis, which has escaped the attention of Taylor's biographers and commentators, is reflected in the very structure of this book. Here Taylor's anthropology is central as found in the third chapter on *Faith and Repentance*. The christological and sacramental dimensions of his thought, and their place of primacy, are expressed in the first chapter on *Jesus Christ, the Great Exemplar,* and in the second chapter on the *Heavenly Sacrifice and Earthly Sacraments*. The ecclesial and eschatological dimensions can be seen respectively in the fourth chapter on *Sermon, Discourse, and Prayer,* and in the fifth chapter on *Holy Living and Holy Dying*. Presented in this way, Taylor's theology can be seen as a whole. It is not just a theology of his age: "a learning which would not preserve his books from oblivion."[116] Ironically, in Bouyer's own words, it is truly "a wisdom drawn from all the ancient sources to which the bible and experience brought the richest contribution!" Taylor, theologian and priest, gave the poet and preacher a new *Word* and a renewed *Ritual*.

No Caroline Divine felt the force of theological tradition more than Taylor. He was not just of his age; he was neither a Continental Schoolman nor a Cambridge Platonist. Like Newman two hundred years later, Taylor, too, could boast that he *followed the Fathers,* a term reserved for Christian writers distinguished by orthodoxy of doctrine, holiness of life, ecclesiastical approval and antiquity. In this context, antiquity is generally understood to include writers down to Gregory the Great (c. 600) or Isodore of Seville (c. 630) in the West, and John Damascene (c. 750) in the East. Taylor was at home in the unseen world of those early Christian writers for their Christ was his—the *Word* . . . *made flesh* (John 1:14) in history . . . *once* (Romans 6:10), but made text for all generations by Matthew, Mark, Luke and John; and made text, too, by Peter and Paul, *an apostle by the grace of God* (1 Corinthians 15:10); by James and Jude, Titus and Timothy, and by the writers of *Hebrews* and *Revelation*. These scriptures shed new light on the scriptures of Israel, and the *Old* and *New* expressions of God's eternal *Testament* became one Bible with different levels of meaning to engage

---

116. A. W. Ward, and A. R. Waller, *The Cambridge History of English Literature,* vol. 7 (London: G. P. Putnam's and Sons, 1907–17), p. 163.

the Fathers, who were the first Christian preachers. Some were literal in their interpretation of the text, and others allegorical, but all saw the intertestamental foreshadowing and realization in history of events that revealed the eternal mystery. Typology soon developed among them as their new and unique mode of knowing, which neither Greek nor Roman could understand. Plato was first invoked to express this Christian faith in a Greek world; afterward, Aristotle's time came round when this faith sought more rational understanding with the *fides quaerens intellectum* of Aquinas and the Schoolmen. Taylor belonged to this tradition of faith and theology as a whole; pilgrim and pastor, he journeyed as a theologian and priest through the ups and downs—political, religious, philosophical—of seventeenth-century England. He was no less a poet and a preacher, for he proclaimed *Paradise Lost* and *Paradise Regained* in prose that rivalled the poetry of Milton, his great Puritan contemporary, a decade before the publication of these epics in 1667 and 1671.

In comparison with Milton, Taylor was a poet in prose and not in verse. He was in the tradition of Cicero and Seneca, Augustine and Chrysostom, who were his masters; he also possessed his own unique gift of handling words, which, according to Matthew Arnold, constituted "the magic of his style." Logan Pearsall Smith calls this "magic of style" a combination of sound and image "which enchants the ear, and fascinates the eye."[117] Taylor's mastery of verbal music, "that felicity of sound and rhythm," can be best noted when he expresses the same idea in a less, and then a more, perfect form. In one passage he compares the death of virtuous men to "the descending of ripe and wholesome fruits from a pleasant and florid tree," but in another "to ripe and pleasant fruit falling from a fair tree, and gathered into baskets for the planter's use."[118] Here, with just a slight change of cadence, a new arrangement of epithets, the miracle happens, the crystallization takes place, and the phrase becomes one of enchantment. This felicity of sound and rhythm is often enhanced by his use of the unexpected and sometimes archaic adjective, which, being out of context, insinuates a remoter meaning, like the receding tide deserting "the *unfaithful* dwelling of the sand."[119]

In addition to this mastery of verbal music, Taylor possessed an

---

117. Smith p. xxx.
118. Ibid. p. xxxi.
119. Ibid. p. xxxii.

INTRODUCTION

extraordinarily rich and wonderful visual imagination; he personifies abstractions and turns them into living creatures; for example, he speaks of sin, "that will look prettily, and talk flattering words, and entice thee with softnesses and easy fallacies."[120] Again, he speaks to grief as to a person: "If you stay but till to-morrow you will be weary, and will lie down to rest."[121] But in his constant creation of simile and metaphor— the most important elements in style, according to Aristotle—he presents visual images, which convey, as only figured diction can, his religious ideas and transcendental experience. Consequently, his sermons are full of poetic images, flashing out in brief similes, as when he speaks of wealth "that flies away like a bird from the hand of a child,"[122] or compares the charity and humility of the Virgin to "the pure leaves of the whitest lily,"[123] or describes her grief at the crucifixion as being "deep as the waters of the abyss, but smooth as the face of a pool."[124] More often, these sermons are decorated with images of the highest poetic beauty, clothed in a soft radiance of words, which can speak even of death in one of the most beautiful similes of the English language:

But so have I seen a Rose newly springing from the clefts of its hood, and at first it was fair as the Morning, and full with the dew of Heaven, as a Lambs fleece; but when a ruder breath had forced open its virgin modesty, and dismantled its too youthful and unripe retirements, it began to put on darknesse, and to decline to softnesse, and the symptomes of a sickly age; it bowed the head, and broke its stalk, and at night having lost some of its leaves, and all its beauty, it fell into the portion of weeds and outworn faces.[125]

Theologians of Taylor's time, under the influence of Calvin, saw God's world under the curse of corruption, but Taylor and his type walked out with sheer delight to suck divinity from nature's flowers; for them, as for the early Fathers who preached the cosmic Christ,

120. Ibid. p. xxxiv.
121. Ibid.
122. Ibid. p. xxxvi.
123. Ibid. p. xxxvii.
124. Ibid.
125. Ibid. p. xxxix, quoting *Works* 3:270.

the beauteous frame of heaven and earth was the glasse in which God beheld his wisdom: he is glorified in the sun and moon, in the rare fabric of the honeycomb, in the discipline of bees, in the economy of ants, in the little houses of birds, in the curiosity of an eye—God being pleased to delight in those little images and reflexes of Himself from those pretty mirrors, which, like a crevice in a wall, through a narrow perspective transmit the species of a vast excellency.[126]

Many of Taylor's similes are drawn from the sun and moon for he delighted in the phenomena of light as he also did in the mystery and magic of water: "Repentance is like the Sun, which enlightens not only the tops of the Eastern hills, or warms the wall-fruits of Italy; it makes the little Balsam tree to weep precious tears with staring upon its beauties; it produces rich spices in Arabia, and warms the cold Hermit in his grot."[127] These images from common things also possess a warmth or tenderness that at times verges on the sentimental, but happily always escapes it:

The gentle stream . . . that begs leave of every turfe to let it passe . . . the little breeze, soft as the breath of heaven, not willing to disturb the softest stalk of a violet . . . the flies that doe rise againe from their little groves in walls, and dance awhile in the sun's winter beams.[128]

But as when the Sun approaches towards the gates of the morning, he first opens a little eye of Heaven, and sends away the spirits of darknesse, and gives light to a cock, and calls up the lark to Mattins, and by and by gilds the fringes of a cloud and peeps over the Eastern hills, thrusting out his golden horns, like those which decked the browes of Moses when he was forced to wear a vail, because himself had seen the face of God; and still while a man tells the story, the sun gets up higher, till he shows a fair face and a full light, and then he shines one whole day, under a cloud often, and sometimes

---

126. Ibid. p. xlvi, quoting *Works* 4:382.
127. Ibid. p. xliii, quoting *Works* 7:668.
128. Ibid. p. xlvii.

weeping great and little showers, and sets quickly: so is a man's reason and his life.[129]

Such was "the magic of style" with which Taylor graced his preaching, although he himself set no special value upon this especial gift. In addition to this felicity of sound and image, he also possessed to an extraordinary degree the gift of dramatic description, which was much favored and fostered by the taste of his times:

The *Contemplations of the State of Man* contain a simile of great power, where the Divine justice is likened to a river of fire, obstructed and dammed up during thirty or forty years, but rushing upon the sinner at the Last Day, with an irresistible inundation, and flooding him, at the same moment, with flame and vengeance. Other sermons display the abundance or the brightness, the wisdom or the tenderness, of his learning and intellect, his experience and sympathy: that on the *Marriage Ring* is more beautiful; that on the *House of Feasting* more varied; that on the *Good and Evil Tongue* more ingenious; that on the *Faith and Patience of the Saints* more pathetic; but the discourses on the Second Advent of Christ unfold the action of his mind in its grandest operations of creative energy. They are the best examples of the sublimity which formed a chief element of his genius; that mysterious faculty of representation and impression which makes dead thoughts to live and move.[130]

To a great degree, Jeremy Taylor was the creator in English of pulpit oratory in its written form. There were, of course, great preachers in England before him, and the power of the pulpit from Fisher to Donne, masters of the spoken word, is well-recorded. The Renaissance gave rise to sermons formed on classical models, for congregations were applying to sermons the criteria they were already applying to Virgil and Horace. These elaborate compositions were perfected by such masters as Bossuet and Massillon in France and Jeremy Taylor in England.

---

129. Ibid. p. xxxviii, *Works* 4:321.
130. Worley, p. 161, quoting Rev. R. A. Willmott, *Bishop Jeremy Taylor, His Predecessors, Contemporaries, and Successors* (London, 1864).

The change was a necessary consequence of the cultivated taste of the time, which required a more elaborate and finished style in such compositions, subject to the test of classic models, and free from the grammatical license of familiar speech which was pardonable, if not necessary, in the fervid exhortation and denunciation of an inspired prophet or revivalist."[131]

Consequently, Taylor's sermons are loaded, and sometimes overloaded, with classical quotations, for his memory was well-stored with all that was wise and beautiful in the ancients: His constant reference to the classics, this borrowing of words and images and phrases from Greek and Latin writers, lends a great distinction, "a kind of Miltonic richness to his style, and fills it with the murmur of far-off overtones and echoes."[132]

The *Eniautos,* or yearly collection of fifty-two sermons, which Taylor published toward the end of the Golden Grove years, were all preached to the select congregation of the Carbery household, where their magic of style, dramatic presentation and classical allusion were appreciated. Nevertheless, there is not one of those sermons that does not lay stress on some homely duty or virtue and point the practical path to possession. Here are no idle flights of fancy or picturesque descriptions of an unattainable sanctity. He is at all times like Chrysostom, his great prototype, driving home his point, for "sermons," he said, "are not like curious enquiries after new nothings, but pursuance of old truths."[133] These truths of his tradition, doctrinal and moral, were the content that inspired the beauty of his style, for in the true artist there is little distinction between manner and meaning: indeed, the form in any work of art expresses the reaction of the artist to the subject, and cannot be separated from that totality of meaning which the work conveys to our senses and imagination. It is Taylor's possession of style in this true sense of poetry—the revelation of a unique vision in the music and magic of words—that makes him a Christian preacher, par excellence, as he dwells on the omnipotence of Christ, "who died not a single or a sudden death, but who dies forever in all the sufferings of His ser-

---

131. Worley, p. 159.
132. Smith, p. liii.
133. Ibid. p. lii.

vants."[134] Indeed this pervading sense of God's presence runs like an undercurrent through his varied pages:

> Always there is Taylor's love of God, His essence, His wisdom, His power; and there is Taylor's consciousness that God is reflected in the forces of nature and in the little creations of the earth, as well as, more clearly, in the actions of a holy life, whereby God is pleased to glorify Himself.[135]

In Taylor, as in Milton, there was that blend and balance of biblical revelation and poetic expression, of vision and of language, that was not yet lost. Even the very titles of his sermons—*Apples of Sodom, The Foolish Exchange, The House of Feasting, The Good and Evil Tongue, The Serpent and the Dove*—were obviously chosen to arouse curiosity by partly revealing and partly concealing the content. Again, in many of his sermons, especially the funeral orations, there is a very happy choice of biblical text, the best possible for his purpose. For example, *for we must needs die, and are as water spilt on the ground, which cannot be gathered up again; yet doth He devise means, that His banished be not expelled from Him* (2 Samuel 14:14) was his text for the funeral sermon of the Countess of Carbery; and at the obsequies of John Bramhall, the lord primate of Ireland, Taylor preached his last funeral oration on the text: *Every man in his own order: Christ the first fruits; afterwards they that are Christ's at His coming (1 Corinthians 15:23)*. Taylor is at his best in those great funeral sermons, which may be distinguished from his other orations by the same marks that distinguish his *Holy Dying* from *Holy Living*: his character and imagination were of that serious cast that is most at home in the solemnities of life and death, which has no inclination to frivolities; his muse was emphatically tragic. There are flashes of wit here and there in his writings; there is that sort of irony that we notice in most writers who have suffered at the hands of the world, and are superior to it; there is plenty of humor, in the proper sense of the word, but there is nothing to raise a laugh.

The combination of Bible and poetry, of which Taylor was the great master in prose, lost its footing in the philosophy of the new world, for neither spoke the scientific truth. Similarly, in the church

---

134. Gest, p. 17.
135. Ibid.

itself "the scriptural and Christian plainness," which George Herbert and some early Carolines preferred, inspired the plea of John Wilkins in his *Ecclesiastes* (1646) "for a plain and simple style of preaching."[136] But the first notable attack on pulpit eloquence after the Restoration was made by Bishop Robert South in a sermon preached at Oxford in 1668. In a well-known passage where he is commending the preaching of St. Paul, he glances posthumously at the works of Jeremy Taylor: "nothing here of *The Fringes of the Northstar* . . . nothing of *The Down of Angels Wings*, or *The Beautiful Locks of Cherebims:* no starched similitudes, introduced with a *Thus have I seen a Cloud rolling in its airy Mansion*, and the like."[137] In this context the plain and simple sermon of the Puritan preacher flourished; it was scriptural in a literal sense and practical in its application, and it had, above all else, a sense of urgency that is perfectly captured in Baxter's couplet:

> I preached as never like to preach again
> And as a dying man to dying men![138]

Few of the Caroline preachers were poets, but all of them were pastors and priests whom, as we have seen, political and religious circumstances sometimes made pilgrims and theologians. However, none of them were simply Puritan preachers for the sermon was an integral part of their *Prayer-Book* worship and, while central in their pastoral practice, was always preceded by catechesis and followed by spiritual guidance:

> Let every minister teach his people the use, practice, methods and benefits of meditation or mental prayer. . . . Let every minister exhort his people to a frequent confession of their sins, and a declaration of the state of their souls; to a conversation with their minister in spiritual things, to an enquiry concerning all parts of their duty: for by preaching, and catechiz-

---

136. D. Bush, *English Literature in the Earlier Seventeenth Century, 1600–1660*, Oxford History of Literature, vol. 5 (Oxford: Clarendon Press, 1945), p. 310ff.

137. J. Sutherland, *English Literature in the Late Seventeenth Century*, Oxford History of Literature, vol. 6 (Oxford: Clarendon Press, 1969), p. 306.

138. H. Davies, *Worship of Theology in England*, vol. 2 (Princeton, NJ: Princeton University Press, 1975), p. 162.

ing, and private intercourse, all the needs of souls can best be served; but by preaching alone they cannot.[139]

Catechism, preaching and guidance together constituted the *Ministry of the Word*, which Taylor performed as pilgrim and pastor, theologian and priest, poet and preacher. In his many volumes, which recount this fundamentally mystagogical ministry, there are places where his practical give-and-take religion anticipates the canonization of commonsense that was destined to dominate eighteenth-century theology and "to replace the ancient and sublime platonic ladder to the serene heavens of eternal peace."[140] Nevertheless, Taylor's vision is not of this world; like the poets Dante and Milton he was *at home* in the unseen world, and consequently in his funeral sermons we breathe at once the air of *Hell, Purgatory* and *Paradise; of Paradise Lost* and *Paradise Regained.* Theologically, he *belonged* both to the world of the early Christian Fathers, who expressed their faith in a Platonic way, and to that of the later Schoolmen, who went the way of Aristotle. Mystically, he *belonged* to Christ, and was *at home* in his kingdom, for he was no stranger along *the other way,* which the classics of Western spirituality call purgative, punitive, unitive:

> The first beginners in religion are employed in the mastering of their first appetites, casting out their devils, exterminating all evil customs, lessening the proclivity of habits, and countermanding the too great forwardness of visious inclinations; and this, which divines call the purgative way, is wholly spent in actions of repentance, mortification, and self-denial. . . .

> After our first step is taken, and the punitive part of repentance is resolved on, and begun, and put forward into good degrees of progress, we then enter into the illuminative way of religion. . . . If a pious soul passes to affections of greater sublimity, and intimate and more immediate, abstracted and immaterial love, it is well; only remember that the love God

---

139. M. Thornton, *English Spirituality* (Cambridge, MA: Cowley Publications, 1986), p. 237.
140. Smith, p. lvi.

requires of us, is an operative, material, and communicative love, "If ye love Me, keep My commandments": so that still a good life is the effect of the sublimest meditation. . . .

Beyond this I have described, there is a degree of meditation so exalted, that it changes the very name, and is called contemplation; and it is in the unitive way of religion, that is, it consists in unions and adherences to God; it is a prayer of quietness and silence, and a meditation extraordinary, a discourse without variety, a vision and intuition of divine excellencies, an immediate entry into an orb of light, and a resolution of all our faculties into sweetness, affections, and starings upon the divine beauty; and is carried on to ecstasies, raptures, suspensions, elevations, abstractions and apprehensions beatifical. . . .

But this is a thing not to be discoursed of, but felt: and although in other sciences the terms must first be known, and then the rules and conclusions scientifical; here it is otherwise: for first, the whole experience of this must be obtained before we can so much as know what it is; and the end must be acquired first, the conclusion before the premises. They that pretend to these heights call them the secrets of the kingdom; but they are such which no man can describe; such which God hath not revealed in the publication of the gospel; such for the acquiring of which there are no means prescribed.[141]

A "vision and intuition of divine excellencies" . . . an "immediate entry into an orb of light" . . . a "resolution of all our faculties into sweetnesses, affections and starings upon the divine beauty," and such other mystical phrases as "a thing not to be discoursed of, but felt" flow gently through Taylor's voluminous pages, refreshing the reader quietly, and peacefully reassuring him, for divine secrets and the human heart are the two sides of Taylor's coinage: "There are some *secreta theologiae* which are only to be understood by persons very holy and spiritual; which are rather to be felt than discoursed of."[142] Such secrets

---

141. Gest, p. 110, quoting *Works* 2: pp. 136–40.
142. Ibid. p. 111.

and the heart that holds them are the stuff that preachers and poets are made of, and Taylor had them both. "God's secrets are to Himself," he says, "and to the sons of His house";[143] in the *Great Exemplar* he speaks of *the secrets of spiritual benediction*, "which are understood only by them to whom they are conveyed, even by the children of the house";[144] elsewhere he refers to the *secret of the spirit*, or the *meaning of the meaning*, which is deep down and heartfelt by any disciple, who is grown old in religion and conversation of the Spirit: "This man best understands the *secret* . . . and feels this unintelligible mystery, and sees with his *heart* what his tongue can never express and his metaphysics can never prove."[145] This vision of the heart—"what heart heard of, ghost guessed"—and which not even the poet's tongue can express— "nor mouth had, no nor mind, expressed"—is God-given:[146] God opens the *heart* and creates a new one, and without this new creation, this new principle of life, we may hear the sound of God's word but never feel its meaning:

> Unless there be in our *hearts* a *secret* conviction by the Spirit of God, the gospel in itself is a dead letter, and worketh not in us the light and righteousness of God . . . for . . . the Scriptures . . . are written within and without . . . and unless there be a light shining within our *hearts*, unfolding the leaves and interpreting the mysterious sense of the Spirit, convincing our consciences and preaching to our *hearts*, to look for Christ in the leaves of the gospel is to look for the living among the dead.[147]

The Caroline scheme of catechism, preaching and guidance was meant to bring to life God's *secret* in man's *heart*, and a heart full of praise and thanksgiving, eucharist or *berekah*, is prayer or the heart's response to the mystery of this pastoral activity. Taylor's every work is laced through and through with a multiplicity and variety of prayers, composed for every conceivable occasion, which are the outpourings of

---

143. Ibid. p. 115.
144. Ibid. p. 113.
145. Ibid. p. 115.
146. G. M. Hopkins, *Poems and Prose,* sel. and ed. W. H. Gardiner, "Spring and Fall," (Middlesex: Penguin, 1953), p. 50.
147. Gest, pp. 114, 112.

a mystic's heart. From Sally Island on Loch Beg, "where the things of the spirit are so plainly shown in the lights and shadows, the colours and shapes of every common day,"[148] he wrote to Evelyn in London about the *secret way* of religion:

> My retirement in this solitary place hath been, I hope, of some advantage to me as to this state of religion, in which I am yet but a novice, but by the goodness of God I see fine things before me whither I am contending. It is a great but a good work, and I beg of you to assist me with your prayers, and to obtaine of God for me that I may arrive at that height of love and union with God, which is given to all those souls who are very deare to God."[149]

It is this mystical quality in the works of Jeremy Taylor, pilgrim and pastor, theologian and priest, poet and preacher, that qualifies them for inclusion in the *Classics of Western Spirituality*, a library of the great spiritual masters:

> Lord, let me be as constant in the ways of religion as the sun in his course, as ready to follow the intimations of Thy Spirit as little birds are to obey the directions of Thy providence and the conduct of Thy hand ... that I may live according to the rules of nature in such things which she teaches, modestly, temperately, and affectionately, in all the parts of my natural and political relations; and that I, proceeding from nature to grace, may henceforth go on from grace to glory, the crown of all obedience, prudent and holy walking, through Jesus Christ our Lord. Amen.[150]

George Rust, dean of Connor and afterward bishop of Dromore, preached the funeral sermon at the obsequies of Jeremy Taylor in Dromore Cathedral on 21 August 1667, and later on September 3 repeated it at a special memorial service at St. Patrick's Cathedral in Dublin.

---

148. M. Cropper, *Flame Touches Flame* (London: Longmans, Green, and Co., 1949), p. 142.

149. Ibid. p. 143.

150. Gest, p. 108, quoting *Works* 2:81.

Courageously, he followed the method Taylor had invented and perfected—a meditation upon the text of scripture first and afterward the biographical details. He was entirely successful; the composition is beautiful in itself, appropriately eloquent and an invaluable contribution to Taylor's biography. In Dromore Cathedral the remains of Jeremy Taylor, bishop of Down and Connor, rest beneath the Episcopal Chair, an appropriate monument with an equally appropriate inscription:

In Piam Memoriam
JEREMY TAYLOR S.T.P.
eruditi Theologi, diserti Oratoris,
fidelis Pastoris,
hujus dioecesis Episcopi.
A.D. 1661–1667.

TEXT

None of the first editions of Jeremy Taylor's works are common. The easiest to come by are *The Worthy Communicant, The Liberty of Prophesying, Unum Necessarium* and *The Great Exemplar,* while many of the others are exceedingly rare. But the Founders Library of Northern Illinois University in DeKalb, Illinois, has in its rare book section the collection of Robert Gathorne-Hardy, the London bookseller and antiquarian. In his book *Recollections of Logan Pearsall Smith,* subtitled *The Story of a Friendship,*[151] he describes his chance meeting in 1928 at his London bookshop with the great American critic and literary epicure. Smith at that time was finishing *The Golden Grove,* his selected passages from the sermons and writings of Jeremy Taylor, and Gathorne-Hardy had his bibliography on Taylor nearing completion; one year later their *Golden Grove* was published. This bibliography was corrected and enlarged in the *Times Literary Supplement,* 25 September, 2 and 9 October 1930, and especially 15 September 1932. A further *Bibliography of the Writings of Jeremy Taylor to 1700,* Gathorne-Hardy's last work, was published in 1971 in collaboration with William Proctor Williams

---

151. R. Gathorne-Hardy, *Recollections of Logan Pearsall Smith* (New York: Macmillan, 1950).

of DeKalb. It provides extensive bibliographical data on all of Taylor's works.

There are three nineteenth-century editions of Taylor's works that most readers accept as standard:

1) *The Whole Works of the Right Reverend Jeremy Taylor, D.D., with a Life of the Author.* 15 volumes. London, 1822 and 1828.

2) *The Whole Works of the Right Rev. Jeremy Taylor, D.D., with an Essay Biographical and Critical.* Edition anonymously revised. 3 volumes. London, 1844 and 1880.

3) *The Whole Works of the Right Reverend Jeremy Taylor, D.D., with a Life of the Author.* Edited by Reginald Heber, revised and corrected by Charles Eden Page. 10 volumes. London, 1847–52.

The third or last of these editions, commonly known as the Heber-Eden, is unquestionably the most critical, but the Bishop Heber fifteen-volume set is probably the most widely distributed. The selections made for this volume are from the Heber-Eden edition [referred to as *Works,* with appropriate volume and page number: any reference to any other edition will be noted accordingly]. The table on the next page of Taylor's major works, designated by their short titles and taken from Harry Boone Porter's recent work, may be of help in locating a text in the most available edition.[152]

A new critical edition of *Holy Living* and *Holy Dying* has been prepared by P. G. Stanwood, professor of English in the University of British Columbia, Vancouver, for publication by Clarendon Press, Oxford. I am grateful for the opportunity of reading the corrected proofsheets of this painstakingly scholarly edition, and for the possibility of using this more critical text. However "the substantive textual variants at the foot of each page as they occur," while important for the *Oxford English Texts* series, were of no significance for an understanding of Taylor's theology and spirituality.[153] Hence, for the sake of uniformity, it seems best to retain throughout this volume the Heber-Eden text.

---

152. H. Boone-Porter, *Jeremy Taylor, Liturgist* (London: Alcuin Club, 1979).
153. From Stanwood's introduction to *Holy Living.*

	Heber's edition	3-volume edition	Eden's edition
Reverence Due to the Altar			5
Sacred Order of Episcopacy	7	2	5
Psalter of David	15	3	
Prayer ex tempore (see Apology for Liturgy)	7	2	
Liberty of Prophesying	7, 8	2	5
Apology for Liturgy	7	2	5
Great Exemplar	2, 3	1	2
Holy Living	4	1	3
Clerus Domini	14	3	1
27 (or 28) Sermons (see Eniautos)	5, 6	1	4
Holy Dying	4	1	3
25 Sermons (see Eniautos)	5	1	4
Eniautos	5, 6	1, 2	4
Real Presence	9, 10	2	6
Golden Grove	15	3	7
Unum Necessarium	8, 9	2	7
Deus Justificatus	9	2	7
Collection of Offices	15	3	8
Ductor Dubitantium	11, 12, 13, 14	3	9, 10
Worthy Communicant	15	3	8
Rules and Advices to Clergy	14	3	1
Discourse of Confirmation	11	3	5
Dissuasive from Popery	10	2	6
Ten (or Eleven) Sermons	6	2	4
Two Prayers, Before and After, Sermon	15	3	1
Rust's Funeral Sermon	1	1	1

Furthermore, the use of Stanwood's understandable and praiseworthy retention of first-edition spelling for *Holy Living* and *Holy Dying* would differ unduly, and without purpose, from the Heber-Eden spelling of the remaining texts.

On the other hand, the updating of Eden's method of reference for the Greek and Latin Fathers would be of considerable help for the study of Taylor's theology and spirituality. Eden's revision of Heber was made between 1847 and 1852, some few years before the publication of Abbé Migne's monumental and still standard Patrologies: the Series Latina (PL), containing 221 volumes was completed in 1864, and the Series Graeca (PG), including 161 volumes of Greek and Latin texts, and 81 volumes of Greek texts only, was begun in 1856 and finished in 1867. Consequently, in this edition references are to Migne's Patrologia Graeca (PG) or Patrologia Latina (PL) with the appropriate number of volume and page. Furthermore, Taylor's frequent use of classical quotations in their original Greek or Latin have been removed from the text, and likewise Eden's cumbersome citation of their sources, for they are always adequately contained and explained in the English text and are usually of stylistic and not theological significance. Classical references, where retained, are updated by the Loeb Classical Library (LCL).

SECONDARY SOURCES

An *Annotated Checklist* of later editions of Taylor's works and a survey of the secondary sources were compiled by Dr. Williams in his *Jeremy Taylor, 1700–1976. Holy Living* and *Holy Dying* have had many modern reprints, for example, Temple Classics. There are also three anthologies of particular importance. In 1923 Martin Armstrong edited *Jeremy Taylor,* a brief selection of well-chosen texts without criticism or commentary. Logan Pearsall Smith's *Golden Grove* was published in 1930, with its brilliant literary introduction to "the Shakespeare of English Divines" and "the magic of his style." But Margaret Gest's *The House of Understanding* (Philadelphia, 1954), with its theological and historical introduction, is the most comprehensive presentation of Taylor, the Caroline divine; her *Selections* show his progress from theological controversy on *The Nature of God, Free Will* and the *Liberty of Conscience,* through Christian reflection on *Living with Others, The Flesh and the Spirit, Reason and Things Reasonable, Time, Death and its Shadow,* to *Prayer, Steps in Mystical Theology* and *The Unitive Way.*

Taylor's biography began with George Rust's funeral sermon, reprinted by Heber-Eden, which also contains the first and best scholarly life. Taylor was fortunate in his biographers. Among those of the nineteenth century, the Reverend Robert Willmott published in 1847 the most charming and sympathetic study of his life and writings. Sir Edmund Gosse, for the *English Men of Letters Series,* attempted for the first time in 1903 to define Taylor's place in literary history, while George Worley, at the same time, published his *Popular Exposition of the Works of Jeremy Taylor*. A more thorough study of Taylor, the divine, was published by Canon Brown in 1925, and in 1952, Canon C. J. Stranks published the final word, so to speak, in the *Life and Writings of Jeremy Taylor,* a work for which every student of Taylor must be grateful.

Taylor has also been the subject of much commentary in literary and theological criticism: Coleridge's extensive comments are in *Literary Remains* (1838), and *Notes on English Divines* (1853); Hazlitt's in *Dramatic Literature of the Age of Elizabeth;* Arnold's in *The Literary Influence of Academics;* Farrar's in *Masters in English Theology* (1877); Henson's in *Typical English Churchmen* (1902); Saintsbury's in *The Golden Age of the English Pulpit* (1920); Mitchell's in *English Pulpit Oratory* (1932). Canon Charles Smyth has briefer remarks in *Art of Preaching* (1940). More recently, Horton Davies in *Worship and Theology in England* (1975) considers his place in Anglican spirituality and preaching, and Louis Bouyer does likewise in *History of Christian Spirituality* (1968).

Finally a new chapter in Anglican and Roman studies was opened with the publication in 1988 of *The Eucharistic Theology of Jeremy Taylor Today* by H. R. McAdoo,[154] former archbishop of Dublin and primate of Ireland, who has brought to light, for the first time, the theological "modernity" of Taylor.

> There are throughout this varied work an interlocking of themes and an underlying unity of thought, so that one must first see his eucharistic theology in the context of his general theology. We shall find throughout, I believe, a vein of moral/ascetic theology and a vein of sacramental theology, which merge and undergird all that he writes, whether it be the *Life of Christ*, the *Liberty of Prophesying,* the devotional works or the sermons, apart altogether from books specifically about the eucharist or about moral theology. All the time and explicitly in all the subjects which he treats Taylor's methodology is that which has created and creates the spirit of Anglicanism, the appeal to scripture, to antiquity and to reason. This is the basis of how he does theology.[155]

---

154. H. R. McAdoo, *The Eucharistic Theology of Jeremy Taylor Today* (Norwich: Canterbury Press, 1988).
155. Ibid. p. 14.

INTRODUCTION

This emphasis on theology by Dr. McAdoo, a bishop-theologian himself, like the pastor-theologians of the Patristic and Caroline churches, safeguards the traditional spirituality of the church from the type of Puritan zeal that, to a certain extent, deprived Anglicanism of its native strength, and postponed the patristic renewal of the whole church. Fortunately, Taylor is also quoted by McAdoo, frequently and at some length, for "the inimitable language" of this "great man of letters" cannot be summarized without "being guilty of a kind of literary vandalism and of theological misprision."[156] I hope that the longer selections of this volume, made in accordance with Taylor's theological substructure, will complement spiritually what McAdoo has so expertly begun theologically.

STRUCTURE

These selections from Taylor's writings were made and structured to illustrate his basic theological synthesis, hence their division into five chapters whose titles respectively express the Christological, sacramental, anthropological, ecclesial and eschatological aspects of his system. Taylor's magic of style, liturgical compositions, cases of conscience, controversies, sermons and devotional writings can never be separated from this corpus, or body of truths, which he theologically accepted, questioned or rejected. Unfortunately, in the past, the approach of his biographers and commentators has been for the most part fragmented, divorced from his theological base, and determined by their own specific purpose; consequently Taylor has been divided, his word has little relevance outside his world, and his world no longer exists.

The structure of this volume with its blend of introduction and text, aims at restoring the balance by situating Taylor's own words in their historical, theological and philosophical world of origin in the hope of recovering their spiritual meaning and vitality for our scientific age. In addition to the general Introduction, the texts of each chapter are briefly introduced with more relevant details and particulars, which enable them to be read in a context that is more spiritual than academic, more popular than professional. At the same time, these texts are, in their length, more typical of *The Essential Jeremy Taylor* than of an

---

156. Ibid. p. 7.

anthology, for they try to preserve the structure of the whole from which they are taken. For example, the first chapter presents Taylor's *Great Exemplar,* or *Life of Christ,* in a truncated but nonetheless continuous narrative form from the annunciation to the ascension, while the final chapter contains not only the principal chapters of his *Holy Living* and *Holy Dying,* but also shows something of their structure and division. In the third chapter on *Faith and Repentance* texts were chosen from his more spiritual than casuistical works to reflect on the positive side his doctrine of holiness, and on the negative side his doctrine of sin. The fourth chapter on *Sermon, Prayer and Discourse* contains the whole text of the *Via Intelligentiae,* Taylor's finest and best sermon, together with shorter treatises in their entirety on the *Lord's Prayer, Via Pacis,* and *Agenda,* rather than a variety of excerpts from other sermons and prayers. Finally, in the second chapter on *Heavenly Sacrifice and Earthly Sacraments* texts were chosen for their magic of style and power of persuasion, for Taylor's use of sacramental language can do much to smooth the polemics of philosophic debate.

CHAPTER ONE

Jesus Christ—
The Great Exemplar

INTRODUCTION

At the outbreak of the Civil War in the summer of 1642 the name of Jeremy Taylor disappeared from the registers of Uppingham in Rutland, where he had been pastor for over four years. In October of that same year he surfaced at Oxford, amid the plaudits of citizens and scholars, as King Charles entered in triumph. For Taylor difficult days had begun to dawn, for his patron, William Laud of Canterbury, was already in the Tower of London, and the House of Lords had ratified the resolution of Commons for "the Abolition of all Bishops" (7 September 1642).

Some years earlier at Oxford, and on the advice of the archbishop, who was also the chancellor, Taylor had published his first work, *A Sermon on Gunpowder Treason*. Around the same time, and again under the influence of Laud, his treatise *On the Reverence Due to the Altar* was probably written. But now, prompted by Sir Christopher Hatton, Laud's cousin and Taylor's new patron, the young clergyman entered the thick of the political struggle by publishing a work of massive erudition, *On the Sacred Order of the Episcopacy*, commonly called *Episcopacy Asserted*. He was rewarded by the king himself with the doctor of divinity degree for this *magnum opus*, which is more a paraphrase of authorities and a concatenation of Greek and Latin quotations than a work of independent authorship or distinct style. Soon afterward Dr. Jeremy Taylor, "the true pastor of Uppingham," was further rewarded for his devotion to king and bishop by having his "house plundered, his

estate seized, and his family driven out of doors."[1] The full significance
of the events that followed in 1644, including the execution of Laud in
January 1645, was later expressed by Taylor in a passage that is more
spiritually revealing than historically telling:

> In this great storm which hath dashed the vessel of the Church
> all in pieces, I have been cast upon the coast of Wales, and in a
> little boat thought to have enjoyed that rest and quietness
> which in England in a greater I could not hope for. Here I cast
> anchor, and thinking to ride safely, the storm followed me
> with so impetuous violence, that it broke a cable, and I lost my
> anchor. And here again I was exposed to the mercy of the sea,
> and the gentleness of an element that could neither distinguish
> things nor persons. And but that He who stilleth the raging
> sea, and the noise of His waves, and the madness of His
> people, had provided a plank for me, I had been lost to all the
> opportunities of content or study. But I know not whether I
> have been more preserved by the courtesies of my friends, or
> the gentleness and mercies of a noble enemy.[2]

The storms of 1645 cast Taylor on the shores of South Wales,
"and in a private corner of the world," where, as Rust tells us in his
panegyric, "a tender providence shrouded him under her wings, and the
prophet was fed in the wilderness."[3] The Earl of Carbery was certainly
the *tender providence*, and probably also the *noble enemy*, for he was a
man more interested in the conflict of sin and grace than in those of
king and Parliament; but Golden Grove, the Carbery Mansion, was by
nature no *wilderness*, for it stood in its own undulating park on the south
side of the Towey River and overlooked the valley to a still lovelier and
more romantic estate, Dynevor Castle. Somewhat to the east of Gron-
gar Hill it shared the view which Dyer described some seventy years
later in his famous poem;

> . . . that long and level lawn,
> On which a dark hill, steep and high,

---

1. Stranks, p. 62.
2. *Works* 5:341.
3. *Works* 1:cccxxiii, Rust's "Funeral Sermon."

Holds and charms the wandering eye;
Deep are his feet in Towey's flood,
His sides are clothed with waving wood;
And ancient towers crown his brow,
That cast an awful look below.[4]

Here Taylor lived for nearly eight years as pastor and priest to the lord and lady of Golden Grove. Such duties allowed him ample time to join two neighboring priests, friends from Oxford days, in their venture at Newtown Hall, where their private school flourished with due recognition in the troubled land. In those circumstances Taylor was sheltered from the storms that surrounded him, and left to the cultivation of his spirit and his eloquence, he rapidly grew in wisdom, grace and in style. It is to this blessed time with the Carberys at Golden Grove that we owe the ripest and liveliest of his compositions; stamped by the grace of his friends and the beauty of their place Taylor's spiritual writings began to flow through the length and breath of an England that had run dry of God's Spirit and His Word.

The abolition of the *Book of Common Prayer* immediately after the execution of Laud deprived the church of her set forms of worship, and the *Westminster Directory* that followed opened the doors to uncontrolled and unrestrained spontaneity, or praying with the spirit, which resulted in chaos:

In very many churches every man uses what he pleases, and all men do not choose well; and where there is nothing regular, and the sacraments themselves are not so solemnly ministered as the sacredness and solemnity of the mysteries do require, and in very many places, where the old excellent forms are not permitted, there is scarce anything at all, but something to show there was a shipwreck—a plank or a cable, a chapter or a psalm.[5]

At this time Taylor published *A Discourse on Prayer,* later called *An Apology for Liturgy,* and it revealed his own spiritual growth and a freedom of style that aptly expressed this spirit. In the *voisinage* of

---

4. Gosse, p. 66.
5. *Works* 5:260.

Golden Grove there were no volumes of the casuistical species, and so the Oxford student had "no other books, or aids, than what a man carries with him on horseback";[6] thus the spiritual master and the master of English were born together at a turbulent time, but in a peaceful place.

The *Liberty of Prophesying*, Taylor's first major work, was published one year later on 28 June 1647, when passions were much aflamed and charity much more extinguished:

> In this world we believe in part, and prophecy in part, and this imperfection shall never be done away till we be transplanted to a more glorious state. Either, then, we must throw our chances and get truth by accident or predestination, or else we must lie safe in a mutual toleration and private liberty of persuasion, unless some other anchor can be thought upon where we may fasten our floating vessels and ride safely.[7]

Here Taylor strikes a note that was absolutely novel in an age altogether given to proscription and persecution. He proposed a toleration not founded upon agreement or concession, but upon a broad basis of practical piety, calling all fanatics back to the humane and merciful doctrine of Jesus Christ, "whose lessons were softer than nard or the juice of Candian olive, and to the Church, which is not a chimera, or a shadow, but a company of men believing in Jesus Christ; hence, the unreasonableness of prescribing to other men's faith, and the iniquity of persecuting differing opinions."[8] Very few people in either camp, including the disappointed king, were content to accept Taylor's position on tolerance and on the liberty of private persuasion: but in a wider field he had begun to plant the good seed he had been gathering in Lord Carbery's Golden Grove.

The death of the king in 1648 removed Taylor from the polemics of those tragic events and inclined him to deeper things. In 1649 he completed *The History of the Life and Death of the Holy Jesus*, generally known by the subtitle *The Great Exemplar*, which was as novel an enterprise in the spiritual and intellectual world as the *Liberty of Proph-*

---

6. Ibid. p. 343.
7. Ibid.
8. Ibid. p. 492.

esying had been in the moral and controversial. Only its excessive length (one thousand pages more or less depending on the edition) can explain its persistent neglect by spiritual writers, theologians, biographers and critics of every age, with the exception, perhaps, of Sir Edmund Gosse, who was truly touched by its flame:

> *The Great Exemplar* is a celebration of the beauty of the Lord Jesus, God and Man. The up-raised, ecstatic movement of the paragraphs betrays the enthusiasm of the writer; he is Christ-possessed. The most gracious voice then to be heard in England is lifted like that of a nightingale above the frogs and ravens of the age. The form he adopts is interesting; it is cunningly devised to sustain and divert the attention, to prevent weariness, to prolong the pleasure of the reader by division and variety. It opens with a preface, one of Taylor's exquisitely winning introductions, in which the great family of Man is described, the necessity of discipline in its organism demonstrated, and Christianity shown to be the most perfect law conceivable for its direction. Then, after an exhortation to the imitation of Jesus, the romance begins.
>
> The string on which the whole sequence of pearls is hung is the narrative of the life of Christ on earth. The author tells the story as he chooses. There is no attempt at Biblical criticism, even as in those days it was understood; no dealing with difficulties of parallel Evangelists; no weighing of evidence. Taylor selects such versions of the narrative as best suits his purpose, not shrinking from the traditions of a later age, if they attract him. For instance, he accepts without a question the legend of the prostration of the Egyptian gods when the Infant crossed the border. If an incident inflames his imagination, he lingers over it as long as he chooses; he weaves his fancy, for instance, for page after page, around the apparition of the Star of the Epiphany. What he dwells upon, exclusively, is the imaginative and the pathetic. He wishes to draw men away from the weariness of controversy to the exquisite mysteries of pure religion.
>
> But he knows that sustained rhetoric fatigues the mind. He is careful to vary his theme. Accordingly, after each section of

his narrative, he applies that fragment of the story to a disquisition on its practical bearing upon life, to general remarks about men's religious duty as illustrated by what he has just described. He rivets the attention of the history to the needs of modern society, to the family, to the state, to friendship, and to the conduct of affairs. Nor is this enough to secure the cunning variety of his design, which is further gained by the introduction of short prayers, each like the gush of music. In these devotions, the most exquisite of their kind in the English language, Jeremy Taylor has no rival. They display, in the most complete manner, the delicate wholesomeness of his conscience and the inimitable distinction of his style. Nowhere does he open a well of English more undefiled than in his admirable private prayers.[9]

As *The History of the Life and Death of the Holy Jesus* this treatise was the first of its kind to appear in the English language; as *The Great Exemplar* it was the beginning in English of a spirituality that is at the same time Christological and biblical, ecclesial and sacramental. At Golden Grove Taylor discovered that divine grace and human style which made this work his unique contribution to English spirituality and to English literature. He combined narrative, meditation, discourse and prayer in a spiritual volume that rivaled in length the heroic novels that were at that time being introduced from France. "Bulk and prolixity were no disadvantage in that age of the Commonwealth, when Puritan asceticism had sealed up the sources of genial enjoyment. . . . The only entertainment left was literature, and people could not have it too elaborately prolonged."[10] Yet not even Jeremy Taylor was ever again so inordinately lengthy. Consequently, in this chapter an attempt is made at brevity for the sake of relevance by allowing the narrative to flow continuously without interruption from discourse, meditation or prayer; as a result the text of the King James is made to dance with the ease and grace of Taylor's style and fancy.

---

9. Gosse, pp. 58–59.
10. Ibid. p. 62.

The Life of Our Blessed Lord
and Saviour Jesus Christ

PART I

BEGINNING AT THE ANNUNCIATION TO THE BLESSED
VIRGIN MARY UNTIL HIS BAPTISM AND
TEMPTATION INCLUSIVELY

Section I
The History of the Conception of Jesus

1. When the fulness of time was come, after the frequent repetition of promises, the expectation of the Jewish nation, the longings and tedious waitings of all holy persons, the departure of the "sceptre from Judah, and the lawgiver from between his feet"; when the number of Daniel's years was accomplished, and the Egyptian and Syrian kingdoms had their period; God, having great compassion towards mankind, remembering His promises, and our great necessities, sent His Son into the world, to take upon Him our nature, and all that guilt of sin which stuck close to our nature, and all that punishment which was consequent to our sin: which came to pass after this manner;—

2. In the days of Herod the king, the angel Gabriel was sent from God to a city of Galilee named Nazareth, to a holy maid called Mary, espoused to Joseph, and found her in a capacity and excellent disposition to receive the greatest honour that ever was done to the daughters of men. Her employment was holy and pious, her person young, her years florid and springing, her body chaste, her mind humble, and a rare repository of divine graces. She was full of grace and excellencies; and God poured upon her a full measure of honour, in making her the mother of the Messias: for the "angel came to her, and said, Hail, thou that art highly favoured, the Lord is with thee; blessed art thou among women."

3. We cannot but imagine the great mixture of innocent disturbances and holy passions, that in the first address of the angel did rather discompose her settledness and interrupt the silence of her spirits, than

dispossess her dominion which she ever kept over those subjects which never had been taught to rebel beyond the mere possibilities of natural imperfection. But if the angel appeared in the shape of a man, it was an unusual arrest to the blessed Virgin, who was accustomed to retirements and solitariness, and had not known an experience of admitting a comely person, but a stranger, to her closet and privacies. But if the heavenly messenger did retain a diviner form, more symbolical to angelical nature and more proportionable to his glorious message, although her daily employment was a conversation with angels, who in their daily ministering to the saints did behold her chaste conversation, coupled with fear, yet they used not any affrighting glories in the offices of their daily attendances, but were seen only by spiritual discernings. However, so it happened, that "when she saw him, she was troubled at his saying, and cast in her mind what manner of salutation this should be."

4. But the angel, who came with designs of honour and comfort to her, not willing that the inequality and glory of the messenger should, like too glorious a light to a weaker eye, rather confound the faculty than enlighten the organ, did, before her thoughts could find a tongue, invite her to a more familiar confidence than possibly a tender virgin, though of the greatest serenity and composure, could have put on in the presence of such a beauty and such a holiness: and "the angel said unto her, Fear not, Mary, for thou hast found favour with God; and behold, thou shalt conceive in thy womb, and bring forth a son, and shalt call His name Jesus."

5. The holy Virgin knew herself a person very unlikely to be a mother; for although the desires of becoming a mother to the Messias were great in every of the daughters of Jacob, and about that time the expectation of His revelation was high and pregnant, and therefore she was espoused to an honest and a just person of her kindred and family, and so might not despair to become a mother; yet she was a person of rare sanctity, and so mortified a spirit, that for all this desponsation of her, according to the desire of her parents and the custom of the nation, she had not set one step toward the consummation of her marriage, so much as in thought; and possibly had set herself back from it by a vow of chastity and holy celibate: for "Mary said unto the angel, How shall this be, seeing I know not a man?"

6. But the angel, who was a person of that nature which knows no conjunctions but those of love and duty, knew that the piety of her soul and the religion of her chaste purposes was a great imitator of angelical

purity, and therefore perceived where the philosophy of her question did consist; and being taught of God, declared that the manner should be as miraculous as the message itself was glorious. For the angel told her, that this should not be done by any way, which our sin and the shame of Adam had unhallowed, by turning nature into a blush, and forcing her to a retirement from a public attesting the means of her own preservation; but the whole matter was from God, and so should the manner be: for "the angel said unto her, The Holy Ghost shall come upon thee, and the power of the Highest shall overshadow thee: therefore also that holy thing which shall be born of thee shall be called the Son of God."

7. When the blessed Virgin was so ascertained that she should be a mother and a maid, and that two glories, like the two luminaries of heaven, should meet in her, that she might in such a way become the mother of her Lord that she might with better advantages be His servant; then all her hopes and all her desires received such satisfaction, and filled all the corners of her heart so much, as indeed it was fain to make room for its reception. But she, to whom the greatest things of religion and the transportations of devotion were made familiar by the assiduity and piety of her daily practices, however she was full of joy, yet she was carried like a full vessel, without the violent tossings of a tempestuous passion or the wrecks of a stormy imagination: and, as the power of the Holy Ghost did descend upon her like rain into a fleece of wool, without any obstreporous noises or violences to nature, but only the extraordinariness of an exaltation; so her spirit received it with the gentleness and tranquillity fitted for the entertainment of the spirit of love, and a quietness symbolical to the holy guest of her spotless womb, the Lamb of God; for she meekly replied, "Behold the handmaid of the Lord; be it unto me according unto thy word: and the angel departed from her," having done his message. And at the same time the Holy Spirit of God did make her to conceive in her womb the immaculate Son of God, the Saviour of the world.

Section II
The Bearing of Jesus in the Womb of the Blessed Virgin

1. Although the blessed Virgin had a faith as prompt and ready, as her body was chaste and her soul pure; yet God, who uses to give full measure, shaken together, and running over, did, by way of confirmation, and fixing the confidence of her assent, give an instance of His omnipotency in the very particular of an extraordinary conception: for the angel said, "Behold thy cousin Elizabeth hath also conceived a son in

her old age, and this is the sixth month with her that was called barren: for with God nothing shall be impossible." A less argument would have satisfied the necessity of a faith which had no scruple; and a greater would not have done it in the incredulity of an ungentle and pertinacious spirit. But the holy maid had complacency enough in the message, and holy desires about her, to carry her understanding as far as her affections, even to the fruition of the angel's message; which is such a sublimity of faith, that it is its utmost consummation, and shall be its crown, when our faith is turned into vision, our hopes into actual possessions, and our grace into glory.

2. And she, who was now full of God, bearing God in her virgin womb, and the Holy Spirit in her heart, who had also overshadowed her, enabling her to a supernatural and miraculous conception, arose with haste and gladness to communicate that joy which was designed for all the world; and she found no breast to pour forth the first emanations of her overjoyed heart so fit as her cousin Elizabeth's, who had received testimony from God to have been "righteous, walking in all the commandments of the Lord blameless"; who also had a special portion in this great honour, for she was designed to be the mother of the Baptist, who was sent as a forerunner, "to prepare the ways of the Lord, and to make His paths straight": "and Mary arose in those days, and went into the hill country with haste, into a city of Judah."

3. Her haste was in proportion to her joy and desires, but yet went no greater pace than her religion: for as in her journey she came near to Jerusalem she turned in, that she might visit His temple, whose temple she herself was now; and there not only to remember the pleasures of religion, which she had felt in continual descents and showers falling on her pious heart, for the space of eleven years' attendance there in her childhood, but also to pay the first fruits of her thanks and joy, and to lay all her glory at His feet, whose humble handmaid she was, in the greatest honour of being His blessed mother: having worshipped, she went on her journey, "and entered into the house of Zacharias, and saluted Elizabeth."

4. It is not easy to imagine what a collision of joys was at this blessed meeting: two mothers of two great princes, the one the greatest that was born of woman, and the other was his Lord, and these made mothers by two miracles, met together with joy and mysteriousness; where the mother of our Lord went to visit the mother of His servant, and the Holy Ghost made the meeting festival, and descended upon Elizabeth, and she prophesied. Never, but in heaven, was there more joy

96

and ecstasy: the persons, who were women whose fancies and affections were not only hallowed, but made pregnant and big with religion, meeting together to compare and unite their joys and their eucharist, and then made prophetical and inspired, must needs have discoursed like seraphims and the most ecstasied order of intelligences; for all the faculties of nature were turned into grace, and expressed in their way the excellent solemnity: "for it came to pass, when Elizabeth heard the salutation of Mary, the babe leaped in her womb; and Elizabeth was filled with the Holy Ghost."

5. After they had both prophesied, and sung their hymns, and resaluted each other with the religion of saints and the joys of angels, "Mary abode with her cousin Elizabeth about three months, and then returned to her own house." Where when she appeared with her holy burden to her husband Joseph, and that he perceived her to be with child, and knew that he had never unsealed that holy fountain of virginal purity, he was troubled. For although her deportment had been pious and chaste to a miracle, her carriage reserved, and so grave, that she drave away temptations and impure visits and all unclean purposes from the neighbourhood of her holy person; yet when he saw she was with child, and had not yet been taught a lesson higher than the principles of nature, "he was minded to put her away," for he knew she was with child; but yet "privily," because he was a good man, and knew her piety to have been such that it had almost done violence to his sense, and made him disbelieve what was visible and notorious, and therefore he would do it privately: "but while he thought on these things, the angel of the Lord appeared unto him in a dream, saying, Joseph, thou son of David, fear not to take unto thee Mary thy wife, for that which is conceived in her is of the Holy Ghost; then Joseph, being raised from sleep, did as the angel of the Lord had bidden him, and took unto him his wife."

Section III
The Nativity of Our Blessed Saviour Jesus

1. The holy maid longed to be a glad mother; and she who carried a burden whose proper commensuration is the days of eternity, counted the tedious minutes, expecting when the Sun of righteousness should break forth from His bed, where nine months He hid Himself as behind a fruitful cloud. About the same time, God, who in His infinite wisdom does concentre and tie together in one end things of disparate and disproportionate natures, making things improbable to co-operate to what wonder or to what truth He pleases, brought the holy Virgin to

97

Bethlehem, the city of David, "to be taxed" with her husband Joseph, according to a decree upon all the world, issuing from Augustus Cæsar.[1] But this happened in this conjunction of time, that it might be fulfilled which was spoken by the prophet Micah, "And thou Bethlehem in the land of Judah art not the least among the princes of Judah, for out of thee shall come a governor that shall rule My people Israel." This rare act of providence was highly remarkable, because this taxing seems wholly to have been ordered by God to serve and minister to the circumstances of this birth.[2] For this taxing was not in order to tribute: Herod was now king, and received all the revenues of the *fiscus,* and paid to Augustus an appointed tribute, after the manner of other kings, friends and relatives of the Roman empire; neither doth it appear that the Romans laid a new tribute on the Jews before the confiscation of the goods of Archelaus. Augustus therefore, sending special delegates to tax every city, made only an inquest after the strength of the Roman empire in men and monies; and did himself no other advantage, but was directed by Him who rules and turns the hearts of princes, that he might, by verifying a prophecy, signify and publish the divinity of the mission and the birth of Jesus.

2. She that had conceived by the operation of that Spirit who dwells within the element of love, was no ways impeded in her journey by the greatness of her burden; but arrived at Bethlehem in the throng of strangers, who had so filled up the places of hospitality and public entertainment, that "there was no room" for Joseph and Mary "in the inn." But yet she felt that it was necessary to retire where she might softly lay her burden, who began now to call at the gates of His prison, and nature was ready to let Him forth. But she that was mother to the king of all the creatures, could find no other but a stable, a cave of a rock, whither she retired; where, when it began to be with her after the manner of women, she humbly bowed her knees, in the posture and guise of worshippers, and in the midst of glorious thoughts and highest speculations "brought forth her first-born into the world."

3. As there was no sin in the conception, so neither had she pains in the production, as the church, from the days of Gregory Nazianzen until now, hath piously believed; though before his days there were some opinions to the contrary, but certainly neither so pious, nor so

---

1. Eusebius, *Ecclesiastical History*, PG 20.81.
2. Chrysostom, *On Matthew*, PG 57.81.

reasonable. For to her alone did not the punishment of Eve extend, that "in sorrow she should bring forth": for where nothing of sin was an ingredient, there misery cannot cohabit. For though amongst the daughters of men many conceptions are innocent and holy, being sanctified by the word of God and prayer, hallowed by marriage, designed by prudence, seasoned by temperance, conducted by religion towards a just, a hallowed, and a holy end, and yet their productions are in sorrow; yet this of the blessed Virgin might be otherwise, because here sin was no relative, and neither was in the principle nor the derivative, in the act nor in the habit, in the root nor in the branch: there was nothing in this but the sanctification of a virgin's womb, and that could not be the parent of sorrow, especially that gate not having been opened by which the curse always entered. And as to conceive by the Holy Ghost was glorious, so to bring forth any of "the fruits of the Spirit" is joyful, and full of felicities. And He that came from His grave fast tied with a stone and signature, and into the college of apostles "the doors being shut," and into the glories of His Father through the solid orbs of all the firmament, came also (as the church piously believes) into the world so without doing violence to the virginal and pure body of His mother, that He did also leave her virginity entire, to be as a seal, that none might open the gate of that sanctuary; that it might be fulfilled which was spoken of the Lord by the prophet, "This gate shall be shut, it shall not be opened, and no man shall enter in by it; because the Lord God of Israel hath entered by it, therefore it shall be shut."[3]

4. Although all the world were concerned in the birth of this great Prince, yet I find no story of any one that ministered at it, save only angels, who knew their duty to their Lord, and the great interests of that person; whom, as soon as He was born, they presented to His mother, who could not but receive Him with a joy next to the rejoicings of glory and beatific vision, seeing Him to be born her son, who was the Son of God, of greater beauty than the sun, purer than angels, more loving than the seraphims, as dear as the eye and heart of God, where He was from eternity engraven, His beloved and His only-begotten.

5. When the virgin mother now felt the first tenderness and yearnings of a mother's bowels, and saw the Saviour of the world born, poor as her fortunes could represent Him, naked as the innocence of Adam, she took Him, and "wrapt Him in swaddling-clothes"; and after

---

3. Ezek. 44:2.

she had a while cradled Him in her arms, she "laid Him in a manger"; for so was the design of His humility; that as the last scene of His life was represented among thieves, so the first was amongst beasts, the sheep and the oxen; according to that mysterious hymn of the prophet Habakkuk, "His brightness was as the light; He had horns coming out of His hand, and there was the hiding of His power."[4]

6. But this place, which was one of the great instances of His humility, grew to be as venerable as became an instrument; and it was consecrated into a church, the crib into an altar, where first lay that "Lamb of God," which afterwards was sacrificed for the sins of all the world. And when Adrian the emperor, who intended a great despite to it, built a temple to Venus and Adonis in that place where the holy virgin-mother, and her more holy Son, were humbly laid; even so he could not obtain but that even amongst the gentile inhabitants of the neighbouring countries it was held in an account far above scandal and contempt. For God can ennoble even the meanest of creatures, especially if it be but a relative and instrumental to religion, higher than the injuries of scoffers and malicious persons. But it was then a temple full of religion, full of glory, when angels were the ministers, the holy Virgin was the worshipper, and Christ the deity.

Section IV
Of the Great and Glorious Accidents Happening about the Birth of Jesus

1. Although the birth of Christ was destitute of the usual excrescences and less necessary pomps which used to signify and illustrate the birth of princes; yet His first humility was made glorious with presages, miracles, and significations from heaven, which did not only, like the furniture of a princely bedchamber, speak the riches of the parent or greatness of the son within its own walls, but did declare to all the world that their prince was born, publishing it with figures and represents almost as great as its empire.

2. For when all the world did expect that in Judea should be born their prince, and that the incredulous world had in their observation slipped by their true prince, because He came not in pompous and secular illustrations; upon that very stock Vespasian[5] was nursed up in

---

4. Hab. 3:4.
5. Suetonius, *Lives of the Caesars* (Vespasian), LCL, vol. 2, p. 286.

hope of the Roman empire, and that hope made him great in designs; and they being prosperous made his fortunes correspond to his hopes, and he was endeared and engaged upon that fortune by the prophecy which was never intended him by the prophet. But the fortune of the Roman monarchy was not great enough for this prince designed by the old prophets. And therefore it was not without the influence of a Divinity that his decessor Augustus, about the time of Christ's nativity, refused to be called "lord,"[6] possibly it was to entertain the people with some hopes of restitution of their liberties, till he had griped the monarchy with a stricter and faster hold: but the Christians were apt to believe that it was upon the prophecy of a sybil foretelling the birth of a greater prince, to whom all the world should pay adoration; and that the prince was about that time born in Judea,[7] the oracle, which was dumb to Augustus's question, told him unasked, the devil having no tongue permitted him but one to proclaim that "an Hebrew child was his lord and enemy."

3. At the birth of which child, there was an universal peace through all the world. For then it was that Augustus Cæsar,[8] having composed all the wars of the world, did the third time cause the gates of Janus's temple to be shut; and this peace continued for twelve years, even till the extreme old age of the prince, until rust had sealed the temple doors, which opened not till the sedition of the Athenians and the rebellion of the Dacians caused Augustus to arm. For He that was born was the Prince of peace, and came to reconcile God with man, and man with his brother; and to make by the sweetness of His example and the influence of a holy doctrine, such happy atonements between disagreeing natures, such confederations and societies between enemies, that "the wolf and the lamb should lie down together, and a little child" boldly and without danger "put his finger in the nest and cavern of an asp."[9] And it could be no less than miraculous, that so great a body as the Roman empire, consisting of so many parts, whose constitutions were differing, their humours contrary, their interests contradicting each other's greatness, and all these violently oppressed by an usurping power, should have no limb out of joint, not so much as an aching tooth, or a rebelling humour, in that huge collection of parts: but so it seemed

---

6. Ibid. (Augustus), vol. 1, p. 206.
7. Orosius, *History Against Paganism*, PL 31. 1057.
8. Ibid.
9. Isa. 11:6.

good in the eye of heaven, by so great and good a symbol to declare not only the greatness, but the goodness, of the Prince that was then born in Judea, the Lord of all the world.

4. But because the heavens as well as the earth are His creatures and do serve Him, at His birth He received a sign in heaven above as well as in the earth beneath, as an homage paid to their common Lord. For as certain shepherds were "keeping watch over their flocks by night," near that part where Jacob did use to feed his cattle when he was in the land of Canaan, "the angel of the Lord came upon them, and the glory of the Lord shone round about them." Needs must the shepherds be afraid, when an angel came arrayed in glory, and clothed their persons in a robe of light, great enough to confound their senses and scatter their understandings. But "the angel said unto them, Fear not; for I bring unto you tidings of great joy, which shall be to all people. For unto you is born this day, in the city of David, a Saviour, which is Christ the Lord." The shepherds needed not be invited to go see this glorious sight; but, lest their fancy should rise up to an expectation of a prince as externally glorious as might be hoped for upon the consequence of so glorious an apparition, the angel, to prevent the mistake, told them of a sign, which indeed was no other than the thing signified; but yet was therefore a sign, because it was so remote from the common probability and expectation of such a birth, that by being a miracle so great a prince should be born so poorly, it became an instrument to signify itself, and all the other parts of mysterious consequence: for the angel said, "this shall be a sign unto you, Ye shall find the babe wrapt in swaddling clothes, lying in a manger."

5. But as light, when it first begins to gild the east, scatters indeed the darknesses from the earth, but ceases not to increase its flame till it hath made perfect day; so it happened now in this apparition of the angel of light: he appeared and told his message, and did shine, but the light arose higher and higher, till midnight was as bright as midday. For, "suddenly there was with the angel a multitude of the heavenly host," and after the angel had told his message in plain song, the whole chorus joined in descant, and sang an hymn to the tune and sense of heaven, where glory is paid to God in eternal and never-ceasing offices, and whence good will descends upon men in perpetual and never-stopping torrents: their song was, "Glory be to God on high, on earth peace, good will towards men"; by this song not only referring to the strange peace which at that time put all the world in ease, but to the great peace which this new-born Prince should make between His Father and all mankind.

6. As soon as these blessed choristers had sung their Christmas carol, and taught the church a hymn to put into her offices for ever in the anniversary of this festivity, "the angels returned into heaven," and "the shepherds went to Bethlehem to see this thing which the Lord had made known unto them: and they came with haste, and found Mary and Joseph, and the babe lying in a manger." Just as the angel had prepared their expectation, they found the narrative verified, and saw the glory and the mystery of it by that representment which was made by the heavenly ministers, seeing God through the veil of a child's flesh, the heir of heaven wrapt in swaddling clothes, and a person to whom the angels did minister, laid in a manger; and they beheld, and wondered, and worshipped.

7. But as precious liquor, warmed and heightened by a flame, first crowns the vessel, and then dances over its brim into the fire, increasing the cause of its own motion and extravagancy; so it happened to the shepherds, whose hearts being filled with the oil of gladness up unto the brim, the joy ran over, as being too big to be confined in their own breasts, and did communicate itself, growing greater by such dissemination: for "when they had seen it, they made known abroad the saying which was told them concerning this child; and," as well they might, "all that heard it, wondered." But Mary, having first changed her joy into wonder, turned her wonder into entertainments of the mystery, and the mystery into a fruition and cohabitation with it: for "Mary kept all these sayings, and pondered them in her heart." And the shepherds having seen what the angels did upon the publication of the news, which less concerned them than us, had learnt their duty, to sing an honour to God for the nativity of Christ: for "the shepherds returned, glorifying and praising God for all the things that they had heard and seen, as it was told unto them."

8. But the angels had told the shepherds that the nativity was "glad tidings of great joy unto all people"; and, that "the heavens might declare the glory of God, and the firmament shew His handy work," this also was told abroad, even to the gentiles, by a sign from heaven, by the message of a star. For there was a prophecy of Balaam, famous in all the eastern country, and recorded by Moses,[10] "there shall come a star out of Jacob, and a sceptre shall arise out of Israel: out of Jacob shall come He that shall have dominion." Which although in its first sense it

---

10. Num. 24:17.

signified David, who was the conqueror of the Moabites, yet in its more mysterious and chiefly intended sense it related to the Son of David; and in expectation of the event of this prophecy,[11] the Arabians, the sons of Abraham by Keturah, whose portion given by their patriarch was gold, frankincense, and myrrh, who were great lovers of astronomy, did with diligence expect the revelation of a mighty prince in Judea at such time when a miraculous and extraordinary star should appear; and therefore, "when Jesus was born in Bethlehem of Judea in the days of Herod the king, there came wise men," inspired by God, taught by art, and persuaded by prophecy, "from the east to Jerusalem, saying, Where is He that is born king of the Jews? for we have seen His star in the east, and are come to worship Him." The Greeks suppose this which was called a star to have been indeed an angel in a pillar of fire, and the semblance of a star; and it is made the more likely, by coming and standing directly over the humble roof of His nativity, which is not discernible in the station of a star, though it be supposed to be lower than the orb of the moon. To which if we add, that they only saw it (so far as we know), and that it appeared as it were by voluntary periods, it will not be very improbable but that it might be like the angel that went before the sons of Israel in a pillar of fire by night; or rather, like the little shining stars sitting upon the bodies of Probus, Tharacus, and Andronicus, martyrs, when their bodies were searched for in the days of Dioclesian, and pointed at by those bright angels.

9. This star did not trouble Herod, till the Levantine princes expounded the mysteriousness of it, and said it declared a "king to be born in Jewry," and that the star was his, not applicable to any signification but of a king's birth.[12] And therefore, although it was no prodigy nor comet, foretelling diseases, plagues, war, and death, but only the happy birth of a most excellent prince, yet it brought affrightment to Herod and all Jerusalem: for "when Herod the king had heard these things, he was troubled, and all Jerusalem with him." And thinking that the question of the kingdom was now in dispute, and an heir sent from heaven to lay challenge to it, who brought a star and the learning of the east with him for evidence and probation of his title, Herod thought there was no security to his usurped possession, unless he could rescind the decrees of Heaven, and reverse the results and eternal counsels of predestina-

---

11. Epiphanius, *An Exposition of the Faith*, PG 42. 786.
12. Ibid.

tion; and he was resolved to venture it, first by craft, and then by violence.

10. And first, "he calls the chief priests and scribes of the people together, and demanded of them where Christ should be born"; and found, by their joint determination, that Bethlehem of Judea was the place designed by ancient prophecy and God's decree. Next, he enquired of the wise men concerning the star, but privily, what time it appeared. For the star had not motion certain and regular, by the laws of nature; but it so guided the wise men in their journey that it stood when they stood, moved not when they rested, and went forward when they were able, making no more haste than they did, who carried much of the business and employment of the star along with them,[13] but when Herod was satisfied in his questions, "he sent them to Bethlehem," with instructions "to search diligently for the young child, and to bring him word," pretending that he would "come and worship him also."

11. The wise men prosecuted the business of their journey, and "having heard the king, they departed; and the star" (which, as it seems, attended their motion) "went before them, until it came and stood over where the young child was"; where "when they saw the star, they rejoiced with exceeding great joy"; such a joy as is usual to wearied travellers when they are entering into their inn; such a joy as when our hopes and greatest longings are laying hold upon the proper objects of their desires; a joy of certainty immediately before the possession: for that is the greatest joy which possesses before it is satisfied, and rejoices with a joy not abated by the surfeits of possession, but heightened with all the apprehensions and fancies of hope and the neighbourhood of fruition; a joy of nature, of wonder, and of religion. And now their hearts laboured with a throng of spirits and passions, and ran into the house, to the embracement of Jesus, even before their feet: but "when they were come into the house, they saw the young child, with Mary His mother." And possibly their expectation was something lessened and their wonder heightened, when they saw their hope empty of pomp and gaiety, the great King's throne to be a manger, a stable to His chamber of presence, a thin court, and no ministers, and the King himself a pretty babe; and, but that He had a star over His head, nothing to distinguish Him from the common condition of children, or to excuse Him from the miseries of a poor and empty fortune.

---

13. Leo, *On Epiphany* (Sermon), PL 54. 244.

12. This did not scandalize those wise persons; but being convinced by that testimony from heaven, and the union of all circumstances, "they fell down and worshipped Him," after the manner of the easterlings when they do veneration to their kings, not with an empty *Ave* and gay blessing of fine words, but "they bring presents and come into His courts"; for "when they had opened their treasures, they presented unto Him gifts, gold, frankincense, and myrrh." And if these gifts were mysterious beyond the acknowledgment of Him to be the king of the Jews, and Christ, that should come into the world; frankincense might signify Him to be acknowledged a God, myrrh to be a man, and gold to be a king: unless we choose by gold to signify the acts of mercy; by myrrh, the chastity of minds and purity of our bodies, to the incorruption of which myrrh is especially instrumental; and by incense we intend our prayers, as the most apt presents and oblations to the honour and service of this young king.[14] But however the fancies of religion may represent variety of ideas, the act of adoration was direct and religious, and the myrrh was medicinal to His tender body; the incense possibly no more than was necessary in a stable, the first throne of His humility: and the gold was a good antidote against the present indigencies of His poverty: presents such as were used in all the Levant (especially in Arabia and Saba, to which the growth of myrrh and frankincense were proper) in their addresses to their God and to their king; and were instruments with which, under the veil of flesh, they worshipped the eternal Word; the wisdom of God, under infant innocency; the almighty power, in so great weakness; and under the lowness of human nature, the altitude of majesty and the infinity of divine glory. And so was verified the prediction of the prophet Esay under the type of the son of the prophetess, "before a child shall have knowledge to cry, My father and my mother, he shall take the spoil of Damascus and Samaria from before the king of Assyria."

13. When they had paid the tribute of their offerings and adoration, "being warned in their sleep by an angel not to return to Herod, they returned into their own country another way"; where, having been satisfied with the pleasures of religion, and taught by that rare demonstration which was made by Christ how man's happiness did nothing at all consist in the affluence of worldly possessions or the tumours of honour; having seen the eternal Son of God poor and weak and un-

---

14. Ambrose, *On Luke*, PL 15. 1649.

clothed of all exterior ornaments; they renounced the world, and retired empty into the recesses of religion and the delights of philosophy.

Section V
Of the Circumcision of Jesus, and His Presentation in the Temple

1. And now the blessed Saviour of the world began to do the work of His mission and our redemption: and because man had prevaricated all the divine commandments, to which all human nature respectively to the persons of several capacities was obliged, and therefore the whole nature was obnoxious to the just rewards of its demerits; first Christ was to put that nature He had assumed into a saveable condition, by fulfilling His Father's preceptive will, and then to reconcile it actually by suffering the just deservings of its prevarications. He therefore addresses Himself to all the parts of an active obedience; "and when eight days were accomplished for the circumcising of the child," He exposed His tender body to the sharpness of the circumcising stone, and shed His blood in drops, giving an earnest of those rivers which He did afterwards pour out for the cleansing all human nature, and extinguishing the wrath of God.

2. He that had no sin, nor was conceived by natural generation, could have no adherences to His soul or body which needed to be pared away by a rite and cleansed by a mystery; neither indeed do we find it expressed that circumcision was ordained for abolition or pardon of original sin; it is indeed presumed so; but it was instituted to be a seal of a covenant between God and Abraham and Abraham's posterity, "a seal of the righteousness of faith," and therefore was not improper for Him to suffer who was the child of Abraham, and who was the prince of the covenant, and "the author and finisher of that faith" which was consigned to Abraham in circumcision. But so mysterious were all the actions of Jesus, that this one served many ends: for first, it gave demonstration of the verity of human nature; secondly, so He began to fulfil the law; thirdly, and took from Himself the scandal of uncircumcision, which would eternally have prejudiced the Jews against His entertainment and communion; fourthly, and then He took upon Him that name, which declared Him to be the Saviour of the world; which, as it was consummate in the blood of the cross, so was it inaugurated in the blood of circumcision: for "when the eight days were accomplished for circumcising of the child, His name was called Jesus."

3. But this holy family, who had laid up their joys in the eyes and heart of God, longed till they might be permitted an address to the

temple, that there they might present the holy babe unto His Father; and indeed that He, who had no other, might be brought to His own house. For although while He was a child He did differ nothing from a servant, yet He was the lord of the place: it was His Father's house, and He was "the Lord of all": and therefore "when the days of the purification were accomplished, they brought Him to Jerusalem to present Him to the Lord," to whom He was holy, as being the first-born; the "first-born of His mother," the "only-begotten Son of His Father," and "the first-born of every creature": and they "did with Him according to the law of Moses, offering a pair of turtle doves" for His redemption.

4. But there was no public act about this holy child but it was attended by something miraculous and extraordinary; and at this instant the Spirit of God directed a holy person into the temple, that he might feel the fulfilling of a prophecy made to himself, that he might before his death "behold the Lord's Christ," and embrace "the glory and consolation of Israel, and the light of the gentiles," in his arms: for old "Simeon came by the Spirit into the temple: and when the parents brought in the child Jesus, then took he Him up in his arms, and blessed God," and prophesied, and spake glorious things of that child, and things sad and glorious concerning His mother; that the "child was set for the rising and falling of many in Israel, for a sign that should be spoken against": and the bitterness of that contradiction should pierce the heart of the holy Virgin-mother like a sword, that her joy at the present accidents might be tempered with present revelation of her future trouble, and the excellent favour of being the mother of God might be crowned with the reward of martyrdom, and a mother's love be raised up to an excellency great enough to make her suffer the bitterness of being transfixed with His love and sorrow, as with a sword.

5. But old Anna the prophetess came also in, full of years and joy, and found the reward of her long prayers and fasting in the temple: the long looked-for redemption of Israel was now in the temple, and she saw with her eyes the light of the world, the heir of heaven, the long looked-for Messias, whom the nations had desired and expected till their hearts were faint and their eyes dim with looking farther and apprehending greater distances. She also prophesied, "and gave thanks unto the Lord. But Joseph and His mother marvelled at those things which were spoken of Him."

Section VI
Of the Death of the Holy Innocents, or the Babes of Bethlehem, and the Flight of Jesus into Egypt

1. All this while Herod waited for the return of the wise men, that they might give directions where the child did lie, and his sword might find Him out with a certain and direct execution. But "when he saw that he was mocked of the wise men, he was exceeding wroth"; for it now began to deserve his trouble, when his purposes, which were most secret, began to be contradicted and diverted with a prevention, as if they were resisted by an all-seeing and almighty Providence. He began to suspect the hand of heaven was in it, and saw there was nothing for his purposes to be acted unless he could dissolve the golden chain of predestination. Herod believed the divine oracles foretelling that a king should be born in Bethlehem, and yet his ambition had made him so stupid that he attempted to cancel the decree of heaven; for if he did not believe the prophecies, why was he troubled? if he did believe them, how could he possibly hinder that event which God had foretold Himself would certainly bring to pass?

2. And therefore since God already had hindered him from the executions of a distinguishing sword, he resolved to send a sword of indiscrimination and confusion, hoping that if he killed all the babes of Bethlehem, this young king's reign also should soon determine. He therefore "sent forth and slew all the children that were in Bethlehem and all the coasts thereof, from two years old and under, according to the time which he had diligently enquired of the wise men." For this execution was in the beginning of the second year after Christ's nativity, as in all probability we guess; not at the two years' end, as some suppose: because as his malice was subtle, so he intended it should be secure; and though he had been diligent in his enquiry, and was near the time in his computation, yet he, that was never sparing of the lives of others, would now, to secure his kingdom, rather overact his severity for some months, than by doing execution but just to the tittle of his account, hazard the escaping of the Messias.

3. This execution was sad, cruel, and universal: no abatements made for the dire shriekings of the mothers, no tender-hearted soldier was employed, no hard-hearted person was softened by the weeping eyes and pity-begging looks of those mothers, that wondered how it was possible any person should hurt their pretty sucklings; no conniv-

ances there, no protections, or friendships, or considerations, or indulgencies; but Herod caused that his own child, which was at nurse in the coasts of Bethlehem, should bleed to death: which made Augustus Cæsar to say that "in Herod's house it were better to be a hog than a child," because the custom of the nation did secure a hog from Herod's knife, but no religion could secure his child. The sword, being thus made sharp by Herod's commission, killed fourteen thousand pretty babes; as the Greeks in their calendar, and the Abyssines of Ethiopia, do commemorate in their offices of liturgy. For Herod, crafty and malicious, that is, perfectly tyrant, had caused all the children to be gathered together; which the credulous mothers, supposing it had been to take account of their age and number in order to some taxing, hindered not, but unwittingly suffered themselves and their babes to be betrayed to an irremediable butchery.

4. "Then was fulfilled that which was spoken by Jeremy the prophet, saying, Lamentation, and weeping, and great mourning; Rachel weeping for her children, and would not be comforted." All the synonymas of sadness were little enough to express this great weeping, when fourteen thousand mothers in one day saw their pretty babes pouring forth their blood into that bosom, whence not long before they had sucked milk; and instead of those pretty smiles which use to entertain the fancy and dear affections of their mothers, nothing but affrighting shrieks, and then ghastly looks. The mourning was great, like "the mourning in the valley of Hinnom, and there was no comforter"; their sorrow was too big to be cured, till it should lie down alone, and rest with its own weariness.

5. But the malice of Herod went also into the hill country; and hearing that of John, the son of Zachary, great things were spoken, by which he was designed to a great ministry about this young prince, he attempted in him also to rescind the prophecies, and sent a messenger of death towards him; but the mother's care had been early with him, and sent him into desert places, where he continued till the time appointed "of his manifestation unto Israel." But as the children of Bethlehem died in the place of Christ, so did the father of the Baptist die for his child; for Herod "slew Zachary between the temple and the altar," because he refused to betray his son to the fury of that rabid bear. Though some persons, very eminent amongst the stars of the primitive church, report a tradition, that a place being separated in the temple for virgins, Zachary suffered the mother of our Lord to abide there after the

birth of her holy Son, affirming her still to be a virgin; and that for this reason, not Herod, but the scribes and pharisees, did kill Zachary.[15]

6. Tertullian reports that the blood of Zachary had so besmeared the stones of the pavement, which was the altar on which the good old priest was sacrificed, that no art or industry could wash the tincture out, the dye and guilt being both indelible; as if, because God did intend to exact of that nation "all the blood of righteous persons from Abel to Zacharias," who was the last of the martyrs of the synagogue, He would leave a character of their guilt in their eyes, to upbraid their irreligion, cruelty, and infidelity.[16] Some there are who affirm these words of our blessed Saviour not to relate to any Zachary who had been already slain, but to be a prophecy of the last of all the martyrs of the Jews, who should be slain immediately before the destruction of the last temple, and the dissolution of the nation. Certain it is that such a Zachary the son of Baruch (if we may believe Josephus) was slain in the middle of the temple, a little before it was destroyed; and it is agreeable to the nature of the prophecy and reproof here made by our blessed Saviour, that "from Abel to Zachary" should take in "all the righteous blood" from first to last, till the iniquity was complete;[17] and it is not imaginable that the blood of our blessed Lord, and of St. James their bishop (for whose death many of themselves thought God destroyed their city), should be left out of the account, which yet would certainly be left out, if any other Zachary should be meant than he whom they last slew: and in proportion to this, Cyprian de Valera expounds that which we read in the past tense, to signify the future, "ye slew," i.e. "shall slay"; according to the style often used by prophets, and as the aorist of an uncertain signification will bear. But the first great instance of the divine vengeance for these executions was upon Herod, who in very few years after was smitten of God with so many plagues and tortures, that himself alone seemed like an hospital of the *incurabili*: for he was tormented with a soft slow fire, like that of burning iron or the cinders of yew, in his body; in his bowels, with intolerable colics and ulcers; in his natural parts, with worms; in his feet, with gout; in his nerves, with convulsions, difficulty of breathing; and out of divers parts of his body

---

15. Gregory Nyssa, *On the Epiphany*, MG 46. 594.
16. Tertullian, *Scorpiace*, PL 2. 136.
17. Josephus, *The Jewish War*, LCL, (bk. 4, ch. 5), vol. 3, p. 98.

issued out so impure and ulcerous a steam, that the loathsomeness, pain, and indignation, made him once to snatch a knife with purpose to have killed himself, but that he was prevented by a nephew of his that stood there in his attendance.

7. But as the flesh of beasts grows callous by stripes and the pressures of the yoke, so did the heart of Herod by the loads of divine vengeance; God began his hell here, and the pains of hell never made any man less impious. For Herod, perceiving that he must now die, first put to death his son Antipater, under pretence that he would have poisoned him; and that the last scene of his life might for pure malice and exalted spite outdo all the rest, because he believed the Jewish nation would rejoice at his death, he assembled all the nobles of the people and put them in prison, giving in charge to his sister Salome that when he was expiring his last all the nobility should be slain, that his death might be lamented with a perfect and universal sorrow.

8. But God, that brings to nought the counsels of wicked princes, turned the design against the intendment of Herod; for when he was dead, and could not call his sister to account for disobeying his most bloody and unrighteous commands, she released all the imprisoned and despairing gentlemen, and made the day of her brother's death a perfect jubilee, a day of joy, such as was that when the nation was delivered from the violence of Haman in the days of Purim.

9. And all this while God had provided a sanctuary for the holy child Jesus. For God, seeing the secret purposes of blood which Herod had, sent His angel, "who appeared to Joseph in a dream, saying, Arise, and take the young child and His mother, and fly into Egypt, and be thou there until I bring thee word; for Herod will seek the young child to destroy Him. Then he arose, and took the young child and His mother by night, and departed into Egypt."[18] And they made their first abode in Hermopolis, in the country of Thebais; whither when they first arrived, the child Jesus being by design or providence carried into a temple, all the statues of the idol-gods fell down, like Dagon at the presence of the ark, and suffered their timely and just dissolution and dishonour, according to the prophecy of Isaiah, "Behold the Lord shall come into Egypt, and the idols of Egypt shall be moved at His presence."[19] And in the life of the prophet Jeremy written by Epiphanius, it

---

18. Matt. 2:13.
19. Isa. 19:1.

is reported "that he told the Egyptian priests, that then their idols should be broken in pieces, when a holy virgin, with her child, should enter into their country"; which prophecy possibly might be the cause that the Egyptians did, besides their vanities, worship also an infant in a manger, and a virgin in her bed.

10. From Hermopolis to Maturea went these holy pilgrims in pursuance of their safety and provisions; where, it was reported, they dwelt in a garden of balsam, till Joseph being at the end of seven years (as it is commonly believed) ascertained by an angel of the death of Herod, and commanded to return to the land of Israel, he was obedient to the heavenly vision and returned. But hearing that Archelaus did reign in the place of his father, and knowing that the cruelty and ambition of Herod was hereditary, or entailed upon Archelaus, being also warned to turn aside into the parts of Galilee, which was of a distinct jurisdiction, governed indeed by one of Herod's sons, but not by Archelaus, thither he diverted; and there that holy family remained in the city of Nazareth, whence the holy Child had the appellative of a Nazarene.

Section VII
Of the Younger Years of Jesus, and His Disputation with the Doctors in the Temple

1. From the return of this holy family to Judea and their habitation in Nazareth, till the blessed child Jesus was twelve years of age, we have nothing transmitted to us out of any authentic record, but that they went to Jerusalem every year at the feast of the passover. And when Jesus was twelve years old, and was in the holy city attending upon the paschal rites and solemn sacrifices of the law, His parents, having fulfilled their days of festivity, went homeward, supposing the child had been in the caravan among His friends; and so they erred for the space of a whole day's journey; "and when they sought Him, and found Him not, they returned to Jerusalem," full of fears and sorrow.

2. No fancy can imagine the doubts, the apprehensions, the possibilities of mischief, and the tremblings of heart, which the holy virgin mother felt thronging about her fancy and understanding, but such a person who hath been tempted to the danger of a violent fear and transportation by apprehension of the loss of a hope greater than a miracle; her discourses with herself could have nothing of distrust, but much of sadness and wonder; and the indetermination of her thoughts was a trouble great as the passion of her love. Possibly an angel might

have carried Him, she knew not whither; or it may be the son of Herod had gotten the prey which his cruel father missed; or He was sick, or detained out of curiosity and wonder, or any thing but what was right. And by this time she was come to Jerusalem; and having spent three days in her sad and holy pursuit of her lost jewel, despairing of the prosperous event of any human diligence, as in all other cases she had accustomed, she made her address to God; and entering into the temple to pray, God, that knew her desires, prevented her with the blessings of goodness; and there her sorrow was changed into joy and wonder; for there she found her holy Son, "sitting in the midst of the doctors, both hearing them, and asking them questions."

3. "And when they saw Him, they were amazed," and so were "all that heard Him, at His understanding and answers"; beyond His education, beyond His experience, beyond His years, and even beyond the common spirits of the best men, discoursing up to the height of a prophet, with the clearness of an angel, and the infallibility of inspiration: for here it was verified, in the highest and most literal signification, that "out of the mouths of babes God had ordained strength"; but this was the strength of argument, and science of the highest mysteries of religion and secret philosophy.

4. Glad were the parents of the Child to find Him illustrated with a miracle, concerning which when He had given them such an account, which they understood not, but yet Mary laid up in her heart, as that this was part of His employment and His Father's business, "He returned with them to Nazareth, and was subject to His parents"; where He lived in all holiness and humility, shewing great signs of wisdom, endearing Himself to all that beheld His conversation; did nothing less than might become the great expectation which His miraculous birth had created of Him; for "He increased in wisdom and stature, and favour with God and man," still growing in proportion to His great beginnings to a miraculous excellency of grace, sweetness of demeanour, and excellency of understanding.

5. They that love to serve God in hard questions, use to dispute whether Christ did truly, or in appearance only, increase in wisdom; for being personally united to the Word, and being the eternal wisdom of the Father, it seemed to them that a plenitude of wisdom was as natural to the whole person as to the divine nature: but others fixing their belief upon the words of the story, which equally affirms Christ as properly to have "increased in favour with God as with man, in wisdom as in stature," they apprehend no inconvenience in affirming it to belong to

the verity of human nature to have degrees of understanding as well as of other perfections: and although the humanity of Christ made up the same person with the divinity, yet they think the divinity still to be free, even in those communications which were imparted to His inferior nature; and the Godhead might as well suspend the emanation of all the treasures of wisdom upon the humanity for a time, as He did the beatifical vision, which most certainly was not imparted in the interval of His sad and dolorous passion. But whether it were truly or in appearance, in habit or in exercise of act, by increase of notion or experience, it is certain the promotions of the holy Child were great, admirable, and as full of wonder as of sanctity, and sufficient to entertain the hopes and expectations of Israel with preparations and dispositions, as to satisfy their wonder for the present, so to accept Him at the time of His publication; they having no reason to be scandalized at the smallness, improbability, and indifferency of His first beginnings.

6. But the holy Child had also an employment, which He undertook in obedience to His supposed father, for exercise and example of humility, and for the support of that holy family, which was dear in the eyes of God, but not very splendid by the opulency of a free and indulgent fortune. He wrought in the trade of a carpenter; and when Joseph died, which happened before the manifestation of Jesus unto Israel, He wrought alone, and was no more called the carpenter's son, but the carpenter himself. "Is not this the carpenter, the son of Mary?" said his offended countrymen.[20] And in this condition the blessed Jesus did abide till He was thirty years old; for He, that came to fulfil the law, would not suffer one tittle of it to pass unaccomplished; for by the law of the nation and custom of the religion, no priest was to officiate or prophet was to preach before He was thirty years of age.

Section VIII
Of the Preaching of John the Baptist, Preparative to the Manifestation of Jesus

1. When Herod had drunk so great a draught of blood at Bethlehem, and sought for more from the hill-country, Elizabeth carried her son into the wilderness, there in the desert places and recesses to hide him from the fury of that beast, where she attended him with as much care and tenderness as the affections and fears of a mother could express

---

20. Mark 6:13.

in the permission of those fruitless solitudes.[21] The child was about eighteen months old when he first fled to sanctuary; but after forty days his mother died, and his father Zachary at the time of his ministration, which happened about this time, was killed in the court of the temple; so that the child was exposed to all the dangers and infelicities of an orphan, in a place of solitariness and discomfort, in a time when a bloody king endeavoured his destruction. But "when his father and mother were taken from him, the Lord took him up." For, according to the tradition of the Greeks,[22] God deputed an angel to be his nourisher and guardian; as he had formerly done to Ishmael[23] who dwelt in the wilderness, and to Elias when he fled from the rage of Ahab,[24] so to this child, who came in the spirit of Elias; to make demonstration that there can be no want where God undertakes the care and provision.

2. The entertainment that St. John's *proveditore* the angel gave him was such as the wilderness did afford, and such as might dispose him to a life of austerity; for there he continued spending his time in meditations, contemplation, prayer, affections and colloquies with God, eating flies and wild honey, not clothed in soft, but a hairy garment and a leathern girdle, till he was thirty years of age. And then, being the fifteenth year of Tiberius, Pontius Pilate being governor of Judea, "the word of God came unto John in the wilderness. And he came into all the country about Jordan, preaching and baptizing."

3. This John, according to the prophecies of him and designation of his person by the holy Ghost, was the fore-runner of Christ, sent to dispose the people for His entertainment, and "prepare His ways"; and therefore it was necessary his person should be so extraordinary and full of sanctity, and so clarified by great concurrences and wonder in the circumstances of his life, as might gain credit and reputation to the testimony he was to give concerning his Lord, the Saviour of the world. And so it happened.

4. For as the Baptist, while he was in the wilderness, became the pattern of solitary and contemplative life, a school of virtue, and example of sanctity and singular austerity; so at his emigration from the places of his retirement he seemed, what indeed he was, a rare and

---

21. Theodoret, *Nativity of John the Baptist*, PG 84. 34.
22. Ibid.
23. Gen. 21:17.
24. 1 Kings 19:5.

excellent personage: and the wonders which were great at his birth, the prediction of his conception by an angel, which never had before happened but in the persons of Isaac and Sampson, the contempt of the world which he bore about him, his mortified countenance and deportment, his austere and eremitical life, his vehement spirit and excellent zeal in preaching, created so great opinions of him among the people, that "all held him for a prophet" in his office, for a heavenly person in his own particular, and a rare example of sanctity and holy life to all others: and all this being made solemn and ceremonious by his baptism, he prevailed so, that he made excellent and apt preparations for the Lord's appearing; for "there went out to him Jerusalem, and all Judea, and all the regions round about Jordan, and were baptized of him, confessing their sins."

5. The Baptist having by so heavenly means won upon the affections of all men, his sermons and his testimony concerning Christ were the more likely to be prevalent and accepted; and the sum of them was "repentance and dereliction of sins," and "bringing forth the fruits of good life"; in the promoting of which doctrine he was a severe reprehender of the pharisees and sadducees, he exhorted the people to works of mercy, the publicans to do justice and to decline oppression, the soldiers to abstain from plundering and doing violence or rapine: and publishing that "he was not the Christ," that he only "baptized with water," but the Messias should "baptize with the holy Ghost and with fire," he finally denounced judgment and great severities to all the world of impenitents, even abscission and "fire unquenchable." And from this time forward, viz. "from the days of John the baptist, the kingdom of heaven suffered violence, and the violent take it by force." For now the gospel began to dawn, and John was like the morning star, or the blushings springing from the windows of the east, foretelling the approach of the Sun of righteousness: and as St. John baptist laid the first rough, hard and unhewn stone of this building in mortification, self-denial, and doing violence to our natural affections; so it was continued by the Master-builder himself, who propounded the glories of the crown of the heavenly kingdom to them only who should climb the cross to reach it. Now it was that multitudes should throng and crowd to enter in at the straight gate, and press into the kingdom; and the younger brothers should snatch the inheritance from the elder, the unlikely from the more likely, the gentiles from the Jews, the strangers from the natives, the publicans and harlots from the scribes and phari-

sees; who, like violent persons, shall by their importunity, obedience, watchfulness, and diligence, snatch the kingdom from them to whom it was first offered; and "Jacob shall be loved, and Esau rejected."

Section IX
Of Jesus Being Baptized, and Going into the Wilderness to be Tempted

1. Now the full time was come, Jesus took leave of His mother and His trade, to begin His Father's work, and the office prophetical, in order to the redemption of the world; and when "John was baptizing in Jordan, Jesus came to John to be baptized of him." The Baptist had never seen His face, because they had been from their infancy driven to several places, designed to several employments, and never met till now. But immediately the holy Ghost inspired St. John with a discerning and knowing spirit, and at His first arrival he knew Him and did Him worship. And when Jesus desired to be baptized, "John forbade Him, saying, I have need to be baptized of Thee, and comest Thou to me?" For the baptism of John, although it was not a direct instrument of the Spirit for the collation of grace, neither find we it administered in any form of words—not so much as in the name of Christ to come, as many dream; because even after John had baptized, the pharisees still doubted if he were the Messias; which they would not, if in his form of ministration he had published Christ to come after him; and also because it had not been proper for Christ himself to have received that baptism, whose form had specified Himself to come hereafter; neither could it consist with the revelation which John had, and the confession which he made, to baptize in the name of Christ to come, whom the Spirit marked out to him to be come already, and himself pointed at Him with his finger—yet it was a ceremonious consignation of the doctrine of repentance, which was one great part of the covenant evangelical; and was a divine institution, the susception of it was in order to the fulfilling all righteousness; it was a sign of humility, the persons baptized confessed their sins; it was a sacramental disposing to the baptism and faith of Christ; but therefore John wondered why the Messias, the Lamb of God, pure and without spot, who needed not the abstersions of repentance or the washings of baptism, should demand it, and of him, a sinner, and His servant. And in the Hebrew gospel of St. Matthew, which the Nazarenes used at Berœa (as St. Hierom reports), these words are added, "The mother of the Lord and His brethren said unto Him, John baptist baptizeth to the remission of sins, let us go and be baptized

of him. He said to them, What have I sinned, that I should go and be baptized of him?"[25] And this part of the story is also told by Justin Martyr. But Jesus wanted not a proposition to consign by His baptism, proportionable enough to the analogy of its institution; for as others professed their return towards innocence, so He avowed His perseverance in it; and though He was never called in scripture a sinner, yet He was made sin for us; that is, He did undergo the shame and the punishment; and therefore it was proper enough for Him to perform the sacrament of sinners.

2. But the holy Jesus, who came (as Himself, in answer to the Baptist's question, professed) "to fulfil all righteousness," would receive that rite which His Father had instituted in order to the manifestation of His Son. For although the Baptist had a glimpse of Him by the first irradiations of the Spirit, yet John professed that he therefore came baptizing with water, that "Jesus might be manifested to Israel"; and it was also a sign given to the Baptist himself, that "on whomsoever he saw the Spirit descending and remaining," He is the person "that baptizeth with the holy Ghost."[26] And God chose to actuate the sign at the waters of Jordan, in great and religious assemblies convened there at John's baptism; and therefore Jesus came to be baptized, and by this baptism became known to John, who, as before he gave to Him an indiscriminate testimony, so now he pointed out the person in his sermons and discourses, and by calling Him the Lamb of God, prophesied of His passion, and preached Him to be the world's Redeemer and the sacrifice for mankind. He was now manifest to Israel: He confirmed the baptism of John; He sanctified the water to become sacramental and ministerial in the remission of sins; He by a real event declared, that to them who should rightly be baptized the kingdom of heaven should certainly be opened; He inserted Himself by that ceremony into the society and participation of holy people, of which communion Himself was head and prince; and He did in a symbol purify human nature, whose stains and guilt He had undertaken.

3. As soon as John had performed his ministry, and Jesus was baptized, He prayed, and the heavens were opened, and the air clarified by a new and glorious light; "and the holy Ghost, in the manner of a

---

25. Jerome, *Against the Pelagians*, PL 23. 570.
26. Clement, *Apostolic Constitutions*, PG 1. 1013.

dove, alighted upon" His sacred head, and God the Father gave "a voice from heaven, saying, Thou art My beloved Son, in whom I am well pleased."[27] This was the inauguration and proclamation of the Messias, when He began to be the great prophet of the new covenant. And this was the greatest meeting that ever was upon earth, where the whole cabinet of the mysterious Trinity was opened and shewn, as much as the capacities of our present imperfections will permit; the second Person in the veil of humanity, the third in the shape or with the motion of a dove; but the first kept His primitive state; and as to the Israelites He gave notice by way of caution, "Ye saw no shape, but ye heard a voice," so now also God the Father gave testimony to His holy Son and appeared, only in a voice without any visible representment.

4. When the rite and the solemnity was over, "Christ ascended up out of the waters," and left so much virtue behind Him, that, as Gregorius Turonensis reports, that creek of the river where His holy body had been baptized, was endued with a healing quality, and a power of curing lepers that bathed themselves in those waters in the faith and with invocation of the holy name of Jesus. But the manifestation of this power was not till afterwards, for as yet Jesus did no miracles.

5. As soon as ever the Saviour of the world was baptized, had opened the heavens, which yet never had been opened to man, and was declared the Son of God, "Jesus was by the Spirit driven into the wilderness," not by an unnatural violence, but by the efficacies of inspiration, and a supernatural inclination and activity of resolution; for it was the holy Spirit that bare Him thither; He was led by the good Spirit to be tempted by the evil: whither also He was pleased to retire, to make demonstration, that even in an active life, such as He was designed to and intended, some recesses and temporary demissions of the world are most expedient, for such persons especially whose office is prophetical and for institution of others, that by such vacancies in prayer and contemplation they may be better enabled to teach others, when they have in such retirements conversed with God.

6. In the desert, which was four miles from the place of His baptism, and about twenty miles from Jerusalem, as the common computations are, He did abide "forty days and forty nights," where He was perpetually disturbed and assaulted with evil spirits, in the midst of wild

----

27. Matt. 3:16; Mark 1:10; Luke 3:22.

beasts, in a continual fast, without eating bread or drinking water; "and the angels ministered to Him," being messengers of comfort and sustentation, sent from His Father for the support and service of His humanity, and employed in resisting and discountenancing the assaults and temporal hostilities of the spirits of darkness.

7. Whether the devils appeared in any horrid and affrighting shapes, is not certain; but it is more likely to a person of so great sanctity and high designation they would appear more angelical and immaterial, in representments intellectual, in words and ideas, temptations and enticements, because Jesus was not a person of those low weaknesses to be affrighted or troubled with an ugly phantasm, which can do nothing but abuse the weak and imperfect conceptions of persons nothing extraordinary. And this was the way which Satan, or the prince of the devils, took, whose temptations were reserved for the last assault, and the great day of trial; for at the expiration of his forty days Jesus being hungry, the tempter invited Him only to eat bread of His own providing, which might refresh His humanity, and prove His divinity, hoping that His hunger, and the desire of convincing the devil, might tempt Him to eat before the time appointed. "But Jesus answered, It is written, Man shall not live by bread alone, but by every word that proceeds out of the mouth of God": meaning, that in every word of God, whether the commandment be general or special, a promise is either expressed or implied of the supply of all provisions necessary for him that is doing the work of God; and that was the present case of Jesus, who was then doing His Father's work, and promoting our interest, and therefore was sure to be provided for: and therefore so are we.

8. The devil, having failed in his assault, tries Him again, requiring but a demonstration of His being the Son of God. He "sets Him upon the battlement of the temple," and invites Him to throw Himself down, upon a pretence that God would send His angels to keep His Son, and quotes scripture for it. But Jesus understood it well; and though He was secured of God's protection, yet He would not tempt God, nor solicit His providence to a dereliction by tempting Him to an unnecessary conservation. This assault was silly and weak. But at last he unites all his powers of stratagem, and places the holy Jesus upon an exceeding high mountain, and by an angelical power draws into one centre species and ideas from all the kingdoms and glories of the world, and makes an admirable map of beauties, and represents it to the eyes of Jesus, saying that all that was put into his power to give, and he "would give it Him if

He would fall down and worship him." But then the holy Lamb was angry as a provoked lion, and commanded him away, when his temptations were violent and his demands impudent and blasphemous. "Then the devil leaveth Him, and the angels came and ministered unto Him," bringing such things as His necessities required, after He had by a forty days' fast done penance for our sins, and consigned to His church the doctrine and discipline of fasting in order to a contemplative life and the resisting and overcoming all the temptations and allurements of the devil and all our ghostly enemies.

The History of the Life and Death of the Holy Jesus

PART II

BEGINNING AT THE TIME OF HIS FIRST MIRACLE UNTIL THE SECOND YEAR OF HIS PREACHING

Section X
Of the First Manifestation of Jesus, by the Testimony of John and a Miracle

1. After that the Baptist by a sign from heaven was confirmed in spirit and understanding that Jesus was the Messias, he immediately published to the Jews what God had manifested to him. And first to the priests and levites, sent in legation from the Sanhedrim, he professed indefinitely, in answer to their question, that himself was "not the Christ, nor Elias, nor that prophet" whom they, by a special tradition, did expect to be revealed, they knew not when: and concerning himself definitely he said nothing, but that he was "the voice of one crying in the wilderness, Make straight the way of the Lord"; He it was who was then "amongst them," but "not known," a person of great dignity, to whom the Baptist was "not worthy" to do the office of the lowest ministry, "who, coming after John, was preferred far before him,"[28] who was to increase,[29] and the Baptist was to decrease, who did "baptize with the holy Ghost and with fire."[30]

2. This was the character of His personal prerogatives; but as yet no demonstration was made of His person till after the descent of the holy Ghost upon Jesus, and then whenever the Baptist saw Jesus, he points Him out with his finger, "Behold the Lamb of God, which taketh away the sins of the world; this is He."[31] Then he shews Him to

---

28. John 1:15.
29. John 3:30.
30. Matt. 3:11.
31. John 1:29.

Andrew, Simon Peter's brother, with the same designation, and to another disciple with him, "who both followed Jesus, and abode with Him all night":[32] Andrew brings his brother Simon with him, and then Christ changes his name from Simon to Peter, or Cephas, which signifies a stone. Then Jesus himself finds out Philip of Bethsaida, and bade him follow Him; and Philip finds out Nathanael, and calls him to see. Thus persons bred in a dark cell, upon their first ascent up to the chambers of light, all run, staring upon the beauties of the sun, and call the partners of their darkness to communicate in their new and stranger revelation.

3. When Nathanael was come to Jesus, Christ saw his heart, and gave him a testimony to be truly honest and full of holy simplicity, "a true Israelite, without guile." And Nathanael being overjoyed that he had found the Messias, believing out of love, and loving by reason of his joy and no suspicion, took that for a proof and verification of His person which was very insufficient to confirm a doubt or ratify a probability: but so we believe a story which we love, taking probabilities for demonstrations, and casual accidents for probabilities: and any thing creates vehement presumptions; in which cases our guides are not our knowing faculties, but our affections; and if they be holy, God guides them into the right persuasions, as He does little birds to make rare nests, though they understand not the mystery of operation, nor the design and purpose of the action.

4. But Jesus took his will and forwardness of affections in so good part, that He promised him greater things; and this gave occasion to the first prophecy which was made by Jesus: for "Jesus said unto him, Because I said I saw thee under the fig-tree, believest thou? thou shalt see greater things than these": and then He prophesied that he should see "heaven open, and the angels of God ascending and descending upon the Son of man"; but being a doctor of the law, Christ chose him not at all to the college of apostles.[33]

5. Much about the same time there happened to be a marriage in Cana of Galilee, in the vicinage of His dwelling, where John the evangelist is by some supposed to have been the bridegroom (but of this there is no certainty); and thither Jesus being with His mother invited, He went, to do civility to the persons espoused, and to do honour to the

---

32. John 1:37.
33. Augustine, *On John's Gospel*, PL 35. 1445.

holy rite of marriage. The persons then married were but of indifferent fortunes, richer in love of neighbours than in the fulness of rich possessions; they had more company than wine. For the master of the feast (whom, according to the order and piety of the nation, they chose from the order of priests to be the president of the feast, by the reverence of his person to restrain all inordination, by his discretion to govern and order the circumstances, by his religious knowledge to direct the solemnities of marriage, and to retain all the persons and actions in the bonds of prudence and modesty) complained to the bridegroom that the guests wanted wine.

6. As soon as the holy Virgin-mother had notice of the want, out of charity, that uses to be employed in supplying even the minutest and smallest articles of necessity, as well as the clamorous importunity of extremities and great indigencies, she complained to her Son by an indefinite address; not desiring Him to make supply, for she knew not how He should; but either out of an habitual commiseration she complained without hoping for remedy, or else she looked on Him, who was a fountain of holiness and of plenty, as expecting a derivation from Him either of discourses or miracles. But "Jesus answered her, woman, what have I to do with thee? Mine hour is not yet come": by this answer intending no denial to the purpose of His mother's intimation, to whom He always bare a religious and pious reverence; but to signify that He was not yet entered into His period and years of miracles; and when He did, it must be not for respect of kindred or civil relations, but as it is a derivation of power from above, so it must be in pursuit of that service and design which He had received in charge together with His power.

7. And so His mother understood Him, giving express charge to the ministers to do whatsoever He commanded. Jesus therefore bade them "fill the water-pots," which stood there for the use of frequent washings which the Jews did use in all public meetings, for fear of touching pollutions or contracting legal impurities; which they did with a curiousness next to superstition, washing the very beds and tables used at their feasts. The ministers "filled them to the brim"; and, as they were commanded, "drew out, and bare unto the governor of the feast," who "knew not of it," till the miracle grew public, and like light, shewed itself; for while they wondered at the economy of that feast in "keeping the best wine till the last," it grew apparent that He, who was the Lord of the creatures, who in their first seeds have an obediential capacity to receive the impresses of what forms He pleases to imprint,

125

could give new natures, and produce new qualities in that subject in which He chooses to glorify His Son.

8. "This beginning of miracles did Jesus in Cana of Galilee." For all those miracles which are reported to be done by Christ in His infancy and interval of His younger years, are apocryphal and spurious; feigned by trifling understandings, who think to serve God with a well-meant lie; and promoted by the credulity of such persons in whose hearts easiness, folly, and credulity, are bound up, and tied fast with silken thread, and easy softnesses of religious affections, not made severe by the rigours of wisdom and experience. This first miracle "manifested His glory, and His disciples believed in Him."

Section XI

Of Christ's Going to Jerusalem to the Passover, the First Time after His Manifestation, and What Followed, till the Expiration of the Office of John the Baptist

1. Immediately after this miracle Jesus abode a few days in Capernaum, but because of the approach of the great feast of passover He ascended to Jerusalem; and the first public act of record that He did was an act of holy zeal and religion in behalf of the honour of the temple. For divers merchants and exchangers of money made the temple to be the market and the bank, and brought beasts thither to be sold for sacrifice against the great paschal solemnity. At the sight of which, Jesus, being moved with zeal and indignation, "made a whip of cords, and drave the beasts out of the temple, overthrew the accounting tables, and commanded them that sold the doves to take them from thence." For His anger was holy, and He would mingle no injury with it; and therefore the doves, which, if let loose, would be detrimental to the owners, he caused to be fairly removed; and published the religion of holy places, establishing their sacredness for ever, by His first gospel sermon that He made at Jerusalem. "Take these things hence: make not My Father's house a house of merchandize; for it shall be called a house of prayer to all nations." And being required to give a sign of His vocation, (for this, being an action like the religion of the zealots among the Jews, if it was not attested by something extraordinary, might be abused into an excess of liberty), He only foretold the resurrection of His body after three days' death, but He expressed it in the metaphor of the temple, "destroy this temple, and I will build it again in three days. He spake of the temple of His body"; and they understood Him of the

temple at Jerusalem; and it was never rightly construed till it was accomplished.

2. At this public convention of the Jewish nation Jesus did many miracles, published Himself to be the Messias, and persuaded many disciples, amongst whom was Nicodemus, a doctor of the law, and a ruler of the nation: "he came by night to Jesus," and affirmed himself to be convinced by the miracles which he had seen; for "no man could do those miracles except God be with him." When Jesus perceived his understanding to be so far disposed, He began to instruct him in the great secret and mysteriousness of regeneration, telling him, "that every production is of the same nature and condition with its parent; from flesh comes flesh and corruption, from the Spirit comes spirit, and life, and immortality; and nothing from a principle of nature could arrive to a supernatural end; and therefore the only door to enter into the kingdom of God, was water, by the manuduction of the Spirit; and by this regeneration we are put into a new capacity, of living a spiritual life in order to a spiritual and supernatural end."

3. This was strange philosophy to Nicodemus; but Jesus bade him not to wonder: for this is not a work of humanity, but a fruit of God's Spirit, and an issue of predestination. For "the Spirit bloweth where it listeth," and is, as the wind, certain and notorious in the effects, but secret in the principle and in the manner of production. And therefore this doctrine was not to be estimated by any proportions to natural principles or experiments of sense, but to the secrets of a new metaphysic, and abstracted, separate speculations. Then Christ proceeds in His sermon, telling him there are yet higher things for him to apprehend and believe; for this, in respect of some other mysteriousness of His Gospel, was but as earth in comparison of heaven. Then He tells of His own descent from heaven, foretells His death and ascension, and the blessing of redemption which He came to work for mankind; He preaches of the love of the Father, the mission of the Son, the rewards of faith, and the glories of eternity; He upbraids the unbelieving and impenitent, and declares the differences of a holy and a corrupt conscience, the shame and fears of the one, the confidence and serenity of the other. And this is the sum of His sermon to Nicodemus, which was the fullest of mystery and speculation and abstracted senses, of any that He ever made, except that which He made immediately before His passion; all His other sermons being more practical.

4. From Jerusalem Jesus goeth into the country of Judea, attended

by divers disciples, whose understandings were brought into subjection and obedience to Christ upon confidence of the divinity of His miracles. There His disciples did receive all comers, and baptized them, as John at the same time did; and by that ceremony admitted them to the discipline and institution; according to the custom of the doctors and great prophets among the Jews, whose baptizing their scholars was the ceremony of their admission. As soon as John heard it, he acquitted himself in public by renewing his former testimony concerning Jesus; affirming Him "to be the Messias," and now the time was come that "Christ must increase, and the Baptist suffer diminution; for Christ came "from above," was "above all," and the sum of His doctrine was "that which He had heard and seen from the Father"; "whom God sent to that purpose," "to whom God had set His seal that He was true," "who spake the words of God," "whom the Father loved, to whom He gave the Spirit without measure," and "into whose hands God had delivered all things"; this was He whose "testimony the world received not." And that they might know not only what person they slighted, but how great salvation also they neglected, he sums up all his sermons, and finishes his mission with this saying, "He that believeth on the Son, hath everlasting life; and he that believeth not on the Son, shall not see life, but the wrath of God abideth on him."[34]

5. For now that the Baptist had fulfilled his office of bearing witness unto Jesus, God was pleased to give him his writ of ease, and bring him to his reward, upon this occasion: John, who had so learned to despise the world, and all its exterior vanities and impertinent relations, did his duty justly, and so without respect of persons, that as he reproved the people for their prevarications, so he spared not Herod for his; but abstaining from all expresses of the spirit of scorn and asperity, mingling no discontents, interests, nor mutinous intimations with his sermons, he told Herod, "it was not lawful for him to have his brother's wife."[35] For which sermon he felt the furies and malice of a woman's spleen, was cast into prison, and about a year after was sacrificed to the scorn and pride of a lustful woman, and her immodest daughter; being, at the end of the second year of Christ's preaching, beheaded by Herod's command, who would not retract his promise, because of his honour, and a rash vow he made in the gaiety of his lust, and compla-

---

34. John 3:36.
35. Tertullian, *Against Marcion*, PL 2. 441.

cencies of his riotous dancings.[36] His head was brought up in a dish, and made a festival present to the young girl, who gave it to her mother: a cruelty that was not known among the barbarisms of the worst of people, to mingle banquetings with blood and sights of death; an insolence and inhumanity, for which the Roman orators accused Q. Flaminius of treason, because to satisfy the wanton cruelty of Placentia, he caused a condemned slave to be killed at supper; and which had no precedent but in the furies of Marius, who caused the head of the consul Antonius to be brought up to him in his feasts, which he handled with much pleasure and insolency.

6. But God's judgments, which sleep not long, found out Herod, and marked him for a curse. For the wife of Herod, who was the daughter of Aretas, a king of Arabia Petræa, being repudiated by paction with Herodias, provoked her father to commence a war with Herod; who prevailed against Herod in a great battle, defeating his whole army, and forcing him to an inglorious flight: which the Jews generally expounded to be a judgment on him for the unworthy and barbarous execution and murder of John the baptist; God, in His wisdom and severity, making one sin to be the punishment of another, and neither of them both to pass without the signature of a curse. And Nicephorus reports that the dancing daughter of Herodias passing over a frozen lake, the ice brake, and she fell up to the neck in water, and her head was parted from her body by the violence of the fragments shaken by the water and its own fall, and so perished; God having fitted a judgment to the analogy and representment of her sin. Herodias herself, with her adulterous paramour Herod, were banished to Lyons in France, by decree of the Roman senate, where they lived ingloriously, and died miserably; so paying dearly for her triumphal scorn, superadded to her crime of murder: for when she saw the head of the Baptist, which her daughter Salome had presented to her in a charger, she thrust the tongue through with a needle as Fulvia had formerly done to Cicero. But herself paid the charges of her triumph.[37]

---

36. Ibid.
37. Josephus (bk. 2, ch. 9), vol. 2, p. 394.

Section XII
Of Jesus' Departure into Galilee; His Manner of Life, Miracles, and Preaching; His Calling of Disciples; and What Happened until the Second Passover

1. "When Jesus understood that John was cast into prison,"[38] and that the Pharisees were envious at Him for the great multitudes of people that resorted to His baptism, which He ministered not in His own person but by the deputation of His disciples, they finishing the ministration which Himself began (who, as Euodius bishop of Antioch reports, baptized the blessed Virgin His mother, and Peter only; and Peter baptized Andrew, James, and John, and they others;) he left Judea and came into Galilee; and in His passage He must touch Sychar a city of Samaria, where in the heat of the day and the weariness of His journey He sat Himself down upon the margin of Jacob's well; whither, when "His disciples were gone to buy meat, a Samaritan woman cometh to draw water," of whom Jesus asked some, to cool His thirst and refresh His weariness.

2. Little knew the woman the excellency of the person that asked so small a charity: neither had she been taught that "a cup of cold water given to a disciple should be rewarded," and much rather such a present to the Lord himself. But she prosecuted the spite of her nation, and the interest and quarrel of the schism; and instead of washing Jesus's feet, and giving Him drink, demanded why He, "being a Jew, should ask water of a Samaritan? for the Jews have no intercourse with the Samaritans?"

3. The ground of the quarrel was this. In the sixth year of Hezekiah, Salmanasar king of Assyria sacked Samaria, transported the Israelites to Assyria, and planted an Assyrian colony in the town and country; who by divine vengeance were destroyed by lions, which no power of man could restrain or lessen. The king thought the cause was, their not serving the God of Israel according to the rites of Moses; and therefore sent a Jewish captive priest to instruct the remanent inhabitants in the Jewish religion; who so learned and practised it that they still retained the superstition of the gentile rites; till Manasses, the brother of Jaddi the high priest of Jerusalem, married the daughter of Sanballat who was the governor under king Darius. Manasses being reproved for marrying a stranger, the daughter of an uncircumcised gentile, and

---

38. Matt. 4:12.

admonished to dismiss her, flies to Samaria, persuades his father-in-law to build a temple in mount Gerizim, introduces the rites of daily sacrifice, and makes himself high priest, and began to pretend to be the true successor of Aaron, and commences a schism, in the time of Alexander the great. From whence the question of religion grew so high, that it begat disaffections, anger, animosities, quarrels, bloodshed, and murders; not only in Palestine, but wherever a Jew and Samaritan had the ill fortune to meet: such being the nature of men, that they think it the greatest injury in the world when other men are not of their minds; and that they please God most when they are most furiously zealous; and no zeal better to be expressed than by hating all those whom they are pleased to think God hates. This schism was prosecuted with the greatest spite that ever any was, because both the people were much given to superstition; and this was helped forward by the constitution of their religion, consisting much in externals and ceremonials, and which they cared not much to hallow and make moral by the intertexture of spiritual senses and charity. And therefore the Jews called the Samaritans "accursed"; the Samaritans at the paschal solemnity would at midnight, when the Jews' temple was open, scatter dead men's bones to profane and desecrate the place;[39] and both would fight, and eternally dispute the question; sometimes referring it to arbitrators, and then the conquered party would decline the arbitration after sentence; which they did at Alexandria, before Ptolomeus Philometor, when Andronicus had by a rare and exquisite oration procured sentence against Theodosius and Sabbeus, the Samaritan advocates: the sentence was given for Jerusalem, and the schism increased, and lasted till the time of our Saviour's conference with this woman.

4. And it was so implanted and woven in with every understanding, that when the woman "perceived Jesus to be a prophet," she undertook this question with Him; "Our fathers worshipped in this mountain; and ye say that Jerusalem is the place where men ought to worship." Jesus knew the schism was great enough already, and was not willing to make the rent wider: and though He gave testimony to the truth, by saying, "salvation is of the Jews"; and "we know what we worship, ye do not"; yet because the subject of this question was shortly to be taken away, Jesus takes occasion to preach the gospel, to hasten an expedient, and by way of anticipation to reconcile the disagreeing inter-

---

39. Josephus, *Jewish Antiquities* (bk. 18, ch. 2), vol. 9, p. 26.

ests, and settle a revelation to be verified for ever. Neither here nor there, by way of confinement; not in one country more than another; but wherever any man shall call upon God "in spirit and in truth," there he shall be heard.

5. But all this while the holy Jesus was athirst, and therefore hastens at least to discourse of water, though as yet He got none. He tells her of "living water," of eternal satisfactions, of "never thirsting again," of her own personal condition of matrimonial relation, and professes Himself to be the Messias; and then was interrupted by the coming of His disciples, who wondered to see Him alone, "talking with a woman," besides His custom and usual reservation. But the woman, full of joy and wonder, left her waterpot, and ran to the city to publish the Messias: and immediately "all the city came out to see; and many believed on Him upon the testimony of the woman, and more when they heard His own discourses." They invited Him to the town, and received Him with hospitable civilities for two days, after which He departed to His own Galilee.

6. Jesus therefore came into the country, where He was received with respect and fair entertainment because of the miracles which the Galileans saw done by Him at the feast; and being at Cana, where He wrought the first miracle, a noble personage—a little king, say some; a palatine, says St. Jerome; a kingly person, certainly—came to Jesus with much reverence, and desired that He would be pleased to come to his house, and cure his son, now ready to die; which he seconds with much importunity, fearing lest his son be dead before He get thither. Jesus, who did not do His miracles by natural operations, cured the child at distance, and dismissed the prince, telling him his son lived; which by narration of his servants he found to be true, and that he recovered at the same time when Jesus spake these salutary and healing words. Upon which accident he and all his house became disciples.

7. And now Jesus left Nazareth, and came to Capernaum, a maritime town and of great resort, choosing that for His scene of preaching and His place of dwelling. For now the time was fulfilled, the office of the Baptist was expired, and the kingdom of God was at hand; He therefore preached the sum of the gospel, faith and repentance, "repent ye, and believe the gospel"; and what that gospel was, the sum and series of all His sermons afterwards did declare.

8. The work was now grown high and pregnant, and Jesus saw it convenient to choose disciples to His ministry and service in the work of preaching, and to be "witnesses of all that He should say, do, or

teach," for ends which were afterwards made public and excellent. Jesus therefore "as He walked by the sea of Galilee," called Simon and Andrew: who knew Him before by the preaching of John, and now "left all," their ship and their net, "and followed Him. And when He was gone a little farther, He calls the two sons of Zebedee, James and John; and they went after Him." And with this family He goes up and down the whole Galilee, preaching the gospel of the kingdom, healing all manner of diseases, curing demoniacs, cleansing lepers, and giving strength to paralytics and lame people.

9. But when "the people pressed on Him to hear the word of God, He stood by the lake of Genesareth," and presently "entering into Simon's ship," commanded him "to launch into the deep," and "from thence He taught the people," and there wrought a miracle; for being lord of the creatures, He commanded the fishes of the sea and they obeyed. For when Simon, who had "fished all night in vain, let down his net at the command of Jesus, he enclosed so great a multitude of fishes that the net brake"; and the fishermen were amazed and fearful at so prodigious a draught. But beyond the miracle, it was intended that a representation should be made of the plenitude of the catholic church, and multitudes of believers who should be taken by Simon and the rest of the disciples, whom by that miracle He consigned to become "fishers of men"; who by their artifices of prudence and holy doctrine might gain souls to God; that when the net should be drawn to shore, and separation made by the angels, they and their disciples might be differenced from the reprobate portion.

10. But the light of the sun uses not to be confined to a province or a kingdom. So great a prophet, and so divine a physician, and so great miracles, created a fame loud as thunder, but not so full of sadness and presage. Immediately the "fame of Jesus went into all Syria, and there came to Him multitudes from Galilee, Decapolis, Jerusalem, and Judea"; and all that had any "sick with divers diseases brought them to Him," and He laid His hands on every one of them "and healed them." And when He cured the "lunatics and persons possessed with evil spirits," the devils cried out, and confessed Him to be "Christ, the Son of God"; but He "suffered them not," choosing rather to work faith in the persuasions of His disciples by moral arguments, and the placid demonstrations of the Spirit; that there might in faith be an excellency in proportion to the choice, and that it might not be made violent by the conviction and forced testimonies of accursed and unwilling spirits.

11. But when Jesus saw His assembly was grown full and His

audience numerous, He "went up into a mountain," and when His disciples came unto Him, He made that admirable sermon called "the sermon upon the mount": which is a divine repository of such excellent truths, and mysterious dictates of secret theology; that contains a breviary of all those precepts which integrate the morality of Christian religion, pressing the moral precepts given by Moses, and enlarging their obligation by a stricter sense and more severe exposition, that their righteousness might "exceed the righteousness of the scribes and pharisees"; preaches perfection, and the doctrines of meekness, poverty of spirit, Christian mourning, desire of holy things, mercy and purity, peace and toleration of injuries, affixing a special promise of blessing to be the guerdon and inheritance of those graces and spiritual excellencies. He explicates some parts of the decalogue, and adds *appendices* and precepts of His own. He teaches His disciples to pray, how to fast, how to give alms, contempt of the world, not to judge others, forgiving injuries, an indifferency and incuriousness of temporal provisions, and a seeking of the kingdom of God and its appendent righteousness.

12. When Jesus had finished His sermon and descended from the mountain, a poor leprous person came and worshipped, and begged to be cleansed; which Jesus soon granted, engaging him not to publish it where he should go abroad, but sending him to the priest, to offer an oblation according to the rites of Moses' law; and then came directly to Capernaum, and "taught in their synagogues upon the sabbath days"; where in His sermons He expressed the dignity of a prophet, and the authority of a person sent from God; not inviting the people by the soft arguments and insinuations of scribes and pharisees, but by demonstrations and issues of divinity. There He cures a demoniac in one of their synagogues; and by and by after going abroad He heals Peter's wife's mother of a fever; insomuch that He grew the talk of all men, and their wonder, till they flocked so to Him to see Him, to hear Him, to satisfy their curiosity and their needs, that after He had healed those multitudes which beset the house of Simon, where He cured his mother of the fever, He retired Himself into a desert place very early in the morning, that He might have an opportunity to pray, free from the oppressions and noises of the multitude.

13. But neither so could He be hid, but, like a light shining by the fringes of a curtain, He was soon discovered in His solitude: for the multitude found Him out, imprisoning Him in their circuits and undeniable attendances: but Jesus told them plainly He must preach the gospel "to other cities also": and therefore resolved to pass to the other

side of the lake of Genesareth, so to quit the throng. Whither as He was going, a scribe offered himself a disciple to His institution; till Jesus told him His condition to be worse than foxes' and birds', for whom an habitation is provided, but none for Him; no, "not a place where to bow His head" and find rest. And what became of this forward professor afterwards, we find not. Others that were probationers of this fellowship, Jesus bound to a speedy profession; not suffering one to go home to bid his friends farewell, nor another so much as to "bury his dead."

14. By the time Jesus got to the ship it was late; and He, heavy to sleep, rested on a pillow, and slept soundly, as weariness, meekness, and innocence could make Him: insomuch that "a violent storm," the chiding of the winds and waters, which then happened, could not awake Him; till the ship being almost covered with broken billows and the impetuous dashings of the waters, the men already sunk in their spirits, and the ship like enough to sink too, the disciples awaked Him, and called for help, "Master, carest Thou not that we perish?" Jesus arising reproved their infidelity, commanded the wind to be still and the seas peaceable, and immediately "there was a great calm"; and they presently arrived in the land of the Gergesenes, or Gerasenes.

15. In the land of Gergesites, or Gergesenes, which was the remaining name of an extinct people, being one of the nations whom the sons of Jacob drave from their inheritance, there were two cities; Gadara, from the tribe of Gad, to whom it fell by lot in the division of the land; which having been destroyed by the Jews was rebuilt by Pompey, at the request of Demetrius Gadarensis. Pompey's freedman: and near to it was Gerasa, as Josephus reports:[40] which diversity of towns and names is the cause of the various recitation of this story by the evangelists. Near the city of Gadara, there were many sepulchres in the hollownesses of rocks, where the dead were buried, and where many superstitious persons used Memphitic and Thessalic rites, invocating evil spirits;[41] insomuch that at the instant of our Saviour's arrival in the country "there met Him two possessed with devils from these tombs, exceeding fierce," and so had been long, "insomuch that no man durst pass that way."

16. Jesus commanded the devils out of the possessed persons: but there were certain men feeding swine, which, though extremely abom-

---

40. Josephus, *Jewish War* (bk. 1, ch. 4), vol. 2, p. 42.
41. Epiphanius, PG 41. 415.

inated by the Jewish religion, yet for the use of the Roman armies and quarterings of soldiers, they were permitted, and divers privileges granted to the masters of such herds:[42] and because Gadara[43] was a Greek city, and the company mingled of Greeks, Syrians, and Jews, these last in all likelihood not making the greatest number, the devils therefore besought Jesus, He would not send them into the abyss, but "permit them to enter into the swine." He gave them leave; "and the swine ran violently down a steep place into the" hot baths which were at the foot of the hill on which Gadara was built (which smaller congregation of waters the Jews used to call "sea"), or else, as others think, into the lake of Genesareth, "and perished in the waters."[44] But this accident so troubled the inhabitants, that they came and "entreated Jesus to depart out of their coasts"; and He did so: leaving "Galilee of the gentiles," He came to the lesser Galilee, and so again to the city of Capernaum.

17. But when He was come thither, He was met by divers "scribes and pharisees" who came from Jerusalem, and "doctors of the law from Galilee"; and while they were sitting in a house, which was encompassed with multitudes, that no business or necessity could be admitted to the door, a poor paralytic was brought to be cured; and they were fain to "uncover the tiles of the house, and let him down in his bed with cords in the midst before Jesus," sitting in conference with the doctors. "When Jesus saw their faith, He said, Man, thy sins be forgiven thee": at which saying the pharisees being troubled, thinking it to be blasphemy, and that "none but God could forgive sins," Jesus was put to verify His absolution, which He did in a just satisfaction and proportion to their understandings. For the Jews did believe that all afflictions were punishments for sin, ("Who sinned, this man or his father, that he was born blind?") and that removing of the punishment was forgiving of the sin: and therefore Jesus, to prove that his sins were forgiven, removed that which they supposed to be the effect of his sin, and by curing the palsy prevented their farther murmur about the pardon; "that ye might know the Son of man hath power on earth to forgive sins, (He saith to

---

42. Josephus, *Jewish War*, LCL, (bk. 2, ch. 18), vol. 2, p. 508.
43. Ibid.
44. 2 Kings 25:13.

the sick of the palsy,) Arise, take up thy bed, and walk: and the man arose, was healed, and glorified God."[45]

18. A while after Jesus went again toward the sea, and on His way, "seeing Matthew" the publican "sitting at the receipt of custom," He bade him "follow Him." Matthew first feasted Jesus, and then became His disciple. But the pharisees that were with Him began to be troubled that He "ate with publicans and sinners." For the office of publican, though amongst the Romans it was honest and of great account, and "the flower of the Roman knights, the ornament of the city, the security of the commonwealth, was accounted to consist in the society of publicans"; yet amongst both the Jews and Greeks the name was odious, and the persons were accursed; not only because they were strangers that were the chief of them, who took in to them some of the nation where they were employed; but because the Jews especially stood upon the charter of their nation and the privilege of their religion, that none of them should pay tribute; and also because they exercised great injustices and oppressions, having a power unlimited, and a covetousness wide as hell, and greedy as the fire or the grave. But Jesus gave so fair an account concerning His converse with these persons that the objection turned to be His apology: for therefore He conversed with them because they were sinners; and it was as if a physician should be reproved for having so much to do with sick persons; for therefore was He "sent, not to call the righteous, but sinners to repentance": to advance the reputation of mercy above the rites of sacrifice.

19. But as the little bubbling and gentle murmurs of the water are presages of a storm, and are more troublesome in their prediction than their violence; so were the arguings of the pharisees symptoms of a secret displeasure and an ensuing war; though at first represented in the civilities of question and scholastical discourses, yet they did but fore-run vigorous objections and bold calumnies, which were the fruits of the next summer. But as yet they discoursed fairly, asking Him "why John's disciples fasted often, but the disciples of Jesus did not fast?" Jesus told them it was because these were the days in which the Bridegroom was come in person to espouse the church unto Himself, and therefore for "the children of the bride-chamber to fast" then, was like

---

45. Luke 5:24.

the bringing of a dead corpse to the joys of a bride or the pomps of coronation; "the days should come that the bridegroom should retire" into His chamber and draw the curtains, "and then they should fast in those days."

20. While Jesus was discoursing with the pharisees, "Jairus, a ruler of the synagogue, came to Him," desiring He would help his daughter, who lay in the confines of death, ready to depart. Whither as He was going, "a woman met Him, who had been diseased with an issue of blood twelve years," without hope of remedy from art or nature; and therefore she runs to Jesus, thinking, without precedent, upon the confident persuasions of a holy faith, "that if she did but touch the hem of His garment, she should be whole." She came trembling, and full of hope and reverence, and "touched His garment, and immediately the fountain" of her unnatural emanation "was stopped," and reverted to its natural course and offices. St. Ambrose says that this woman was Martha.[46] But it is not likely that she was a Jewess, but a gentile; because of that return which she made, in memory of her cure and honour of Jesus, according to the gentile rites. For Eusebius reports that himself saw at Cæsarea Philippi a statue of brass, representing a woman kneeling at the feet of a goodly personage, who held his hand out to her in a posture of granting her request, and doing favour to her;[47] and the inhabitants said it was erected by the care and cost of this woman; adding (whether out of truth or easiness is not certain) that at the pedestal of this statue an unusual plant did grow, which when it was come up to that maturity and height as to arrive at the fringes of the brass monument, it was medicinal in many dangerous diseases: so far Eusebius. Concerning which story I shall make no censure but this, that since St. Mark and St. Luke affirm,[48] that this woman before her cure "had spent all her substance upon physicians," it is not easily imaginable how she should become able to dispend so great a sum of money as would purchase two so great statues of brass: and if she could, yet it is still more unlikely that the gentile princes and proconsuls, who searched all places public and private, and were curiously diligent to destroy all honorary monuments of Christianity, should let this alone;

---

46. Ambrose, *On Luke's Gospel*, PL 15. 1768.
47. Eusebius, PG 20. 679.
48. Mark 5:26; Luke 8:43.

and that this should escape not only the diligence of the persecutors, but the fury of such wars and changes as happened in Palestine; and that for three hundred years together it should stand up in defiance of all violences and changeable fate of all things. However it be, it is certain that the book against images, published by the command of Charles the great eight hundred and fifty years ago, gave no credit to the story; and if it had been true, it is more than probable that Justin Martyr, who was born and bred in Palestine, and Origen, who lived many years in Tyre, in the neighbourhood of the place where the statue is said to stand, and were highly diligent to heap together all things of advantage and reputation to the Christian cause, would not have omitted so notable an instance. It is therefore likely that the statues which Eusebius saw, and concerning which he heard such stories, were first placed there upon the stock of a heathen story or ceremony; and in process of time, for the likeness of the figures, and its capacity to be translated to the Christian story, was by the Christians in after ages attributed by a fiction of fancy, and afterwards by credulity confidently applied, to the present narrative.

21. "When Jesus was come to the ruler's house," He found the minstrels making their funeral noises for the death of Jairus's daughter, and his servants had met him and acquainted him of "the death of the child"; yet Jesus turned out the minstrels, and "entered with the parents of the child into her chamber, and taking her by the hand, called her," and awakened her from her sleep of death, and "commanded them to give her to eat," and enjoined them not to publish the miracle.[49] But as flames, suppressed by violent detentions, break out and rage with a more impetuous and rapid motion; so it happened to Jesus; who, endeavouring to make the noises and reports of him less popular, made them to be œcumenical; for not only we do that most greedily from which we are most restrained, but a great merit, enamelled with humility, and restrained with modesty, grows more beauteous and florid, up to the heights of wonder and glories.

22. As He came from Jairus's house, He cured two blind men, upon their petition, and confession that they did believe in Him; and cast out a dumb devil, so much to the wonder and amazement of the people, that the pharisees could hold no longer, being ready to burst with envy, but said "He cast out devils by help of the devils": their

---

49. Luke 8:56.

malice being, as usually it is, contradictory to its own design by its being unreasonable; nothing being more sottish than for the devil to divide his kingdom upon a plot, to ruin his certainties upon hopes future and contingent. But this was but the first eruption of their malice; all the year last past, which was the first year of Jesus's preaching, all was quiet; neither the Jews, nor the Samaritans, nor the Galileans, did malign His doctrine or person, but He preached with much peace on all hands;[50] for this was the year which the prophet Isaiah called in his prediction "the acceptable year of the Lord."

---

50. Epiphanius, PG 41. 890.

The History of the Life and Death of the Holy Jesus

PART III
BEGINNING AT THE SECOND YEAR OF HIS PREACHING UNTIL HIS ASCENSION

Section XIII
Of the Second Year of the Preaching of Jesus

1. When the first year of Jesus, the year of peace and undisturbed preaching, was expired, "there was a feast of the Jews, and Jesus went up to Jerusalem."[51] This feast was the second passover He kept after He began to preach;[52] not the feast of pentecost, or tabernacles, both which were past before Jesus came last from Judea: whither when He was now come, He finds an "impotent person lying at the pool of Bethesda, waiting till the angel should move the waters, after which whosoever first stepped in was cured of his infirmity." The poor man had waited thirty-eight years, and still was prevented by some other of the hospital that needed a physician. But Jesus seeing him had pity on him, cured him, and bade him "take up his bed and walk." This cure happened to be wrought "upon the sabbath," for which the Jews were so moved with indignation, that they "thought to slay Him": and their anger was enraged by His calling Himself "the Son of God," and "making Himself equal with God."

2. Upon occasion of this offence, which they snatched at before it was ministered, Jesus discourses upon His mission and derivation of His authority from the Father;[53] of the union between them, and the excellent communications of power, participation of dignity, delegation of judicature, reciprocations and reflections of honour from the Father

---

51. John 5:1.
52. Irenaeus, *Against Heresy*, PG 7. 783.
53. John 5:19.

to the Son, and back again to the Father. He preaches of life and salvation to them that believe in Him; prophesies of the resurrection of the dead by the efficacy of the voice of the Son of God; speaks of the day of judgment, the differing conditions after, of salvation and damnation respectively; confirms His words and mission by the testimony of John the baptist, of Moses, and the other scriptures, and of God himself. And still the scandal rises higher: for "in the second sabbath after the first," that is, in the first day of unleavened bread, which happened the next day after the weekly sabbath, the disciples of Jesus pull ripe ears of corn, rub them in their hands, and eat them, to satisfy their hunger; for which He offered satisfaction to their scruples, convincing them, that works of necessity are to be permitted, even to the breach of a positive temporary constitution; and that works of mercy are the best serving of God upon any day whatsoever, or any part of the day, that is vacant to other offices, and proper for a religious festival.

3. But when neither reason nor religion would give them satisfaction, but that they went about to kill Him, He withdrew Himself from Jerusalem, and returned to Galilee; whither the scribes and pharisees followed Him, observing His actions, and whether or not He would prosecute that which they called profanation of their sabbath, by doing acts of mercy upon that day. He still did so: for entering into one of the synagogues of Galilee upon the sabbath, Jesus saw a man (whom St. Hierom reports to have been a mason) coming to Tyre, and complaining that his hand was withered, and desiring help of Him, that he might again be restored to the use of his hands, lest he should be compelled with misery and shame to beg his bread. Jesus restored his hand as whole as the other, in the midst of all those spies and enemies. Upon which act being confirmed in their malice, the pharisees went forth and joined with the herodians (a sect of people who said Herod was the Messias, because by the decree of the Roman senate, when the sceptre departed from Judah, he was declared king) and both together took counsel how they might kill Him.[54]

4. Jesus therefore departed again to the sea coast, and His companies increased as His fame; for He was now followed by new "multitudes from Galilee, from Judea, from Jerusalem, from Idumea, from beyond Jordan, from about Tyre and Sidon"; who hearing the report of His miraculous power to cure all diseases by the word of His mouth, or

---

54. Epiphanius, PG 41. 269.

the touch of His hand, or the handling His garment, came with their ambulatory hospital of sick, and their possessed; and they pressed on Him but to touch Him, and were all immediately cured: the devils confessing publicly that He was "the Son of God," till they were upon all such occasions restrained, and compelled to silence.

5. But now Jesus, having commanded a ship to be in readiness against any inconvenience or troublesome pressures of the multitude, "went up into a mountain to pray, and continued in prayer all night," intending to make the first ordination of apostles; which the next day He did, choosing out of the number of His disciples these twelve to be apostles: Simon Peter and Andrew; James and John, the sons of thunder; Philip and Bartholomew; Matthew and Thomas; James the son of Alpheus, and Simon the zelot; Judas the brother of James, and Judas Iscariot. With these descending from the mountain to the plain, He repeated the same sermon, or much of it, which He had before preached in the first beginning of His prophesyings; that He might publish His gospel to these new auditors, and also more particularly inform His apostles in "the doctrine of the kingdom": for now, because He "saw Israel scattered like sheep having no shepherd," He did purpose to send these twelve abroad, to preach repentance and the approximation of the kingdom; and therefore first instructed them in the mysterious parts of His holy doctrine, and gave them also particular instructions together with their temporary commission for that journey.[55]

6. For Jesus "sent them out by two and two, giving them power over unclean spirits," and to heal all manner of sickness and diseases; telling them they were "the light," and "the eyes," and "the salt of the world," so intimating their duties of diligence, holiness, and incorruption; giving them in charge to preach the gospel, to dispense their power and miracles freely as they had received it, to anoint sick persons with oil, not to enter into any Samaritan town, but to "go rather to the lost sheep of the house of Israel," to provide no *viaticum* for their journeys, but to put themselves upon the religion and piety of their proselytes: He arms them against persecutions, gives them leave to fly the storm from city to city, promises them the assistances of His Spirit, encourages them by His own example of long-suffering, and by instances of divine providence expressed even to creatures of smallest value, and by promise of great rewards to the confident confession of

---

55. Matt. 10:1; Mark 6:7; Luke 9:1.

His name; and furnishes them with some propositions, which are like so many bills of exchange, upon the trust of which they might take up necessaries; promising great retributions, not only to them who quit any thing of value for the sake of Jesus, but to them that offer a cup of water to a thirsty disciple. And with these instructions they departed to preach in the cities.

7. And Jesus, returning to Capernaum, received the address of a faithful centurion of the legion called the Iron legion (which usually quartered in Judea), in behalf of his servant whom he loved, and who was grievously afflicted with the palsy; and healed him, as a reward and honour to his faith. And from thence going to the city Naim, He raised to life the only son of a widow, whom the mourners followed in the street, bearing the corpse sadly to his funeral. Upon the fame of these and divers other miracles, John the baptist, who was still in prison (for he was not put to death till the latter end of this year), sent two of his disciples to Him, by divine providence, or else by John's designation, to minister occasion of His greater publication, enquiring if He was the Messias. To whom Jesus returned no answer but a demonstration taken from the nature of the thing, and the glory of the miracles, saying, "Return to John, and tell him what ye see; for the deaf hear, the blind see, the lame walk, the dead are raised, and the lepers are cleansed, and to the poor the gospel is preached": which were the characteristic notes of the Messias according to the predictions of the holy prophets.[56]

8. When John's disciples were gone with this answer, Jesus began to speak concerning John; of the austerity and holiness of his person, the greatness of his function, the divinity of his commission, saying, that he was greater than a prophet, a burning and shining light, the Elias that was to come, and the consummation or ending of the old prophets: adding withal, that the perverseness of that age was most notorious in the entertainment of Himself and the Baptist: for neither could the Baptist, who came neither eating nor drinking, that by his austerity and mortified deportment he might invade the judgment and affections of the people, nor Jesus, who came both eating and drinking, that by a moderate and an affable life, framed to the compliance and common use of men, He might sweetly insinuate into the affections of the multitude, obtain belief amongst them. They could object against every thing, but nothing could please them. But wisdom and righteousness had a theatre

---

56. Isa. 35;4.

in its own family, and is justified of all her children. Then He proceeds to a more applied reprehension of Capernaum, and Chorazin, and Bethsaida, for being pertinacious in their sins and infidelity, in defiance and reproof of all the mighty works which had been wrought in them. But these things were not revealed to all dispositions; the wise and the mighty of the world were not subjects prepared for the simplicity and softer impresses of the gospel, and the downright severity of its sanctions. And therefore Jesus glorified God for the magnifying of His mercy, in that these things which were hid from the great ones, were revealed to babes; and concludes this sermon with an invitation of all wearied and disconsolate persons loaded with sin and misery, to come to Him, promising ease to their burdens, and refreshment to their weariness, and to exchange their heavy pressures into an easy yoke, and a light burden.

9. When Jesus had ended this sermon, one of the pharisees[57] named Simon invited Him to "eat with him"; into whose house when He was entered, a certain "woman that was a sinner," abiding there in the city, heard of it; her name was Mary: she had been married to a noble personage, a native of the town and castle of Magdal, from whence she had her name of Magdalen, though she herself was born in Bethany; a widow she was, and prompted by her wealth, liberty, and youth, to an intemperate life, and too free entertainments. She came to Jesus into the pharisee's house: not, as did the staring multitude, to glut her eyes with the sight of a miraculous and glorious person; nor, as did the centurion, or the Syrophœnician, or the ruler of the synagogue, for cure of her sickness, or in behalf of her friend, or child, or servant; but (the only example of so coming) she came in remorse and regret for her sins, she came to Jesus to lay her burden at His feet, and to present Him with a broken heart, and a weeping eye, and great affection, and a box of nard pistic, salutary and precious. For she came trembling, and fell down before Him, weeping bitterly for her sins, pouring out a flood great enough to "wash the feet" of the blessed Jesus, and "wiping them with the hairs of her head"; after which she "brake the box," and "anointed His feet with ointment." Which expression was so great an ecstasy of love, sorrow, and adoration, that to anoint the feet even of the greatest monarch was long unknown, and in all the pomps and greatnesses of the Roman prodigality it was not used, till Otho taught it to Nero; in whose

---

57. Luke 7:36.

instance it was by Pliny reckoned for a prodigy of unnecessary profusion: and in itself, without the circumstance of so free a dispensation, it was a present for a prince, and an alabaster box of nard pistic was sent as a present from Cambyses to the king of Ethiopia.

10. When Simon observed this sinner so busy in the expresses of her religion and veneration to Jesus, he thought with himself that this was no prophet that did not know her to be a sinner: or no just person, that would suffer her to touch him. For although the Jews' religion did permit harlots of their own nation to live, and enjoy the privileges of their nation, save that their oblations were refused: yet the pharisees, who pretended to a greater degree of sanctity than others, would not admit them to civil usages, or the benefits of ordinary society; and thought religion itself, and the honour of a prophet, was concerned in the interests of the same superciliousness: and therefore Simon made an objection within himself. Which Jesus knowing, (for He understood his thoughts as well as his words,) made her apology and His own in a civil question, expressed in a parable of two debtors, to whom a greater and a less debt respectively was forgiven:[58] both of them concluding that they would love their merciful creditor in proportion to his mercy and donative: and this was the case of Mary Magdalen; to whom because "much was forgiven, she loved much," and expressed it in characters so large, that the pharisee might read his own incivilities and inhospitable entertainment of the Master, when it stood confronted with the magnificency of Mary Magdalen's penance and charity.

11. When Jesus had dined, He was presented with the sad sight of a poor demoniac possessed with a blind and a dumb devil, in whose behalf his friends entreated Jesus that He would cast the devil out; which He did immediately, and "the blind man saw, and the dumb spake," so much to the amazement of the people that they ran in so prodigious companies after Him, and so scandalized the pharisees, who thought that by means of this prophet their reputation would be lessened and their schools empty, that first a rumour was scattered up and down, from an uncertain principle, but communicated with tumult and apparent noises, that Jesus was "beside Himself": upon which rumour His friends and kindred came together to see, and to make provisions accordingly; and the holy Virgin-mother came herself, but without any apprehensions of any such horrid accident. The words and things she

---

58. Luke 7:40.

had from the beginning laid up in her heart would furnish her with principles exclusive of all apparitions of such fancies; but she came to see what that persecution was which under that colour it was likely the pharisees might commence.

12. When the mother of Jesus and His kindred came, they found Him in a house encircled with people full of wonder and admiration: and there the holy Virgin-mother might hear part of her own prophecy verified, that the generations of the earth should call her blessed; for a woman, worshipping Jesus, cried out, "Blessed is the womb that bare Thee, and the paps that gave Thee suck." To this Jesus replied, not denying her to be highly blessed who had received the honour of being the mother of the Messias, but advancing the dignities of spiritual excellencies far above this greatest temporal honour in the world: "Yea rather blessed are they that hear the word of God, and do it." For in respect of the issues of spiritual perfections and their proportionable benedictions, all immunities and temporal honours are empty and hollow blessings; and all relations of kindred disband and empty themselves into the greater channels and floods of divinity.

13. For when, Jesus being in the house, they told Him "His mother and His brethren staid for Him without," He told them those relations were less than the ties of duty and religion: for those dear names of mother and brethren, which are hallowed by the laws of God and the endearments of nature, are made far more sacred when a spiritual cognation does supervene, when the relations are subjected in persons religious and holy: but if they be abstract and separate, the conjunction of persons in spiritual bands, in the same faith, and the same hope, and the union of them in the same mystical head, is an adunation nearer to identity than those distances between parents and children, which are only cemented by the actions of nature as it is of distinct consideration from the spirit. For Jesus, pointing to His disciples, said, "Behold My mother and My brethren; for whosoever doeth the will of My Father which is in heaven, he is My brother, and sister, and mother."

14. But the pharisees upon the occasion of the miracles renewed the old quarrel: "He casteth out devils by Beelzebub." Which senseless and illiterate objection Christ having confuted, charged them highly upon the guilt of an unpardonable crime, telling them that the so charging those actions of His, done in the virtue of the divine Spirit, is a sin against the holy Ghost; and however they might be bold with the Son of man, and prevarications against His words or injuries to His person

147

might upon repentance and baptism find a pardon, yet it was a matter of greater consideration to sin against the holy Ghost; that would find no pardon here nor hereafter. But taking occasion upon this discourse, He by an ingenious and mysterious parable gives the world great caution of recidivation and backsliding after repentance: for if "the devil returns into a house once swept and garnished, he bringeth seven spirits more impure than himself; and the last estate of that man is worse than the first."[59]

15. After this, Jesus went from the house of the pharisee, and coming to the sea of Tiberias or Gennesareth (for it was called the sea of Tiberias from a town on the banks of the lake) taught the people upon the shore, Himself sitting in the ship; but He taught them by parables, under which were hid mysterious senses, which shined through their veil, like a bright sun through an eye closed with a thin eye-lid; it being light enough to shew their infidelity, but not to dispel those thick Egyptian darknesses which they had contracted by their habitual indispositions and pertinacious aversations. By the parable of the sower scattering his seed by the wayside, and some on stony, some on thorny, some on good ground, He intimated the several capacities or indispositions of men's hearts, the carelessness of some, the forwardness and levity of others, the easiness and softness of a third; and how they are spoiled with worldliness and cares, and how many ways there are to miscarry, and that but one sort of men receive the word and bring forth the fruits of a holy life. By the parable of tares permitted to grow amongst the wheat, He intimated the toleration of dissenting opinions not destructive of piety or civil societies. By the three parables of the seed growing insensibly, of the grain of mustard seed swelling up to a tree, of a little leaven qualifying the whole lump, He signified the increment of the gospel and the blessings upon the apostolical sermons.

16. Which parables when He had privately to His apostles rendered into their proper senses, He added to them two parables concerning the dignity of the gospel, comparing it to treasure hid in a field, and a jewel of great price, for the purchase of which every good merchant must quit all that he hath, rather than miss it: telling them withal, that however purity and spiritual perfections were intended by the gospel, yet it would not be acquired by every person; but the public professors of christianity should be a mixed multitude, like a net, en-

---

59. Matt. 12:45; Luke 9:25.

closing fishes good and bad. After which discourses, He retired from the sea-side, and went to His own city of Nazareth; where He preached so excellently upon certain words of the prophet Isaiah,[60] that all the people wondered at the wisdom which He expressed in His divine discourses. But the men of Nazareth did not do honour to the Prophet that was their countryman, because they knew Him in all the disadvantages of youth, and kindred, and trade, and poverty; still retaining in their minds the infirmities and humilities of His first years, and keeping the same apprehensions of Him, a man, and a glorious prophet, which they had to Him, a child, in the shop of a carpenter. But when Jesus in His sermon had reproved their infidelity (at which He wondered, and therefore did but few miracles there in respect of what He had done at Capernaum), and intimated the prelation of that city before Nazareth, "they thrust Him out of the city, and led Him to the brow of the hill on which the city was built," intending to "throw Him down headlong." But His work was not yet finished; therefore He, "passing through the midst of them, went His way."

17. Jesus therefore, departing from Nazareth, went up and down to all the towns and castles of Galilee, attended by His disciples, and certain women, out of whom He had cast unclean spirits; such as were Mary Magdalen, Johanna wife to Chuza Herod's steward, Susanna, and some others, who did for Him offices of provision, and "ministered to Him out of their own substance," and became parts of that holy college, which about this time began to be full; because now the apostles were returned from their preaching, full of joy that the devils were made subject to the word of their mouth, and the empire of their prayers, and invocation of the holy name of Jesus. But their Master gave them a lenitive to assuage the tumour and excrescency, intimating that such privileges are not solid foundations of a holy joy, but so far as they co-operate toward the great end of God's glory, and their own salvation, to which when they are consigned, and "their names written in heaven," in the book of election and registers of predestination, then their joy is reasonable, holy, true, and perpetual.

18. But when Herod had heard these things of Jesus, presently his apprehensions were such as derived from his guilt; he thought it was John the baptist who was risen from the dead, and that these mighty works were demonstrations of his power, increased by the superaddi-

---

60. Isa. 61:1.

149

tions of immortality and diviner influences made proportionable to the honour of a martyr, and the state of separation. For a little before this time, Herod had sent to the castle of Machæruns, where John was prisoner, and caused him to be beheaded. His head Herodias buried in her own palace, thinking to secure it against a re-union, lest it should again disturb her unlawful lusts, and disquiet Herod's conscience. But the body the disciples of John gathered up, and carried it with honour and sorrow, and buried it in Sebastet, in the confines of Samaria, making his grave between the bodies of Elizeus and Abdias, the prophets. And about this time was the passover of the Jews.

Section XIV
Of the Third Year of the Preaching of Jesus

1. But Jesus, knowing of the death of the Baptist, Herod's jealousy, and the envy of the pharisees, retired into a desert place beyond the lake, together with His apostles: for the people pressed so upon them they had not leisure to eat. But neither there could He be hid, but great multitudes flocked thither also; to whom He preached many things. And afterwards because there were no villages in the neighbourhood, lest they should faint in their return to their houses, He caused them to sit down upon the grass, and, with five loaves of barley and two small fishes He satisfied five thousand men, besides women and children, and caused the disciples to gather up the fragments, which, being amassed together, filled twelve baskets. Which miracles had so much proportion to the understanding, and met so happily with the affections of the people, that they were convinced that this was the "Messias who was to come into the world," and had a purpose to have "taken Him by force and made Him a king."

2. But He that left His Father's kingdom to take upon Him the miseries and infelicities of the world, fled from the offers of a kingdom, and their tumultuary election, as from an enemy; and therefore sending His disciples to the ship before towards Bethsaida, He ran into the mountains to hide Himself till the multitude should scatter to their several habitations; He in the meantime taking the opportunity of that retirement for the advantage of His prayers. But when the apostles were far engaged in the deep, a great tempest arose, with which they were pressed to the extremity of danger and the last refuges, labouring in sadness and hopelessness till "the fourth watch of the night," when in the midst of their fears and labour "Jesus comes, walking on the sea," and appeared to them; which turned their fears into affrightments, for

"they supposed it had been a spirit"; but He appeased their fears, with His presence, and manifestation who He was. Which yet they desired to have proved to them by a sign; for "Simon Peter said unto Him, Master, if it be Thou, command me to come to Thee on the waters": the Lord did so: and Peter, throwing himself upon the confidence of His Master's power and providence, came out of the ship; and his fear began to weigh him down, and "he cried, saying, Lord, save me: Jesus took him by the hand," reproved the timorousness of his faith, and "went with him into the ship": where when they had "worshipped Him," and admired the divinity of His power and person, they presently "came into the land of Genesareth," the ship arriving "at the port immediately." And "all that were sick," or possessed with unclean spirits, "were brought to Him, and as many as touched the border of His garment were made whole."

3. By this time, they whom Jesus had left on the other side of the lake had come as far as Capernaum to seek Him, wondering that He was there before them: but upon the occasion of their so diligent inquisition, Jesus observes to them, that it was not the divinity of the miracle that provoked their zeal, but the satisfaction they had in the loaves, a carnal complacency in their meal; and upon that intimation, speaks of celestial bread, the divine nutriment of souls; and then discourses of the mysterious and symbolical manducation of Christ himself, affirming that He himself was "the bread of life, that came down from heaven," that He would give His disciples "His flesh to eat, and His blood to drink," and all this should be "for the life of the world," to nourish unto life eternal; so that without it a happy eternity could not be obtained. Upon this discourse "divers of His disciples" (amongst whom St. Mark the evangelist is said to be one, though he was afterwards recalled by Simon Peter)[61] "forsook Him," being scandalized by their literal and carnal understanding of those words of Jesus which He intended in a spiritual sense. For "the words that He spake" were not profitable in the sense of flesh and blood, but "they are spirit, and they are life," Himself being the expounder, who best knew His own meaning.

4. When Jesus saw this great defection of His disciples from Him, He turned Him to the twelve apostles, and asked if they "also would go away? Simon Peter answered, Lord, whither shall we go? Thou hast the words of eternal life; and we believe, and are sure, Thou art that Christ,

---

61. Epiphanius, PG 41. 895.

the Son of the living God." Although this public confession was made
by Peter in the name and confidence of the other apostles, yet Jesus told
them that even amongst the twelve there was "one devil"; meaning
Judas Iscariot, "who afterwards betrayed Him." This He told them
prophetically, that they might perceive the sad accidents which afterwards happened did not invade and surprise Him in the disadvantages
of ignorance or improvision, but came by His own knowledge and
providence.

5. Then came to Him the pharisees, and some scribes, which came
from Jerusalem and Galilee, (for "Jesus would not go to Judea, because
the Jews laid wait to kill Him,") and quarrelled with Him about certain
impertinent, unnecessary rites, derived to them not by divine sanction,
but "ordinances of man": such as were washing their hands oft when
they eat, baptizing cups and platters, and washing tables and beds; which
ceremonies the apostles of Jesus did not observe, but attended diligently
to the simplicity and spiritual holiness of their Master's doctrine. But in
return to their vain demands Jesus gave them a sharp reproof, for
prosecuting these and many other traditions to the discountenance of
divine precepts; and in particular, they taught men to give to the *corban*,
and refused to supply the necessity of their parents, thinking it to be
religion though they neglected piety and charity. And again He
thunders out woes and sadnesses against their impieties, for being curious of minutes, and punctual in rites and ceremonials, but most negligent and incurious of judgment and the love of God; for their pride, for
their hypocrisy, for their imposing burdens upon others, which themselves helped not to support; for taking away the key of knowledge
from the people, obstructing the passages to heaven; for approving the
acts of their fathers in persecuting the prophets. But for the question
itself concerning washings, Jesus taught the people that no outward
impurity did stain the soul in the sight of God, but all pollution is from
within, from the corruption of the heart, and impure thoughts, unchaste
desires, and unholy purposes, and that charity is the best purifier in
the world.

6. And thence "Jesus departed into the coasts of Tyre and Sidon,
and entered into a house" that He might "not be known." The diligence
of a mother's love, and sorrow and necessity, found Him out in His
retirement; for a "Syrophœnician woman came and besought Him that
He would cast the devil out of her daughter." But Jesus discoursed to
her by way of discomfort and rejection of her, for her nation's sake. But
the seeming denial did but enkindle her desires, and made her impor-

tunity more bold and undeniable; she begged but "some crumbs that fell from the children's table," but one instance of favour to her daughter, which He poured forth without measure upon the sons and daughters of Israel. Jesus was pleased with her zeal and discretion, and pitied her daughter's infelicity, and dismissed her with saying "the devil was gone out of her daughter."

7. But Jesus staid not long here, but returning "to the sea of Galilee, through the midst of Decapolis, they brought unto Him a man deaf and dumb," whom Jesus cured by "touching his tongue, and putting His fingers in his ears": which caused the people to give a large testimony in approbation of all His actions. And they followed Him unto a mountain, bringing to Him multitudes of diseased people, and He healed them all. But because the people had followed Him "three days, and had nothing to eat," Jesus in pity to their need resolved to feast them once more at the charge of a miracle; therefore taking "seven loaves and a few small fishes, He blessed them, and satisfied four thousand men, besides women and children"; and there remained "seven baskets full" of broken bread and fish. From whence Jesus departed by ship to the coasts of Mageddon and Dalmanutha: whither "the pharisees and sadducees came, seeking of Him a sign": but Jesus rejected their impertinent and captious demand, knowing they did it to ill purposes, and with disaffection; reproving them, that they "discerned the face of the sky," and the prognostics of "fair or foul weather," but "not the signs of the times" of the Son of man. However, since they had neglected so great demonstrations of miracles, gracious discourses, holy laws and prophecies, they must expect "no other sign but the sign of the prophet Jonas," meaning the resurrection of His body after three days' burial; and so He dismissed the impertinent inquisitors.

8. And passing again over the lake, as His disciples were solicitous because "they had forgot to take bread," He gave them caution to "beware of the leaven of the pharisees and sadducees, and the leaven of Herod"; meaning, the hypocrisy and vanities of the one, and the heresy of the other: for Herod's leaven was the pretence that he was the Messias, which the sect of the Herodians did earnestly and spitefully promote. And after this entertainment of themselves by the way, they came together to Bethsaida, where Jesus cured a blind man with a collyrium of spittle, salutary as balsam or the purest eye-bright, when His divine benediction once had hallowed it. But Jesus staid not there, but departing thence into the coasts of Cæsarea Philippi, out of Herod's power (for it was in Philip's jurisdiction), after He had "prayed with

153

His disciples," He enquired what opinion the world had of Him, and "whom they reported Him to be? they answered, Some say thou art John the baptist, some that thou art Elias, or Jeremias, or one of the prophets." For in Galilee especially the sect of the pharisees was mightily disseminated, whose opinion it was that the souls of dead men, according to their several merits, did transmigrate into other bodies of very perfect and excellent persons; and therefore in all this variety none hit upon the right, or fancied Him to be a distinct person from the ancients, but although they differed in the assignation of His name, yet generally they agreed it was the soul of a departed prophet which had passed into another body. But Jesus asked the apostles their opinion; and Peter in the name of all the rest made an open and confident confession, "Thou art Christ, the Son of the living God."

9. This confession Jesus not only confirmed as true, but as "revealed by God," and of fundamental necessity: for after the blessing of Peter's person, upon allusion of Peter's name, Jesus said that "upon this rock (the article of Peter's confession) He would build His church," promising to it assistances, even to perpetuity, insomuch that "the gates of hell," that is, persecution, and death, and the grave, "should never prevail against it": adding withal a promise to Peter, in behalf of all the rest, as he had made a confession for them all, that He would "give unto him the keys of the kingdom of heaven, so that whatsoever He should bind on earth, should be bound in heaven: and whatsoever he should loose on earth, should be loosed in heaven": a power which He never communicated before or since, but to their successors; greater than the large charter of nature, and the donative of creation, in which all the creatures under heaven were made subject to man's empire, but till now heaven itself was never subordinate to human ministration.

10. And now the days from henceforward to the death of Jesus we must reckon to be like the vigils or eves of His passion; for now He began, and often did ingeminate, those sad predictions of His unhandsome usage He should shortly find; that He should be "rejected of the elders and chief priests and scribes, and suffer many things at Jerusalem, and be killed, and be raised up the third day." But Peter, hearing that sad discourse, so contrary to his hopes, which he had blended with temporal expectances (for he had learned the doctrine of Christ's advent, but not the mystery of the cross), in great and mistaken civility took Jesus aside, "and began to rebuke Him, saying, Be it far from Thee, Lord: this shall not be unto Thee." But Jesus, full of zeal against so soft and human

154

admonition, that savoured nothing of God, or of abstracted immaterial considerations, chid Peter bitterly; "Get thee behind Me, Satan, thou art an offence unto Me"; and calling His disciples to Him, told them a second part of a sad doctrine, that not only Himself, but all they also must suffer. For when the head was to be crowned with thorns, if the members were wrapt in softnesses, it was an unhandsome undecency, and a disunion too near an antipathy: and therefore whoever will be the disciple of Jesus, must "take up his cross, deny himself" and his own fonder appetites, and trace his Master's footsteps, marked out with blood, that He shed for our redemption and restitution. And that there be no escape from the participation of Christ's suffering, Jesus added this dilemma; "He that will save his life, shall lose it; and he that will lose it, shall save it" to eternity. Which part soever we choose, there is a life to be lost; but as the first are foolish to the extremest misery that will lose their souls to gain the world, so they are most wise and fortunate that will give their lives for Him; because when "the Son of man shall come in His own glory and His Father's and of His angels, He shall reward every man according to his works." This discourse Jesus concluded with a prophecy, that "some standing" in that presence "should not die till they saw the Son of man coming in His kingdom."

11. Of the greater glories of which, in due time to be revealed, "Jesus after eight days" gave a bright and excellent probation. For "taking with Him Peter, and James, and John, He went up into the mountain Tabor to pray; and while He prayed, He was transfigured before them, and His face did shine like the sun, and His garments were white and glistering: and there appeared talking with Him Moses and Elias gloriously, speaking of the decease which He should accomplish at Jerusalem"; which glory these apostles, after they had awaked from sleep, did behold. And the interlocutors with Jesus, having finished their embassy of death, which they delivered in forms of glory, representing the excellencies of the reward together with the sharpness of the passage and interval, departed, leaving the apostles "full of fear" and wonder and ecstasy; insomuch that "Peter talked, he knew not what," but nothing amiss, something prophetical, saying, "Master, it is good to be here; let us build three tabernacles": and some devout persons, in memory of the mystery, did erect three churches in the same place in after ages. But after the departure of those attendant saints, "a cloud encircled Jesus" and the disciples, "and a voice came from the excellent glory, This is My beloved Son, hear Him." The cloud quickly disap-

peared, and freed the disciples from the fear it had put them in. So they attended Jesus, and "descended from the mountain," being commanded silence, which they observed, "till the resurrection."[62]

12. The next day came to Jesus a man praying in behalf of his son, "lunatic and sore troubled with a devil," who sought oft "to destroy him in fire and water," that Jesus would be pleased to deliver him. For His apostles tried, and "could not," by reason of the want of faith: for this grace, if it be true, though in a less degree, is of power to "remove mountains," to pluck up trees by the roots, and to give them solid foundation in the waters. "And Jesus rebuked the devil, and he departed out of him" from that very hour. Thence Jesus departed privately into Galilee, and in His journey repeated those sadnesses of His approaching passion: which so afflicted the spirits of the disciples that they durst no more provoke Him to discourse, lest He should take occasion to inter-weave something of that unpleasant argument with it. For sad and disconsolate persons use to create comforts to themselves by fiction of fancy, and use arts of avocation to remove displeasure from them, and stratagems to remove it from their presence by removing it from their apprehensions, thinking the incommodity of it is then taken away when they have lost the sense.

13. When Jesus was now come to Capernaum, the exactors of rates came to Simon Peter, asking him if his Master paid the accustomed imposition, viz. a sicle, or didrachm, the fourth part of an ounce of silver, which was the tribute which the Lord imposed upon all the sons of Israel, from twenty years old and above, to pay for redemption and propitiation, and for the use of the tabernacle.[63] "When Peter came into the house, Jesus," knowing the message that he was big with, "pre-vented him," by asking him, "Of whom do the kings of the nations take tribute? of their own children or of strangers? Peter answered, Of strangers": then "said Jesus, then are the children free"; meaning, that since the gentile kings do not exact tribute of their sons, neither will God of His; and therefore this pension to be paid for the use of the tabernacle, for the service of God, for the redemption of their souls, was not to be paid by Him who was the Son of God, but by strangers: "yet to avoid offence," He sent Peter a-fishing, and provided a fish with two didrachms of silver in it, which He commanded Peter to pay for them two.

---

62. Matt. 17:1; Mark 9:2; Luke 9:29.
63. Exod. 30:13.

14. But when the disciples were together with "Jesus in the house, He asked them what they discoursed of upon the way"; for they had fallen upon an ambitious and mistaken quarrel, "which of them should be greatest in their Master's kingdom," which they still did dream should be an external and secular royalty, full of fancy and honour. But the Master was diligent to check their forwardness, establishing a rule for clerical deportment, "he that will be greatest among you, let him be your minister": so supposing a greater and a lesser, a minister, and a person to be ministered unto; but dividing the grandeur of the person from the greatness of office, that the higher the employment is, the more humble should be the man. Because in spiritual prelation it is not as in secular pomps, where the dominion is despotic, the coercion bloody, the dictates imperious, the laws externally compulsory, and the titles arrogant and vain; and all the advantages are so passed upon the person, that making that first to be splendid, it passes from the person to the subjects, who in abstracted essences do not easily apprehend regalities in veneration, but as they are subjected in persons made excellent by such superstructures of majesty; but in dignities ecclesiastical the dominion is paternal, the regiment persuasive and argumentative, the coercion by censures immaterial, by cession and consent, by denial of benefits, by the interest of virtues, and the efficacy of hopes, and impresses upon the spirit; the laws are full of admonition and sermon; the titles of honour monitors of duty, and memorials of labour and offices; and all the advantages which from the office usually pass upon the person, are to be divested by the humility of the man; and when they are of greatest veneration, they are abstracted excellencies and immaterial, not passing through the person to the people, and reflected to his lustre, but transmitted by his labour and ministry, and give him honour for his labour's sake (which is his personal excellency), not for his honour and title, which is either a derivative from Christ, or from the constitution of pious persons estimating and valuing the relatives of religion.

15. Then "Jesus taketh a little child, and setteth him in the midst," propounding him by way of emblem a pattern of humility and simplicity, without the mixtures of ambition or caitive distempers; such infant candour, and lowliness of spirit, being the necessary port through which we must pass if we will enter into the courts of heaven. But as a current of wholesome waters, breaking from its restraint, runs out in a succession of waters, and every preceding draught draws out the next; so were the discourses of Jesus excellent and opportune, creating occasions for others; that the whole doctrine of the gospel, and the entire

157

will of the Father, might be communicated upon design, even the chances of words and actions being made regular and orderly by divine providence. For from the instance of humility in the symbol and hiero-glyphic of the child, Jesus discourses of the care God takes of little children, whether naturally or spiritually such; the danger of doing them scandal and offences; the care and power of their angels guardian; of the necessity in the event that scandals should arise, and of the great woe and infelicity of those persons who were the active ministers of such offences.

16. But if in the traverses of our life discontents and injuries be done, Jesus teaches how the injured person should demean himself; first, reprove the offending party privately; if he repent, forgive him for ever, with a mercy as unwearied and as multiplied as his repentance; for the servant to whom his lord had forgiven ten thousand talents, because he refused to forgive his fellow-servant one hundred pence was deliv-ered to the tormentors till he should pay that debt, which his lord once forgave, till the servant's impiety forced him to repent his donative and remission. But if he refuses the charity of private correction, let him be reproved before a few witnesses; and in case he be still incorrigible, let him be brought to the tribunal of the church; against whose advices if he shall kick, let him feel her power, and be cut off from the communion of saints, becoming a pagan or a publican. And to make that the church shall not have a dead and ineffectual hand in her animadversions, Jesus promises to all the apostles, what before He promised to Peter, a power of "binding and loosing on earth," and that it should be ratified in heaven, what they shall so dispose on earth with an unerring key.

17. But John interrupted Him, telling Him of a stranger that "cast out devils in the name of Jesus," but because he was not of the family he had "forbidden him." To this Jesus replied that he should "in no wise have forbidden him," for in all reason he would do veneration to that Person whose name he saw to be energetical and triumphant over devils, and in whose name it is almost necessary that man should believe who used it as an instrument of ejection of impure spirits. Then Jesus proceeded in His excellent sermon and union of discourses, adding holy precepts concerning "offences" which a man might do to himself; in which case he is to be severe, though most gentle to others: for in his own case he must shew no mercy, but abscission: for it is better to "cut off the offending hand or foot," or "extinguish the offending eye," rather than upon the support of a troublesome foot, and by the light of an offending eye, walk into ruin and a sad eternity, "where the worm

dieth not, and the fire is not quenched." And so Jesus ended this chain of excellent discourses.

18. About this time was the Jews' feast of tabernacles, whither Jesus went up as it were in secret. And passing through Samaria, He found the inhabitants of a little village so inhospitable as to refuse to give Him entertainment; which so provoked the intemperate zeal of James and John, that they would fain have "called for fire to consume them, even as Elias did": but Jesus rebuked the furies of their anger, teaching them to distinguish the spirit of christianity from the ungentleness of the decretory zeal of Elias; for since "the Son of man came" with a purpose "to seek and save what was lost," it was but an indiscreet temerity, suddenly upon the lightest umbrages of displeasure to destroy a man, whose redemption cost the effusion of the dearest blood from the heart of Jesus. But contrariwise Jesus does a miracle upon the ten leprous persons, which came to Him from the neighbourhood crying out with sad exclamations for help; but Jesus sent them to the priest, to offer for their cleansing: thither they went, and but one only returned to give thanks, and he a stranger, who "with a loud voice glorified God," and with humble adoration worshipped and gave thanks to Jesus.[64]

19. When Jesus had finished His journey and was now come to Jerusalem, for the first days He was undiscerned in public conventions, but heard of the various opinions of men concerning Him, "some saying He was a good man, others that He deceived the people." And the pharisees sought for Him, to do Him a mischief; but when they despaired of finding Him in the midst of the feast and the people, He made sermons openly, in the midst of the temple. Whom when He had convinced by the variety and divinity of His miracles and discourses, they gave the greatest testimony in the world of human weakness, and how prevalent a prejudice is above the confidence and conviction of a demonstration: for a proverb, a mistake, an error in matter of circumstance, did in their understandings outweigh multitudes of miracles and arguments; and because "Christ was of Galilee," because they "knew whence He was," because of the proverb that "out of Galilee comes no prophet," because "the rulers did not believe in Him," these outweighed the demonstrations of His mercy, and His power, and divinity. But yet "very many believed on Him; and no man durst lay hands to take Him, for as yet His time was not come" in which He meant to give

---

64. Luke 17:15.

159

Himself up to the power of the Jews; and therefore when the pharisees sent officers to seize Him, they also became His disciples, being themselves surprised by the excellency of His doctrine.

20. After this "Jesus went to the mount of Olivet," on the east of Jerusalem; and "the next day returned again into the temple," where "the scribes and pharisees brought Him a woman taken in the act of adultery," tempting Him to give sentence, that they might accuse Him of severity or intermeddling if He condemned her, or of remissness and popularity if He did acquit her: but Jesus found out an expedient for their difficulty, and changed the scene, by bidding "the innocent person among them cast the first stone" at the adulteress; and then "stooping down," to give them fair occasion to withdraw, "He wrote upon the ground with His finger," whilst they left the woman and her crime to a more private censure: "Jesus was left alone, and the woman in the midst"; whom Jesus dismissed, charging her to "sin no more." And a while after Jesus begins again to discourse to them, "of His mission from the Father, of His crucifixion and exaltation from the earth, of the reward of believers, of the excellency of truth, of spiritual liberty and relations; who are the sons of Abraham, and who the children of the devil; of His own eternal generation, of the desire of Abraham to see His day." In which sermon He continued, adding still new excellencies, and confuting their malicious and vainer calumnies, till they, that they also might confute Him, "took up stones to cast at Him"; but He "went out of the temple, going through the midst of them, and so passed by."

21. But in His passage He met a man who had been born blind: and after He had discoursed cursorily of the cause of that blindness, it being a misery not sent as a punishment to "his own or his parent's sin," but as an occasion to make public "the glory of God"; He, to manifest that Himself was "the light of the world" in all senses, said it now, and proved it by a miracle: for sitting down, "He made clay of spittle," and "anointing the eyes of the blind man," bade him "go wash in Siloam"; which was a pool of limpid water which God sent at the prayer of Isaiah the prophet a little before his death, to satisfy the necessities of His people oppressed with thirst and a strict siege; and it stood at the foot of Mount Sion, and gave its water at first by returns and periods, always to the Jews, but not to the enemies: and those intermitted springings were still continued, but only a pool was made from the frequent effluxes. The blind man "went, and washed, and returned seeing"; and was incessantly vexed by the pharisees, to tell them the manner and circumstances of the cure: and when the man had averred the truth, and named

his physician, giving Him a pious and charitable testimony, the pharisees, because they could not force him to disavow his good opinion of Jesus, "cast him out of the synagogue." But Jesus meeting him received him into the church, told him He was Christ; and the man became again enlightened, and he "believed and worshipped." But the pharisees blasphemed: for such was the dispensation of the divine mysteries, that the blind should see, and they which think they see clearly should become blind, because they had not the excuse of ignorance to lessen or take off the sin, but in the midst of light they shut their eyes, and doted upon darkness, and "therefore did their sin remain."

22. But Jesus continued His sermon among the pharisees, insinuating reprehensions in His dogmatical discourses, which, like light, shined, and discovered error. For by discoursing the properties of a "good shepherd" and the lawful way of intromission, He proved them to be "thieves and robbers," because they refused to "enter in by Jesus," who is "the door of the sheep"; and upon the same ground reproved all those false Christs which before Him usurped the title of Messias; and proved His own vocation and office by an argument which no other shepherd would use, because He "laid down His life for His sheep": others would take the fleece and eat the flesh, but none but Himself would die for His sheep; but He would first die, and then gather His "sheep" together "into one fold" (intimating the calling of the gentiles); to which purpose He was "enabled by His Father to lay down His life, and to take it up"; and had also endeared them to His Father, that they should be "preserved unto eternal life"; and "no power should be able to take them out of His hand or the hand of His Father," for because Jesus was "united to the Father," the Father's care preserved the Son's flocks.

23. But the Jews, to requite Him for His so divine sermons, betook themselves to their old argument: "they took up stones again to cast at Him," pretending He had blasphemed: but Jesus proved it to be no blasphemy to call Himself "the Son of God," because "they to whom the word of God came, are" in scripture "called gods"; but nothing could satisfy them, whose temporal interest was concerned not to consent to such doctrine which would save their souls by ruining their temporal concernments. But when they sought again to take Him, Jesus escaped out of their hands, and went away beyond Jordan where John at first baptized: which gave the people occasion to remember that "John did no miracle," but this man does many; and John, whom all men did revere and highly account of for his office and sanctity, gave testimony to Jesus: "and many believed on Him there."

161

24. After this Jesus, knowing that the harvest was great, and as yet the labourers had been few, sent out seventy-two of His disciples, with the like commission as formerly the twelve apostles, that they might "go before to those places whither Himself meant to come": of which number were the seven whom afterwards the apostles set over the widows, and Matthias, Mark, and some[65] say Luke, Justus, Barnabas, Apelles, Rufus, Niger, Cephas, (not Peter,) Thaddæus, Aristion, and John; the rest of the names could not be recovered by the best diligence of Eusebius and Epiphanius.[66] But when they returned from their journey, they rejoiced greatly in the legation and power, and Jesus also "rejoiced in spirit," giving glory to God that He had "made His revelations to babes" and the more imperfect persons; like the lowest valleys, which receive from heaven the greatest floods of rain and blessings, and stand thick with corn and flowers, when the mountains are unfruitful in their height and greatness.

25. And now a doctor of the law came to Jesus, asking Him a question of the greatest consideration that a wise man could ask, or a prophet answer, "master, what shall I do to inherit eternal life?" Jesus referred him to the scriptures, and declared the way to heaven to be this only, "to love the Lord with all our powers and faculties, and our neighbour as ourself." But when the lawyer, being captious, made a scruple in a smooth rush, asking what is meant by "neighbour"; Jesus told him, by a parable of a traveller fallen into the hands of robbers, and neglected by a priest and by a Levite, but relieved by a Samaritan, that no distance of country or religion destroys the relation of neighbourhood; but every person with whom we converse in peace and charity, is that neighbour whom we are to love as ourselves.

26. Jesus, having departed from Jerusalem upon the fore-mentioned danger, came to a village called Bethany, where Martha, making great and busy preparation for His entertainment, to express her joy and her affections to His person, desired Jesus to dismiss her sister Mary from His feet, who sate there feasting herself with the viands and sweetnesses of His doctrine, incurious of the provisions for entertainment. But Jesus commended her choice; and though He did not expressly disrepute Martha's civility, yet He preferred Mary's religion and sanctity of affections.—In this time, because "the night drew on in

---

65. Epiphanius, PG 41. 908.
66. Eusebius, op. cit., PG 2. 118.

which no man could work," Jesus hastened to do His Father's business, and to pour out whole cataracts of holy lessons; like the fruitful Nilus swelling over the banks, and filling all the trenches, to make a plenty of corn and fruits great as the inundation. Jesus therefore teaches His disciples that form of prayer the second time, which we call the Lord's prayer: teaches them assiduity and indefatigable importunity in prayer, by a parable of an importunate neighbour borrowing loaves at midnight, and a troublesome widow who forced an unjust judge to do her right by her clamorous and hourly addresses: encourages them to pray by consideration of the divine goodness and fatherly affection, far more indulgent to His sons than natural fathers are to their dearest issue; and adds a gracious promise of success to them that pray. He reproves pharisaical ostentation; arms His disciples against the fear of men and the terrors of persecution, which can arrive but to the incommodities of the body; teaches the fear of God, who is Lord of the whole man, and can accurse the soul as well as punish the body. He refuses to divide the inheritance between two brethren, as not having competent power to become lord in temporal jurisdictions. He preaches against covetousness and the placing felicities in worldly possessions, by a parable of a rich man, whose riches were too big for his barns, and big enough for his soul, and he ran over into voluptuousness and stupid complacencies in his perishing goods; he was snatched from their possession, and his soul taken from him, in the violence of a rapid and hasty sickness, in the space of one night. He discourses of divine providence and care over us all, and descending even as low as grass. He exhorts to alms-deeds, to watchfulness, and preparation against the sudden and unexpected coming of our Lord to judgment, or the arrest of death: tells the offices and sedulity of the clergy, under the apologue of stewards and governors of their Lord's houses; teaches them gentleness and sobriety, and not to do evil upon confidence of their Lord's absence and delay; and teaches the people even of themselves to judge what is right concerning the signs of the coming of the Son of man. And the end of all these discourses was, that all men should repent, and live good lives, and be saved.

27. At this sermon "there were present some that told Him of the Galileans, whose blood Pilate mingled with their sacrifices." For the Galileans were a sort of people that taught it to be unlawful to pay tribute to strangers, or to pray for the Romans; and because the Jews did both, they refused to communicate in their sacred rites, and would sacrifice apart: at which solemnity when Pilate the Roman deputy had apprehended many of them, he caused them all to be slain, making them

163

to die upon the same altars. These were of the province of Judea, but of the same opinion with those who taught in Galilee, from whence the sect had its appellative. But to the story: Jesus made reply that these external accidents, though they be sad and calamitous, yet they are no arguments of condemnation against the persons of the men, to convince them of a greater guilt than others upon whom no such visible signatures have been imprinted; the purpose of such chances is that we should "repent, lest we perish" in the like judgment.

28. About this time a certain ruler of a synagogue renewed the old question about the observation of the sabbath, repining at Jesus that He cured a woman that was crooked, loosing her from her infirmity with which she had been afflicted eighteen years; but Jesus made the man ashamed by an argument from their own practice, who themselves "loose an ox from the stall on the sabbath, and lead him to watering." And by the same argument He also stopped the mouths of the scribes and pharisees, which were open upon Him, for curing an hydropic person upon the sabbath. For Jesus, that He might draw off and separate christianity from the yoke of ceremonies by abolishing and taking off the strictest mosaical rites, chose to do very many of His miracles upon the sabbath, that He might do the work of abrogation and institution both at once; not much unlike the sabbatical pool in Judea, which was dry six days, but gushed out in a full stream upon the sabbath:[67] for though upon all days Christ was operative and miraculous, yet many reasons did concur and determine Him to a more frequent working upon those days of public ceremony and convention. But going forth from thence, He went up and down the cities of Galilee, re-enforcing the same doctrine He had formerly taught them, and daily adding new precepts, and cautions, and prudent insinuations; advertizing of the multitudes of them that perish, and the paucity of them that shall be saved, and that we should "strive to enter in at the straight gate"; that "the way to destruction is broad" and plausible, "the way to heaven" nice and austere, "and few there be that find it": teaches them modesty at feasts, and entertainments of the poor: discourses of the many excuses and unwillingnesses of persons who were invited to the feast of the kingdom, the refreshments of the gospel; and tacitly insinuates the rejection of the Jews, who were the first "invited," and the calling of the gentiles, who were the persons "called in from the highways and

---

67. Josephus, *Jewish War*, LCL, (bk. 7, ch. 5), vol. 3, p. 534.

hedges." He reprehends Herod for his subtilty and design to kill Him; prophesies that He should die at Jerusalem; and intimates great sadnesses future to them, for neglecting "this their day" of visitation, and for "killing the prophets and the messengers sent from God."

29. It now grew towards winter, and the Jews' feast of dedication was at hand; therefore Jesus went up to Jerusalem to the feast, where He preached in Solomon's porch (which part of the temple stood entire from the first ruins), and the end of His sermon was that the Jews had liked to have stoned Him. But retiring from thence, He went beyond Jordan; where He taught the people, in a most elegant and persuasive parable, concerning the mercy of God in accepting penitents, in the parable of the "prodigal son" returning; discourses of the design of the Messias coming into the world, to recover erring persons from their sin and danger, in the apologues of the "lost sheep," and "groat"; and under the representment of an unjust but prudent steward, He taught us so to employ our present opportunities and estates, by laying them out in acts of mercy and religion, that when our souls shall be dismissed from the stewardship and custody of our body we "may be entertained in everlasting habitations." He instructeth the pharisees in the question of divorces, limiting the permissions of separations to the only cause of fornication: preferreth holy celibate before the estate of marriage, in them to whom the gift of continency is given, in order to the kingdom of heaven. He telleth a story or a parable (for which is uncertain) of a rich man (whom Euthymius out of the tradition of the Hebrews nameth Nymensis) and Lazarus; the first a voluptuous person, and uncharitable; the other, pious, afflicted, sick, and a beggar; the first died, and went to hell; the second, to Abraham's bosom: God so ordering the dispensation of good things, that we cannot easily enjoy two heavens; nor shall the infelicities of our lives, if we be pious, end otherwise than in a beatified condition. The epilogue of which story discovered this truth also, that the ordinary means of salvation are the express revelations of scripture, and the ministries of God's appointment; and whosoever neglects these, shall not be supplied with means extraordinary, or if he were, they would be totally ineffectual.

30. And still the people drew water from the fountains of our Saviour, which streamed out in a full and continual emanation. For adding wave to wave, "line to line, precept upon precept," He reproved the fastidiousness of the pharisee, that came with eucharist to God, and contempt to his brother; and commended the humility of the publican's address, who came deploring his sins, and with modesty and penance, and

importunity, begged, and obtained a mercy. Then He laid hands upon certain young children, and gave them benediction, charging His apostles to admit infants to Him, because to them in person, and to such in emblem and signification, the kingdom of heaven does appertain. He instructs a young man in the ways and counsels of perfection, besides the observation of precepts, by heroical renunciations, and acts of munificent charity. Which discourse because it alighted upon an indisposed and an unfortunate subject (for the young man was very rich), Jesus discourses, how hard it is for a rich man to be saved; but He expounds Himself to mean, "they that trust in riches"; and however it is a matter of so great temptation that it is almost impossible to escape, yet "with God nothing is impossible." But when the apostles heard the Master bidding the young man "sell all, and give to the poor, and follow Him," and for his reward promised him "a heavenly treasure"; Peter, in the name of the rest, began to think that this was their case, and the promise also might concern them; but they asked the question, What shall we have, who have forsaken all, and followed Thee? Jesus answered that they should "sit upon twelve thrones, judging the twelve tribes of Israel."

31. And Jesus extended this mercy to every disciple that should forsake either house, or wife, or children, or any thing, for His sake and the gospel's, and that they should receive a hundredfold in this life by way of comfort and equivalency, and in the world to come, thousands of glories and possessions in fruition and redundancy. For "they that are last shall be first, and the first shall be last": and the despised people of this world shall reign like kings, and contempt itself shall swell up into glory, and poverty into an eternal satisfaction. And these rewards shall not be accounted according to the privileges of nations or priority of vocation, but readiness of mind and obedience, and sedulity of operation after calling: which Jesus taught His disciples in the parable of the labourers in the vineyard, to whom the master gave the same reward, though the times of their working were different; as their calling and employment had determined the opportunity of their labours.

Section XV
Of the Accidents Happening from the Death of Lazarus until the Death and Burial of Jesus

1. While Jesus was in Galilee, messengers came to Him from Martha and her sister Mary, that He would hasten into Judea, to Bethany, to relieve the sickness and imminent dangers of their brother Lazarus. But He deferred His going till Lazarus was dead; purposing to

give a great probation of His divinity, power, and mission, by a glorious miracle; and to give God glory, and to receive reflections of the glory upon Himself. For after He had staid two days, He called His disciples to go with Him into Judea, telling them that Lazarus was dead, but He would raise him out of that sleep of death. But by that time Jesus was arrived at Bethany, "He found that Lazarus had been dead four days," and now near to putrefaction. But when Martha and Mary met Him, weeping their pious tears for their dead brother, Jesus suffered the passions of piety and humanity, and wept, distilling that precious liquor into the grave of Lazarus; watering the dead plant, that it might spring into a new life, and raise his head above the ground.

2. When Jesus had by His words of comfort and institution strengthened the faith of the two mourning sisters, and commanded "the stone to be removed" from the grave, He made an address of adoration and eucharist to His Father, confessing His perpetual propensity to hear Him, and then cried out, "Lazarus, come forth! and he that was dead came forth" from his bed of darkness, with his night-clothes on him; whom when the apostles had unloosed at the command of Jesus, he went to Bethany: and many that were present "believed on Him"; but others, wondering and malicious, went and told the pharisees the story of the miracle, who upon that advice called their great council, whose great and solemn cognizance was of the greater causes of prophets, of kings, and of the holy law. At this great assembly it was that Caiaphas the high-priest prophesied that it was "expedient one should die for the people." And thence they determined the death of Jesus; but He, knowing they had passed a decretory sentence against Him, retired to the city Ephraim in the tribe of Judah, near the desert, where He staid a few days, till the approximation of the feast of Easter.

3. Against which feast when Jesus with His disciples was going to Jerusalem, He told them the event of the journey would be that the Jews should "deliver Him to the gentiles"; that they should "scourge Him, and mock Him, and crucify Him, and the third day He should rise again." After which discourse the mother of Zebedee's children begged of Jesus for her two sons, that "one of them might sit at His right hand, the other at the left, in His kingdom." For no discourses of His passion, or intimations of the mysteriousness of His kingdom, could yet put them into right understandings of their condition. But Jesus, whose heart and thoughts were full of fancy and apprehensions of the neighbour passion, gave them answer in proportion to His present conceptions and their future condition. For if they desired the honours of His

167

kingdom such as they were, they should have them, unless themselves did decline them; they should "drink of His cup," and dip in His lavatory, and be "washed with His baptism," and "sit in His kingdom," if the heavenly "Father had prepared" it for them; but the donation of that immediately was an issue of divine election and predestination, and was only competent to them who by holy living and patient suffering put themselves into a disposition of becoming vessels of election.

4. But as Jesus in this journey came near Jericho, He cures a blind man, who sat begging by the way-side: and espying Zaccheus, the chief of the publicans, upon a tree, that he being low of stature might upon that advantage of station see Jesus passing by, He invited Himself to his house; who received Him with gladness, and repentance of his crimes, purging his conscience, and filling his heart and house with joy and sanctity; for immediately upon the arrival of the Master at his house, he offered restitution to all persons whom he had injured, and satisfaction; and half of his remanent estate he gave to the poor, and so gave the fairest entertainment to Jesus, who brought along with Him salvation to his house. There it was that He spake the parable of the king, who concredited divers talents to his servants, and having at his return exacted an account, rewarded them who had improved their bank, and been faithful in their trust, with rewards proportionable to their capacity and improvement; but the negligent servant who had not meliorated his stock, was punished with ablegation and confinement to outer darkness. And from hence sprang up that dogmatical proposition, which is mysterious and determined in christianity, "to him that hath shall be given, and from him that hath not shall be taken away even what he hath." After this, going forth of Jericho, He cured two blind men upon the way.

5. Six days before Easter, Jesus came to Bethany, where He was feasted by Martha and Mary, and accompanied by Lazarus, who "sat at the table with Jesus." But Mary brought a pound of nard pistic, and, as formerly she had done, again "anoints the feet of Jesus, and fills the house with the odour," till God himself smelt thence a savour of a sweet-smelling sacrifice. But Judas Iscariot, the thief and the traitor, repined at the vanity of the expense, as he pretended, because it might have been "sold for three hundred pence, and have been given to the poor."[68] But Jesus in His reply taught us, that there is an opportunity

68. John 12:5.

for actions of religion as well as of charity; "Mary did this against the burial of Jesus," and her religion was accepted by Him, to whose honours the holocaust of love and the oblations of alms-deeds are in their proper seasons direct actions of worship and duty. But at this meeting there came many Jews to see Lazarus, who was raised from death, as well as to see Jesus; and because by occasion of his resurrection, "many of them believed on Jesus," therefore the pharisees deliberated about putting him to death; but God in His glorious providence was pleased to preserve him as a trumpet of His glories, and a testimony of the miracle, thirty years after the death of Jesus.[69]

6. The next day, being the fifth day before the passover, Jesus came to the foot of the Mount of olives, and sent His disciples to Bethphage, a village in the neighbourhood, commanding them to unloose an ass and a colt, and bring them to Him, and to tell the owners it was done for the Master's use; and they did so: and when they brought the ass to Jesus, He rides on him to Jerusalem; and the people, having notice of His approach, took branches of palmtrees and went out to meet Him, strewing branches and garments in the way, crying out, Hosanna to the Son of David! which was a form of exclamation used to the honour of God, and in great solemnities, and signifies "adoration" to the Son of David, by the rite of carrying branches; which when they used in procession about their altars, they used to pray, "Lord, save us; Lord prosper us"; which hath occasioned the reddition of "Hoschiannah" to be amongst some that prayer which they repeated at the carrying of the "Hoschiannah," as if itself did signify, "Lord, save us." But this honour was so great and unusual to be done even to kings, that the pharisees, knowing this to be an appropriate manner of address to God, said one to another by way of wonder, "Hear ye what these men say?" For they were troubled to hear the people revere Him as a God.

7. When Jesus from the Mount of olives beheld Jerusalem, He "wept over it," and foretold great sadnesses and infelicities futurely contingent to it: which not only happened in the sequel of the story according to the main issues and significations of this prophecy, but even to minutes and circumstances it was verified; for in the Mount of olives where Jesus shed tears over perishing Jerusalem, the Romans first pitched their tents when they came to its final overthrow.[70] From

---

69. Epiphanius, PG 42. 85.
70. Josephus, *Jewish War*, LCL, (bk. 5, ch. 2), vol. 3, p. 220.

thence descending to the city He went into the temple, and still the acclamations followed Him, till the pharisees were ready to burst with the noises abroad, and the tumults of envy and scorn within, and by observing that all their endeavours to suppress His glories were but like clapping their hands to veil the sun, and that in despite of all their stratagems the whole nation was become disciple to the glorious Nazarene. And there He cured certain persons that were "blind and lame."

8. But whilst He abode at Jerusalem, "certain Greeks who came to the feast to worship" made their address to Philip that they might be brought to Jesus. Philip tells Andrew, and they both tell Jesus; who, having admitted them, discoursed many things concerning His passion, and then prayed a petition, which is the end of His own sufferings, and of all human actions, and the purpose of the whole creation, "Father, glorify Thy name"; to which He was answered by a voice from heaven, "I have both glorified it, and will glorify it again." But this, nor the whole series of miracles that He did, the mercies, the cures, nor the divine discourses, could gain the faith of all the Jews, who were determined by their human interest; for "many of the rulers who believed on Him durst not confess Him, because they loved the praise of men more than the praise of God." Then Jesus again exhorted all men to believe on Him, that so they might in the same act believe on God; that they might approach unto the light, and not abide in darkness; that they might obey the commandments of the Father, whose express charge it was that Jesus should preach this gospel; and that they might not be judged at the last day by the word which they have rejected, which word to all its observers is everlasting life. After which sermon retiring to Bethany He abode there all night.

9. On the morrow returning to Jerusalem, on the way being hungry He passed by a fig-tree; where expecting fruit, He found none, and cursed the fig-tree, which by the next day was dried up and withered; upon occasion of which preternatural event Jesus discoursed of the power of faith, and its power to produce miracles. But upon this occasion others, the disciples of Jesus in after ages, have pleased themselves with fancies and imperfect descants, as that He cursed this tree in mystery and secret intendment; it having been the tree in the eating whose fruit Adam, prevaricating the divine law, made an inlet to sin, which brought in death, and the sadnesses of Jesus' passion. But Jesus having entered the city came into the temple and preached the gospel: and the chief priests and scribes questioned His commission, and by what authority He did those things; but Jesus, promising to answer

them if they would declare their opinions concerning John's baptism, which they durst not for fear of "displeasing the people" or throwing dirt in their own faces, was acquitted of His obligation by their declining the proposition.

10. But there He reproved the pharisees and rulers, by the parable of two sons; the first whereof said to his father he would not obey, but repented and did his command; the second gave good words, but did nothing; meaning that persons of the greatest improbability were more heartily converted than they whose outside seemed to have appropriated religion to the labels of their frontlets. He added a parable of the vineyard let out to husbandmen, who killed the servants sent to demand the fruits, and at last the son himself, that they might invade the inheritance; but made a sad commination to all such who should either stumble at this stone, or on whom this stone should fall. After which and some other reprehensions, (which He so veiled in parable, that it might not be expounded to be calumny or declamation, although such sharp sermons had been spoken in the people's hearing, but yet so transparently that themselves might see their own iniquity in those modest and just representments,) the pharisees would fain have seized Him, but they durst not for the people, but resolved if they could to entangle Him in His talk; and therefore sent out spies, who should pretend sanctity and veneration of His person, who, with a goodly insinuating preface, that "Jesus regarded no man's person, but spake the word of God" with much simplicity and justice, desired to know if it were "lawful to pay tribute to Cæsar, or not." A question which was of great dispute, because of the numerous sect of the Galileans, who denied it, and of the affections of the people, who loved their money, and their liberty, and the privileges of their nation. And now in all probability He should fall under the displeasure of the people or of Cæsar, but Jesus called to "see a penny," and finding it to be superscribed with Cæsar's image, with incomparable wisdom He brake their snare, and established an evangelical proposition for ever, saying, "Give to Cæsar the things that are Cæsar's, and to God the things that are God's."[71]

11. Having so excellently, and so much to their wonder, answered the pharisees, the sadducees bring their great objection to Him against the resurrection, by putting case of a woman married to seven husbands, and "whose wife should she be in the resurrection?" thinking that to be

---

71. Matt. 22:21.

an impossible state which engages upon such seeming incongruities that a woman should at once be wife to seven men. But Jesus first answered their objection, telling them that all those relations, whose foundation is in the imperfections and passions of flesh and blood, and duties here below, shall cease in that state which is so spiritual that it is like to the condition of angels, amongst whom there is no difference of sex, no cognations, no genealogies or derivation from one another; and then by a new argument proves the resurrection, by one of God's appellatives, who did then delight to be called "the God of Abraham, Isaac, and Jacob": for since "God is not the God of the dead but of the living," unto Him even these men are alive; and if so, then either they now exercise acts of life, and therefore shall be restored to their bodies, that their actions may be complete, and they not remain in a state of imperfection to all eternity; or if they be alive, and yet cease from operation, they shall be much rather raised up to a condition which shall actuate and make perfect their present capacities and dispositions, lest a power and inclination should for ever be in the root and never rise up to fruit or herbage, and so be an eternal vanity, like an old bud or an eternal child.

12. After this, the pharisees being well pleased, not that Jesus spake so excellently, but that the sadducees were confuted, came to Him, asking, "which was the great commandment?" and some other things, more out of curiosity than pious desires of satisfaction. But at last Jesus was pleased to ask them concerning Christ, "whose son He was?" They answered, "the Son of David": but He replying, "How then doth David call Him Lord?"—"the Lord said unto my Lord, Sit thou on my right hand," etc.—they had nothing to answer. But Jesus then gave His disciples caution against the pride, the hypocrisy, and the oppression of the scribes and pharisees; and commended the poor widow's oblation of her two mites into the treasury, it being a great love in a little print, for it was all her living. All this was spoken in the temple, the goodly stones of which when the apostles beheld with wonder, they being white and firm, twenty cubits in length, twelve in breadth, eight in depth, as Josephus reports,[72] Jesus prophesies the destruction of the place: concerning which prediction when the apostles, being with Him at the Mount of olives, asked Him privately concerning

---

72. Josephus, *Jewish Antiquities*, LCL, (bk. 15, ch. 11), vol. 8, p. 190.

the time and the signs of so sad event, He discoursed largely of His coming to judgment against that city, and interweaved predictions of the universal judgment of all the world; of which this, though very sad, was but a small adumbration: adding precepts of watchfulness, and standing in preparation, with hearts filled with grace, our lamps always shining, that when the bridegroom shall come we may be ready to enter in: which was intended in the parable of the five wise virgins: and concluded His sermon with a narrative of His passion, foretelling that within two days He should be crucified.

13. Jesus descended from the mount, and came to Bethany: and turning into the house of Simon the leper, Mary Magdalen, having been reproved by Judas for spending ointment upon Jesus' feet, it being so unaccustomed and large a profusion, thought now to speak her love once more, and trouble nobody, and therefore she poured ointment on His sacred head, believing that, being a pompousness of a more accustomed festivity, would be indulged to the expressions of her affection: but now all the disciples murmured, wondering at the prodigiousness of the woman's religion, great enough to consume a province in the overflowings of her thankfulness and duty. But Jesus now also entertained the sincerity of her miraculous love, adding this prophecy, that where the gospel should be preached, there also a record of this act should be kept, as a perpetual monument of her piety, and an attestation of His divinity who could foretell future contingencies; christianity receiving the greatest argument from that which St. Peter calls, "the surer word of prophecy," meaning it to be greater than the testimony of miracles, not easy to be dissembled by impure spirits, and whose efficacy should descend to all ages: for this prophecy shall for ever be fulfilling, and being every day verified, does every day preach the divinity of Christ's person, and of His institution.

14. Two days before the passover, the scribes and pharisees called a council to contrive crafty ways of destroying Jesus, they not daring to do it by open violence. Of which meeting when Judas Iscariot had notice (for those assemblies were public and notorious), he ran from Bethany, and offered himself to betray his master to them, if they would give him a considerable reward: they agreed for "thirty pieces of silver." Of what value each piece was, is uncertain; but their own nation hath given a rule, that when a piece of silver is named in the pentateuch, it signifies a sicle; if it be named in the prophets, it signifies a pound; if in the other writings of the Old testament, it signifies a talent. This therefore being alleged out of the prophet Jeremy by one of the evan-

gelists,[73] it is probable the price at which Judas sold his Lord was thirty pound weight of silver; "a goodly price" for the Saviour of the world to be prized at by His undiscerning and unworthy countrymen.

15. The next day was the first day of unleavened bread, on which it was necessary they should kill the passover: therefore Jesus sent Peter and John to the city to a certain man whom they should find carrying a pitcher of water to his house; him they should follow, and there prepare the passover. They went, and found the man in the same circumstances, and prepared for Jesus and His family, who at the even came to celebrate the passover. It was the house of John, surnamed Mark, which had always been opened to this blessed family, where He was pleased to finish His last Supper and the mysteriousness of the vespers of His passion.

16. When evening was come, Jesus stood with His disciples, and ate the paschal lamb; after which He girt Himself with a towel, and, taking a basin, washed the feet of His disciples, not only by the ceremony, but in His discourses, instructing them in the doctrine of humility, which the Master, by His so great condescension to His disciples, had made sacred, and imprinted the lesson in lasting characters by making it symbolical. But Peter was unwilling to be washed by his Lord, until he was told he must renounce his part in Him unless he were washed; which option being given to Peter, he cried out, "Not my feet only, but my hands and my head." But Jesus said the ablution of the feet was sufficient for the purification of the whole man; relating to the custom of those countries, who used to go to supper immediately from the baths, who therefore were sufficiently clean, save only on their feet by reason of the dust contracted in their passage from the baths to the dining-rooms; from which when by the hospitable master of the house they were caused to be cleansed, they needed no more ablution: and by it Jesus, passing from the letter to the spirit, meant that the body of sin was washed in the baths of baptism; and afterwards, if we remained in the same state of purity, it was only necessary to purge away the filth contracted in our passage from the font to the altar; and then we are clean all over, when the baptismal state is unaltered, and the little adherencies of imperfection and passions are also washed off.

17. But, after the manducation of the paschal lamb, it was the

---

73. Matt. 27:9.

custom of the nation to sit down to a second supper, in which they ate herbs and unleavened bread, the *major-domo* first dipping his morsel, and then the family; after which the father brake bread into pieces, and distributed a part to every of the guests, and first drinking himself, gave to the rest the chalice filled with wine, according to the age and dignity of the person, adding to each distribution a form of benediction proper to the mystery, which was eucharistical and commemorative of their deliverance from Egypt. This supper Jesus being to celebrate, changed the forms of benediction, turned the ceremony into mystery, and gave His body and blood in sacrament and religious configuration; so instituting the venerable sacrament which from its time of institution is called the "Lord's Supper": which rite Jesus commanded the apostles to perpetuate in commemoration of Him their Lord, until His second coming. And this was the first delegation of a perpetual ministry which Jesus made to His apostles, in which they were to be succeeded to in all generations of the church.

18. But Jesus being troubled in spirit, told His apostles that one of them should betray Him; which prediction He made that they might not be scandalized at the sadness of objection of the passion, but be confirmed in their belief, seeing so great demonstration of His wisdom and spirit of prophecy. The disciples were all troubled at this sad arrest, "looking one on another, and doubting of whom He spake"; but they beckoned to the beloved disciple, leaning on Jesus' breast, that he might ask: for they, who knew their own innocency and infirmity, were desirous to satisfy their curiosity, and to be rid of their indetermination and their fear. But Jesus, being asked, gave them a sign, and a sop to Judas, commanding him to do what he list speedily; for Jesus was extremely "straitened," till He had drunk the chalice off, and accomplished His mysterious and afflictive baptism. After Judas received the sop, the devil entered into him; and Judas went forth immediately, it being now night.

19. When he was gone out, Jesus began His farewell sermon, rarely mixed of sadness and joys, and studded with mysteries as with emeralds, discoursing of the glorification of God in His Son, and of those glories which the Father had prepared for Him; of His sudden departure, and His migration to a place whither they could not come yet, but afterwards they should; meaning, first to death, and then to glory; commanding them to love one another; and foretelling to Peter, who made confident protests that he would die with his Master, that before the cock should crow twice, he should deny Him thrice. But lest

He should afflict them with too sad representments of His present condition, He comforts them with the comforts of faith, with the intendments of His departure to prepare places in heaven for them, whither they might come by Him, who is the way, the truth, and the life; adding a promise in order to their present support and future felicities, that if they should ask of God any thing in His name, they should receive it; and upon condition they would love Him and keep His commandments, He would pray for the holy Ghost to come upon them, to supply His room, to furnish them with proportionable comforts, to enable them with great gifts, to lead them into all truth, and to abide with them for ever. Then arming them against future persecutions, giving them divers holy precepts, discoursing of His emanation from the Father, and of the necessity of His departure, He gave them His blessing, and prayed for them; and then having sung a hymn, which was part of the great Allelujah beginning at the hundred and fourteenth psalm, "When Israel came out of Egypt," and ending at the hundred and eighteenth inclusively, went forth with His disciples over the brook Cedron unto the Mount of olives, to a village called Gethsemane, where there was a garden, into which He entered to pray together with His disciples.

20. But taking Peter, James, and John, apart with Him about a stone's cast from the rest, He began to be exceeding sorrowful, and sad even unto death. For now He saw the ingredients of His bitter draught pouring into the chalice, and the sight was full of horror and amazement; He therefore "fell on His face, and prayed, O My Father, if it be possible, let this cup pass from Me." In this prayer He fell into so sad an agony, that the pains, inflicted by His Father's wrath, and made active by His own apprehension, were so great, that a sweat distilled from His sacred body as great and conglobated as drops of blood; and God, who heard His prayer, but would not answer Him in kind, sent an angel to comfort Him in the sadness which He was pleased not to take away. But knowing that the drinking this cup was the great end of His coming into the world, He laid aside all His own interests, and devested Himself of the affections of flesh and blood, willing His Father's will; and because His Father commanded, He in defiance of sense and passion was desirous to suffer all our pains. But as, when two seas meet, the billows contest in ungentle embraces, and make violent noises, till, having wearied themselves into smaller waves and disunited drops, they run quietly into one stream: so did the spirit and nature of Jesus assault each other with disagreeing interests and distinguishing disputations, till the

earnestness of the contention was diminished by the demonstrations of the Spirit and the prevailings of grace, which the sooner got the victory because they were not to contest with an unsanctified or a rebellious nature, but a body of affections which had no strong desires but of its own preservation: and therefore Jesus went thrice and prayed the same prayer, that if it were possible the cup might pass from Him, and thrice made an act of resignation, and in the intervals came and found His apostles asleep, gently chiding their incuriousness, and warning them to watch and pray, that they enter not into temptation; till the time that the traitor came with a multitude armed with swords and staves from the priests and elders of the people to apprehend Him.

21. Judas gave them the opportunity of the night; that was all the advantage they had by him, because they durst not seize Him by day for fear of the people; and he signified the person of his Master to the soldiers by a kiss, and an address of seeming civility.[74] But when they came towards Him, "Jesus said, Whom seek ye? they said, Jesus of Nazareth. He said, I am He." But there was a divinity upon Him, that they could not seize Him at first: but as a wave climbing of a rock is beaten back and scattered into members, till falling down it creeps with gentle waftings, and kisses the feet of the stony mountain, and so encircles it: so the soldiers, coming at first with a rude attempt, were twice repelled by the glory of His person, till they, falling at His feet, were at last admitted to the seizure of His body, having by those involuntary prostrations confessed His power greater than theirs, and that the lustre and influence of a God are greater than the violences and rudenesses of soldiers.[75] And still they, like weak eyes, durst not behold the glory of this Sun, till a cloud, like a dark veil, did interrupt the emissions of His glories; they could not seize upon Him, till they had thrown a veil upon His holy face: which, although it was a custom of the easterlings, and of the Roman empire generally, yet in this case was violence and necessity, because a certain impetuosity and vigorousness of spirit, and divinity, issuing from His holy face, made them to take sanctuary in darkness, and to throw a veil over Him in that dead time of a sad and dismal night. But Peter, a stout Galilean, bold and zealous, attempted a rescue, and smote a servant of the high priest, and cut off his ear; but Jesus rebuked the intemperance of his passion, and com-

---

74. Jerome, *On Matthew's Gospel*, PL 26. 54.
75. Ibid.

manded him to put up his sword, saying, "all they that strike with the sword shall perish with the sword"; so putting a bridle upon the illegal inflictions and expresses of anger or revenge from an incompetent authority: but "Jesus touched Malchus's ear, and cured it."

22. When Jesus had yielded Himself into their power, and was now led away by the chief priests, captains of the temple, elders of the people, and soldiers, who all came in combination and covenant to surprise Him, His disciples fled; and John the evangelist, who with grief and an overrunning fancy had forgot to lay aside his upper garment which in festivals they are used to put on, began to make escape, but being arrested by his linen upon his bare body, was forced to leave that behind him that himself might escape his Master's danger: for now was verified the prophetical saying, "I will smite the Shepherd, and the sheep shall be scattered." But Peter followed afar off; and the greatness of John's love, when he had mastered the first inconsiderations of his fear, made him to return a while after into the high priest's hall.

23. Jesus was first led to Annas, who was the prince of the Sanhedrim, and had cognizance of prophets and public doctrines; who therefore enquired of Jesus concerning His disciples and His discipline: but He answered, that His doctrine had been public or popular, that He never taught in conventicles; and therefore referred him to the testimony of all the people. For which free answer a servant standing by smote Him on the face; and Jesus meekly asked him, What evil He had done? But Annas without the seventy assessors could judge nothing, and therefore sent Him bound to Caiaphas, who was high priest that year, president of the rites of the temple, as the other high priest was of the great council. Thither Peter came, and had admission by the means of another disciple, supposed to be John, who, having sold his possessions in Galilee to Caiaphas, came and dwelt near mount Sion, but was by intervention of that bargain made known to the high priest, and brought Peter into the house: where when Peter was challenged three times by the servants to be a Galilean, and of Jesus's family, he denied and forswore it; till Jesus, looking back, reminded him of His prediction, and the foulness of the crime; and the cock crew: for it was now the second cock-crowing after ten of the clock in the fourth watch: "and Peter went out, and wept bitterly," that he might cleanse his soul, washing off the foul stains he had contracted in his shameful perjury and denying of his Lord. And it is reported of the same holy person, that ever after, when he heard the cock crow, he wept, remembering the old

instrument of his conversion, and his own unworthiness, for which he never ceased to do actions of sorrow and sharp repentance.

24. On the morning the council was to assemble; and whilst Jesus was detained in expectation of it, the servants mocked Him, and did all actions of affront and ignoble despite to His sacred head: and because the question was whether He were a prophet, they covered His eyes and smote Him in derision, calling on Him to prophesy, who smote Him. But in the morning, when the high priests and rulers of the people were assembled, they sought false witness against Jesus, but found none to purpose; they railed boldly, and could prove nothing; they accused vehemently, and the allegations were of such things as were no crimes; and the greatest article which the united diligence of all their malice could pretend, was that He said He would destroy the temple and in three days build it up again. But Jesus neither answered this nor any other of their vainer allegations, for the witnesses destroyed each other's testimony by their disagreeing; till at last Caiaphas, who, to verify his prophecy, and to satisfy his ambition, and to bait his envy, was furiously determined Jesus should die, adjures Him by the living God to say whether He were the Christ, the Son of the living God. Jesus knew his design to be an inquisition of death, not of piety or curiosity; yet because His hour was now come, openly affirmed it, without any expedient to elude the high priest's malice or to decline the question.

25. When Caiaphas heard the saying, he accused Jesus of blasphemy, and pretended an apprehension so tragical, that he over-acted his wonder and feigned detestation; for he rent his garments (which was the interjection of the country, and custom of the nation, but forbidden to the high priest) and called presently to sentence: and, as it was agreed beforehand, they all condemned Him as guilty of death, and, as far as they had power, inflicted it; for they beat Him with their fists, smote Him with the palms of their hands, spit upon Him, and abused Him beyond the licence of enraged tyrants. When Judas heard that they had passed the final and decretory sentence of death upon his Lord, he, who thought not it would have gone so far, repented him to have been an instrument of so damnable a machination, and came and brought the silver which they gave him for hire, threw it in amongst them, and said, "I have sinned in betraying the innocent blood." But they, incurious of those hell torments Judas felt within him, because their own fires burnt not yet, dismissed him, and upon consultation bought with the money a field to bury strangers in. And Judas went and hanged himself: and the

judgment was made more notorious and eminent by an unusual accident at such deaths, for he so swelled, that he burst, and his bowels gushed out. But the Greek scholiast, and some others,[76] report out of Papias, St. John's scholar, that Judas fell from the fig-tree on which he hanged before he was quite dead, and survived his attempt some while, being so sad a spectacle of deformity, and pain, and a prodigious tumour, that his plague was deplorable, and highly miserable, till at last he burst in the very substance of his trunk, as being extended beyond the possibilities and capacities of nature.

26. But the high priests had given Jesus over to the secular power, and carried Him to Pilate to be put to death by his sentence and military power: but coming thither, they would not enter into the judgment-hall because of the feast; but Pilate met them, and willing to decline the business bade them judge Him according to their own law. They replied, it was not lawful for them to put any man to death; meaning, during the seven days of unleavened bread, (as appears in the instance of Herod, who detained Peter in prison, intending after Easter to bring him out to the people,) and their malice was restless till the sentence they had passed were put into execution; others thinking, that all the right of inflicting capital punishments was taken from the nation by the Romans; and Josephus writes, that when Ananias, their high priest, had by a council of the Jews condemned St. James the brother of our Lord, and put him to death, without the consent of the Roman president, he was deprived of his priesthood. But because Pilate, who, either by common right, or at that time, was the judge of capital inflictions, was averse from intermeddling in the condemnation of an innocent person, they attempted him with excellent craft; for knowing that Pilate was a great servant of the Roman greatness, and a hater of the sect of the Galileans, the high priest accused Jesus that He was of that sect, that He denied paying tribute to Cæsar, that He called Himself king. Concerning which when Pilate interrogated Jesus, He answered, that His kingdom was not of this world; and Pilate, thinking he had nothing to do with the other, came forth again, and gave testimony that he found nothing worthy of death in Jesus. But hearing that He was a Galilean, and of Herod's jurisdiction, Pilate sent Him to Herod, who was at Jerusalem at the feast. And Herod was glad, because he had heard much of Him, and since his return from Rome had desired to see Him, but

---

76. Euthymius, *On Matthew's Gospel*, PG 129. 704.

could not, by reason of his own avocations, and the ambulatory life of Christ; and now he hoped to see a miracle done by Him, of whom he had heard so many. But the event of this was that Jesus did there no miracle; Herod's soldiers set Him at nought, and mocked Him: and that day Herod was reconciled to Pilate. And Jesus was sent back, arrayed in a white and splendid garment: which though possibly it might be intended for derision, yet was a symbol of innocence, condemned persons usually being arrayed in black.[77] And when Pilate had again examined Him, Jesus, meek as a lamb, and as a sheep before the shearers, opened not His mouth; insomuch that Pilate wondered, perceiving the greatest innocence of the man by not offering to excuse or lessen any thing: for though Pilate had power to release Him or crucify Him, yet His contempt of death was in just proportion to His innocence: which also Pilate concealed not, but published Jesus' innocence by Herod's and his own sentence; to the great regret of the rulers, who like ravening wolves thirsted for a draught of blood, and to devour the morning-prey.

27. But Pilate hoped to prevail upon the rulers, by making it a favour from them to Jesus, and an indulgence from him to the nation, to set Him free: for oftentimes even malice itself is driven out by the devil of self-love, and so we may be acknowledged the authors of a safety, we are content to rescue a man even from our own selves. Pilate therefore offered that according to the custom of the nation Jesus should be released, for the honour of the present festival, and as a donative to the people. But the spirit of malice was here the more prevalent, and they desired that Barabbas, a murderer, a thief, and a seditious person, should be exchanged for Him. Then Pilate, casting about all ways to acquit Jesus of punishment, and himself of guilt, offered to scourge Him and let Him go, hoping that a lesser draught of blood might stop the furies and rabidness of their passion, without their bursting with a river of His best and vital liquor. But these leeches would not so let go; they cry out, Crucify Him; and to engage him finally, they told him, if he did let this man go, he was no friend to Cæsar.

28. But Pilate called for water and washed his hands, to demonstrate his own unwillingness, and to reject and transmit the guilt upon them, who took it on them as greedily as they sucked the blood; they cried out, "His blood be on us and our children." As Pilate was going to give sentence, his wife, being troubled in her dreams, sent, with the

---

77. Josephus, *Jewish Antiquities*, LCL, (bk. 16, ch. 8), vol. 8, p. 312.

earnestness and passion of a woman, that he should have nothing to do with that just person: but he was engaged: Cæsar and Jesus, God and the king, did seem to have different interests; or at least he was threatened into that opinion; and Pilate, though he was satisfied it was but calumny and malice, yet he was loath to venture upon his answer to Rome, in case the high priest should have accused him. For no man knows whether the interest or the mistake of his judge may cast the sentence; and whoever is accused strongly is never thought entirely innocent: and therefore, not only against the divine laws, but against the Roman too, he condemned an innocent person, upon objections notoriously malicious; he adjudged Him to a death which was only due to public thieves and homicides (crimes with which He was not charged), upon a pretence of blasphemy, of which He stood accused, but not convicted, and for which by the Jewish law He should have been stoned if found guilty. And this he did put into present execution, against the Tiberian law, which about twelve years before decreed in favour of condemned persons that, after sentence, execution should be deferred ten days.[78]

29. And now was the holy Lamb to bleed. First therefore Pilate's soldiers array Him in a kingly robe, put a reed in His hand for a sceptre, plait a crown of thorns and put it on His head; they bow the knee, and mock Him; they smite Him with His fantastic sceptre, and instead of tribute pay Him with blows and spittings upon His holy head: and when they had emptied the whole stock of poisonous contempt, they devest Him of the robes of mockery, and put Him on His own; they lead Him to a pillar, and bind Him fast, and scourge Him with whips, a punishment that slaves only did use to suffer (free persons being in certain cases beaten with rods and clubs), that they might add a new scorn to His afflictions, and make His sorrows, like their own guilt, vast and mountainous: after which, Barabbas being set free, Pilate delivered Jesus to be crucified.

30. The soldiers therefore, having framed a cross, sad and heavy, laid it upon Jesus' shoulders (who like Isaac bore the wood with which He was to be sacrificed Himself), and they drive Him out to crucifixion, who was scarce able to stand under that load. It is generally supposed that Jesus bore the whole tree, that is, both the parts of His cross; but to him that considers it, it will seem impossible: and therefore it is more likely, and agreeable to the old manner of crucifying malefactors,

---

78. Dio, *Roman History*, LCL, vol. 7, p. 112.

that Jesus only carried the cross part; the body of it being upon the place either already fixed, or prepared, for its station. Even that lesser part was grievous and intolerable to His tender, virginal, and weakened body; and when He fainted, they compel Simon, a Cyrenian, to help Him. A great and a mixed multitude followed Jesus to Golgotha, the charnel house of the city, and the place of execution. But the women wept with bitter exclamations, and their sadness was increased by the sad predictions Jesus then made of their future misery, saying, "Ye daughters of Jerusalem, weep not for Me, but weep for yourselves and for your children: for the time shall come that men shall say, Blessed are the barren that never bare, and the paps that never gave suck; for they shall call on the hills to cover them, and on the mountains to fall upon them," that by a sudden ruin they may escape the lingering calamities of famine and fear, and the horror of a thousand deaths.

31. When Jesus was come to Golgotha, a place in the mount of Calvary, (where according to the tradition of the ancients Adam was buried, and where Abraham made an altar for the sacrifice of his son)[79] by the piety of His disciples, and, it is probable, of those good women which did use to minister to Him, there was provided wine mingled with myrrh, which among the Levantines is an excellent and pleasant mixture, and such as the piety and indulgence of the nations used to administer to condemned persons.[80] But Jesus, who by voluntary susception did choose to suffer our pains, refused that refreshment which the piety of the women presented to Him. The soldiers, having stripped Him, nailed Him to the cross with four nails, and divided His mantle into four parts, giving to each soldier a part; but for His coat, because it would be spoiled if parted, it being weaved without seam, they cast lots for it.

32. Now Pilate had caused a title, containing the cause of His death, to be superscribed on a table, in Latin, Greek and Hebrew, the Hebrew being first, the Greek next, and the Latin nearest to the holy body; but all written after the Jewish manner, from the right hand to the left; for so the title is shewn in the church of Santa Croce in Rome, the Latin letters being to be read as if it were Hebrew; the reason of which I could never find sufficiently discovered, unless it were to make it more legible to the Jews, who by conversing with the Romans began to

---

79. Augustine, *Sermons*, PL 39. 1750.
80. Origen, *On Matthew's Gospel*, PG 13. 1593.

understand a little Latin. The title was, JESUS OF NAZARETH, KING OF THE JEWS: but the Pharisees would have it altered, and that He said He was king of the Jews. But Pilate, out of wilfulness, or to do despite to the nation, or in honour to Jesus whom he knew to be a "just person," or being overruled by divine providence, refused to alter it. And there were crucified with Jesus two thieves, Jesus being in the midst, according to the prophecy, "He was reckoned with the transgressors." Then Jesus prayed for His persecutors, "Father, forgive them, for they know not what they do." But while Jesus was full of pain and charity, and was praying and dying for His enemies, the rulers of the Jews mocked Him, upbraiding Him with the good works He did, and the expresses of His power, saying, "He saved others, Himself He cannot save"; others saying, "Let Him come down from the cross, if He be the king of the Jews, and we will believe in Him": and others, according as their malice was determined by fancy and occasion, added weight and scorn to His pains; and of the two malefactors that were crucified with Him, one reviled Him, saying, "If Thou be the Christ, save Thyself and us." And thus far the devil prevailed, undoing himself in riddle, provoking men to do despite to Christ, and to heighten His passion out of hatred to Him; and yet doing and promoting that which was the ruin of all his own kingdom and potent mischiefs: like the Jew, who in indignation against Mercury threw stones at his image, and yet was by his superior judged idolatrous, that being the manner of doing honour to the idol among the gentiles. But then Christ, who had upon the cross prayed for His enemies, and was heard of God in all that He desired, felt now the beginnings of success: for the other thief, whom the present pains and circumstances of Jesus' passion had softened and made believing, reproved his fellow for not fearing God, confessed that this death happened to them deservedly, but to Jesus causelessly; and then prayed to Jesus, "Lord, remember me when Thou comest into Thy kingdom": which combination of pious acts and miraculous conversion Jesus entertained with a speedy promise of a very great felicity, promising that upon that very day he should be with Him in paradise.

33. "Now, there were standing by the cross the mother of Jesus, and her sister, and Mary Magdalen and John": and Jesus, being upon His death-bed, although He had no temporal estate to bestow, yet He would make provision for His mother, who being a widow, and now childless, was likely to be exposed to necessity and want; and therefore He did arrogate John, the beloved disciple, into Mary's kindred, making him to be her adopted son and her to be his mother, by fiction of law:

"Woman, behold thy son"; and, "Man, behold thy mother"; and from that time forward John took her home to his own house, which he had near mount Sion, after he had sold his inheritance in Galilee to the high priest.

34. While these things were doing, the whole frame of nature seemed to be dissolved and out of order, while their Lord and Creator suffered. For the sun was so darkened that the stars appeared; and the eclipse was prodigious in the manner as well as in degree, because the moon was not then in conjunction, but full: and it was noted by Phlegon,[81] the freed man of the emperor Hadrian, by Lucian out of the acts of the Gauls, and Dionysius, while he was yet a heathen, excellent scholars all, great historians and philosophers; who also noted the day of the week, and hour of the day, agreeing with the circumstances of the cross.[82] For the sun hid his head from beholding such a prodigy of sin and sadness, and provided a veil for the nakedness of Jesus, that the women might be present, and Himself die, with modesty.[83]

35. The eclipse and the passion began at the sixth hour, and endured till the ninth, about which time Jesus, being tormented with the unsufferable load of His Father's wrath due for our sins, and wearied with pains and heaviness, cried out, "My God, My God, why hast Thou forsaken Me?" and, as it is thought, repeated the whole two and twentieth psalm, which is an admirable narrative of the passion, full of prayer and sadness, and description of His pains at first, and of eucharist, and joy, and prophecy at the last. But these first words, which it is certain and recorded that He spake, were in a language of itself, or else by reason of distance, not understood, for they thought He had called for Elias, to take Him down from the cross. Then Jesus, being in the agonies of a high fever, said, "I thirst"; and one ran and filled a sponge with vinegar, wrapping it with hyssop, and put it on a reed, that He might drink. The vinegar and the sponge were, in executions of condemned persons, set to stop the too violent issues of blood, and to prolong the death, but were exhibited to him in scorn; mingled with gall, to make the mixture more horrid and ungentle: but Jesus tasted it only, and refused the draught. And now, knowing that the prophecies were fulfilled, His Father's wrath appeased, and His torments satisfac-

---

81. Eusebius, *The Chronicle*, PG 19. 101.
82. Origen, *Against Celsus*, PG 11. 854.
83. Ibid.

tory, He said, "It is finished"; and crying with a loud voice, "Father, into Thy hands I commend My spirit," He bowed His head, and yielded up His spirit into the hands of God, and died hastening to His Father's glories. Thus did this glorious Sun set in a sad and clouded west, running speedily to shine in the other world.

36. Then was the veil of the temple, which separated the secret Mosaic rites from the eyes of the people, rent in the midst, from the top to the bottom; and the angels, presidents of the temple, called to each other to depart from their seats; and so great an earthquake happened, that the rocks did rend, the mountains trembled, the graves opened, and the bodies of dead persons arose, walking from their cemeteries to the holy city, and appeared unto many; and so great apprehensions and amazements happened to them all that stood by, that they departed, smiting their breasts with sorrow and fear; and the centurion that ministered at the execution, said, "Certainly this was the Son of God"; and he became a disciple, renouncing his military employment, and died a martyr.[84]

37. But because the next day was the Jews' sabbath, and a paschal festival besides, the Jews hastened that the bodies should be taken from the cross; and therefore sent to Pilate to hasten their death by breaking their legs, that before sunset they might be taken away, according to the commandment, and be buried. The soldiers therefore came and brake the legs of the two thieves; but espying, and wondering that Jesus was already dead, they brake not His legs; for the scripture foretold that a bone of Him should not be broken: but a soldier with his lance pierced His side, and immediately there streamed out two rivulets of water and blood. But the holy Virgin-mother (whose soul during this whole passion was pierced with a sword and sharper sorrows, though she was supported by the comforts of faith, and those holy predictions of His resurrection and future glories which Mary had laid up in store against this great day of expense) now that she saw her holy Son had suffered all that our necessities, and their malice, could require or inflict, caused certain ministers, with whom she joined, to take her dead Son from the cross; whose body when she once got free from the nails, she kissed, and embraced with entertainments of the nearest vicinity that could be expressed by a person that was holy and sad, and a mother weeping for her dead son.

---

84. Jerome, *Letters*, PL 22. 480.

38. But she was highly satisfied with her own meditations, that now that great mystery determined by divine predestination before the beginning of all ages, was fulfilled in her Son; and the passion, that must needs be, was accomplished: she therefore first bathes His cold body with her warm tears, and makes clean the surface of the wounds, and, delivering a winding napkin to Joseph of Arimathea, gave to him in charge to enwrap the body, and embalm it, to compose it to the grave, and to do it all the rites of funeral, having first exhorted him to a public confession of what he was privately, till now: and he obeyed the counsel of so excellent a person, and ventured upon the displeasure of the Jewish rulers, and went confidently to Pilate, and begged the body of Jesus. And Pilate gave him the power of it.

39. Joseph therefore takes the body, binds His face with a napkin, washes the body, anoints it with ointment, enwraps it in a composition of myrrh and aloes, and puts it into a new tomb which he for himself had hewn out of a rock (it not being lawful among the Jews to inter a condemned person in the common cemeteries), for all these circumstances were in the Jews' manner of burying. But when the sun was set, the chief priests and pharisees went to Pilate, telling him that Jesus whilst He was living foretold His own resurrection upon the third day; and lest His disciples should come and steal the body, and say He was risen from the dead, desired that the sepulchre might be secured against the danger of any such imposture. Pilate gave them leave to do their pleasure, even to the satisfaction of their smallest scruples; they therefore sealed the grave, rolled a great stone at the mouth of it, and, as an ancient tradition says, bound it about with labels of iron, and set a watch of soldiers, as if they had intended to have made it surer than the decrees of fate, or the never-failing laws of nature.

Section XVI
Of the Resurrection and Ascension of Jesus

1. While it was yet "early in the morning, upon the first day of the week, Mary Magdalen, and Mary the mother of James, and Salome, brought sweet spices to the sepulchre," that they might again embalm the holy body (for the rites of embalming among the Hebrews used to last forty days), and their love was not satisfied with what Joseph had done. They therefore hastened to the grave; and after they had expended their money and bought the spices, then begin to consider "who shall remove the stone": but yet they still go on, and their love answers the objection, not knowing how it should be done, but yet resolving to

go through all the difficulties; but never remember or take care to pass the guards of soldiers. But when they came to the sepulchre, they found the guard affrighted and removed, and the stone rolled away; for there had a little before their arrival been a great earthquake; and an angel descending from heaven, rolled away the stone, and sat upon it; and for fear of him the guards about the tomb became astonished with fear, and were like dead men: and some of them ran to the high priests, and told them what happened. But they, now resolving to make their iniquity safe and unquestionable by a new crime, hire the soldiers to tell an incredible and a weak fable, that His disciples came by night and stole Him away, against which accident the wit of man could give no more security than themselves had made. The women entered into the sepulchre, and missing the body of Jesus, Mary Magdalen ran to the eleven apostles, complaining that the body of our Lord was not to be found. Then Peter and John ran as fast as they could to see: for the unexpectedness of the relation, the wonder of the story, and the sadness of the person, moved some affections in them, which were kindled by the first principles and sparks of faith, but were not made actual and definite, because the faith was not raised to a flame: they looked into the sepulchre, and finding not the body there, they returned. By this time Mary Magdalen was come back; and the women who staid weeping for their Lord's body, saw two angels sitting in white, the one at the head, and the other at the feet: at which unexpected sight they trembled, and bowed themselves: but an angel bid them not to fear, telling them that Jesus of Nazareth, who was crucified, was also risen, and was not there: and called to mind what Jesus had told them in Galilee concerning His crucifixion, and resurrection the third day.

2. And Mary Magdalen turned herself back, and saw Jesus; but supposing Him to be the gardener, she said to Him, "Sir, if thou have borne Him hence, tell me where thou hast laid Him, and I will take Him away." But Jesus said unto her, "Mary!" Then she knew His voice, and with ecstasy of joy and wonder was ready to have crushed His feet with her embraces: but He commanded her not to touch Him, but go to His brethren, and say, "I ascend unto My Father and to your Father, to My God and your God." Mary departed with satisfaction, beyond the joys of a victory or a full vintage, and told these things to the apostles; but the narration seemed to them as talk of abused and fantastic persons.—About the same time Jesus also appeared unto Simon Peter.—Towards the declining of the day, two of His disciples going to Emmaus, sad, and discoursing of the late occurrences, Jesus puts Himself into their com-

pany, and upbraids their incredulity; and expounds the scriptures, that Christ ought to suffer, and rise again the third day; and in the breaking of bread disappeared, and so was known to them by vanishing away, whom present they knew not: and instantly they hasten to Jerusalem, and told the apostles what had happened.

3. And while they were there, that is, the same day at evening, when the apostles were assembled, all save Thomas, secretly, for fear of the Jews, the doors being shut, Jesus came and stood in the midst of them. They were exceedingly troubled, supposing it had been a spirit. But Jesus confuted them by the philosophy of their senses, by feeling His flesh and bones, which spirits have not. For He gave them His benediction, shewing them His hands and His feet. At which sight they rejoiced with exceeding joy, and began to be restored to their indefinite hopes of some future felicity by the return of their Lord to life: and there He first breathed on them, giving them the holy Ghost, and performing the promise twice made before His death; the promise of the keys, or of binding and loosing, saying, "whosoever sins ye remit, they are remitted to them: and whosoever sins ye retain, they are retained": and that was the second part of clerical power with which Jesus instructed His disciples, in order to their great commission of preaching and government ecclesiastical. These things were told to Thomas, but he believed not, and resolved against the belief of it, unless he might put his finger into His hands, and his hand into His side. Jesus therefore on the octaves of His resurrection appeared again to the apostles met together, and makes demonstration to Thomas; in conviction and reproof of his unbelief promising a special benediction to all succeeding ages of the church; for they are such who "saw not, and yet have believed."

4. But Jesus at His early appearing had sent an order by the women, that the disciples should go into Galilee; and they did so after a few days. And Simon Peter being there, went a fishing, and six other of the apostles with him, to the sea of Tiberias; where they laboured all night and caught nothing. Towards the morning, Jesus appeared to them, and bade them cast the net on the right side of the ship; which they did, and enclosed an hundred and fifty-three great fishes: by which prodigious draught John, the beloved disciple, perceived it was the Lord. At which instant, Peter threw himself into the sea, and went to Jesus; and when the rest were come to shore, they dined with broiled fish. After dinner Jesus, taking care for those scattered sheep which were dispersed over the face of the earth, that He might gather them

189

into one sheepfold under one Shepherd, asked Peter, "Simon, son of Jonas, lovest thou Me more than these? Peter answered, Yea, Lord; Thou, that knowest all things, knowest that I love Thee; then Jesus said unto him, Feed My lambs." And Jesus asked him the same question, and gave him the same precept the second time, and the third time: for it was a considerable and a weighty employment, upon which Jesus was willing to spend all His endearments and stock of affections that Peter owed Him, even upon the care of His little flock. And after the intrusting of this charge to him, He told him that the reward he should have in this world, should be a sharp and an honourable martyrdom; and withal checks at Peter's curiosity, in busying himself about the temporal accidents of other men, and enquiring what should become of John, the beloved disciple. Jesus answered his question with some sharpness of reprehension; and no satisfaction: "If I will that he tarry till I come, what is that to thee?" Then they fancied that he should not die; but they were mistaken, for the intimation was expounded and verified by St. John's surviving the destruction of Jerusalem; for after the attempts of persecutors, and the miraculous escape of prepared torments, he died a natural death in a good old age.

5. After this Jesus, having appointed a solemn meeting for all the brethren that could be collected from the dispersion, and named a certain mountain in Galilee, appeared to five hundred brethren at once; and this was His most public and solemn manifestation; and while some doubted, Jesus came according to the designation, and spake to the eleven; sent them to preach to all the world repentance, and remission of sins in His name; promising to be with them to the end of the world.—He appeared also unto James, but at what time is uncertain, save that there is something concerning it in the gospel of St. Matthew which the Nazarenes of Berœa used; and which it is likely themselves added out of report, for there is nothing of it in our Greek copies. The words are these: "When the Lord had given the linen in which He was wrapped to the servant of the high priest, He went and appeared unto James; for James had vowed after he received the Lord's supper, that he would eat no bread till he saw the Lord risen from the grave: then the Lord called for bread: He blessed it, and brake it, and gave it to James the just, and said, 'My brother, eat bread, for the Son of man is risen from the sleep of death' ": so that by this it should seem to be done upon the day of the resurrection; but the relation of it by St. Paul puts it between the appearance which He made to the five hundred, and that last to the apostles when He was to ascend into heaven.—Last of all,

when the apostles were at dinner, He appeared to them, upbraiding their incredulity; and then He opened their understanding that they might discern the sense of scripture, and again commanded them to preach the gospel to all the world, giving them power to do miracles, to cast out devils, to cure diseases; and instituted the sacrament of baptism, which He commanded should, together with the sermons of the gospel, be administered to all nations, In the name of the Father, and of the Son, and of the Holy Ghost. Then He led them into Judea, and they came to Bethany, and from thence to the mount Olivet; and He commanded them to stay in Jerusalem, till the holy Ghost, the promise of the Father, should descend upon them, which should be accomplished in few days; and then they should know the times, and the seasons, and all things necessary for their ministration and service, and propagation of the gospel. And while He discoursed many things concerning the kingdom, behold a cloud came and parted Jesus from them, and carried Him in their sight up into heaven; where He sits at the right hand of God, blessed for ever. Amen.

6. While His apostles stood gazing up to heaven, two angels appeared to them, and told them that Jesus should come in like manner as He was taken away, viz. with glory and majesty, and in the clouds, and with the ministry of angels.

"Amen. Come, Lord Jesus; come quickly."

191

CHAPTER TWO

The Heavenly Sacrifice and Earthly Sacraments

INTRODUCTION

The selections in this second chapter are made from writings of Taylor that span the greater part of his public life from his treatise *On the Reverence Due the Altar*, written at Oxford around 1643, to the *Discourse on Confirmation*, prepared at the request of his brother bishops in Ireland some twenty years later. *Clerus Domini* (1651), or the *Divine Institution and Necessity of the Office Ministerial,* together with his sermon entitled *The Marriage Ring* (1653), and his discourse on baptism from *The Great Exemplar* belong to his time of retreat at Golden Grove and bear that stamp, while the *Preface, Apology* and *Collection of Offices* mark his re-entry into the world of politics and polemics after the quiet of Golden Grove.

Taylor's years of conflict and affliction, the storm after the calm, began with his departure from Golden Grove in 1654 and never really ended. Consequently, the writings of this period show their wounds, and are, for the most part, defensive and polemical, while at the same time liturgical and theological. "A variety of circumstances," according to Gosse, "without immediately severing his connection with Golden Grove, was now to draw him out into the light of common day, and cause him to take part in the anxieties and afflictions of his fellow-men."[1] But these circumstances, which drove him from his place of baptism into the desert of the Commonwealth, included his zeal for the

---

1. Gosse, p. 105.

Temple, for like Jeremiah he stood amid the ruins and made loud lamentation:

> I shall only crave leave that I may remember Jerusalem, and call to mind the pleasures of the temple, the order of her service, the beauty of her buildings, the sweetness of her songs, the decency of her ministrations, the assiduity and economy of her priests and levites, the daily sacrifice, and that eternal fire of devotion that went not out by day nor by night: these were the pleasures of our peace and there is a remanent felicity in the very memory of those spiritual delights, which we then enjoyed, as antepasts of heaven, and consignations of an immortality of joys. And it may be so again, when it shall please God, and when men will consider the invaluable loss that is consequent, and the danger of sin that is appendant to the destroying forms of discipline and devotion in which God was purely worshipped and the Church was edified and the people instructed to great degrees of piety, knowledge and devotion.[2]

Taylor's experience as a pastor and priest, at this time in a sort of underground church, showed him, on the one hand, the need for liturgical tradition, since the *Book of Common Prayer* was forbidden, and, on the other hand, the need for debate, if puritan excesses were to be curtailed. Hence his *Collection of Offices*, published in 1658 under an actively persecuting government and composed from the ancient liturgies of the Greeks, the church's earliest celebrations of her divine mysteries or sacraments, which "make better fuel for the fires of devotion than the straw and stubble which some men did suddenly or weakly rake together whenever they were to dress their sacrifice."[3] The "straw and stubble" to which the *Westminster Directory* gave rise are described in his expanded *Preface*, which accompanied the republication at this time of his earlier work, the *Apology for Liturgy*. He concludes this *Preface* by describing the *Directory* as

> a direction without a rule; a rule without restraint; an office that leaves the form of ministration of sacraments so indiffer-

---

2. *Works* 5:232.
3. Ibid. p. 252.

ently, that if there be any form of words essential, the sacrament is in much danger to become invalid, for want of provision of due forms of ministration: an office that complies with no precedent of scripture or the ancient Church; that hath no external forms to entertain the fancy of the more common spirits; an office that permits children to be unbaptized; that will not suffer them to be confirmed; that joins in marriage as Cacus did his oxen; that will not do piety to the dead, nor comfort to the living, by solemn and honorary offices of funeral; an office that never thinks of absolving penitents or exercising the power of the keys, after the custom and rites of priests: a liturgy that recites no creed; that consigns no public canon of communion but leaves that as casual and fantastic as any of the lesser offices; an office that takes no more care than chance does for the reading of the Holy Scriptures; that never commemorates a departed saint: that hath no communion with the Church triumphant anymore than with the other parts of the militant: that never thanks God for the redemption of the world by the nativity, passion, resurrection and Ascension of our blessed Saviour.[4]

Taylor's theological works at this time of controversy, especially those like the *Worthy Communicant* (1660), which deals with the sacraments, introduce us to the world of the Greek and Latin Fathers of the early centuries with their emphasis on divine mystery and sacramental presence, the realm of the Spirit where the limitations of time and place are no more, and where holy men can represent on earth the realities of paradise:

When the holy man stands at the table of blessing and ministers the rite of consecration, then do as the angels do, who behold, and love, and wonder that the Son of God should become food to the souls of his servants; that he, who cannot suffer any change or lessening, should be broken into pieces, and enter into the body to support and nourish the spirit, and yet at the same time remain in heaven, while he descends to thee upon earth; that he who hath essential felicity should

---

4. Ibid.

become miserable and die for thee, and then give himself to thee for ever to redeem thee from sin and misery; that by his wounds he should procure health to thee, by his affronts he should entitle thee to glory, by his death, he should bring thee to life and by becoming a man he should make thee partaker of the Divine nature.[5]

In his reading of the Fathers Taylor sensed that unity of symbol and mystery that the Ancients enjoyed in the Greek East and in the Latin West, and his theory of *Sacramental Representation*, or earthly manifestations of heavenly realities, *Epiphanies of Mysteries*, was a unique insight at the time. This clear vision of mystery gave divine content to his prose which took instant flight and told of things in heaven and on earth, as Chrysostom did when mysteries were real and language sacramental:

Taylor: When the holy man reacheth forth his hands upon the symbols, and prays over them, and intercedes for the sins of the people, and breaks the holy bread, and pours forth the sacred chalice, place thyself, by faith and meditation, in heaven, and see Christ doing, in his glorious manner, this very thing which thou seest ministered and imitated upon the table of the Lord; and then remember, that it is impossible thou shouldst miss of eternal blessings, which are so powerfully procured for thee by the Lord himself.

Chrysostom: For when thou seest the Lord sacrificed, and laid upon the altar, and the priest standing and praying over the victim, and all the worshippers empurpled with that precious blood, canst thou then think that thou art still amongst men, and standing upon the earth? Art thou not, on the contrary, straightway translated to Heaven, and casting out every carnal thought from the soul, dost thou not with disembodied spirit and pure reason contemplate the things which are in Heaven? Oh! what a marvel! what love of God to man! He who sitteth on high with the Father is at that hour held in the hands of all,

---

5. Ibid.

and gives Himself to those who are willing to embrace and grasp Him.[6]

These passages show the unity in Taylor's mind of the heavenly sacrifice of Christ, the altar on earth and the holy man of blessing and consecration. Accordingly, the order of readings in this chapter from (1) *The Worthy Communicant,* (2) *Reverence Due to the Altar,* and (3) *Clerus Domini* was chosen to reflect this unity of heavenly sacrifice and earthly sacrament. Angels abound around Taylor's altar, for it is on earth a place of God's presence, the throne of his memorial, and the table of Christ's body and blood. It is also a place "in which the clergy in their appointed ministry do stand between God and the people and do fulfill a special and incomprehensible ministry, which the angels themselves do look into with admiration."[7] In *Clerus Domini* Taylor the theologian argues pedantically from the scriptures, the fathers, history and reason for the divine institution of the priesthood, as he did for the episcopacy in *Episcopacy Asserted.* But in a sermon on *The Minister's Duty in Life and Doctrine,* Taylor the preacher reaches mystical heights and never stumbles for the word. So often he begins in his sermons as God begins in the Bible with the separation of light and darkness, and then everything comes to life: the baptized are a separation from Israel, and the clergy become a church within a church in response to God's word of light and life calling forth and into, and all philosophical explanations become irrelevant, and Taylor is no longer "weary and toiled with rowing up and down in the seas of questions which the interests of Christendom had commenced."[8]

The *Discourse on Baptism,* which follows *Clerus Domini,* is taken from *The Great Exemplar,* which at its best is written with enchanting fluidity and vitality, the bright elastic phrase always leaping into light. For such prose baptism is indeed an apt mystery:

Out of the waters God produced every living creature; and when at first "the Spirit moved upon the waters" and gave life, it was the type of what was designed in renovation. Ev-

---

6. Boone-Porter, p. 47.
7. *Works* 5:330.
8. *Works* 2:3.

erything that lives now is born of water and the Spirit, and Christ, who is our creator and Redeemer is the new birth, opened the fountains and hallowed the stream. . . . For when the family of God's Church grew separate, notorious, numerous and distinct, He sent them into their own country by a baptism, through which the whole nation passed; for all were baptised unto Moses in the cloud above and in the sea below: so should all the persons of the church be initiated unto Christ by the Spirit from above and the water from below.[9]

In 1664 Taylor published his *Discourse on Confirmation* to convince his Presbyterian clergy and flock of the divine origin of the Rite, its continuous use from the earliest times and the necessity of bishops to administer it. Scholars have regarded this work as the fullest treatment of confirmation on its doctrinal, historical and practical sides, put forth by any theologian of the English Church. But the spirituality of his approach is powerfully felt in every word as it was in his writings on baptism. Again, "We are a new mass . . . rescued from an evil portion . . . candidates of heaven and immortality . . . an embryo in the regeneration until the Spirit of God enlivens us and moves again upon the waters."[10]

Taylor preached two sermons on *The Marriage Ring*, which were published in the *Eniatos, Collection of Sermons* in 1653. This was the year in which his first wife died. This is the only treatment of marriage found in all of Taylor's works, but the presentation is completely pastoral or moral, and in no way theological in the strict sense. He makes no reference to Milton's acrimonious pamphlets on divorce, which were already in circulation, or to any of the theories of marriage that were being discussed at that time. Neither does he think it necessary to make more than the slightest reference to the church's right to bless the union of her children; this might have been expected since the sectaries, who were now strongly in power, hated all religious ceremonies and were soon to enact that only marriages performed by a justice of the peace were legal. On the contrary, the sermons were delightful outpourings of a heart happily married in spite of worldly misfortunes. These two sermons have attracted a good deal of attention, both because

9. *Works* 2:229.
10. *Works* 5:615.

of the unusual charm of the thought and the carefully wrought literary beauty with which they abound. In them, we get one of those all too rare glimpses into his own home life:

> No man can tell but that he loves his children, how many delicious accents make a man's heart dance in the pretty conversation of these pledges; their childishness, their stammering, their little angers, their innocence, their imperfections, their necessities, are so many little emanations of joy and comfort to him that delights in their persons and society; but he that loves not his wife and children, feeds a lioness at home, and broods a nest of sorrows.[11]

The Reformation theologians had debated the nature and number of the sacraments, and the Roman number seven, which Trent canonized, found Anglican expression in the 25th of the *Thirty-Nine Articles*, which distinguished between the two sacraments of the gospel and "those five commonly called sacraments." Taylor was of this tradition, and consequently his understanding of *Ecclesiastical Penance* and the *Anointing of the Sick* will be considered in Chapters 3 and 5 respectively, where they more naturally belong. But Taylor was also wider than this tradition and the medieval world from which it sprang; he belonged to the world of the Fathers, to their symbolic mode of knowing and saying, and it suited well his mystic soul and eloquent speech.

> "All those things that now please us shall pass from us, or we from them"; but those things that concern the other life are permanent as the numbers of eternity: and although at the resurrection there shall be no relation of husband and wife, and no marriage shall be celebrated but the marriage of the Lamb; yet then shall be remembered how men and women passed through this state which is a type of that, and from this sacramental union all holy pairs shall pass to the spiritual and eternal, where love shall be their portion, and joys shall crown their heads, and they shall lie in the bosom of Jesus and in the heart of God to eternal ages. Amen.[12]

---

11. *Works* 4:224.
12. *Works* 4:232.

The Worthy Communicant[1]

INTRODUCTION

. . . The holy communion or supper of the Lord is the most sacred, mysterious, and useful conjugation of secret and holy things and duties in the religion. It is not easy to be understood, it is not lightly to be received: it is not much opened in the writings of the New testament, but still left in its mysterious nature; it is too much untwisted and nicely handled by the writings of the doctors; and by them made more mysterious, and like a doctrine of philosophy made intricate by explications, and difficult by the aperture and dissolution of distinctions. So we sometimes espy a bright cloud formed into an irregular figure; when it is observed by unskilful and fantastic travellers, looks like a centaur to some, and as a castle to others; some tell that they saw an army with banners, and it signifies war; but another wiser than his fellow says it looks for all the world like a flock of sheep, and foretells plenty; and all the while it is nothing but a shining cloud by its own mobility and the activity of a wind cast into a contingent and inartificial shape. So it is in this great mystery of our religion; in which some espy strange things which God intended not, and others see not what God hath plainly told: some call that part of it a mystery which is none, and others think all of it nothing but a mere ceremony and a sign: some say it signifies, and some say it effects; some say it is a sacrifice, and others call it a sacrament; some schools of learning make it the instrument of grace in the hand of God; others say that it is God himself in that instrument of grace; some call it venerable, and others say as the vain men in the prophet[2] that "the table of the Lord is contemptible": some come to it with their sins on their heads, and others with their sins in their mouth: some come to be cured, some to be quickened; some to be nourished, and others to be made alive; some out of fear and reverence take it but

---

1. *Works* 8:8ff.
2. Mal. 1:7.

201

seldom, others out of devotion take it frequently; some receive it as a means to procure great graces and blessings, others as an eucharist, and an office of thanksgiving for what they have received: some call it an act of obedience merely, others account it an excellent devotion and the exercising of the virtue of religion; some take it to strengthen their faith, others to beget it, and yet many affirm that it does neither, but supposes faith beforehand as a disposition; faith in all its degrees according to the degree of grace whither the communicant is arrived. Some affirm the elements are to be blessed by prayers of the bishop or other minister; others say it is only by the mystical words, the words of institution; and when it is blessed, some believe it to be the natural body of Christ; others to be nothing of that, but the blessings of Christ, His word and His spirit, His passion in representment, and His grace in real exhibition: and all these men have something of reason for what they pretend; and yet the words of scripture from whence they pretend, are not so many as are the several pretensions.

My purpose is not to dispute, but to persuade; not to confute any one, but to instruct those that need; not to make a noise, but to excite devotion; not to enter into curious, but material enquiries; and to gather together into an union all those several portions of truth, and differing apprehensions of mysteriousness, and various methods and rules of preparation, and seemingly opposed doctrines, by which even good men stand at distance and are afraid of each other. For since all societies of Christians pretend to the greatest esteem of this above all the rites or external parts and ministries of religion, it cannot be otherwise but that they will all speak honourable things of it, and suppose holy things to be in it, and great blessings one way or other to come by it; and it is contemptible only among the profane and the atheistical; all the innumerable differences which are in the discourses and consequent practices relating to it, proceed from some common truths and universal notions and mysterious or inexplicable words, and tend all to reverential thoughts and pious treatment of these rites and holy offices; and therefore it will not be impossible to find honey or wholesome dews upon all this variety of plants; and the differing opinions and several understandings of this mystery, which (it may be) no human understanding can comprehend, will serve to excellent purposes of the spirit, if, like men of differing interest, they can be reconciled in one communion; at least the ends and designs of them all can be conjoined in the design and ligatures of the same reverence and piety and devotion.

My purpose therefore is to discourse of the nature, excellencies, uses and intention of the holy sacrament of the Lord's supper, the blessings and fruits of the sacrament; all the advantages of a worthy communion, the public and the private, the personal and the ecclesiastical, that we may understand what it is that we go about, and how it is to be treated. . . .

CHAPTER I
OF THE NATURE, EXCELLENCIES, USES AND INTENTION OF THE HOLY SACRAMENT OF THE LORD'S SUPPER

Section I
Of the Several Apprehensions of Men Concerning It

When our blessed Lord was to nail the handwriting of ordinances to His cross, He was pleased to retain two ceremonies, baptism and the holy supper; that Christians may first wash and then eat; first be made clean, and then eat of the supper of the Lamb: and it cannot be imagined but that this so signal and peculiar retention of two ceremonies is of great purpose and remarkable virtues. The matter is evident in the instance of baptism; and as the mystery is of the foundation of religion; so the virtue of it is inserted into our creed, and we all "believe one baptism for the remission of our sins";[3] and yet the action is external, the very mystery is by a ceremony, the allusion is bodily, the element is pure water, the minister a sinful man, and the effect is produced out of the sacrament in many persons and in many instances, as well as in it; and yet that it is effected also by it and with it, in the conjunction with due dispositions of him that is to be baptized, we are plainly taught by Christ's apostles[4] and the symbols of the church.

But concerning the other sacrament there are more divisions and thoughts of heart; for it is never expressly joined with a word of promise, and where mention is made of it in the gospels, it is named only as a duty and a commandment, and not as a grace, or treasure of holy blessings; we are bidden to do it, but promised nothing for a reward, it is commanded to us, but we are not invited to obedience by consideration of any consequent blessing; and when we do it, so many holy things are

---

3. Heb. 6:1.
4. Acts 2:38.

required of us, which as they are fit to be done even when we do not receive the blessed sacrament; so they effect salvation to us by virtue of their proper and proportioned promises in the virtue of Christ's death however apprehended and understood.

Upon this account some say that "we receive nothing in the blessed eucharist, but we commemorate many blessed things which we have received; that it is affirmed in no scripture that in this mystery we are to call to mind the death of Christ, but because we already have it in our mind, we must also have it in our hearts, and publish it in our confessions and sacramental representment; and therefore it is not the memory, but the commemoration of Christ's death; that as the anniversary sacrifices in the law were a commemoration of sins every year; not a calling them to mind, but a confession of their guilt and of our deserved punishment; so this sacrament is a representation of Christ's death by such symbolical actions as Himself graciously hath appointed: but then, excepting that to do so is an act of obedience, it exercises no other virtue, it is an act of no other grace, it is the instrument of no other good; it is neither virtue nor gain, grace nor profit. And whereas it is said to confirm our faith, this also is said to be unreasonable; for this being our own work, cannot be the means of a divine grace—not naturally; because it is not of the same kind, and faith is no more the natural effect of this obedience than chastity can be the product of christian fortitude—not by divine appointment; because we find no such order; no promise, no intimation of any such event; and although the thing itself indeed shall have what reward God please to apportion to it as it is obedience; yet of itself it hath no other worthiness; it is not so much as an argument of persuasion; for the pouring forth of wine can no more prove or make faith that Christ's blood was poured forth for us, than the drinking the wine can effect this persuasion in us that we naturally, though under a veil, drink the natural blood of Christ; which the angels gathered as it ran into golden phials, and Christ multiplied to a miracle like the loaves and fishes in the gospel. But because nothing that naturally remains the same in all things as it was before, can do anything that it could not do before; the bread and wine which have no natural change, can effect none; and therefore we are not to look for an egg where there is nothing but order; and a blessing where there is nothing but an action; and a real effect where there is nothing but an analogy, a sacrament, a mystical representment, and something fit to signify, and many things past, but nothing that is to come." This is the sense and discourse of some persons that call for an express word, or a manifest reason to the contrary, or else resolve that their belief shall be as unactive as the scriptures are silent in the effects of this mystery. Only these men will allow the sacraments to be "marks of christianity," "symbols of mutual charity," "testimonies of a thankful mind to God," "allegorical admonitions of christian mortification," and "spiritual alimony," "symbols of grace conferred before the sacrament," and "rites instituted to stir up faith by way of object and representation"; that is, occasionally and morally, but neither by any divine or physical, by natural or supernatural power, by the work done, or by the divine institution. This indeed is something, but very much too little.

But others go as far on the other hand, and affirm that "in the blessed sacrament we receive the body and blood of Christ; we chew His flesh, we drink His blood; for 'His flesh is meat indeed, and His blood is drink indeed'; and this is the *manna* which came down from heaven; our bodies are nourished, our souls united to Christ; and the sacrament is the infallible instrument of pardon to all persons that do not maliciously hinder it; and it produces all its effects by virtue of the sacrament itself so appointed; and that the dispositions of the communicants are only for removing obstacles and impediments, but effect nothing; the sumption of the mysteries does all in a capable subject; as in infants who do nothing, in penitents who take away what can hinder; for it is nothing but Christ himself; the body that died upon the cross is broken in the hand of him that ministers, and by the teeth of him that communicates; and when God gives us His Son in this divine and glorious manner, with heaps of miracles to verify heaps of blessings, how shall not He with Him give us all things else?" They who teach this doctrine call the holy sacrament, "the host," "the unbloody sacrifice," "the flesh of God," "the body of Christ," "God himself," "the mass," "the sacrament of the altar." I cannot say that this is too much; but, that these things are not true: and although all that is here said that is of any material benefit and real blessing is true; yet the blessing is not so conferred, it is not so produced.

A third sort of Christians speak indefinitely and gloriously of this divine mystery; they speak enough, but they cannot tell what; they publish great and glorious effects; but such which they gather by similitude and analogy, such which they desire but cannot prove; which indeed they feel, but know not whence they do derive them: they are blessings which come in company of the sacraments, but are not always to be imputed to them; they confound spiritual senses with mystical expressions, and expound mysteries to natural significations: that is, they mean well but do not always understand that part of christian philosophy which explicates the secret nature of this divine sacrament: and the effect of it is this; that they sometimes put too great confidence in the mystery, and look for impresses which they find not, and are sometimes troubled that their experience does not answer to their sermons; and meet with scruples instead of comforts, and doubts instead of rest, and anxiety of mind in the place of a serene and peaceful conscience. But these men both in their right and in their wrong enumerate many glories of the holy sacrament, which they usually signify in these excellent appellatives, calling it "the supper of the Lord"; "the bread of elect souls" and "the wine of angels," "the Lord's body," "the New testament" and the "calice of benediction," "spiritual food," "the great supper," "the divinest and archi-symbolical feast"; "the banquet of the church," "the celestial dinner," "the spiritual, the sacred, the mystical, the formidable, the rational table," "the supersubstantial bread," "the bread of God," "the bread of life"; "the Lord's mystery," "the great mystery of salvation," "the Lord's sacrament," "the sacrament of piety," "the sign of unity," "the contesseration of the christian communion," "the divine grace," "the divine-making grace," "the holy thing," "the desirable," "the communication of good," "the perfection and consummation of a Christian," "the holy particles," "the gracious symbols," "the holy gifts," "the sacrifice of commemoration," "the intellectual and mystical good," "the hereditary donative of the New testament," "the sacrament of the Lord's body," "the sacrament of the calice," "the paschal oblation," "the christian passport," "the mystery of perfection," "the great oblation," "the worship of God," "the life of souls," "the sacrament of our price and our redemption," and some few others much to the same purposes: all which are of great and useful signification, and if the explications and consequent propositions were as justifiable as the titles themselves are sober and useful, they would be apt only for edification and to minister to the spirit of devotion. That therefore is to be the design of the present meditations, to represent the true and proper and mysterious nature of this divine nutriment of our souls; to account what are the blessings God reacheth forth to us in the mysteries, and what returns of duty He expects from all to whom He gives His most holy Son.

I shall only here add the names and appellatives which the scripture gives to these mysteries, and place it as a part of the foundation of the following doctrines. It is by the Spirit of God called, "the bread that is broken," and "the cup of blessing," "the breaking of bread"; "the body and blood of the Lord"; "the communication of His body" and "the communication of His blood"; "the feast of charity or love";[5] "the Lord's table," and "the supper of the Lord." Whatsoever is consequent to these titles we can safely own, and our faith may dwell securely, and our devotion, like a pure flame, with these may feed as with the spices and gums upon the altar of incense.

. . . In conclusion, the sum is this. The sacraments and symbols, if they be considered in their own nature, are just such as they seem, water, and bread, and wine; they retain the names proper to their own natures; but because they are made to be signs of a secret mystery, and water is the symbol of purification of the soul from sin, and bread and wine of Christ's body and blood, therefore the symbols and sacraments receive the names of what themselves do sign; they are the body and they are the blood of Christ; they are metonymically such. But because yet further; they are instruments of grace in the hand of God, and by these His holy spirit changes our hearts and translates us into a divine nature; therefore the whole work is attributed to them by a synecdoche; that is, they do in their manner the work for which God ordained them, and they are placed there for our sakes, and speak God's language in our accent, and they appear in the outside; we receive the benefit of their ministry, and God receives the glory.

Section IV[6]
The Blessings and Graces of the Holy Sacrament
In the reception of the blessed sacrament, there are many blessings which proceed from our own actions, the conjugations of moral duties, the offices of preparation and reception, the reverence and the devotion; of which I shall give account in the following chapters. Here I am to enumerate those graces which are intended to descend upon us from the Spirit of God in the use of the sacrament itself precisely.

But first I consider, that it must be infinitely certain that great spiritual blessings are consequent to the worthy receiving of this divine sacrament, because it is not at all received but by a spiritual hand. For it is either to be understood in a carnal sense that Christ's body is there eaten, or in a spiritual sense. If in a carnal, it profits nothing. If in a spiritual He be eaten, let the meaning of that be considered, and it will

---

5. 1 Cor. 11:20, 10:16; Acts 16:2.
6. *Works* 8:32ff.

207

convince us that innumerable blessings are in the very reception and communion. . . . Faith is the inward applicatory, and if there be any outward at all, it must be the sacraments; and both of them are of remarkable virtue in this particular; for by baptism we are baptized into the death of Christ; and the Lord's supper is an appointed enunciation and declaration of Christ's death, and it is a sacramental participation of it. Now to partake of it sacramentally, is by sacrament to receive it; that is, so to apply it to us, as that can be applied: it brings it to our spirit, it propounds it to our faith, it represents it as the matter of eucharist, it gives it as meat and drink to our souls, and rejoices in it in that very formality in which it does receive it, viz., as broken for, as shed for the remission of our sins. Now then what can any man suppose a sacrament to be, and what can be meant by sacramental participation? For unless the sacraments do communicate what they relate to, they are no communion or communication at all; for it is true that our mouth eats the material signs; but at the same time, faith eats too; and therefore must eat, that is, must partake of the thing signified. Faith is not maintained by ceremonies: the body receives the body of the mystery; we eat and drink the symbols with our mouths; but faith is not corporeal, but feeds upon the mystery itself; it entertains the grace, and enters into that secret which the Spirit of God conveys under that signature. Now since the mystery is perfectly and openly expressed to be the remission of sins; if the soul does the work of the soul, as the body the work of the body, the soul receives remission of sins, as the body does the symbols of it, and the sacrament.

But we must be infinitely careful to remember that even the death of Christ brings no pardon to the impenitent persevering sinner, but to him that repents truly: and so does the sacrament of Christ's death; this can do no more than that: and therefore let no man come with his guilt about him, and in the heat and in the affections of his sin, and hope to find his pardon by this ministry. He that thinks so will but deceive, will but ruin himself. They are excellent but very severe words which God spake to the Jews, and which are a prophetical reproof of all unworthy communicants in these divine mysteries, "What hath My beloved to do in My house, seeing she hath wrought lewdness with many? The holy flesh hath passed from thee when thou doest evil"; that is, this holy sacrifice, the flesh and blood of thy Lord, shall slip from thee without doing thee any good, if thou hast not ceased from doing evil. But the vulgar Latin reads these words much more emphatically to our purpose, "Shall the holy flesh take from thee thy wickedness in which thou rejoicest?" Deceive not thyself; thou hast no part nor portion in this matter. For the holy sacrament operates indeed and consigns our pardon, but not alone, but in conjunction with all that Christ requires as conditions of pardon; but when the conditions are present, the sacrament ministers pardon, as pardon is ministered in this world; that is, by parts, and in order to several purposes, and with power of revocation, by suspending the divine wrath, by procuring more graces, by obtaining time of repentance, and powers and possibilities of working out our salvation; and by setting forward the method and economy of our salvation. For in the usual methods of God, pardon of sins is proportionable to our repentance; which because it is all that state of piety we have in this whole life after our first sin, pardon of sins is all that effect of grace which is consequent to that repentance; and the worthy receiving of the holy communion is but one conjugation of holy actions and parts of repentance, but indeed it is the best and the noblest, and such in which man does best co-operate towards pardon, and the grace of God does the most illustriously consign it. But of these particulars I shall give full account when I shall discourse of the preparations of repentance.

4. It is the greatest solemnity of prayer, the most powerful liturgy and means of impetration in this world. For when Christ was consecrated on the cross and became our high-priest, having reconciled us to God by the death of the cross, He became infinitely gracious in the eyes of God, and was admitted to the celestial and eternal priesthood in heaven; where in the virtue of the cross He intercedes for us, and represents an eternal sacrifice in the heavens on our behalf. That He is a priest in heaven, appears in the large discourses and direct affirmatives of S. Paul;[7] that there is no other sacrifice to be offered but that on the cross, it is evident, because "He hath but once appeared in the end of the world to put away sin by the sacrifice of Himself"; and therefore since it is necessary that He hath something to offer so long as He is a priest[8] and there is no other sacrifice but that of Himself offered upon the cross; it follows that Christ in heaven perpetually offers and represents that sacrifice to His heavenly Father, and in virtue of that obtains all good things for His church.

Now what Christ does in heaven, He hath commanded us to do on

7. Heb. 7:24.
8. Heb. 8:3.

earth, that is, to represent His death, to commemorate this sacrifice, by humble prayer and thankful record; and by faithful manifestation and joyful eucharist to lay it before the eyes of our heavenly Father, so ministering in His priesthood, and doing according to His commandment and His example; the church being the image of heaven, the priest the minister of Christ; the holy table being a copy of the celestial altar, and the eternal sacrifice of the lamb slain from the beginning of the world being always the same; it bleeds no more after the finishing of it on the cross; but it is wonderfully represented in heaven, and graciously represented here; by Christ's action there, by His commandment here. And the event of it is plainly this; that as Christ in virtue of His sacrifice on the cross intercedes for us with His Father, so does the minister of Christ's priesthood here, that the virtue of the eternal sacrifice may be salutary and effectual to all the needs of the church both for things temporal and eternal. And therefore it was not without great mystery and clear signification that our blessed Lord was pleased to command the representation of His death and sacrifice on the cross should be made by breaking bread and effusion of wine; to signify to us the nature and sacredness of the liturgy we are about; and that we minister in the priesthood of Christ, who is "a priest for ever after the order of Melchisedec"; that is, we are ministers in that unchangeable priesthood, imitating in the external ministry the prototype Melchisedec, of whom it was said, "he brought forth bread and wine, and was the priest of the most high God"; and in the internal, imitating the antitype or the substance, Christ himself; who offered up His body and blood for atonement for us, and by the sacraments of bread and wine, and the prayers of oblation and intercession commands us to officiate in His priesthood, in the external ministering like Melchisedec; in the internal after the manner of Christ himself.

This is a great and a mysterious truth, which as it is plainly manifested in the epistle to the Hebrews, so it is understood by the ancient and holy doctors of the church. So S. Ambrose,[9] "Now Christ is offered, but He is offered as a man, as if He received His passion; but He offers Himself as a priest, that He may pardon our sins; here in image or representation; there in truth, as an advocate interceding with His Father for us." So S. Chrysostom,[10] "In Christ once the sacrifice was

---

9. Ambrose, *On the Duties of the Clergy*, PL 16. 92.
10. Chrysostom, *Homilies on Hebrews*, PG 63. 130.

offered, which is powerful to our eternal salvation"; "but what then do we? do not we offer every day? what we daily offer is at the memorial of His death, and the sacrifice is one, not many; . . . because Christ was once offered: but this sacrifice is the example or representation of that." And another, "Christ is not impiously slain by us, but piously sacrificed; and by this means we declare the Lord's death till He come; for here through Him we humbly do in earth, which He as a Son who is heard according to His reverence, does powerfully for us in heaven; where as an advocate He intercedes with His Father, whose office or work it is, for us to exhibit and interpose His flesh which He took of us and for us, and as it were to press it upon His Father." To the same sense is the meditation of S. Austin,[11] "By this He is the priest and the oblation, the sacrament of which He would have the daily sacrifice of the church to be: which because it is the body of that head, she learns from Him to offer herself to God by Him, who offered Himself to God for her." And therefore this whole office is called by S. Basil[12] "the prayer of oblation"; the great christian sacrifice and oblation, in which we present our prayers and the needs of ourselves and of our brethren unto God in virtue of the great sacrifice, Christ upon the cross, whose memorial we then celebrate in a divine manner by divine appointment.

The effect of this I represent in the words of Lyra,[13] "That which does purge and cleanse our sins must be celestial and spiritual, and that which is such hath a perpetual efficacy, and needs not to be done again"; but that which "is daily offered in the church . . . is a daily commemoration of that one sacrifice which was offered on the cross, according to the command of Christ, Do this in commemoration of Me."

Now this holy ministry and sacrament of this death, being according to Christ's commandment, and in our manner a representation of that eternal sacrifice, an imitation of Christ's intercession in heaven in virtue of that sacrifice, must be "after the pattern in the mount"; it must be as that is, *pura prece*, as Tertullian's[14] phrase is, "by pure prayer"; it is an intercession for the whole church present and absent, in the virtue of that sacrifice.—I need add no more; but leave it to the meditation, to the joy and the admiration of all christian people, to think and to enumerate the blessings of this sacrament; which is so excellent a representation of

---

11. Augustine, *City of God,* PL 41. 298.
12. Basil, *Liturgy of St. Basil,* PG 31. 1635.
13. "Lyra" = a gloss on Heb. 10:3.
14. Tertullian, *To Scapula,* PL 1. 699.

Christ's death by Christ's commandment, and so glorious an imitation of that intercession which Christ makes in heaven for us all. It is all but the representment of His death, in the way of prayer and interpellation, Christ as head, and we as members; He as high-priest, and we as servants His ministers; and therefore I shall stop here, and leave the rest for wonder and eucharist. We may pray here with all the solemnity and advantages imaginable: we may with hope and comfort use the words of David,[15] "I will take the cup of salvation, and call upon the name of the Lord": we are here very likely to prevail for all blessings, for this is by way of eminency, glory and singularity,[16] *calix benedictionis*, "the cup of blessing, which we bless," and by which God will bless us, and for which He is to be blessed for evermore.

5. By the means of this sacrament, our bodies are made capable of the resurrection to life and eternal glory. For when we are externally and symbolically in the sacrament, and by faith and the Spirit of God internally united to Christ and made partakers of His body and His blood, we are joined and made one with Him who did rise again; and when the head is risen, the members shall not see corruption for ever, but rise again after the pattern of our Lord. If by the sacrament we are really united and made one with Christ, then it shall be to us in our proportion as it was to Him; we shall rise again, and we shall enter into glory. But it is certain we are united to Christ by it; we eat His body and drink His blood sacramentally by our mouths, and therefore really and spiritually, by our spirits and by spiritual actions co-operating.[17] For what good will it do us to partake of His body, if we do not also partake of His spirit? But certain it is, if we do one we do both; *cum naturalis per sacramentum proprietas perfecta sacramentum sit unitatis*, as S. Hilary's[18] expression is, "the natural propriety," viz., the outward elements, "by the sacrament," that is, by the institution and blessing of God, "become the sacrament of a perfect unity"; which, beside all the premises, is distinctly affirmed in the words of the apostle, "We which are sanctified and He which sanctifies are all of one"; and again, "The bread which we break, is it not the communication of the body of Christ; and the cup which we drink, is it not the communication of the blood of Christ?" Plainly saying, that by this holy ministry we are

---

15. Ps. 116:12.
16. Gregory, (Pope) *The Dialogues*, PL 77. 425.
17. Cyril of Alexandria, *On John's Gospel*, PG 74. 542.
18. Hilary, *The Trinity*, PL 10. 246.

joined and partake of Christ's body and blood; and then we become spiritually one body; and therefore shall receive in our bodies all the effects of that spiritual union; the chief of which in relation to our bodies, is resurrection from the grave. And this is expressly taught by the ancient church. So S. Irenaeus[19] teaches us, "As the bread which grows from the earth, receiving the calling of God," that is, blessed by prayer and the word of God, "is not now common bread, but the eucharist, consisting of two things, an earthly and an heavenly: so also our bodies receiving the eucharist, are not now corruptible, but have the hope of resurrection." And again,[20] "When the mingled calice and the made bread receives the word of God," viz., is consecrated and blessed, "it is made the eucharist of the body and blood of Christ out of those things by which our body is nourished, and our substance does consist: and how shall any one deny that the flesh is capable of the gift of God, which is eternal life, which is nourished by the body and blood of Christ?" And S. Ignatius[21] calls the blessed eucharist "the medicine of immortality"; for the drink is His blood who is "incorruptible love and eternal life": so the fathers of the Nicene council,[22] "the symbols of our resurrection"; "the meat nourishing to immortality and eternal life," so S. Cyril of Alexandria[23]; "for this is to drink the blood of Jesus, to be partakers of the Lord's incorruptibility," said S. Clement. For "bread is food, and blood is life; but we drink the blood of Christ, Himself commanding us, that together with Him we may by Him be partakers of eternal life," so S. Cyprian, *aut quicunque sit auctor sermon. de cœna Domini.*[24]

---

19. Irenaeus, *Against Heresy*, PG 7. 1029.
20. Ibid. PG 7. 1125.
21. Ignatius of Antioch, *To the Ephesians*, PG 5. 755.
22. Gelasius, *History of Nicea*, PG 85. 1315.
23. Cyril of Alexandria, PG 73. 582.
24. Cyprian, *Sacrament of the Lord's Cup*, PL 4. 572.

A Communion Office[25]

After a decent pause for short meditation, the minister shall
with a loud voice say,
Our Father, etc.
And then this EKPHŌNĒSIS, *or denunciation*

Let all corruptible flesh be silent, and stand with fear and trembling, and think within itself nothing that is earthly, nothing that is unholy. The Kind of kings and the Lord of lords, Christ our God comes down from heaven unto us, and gives Himself to be meat for the souls of all faithful people. All the glorious companies of angels behold this and wonder, and love and worship Jesus. Every throne and dominion, the cherubims with many eyes, and the seraphims with many wings cover their faces before the majesty of His glory, and sing a perpetual song for ever,

Alleluiah, Alleluiah!
Glory be to God on high,
and in earth peace, good will towards men.
Alleluiah.

Then shall follow this prayer of consecration, to be said by
the minister standing

I.

Have mercy upon us, O heavenly Father, according to Thy glorious mercies and promises, send Thy holy Ghost upon our hearts, and let Him also descend upon these gifts, that by His good, His holy, His glorious presence, He may sanctify and enlighten our hearts, and He may bless and sanctify these gifts.

That this bread may become the holy body of Christ.

---

25. *Works* 8:624ff.

Amen.

And this chalice may become the life-giving blood of Christ.

Amen.

That it may become unto us all that partake of it this day, a blessed instrument of union with Christ, of pardon and peace, of health and blessing, of holiness and life eternal, through Jesus Christ our Lord.

Amen.

II.

Holy and blessed art Thou, O king of eternal ages, fountain and giver of all righteousness.

Holy art Thou, the eternal and only-begotten Son of God, our Lord Jesus Christ, Redeemer of the world.

Holy art Thou, O blessed Spirit, that searchest all things, even the depths and hidden things of God.

Thou, O God, art almighty: Thou art good and gracious, dreadful and venerable, holy and merciful to the work of Thine own hands.

Thou didst make man according to Thine image; Thou gavest him the riches and the rest of paradise: when he fell and broke Thy easy commandment, Thou didst not despise his folly, nor leave him in his sin, but didst chastise him with Thy rod, and restrain him by Thy law, and instruct him by Thy prophets, and at last didst send Thy holy Son into the world, that He might renew and repair Thy broken image.

The people shall answer, Blessed be God!

He coming from heaven, and taking our flesh, by the power of the holy Ghost, of the virgin Mary, conversed with men, and taught us the way of God, and the dispensation of eternal life.

People. Holy Jesus! blessed be God.

But when for the redemption of us sinners He would suffer death upon the cross, without sin, for us who were nothing but sin and misery, in the night in which He was betrayed, He took bread, He looked up to heaven, He gave thanks, He sanctified it, He brake it, * The minister at those and gave it to His apostles, saying, Take, eat, this* words shall touch the is My body which is broken for you; do this in bread. remembrance of Me.

Likewise after supper He took the cup, and when He had given

215

thanks and blessed it, He gave it to them, saying, Drink ye all of
this, for this* is My blood of the New testament, which
is shed for you and for many for the remission of sins;
do this in remembrance of Me.

*Here he must touch or handle the chalice.

For as often as ye shall eat this bread, and drink this cup, ye shall shew forth the Lord's death till He come.

The people shall answer, Amen.
Minister. We believe, and we confess.
People. We declare Thy death, and confess Thy resurrection.

Then the minister kneeling shall say this prayer of oblation

I.

We sinners, Thy unworthy servants, in remembrance of Thy life-giving passion, Thy cross and Thy pains, Thy death and Thy burial, Thy resurrection from the dead and Thy ascension into heaven, Thy sitting at the right hand of God, making intercession for us; and expecting with fear and trembling Thy formidable and glorious return to judge the quick and dead, when Thou shalt render to every man according to his works; do humbly present to Thee, O Lord, this present sacrifice of remembrance and thanksgiving, humbly and passionately praying Thee not to deal with us according to our sins, nor recompense us after our transgressions; but according to Thy abundant mercy and infinite goodness to blot out and take away the hand-writing that is against us in the book of remembrances which Thou hast written: and that Thou wilt give unto us spiritual, celestial and eternal gifts, which neither eye hath seen nor ear hath heard, neither hath it entered into the heart of man to understand, which God hath prepared for them that love Him, through Jesus Christ our Lord. *Amen.*

Then shall follow the reception and distribution of the holy
sacrament

The minister first receiving, and privately saying this short
prayer

O blessed Jesus, my Lord and my God, Thou art the celestial food and the life of every man that cometh unto Thee. I have sinned against heaven and before Thee, and am not worthy to partake of these holy

216

mysteries: but Thou art my merciful Saviour; grant that I may religiously, thankfully, and without reproof partake of Thy blessed body and blood, for the remission of my sins, and unto life eternal. Amen.

Then reverently taking in his hand the consecrated bread that he means to eat, let him say,

The body of our Lord Jesus which was broken for me, preserve my body and soul into everlasting life. Amen.

Then praying awhile privately, let him receive the chalice, saying,

The blood of our Lord Jesus Christ which was shed for the remission of my sins, cleanse my soul, and preserve it into everlasting life. Amen.

Then let him pray awhile privately, and recommend to God his own personal necessities spiritual and temporal, and the needs of all his relatives, etc.
After that, let him distribute it first to the clergy that helps to officiate, and after that, to the whole congregation that offers themselves, saying the same words, changing the person
While the minister of the mysteries is praying privately, the people may secretly pray thus, or to this purpose

I believe, O God, and confess that Thou art Christ the Son of the living God, who came into the world to save sinners, whereof I am chief. Lord, make me this day partaker of Thy heavenly table; for Thou dost not give Thy secrets to Thy enemies, but to the sons of Thine own house. Let me never give Thee a Judas kiss; I confess Thee and Thy glories, I invocate Thee and Thy mercies, I trust upon Thee and Thy goodness, like the thief upon the cross; Lord, remember me in Thy kingdom, with the remembrances of an everlasting love.

Lord, I am not worthy that Thou shouldest come under my roof; but as Thou didst vouchsafe to lie in a manger with beasts, and to enter into the house of Simon the leper, nor didst despise the repenting harlot when she kissed Thy feet; so vouchsafe to lodge in my soul, though it be a place of beastly affections and unreasonable passions; throw them out and dwell there for ever; purify my soul, accept the sinner, cleanse the leper, so shall I be worthy to partake of this divine banquet. Amen.

HEAVENLY SACRIFICE AND EARTHLY SACRAMENTS

When every of the communicants hath received in both kinds, let the paten and chalice (if any of the consecrated elements remain) be decently covered, and then shall follow these prayers

THE POST-COMMUNION

The minister and people devoutly kneeling shall say the Lord's prayer, the people repeating every petition after the minister

Our Father, which art in heaven; hallowed be Thy name. Thy kingdom come. Thy will be done in earth as it is in heaven. Give us this day our daily bread. And forgive us our trespasses, as we forgive them that trespass against us. And lead us not into temptation; but deliver us from evil. For Thine is the kingdom, the power and the glory, for ever and ever. Amen.

Then the minister shall pray this prayer for the catholic church

I.

Receive, O eternal God, this sacrifice for and in behalf of all christian people, whom Thou hast redeemed with the blood of Thy Son, and purchased as Thine own inheritance. From the fountains of mercy, the springs of our blessed Saviour, let all Thy people upon whom the name of Jesus is called, receive confirmation and increase of grace, fruitfulness in good works, and perfect understanding in the way of godliness; defend, O God, Thy church, and preserve her from all heresy and scandal, from sacrilege and simony, from covetousness and pride, from factions and schism, from atheism and irreligion, from all that persecute the truth, and from all that work wickedness, and let not the gates of hell prevail against her, nor any evil come near to hurt her.

II.

Give Thy blessing, O God, to this nation; remember us for good and not for evil; be reconciled unto us in the Son of Thy love, and let not Thine anger be any longer upon us, nor Thy jealousy burn like fire. Send us health and peace, justice and truth, good laws and good government; an excellent religion, undivided, undisturbed; temperate air, seasonable showers, wholesome dews, fruitful seasons: crown the year

218

with goodness, and let the clouds drop fatness, that we may glorify Thy name, and confess Thy goodness, while Thou bearest witness to us from heaven, filling our hearts with food and gladness.

III.

With a propitious eye and a great pity behold the miseries of mankind; put a speedy period to all our sins and to all our calamities: hear the sighings of the distressed, the groans of the sick, the prayers of the oppressed, the desires of the poor and needy; support the weakness of them that languish and faint, ease the pains of them that are in affliction and call to Thee for help. Take from the miserable all tediousness of spirit and despair: pardon all the penitents, reform the vicious, confirm the holy, and let them be holy still; pity the folly of young men, their little reason and great passion; succour the infirmities and temptations of the aged, preserving them that they may not sin towards the end of their lives, for Jesus Christ his sake.

IV.

Admit, O blessed God, into the society of our prayers, and the benefits of this eucharist, our fathers and brethren, our wives and children, our friends and benefactors, our charges and relatives, all that have desired our prayers and all that need them, all that we have and all that we have not remembered; thou knowest all their necessities and all their dwellings, their joys and their sorrows, their hopes and their fears, the number of their sins and the measures of their repentances; O dear God, sanctify them and us, let our portion be in the good things of God, in religion and purity, in the peace of conscience, and the joys of the holy Ghost, in the love of God and of our neighbours. O gather us to the feet of Thy elect, when Thou wilt, and in what manner Thou art pleased; only let us appear before Thee without shame and without sins, through the merits of Jesus Christ, our most merciful Saviour and Redeemer. *Amen.*

Then shall follow the eucharistical prayers

I.

Glory be to Thee, O God our Father, who hast vouchsafed to make us at this time partakers of the body and blood of Thy holy Son: we offer unto Thee, O God, ourselves, our souls and bodies, to be a reasonable, holy, and living sacrifice unto Thee: keep us under the shadow of Thy wings, and defend us from all evil, and conduct us by Thy holy spirit of grace into all good; for Thou who hast given Thy holy Son unto us, how shalt not Thou with Him give us all things else? Blessed be the name of our God for ever and ever. *Amen.*

II.

Glory be to Thee, O Christ, our king, the only-begotten Son of God, who wert pleased to become a sacrifice for our sins, a redemption from calamity, the physician and the physic, the life and the health, the meat and the drink of our souls; Thou by Thy unspeakable mercy didst descend to the weakness of sinful flesh, remaining still in the perfect purity of spirit, and hast made us partakers of Thy holy body and blood: O condemn us not when Thou comest to judgment, but keep us ever in Thy truth, in Thy fear, and in Thy favour, that we may have our portion in Thine inheritance, where holiness and purity, where joy and everlasting praises do dwell for ever and ever. *Amen.*

III.

Proceeding from glory to glory, we still glorify Thee, O Father of spirits, and pray Thee for ever to continue Thy goodness towards us. Direct our way aright, establish us in holy purposes, keep us unspotted in Thy faith, let the enemy have no part in us, but conform us for ever to the likeness of Thy holy Son; lead us on to the perfect adoption of our souls, and to the redemption of our bodies from corruption, and fill our hearts and tongues with everlasting praises of Thy name, through Jesus Christ our Lord. *Amen.*

The blessing

The peace of God, which passeth all understanding, keep your hearts and minds in the knowledge and love of God, and of His Son Jesus Christ our Lord: and the blessing of God almighty, Father, Son and holy Spirit, be upon you, and abide with you, and be your portion for ever and ever. *Amen.*

THE END OF THE COMMUNION OFFICE

The Reverence
Due to the Altar[26]

. . . understand all those places of Scripture, where we are called on to worship God, to bow downe to him, to fall downe before his footstoole, of externall, or corporall adoration. For where the externall is onely expressed, there although the internall be also meant, as being the root from whence the externall must come, yet there the externall is not excluded. That which is onely nam'd is not onely to be left out, especially since externall worshippings are expresse acts of duty, and subordination to the person worshipped. Thus to be uncovered in these Westerne parts is a tendry of our service, and ever was since *donare pileo* was to make a free man of a slave. But among all nations inclining of the head, or bowing of the face to the ground, nay even in nature it selfe it is a duty of inferiours to Superiours, for it is *deponere magnificentiam propriam*, to lay our glory at the feet of another, that's a true . . . worship, or adoration. And this not to be given to God, or to be given to an Idol, does promerit God's anger (Esa. 2.9) They *worship* the worke of their owne hands. How doe they worship it? The meane man boweth downe, and the great man humbleth himselfe, therefore forgive them not. I think it is cleare that worship of God supposes externall, and to worship God in spirit is not opposed to worship him in body; for it might as well exclude honouring God with our Substance (as Solomon bids[27]), for of themselves our bodyes are as spirituall as our money; and then as we should not come, and bow down low before his footstoole,[28] so neither should we bring[29] an offering, and come into his courts. Nay

---

26. *Works* 5:319ff. A manuscript, entitled *The Reverence Due to the Altar*, was discovered in the Library of Queen's College, Oxford, early in the nineteenth century. Printed first as a separate booklet, and only later included in the Heber-Eden edition of Taylor's works, it remains here in its unedited and undeveloped form.

27. Prov. 10:3.

28. Ps. 95:6.

29. Ps. 96:8.

spirituall worship no more excludes bodily, then *corde creditur* does exclude *ore fit confessio;* unlesse we say that faith is no part of divine worship: for if it be, then spirituall is not onely internall, or at least excludes not the other.

The next step to the Altar is, that God is there specially to be worshipped, where he is most praesentiall. For although God bee present in all places alike in respect of his essence, yet he exhibits the issues, and effects of his presence more in some then in others. And that thither the addresses of our adorations must be where God is specially present, nature teaches us. We looke men in the face when we speake to them, and if we may any where pray to God, and adore him because he is every where present and heares us, then by the same reason we must specially adore him where he is specially present, (because his presence is the determination of our addresse) that is in Heaven, and in all Holy places; And therefore the generall addresse of our devotion is towards heaven; so Christ taught us to say, *Pater noster qui es in Cœlis* etc. so we doe in lifting up our eyes, and hands for there is his court, and his glorious *satellitium* of Angells, and his royall throne. But this generall addresse is limited by a more speciall, and that is in Holy places, places consecrate to the service of God by acts of publike, and religious solemnity, in them, and from them to Heaven. Thus it was in Solomon's Temple;[30] If they pray towards this place, then heare thou in Heaven etc. *Est ergo Altare in Cœlis. Illuc enim preces nostræ, et oblationes nostræ diriguntur: et ad Templum quemadmodum Johannes in Apocalypsi ait, et apertum est Templum Dei, et Tabernaculum. Ecce enim inquit, Tabernaculum Dei in quo habitabit cum hominibus* saith S. Irenaeus.[31] For Gods seat is in Holy places: his presence is there: his face is there: his feet is there: his throne is there.

See this by constant testimony of Scripture: Jacob in Bethel, surely saith he God is in this place: how know you Jacob? Oh, says he, it is the house of God, and the Gate of Heaven. *Quam reverenda sunt hæc loca!* When God had given direction to Moses for the Tabernacle and to place the Cherubims before the Mercy seat, that God tooke up his residence there was so knowne a thing, that it became to him like an attribute, or an appellative; Oh thou that sittest betweene the Cherubims, said David.[32] The Philistins had soone learnd that; for when the

---

30. 1 Kings 8:35.
31. Irenaeus, PG 7. 1083.
32. Ps. 80:1.

Arke was come into the campe of the Hebrews they were affrayd, for they sayd, God is come into the Campe.[33]

Gods presence is there. Serve the Lord with gladnesse, and come before his "presence" with a song (Ps. 100) for though this be the same with the former, yet they are severall expressions us'd by God himselfe. And therefore the Arke was called the Tabernacle of the Congregation, not because of the peoples meeting with the priest, and one with another, but Gods meeting with the people (Num. 7.4). And thou shalt lay them in the tabernacle of the congregation where I will meet with you. And when Moses had any businesse of particular consequence with God, thither he went, for there he knew he was. And when Moses was gone into the Tabernacle of the Congregation "to speake with him," he heard the voyce etc.

His face is there. This is intimated to us in the shewbread layd upon the table of the proposition in the Tabernacle, which was called amongst the Hebrews, Facebread; and the 70 expressly reads it countenance loaves, bread set there where Gods countenance is present.

His throne, and feet are there. The place of my throne, and the soles of my feet, where I will dwell in the midst of the children of Israel for ever, and my holy name shall they no more defile, in setting their threshold by my threshold, and their posts by my posts (Ezek: 43.7). And againe, The glory of Lebanon . . . shall beautify the place of my Sanctuary, and I will make the place of my feet glorious.

God's memoriall is there. An Altar of earth shalt thou make mee . . . in all places where "I record my name" I will come and blesse thee.[34] In the places where he appoints himselfe to be worshipped, there he records his name, and there he promises his presence, and that will bring a blessing, where I record my name "I will come" and blesse thee. All these are but various expressions of that which the prophet David speakes in plaine termes,[35] The Lord is in his Holy Temple the Lord's seat is in Heaven.

The consequence of these is playnely thus much; therefore these places are holy, therefore proper for Divine adoration. That they are holy is plaine, not onely by consequence, but in direct terms: God's Sanctuary is called the beauty of Holiness,[36] and the beauty of Holinesse

---

33. 1 Sam. 4:7.
34. Exod. 20:24.
35. Ps. 11:4.
36. Ps. 96:9.

must needs be Holy, and therefore *Adorate Dominum,* worship the Lord in the beauty of Holinesse. There they are together. And againe Holinesse becommeth thy house for ever, Holinesse for Holy places, *Sancta Sanctis:* Holinesse is its ornament, and beauty (Ps. 93). That's one of them, the other is in psalm 99. Exalt the Lord our God, and fall downe before his footstoole. Nay at God's approximation to Moses in the Bush, God commanded him to be discalceate, and gives no other reason for it, but because the ground was Holy. . . .[37]

---

37. Exod. 3:5.

Clerus Domini
or
The Office Ministerial
and
The Nature and Manner of Its Power
and Operation[38]

Section IV

... One thing I offer to consideration; that since the keys of the kingdom of heaven be most notoriously and signally used in baptism, in which the kingdom of heaven, the gospel and all its promises, is opened to all believers, and though as certainly yet less principally in reconciling penitents, and admitting them to the communion of the faithful; it may be of ill consequence to let them be usurped by hands to whom they were not consigned. Certain it is, S. Peter used his keys, and opened the kingdom of heaven first, when he said,[39] "Repent and be baptized every one of you in the name of Jesus Christ for the remission of sins, and ye shall receive the gift of the holy Ghost." However, as to the main question, we have not only the universal doctrine of christendom, but also express authority and commission in scripture, sending out apostles and apostolical men, persons of choice and special designation to "baptize all nations," and to entertain them into the services and institution of the holy Jesus.

Section V

1. I shall instance but once more, but it is in the most solemn, sacred, and divinest mystery in our religion; that in which the clergy in

---

38. *Works* 1:3ff.
39. Acts 2:38.

225

their appointed ministry do "stand between God and the people," and do fulfil a special and incomprehensible ministry, which "the angels themselves do look into"[40] with admiration, to which the people if they come without fear, cannot come without sin; and this of so sacred and reserved mysteriousness, that but few have dared to offer at with unconsecrated hands: some have. But the EUCHARIST is the fulness of all the mysteriousness of our religion; and the clergy, when they officiate here, are most truly in the phrase of S. Paul,[41] *dispensatores mysteriorum Dei,* "dispensers of the great mysteries of the kingdom." For, to use the words of S. Cyprian,[42] "Jesus Christ is our high-priest, and Himself become our sacrifice, which He finished upon the cross in a real performance, and now in His office of mediatorship makes intercession for us by a perpetual exhibition of Himself, of His own person in heaven, which is a continual actually represented argument to move God to mercy to all that believe in and obey the holy Jesus."

2. Now Christ did also establish a number of select persons, to be ministers of this great sacrifice, finished upon the cross; that they also should exhibit and represent to God, in the manner which their Lord appointed them, this sacrifice, commemorating the action and suffering of the great Priest; and by way of prayers and impetration, offering up that action in behalf of the people, *EPI TO ANŌ THYSIASTĒRION ANA-PEMPSAS TAS THYSIAS,* (as Gregory Nazianzen[43] expresses it) sending up sacrifices to be laid upon the altar in heaven, that the church might be truly united unto Christ their head, and, in the way of their ministry, may do what He does in heaven; for He exhibits the sacrifice, that is, Himself, actually and presentially in heaven: the priest on earth commemorates the same, and by his prayers represents it to God in behalf of the whole catholic church; presentially too, by another and more mysterious way of presence; but both Christ in heaven, and His ministers on earth do actuate that sacrifice, and apply it to its purposed design by praying to God in the virtue and merit of that sacrifice; Christ himself, in a high and glorious manner; the ministers of His priesthood (as it becomes ministers) humbly, sacramentally, and according to the energy of human advocation and intercession. This is the sum and great mysteriousness of christianity, and is now to be proved.

---

40. 1 Pet. 1:12.
41. 1 Cor. 4:1.
42. Cyprian, PL 4. 372.
43. Gregory Nazianzen, *The Orations,* PG 35. 831.

3. This is expressly described in scripture; that part concerning Christ is the doctrine of S. Paul, who disputes largely concerning Christ's priesthood; affirming[44] that "Christ is a priest for ever"; He hath therefore "an unchangeable priesthood," because "He continueth for ever," and "He lives for ever to make intercession for us"; this He does as priest, and therefore it must be by offering a sacrifice, "for every high-priest is ordained to offer gifts and sacrifices," and therefore "it is necessary He also have something to offer," as long as He is a priest, that is, "for ever," till the consummation of all things; since therefore He hath nothing new to offer, and something He must continually offer, it is evident He offers himself as the medium of advocation, and the instance and argument of a prevailing intercession; and this He calls "a more excellent ministry," and by it Jesus is "a minister of the sanctuary, and of the true tabernacle"; that is, He as our high-priest officiates in heaven in the great office of a mediator, in the merit and power of His death and resurrection. Now what Christ does always in a proper and most glorious manner, the ministers of the gospel also do in theirs: commemorating the sacrifice upon the cross, "giving thanks," and celebrating a perpetual eucharist for it, and by "declaring the death of Christ," and praying to God in the virtue of it, for all the members of the church, and all persons capable; it is *in genere orationis* a sacrifice, and an instrument of propitiation, as all holy prayers are in their several proportions.

4. And this was by a precept of Christ; *Hoc facite,* "do this in remembrance of Me." Now this precept is but twice reported of in the New testament, though the institution of the sacrament be four times. And it is done with admirable mystery; to distinguish the several interests and operations which concern several sorts of Christians in their distinct capacities: S. Paul thus represents it, "Take, eat," "This do in remembrance of Me"; plainly referring this precept to all that are to eat and drink the symbols: for they also do in their manner enunciate, declare, or represent the Lord's death till He come. And S. Paul prosecutes it with instructions particular to "them that do communicate," as appears in the succeeding cautions against unworthy manducation, and for due preparation to its reception. But S. Luke reports it plainly to another purpose, "And He took bread, and gave thanks, and brake it, and gave it unto them, saying, This is My body which is given for you;

---

44. Heb. 7:23ff, 8:2ff.

Hoc facite, this do in remembrance of Me." "This" cannot but relate to *accepit, gratias egit, fregit, distribuit. Hoc facite;* here was no manducation expressed, and therefore *Hoc facite* concerns the apostles in the capacity of ministers; not as receivers, but as consecrators and givers; and if the institution had been represented in one scheme without this mysterious distinction, and provident separation of employment, we had been eternally in a cloud, and have needed a new light to guide us; but now the Spirit of God hath done it in the very first fountains of scripture.

5. And this being the great mystery of christianity, and the only remanent express of Christ's sacrifice on earth, it is most consonant to the analogy of the mystery, that this commemorative sacrifice be presented by persons as separate and distinct in their ministry, as the sacrifice itself is from and above the other parts of our religion. . . .

Section VII

By this ordination the persons ordained are made "ministers of the gospel," "stewards of all its mysteries," the "light," the "salt of the earth," the "shepherd of the flock," "curates of souls"; these are their offices, or their appellatives (which you please) for the clerical ordination is no other but a sanctification of the person in both senses; that is, 1) A separation of him to do certain mysterious actions of religion; which is that sanctification by which Jeremy and S. John the baptist were sanctified from their mothers' wombs. 2) It is also a sanctification of the person, by the increasing or giving respectively to the capacity of the suscipient, such graces as make the person meet to speak to God, to pray for the people, to handle the mysteries, and to have influence upon the cure.

I. The first sanctification, of a designation of the person; which must of necessity be some way or other by God: because it is a nearer approach to Him, a ministry of His graces, which without His appointment a man must not, cannot any more do, than a messenger can carry pardon to a condemned person which his prince never sent. But this separation of the person is not only a naming of the man (for so far the separation of the person may be previous to the ordination: for so it was in the ordinations of Matthias and the seven deacons; the apostles . . . "they appointed two" before God chose by lot; and the whole church chose the seven deacons before the apostles imposed hands) but the separation, or this first sanctification of the person, is a giving him a power to do such offices which God hath appointed to be done to Him

228

and for the people; which we may clearly see and understand in the instance of Job[45] and his friends; for when God would be entreated in behalf of Eliphaz and his companions, He gave order that Job should make the address, "Go to My servant, he shall pray for you, and him will I accept." This separation of a person for the offices of advocation is the same thing which I mean by this "first sanctification." . . . And therefore in the office of consecration in the Greek church, this power passes upon the person ordained, "that he may be worthy to ask things of Thee for the salvation of the people," that is, to celebrate the sacraments and rites, "and that Thou wilt hear him": which fully expresses the sense of the present discourse, that the first part of that grace of the holy Spirit which consecrates the priest, the first part of his sanctification, is a separation of the person to the power of intercession for the people, and a ministerial mediation, by the ministration of such rites and solemn invocations which God hath appointed or designed.

And now this sanctification which is so evident in scripture, tradition, and reason, taken from proportion and analogy to religion, is so far from making the power of the holy man less than is supposed, that it shews the greatness of it by a true representment; and preserves the sacredness of it so within its own cancels, that it will be the greatest sacrilege in the world to invade it; for, whoever will boldly enter within this veil, *nisi qui vocatur sicut Aaron,* "unless he be sanctified as is the priest," who is SYNIEREYSAS TŌ CHRISTŌ, as Nazianzen calls him, "a minister co-operating with Christ," he does without leave call himself "a man of God," "a mediator between God and the people under Christ," he boldly thrusts himself into the participation of that glorious mediation which Christ officiates in heaven; all which things as they are great honours to the person rightly called to such vicinity and endearments with God, so they depend wholly upon divine dignation of the grace and vocation of the person.

II. Now for the other part of spiritual emanation or descent of graces in sanctification of the clergy, that is in order to the performance of the other . . . certainly they who are honoured with so great a grace as to be called to officiate in holy and useful ministries have need also of other graces to make them persons holy in habit and disposition, as well as holy in calling, and therefore God hath sent His spirit to furnish His emissaries with excellencies proportionable to their need and the use-

---

45. Job 42:8.

fulness of the church. At the beginning of christianity God gave gifts extraordinary, as boldness of spirit, fearless courage, freedom of discourse, excellent understanding, discerning of spirits, deep judgment, innocence and prudence of deportment, the gift of tongues; these were so necessary at the institution of the christian church, that if we had not had testimony of the matter of fact, the reasonableness of the thing would prove the actual dispensation of the Spirit; because God never fails in necessaries: but afterward, when all the extraordinary needs were served, the extraordinary stock was spent, and God retracted those issues into their fountains, and then the graces that were necessary for the well discharging . . . "the priestly function," were such as make the person of more benefit to the people, not only by being exemplary to them, but gracious and loved by God: and those are spiritual graces of sanctification.

And therefore ordination is a collation of holy graces of sanctification; of a more excellent faith, of fervent charity, of providence and paternal care: gifts which now descend not by way of miracle, as upon the apostles, are to be acquired by human industry, by study and good letters, and therefore are pre-supposed in the person to be ordained: to which purpose the church now examines the abilities of the man before she lays on hands: and therefore the church does not suppose that the Spirit in ordination descends in gifts, and in the infusion of habits, and perfect abilities, though then also it is reasonable to believe that God will assist the pious and careful endeavours of holy priests, and bless them with special aids and co-operation, because a more extraordinary ability is needful for persons so designed: but the proper and great aid which the Spirit of ordination gives, is such instances of assistance which make the person more holy.

And this is so certainly true, that even when the apostle had ordained Timothy to be bishop of Ephesus, he calls upon him[46] to "stir up the gift of God which was in him by the putting on of his hands," and that gift is a "rosary of graces"; what graces they are he enumerates in the following words, "God hath not given us the spirit of fear, but of power, of love, and of a modest and sober mind," (and these words are made part of the form of collating the episcopal order in the church of England). Here is all that descends from the Spirit in ordination: *DYN-AMIS* "power," that is, to officiate and intercede with God in the parts

---

46. 2 Tim. 1:6ff.

of ministry; and the rest are such as imply duty, such as make him fit to be a ruler in paternal and sweet government, "modesty," "sobriety," "love"; and therefore in the forms of ordination of the Greek church (which are therefore highly to be valued, because they are most ancient, have suffered the least change, and been polluted with fewer interests) the mystical prayer of ordination names graces in order to holiness. "We pray Thee that the grace of the ever-holy Spirit may descend upon him; fill him full of all faith and love and power and sanctification by the illumination of Thy holy and life-giving Spirit": and the reason why these things are desired and given, is in order to the right performing his holy offices, "that he may be worthy to stand without blame at Thy altar, to preach the gospel of Thy kingdom, to minister the words of Thy truth, to bring to Thee gifts and spiritual sacrifices, to renew the people with the laver of regeneration."

And therefore S. Cyril[47] says that Christ's saying, "Receive ye the holy Ghost," signifies grace given by Christ to the apostles, whereby they were sanctified: that by the holy Ghost they might be absolved from their sins, saith Haymo,[48] and S. Austin[49] says that many persons that were snatched violently to be made priests or bishops, who had in their former purposes determined to marry and live a secular life, have in their ordination received the gift of continency. And therefore there was reason for the greatness of the solemnities used in all ages in separation of priests from the world, insomuch that whatsoever was used in any sort of sanctification or solemn benediction by Moses's law, all that was used in consecration of the priest, who was to receive the greatest measure of sanctification. *Eadem item vis etiam sacerdotem augustum et honorandum facit, novitate benedictionis a communitate vulgi segregatum; cum enim heri unus e plebe esset, repente redditur præceptor, præses, doctor pietatis, mysteriorum latentium præsul, etc.; invisibili quadam vi ac gratia invisibilem animam in melius transformatam gerens,* that is, "improved in all spiritual graces"; which is highly expressed by Martyrius[50] who said to Nectarius, *Tu, o beate, recens baptizatus et purificatus, et mox insuper sacerdotio auctus es; utraque autem hæc peccatorum expiatoria esse Deus constituit:* which are not to be expounded as if ordination did confer the first grace, which in the schools

---

47. Cyril of Alexandria, PG 74. 710.
48. Haymo, *On the Octave of the Pasch,* PL 118. 489.
49. Augustine, *Adulterous Marriages,* PL 40. 451.
50. Sozomen *Ecclesiastical History,* PG 67. 1439.

is understood only to be expiatorious; but the increment of grace and sanctification; and that also is remissive of sins, which are taken off by parts as the habit decreases; and we grow in God's favour as our graces multiply or grow.

Now that these graces being given in ordination, are immediate emanations of the holy Spirit, and therefore not to be usurped or pretended to by any man upon whom the holy Ghost in ordination hath not descended, I shall less need to prove, because it is certain upon the former grounds, and will be finished in the following discourses. . . .

Sermon X[51]
The Minister's Duty In Life and Doctrine

TIT. II. 7, 8

In all things shewing thyself a pattern of good works: in doctrine
shewing uncorruptness, gravity, sincerity;
Sound speech that cannot be condemned, that he that is of the
contrary part may be ashamed, having no evil thing to say of
you.

As God in the creation of the world first produced a mass of matter, having nothing in it but an obediential capacity and passivity; which God separating into classes of division, gave to every part a congruity to their respective forms, which in their distinct orbs and stations they did receive in order, and then were made beauteous by separations and a new economy; and out of these He appointed some for servants, and some for government; and some to eat, and some to be eaten; some above, and some below; some to be useful to all the rest, and all to minister to the good of man, whom He made the prince of the creation, and a minister of the divine glory: so God hath also done in the new creation; all the world was concluded under sin, it was a corrupt mass, all mankind "had corrupted themselves"; but yet were capable of divine influences, and of a nobler form, producible in the new birth: here then God's spirit moves upon the waters of a divine birth, and makes a separation of part from part, of corruption from corruption; and first chose some families to whom He communicated the divine influences and the breath of a nobler life; Seth and Enoch, Noah and Abraham, Job and Bildad: and these were the special repositories of the divine grace, and prophets of righteousness to glorify God in them-

51. *Works* 8:497ff.

selves, and in their sermons unto others. But this was like enclosing of the sun; he that shuts him in, shuts him out; and God who was and is an infinite goodness, would not be circumscribed and limited to a narrow circle; goodness is His nature, and infinite is His measure, and communication of that goodness is the motion of that eternal being: God *g.*,[52] breaks forth as out of a cloud, and picks out a whole nation; the sons of Israel became His family, and that soon swelled into a nation, and that nation multiplied till it became too big for their country, and by a necessary dispersion went, and did much good, and gained some servants to God out of other parts of mankind. But God was pleased to cast lots once more, and was like the sun already risen upon the earth, who spreads his rays to all the corners of the habitable world, that all that will open their eyes and draw their curtains, may see and rejoice in his light. Here God resolved to call all the world; He sent into the high-ways and hedges, to the corners of the gentiles, and the high-ways of the Jews, all might come that would; for "the sound of the gospel went out into all lands";[53] and God chose all that came, but all would not; and those that did, He gathered into a fold, marked them with His own mark, sent His Son to be the great "Shepherd and bishop of their souls";[54] and they became "a peculiar people" unto God, a "little flock," a "new election."

And here is the first separation and singularity of the gospel; all that hear the voice of Christ's first call, all that profess themselves His disciples, all that take His signature, they and their children are the church, "called out" from the rest of the world, the "elect" and the "chosen of God."

Now these being thus chosen out, culled and picked from the evil generations of the world, He separates them from others, to gather them to Himself; He separates them and sanctifies them to become holy; to come out (not of the companies so much, as) from the evil manners of the world: God chooses them unto holiness, they are "put in the right order to eternal life."[55]

All Christians are "holy unto the Lord," and therefore must not be unholy in their conversation; for nothing that is unholy shall come near to God: that's the first great line of our duty, but God intends it further; all Christians must not be only holy, but eminently holy. For "John

---

52. *g.* = *ergo.*
53. Ps. 19:4, Rom. 10:18.
54. 1 Pet. 2:25.
55. Acts 13:48.

indeed baptized with water";[56] but that's but a dull and unactive element, and moves by no principle, but by being ponderous; Christ "baptizes with the holy Ghost and with fire," and God hates lukewarmness; and when He chooses to Him a "peculiar people," He adds, they must be "zealous of good works."[57]

...THE SPECIAL SEPARATION OF THE CLERGY...

For God hath made a separation of you even beyond this separation: He hath separated you yet again; He hath put you anew into the crucible, He hath made you to pass through the fire seven times more. For it is true that the whole community of the people is the church; *ecclesia sancta est communio sanctorum*, "the holy catholic church is the communion of saints"; but yet by the voice and consent of all christendom, you are the church by way of propriety, and eminency, and singularity. "Churchmen," that's your appellative: all are ANDRES PNEUMATIKOI,[58] "spiritual men," all have received the Spirit, and all walk in the Spirit, and ye are all "sealed by the Spirit unto the day of redemption," and yet there is a spirituality peculiar to the clergy. "If any man be overtaken in a fault, ye which are spiritual restore such a one in the spirit of meekness":[59] you who are spiritual by office and designation, of a spiritual calling, and spiritual employment; you who have the Spirit of the Lord Jesus, and minister the Spirit of God, you are more eminently spiritual; you have the Spirit in graces and in powers, in sanctification and abilities, in office and in person; the "unction from above" hath descended upon your heads and upon your hearts; you are, by way of eminency and prelation, "spiritual men." "All the people of God were holy"; Corah and his company were in the right so far,[60] but yet Moses and Aaron were more holy, and stood nearer to God. All the people are prophets: it is now more than Moses' wish,"[61] for the Spirit of Christ hath made them so. "If any man prayeth or prophesieth with his

---

56. Matt. 3:11.
57. Titus 2:14.
58. 1 Cor. 2:15, 3:1.
59. Gal. 6:1.
60. Num. 16:3.
61. Num. 11:29.

head covered," or "if any woman prophesieth with her head uncovered,"[62] they are dishonoured; but either man or woman may do that work in time and place; for "in the latter days I will pour out of My spirit, and your daughters shall prophesy":[63] and yet God hath appointed in His church prophets above these, to whose spirit all the other prophets are subject; and as God said to Aaron and Miriam[64] concerning Moses, "To you I am known in a dream or a vision, but to Moses I speak face to face"; so it is in the church, God gives of His spirit to all men, but you He hath made the ministers of His spirit. Nay, the people have their portion of the keys of the kingdom of heaven, so said S. Paul,[65] "to whom ye forgive any thing, to him I forgive also"; and to the whole church of Corinth he gave a commission, "in the name of Christ, and by His Spirit, to deliver the incestuous person unto Satan"; and when the primitive penitents stood in their penitential stations, they did *caris Dci adgeniculari, et toti populo legationem orationis suæ commendare;*[66] and yet the keys were not only promised, but given to the apostles to be used then, and transmitted to all generations of the church; and we are "ministers of Christ, and stewards of the manifold mysteries of God";[67] and "to us is committed the word of reconciliation."[68] And thus in the consecration of the mysterious sacrament, the people have their portion; for the bishop or the priest blesses, and the people by saying "Amen" to the mystic prayer is partaker of the power, and the whole church hath a share in the power of spiritual sacrifice; "ye are a royal priesthood," "kings and priests unto God";[69] that is, so ye are priests as ye are kings; but yet kings and priests have a glory conveyed to them, of which the people partake but in minority, and allegory, and improper communication: but you are, and are to be respectively that considerable part of mankind by whom God intends to plant holiness in the world; by you God means to reign in the hearts of men; and therefore you are to be the first in this kind, and consequently the measure of all the rest. To you therefore I intend this, and some

---

62. 1 Cor. 11:5.
63. Joel 2:28.
64. Num. 12:6ff.
65. 2 Cor. 2:10.
66. Tertullian, *On Penance*, PL 1. 1243.
67. 1 Cor. 4:1.
68. 2 Cor. 5:19.
69. 1 Pet. 2:9; Rev. 1:6.

following discourses in order to this purpose; I shall but now lay the first stone, but it is the corner stone in this foundation.

But to you, I say, of the clergy, these things are spoken properly; to you these powers are conveyed really; upon you God hath poured His spirit plentifully; you are the choicest of His choice, the elect of His election, a church picked out of the church, vessels of honour for your Master's use, appointed to teach others, authorized to bless in His name; you are the ministers of Christ's priesthood, underlabourers in the great work of mediation and intercession, *medii inter Deum et populum*, you are "for the people towards God,"[70] and convey answers and messages from God to the people. These things I speak, not only to magnify your office, but to enforce and heighten your duty; you are holy by office and designation; for your very appointment is a sanctification and a consecration, and therefore whatever holiness God requires of the people, who have some little portions in the priesthood evangelical, He expects it of you, and much greater, to whom He hath conveyed so great honours, and admitted so near unto Himself, and hath made to be the great ministers of His kingdom and His spirit: and now as Moses[71] said to the levitical schismatics, Corah and his company, so I may say to you, "Seemeth it but a small thing unto you that the God of Israel hath separated you from the congregation of Israel to bring you to Himself, to do the service of the tabernacle of the Lord, and to stand before the congregation to minister to them? And He hath brought thee near to Him." Certainly if of every one of the christian congregation God expects a holiness that mingles with no unclean thing; if God will not suffer of them a lukewarm and an indifferent service, but requires zeal of His glory, and that which S. Paul calls the "labour of love"; if He will have them to be without spot or wrinkle, or any such thing; if He will not endure any pollution in their flesh or spirit; if He requires that their bodies, and souls, and spirits be kept blameless unto the coming of the Lord Jesus; if He accepts of none of the people unless they have within them the conjugation of all christian graces; if He calls on them to abound in every grace, and that in all the periods of their progression unto the ends of their lives, and to the consummation and perfection of grace; if He hath made them lights in the world, and the salt of the earth, to enlighten others by their good example, and to teach them and invite

---

70. Exod. 18:19.
71. Num. 16:9.

them by holy discourses, and wise counsels, and speech seasoned with salt; what is it think ye, or with what words is it possible to express what God requires of you? They are to be examples of good life to one another, but you are to be examples even of the examples themselves; that's your duty, that's the purpose of God, and that's the design of my text, that "in all things ye shew yourselves a pattern of good works; in doctrine shewing uncorruptness, gravity, sincerity, sound speech that cannot be condemned; that he that is of the contrary part may be ashamed, having no evil thing to say of you."

A Form of Administration
of the Holy Sacrament
of Baptism[72]

Pure water being provided and put into the fount, or into a lavatory of silver, or some other clean vessel, fit and decent for this sacred action; the minister being vested in an ecclesiastical habit, shall begin with this exhortation.

Dearly Beloved Brethren,

Forasmuch as from our first parents we derive nothing but flesh and corruption: and that flesh and blood cannot inherit the kingdom of heaven; it is necessary that every man who is reckoned in Adam should be also reckoned in Christ, that every one who is born of the flesh be also born again, and born of the Spirit, that every son of man by nature may become the son of God by adoption, be incorporated into Christ, intitled to the promises, and become heir of heaven by grace and faith in Jesus Christ: and that this cannot be done but by being admitted to the covenant of grace in baptism, our blessed Saviour saying that "except a man be born again of water and of the Spirit, he cannot enter into the kingdom of God": Let us humbly and devoutly pray unto God in the name of our Lord Jesus Christ, that He will be pleased to send down His holy spirit upon these waters of baptism, that they may become to this infant a laver of regeneration, and a well of water springing up to life eternal; and that this infant may be admitted to the covenant of grace and pardon, of mercy and holiness, receiving from grace what by nature he cannot have, that being baptized in water to the remission of sins, he may all his life walk in this covenant of grace and holiness, as a lively member of the holy church, which is the mystical body of Christ our head.

---

72. *Works* 8:631ff.

I.

O Almighty and eternal God, Father of men and angels, Lord of heaven and earth, whose Spirit moving upon the waters at the beginning of the world produced every living and every moving creature: Thou by the flood of waters didst wash away the iniquity of the old world, and by preserving to Thyself a generation of holy persons, whom Thou didst bring up from those waters, didst consign to us a type of regeneration: Look, O Lord, graciously upon the face of Thy church, and multiply in her Thy regenerations, and the new-births of Thy spirit. With the abundance of Thy grace make Thy holy city to rejoice, and still open this holy fountain of baptism, for the reformation and sanctification of all the nations of the world; that Thy blessed spirit sanctifying these waters, a new and heavenly offspring may hence arise, full of health and light; that human nature, which was made after Thy own image, being reformed and restored to the honour of its first beginning, may be cleansed from all the impure adherencies of sin, preserved from the dominion of it, and rescued from all its sad effects, that what shall be so born in the womb of the church, may dwell in the house of God, and reign with Thee for ever in the inheritance of our blessed Lord and Saviour Jesus. *Amen.*

II.

Our blessed Lord and Saviour Jesus, who was baptized of John in Jordan, who walked upon the waters, who converted water into wine, who out of His precious side shed forth blood and water, the two sacraments of life, unto His holy church, and commanded His disciples to teach all nations, baptizing them with water in the name of the Father, of the Son, and of the holy Ghost: He bless and sanctify by His holy spirit this water, that it may be instrumental and effective of grace, of pardon and sanctification: hear us, O most gracious God, that whosoever shall be baptized in this water may be renewed by Thy grace, justified by Thy mercy, sanctified by Thy spirit, preserved by Thy providence, and guided by Thy word, that in this water, springing from the paradise of God, the soul [or souls] presented unto Thee may be cleansed and purified, and that there may be added to Thy church daily such as shall be saved in the day of Thy glorious appearing, O blessed Lord and Saviour Jesus. *Amen.*

Then the minister and people arising from their knees, the
following gospel shall be read

Hear the words of the holy gospel written by S. Matthew, in the
third chapter, etc.

Verse 13 to verse 17 inclusively

"Then cometh Jesus from Galilee to Jordan unto John to be baptized of him. But John forbad Him, saying, I have need to be baptized of
Thee, and comest Thou to me? And Jesus answering said unto him,
Suffer it to be so now, for thus it becometh us to fulfil all righteousness.
Then he suffered Him. And Jesus when He was baptized went up
straightway out of the water, and lo, the heavens were opened unto
Him, and He saw the Spirit of God descending like a dove, and lighting
upon Him. And lo, a voice from heaven saying, This is My beloved Son,
in whom I am well pleased."
Hear likewise what S. Mark writeth in his tenth chapter.

Verse 13 and 17 exclusively

"The Jews brought children [to Christ] that He should touch them:
and His disciples rebuked those that brought them; but when Jesus saw
it, He was much displeased, and said unto them, Suffer the little children to come unto Me, and forbid them not, for of such is the kingdom
of God. Verily I say unto you, whosoever shall not receive the kingdom
of God as a little child, he shall not enter therein. And He took them up
in His arms, put His hands upon them and blessed them."

Friends,
In these gospels you see the actions and hear the words of our
blessed Saviour; how He commanded little children to be brought unto
Him, how He rebuked those that would have kept them away, how
readily He blessed them, how kindly He embraced them, how He
pronounced them capable of and entitled to the kingdom of God; how
He commanded us to receive the kingdom as infants received it, and
affirmed that we can no way receive it but by being like them. You
know also that although Christ commanded them to be brought unto
Him, there is no ordinary and appointed way for infants to come to

Christ, and no way possible for them to be brought to Christ, but by this new birth and regeneration in the laver of baptism. You see also by the example and words of our blessed Lord himself, that even the most innocent persons ought to be baptized; for He himself who knew no sin, was yet baptized in the baptism of repentance, and so to do was the fulfilling of righteousness: We may therefore easily perceive that the innocence of infants, and their freedom from actual sin, cannot excuse them from baptism; and if we remember, that although our blessed Saviour required faith of them who came to be healed of their diseases, yet by the faith of others[73] who came in behalf of such as could not be brought, or could not come, the sick person was healed; we are sufficiently instructed, that although infants have no more actual faith than they have actual sin, yet the faith of others can be, and is by the usual and revealed method of the divine mercy, as well imputed to them to the purposes of grace and life, as the sin of Adam can be imputed to the purposes of death; that as in Adam all die, so in Christ all should be made alive. We may therefore from these certain evidences conclude that God alloweth in you this obedience and charity, in bringing this child to Christ to receive all blessings of which he is capable, a title to the promises, and adoption to be the child of God, a sanctification by the Spirit, a designation to the service of Christ, and putting him into the order of eternal life. Therefore "The uncircumcised child, whose flesh is not circumcised, that soul shall be cut off from his people": so baptism, which is now the seal of the same faith[74] and the same righteousness, and a figure like unto the former, is to be administered to infants, although they have no more actual faith than the children of the Israelites had; our blessed Saviour having made baptism as necessary in the New testament, as circumcision in the Old. For because little children can receive the kingdom of God, and in infants there is no incapacity of receiving the mercies of God, the adoption to be children of God, a title to the promises, the covenant of repentance, and a right to pardon; whosoever shall deny to baptize infants, when he is justly required, is sacrilegious and uncharitable. Since therefore the church of God hath so great, so clear, so indubitable a warrant to baptize infants, and therefore did always practise it let us humbly and charitably give thanks to God for His great mercies unto us all, and with meekness and love recommend this child to the grace of God.

---

73. Matt. 8:13, 9:28; John 4:50; Mark 9:23.
74. Rom. 4:11–13; Gal. 3:14.

HEAVENLY SACRIFICE AND EARTHLY SACRAMENTS

I.

O Almighty and eternal God, who hast redeemed us from sin and shame, from the gates of hell and the sting of death, and from ignorance and darkness, by Thy holy Son, who is that light which lighteneth every man that cometh into the world; we praise and glorify Thy name, that Thou hast called us to the knowledge of Thy will, and the love of Thy name, and the service of Thy majesty, which is perfect freedom, the freedom of the sons of God.

II.

As Thou hast dealt graciously with us, so deal with this infant, whom we humbly bring and offer to our blessed Saviour Jesus, that He should receive him, and bless him with the blessings of an everlasting love. Receive him, O most gracious Lord, who is Thy child by creation, make him Thine also by adoption into Thy covenant of grace and favour; let him be consigned with Thy sacrament, be admitted into Christ's kingdom, enter into His warfare, believe His doctrine, labour and hope for His promises; that this child, witnessing here a good confession, may have his understanding for ever brought unto the obedience, his affections to the love, and all his faculties to the service of Christ; and after he hath served Thee in his generation, he may receive his part and portion in Thy glory, through Jesus Christ our Lord.

Then arising from their knees, the minister shall say unto the godfathers and godmothers as followeth:

Well-beloved friends, you have brought this child to be presented unto Christ as a servant of His laws and a disciple of His doctrine, ye have prayed that God would receive him and give him a portion in the gospel and kingdom of His Son; ye have heard what promises God hath made on His part, and ye believe and know all His words are yea and amen, and not one tittle of them shall pass unaccomplished; now therefore because it is a covenant of grace and favour on God's part, and of faith and obedience on ours, though God prevents us with His grace, and begins to do for us before we can do any thing for Him, yet you, under whose power this child is, and by whose faith and charity this child comes to Christ in holy baptism, must also on his [or her] behalf promise that he will forsake the devil and all his wicked works, that he

243

will faithfully believe Christ's holy gospel, and dutifully keep all Christ's commandments.

Minister. Dost thou abjure and renounce and promise to forsake the devil and all his wicked works, not to listen to his temptations, not to be led by the flesh, by the vain powers of the world, by carnal or covetous desires, but thou wilt be the servant of the Lord Jesus?

Answer. I forsake them all, and will be a servant of Jesus.

Minister. Dost thou believe in God the Father almighty, maker of heaven and earth? And in Jesus Christ His only-begotten Son our Lord; and that He was conceived by the holy Ghost, born of the virgin Mary; that He suffered under Pontius Pilate, was crucified, dead, and buried; that He went down into hell, and also did rise again the third day; that He ascended into heaven, and sitteth at the right hand of God the Father almighty; and from thence He shall come again at the end of the world to judge the quick and the dead? And dost thou believe in the holy Ghost; the holy catholic church; the communion of saints; the remission of sins; the resurrection of the flesh; and everlasting life after death?

Answer. All this I will profess and stedfastly believe.

Minister. Wilt thou be baptized into this faith?

Answer. That is my desire.

LET US PRAY.

O Almighty God, who hast given the promise of Thy spirit to us and to our children, even to as many as the Lord our God shall call; Give Thy holy spirit to this infant, that the evil spirits of darkness may not take Thy portion from Thee, nor hurt the body, nor deceive the understanding, nor corrupt the will, nor tempt the affections of this infant; but that Thy spirit, who bloweth where it listeth, and no man knows whence He cometh nor whither He goeth, may be in this child as the seed of God springing up to life eternal, that the kingdom of God which is within, and cometh not with observation, may early rule and conduct this infant, prevent the folly of his childhood from growing up to sins in his youth, and may work strongly in him when his weakness, his ignorances, and temptations are most powerful to prevail upon him; that from his cradle to his grave he may be guided by the Spirit of God in the paths of the divine commandments. Admit him, O God, into the bosom of the church, into the arms of Thy mercy, into a right of the promises, into the service of Christ, into the communion of saints; and give him power to become the son of God: that being buried with Christ in baptism, he may also rise with Him through the faith of the operation of God, through the same our blessed Lord and Saviour Jesus Christ. *Amen.*

Then the minister of the sacrament shall take the child in his arms, and ask the name.

Then naming the child aloud, he shall dip the head or face or body of the child in the water, saying,

N. I baptize thee in the name of the Father, and of the Son, and of the holy Ghost;

dipping the head at the naming of the holy Trinity.

If the child be weak, or any other great cause intervene, it may suffice, instead of dipping, to sprinkle water on the face, using the same form of words.

Then shall the priest make the sign of the cross upon the child's forehead, saying,

We sign this child with the sign of the cross, and enrol him a soldier under the banner of Christ, to signify, and as a ceremony to represent, that the duty of this and all baptized persons is manfully to fight under the banner of Christ against the flesh, the world, and the devil, all the days of their life; and by the power which Christ our blessed Lord, who hath the key of David, hath given unto me, I admit this child into the communion of saints, into the bosom of the visible church, the kingdom of grace, and the title to the promises evangelical, and the hopes of glory.

Our blessed Lord and Saviour Jesus, who when He had overcome the sharpness of death did open the kingdom of heaven to all believers, and gave unto His church the keys of the kingdom, that His ministers might let into it all that come to Him: He of His infinite goodness and truth make good His gracious promises upon this infant, that what we do on earth according to His will He may confirm in heaven by His spirit and by His word, to the glory of the blessed and undivided Trinity, God the Father Son, and holy Ghost. *Amen.*

Then shall the minister add this invitation

Seeing now, dearly beloved, that this infant hath received holy baptism, and is washed in the laver of regeneration, admitted into the bosom of the church, into the covenant of faith and repentance, pardon and holiness; let us give thanks to God for these graces, and pray that this child may lead his life according to the present undertaking.

I.

We give thee thanks and praise, O heavenly and most gracious Father, that it hath pleased Thee to call this child to Thy holy baptism, to renew him with Thy holy spirit, to admit him into the church, to adopt him for Thy child, and to receive him unto the profession of Thy faith: and we humbly beseech Thee to grant unto him Thy grace to accompany him all the days of his life, that he may hold fast the profession of his faith, making his calling and election sure, that his body being washed in pure water, and he tasting of the heavenly gift, being made partaker of the holy Ghost, and sprinkled in his heart from an evil conscience, he may follow Thee in the regeneration, and after the end of this life he may for ever be with them who have washed their robes and made them white in the blood of the Lamb. Grant this, O God our Father, through Jesus Christ our blessed Saviour and Redeemer.

II.

O most holy, most gracious Saviour Jesus, who lovest Thy church and hast given Thyself for it, that Thou mayest sanctify and cleanse it with the washing of water in the word: Do Thou with Thy holy spirit enlighten, and with Thy word instruct the understanding of this child, that he may live by faith, and may receive the secrets of Thy kingdom, and know Thy will, and obey Thy laws, and promote Thy glory.

III.

O God, be Thou his father for ever, Christ his elder brother and his Lord, the church his mother; let the body of Christ be his food, the blood of Christ his drink, and the Spirit the earnest of his inheritance. Let faith be his learning, religion his employment, his whole life be spiritual, heaven the object of his hopes and the end of his labours; let him be Thy servant in the kingdom of grace, and Thy son in the kingdom of glory, through Jesus Christ our Lord. *Amen.*

Then shall the priest add this blessing

Our blessed Lord God, the Father of men and angels, who hath sent forth His angels ministers, appointing them to minister to the good of them who shall be heirs of salvation: He of His mercy and goodness send His holy angel to be the guardian of this child, and keep him from the danger and violence of fire and water, of falls and sad accidents, from evil tongues and evil eyes, from witchcraft and all impressions of the spirits of darkness, from convulsions and rickets, from madness and stupidity, from folly and evil principles, from bad examples and from evil teachers, from crookedness and deformity, from the mutilation of a member or the loss of sense, from being useless and unprofitable, from being impious, harsh-natured, and unreasonable; and make him a wise, useful, and a holy person, beloved of men and beloved of God, through Jesus Christ our Lord. Amen. Amen.

You the godfathers and godmothers of the child, as you have done this charity to the infant to bring him to holy baptism, so you must be sure to continue your care over him till he be instructed in his duty, taught what vow he hath made by you, and how he shall perform it. To this purpose you shall take care that he may learn the Lord's prayer, the apostles' creed, and the commandments of our Lord; that he may know how to pray, what to believe, and what to practise: and when he is in all these things competently instructed, neglect not any opportunity of bringing him to the bishop, that he, by imposition of hands and invocation of the holy Spirit of God, may procure blessing and spiritual strength to this child. Which duty when you have done, you are discharged of this trust, and from the mercies of God may humbly hope for the reward of your charity.

SO ENDS THE OFFICE OF BAPTISM.

Baptism[75]

Considerations upon the baptizing of the holy Jesus.

1. When the day did break, and the Baptist was busy in his offices, the Sun of righteousness soon entered upon our hemisphere; and after He had lived a life of darkness and silence for thirty years together, yet now that He came to do the greatest work in the world, and to minister in the most honourable embassy, He would do nothing of singularity, but fulfil all righteousness, and satisfy all commands, and join in the common rites and sacraments which all people, innocent or penitent, did undergo, either as deleteries of sin or instruments of grace. For so He would needs be baptized by His servant; and though He was of purity sufficient to do it, and did actually by His baptism purify the purifier, and sanctify that and all other streams to a holy ministry and effect, yet He went in, bowing His head like a sinner, unclothing Himself like an imperfect person, and craving to be washed as if He had been crusted with an impure leprosy; thereby teaching us to submit ourselves to all those rites which He would institute; and although some of them be, like the baptism of John, joined with confession of sins and publication of our infirmities, yet it were better for us to lay by our loads and wash our ulcers, than by concealing them out of vainer desires of impertinent reputation, cover our disease till we are heartsick and die. But when so holy a person does all the pious ministries of the more imperfect, it is a demonstration to us that a life common and ordinary, without affectation or singularity, is the most prudent and safe. Every great change, every violence of fortune, all eminencies and uneven-nesses whatsoever, whether of person, or accident, or circumstance, puts us to a new trouble, requires a distinct care, creates new dangers, objects more temptations, marks us out the object of envy, makes our standing more insecure, and our fall more contemptible and ridiculous. But an even life, spent with as much rigour of duty to God as ought to

---

75. *Works* 2:193ff.

be, yet in the same manner of devotions, in the susception of ordinary offices, in bearing public burdens, frequenting public assemblies, performing offices of civility, receiving all the rites of an established religion, complying with national customs and hereditary solemnities of a people; in nothing disquieting public peace, or disrelishing the great instruments of an innocent communion, or dissolving the circumstantial ligaments of charity, or breaking laws and the great relations and necessitudes of the world out of fancy or singularity, is the best way to live holily, and safely, and happily; safer from sin and envy, and more removed from trouble and temptation.

2. When Jesus came to John to be baptized, John out of humility and modesty refused Him; but when Jesus by reduplication of His desire, fortifying it with a command, made it in the Baptist to become a duty, then he obeyed. And so also did the primitive clerks refuse to do offices of great dignity and highest ministry; looking through the honour upon the danger, and passing by the dignity, they considered the charge of the cure, and knew that the eminency of the office was in all senses insecure to the person, till by command and peremptory injunction of their superiors it was put past a dispute, and became necessary, and that either they must perish instantly in the ruins and precipices of disobedience, or put it to the hazard and a fair venture, for a brighter crown or a bigger damnation. I wish also this care were entailed, and did descend upon all ages of the church; for the ambitious seeking of dignities and prelacies ecclesiastical is grown the pest of the church, and corrupts the salt itself, and extinguishes the lights, and gives too apparent evidences to the world that neither the end is pure, nor the intention sanctified, nor the person innocent, but the purpose ambitious or covetous, and the person vicious; and the very entrance into church offices is with an impure torch, and a foul hand, or a heart empty of the affections of religion, or thoughts of doing God's work. I do not think the present age is to be treated with concerning denying to accept rich prelacies and pompous dignities; but it were but reasonable that the main intention and intellectual design should be, to appreciate and esteem the office and employment to be of greatest consideration. It is lawful to desire a bishoprick; neither can the unwillingness to accept it be in a prudent account adjudged the aptest disposition to receive it, (especially if done in ceremony, just in the instant of their entertainment of it, and possibly after a long ambition:) but yet it were well if we remember that such desires must be sanctified with holy care and diligence in the office; for the honey is guarded with thousands of little sharp stings and dangers;

and it will be a sad account if we be called to audit for the crimes of our diocese, after our own tallies are made even; and he that believes his own load to be big enough, and trembles at the apprehension of the horrors of doom's day, is not very wise if he takes up those burdens which he sees have crushed their bearers, and presses his own shoulders till the bones crack, only because the bundles are wrapped in white linen and bound with silken cords. "He that desires the office of a bishop, desires a good work," saith St. Paul; and therefore we must not look on it for the fair-spreading sails and the beauteous streamers which the favour of princes hath put to it to make it sail fairer and more secure against the dangers of secular discomforts, but upon the burden it bears. Prelacy is a good work; and a good work well done is very honourable, and shall be rewarded; but he that considers the infinite dangers of miscarrying, and that the loss of the ship will be imputed to the pilot, may think it many times the safest course to put God or his superiors to the charge of a command, before he undertakes such great ministries: and he that enters in by the force of authority, as he himself receives a testimony of his worth and aptness to the employment, so he gives the world another, that his search for it was not criminal nor his person immodest; and by his weighty apprehension of his dangers he will consider his work, and obtain a grace to do it diligently and to be accepted graciously: and this was the modesty and prudence of the Baptist.

3. "When Jesus was baptized, He prayed, and the heavens were opened." External rites of divine institution receive benediction and energy from above, but it is by the mediation of prayer; for there is nothing ritual, but it is also joined with something moral,[76] and required on our part, in all persons capable of the use of reason; that we may understand that the blessings of religion are works and graces too, God therefore requiring us to do something, not that we may glory in it, but that we may estimate the grace, and go to God for it in the means of His own hallowing. Naaman had been stupid, if when the prophet bade him wash seven times in Jordan for his cure, he had not confessed the cure to be wrought by the God of Israel and the ministry of His prophet, but had made himself the author because of his obedience to the enjoined condition; and it is but a weak fancy to derogate from God's grace and

---

76. 1 Cor. 10:1–3; Gal. 3:14; 1 Pet. 3:21; 1 Cor. 12:7.

the glory and the freedom of it, because He bids us wash before we are cleansed, and pray when we are washed, and commands us to ask before we shall receive. But this also is true from this instance, that the external rite of sacrament is so instrumental in a spiritual grace, that it never does it but with the conjunction of something moral: and this truth is of so great persuasion in the Greek church;[77] that the mystery of consecration in the venerable eucharist is amongst them attributed not to any mystical words and secret operations of syllables, but to the efficacy of the prayers of the church in the just imitation of the whole action and the rite of institution. And the purpose of it is, that we might secure the excellence and holiness of such predispositions and concomitant graces, which are necessary to the worthy and effectual susception of the external rites of Christianity.

4. After the holy Jesus was baptized, and had prayed, the heavens opened, the holy Ghost descended, and a voice from heaven proclaimed Him to be the Son of God, and one in whom the Father was well pleased; and the same ointment that was cast upon the head of our High priest, went unto His beard, and thence fell to the borders of His garment: for as Christ our Head felt these effects in manifestation, so the church believes God does to her and to her meanest children, in the susception of the holy rite of baptism in right, apt, and holy dispositions. For the heavens open too upon us; and the holy Ghost descends, to sanctify the waters, and to hallow the catechumen, and to pardon the past and repented sins, and to consign him to the inheritance of sons, and to put on his military girdle, and give him the sacrament and oath of fidelity; for all this is understood to be meant by those frequent expressions of scripture, calling baptism, "the laver of regeneration, illumination, a washing away the filth of the flesh, and the answer of a good conscience, a being buried with Christ,"[78] and many others of the like purpose and signification. But we may also learn hence, sacredly to esteem the rites of religion, which He first sanctified by His own personal susception, and then made necessary by His own institution and command; and God hath made to be conveyances of blessing, and ministries of the holy Spirit.

5. "The holy Ghost descended upon Jesus in the manner or visible

---

77. Justin, *Apology*, PG 6. 427.
78. Eph. 5:26; Heb. 10:32; 1 Pet. 3:21; Rom. 6:4.

representment of a dove"; either in similitude of figure which He was pleased to assume, as the church more generally hath believed; or at least He did descend like a dove, and in His robe of fire hovered over the Baptist's head, and then "sat upon him," as the dove uses to sit upon the house of her dwelling; whose proprieties of nature are pretty and modest hieroglyphics of the duty of spiritual persons, which are thus observed in both philosophies. The dove sings not, but mourns; it hath no gall, strikes not with its bill, hath no crooked talons, and forgets its young ones soonest of any of the inhabitants of the air. And the effects of the holy Spirit are symbolical in all the sons of sanctification: for the voice of the church is sad in those accents which express her own condition; but as the dove is not so sad in her breast as in her note, so neither is the interior condition of the church wretched and miserable, but indeed her song is most of it elegy within her own walls; and her condition looks sad, and her joys are not pleasures in the public estimate, but they that afflict her think her miserable because they know not the sweetnesses of a holy peace and serenity which supports her spirit, and plains the heart under a rugged brow, making the soul festival under the noise of a threne and sadder groanings. But the sons of consolation are also taught their duty by this apparition; for upon whomsoever the Spirit descends, He teaches him to be meek and charitable, neither offending by the violence of hands or looser language. For the dove is inoffensive in beak and foot, and feels no disturbance and violence of passions when its dearest interests are destroyed; that we also may be of an even spirit in the saddest accidents which usually discompose our peace: and however such symbolical intimations receive their efficacy from the fancy of the contriver; yet here, whether this apparition did intend any such moral representment or no, it is certain that wherever the holy Spirit does dwell, there also peace and sanctity, meekness and charity, a mortified will and an active dereliction of our desires, do inhabit. But besides this hieroglyphical representment, this dove, like that which Noah sent out from the ark, did aptly signify the world to be renewed, and all to be turned to a new creation; and God hath made a new covenant with us, that unless we provoke Him, He will never destroy us any more.

6. No sooner had the voice of God pronounced Jesus to be the well-beloved Son of God, but the devil thought it of great concernment to attempt Him with all his malice and his art; and that is the condition of all those whom God's grace hath separated from the common expectations and societies of the world: and therefore the son of Sirach gave

good advice, "My son, if thou come to serve the Lord, prepare thy soul for temptation";[79] for not only the spirits of darkness are exasperated at the declension of their own kingdom, but also the nature and constitution of virtues and eminent graces which holy persons exercise in their lives, is such as to be easily assailable by their contraries, apt to be lessened by time, to be interrupted by weariness, to grow flat and insipid by tediousness of labour, to be omitted and grow infrequent by the impertinent diversions of society and secular occasions; so that to rescind the ligaments of vice made firm by nature and evil habits, to acquire every new degree of virtue, to continue the holy fires of zeal in their just proportion, to overcome the devil, and to reject the invitations of the world and the softer embraces of the flesh, which are the proper employment of the sons of God, is a perpetual difficulty; and every possibility of prevaricating the strictnesses of a duty, is a temptation and an insecurity to them who have begun to serve God in hard battles. . . .

---

79. Eccles. 2:1.

A Discourse
of Confirmation[80]

INTRODUCTION

Next to the incarnation of the Son of God and the whole economy of our redemption wrought by Him in an admirable order and conjugation of glorious mercies, the greatest thing that ever God did to the world is the giving to us the Holy Ghost; and possibly this is the consummation and perfection of the other. For in the work of redemption Christ indeed made a new world; we are wholly a new creation, and we must be so: and therefore when S. John began the narrative of the gospel, he began in a manner and style very like to Moses in his history of the first creation; "In the beginning was the Word," etc. "All things were made by Him, and without Him was not any thing made that was made." But as in the creation the matter was first; there were indeed heavens and earth and waters, but all this was rude and "without form," till "the Spirit of God moved upon the face of the waters": so it is in the new creation. We are a new mass, redeemed with the blood of Christ, rescued from an evil portion and made candidates of heaven and immortality; but we are but an embryo in the regeneration until the Spirit of God enlivens us and moves again upon the waters, and then every subsequent motion and operation is from the Spirit of God. "We cannot say that Jesus is the Lord, but by the Holy Ghost"; by Him we live, in Him we walk, by His aids we pray, by His emotions we desire; we breathe, and sigh, and groan by Him; He "helps" us in all "our infirmities," and He gives us all our strengths; He reveals mysteries to us and teaches us all our duties; He stirs us up to holy desires and He actuates those desires; He "makes us to will and to do of His good pleasure."

For the Spirit of God is that in our spiritual life that a man's soul is in his natural, without it we are but a dead and lifeless trunk. But then as

---

80. *Works* 5:615ff.

a man's soul in proportion to the several operations of life obtains several appellatives; it is vegetative and nutritive, sensitive and intellective, according as it operates: so is the Spirit of God. He is the spirit of regeneration in baptism, of renovation in repentance; the spirit of love and the spirit of holy fear; the searcher of the hearts and the spirit of discerning; the spirit of wisdom and the spirit of prayer. In one mystery He illuminates and in another He feeds us; He begins in one and finishes and perfects in another. It is the same spirit working divers operations. For He is all this now reckoned and He is every thing else that is the principle of good unto us; He is the beginning and the progression, the consummation and perfection of us all; and yet every work of His is perfect in its kind and in order to His own designation, and from the beginning to the end is perfection all the way. Justifying and sanctifying grace is the proper entitative product in all, but it hath divers appellatives and connotations in the several rites; and yet even then also because of the identity of the principle, the similitude and general consonancy in the effect, the same appellative is given, and the same effect imputed to more than one; and yet none of them can be omitted, when the great master of the family hath blessed it and given it institution. Thus S. Dionys[81] calls baptism "the perfection of the divine birth"; and yet the baptized person must receive other mysteries which are more signally perfective: *HĒ TOY MYROY CHRISIS TELEIOTIKĒ* confirmation is yet more "perfective," and is properly the perfection of baptism.

By baptism we are heirs, and are adopted to the inheritance of sons, admitted to the covenant of repentance, and engaged to live a good life; yet this is but the solemnity of the covenant, which must pass into after-acts by other influences of the same divine principle. Until we receive the spirit of obsignation or confirmation, we are but "babes in Christ" in the meanest sense, infants that can do nothing, that cannot speak, that cannot resist any violence, exposed to every rudeness and perishing by every temptation.

But therefore as God at first appointed us a ministry of a new birth, so also hath He given to His church the consequent ministry of a new strength. The Spirit moved a little upon the waters of baptism, and gave us the principles of life, but in confirmation He makes us able to move ourselves. In the first He is the spirit of life, but in this He is the spirit

---

81. Pseudo-Dionysius, *On Church Hierarchy*, PG 3. 391.

of strength and motion. *Baptisma est nativitas, unguentum vero est nobis actionis instar et motus,* said Cabasilas.[82] "In baptism we are intitled to the inheritance; but because we are in our infancy and minority, the father gives unto his sons a tutor, a guardian and a teacher in confirmation," said Rupertus:[83] that as we are baptized into the death and resurrection of Christ, so in confirmation we may be renewed in the inner man, and strengthened in all our holy vows and purposes by the Holy Ghost ministered according to God's ordinance. . . .

Now if we will understand in general what excellent fruits are consequent to this dispensation, we may best receive the notice of them from the fountain itself, our blessed Saviour. "He that believes, out of his belly, as the scripture saith, shall flow rivers of living waters. But this He spake of the Spirit, which they that believe on Him should receive."[84] This is evidently spoken of the Spirit which came down in Pentecost, which was promised to all that should believe in Christ, and which the apostles ministered by imposition of hands, the Holy Ghost himself being the expositor; and it can signify no less but that a spring of life should be put into the heart of the confirmed, to water the plants of God; that they should become trees, not only planted by the water side (for so it was in David's time and in all the ministry of the Old testament) but having a river of living water within them to make them fruitful of good works, and bringing their fruit in due season, fruits worthy of amendment of life.

1. But the principal thing is this: confirmation is the consummation and perfection, the corroboration and strength of baptism and baptismal grace; for in baptism we undertake to do our duty, but in confirmation we receive strength to do it; in baptism others promise for us, in confirmation we undertake for ourselves, we ease our godfathers and godmothers of their burden, and take it upon our own shoulders, together with the advantage of the prayers of the bishop and all the church made then on our behalf; in baptism we give up our names to Christ, but in confirmation we put our seal to the profession, and God puts His seal to the promise. It is very remarkable what S. Paul says of the beginnings of our being Christians, "the word of the beginning of Christ"; Christ begins with us, He gives us His word and admits us, and

---

82. Cabasilas, *Life in Christ*, PG 150. 522.
83. Rupert of Deutz (†1129), *Liturgical Observances*, PL 170. 139.
84. John 7:33.

we by others' hands are brought in; it is "the form of doctrine unto which ye were delivered."[85] Cajetan observes right, that this is a new and emphatical way of speaking: we are wholly immerged in our fundamentals; other things are delivered to us, but we are delivered up unto these. This is done in baptism and catechism; and what was the event of it? "Being then made free from sin, ye became the servants of righteousness."[86] Your baptism was for the remission of sins there, and then ye were made free from that bondage; and what then? why then in the next place, when ye came to consummate this procedure, when the baptized was confirmed, then he became a servant of righteousness, that is, then the Holy Ghost descended upon you, and enabled you to walk in the Spirit; then the seed of God was first thrown into your hearts by a celestial influence. *Spiritus sanctus in baptisterio plenitudinem tribuit ad innocentiam, sed in confirmatione augmentum præstat ad gratiam,* said Eusebius Emissenus[87]: in baptism we are made innocent, in confirmation we receive the increase of the Spirit of grace; in that we are regenerated unto life, in this we are strengthened unto battle. *Dono sapientiæ illuminamur, ædificamur, erudimur, instruimur, confirmamur, ut illam sancti Spiritus vocem audire possimus, Intellectum tibi dabo, et instruam te in hac via qua gradieris,* said P. Melchiades, "we are enlightened by the gift of wisdom, we are built up, taught, instructed and confirmed, so that we may hear that voice of the Holy Spirit, 'I will give unto thee an understanding heart, and teach thee in the way wherein thou shalt walk.' " For so,

> Signari populos effuso pignore sancto,
> Mirandæ virtutis opus,[88]

"it is a work of great and wonderful power when the holy pledge of God is poured forth upon the people." This is that power from on high which first descended in Pentecost, and afterward was ministered by prayer and imposition of the apostolical and episcopal hands, and comes after the other gift of remission of sins. *Vides quod non simpliciter hoc fit, sed multa opus est virtute ut detur Spiritus sanctus, non enim idem est assequi remissionem peccatorum et accipere virtutem illam,* said S. Chry-

---

85. Rom. 6:17.
86. Rom. 6:18.
87. Eusebius, quoting Pope Melchiades, PG 20. 879.
88. Tertullian, *Against Marcion,* PL 2. 249.

sostom[89] "you see that this is not easily done, but there is need of much power from on high to give the Holy Spirit, for it is not all one to obtain remission of sins and to have received this virtue or power from above." *Quamvis enim continuo transituris sufficiant regenerationis beneficia, victuris tamen necessaria sunt confirmationis auxilia,* said Melchiades; "although to them that die presently the benefits of regeneration (baptismal) are sufficient, yet to them that live the auxiliaries of confirmation are necessary." For according to the saying of S. Leo[90] in his epistle to Nicetas the bishop of Aquileia, commanding that heretics returning to the church should be confirmed with invocation of the Holy Spirit and imposition of hands, "they have only received the form of baptism *sine sanctificationis virtute,* without the virtue of sanctification"; meaning that this is the proper effect of confirmation. For in short, "although the newly-listed soldiers in human warfare are enrolled in the number of them that are to fight, yet they are not brought to battle till they be more trained and exercised: so although by baptism every one is ascribed into the catalogue of believers, yet he receives more strength and grace for the sustaining and overcoming the temptations of the flesh, the world, and the devil, only by imposition of the bishop's hands." They are words which I borrowed from a late synod at Rhemes.[91] That's the first remark of blessing; in confirmation we receive strength to do all that which was for us undertaken in baptism: for the apostles themselves (as the holy fathers observe) were timorous in the faith until they were confirmed in Pentecost, but after the reception of the Holy Ghost they waxed valiant in the faith and in all their spiritual combats.

2. In confirmation we receive the Holy Ghost as the earnest of our inheritance, as the seal of our salvation: "we therefore call it a seal or signature, as being a guard and custody to us, and a sign of the Lord's dominion over us."[92] The confirmed person is "a sheep that is marked," which thieves do not so easily steal and carry away. To the same purpose are those words of Theodoret[93]: "remember that holy mystagogy, in which they who were initiated, after the renouncing that tyrant (the devil and all his works) and the confession of the true king (Jesus

---

89. Chrysostom, *Homily on Acts*, PG 60. 141.
90. Leo, *Letters*, PL 54. 1135.
91. Flodoard of Reims, *The Annals of Flodoard*, PL 135. 491.
92. Gregory Nazianzen, *Orations*, PG 36. 362.
93. Theodoret of Cyrus, *Canticle of Canticles*, PG 81. 27.

Christ), have received the chrism of spiritual unction like a royal signature, by that unction, as in a shadow, perceiving the invisible grace of
the most Holy Spirit." That is, in confirmation we are sealed for the
service of God and unto the day of redemption; then it is that the seal of
God is had by us, "The Lord knoweth who are His." *Quomodo vero
dices, Dei sum, si notas non produxeris?* said S. Basil,[94] "How can any man
say I am God's sheep unless he produce the marks?" *Signati estis Spiritu
promissionis per sanctissimum divinum Spiritum, Domini grex effecti
sumus,* said Theophylact.[95] "When we are thus sealed by the most holy
and divine Spirit of promise, then we are truly of the Lord's flock, and
marked with His seal": that is, when we are rightly confirmed, then He
descends into our souls; and though He does not operate (it may be)
presently, but as the reasonable soul works in its due time and by the
order of nature, by opportunities and new fermentations and actualities;
so does the Spirit of God; when He is brought into use, when He is
prayed for with love and assiduity, when He is caressed tenderly, when
He is used lovingly, when we obey His motions readily, when we
delight in His words greatly, then we find it true that the soul had a new
life put into her, a principle of perpetual actions: but the "tree planted
by the water's side" does not presently bear fruit, but "in its due
season. . . ."

To Christians that sin after these ministrations there is only left a
expergiscimini, that they "arise from slumber," and stir up the graces of
the Holy Ghost. Every man ought to be careful that he "do not grieve
the Holy Spirit"; but if he does, yet let him not quench Him, for that is a
desperate case. *PHYLATTE TON PHYLAKTIKON* the Holy Spirit is the great
conservative of the new life; only "keep the keeper," take care that the
Spirit of God do not depart from you: for the great ministry of the Spirit
is but once; for as baptism is, so is confirmation.

I end this discourse with a plain exhortation out of S. Ambrose[96]
upon those words of S. Paul, "He that confirmeth us with you in Christ
is God." "Remember that thou, who hast been confirmed, hast received
the spiritual signature, the spirit of wisdom and understanding, the
spirit of counsel and strength, the spirit of knowledge and godliness, the
spirit of holy fear; keep what thou hast received: the Father hath sealed

---

94. Basil, *On the Holy Spirit,* PG 32. 67.
95. Theophylact, *On Ephesians,* PG 124. 1042.
96. Ambrose, *The Mysteries,* PL 16. 402.

thee, and Christ thy Lord hath confirmed thee" by His divine Spirit, and He will never depart from thee, "unless by evil works we estrange Him from us." The same advice is given by Prudentius,[97]

> Cultor Dei, memento
> Te fontis et lavacri
> Rorem subîsse sanctum,
> Et chrismate innotatum

Remember how great things ye have received, and what God hath done for you: ye are of His flock and His militia; ye are now to fight His battles, and therefore to put on His armour, and to implore His auxiliaries, and to make use of His strengths, and always to be on His side against all His and all our enemies. But he that desires grace must not despise to make use of all the instruments of grace. For though God communicates His invisible Spirit to you, yet that He is pleased to do it by visible instruments is more than He needs, but not more than we do need. And therefore since God descends to our infirmities, let us carefully and lovingly address ourselves to His ordinances: that as we receive remission of sins by the washing of water, and the body and blood of Christ by the ministry of consecrated symbols; so we may receive the Holy Ghost *sub ducibus christianæ militiæ,* by the prayer and imposition of the bishop's hands, whom our Lord Jesus hath separated to this ministry. . . .

---

97. Prudentius, *The Cathemerinon Book,* PL 59. 858.

Sermon XVII[98]
The Marriage Ring; or,
the Mysteriousness and Duties of Marriage

EPH. V. 32, 33

This is a great mystery, but I speak concerning Christ and the church. Nevertheless, let every one of you in particular so love his wife even as himself, and the wife see that she reverence her husband.

The first blessing God gave to man was society, and that society was a marriage, and that marriage was confederate by God himself, and hallowed by a blessing: and at the same time, and for very many descending ages, not only by the instinct of nature, but by a superadded forwardness, God himself inspiring the desire, the world was most desirous of children, impatient of barrenness, accounting single life a curse, and a childless person hated by God. The world was rich and empty, and able to provide for a more numerous posterity than it had. . . .

Poor men are not so fond of children, but when a family could drive their herds, and set their children upon camels, and lead them till they saw a fat soil watered with rivers, and there sit down without paying rent, they thought of nothing but to have great families, that their own relations might swell up to a patriarchate, and their children be enough to possess all the regions that they saw, and their grandchildren become princes, and themselves build cities and call them by the name of a child, and become the fountain of a nation. This was the consequent of the first blessing, "increase and multiply." The next blessing was the promise of the Messias, and that also increased in men and women a wonderful desire of marriage: for as soon as God had

98. *Works* 4:207 ff.

chosen the family of Abraham to be the blessed line from whence the world's Redeemer should descend according to the flesh, every of his daughters hoped to have the honour to be His mother or His grandmother or something of His kindred: and to be childless in Israel was a sorrow to the Hebrew women great as the slavery of Egypt or their dishonours in the land of their captivity.

But when the Messias was come, and the doctrine was published, and His ministers but few, and His disciples were to suffer persecution and to be of an unsettled dwelling, and the nation of the Jews, in the bosom and society of which the church especially did dwell, were to be scattered and broken all in pieces with fierce calamities, and the world was apt to calumniate and to suspect and dishonour Christians upon pretences and unreasonable jealousies, and that to all these purposes the state of marriage brought many inconveniences; it pleased God in this new creation to inspire into the hearts of His servants a disposition and strong desires to live a single life, lest the state of marriage should in that conjunction of things become an accidental impediment to the dissemination of the gospel, which called men from a confinement in their domestic charges to travel, and flight, and poverty, and difficulty, and martyrdom: upon this necessity the apostles and apostolical men published doctrines declaring the advantages of single life, not by any commandment of the Lord, but by the spirit of prudence ... and in order to the advantages which did accrue to the public ministries and private piety. "There are some," said our blessed Lord,[99] "who make themselves eunuchs for the kingdom of heaven," that is, for the advantages and the ministry of the gospel; *non ad vitæ bonæ meritum,* as St. Austin in the like case;[100] not that it is a better service of God in itself, but that it is useful to the first circumstances of the gospel and the infancy of the kingdom, because the unmarried person ... "is apt to spiritual and ecclesiastical employments": first *HAGIOS,* and then *HAGIAZOMENOS,* holy in his own person, and then sanctified to public ministries; and it was also of ease to the Christians themselves, because as then it was, when they were to flee, and to flee for aught they knew in winter, and they were persecuted to the four winds of heaven, and the nurses and the women with child were to suffer a heavier load of

---

99. Matt. 19:12.
100. Augustine, *The Good Spouse,* PL 40. 587.

sorrow because of the imminent persecutions, and above all because of the great fatality of ruin upon the whole nation of the Jews, well it might be said by St. Paul,[101] "such shall have trouble in the flesh," that is, they that are married shall, and so at that time they had: and therefore it was an act of charity to the Christians to give that counsel, "I do this to spare you," and, *THELŌ HYMAS AMERIMNOYS EINAI*[102]: for when the case was altered, and that storm was over, and the first necessities of the gospel served, and "the sound was gone out into all nations";[103] in very many persons it was wholly changed, and not the married but the unmarried had "trouble in the flesh"; and the state of marriage returned to its first blessing, *et non erat bonum homini esse solitarium*,[104] "and it was not good for man to be alone."

But in this first interval, the public necessity and the private zeal mingling together did sometimes overact their love of single life, even to the disparagement of marriage, and to the scandal of religion: which was increased by the occasion of some pious persons renouncing their contract of marriage, not consummate, with unbelievers. For when Flavia Domitilla being converted by Nereus and Achilleus the eunuchs, refused to marry Aurelianus to whom she was contracted, if there were not some little envy and too sharp hostility in the eunuchs to a married state, yet Aurelianus thought himself an injured person, and caused St. Clemens, who veiled her, and his spouse both, to die in the quarrel.[105] St. Thecla[106] being converted by St. Paul grew so in love with virginity, that she leaped back from the marriage of Tamyris where she was lately engaged. St. Iphigenia[107] denied to marry king Hyrtacus, and it is said to be done by the advice of St. Matthew. And Susanna[108] the niece of Dioclesian refused the love of Maximianus the emperor; and these all had been betrothed; and so did St. Agnes,[109] and St. Felicula, and divers others then and afterwards: insomuch that it was reported among the

---

101. 1 Cor. 7:28.
102. 1 Cor. 7:32.
103. Ps. 14:4.
104. Gen. 2:18.
105. D. Attwater, *The Legends of the Saints* (New York, 1962), p. 230.
106. Ibid.
107. Ibid.
108. Ibid.
109. Ibid.

gentiles, that the Christians did not only hate all that were not of their persuasion, but were enemies of the chaste laws of marriage; and indeed some that were called Christians were so, "forbidding to marry, and commanding to abstain from meats."[110] Upon this occasion it grew necessary for the apostle to state the question right, and to do honour to the holy rite of marriage, and to snatch the mystery from the hands of zeal and folly, and to place it in Christ's right hand, that all its beauties might appear, and a present convenience might not bring in a false doctrine and a perpetual sin and an intolerable mischief. The apostle therefore, who himself had been a married man, but was now a widower, does explicate the mysteriousness of it, and describes its honours, and adorns it with rules and provisions of religion, that as it begins with honour, so it may proceed with piety and end with glory.

For although single life hath in it privacy and simplicity of affairs, such solitariness and sorrow, such leisure and unactive circumstances of living, that there are more spaces for religion if men would use them to these purposes; and because it may have in it much religion and prayers, and must have in it a perfect mortification of our strongest appetites, it is therefore a state of great excellency; yet concerning the state of marriage we are taught from scripture and the sayings of wise men great things and honourable. "Marriage is honourable in all men";[111] so is not single life; for in some it is a snare and a *PYRŌSIS,* "a trouble in the flesh," a prison of unruly desires which is attempted daily to be broken. Celibate or single life is never commanded, but in some cases marriage is, and he that burns sins often if he marries not; he that cannot contain must marry, and he that can contain is not tied to a single life, but may marry and not sin. Marriage was ordained by God, instituted in paradise, was the relief of a natural necessity and the first blessing from the Lord; He gave to man not a friend, but a wife, that is, a friend and a wife too; for a good woman is in her soul the same that a man is, and she is a woman only in her body; that she may have the excellency of the one, and the usefulness of the other, and become amiable in both. It is the seminary of the church, and daily brings forth sons and daughters unto God; it was ministered to by angels, and Raphael[112] waited upon a

---

110. Ibid. Cf. 1 Tim. 4:3.
111. Heb. 13:4.
112. Tob. 5:1ff.

young man that he might have a blessed marriage, and that that marriage might repair two sad families, and bless all their relatives. Our blessed Lord though He was born of a maiden, yet she was veiled under the cover of marriage, and she was married to a widower: for Joseph the supposed father of our Lord had children by a former wife. The first miracle that ever Jesus did was to do honour to a wedding. Marriage was in the world before sin, and is in all ages of the world the greatest and most effective antidote against sin, in which all the world had perished if God had not made a remedy: and although sin hath soured marriage, and stuck the man's head with cares, and the woman's bed with sorrows in the production of children; yet these are but throes of life and glory, and "she shall be saved in child-bearing, if she be found in faith and righteousness."[113] Marriage is a school and exercise of virtue; and though marriage hath cares, yet the single life hath desires which are more troublesome and more dangerous, and often end in sin, while the cares are but instances of duty and exercises of piety; and therefore if single life hath more privacy of devotion, yet marriage hath more necessities and more variety of it, and is an exercise of more graces. In two virtues celibate or single life may have the advantage of degrees ordinarily and commonly, that is, in chastity and devotion; but as in some persons this may fail, and it does in very many, and a married man may spend as much time in devotion as any virgins or widows do; yet as in marriage even those virtues of chastity and devotion are exercised, so in other instances this state hath proper exercises and trials for those graces for which single life can never be crowned. Here is the proper scene of piety and patience, of the duty of parents and the charity of relatives; here kindness is spread abroad, and love is united and made firm as a centre: marriage is the nursery of heaven; the virgin sends prayers to God, but she carries but one soul to Him; but the state of marriage fills up the numbers of the elect, and hath in it the labour of love, and the delicacies of friendship, the blessing of society, and the union of hands and hearts;[114] it hath in it less of beauty, but more of safety, than the single life; it hath more care, but less danger; it is more merry, and more sad; is fuller of sorrows, and fuller of joys; it lies under more burdens, but it is supported by all the strengths of love and charity,

---

113. 1 Tim. 2:15.
114. Plato, *The Laws*, LCL, vol. 9, pp. 459ff.

and those burdens are delightful. Marriage is the mother of the world, and preserves kingdoms, and fills cities, and churches, and heaven itself. Celibate, like the fly in the heart of an apple, dwells in a perpetual sweetness, but sits alone, and is confined and dies in singularity; but marriage, like the useful bee, builds a house and gathers sweetness from every flower, and labours and unites into societies and republics, and sends out colonies, and feeds the world with delicacies, and obeys their king, and keeps order, and exercises many virtues, and promotes the interest of mankind, and is that state of good things to which God hath designed the present constitution of the world.

Single life makes men in one instance to be like angels, but marriage in very many things makes the chaste pair to be like to Christ. "This is a great mystery," but it is the symbolical and sacramental representment of the greatest mysteries of our religion. Christ descended from His Father's bosom, and contracted His divinity with flesh and blood, and married our nature, and we became a church, the spouse of the Bridegroom, which He cleansed with His blood, and gave her His holy spirit for a dowry, and heaven for a jointure, begetting children unto God by the gospel. This spouse He hath joined to Himself by an excellent charity, He feeds her at His own table, and lodges her nigh His own heart, provides for all her necessities, relieves her sorrows, determines her doubts, guides her wanderings; He is become her head, and she as a signet upon His right hand; He first indeed was betrothed to the synagogue and had many children by her, but she forsook His love, and then He married the church of the gentiles, and by her as by a second venter had a more numerous issue, *atque una domus est omnium filiorum ejus,* "all the children dwell in the same house," and are heirs of the same promises, entitled to the same inheritance. Here is the eternal conjunction, the indissoluble knot, the exceeding love of Christ, the obedience of the spouse, the communicating of goods, the uniting of interests, the fruit of marriage, a celestial generation, a new creature: *Sacramentum hoc magnum est,* "this is the sacramental mystery" represented by the holy rite of marriage; so that marriage is divine in its institution, sacred in its union, holy in the mystery, sacramental in its signification, honourable in its appellative, religious in its employments; it is advantage to the societies of men, and it is "holiness to the Lord."

Dico autem in Christo et ecclesia, it must be "in Christ and the church." If this be not observed, marriage loses its mysteriousness; but because it is to effect much of that which it signifies, it concerns all that enter into those golden fetters to see that Christ and His church be in at every of its periods, and that it be entirely conducted and overruled by religion; for so the apostle passes from the sacramental rite to the real duty; "Nevertheless," that is, although the former discourse were wholly to explicate the conjunction of Christ and His church by this similitude, yet it hath in it this real duty, "that the man love his wife, and the wife reverence her husband. . . ."

CHAPTER THREE

Faith and Repentance

INTRODUCTION

Jeremy Taylor, in spite of the turmoil of his times, political, religious and philosophical, understood all time in the light of eternity. Revelation was his faith and redemption his hope in an age when there was much hatred and little love. Like the Countess of Carbery amid her many afflictions, Taylor too "had a strange evenness . . . sliding toward his ocean of God and of infinity with a certain and silent motion. So have I seen a river deep and smooth passing with a still foot and a sober face, and paying to . . . the great exchequer of the sea, the prince of all the watery bodies, a tribute large and full."[1]

> "Faith is a certain image of eternity; all things are present to it, things past and things to come are all so before the eyes of faith," that he in whose eye that candle is enkindled beholds heaven as present, and sees how blessed a thing it is to die in God's favour and to be chimed to our grave with the music of a good conscience. Faith converses with the angels and antedates the hymns of glory; every man that hath this grace is as certain that there are glories for him if he perseveres in duty, as if he had heard and sung the thanksgiving-song for the blessed sentence of domesday. And therefore it is no matter if these things are separate and distant objects; none but children and fools are taken with the present trifle, and neglect a distant blessing of which they have credible and believed notices. Did the merchant see the pearls and the wealth he designs to

---

1. *Works* 8:447.

get in the trade of twenty years? And is it possible that a child should, when he learns the first rudiments of grammar, know what excellent things there are in learning, whither he designs his labour and his hopes? We labour for that which is uncertain, and distant, and believed, and hoped for with many allays, and seen with diminution and a troubled ray. . . . [Faith] will, if we let it do its first intention, chastise our errors, and discover our follies; it will make us ashamed of trifling interests and violent prosecutions, of false principles and the evil disguises of the world; and then our nature will return to the innocence and excellency in which God first estated it: that is, our flesh will be a servant of the soul, and the soul a servant to the spirit.[2]

Such faith lights another way and inspires, amid trials and tribulations, the conjectures and expectations of hope, which Taylor described as "a helmet against the scorchings of despair in temporal things." For such as Taylor there were indeed these three, faith, hope and charity, "which is the vertical top of all religion, and is nothing else but a union of joys concentred in the heart, and reflected from all the angles of our life and entercourse. It is a rejoicing in God, a gladness in our neighbour's good, a pleasure in doing good, a rejoicing with him."[3]

I am fallen into the hands of publicans and sequestrators, and they have taken all from me; what now? let me look about me. They have left me the sun and moon, fire and water, a loving wife, and many friends to pity me and some to relieve me, and I can still discourse. And unless I list they have not taken away my merry countenance and my cheerful spirit and a good conscience: they still have left me the providence of God, and all the promises of the gospel, and my religion, and my hopes of heaven, and my charity to them, too; and still I sleep and digest, I eat and drink, I read and meditate; I can walk in my neighbour's pleasant fields, and see the varieties of natural beauties, and delight in all that in which God delights: that is,

---

2. *Works* 4:134.
3. *Works* 4:291.

in virtue and wisdom, in the whole creation, and in God himself.[4]

This sort of writing situates Taylor among the great masters of the spiritual life. In this tradition he was first and foremost concerned with the world around him and its power to corrupt; secondly, he believed the victory of Christ and the triumph of Christianity to be man's only hope; thirdly, he saw eternal things in time; but fourthly, he also realized man's need of repentance to possess now those things that will be forever. Hence the texts of this chapter are arranged within this theological framework and reflect on the positive side his doctrine of holiness, and on the negative side his doctrine of sin.

Conflict and affliction marked Taylor's return to the world in 1654, after his Golden Grove retreat of ten years, and, appropriately, sin and repentance became his new theme. In 1655 he published *Unum Necessarium,* his call for repentance to a world in sin. He was immediately drawn into conflict with friend and foe alike and discredited in the eyes of all for his comments on original sin. Ironically, his passion for piety and his desire to perfect men in holiness led to the accusations against him, and he who drew a strict line between mortal and venial sins and practically denied the value of a death-bed repentance was accused of Pelagianism. In the words of John Warner, the bishop of Rochester to whom Taylor had inscribed the book, "Pelagius had puddled the stream of Taylor's faith."

Golden Grove was in a sense poor preparation for the world Taylor now entered; yet in another way it prepared him for the long haul that would end where all Christian roads must ultimately end in the triumph of failure. Without wife and home Taylor had now to cope with the deaths of three young sons, the loss of friends and the consequences of controversy, rejection and isolation, poverty and prison. Such experiences suddenly shaped his attitude to the world and its power, to Christ and his triumph. In these times of turmoil Taylor was as given to the composition of prayers as he had been in the peace and quiet of Golden Grove. The controversial works of this period, like the devotional works of the former, are laced through and through with prayers and a spirit of prayer that brings us beyond the words of men and their divisions to the Word of God and communion:

---

4. *Works* 3:91.

Have mercy upon me, O God, according to Thy loving-kindness: according to the multitude of Thy tender mercies blot
out my transgressions.

For our transgressions are multiplied before Thee, and
our sins testify against us: our transgressions are with us, and
as for our iniquities, we know them;

In transgressing and lying against the Lord, and departing
away from our God, speaking oppression and revolt, con-
ceiving and uttering from the heart words of falsehood.

Our feet have run to evil, our thoughts are thoughts of
iniquity. The way of peace we have not known: we have made
us crooked paths, whosoever goeth therein shall not know
peace. Therefore do we wait for light, but behold obscurity
for brightness, but we walk in darkness.

Lord make me to know mine end, and the measure of my
days, what it is: that I may know how frail I am, and that I may
apply my heart unto wisdom.

Withhold not Thou thy tender mercies from me, O
Lord: let Thy loving-kindness and Thy truth continually preserve me.

For innumerable evils have compassed me about, mine
iniquities have taken hold upon me, so that I am not able to
look up: for they are more than the hairs of my head, therefore
my heart faileth me.

But Thou, O Lord, though mine iniquities testify against
me, save me for Thy name sake: for our backslidings are
many, we have sinned grievously against Thee.

But the Lord God will help me, therefore shall I not be
confounded: therefore have I set my face like a flint, and I
know that I shall not be ashamed.

He is near that justifieth me, who will contend with me?
The Lord God will help me, who is he that shall condemn me?
I will trust in the Lord, and stay upon my God.

O let me have this of Thine hand, that I may not lie down
in sorrow.[5]

---

5. *Works* 7:79.

Taylor's vision of the world and its power to corrupt, and of the triumph of Christianity, which revealed to man eternal things, leads him in his unlucky volume to a consideration of sin and repentance, as the full title of the book shows: *Unum Necessarium: The Doctrine and Practice of Repentance, describing the necessities and measures of a strict, a holy and a Christian life and rescued from popular errors.* The church's preaching and practice of repentance from its beginnings led Taylor to emphasize the reality of sin in this world more than its origins in another, but the heat of the controversy obscured this fact. However, by appealing to the Greek Fathers, the Scotists and the Arminians, who held that man could and should rise to his responsibilities, Taylor defended his more liberal view of man and his fall and published it in another work, *Deus Justificatus* or *A Vindication of the Glory of the Divine Attributes in the Question of Original Sin.* But *Unum Necessarium* remains his call to sinners or his gospel of repentance:

> The duty of repentance is of so great and universal concernment, a *catholicon* to the evils of the soul of every man, that if there be any particular in which it is worthy the labours of the whole ecclesiastical calling to be "instant in season and out of season," it is in this duty; and therefore I hope I shall be excused in my Discourses of Repentance, like the duty itself, be perpetually increasing; and I may, like the widow in the gospel to the unjust judge, at least hope to prevail with some men by my importunity. Men have found out so many devices and arts to cozen themselves, that they will rather admit any weak discourses and images of reason, than think it necessary to repent speedily, severely and effectively. We find that sinners are prosperous, and God is long before He strikes; and it is always another man's case when we see a judgement happen upon a sinner, we feel it not ourselves, for when we do, it is commonly past remedy. . . . For repentance is thought to be just as other graces, fit for their proper season, like fruits in their own month; but then everything else must have its day too: we shall sin, and we must repent; but sin will come again, and so may repentance: for "there is a time for everything under the sun"; and the time for repentance is when we can sin no more, when every objection is answered, when we can

have no more excuse; and they who go upon that principle will never do it till it be too late: for every age hath temptations of its own, and they that have been used to the yoke all their life time, will obey their sin when it comes in any shape in which they can take any pleasure. But men are infinitely abused, and by themselves most of all. For repentance is not like the summer fruits, fit to be taken a little in their own time; it is like bread, the provisions and support of our life, the entertainment of every day, but it is "the bread of affliction" to some, and "the bread of carefulness" to all; and he who preaches this with the greatest zeal and the greatest severity, it may be he takes the liberty of an enemy, but he gives the counsel and the assistance of a friend.[6]

In the tenth and final chapter of *Unum Necessarium*, a section of which concludes this third chapter, Taylor treats of ecclesiastical penance, one of "those five commonly called sacraments." He has little doubt about the efficacy or spiritual power of the tradition:

Confession of sins is so necessary a duty that in all scriptures it is the immediate preface to pardon: that in all ages of the Gospel it hath been taught and practised; that it is by all churches esteemed a duty necessary to be done in cases of a troubled conscience; that St. James gives an express precept that we Christians should confess our sins to each other, that is, christian to christian, brother to brother and the people to their minister: and that the ministers of the Gospel are the ministers of reconciliation and are commanded to restore such persons as are overtaken in a fault, if they may take cognizance of the fault.[7]

Confession of sin was for Taylor an integral part of prayer, private and public, and his many liturgical compositions have substantial prayers of confession and petitions for forgiveness. He was particularly interested in the practice of auricular confession to a priest and found himself in

---

6. *Works* 7:3.
7. *Works* 7:480.

the ambiguous position of denouncing it in Romanism and advocating it in Anglicanism:

> The spiritual man is appointed to restore us and to pray for us and to receive our confessions and to inquire into our wounds, and to infuse oil and remedy and to pronounce pardon: if we be cut off from the communion of the faithful by our own demerits, their holy hands must reconcile us and give us peace; they are our appointed comforters, our instructors, our ordinary judges.[8]

Taylor had a noble view of man, and saw him as accountable and responsible for his moral freedom; thus, "the sick man who has seen in his illness God's correcting rod, and has been driven to change his way of life as a result of it, emerges the better man." Consequently, repentance is a means of redeeming life, a way of giving purpose and meaning to what is otherwise a chaos of misadventure. Ultimately, repentance in this world of sin is the final triumph of Christianity—the possession of eternal things, both now and forever.

> Repentance is like the sun, which enlightens not only the tops of the eastern hills, or warms the wall-fruits of Italy. It makes the little balsam tree to weep precious tears with staring upon its beauties; it produces rich spices in Arabia, and warms the cold hermit in his grot, and calls the religious man from his dorter [dormitory] in all the parts of the world where holy religion dwells. At the same time it digests the American gold and melts the snow from the Riphaean mountains, because he darts his rays in every portion of the air; and the smallest atom that dances in the air is tied to a little thread of light, which by equal emanations fills all the capacities of every region. So is repentance; it scatters its beams and holy influences.[9]

---

8. *Works* 7:482.
9. *Works* 7:478.

Discourse VII[1] of Faith

THE PRAYER

I.

O eternal God, fountain of all truth and holiness, in whom to believe is life eternal; let Thy grace descend with a mighty power into my soul, beating down every strong hold and vainer imagination, and bringing every proud thought, and my confident and ignorant understanding, into the obedience of Jesus. Take from me all disobedience and refractariness of spirit, all ambition, and private and baser interests; remove from me all prejudice and weakness of persuasion, that I may wholly resign my understanding to the persuasions of Christianity, acknowledging Thee to be the principle of truth, and Thy word the measure of knowledge, and Thy laws the rule of my life, and Thy promises the satisfaction of my hopes, and an union with Thee to be the consummation of charity in the fruition of glory. Amen.

II.

Holy Jesus, make me to acknowledge Thee to be my Lord and Master, and myself a servant and disciple of Thy holy discipline and institution; let me love to sit at Thy feet, and suck in with my ears and heart the sweetness of Thy holy sermons. Let my soul be shod with the preparation of the gospel of peace, with a peaceable and docile disposition. Give me great boldness in the public confession of Thy name and the truth of Thy gospel, in despite of all hostilities and temptations. And grant I may always remember that Thy name is called upon me, and I may so behave myself, that I neither give scandal to others, nor cause disreputation to the honour of religion; but that Thou mayest be glorified in me, and I by Thy mercies, after a strict observance of all the holy laws of Christianity. Amen.

---

1. *Works* 2:294ff.

Of Faith

1. Nathanael's faith was produced by an argument not demonstrative, not certainly concluding; Christ knew him when He saw him first, and he believed Him to be the Messias: his faith was excellent, whatever the argument was. And I believe a God, because the sun is a glorious body; or because of the variety of plants, or the fabric and rare contexture of a man's eye: I may as fully assent to the conclusion as if my belief dwelt upon the demonstrations made by the prince of philosophers in the eighth of his physics and twelfth of his metaphysics. This I premise as an inlet into the consideration concerning the faith of ignorant persons. For if we consider upon what easy terms most of us now are Christians, we may possibly suspect that either faith hath but little excellence in it, or we but little faith, or that we are mistaken generally in its definition. For we are born of Christian parents, made Christians at ten days old, interrogated concerning the articles of our faith by way of anticipation, even then when we understand not the difference between the sun and a tallow-candle: from thence we are taught to say our catechism as we are taught to speak, when we have no reason to judge, no discourse to discern, no arguments to contest against a proposition, in case we be catechized into false doctrine; and all that is put to us we believe infinitely and without choice, as children use not to choose their language. And as our children are made Christians, just so are thousand others made Mahometans, with the same necessity, the same facility. So that thus far there is little thanks due to us for believing the Christian creed; it was indifferent to us at first, and at last our education had so possessed us, and our interest, and our no temptation to the contrary, that as we were disposed into this condition by Providence, so we remain in it without praise or excellency. For as our beginnings are inevitable, so our progress is imperfect and insufficient; and what we began by education, we retain only by custom: and if we be instructed in some slighter arguments to maintain the sect or faction of our country religion, as it disturbs the unity of Christendom; yet if we examine and consider the account, upon what slight arguments we have taken up Christianity itself (as, that it is the religion of our country, or that our fathers before us were of the same faith, or because the priest bids us, and he is a good man, or for something else, but we know not what) we must needs conclude it the good providence of God, not our choice, that made us Christians.

2. But if the question be, Whether such a faith be in itself good

and acceptable that relies upon insufficient and unconvincing grounds? I suppose this case of Nathanael will determine us: and when we consider that faith is an infused grace, if God pleases to behold His own glory in our weakness of understanding, it is but the same thing He does in the instances of His other graces. For as God enkindles charity upon variety of means and instruments, by a thought, by a chance, by a text of scripture, by a natural tenderness, by the sight of a dying or a tormented beast: so also He may produce faith by arguments of a differing quality, and by issues of His providence He may engage us in such conditions in which, as our understanding is not great enough to choose the best, so neither is it furnished with powers to reject any proposition: and to believe well is an effect of a singular predestination, and is a gift in order to a grace, as that grace is in order to salvation. But the insufficiency of an argument, or disability to prove our religion, is so far from disabling the goodness of an ignorant man's faith, that as it may be as strong as the faith of the greatest scholar, so it hath full as much excellency, not of nature, but in order to divine acceptance. For as he who believes upon the only stock of education made no election of his faith, so he who believes what is demonstrably proved is forced by the demonstration to his choice. Neither of them did choose, and both of them may equally love the article.

3. So that since a small argument in a weak understanding does the same work that a strong argument in a more sober and learned, that is, it convinces and makes faith, and yet neither of them is matter of choice; if the thing believed be good and matter of duty or necessity, the faith is not rejected by God upon the weakness of the first, nor accepted upon the strength of the latter principles; when we are once in, it will not be enquired by what entrance we passed thither; whether God leads us or drives us in, whether we come by discourse or by inspiration, by the guide of an angel or the conduct of Moses, whether we be born or made Christians, it is indifferent, so we be there where we should be; for this is but the gate of duty, and the entrance to felicity. For thus far faith is but an act of the understanding, which is a natural faculty, serving indeed as an instrument to godliness, but of itself no part of it; and it is just like fire producing its act inevitably, and burning as long as it can, without power to interrupt or suspend its action; and therefore we cannot be more pleasing to God for understanding rightly than the fire is for burning clearly: which puts us evidently upon this consideration, that Christian faith, that glorious duty which gives to Christians a great

degree of approximation to God by Jesus Christ, must have a great proportion of that ingredient which makes actions good or bad, that is, of choice and effect.

4. For the faith of a Christian hath more in it of the will than of the understanding. Faith is that great mark of distinction which separates and gives formality to the covenant of the gospel, which is a "law of faith." The faith of a Christian is his religion, that is, it is that whole conformity to the institution or discipline of Jesus Christ which distinguishes him from the believers of false religions. And to be one of the faithful signifies the same with being a disciple; and that contains obedience as well as believing. For to the same sense are all those appellatives in scripture, "the faithful, brethren, believers, the saints, disciples," all representing the duty of a Christian. A believer, and a saint, or a holy person, is the same thing; "brethren" signifies charity, and "believers," faith in the intellectual sense: the "faithful" and "disciples" signify both; for besides the consent to the proposition, the first of them is also used for perseverance and sanctity, and the greatest of charity mixed with a confident faith up to the height of martyrdom. "Be faithful unto the death," said the holy Spirit, "and I will give thee the crown of life."[2] And when the apostles, by way of abbreviation, express all the body of Christian religion, they call it "faith working by love";[3] which also St. Paul in a parallel place calls a "new creature";[4] it is "a keeping of the commandments of God."[5] That is the faith of a Christian, into whose definition charity is ingredient, whose sense is the same with keeping of God's commandments; so that if we define faith, we must first distinguish it. The faith of a natural person, or the faith of devils, is a mere believing a certain number of propositions upon conviction of the understanding: but the faith of a Christian, the faith that justifies and saves him, is "faith working by charity," or "faith keeping the commandments of God." They are distinct faiths, in order to different ends, and therefore of different constitution; and the instrument of distinction, is charity or obedience.

5. And this great truth is clear in the perpetual testimony of holy scripture. For Abraham is called the "father of the faithful"; and yet our blessed Saviour told the Jews that if they had been "the sons of Abra-

---

2. Rev. 2:10.
3. Gal. 5:6.
4. Gal. 6:15.
5. 1 Cor. 7:19.

ham, they would have done the works of Abraham";[6] and therefore good works are by the apostle called "the footsteps of the faith of our father Abraham."[7] For faith, in every of its stages, at its first beginning, at its increment, at its greatest perfection, is a duty made up of the concurrence of the will and the understanding, when it pretends to the divine acceptance. Faith and repentance begin the Christian course; "repent and believe the gospel," was the sum of the apostle's sermons: and all the way after it is, "faith working by love." Repentance puts the first spirit and life into faith, and charity preserves it and gives it nourishment and increase; itself also growing by a mutual supply of spirits and nutriment from faith. Whoever does heartily believe a resurrection and life eternal upon certain conditions, will certainly endeavour to acquire the promises by the purchase of obedience and observation of the conditions. For it is not in the nature or power of man directly to despise and reject so infinite a good: so that faith supplies charity with argument and maintenance, and charity supplies faith with life and motion; faith makes charity reasonable, and charity makes faith living and effectual. And therefore the old Greeks called faith and charity a miraculous chariot or yoke, they bear the burden of the Lord with an equal confederation: these are like Hippocrates' twins, they live and die together. Indeed faith is the first born of the twins; but they must come both at a birth, or else they die, being strangled at the gates of the womb. But if charity, like Jacob, lays hold of his elder brother's heel, it makes a timely and a prosperous birth, and gives certain title to the eternal promises: for let us give the right of primogeniture to faith, yet the blessing, yea, and the inheritance too, will at last fall to charity; not that faith is disinherited, but that charity only enters into the possession. The nature of faith passes into the excellency of charity before they can be rewarded; and that both may have their estimate, that which justifies and saves us keeps the name of faith, but doth not do the deed till it hath the nature of charity. For to think well, or to have a good opinion, or an excellent or a fortunate understanding, entitles us not to the love of God and the consequent inheritance; but to choose the ways of the Spirit, and to relinquish the paths of darkness, this is the way of the kingdom, and the purpose of the gospel, and the proper work of faith.

6. And if we consider upon what stock faith itself is instrumental

---

6. John 8:39.
7. Rom. 4:12.

and operative of salvation, we shall find it is in itself acceptable, because it is a duty, and commanded; and therefore it is an act of obedience, a work of the gospel, a submitting the understanding, a denying the affections, a laying aside all interests, and a bringing our thoughts under the obedience of Christ. This the apostle calls "the obedience of faith."[8] And it is of the same condition and constitution with other graces, all which equally relate to Christ, and are as firm instruments of union, and are washed by the blood of Christ, and are sanctified by His death, and apprehend Him in their capacity and degrees, some higher, and some not so high: but hope and charity apprehend Christ in a measure and proportion greater than faith, when it distinguishes from them. So that if faith does the work of justification, as it is a mere relation to Christ, then so also does hope and charity; or if these are duties and good works, so also is faith: and they all being alike commanded in order to the same end, and encouraged by the same reward, are also accepted upon the same stock, which is, that they are acts of obedience and relation too; they obey Christ, and lay hold upon Christ's merits, and are but several instances of the great duty of a Christian, but the actions of several faculties of the new creature. But because faith is the beginning grace, and hath influence and causality in the production of the other, therefore all the other as they are united in duty, are also united in their title and appellative; they are all called by the name of faith, because they are parts of faith, as faith is taken in the larger sense: and when it is taken in the strictest and distinguishing sense, they are effects and proper products by way of natural emanation.

7. That a good life is the genuine and true-born issue of faith, no man questions that knows himself the disciple of the holy Jesus: but that obedience is the same thing with faith, and that all Christian graces are parts of its bulk and constitution, is also the doctrine of the holy Ghost, and the grammar of scripture, making faith and obedience to be terms coincident and expressive of each other. For faith is not a single star, but a constellation, a chain of graces, called by St. Paul "the power of God unto salvation to every believer";[9] that is, faith is all that great instrument by which God intends to bring us to heaven: and he gives this reason, "in the gospel the righteousness of God is revealed from faith to faith"; for "it is written, The just shall live by faith." Which discourse

---

8. Rom. 16:26.
9. Rom. 1:16–17.

makes faith to be a course of sanctity and holy habits, a continuation of a Christian's duty, such a duty as not only gives the first breath, but by which a man lives the life of grace. "The just shall live by faith"; that is, such a faith as grows from step to step till the whole righteousness of God be fulfilled in it. "From faith to faith," saith the apostle; which St. Austin expounds, from faith believing, to faith obeying;[10] from imperfect faith, to faith made perfect by the animation of charity; that "he who is justified, may be justified still." For as there are several degrees and parts of justification, so there are several degrees of faith answerable to it; that in all senses it may be true that "by faith we are justified, and by faith we live, and by faith we are saved." For if we proceed "from faith to faith," from believing to obeying, from faith in the understanding to faith in the will, from faith barely assenting to the revelations of God to faith obeying the commandments of God, from the body of faith to the soul of faith, that is, to faith formed and made alive by charity; then we shall proceed from justification to justification, that is, from remission of sins to become the sons of God, and at last to an actual possession of those glories to which we were here consigned by the fruits of the holy Ghost.

8. And in this sense the holy Jesus is called by the apostle "the author and finisher of our faith."[11] He is the principle, and He is the promoter; He begins our faith in revelations, and perfects it in commandments; He leads us by the assent of our understanding, and finishes the work of His grace by a holy life: which St. Paul there expresses by its several constituent parts; as "laying aside every weight and the sin that so easily besets us, and running with patience the race that is set before us ... resisting unto blood, striving against sin,"[12] for in these things Jesus is therefore made our example, because He is "the author and finisher of our faith"; without these faith is imperfect. But the thing is something plainer yet, for St. James says that faith lives not but by charity;[13] and the life or essence of a thing is certainly the better part of its constitution, as the soul is to a man. And if we mark the manner of his probation, it will come home to the main point: for he proves that Abraham's faith was therefore imputed to him for righteousness, because he was justified by works; "was not Abraham our father justified

---

10. Augustine, *On the Spirit and Letter*, PL 44.211.
11. Heb. 12:2.
12. Heb. 12:1–4.
13. James 2:20–3:6.

by works, when he offered up his son? and the scripture was fulfilled, saying, Abraham believed God, and it was imputed to him for righteousness; for faith wrought with his works, and made his faith perfect." It was a dead and an imperfect faith, unless obedience gave it being, and all its integral or essential parts. So that faith and charity, in the sense of a Christian, are but one duty, as the understanding and the will are but one reasonable soul; only they produce several actions in order to one another, which are but "divers operations and the same spirit."

9. Thus St. Paul, describing the faith of the Thessalonians, calls it that whereby they "turned from idols," and whereby they "served the living God";[14] and the faith of the patriarchs "believed the world's creation, received the promises, did miracles, wrought righteousness,"[15] and did and suffered so many things as make up the integrity of a holy life. And therefore disobedience and unrighteousness is called "want of faith,"[16] and heresy, which is opposed to faith, is "a work of the flesh,"[17] because faith itself is a work of righteousness. And that I may enumerate no more particulars, the thing is so known, that the word *APEITHEIA*,[18] which in propriety of language signifies mispersuasion or infidelity, is rendered disobedience; and the "not providing for our families" is an act of infidelity, by the same reason and analogy that obedience, or charity, and a holy life, are the duties of a Christian, of a justifying faith. And although in the natural or philosophical sense, faith and charity are distinct habits; yet in the sense of a Christian, and the signification of duty, they are the same; for we cannot believe aright, as believing is in the commandment, unless we live aright; for our faith is put upon the account just as it is made precious by charity; according to that rare saying of St. Bartholomew, recorded by the supposed St. Denis, "Charity is the greatest and the least theology";[19] all our faith, that is, all our religion, is completed in the duties of universal charity; as our charity or our manner of living is, so is our faith. If our life be unholy, it may be the faith of devils, but not the faith of Christians. For this is the difference;

10. The faith of the devils hath more of the understanding in it,

---

14. 1 Thess. 1:8–9.
15. Heb. 11:1ff.
16. Col. 3:6; 2 Thess. 3:2.
17. Gal. 5:20.
18. Eph. 2:2, 5:6; 1 Tim. 5:8.
19. Dionysius the Areopagite, *Mystical Theology*, PG 3.998.

the faith of Christians more of the will; the devils in their faith have better discourse, the Christians better affections; they in their faith have better arguments, we more charity. So that charity or a good life is so necessary an ingredient into the definition of a Christian's faith, that we have nothing else to distinguish it from the faith of devils; and we need no trial of our faith but the examination of our lives. If you "keep the commandments of God," then have you the faith of Jesus; they are immediate, in St. John's expression[20]: but if you be importune and ungodly, you are in St. Paul's list[21] amongst them that have no faith. Every vice that rules amongst us, and sullies the fair beauty of our souls, is a conviction of infidelity.

11. For it was the faith of Moses that made him despise the riches of Egypt; the faith of Joshua, that made him valiant; the faith of Joseph, that made him chaste; Abraham's faith made him obedient; St. Mary Magdalen's faith made her penitent; and the faith of St. Paul made him travel so far and suffer so much, till he became a prodigy both of zeal and patience. Faith is a *catholicon,* and cures all the distemperatures of the soul; it "overcomes the world,"[22] saith St. John; it "works righteousness,"[23] saith St. Paul; it "purifies the heart,"[24] saith St. Peter; "it works miracles," saith our blessed Saviour; miracles in grace always, as it did miracles in nature at its first publication: and whatsoever is good, if it be a grace, it is an act of faith; if it be a reward, it is the fruit of faith. So that as all the actions of man are but the productions of the soul, so are all the actions of the new man the effects of faith. For faith is the life of Christianity, and a good life is the life of faith.

12. Upon the grounds of this discourse, we may understand the sense of that question of our blessed Saviour; "when the Son of man comes, shall He find faith on earth?"[25] truly, just so much as He finds charity and holy living, and no more. For then only we can be confident that faith is not "failed from among the children of men," when we feel the heats of the primitive charity return, and the calentures of the first old devotion are renewed; when it shall be accounted honourable to be a servant of Christ, and a shame to commit a sin. Then, and then only, our

---

20. Rev. 14:12.
21. 2 Thess. 3:2.
22. 1 John 5:4.
23. Heb. 11:33.
24. Acts 15:9.
25. Luke 18:8.

churches shall be assemblies of the faithful, and the kingdoms of the world Christian countries. But so long as it is notorious that we have made Christian religion another thing than what the holy Jesus designed it to be; when it does not make us live good lives, but itself is made a pretence to all manner of impiety, a stratagem to serve ends, the ends of covetousness, of ambition, and revenge; when the Christian charity ends in killing one another for conscience sake, so that faith is made to cut the throat of charity, and our faith kills more than our charity preserves; when the humility of a Christian hath indeed a name amongst us, but it is like a mute person, talked of only; while ambition and rebellion, pride and scorn, self-seeking and proud undertakings, transact most of the great affairs of Christendom; when the custody of our senses is to no other purposes but that no opportunity of pleasing them pass away; when our oaths are like the fringes of our discourses, going round about them as if they were ornaments and trimmings; when our blasphemies, profanation, sacrilege, and irreligion, are become scandalous to the very Turks and Jews; while our lusts are always habitual, sometimes unnatural; will any wise man think that we believe those doctrines[26] of humility and obedience, of chastity and charity, of temperance and justice, which the Saviour of the world made sacred by His sermon and example, or indeed any thing He either said or did, promised or threatened? For is it possible a man with his wits about him, and believing that he should certainly be damned (that is, be eternally tormented in body and soul with torments greater than can be in this world) if he be a swearer, or liar, or drunkard, or cheats his neighbour; that this man should dare to do these things to which the temptations are so small, in which the delight is so inconsiderable, and the satisfaction so none at all?

13. We see by the experience of the whole world, that the belief of an honest man, in a matter of temporal advantage, makes us do actions of such danger and difficulty, that half so much industry and sufferance would ascertain us into a possession of all the promises evangelical. Now let any man be asked, whether he had rather be rich or be saved? he will tell you without all doubt, heaven is the better option by infinite degrees: for it cannot be that riches, or revenge, or lust, should be directly preferred, that is, be thought more eligible than the

---

26. Chrysostom, *On Compunction*, PG 47.397.

glories of immortality. That therefore men neglect so great salvation, and so greedily run after the satisfaction of their baser appetites, can be attributed to nothing but want of faith; they do not heartily believe that heaven is worth so much; there is upon them a stupidity of spirit, and their faith is dull, and its actions suspended most commonly, and often interrupted, and it never enters into the will: so that the propositions are considered nakedly and precisely in themselves, but not as referring to us or our interests; there is nothing of faith in it, but so much as is the first and direct act of understanding; there is no consideration or reflection upon the act, or upon the person, or upon the subject. So that even as it is seated in the understanding, our faith is commonly lame, mutilous, and imperfect; and therefore much more is it culpable, because it is destitute of all co-operation of the rational appetite.

14. But let us consider the power and efficacy of worldly belief. If a man believes that there is gold to be had in Peru for fetching, or pearls and rich jewels in India for the exchange of trifles, he instantly, if he be in capacity, leaves the wife of his bosom, and the pretty delights of children, and his own security, and ventures into the dangers of waters and unknown seas, and freezings and calentures, thirst and hunger, pirates and shipwrecks; and hath within him a principle strong enough to answer all objections, because he believes that riches are desirable, and by such means likely to be had. Our blessed Saviour, comparing the gospel to "a merchantman, that found a pearl of great price," and "sold all to buy it," hath brought this instance home to the present discourse. For if we did as verily believe that in heaven those great felicities which transcend all our apprehensions, are certainly to be obtained by leaving our vices and lower desires, what can hinder us but we should at least do as much for obtaining those great felicities as for the lesser, if the belief were equal? for if any man thinks he may have them without holiness and justice and charity, then he wants faith, for he believes not the saying of St. Paul, "follow peace with all men, and holiness, without which no man shall ever see God."[27] If a man believes learning to be the only or chiefest ornament and beauty of souls, that which will ennoble him to a fair employment in his own time, and an honourable memory to succeeding ages; this if he believes heartily, it hath power to make him endure catarrhs, gouts, hypochondriacal passions, to read till his eyes

---

27. Heb. 12:14.

almost fix in their orbs, to despise the pleasures of idleness or tedious sports, and to undervalue whatsoever does not co-operate to the end of his faith, the desire of learning. Why is the Italian so abstemious in his drinkings, or the Helvetian so valiant in his fight or so true to the prince that employs him, but that they believe it to be noble so to be? If they believed the same and had the same honourable thoughts of other virtues, they also would be as national as these. For faith will do its proper work. And when the understanding is peremptorily and fully determined upon the persuasion of a proposition, if the will should then dissent and choose the contrary, it were unnatural and monstrous: and possibly no man ever does so; for that men do things without reason and against their conscience, is because they have put out their light, and discourse their wills into the election of a sensible good, and want faith to believe truly all circumstances which are necessary by way of predisposition for choice of the intellectual.

15. But when men's faith is confident, their resolution and actions are in proportion: for thus the faith of Mahometans makes them to abstain from wine for ever; and therefore, if we had the Christian faith, we should much rather abstain from drunkenness for ever; it being an express rule apostolical, "be not drunk with wine, wherein is excess."[28] The faith of the Circumcellians made them to run greedily to violent and horrid deaths, as willingly as to a crown; for they thought it was the king's highway to martyrdom. And there was never any man zealous for his religion, and of an imperious bold faith, but he was also willing to die for it; and therefore also by as much reason to live in it, and to be a strict observer of its prescriptions. And the stories of the strict sanctity, and prodigious sufferings, and severe disciplines, and expensive religion, and compliant and laborious charity, of the primitive Christians, is abundant argument to convince us that the faith of Christians is infinitely more fruitful and productive of its univocal and proper issues, than the faith of heretics, or the false religions of misbelievers, or the persuasions of secular persons, or the spirit of antichrist. And therefore when we see men serving their prince with such difficult and ambitious services, because they believe him able to reward them, though of his will they are not so certain, and yet so supinely negligent and incurious of their services to God, of whose power and will to reward us infi-

---

28. Eph. 5:18.

nitely there is certainty absolute and irrespective; it is certain probation that we believe it not: for if we believe there is such a thing as heaven, and that every single man's portion of heaven is far better than all the wealth in the world, it is morally impossible we should prefer so little before so great profit.

16. I instance but once more. The faith of Abraham was instanced in the matter of confidence or trust in the divine promises; and he being "the father of the faithful," we must imitate his faith by a clear dereliction of ourselves and our own interests, and an entire confident relying upon the divine goodness in all cases of our needs or danger. Now this also is a trial of the verity of our faith, the excellency of our condition, and what title we have to the glorious names of Christians, and faithful, and believers. If our fathers when we were in pupilage and minority, or a true and an able friend when we were in need, had made promises to supply our necessities, our confidence was so great that our care determined. It were also well that we were as confident of God, and as secure of the event when we had disposed ourselves to reception of the blessing, as we were of our friend or parents. We all profess that God is almighty, that all His promises are certain, and yet when it comes to a pinch, we find that man to be more confident that hath ten thousand pounds in his purse, than he that reads God's promises over ten thousand times. "Men of a common spirit," saith St. Chrysostom, "of an ordinary sanctity, will not steal, or kill, or lie, or commit adultery; but it requires a rare faith and a sublimity of pious affections, to believe that God will work a deliverance which to me seems impossible." And indeed St. Chrysostom hit upon the right. He had need be a good man, and love God well, that puts his trust in Him. For those we love, we are most apt to trust, and although trust and confidence is sometimes founded upon experience, yet it is also begotten and increased by love, as often as by reason and discourse. And to this purpose it was excellently said by St. Basil, that "the knowledge which one man learneth of another is made perfect by continual use and exercise; but that which through the grace of God is engrafted in the mind of man, is made absolute by justice, gentleness, and charity." So that if you are willing even in death to confess not only the articles, but in affliction and death to trust the promises; if in the lowest nakedness of poverty you can cherish yourselves with the expectation of God's promises and dispensation, being as confident of food and raiment, and deliverance or support, when all is in God's hand, as you are when it is in your own; if you can be cheerful in a storm, smile when the world frowns, be content

in the midst of spiritual desertions and anguish of spirit, expecting all should work together for the best, according to the promise; if you can strengthen yourselves in God when you are weakest, believe when you see no hope, and entertain no jealousies or suspicious of God, though you see nothing to make you confident; then, and then only, you have faith, which, in conjunction with its other parts, is able to save your souls. For in this precise duty of trusting God there are the rays of hope, and great proportions of charity and resignation.

Credenda[29]
An Exposition of the
Apostles' Creed

I BELIEVE IN GOD,

I believe that there is a God who is one, true, supreme and alone, infinitely wise, just, good, free, eternal, immense, and blessed, and in Him alone we are to put our trust.[30]

THE FATHER ALMIGHTY,

I believe that He is the Father (1) of our Lord Jesus Christ; and (2) of all that believe in Him, whom He hath begotten by His word, and adopted to the inheritance of sons; and because He is our Father, He will do us all that good to which we are created and designed by grace; and because He is almighty, He is able to perform it all; and therefore we may safely believe in Him, and rely upon Him.[31]

MAKER OF HEAVEN AND EARTH.

He made the sun and the moon, the stars, and all the regions of glory; He made the air, the earth, and the water, and all that live in them; He made angels and men, and He who made them does, and He only can

---

29. Taylor, *Works,* Vol. 7, pp. 600ff.

30. Luke 7:35; Deut. 10:17; Mark 12:29–32; 1 Cor. 8:4; John 17:3; 1 Thess. 1:9; Ps. 90:2; Ps. 93:2; Ps. 77:13; Ps. 95:3; Ps. 147:5; Rom. 16:7; 1 Tim. 1:17; 2 Chr. 19:7; Ps. 119:137; 1 Chr. 16:3–4; Ps. 34:8; Ps. 135:6; Exod. 33:19; 1 Tim. 1:11.

31. John 8:54; Rom. 8:29–32; 1 Cor. 8:6; Matt. 24:36; Heb. 2:11; 1 Pet. 1:23; Gal. 4:4.

preserve them in the same being, and thrust them forwards to a better; He that preserves them does also govern them, and intends they should minister to His glory; and therefore we are to do worship and obedience to Him in all that we can, and that He hath commanded.[32]

AND IN JESUS CHRIST,

I also believe in Jesus Christ, who is, and is called a Saviour, and the anointed of the Lord, promised to the patriarchs, whom God anointed with the holy Spirit, and with power, to become the great prophet, and declarer of His Father's will to all the world, telling us how God will be worshipped and served; He is anointed to be the mediator of the new covenant, and our high-priest, reconciling us to His Father by the sacrifice of Himself; and to be the great king of all the world: and by this article we are Christians, who serve and worship God the Father through Jesus Christ.[33]

HIS ONLY SON,

Jesus Christ is the Son of God, He alone of Him alone: for God by His holy Spirit caused Him to be born of a virgin: by His power He raised Him from the dead and gave Him a new birth, or being in the body: He gave Him all power, and all excellency; and beyond all this, He is the express image of His person, the brightness of His glory, equal to God, beloved before the beginning of the world, of a nature perfectly divine; very God by essence and very man by assumption; as God, all one in nature with the Father; and as man, one person in Himself.[34]

---

32. Isa. 65:17; Isa. 66:22; Acts 4:24; Ps. 36:7–8; Matt. 6:26; Matt. 10:29–30; Matt. 4:10; Rev. 14:7.

33. Matt. 1:20; John 3:34; Acts 10:28; Heb. 12:34; Rev. 1:5; Acts 11:26; Acts 26:28; 1 Pet. 4:16.

34. Luke 1:32; Rom. 1:3–4; 1 John 5:9; John 1:1ff.; Col. 1:15–18; Heb. 1:3–5; Phil. 2:6; John 3:35; John 5:19; Col. 2:9–10; John 17:24.

FAITH AND REPENTANCE

OUR LORD;

Jesus Christ, God's only Son, is the heir of all things and persons in His Father's house: all angels and men are His servants, and all the creatures obey Him; we are to believe in Him, and by faith in Him only, and in His name, we shall be saved.[35]

WHO WAS CONCEIVED BY THE HOLY GHOST,

I believe that Jesus Christ was not begotten of a man, nor born by natural means, but that a divine power from God (God's holy Spirit) did overshadow the virgin mother of Christ, and made her in a wonderful manner to conceive Jesus in her womb; and by this His admirable manner of being conceived, He was the Son of God alone, and no man was His father.[36]

BORN OF THE VIRGIN MARY;

Though God was His Father, and He begat Him by the power of the Holy Ghost, and caused Him miraculously to begin in the womb of His mother, yet from her He also derived His human nature, and by His mother He was of the family of king David, and called the son of man, His mother being a holy person, not chosen to this great honour for her wealth or beauty, but by the good will of God, and because she was of a rare exemplar modesty and humility: and she received the honour of being a mother to the Son of God, and ever a virgin, and all generations shall call her blessed.[37]

SUFFERED UNDER PONTIUS PILATE;

After that Jesus passed through the state of infancy and childhood, being subject to His parents, and working in an humble trade to serve

---

35. Matt. 28:18; Acts 2:36; Ps. 2:6–7; 1 Cor. 8:6; Heb. 1:6–14; 1 Pet. 1:21.
36. Luke 1:35; Gal. 4:4; Luke 1:32.
37. Luke 1:26; Matt. 1:18; Luke 1:45–48; Matt. 1:25.

His own and His mother's needs, He grew to the state of a man, He began to preach at the age of thirty years, and having for about three years and a half preached the gospel, and taught us His Father's will, having spoken the gospel of His kingdom, and revealed to us the secrets of eternal life, and resurrection of the dead, regeneration, and renewing by the Holy Spirit, perfect remission of sins, and eternal judgment: at last, that He might reconcile the world to His Father, He became a sacrifice for all our sins, and suffered Himself to be taken by the malicious Jews, and put to a painful and shameful death; they being envious at Him for the number of His disciples, and the reputation of His person, the innocence of His life, the mightiness of His miracles, and the power of His doctrine: and this death He suffered when Pontius Pilate was governor of Judea.[38]

WAS CRUCIFIED,

Jesus Christ being taken by the rulers of the Jews, bound, and derided, buffeted, and spit upon, accused weakly, and persecuted violently; at last, wanting matter and pretences to condemn Him, they asked Him of His person and office; and because He affirmed that great truth which all the world of good men longed for, that He was the Messias, and designed to sit at the right hand of the majesty on high, they resolved to call it blasphemy, and delivered Him over to Pilate, and by importunity and threats forced him against his conscience to give Him up to be scourged, and then to be crucified. The soldiers therefore mocking Him with a robe and a reed, and pressing a crown of thorns upon His head, led Him to the place of His death; compelling Him to bear His cross, to which they presently nailed Him; on which for three hours He hanged in extreme torture, being a sad spectacle of the most afflicted and the most innocent person of the whole world.[39]

---

38. Luke 2:51–52; Luke 3:23; John 3:4; Acts 13:39; Matt. 25:31–32; Luke 12:63; John 18:4–12; Matt. 26:1ff.
39. Matt. 27:1ff.; Mark 15:1ff.; Luke 23:1ff.; John 19:1ff.

DEAD,

When the holy Jesus was wearied with tortures, and He knew all things were now fulfilled, and His Father's wrath appeased towards mankind: His Father pitying His innocent Son groaning under such intolerable miseries, hastened His death; and Jesus commending His spirit into the hands of His Father, cried with a loud voice, bowed His head, and died; and by His death sealed all the doctrines and revelations which He first taught the world, and then confirmed by His blood: He was consecrated our merciful high-priest, and by a feeling of our miseries and temptations became able to help them that are tempted: and for these His sufferings was exalted to the highest throne and seat of the right hand of God: and hath shewn that to heaven there is no surer way than suffering for His name, and hath taught us willingly to suffer for His sake what Himself hath already suffered for ours: He reconciled us to God by His death, led us to God, drew us to Himself, redeemed us from all iniquity, purchased us for His Father, and for ever made us His servants and redeemed ones, that we being dead unto sin might live unto God: and this death being so highly beneficial to us, He hath appointed means to apply to us, and to represent to God for us, in the holy sacrament of His last supper. And upon all these considerations, that cross which was a smart and shame to our Lord, is honour to us, and as it turned to His glory, so also to our spiritual advantages.[40]

AND BURIED;

That He might suffer every thing of human nature, He was by the care of His friends and disciples, by the leave of Pilate, taken from the cross, and embalmed (as the manner of the Jews was to bury) and wrapt in linen, and buried in a new grave, hewn out of a rock; and this was the last and lowest step of His humiliation.[41]

---

40. John 18:37; Phil. 2:8; Col. 1:20; Isa. 53:10; Heb. 7:25; Heb. 9:12; Heb. 2:17–18; Heb. 4:15; Luke 23:46; John 10:17–18; John 12:32; John 11:51; Eph. 2:13–14; Heb. 2:10; Col. 1:21; Titus 2:14; John 6:51; 1 Pet. 2:24; 1 Pet. 4:13; 2 Tim. 2:11; Gal. 6:14.
41. Matt. 27:57ff.

FAITH AND REPENTANCE

HE DESCENDED INTO HELL,

That is, He went down into the lower parts of the earth, or (as Himself called it) into the heart of the earth; by which phrase the scripture understands the state of separation, or of souls severed from their bodies: by this His descending to the land of darkness, where all things are forgotten, He sanctified the state of death and separation, that none of His servants might ever after fear the jaws of death and hell; whither He went, not to suffer torment (because He finished all that upon the cross) but to triumph over the gates of hell, to verify His death, and the event of His sufferings, and to break the iron bars of those lower prisons, that they may open and shut hereafter only at His command.[42]

THE THIRD DAY HE ROSE AGAIN FROM THE DEAD,

After our Lord Jesus had abode in the grave the remaining part of the day of His passion and all the next day, early in the morning upon the third day, by the power of God, He was raised from death and hell to light and life, never to return to death any more, and is become the first-born from the dead, the first-fruits of them that slept; and although He was put to death in the flesh, yet now being quickened in the spirit He lives for ever; and as we all die in Adam, so in Christ we all shall be made alive; but every man in his own order: Christ is the first, and we, if we follow Him in the regeneration, shall also follow Him in the resurrection.[43]

HE ASCENDED INTO HEAVEN,

When our dearest Lord was risen from the grave, He conversed with His disciples for forty days together, often shewing Himself alive

---

42. Eph. 4:9; Matt. 12:40; Acts 2:27; Hos. 13:14; 1 Cor. 15:54ff.; Rev. 20:13–14; Matt. 16:18.

43. Mark 16:1; Acts 10:10; Rom. 14:9; Acts 5:30ff.; Col. 1:18; Matt. 28:1; 1 Pet. 3:18; 1 Pet. 1:3; Eph. 1:17.

by infallible proofs, and once to five hundred of His disciples at one appearing. Having spoken to them fully concerning the affairs of the kingdom, and the promise of the Father; leaving them some few things in charge for the present, He solemnly gave them His blessing, and in the presence of His apostles was taken up into heaven, by a bright cloud and the ministry of angels, being gone before us to prepare a place for us above all heavens, in the presence of His Father, and at the foot of the throne of God; from which glorious presence we cannot be kept by the change of death and the powers of the grave, nor the depth of hell, nor the height of heaven, but Christ being lifted up shall draw all His servants unto Him.[44]

AND SITTETH AT THE RIGHT HAND OF GOD THE FATHER ALMIGHTY;

I believe that Jesus Christ sitteth in heaven above all principalities and powers, being exalted above every name that is named in heaven and earth, that is, above every creature above and below, all things being put under His feet: He is always in the presence of His Father, interceding for us, and governs all things in heaven and earth, that He may defend His church, and adorn her with His spirit, and procure and effect her eternal salvation. There He sits and reigns as king, and intercedes as our high-priest; He is a minister of the sanctuary, and of the true tabernacle which God made and not man, the author and finisher of our faith, the captain of our confession, the great apostle of our religion, the great bishop of our souls, the head of the church, and the Lord of heaven and earth: and therefore to Him we are to pay divine worship, service and obedience, and we must believe in Him, and in God by Him, and rely entirely on the mercies of God through Jesus Christ.[45]

---

44. Luke 24:45–50; Matt. 21:17; John 20:1ff.; John 21:1ff.; Acts 1:9; 1 Cor. 15:6; 1 Cor. 15:45–47; Heb. 6:19; Rom. 8:38–39; 1 John 3:3.
45. Phil. 2:8–9; Eph. 1:17–22; Rom. 8:34; Heb. 7:27; 2 Pet. 1:4; Heb. 12:2; 1 Pet. 1:20–21; Heb. 1:6.

FAITH AND REPENTANCE

FROM THENCE HE SHALL COME

In the clouds, shining, and adorned with the glory of His Father, attended by millions of bright angels, with the voice of an archangel, and a shout of all the heavenly army, the trump of God; and every eye shall see Him, and they that pierced His hands and His feet shall behold His majesty, His terror, and His glory; and all the families of the earth shall tremble at His presence; and the powers of heaven shall be shaken, and the whole earth and sea shall be broken in pieces and confusion: for then He shall come to put an end to this world,[46] and

TO JUDGE THE QUICK AND DEAD.

For the Father judgeth no man, but hath given all judgment to the Son; and at this day of judgment the Lord Jesus shall sit in the air in a glorious throne; and the angels having gathered together God's elect from the four corners of the world, and all the kindreds of the earth being brought before the judgment-seat, shall have the records of their conscience laid open; that is, all that ever they thought, or spake, or did, shall be brought to their memory, to convince the wicked of the justice of the Judge in passing the fearful sentence upon them, and to glorify the mercies of God towards His redeemed ones: and then the righteous Judge shall condemn the wicked to the portion of devils for ever, to a state of torments, the second, and eternal, and intolerable death; and the godly being placed on His right hand, shall hear the blessed sentence of absolution, and shall be led by Christ to the participation of the glories of His Father's kingdom for ever and ever.[47] Amen.

I BELIEVE IN THE HOLY GHOST (OR THE HOLY SPIRIT),

Who is the third Person of the holy, undivided, ever-blessed Trinity, which I worship, and adore, and admire, but look upon with wonder, and am not in a capacity to understand. I believe that the holy

---

46. John 14:3; Matt. 24:30; 1 Thess. 4:16; Rev. 1:7; Acts 1:11; 2 Tim. 4:1.
47. John 5:22–23; 1 Thess. 4:16–17; Matt. 25:32; Acts 10:42; Matt. 25:34ff.

Spirit, into whose name, as of the Father and the Son, I was baptized, is the heavenly author, the captain, the teacher, and the witness of all the truths of the gospel: that as the Father sent the Son, so the Son from heaven sent the holy Spirit to lead the church into all truth; to assist us in all temptations, and to help us in the purchase of all virtue. This holy Spirit proceeds from the Father, and our Lord Jesus received Him from His Father, and sent Him into the world, who receiving the things of Christ, and declaring the same excellent doctrines, speaks whatsoever He hath heard from Him; and instructed the apostles, and builds the church, and produces faith, and confirms our hope, and increases charity: and this holy Spirit our blessed Lord hath left with His church for ever, by which all the servants of God are enabled to do all things necessary to salvation, which by the force of nature they cannot do: and we speak by the Spirit, and work by the Spirit, when by His assistances any ways imparted to us we speak or do any thing of our duty. He it is who enlightens our understandings, sanctifies our will, orders and commands our affections; He comforts our sorrows, supports our spirits in trouble, and enables us by promises and confidences, and gifts, to suffer for the Lord Jesus and the gospel: and all these things God the Father does for us by His Son, and the Son by the holy Spirit, and the holy Spirit by all means within and without, which are operative upon, and proportionable to, the nature of reasonable creatures. This is He who works miracles, gives the gifts of prophecy and of interpretation; that teaches us what and how to pray; that gives us zeal and holy desires; who sanctifies children in baptism, and confirms them with His grace in confirmation, and reproves the world, and consecrates bishops and all the ministers of the gospel, and absolves the penitent, and blesses the obedient, and comforts the sick, and excommunicates the refractary, and makes intercession for the saints, that is, the church; and those whom He hath blessed, appointed, and sanctified to these purposes, do all these ministries by His authority, and His commandment, and His aids. This is He that testifies to our spirits that we are the sons of God, and that makes us to cry, Abba, Father; that is, who inspires into us such humble confidences of our being accepted in our hearty and constant endeavours to please God, that we can with cheerfulness and joy call God our Father, and expect and hope for the portion of sons both here and hereafter, and in the certainty of this hope, to work out our salvation with fear and reverence, with trembling and joy, with distrust of ourselves, and mighty confidence in God. By this holy and ever-blessed Spirit several persons in the church, and every man in his proportion, receives the gifts of wisdom, and utterance, and knowledge, and interpretation, and prophecy, and healing, and government, and discerning of spirits, and faith, and tongues, and whatsoever can be necessary for the church in several ages and periods, for her beginning, for her continuance, for her in prosperity, and for her in persecution. This is the great promise of the Father, and it is the gift of God which He will give to all them that ask Him, and who live piously and chastely, and are persons fit to entertain so divine a grace. This holy Spirit God gives to some more, to some less, according as they are capable. They who obey His motions, and love His presence, and improve His gifts, shall have Him yet more abundantly: but they that grieve the holy Spirit shall lose that which they have: and they that extinguish Him belong not to Christ, but are in the state of reprobation: and they that blaspheme this holy Spirit, and call Him the spirit of the devil, or the spirit of error, or folly, or do malicious despites to Him, that is, they who on purpose, considering and choosing, do Him hurt by word or by deed so far as lies in them, shall for ever be separated from the presence of God and of Christ, and shall never be forgiven in this world, nor in the world to come. Lastly, this holy Spirit seals us to the day of redemption; that is, God gives us His holy Spirit as a testimony that He will raise us again at the last day, and give us a portion in the glories of His kingdom, in the inheritance of our Lord Jesus.[48]

THE HOLY CATHOLIC CHURCH,

I believe that there is and ought to be a visible company of men, professing the service and discipline, that is, the religion of the gospel, who agree together in the belief of all the truths of God revealed by Jesus Christ, and in confession of the articles of this creed, and agree together in praying and praising God through Jesus Christ; to read and hear the scriptures read and expounded; to provoke each other to love and to good works; to advance the honour of Christ, and to propagate

---

48. Matt. 28:19; John 15:26; John 16:13; John 6:45; John 7:16–17; John 5:37; Acts 15:32; Acts 3:33; Acts 13:1–3; Acts 22:28; Luke 12:12; John 17:3; John 14:16; John 16:13; Matt. 10:19; Eph. 1:17; Eph. 3:16; 1 Cor. 2:10–12; Rom. 8:14–16; Rom. 15:13–19; 1 Thess. 1:6; Luke 24:49; Luke 4:18; Acts 2:33–38; Eph. 4:7–30; 1 Cor. 3:16; Eph. 1:13; Acts 7:51; Rom. 1:14; 1 Thess. 5:19; Mark 3:26; 2 Cor. 1:22; 2 Cor. 5:5.

His faith and worship. I believe this to be a holy church, spiritual, and not civil and secular, but sanctified by their profession, and the solemn rites of it, professing holiness, and separating from the evil manners of heathens and wicked persons, by their laws and institutions. And this church is catholic, that is, it is not confined to the nation of the Jews, as was the old religion; but it is gathered out of all nations, and is not of a differing faith in differing places, but always did, doth, and ever shall profess the faith which the apostles preached, and which is contained in this creed; which whosoever believes, is a catholic and a Christian, and he that believes not, is neither. This catholic church I believe, that is, I believe whatsoever all good Christians in all ages and in all places did confess to be the catholic and apostolic faith.[49]

THE COMMUNION OF SAINTS,

That is, the communion of all Christians: because by reason of their holy faith, they are called saints in scripture; as being begotten by God into a lively faith, and cleansed by believing; and by this faith, and the profession of a holy life in obedience to Jesus Christ, they are separated from the world, called to the knowledge of the truth, justified before God, and endued with the holy Spirit of grace, foreknown from the beginning of the world, and predestinated by God to be made conformable to the image of His Son, here in holiness of life, hereafter in a life of glory. And they who are saints in their belief and profession, must be so also in their practice and conversation, that so they may make their calling and election sure, lest they be saints only in name and title, in their profession and institution, and not in manners and holiness of living, that is, lest they be so before men, and not before God. I believe that all people who desire the benefit of the gospel, are bound to have a fellowship and society with these saints, and communicate with them in their holy things, in their faith and in their hope, and in their sacraments, and in their prayers, and in their public assemblies, and in their government: and must do to them all the acts of charity and mutual help which they can and are required to: and without this communion of saints, and a conjunction with them who believe in God through Jesus

---

49. 1 Tim. 3:15; Eph. 3:21; Heb. 2:12; Heb. 10:24; 1 Cor. 14:26; Matt. 18:17–18; Acts 12:5; 1 Cor. 14:4; Gal. 1:8–9; Col. 2:8–9; Heb. 13:8–9.

Christ, there is no salvation to be expected: which communion must be kept in inward things always, and by all persons, and testified by outward acts always, when it is possible, and may be done upon just and holy conditions.[50]

THE FORGIVENESS OF SINS,

I believe that all the sins I committed before I came to the knowledge of the truth, and all the slips of human infirmity, against which we heartily pray, and watch and labour, and all the evil habits, of which we repent so timely and effectually, that we obtain their contrary graces, and live in them, are fully remitted by the blood of Christ: which forgiveness we obtain by faith and repentance, and therefore are not justified by the righteousness of works, but by the righteousness of faith: and we are preserved in the state of forgiveness or justification by the fruits of a lively faith, and a timely active repentance.[51]

THE RESURRECTION OF THE BODY,

I believe at the last day all they whose sins are forgiven, and who lived and died in the communion of saints, and in whom the holy Spirit did dwell, shall rise from their graves, their dead bones shall live, and be clothed with flesh and skin, and their bodies together with their souls shall enter into the portion of a new life: and that this body shall no more see corruption, but shall rise to an excellent condition; it shall be spiritual, powerful, immortal and glorious, like unto His glorious body, who shall then be our judge, is now our advocate, our Saviour, and our Lord.[52]

---

50. Acts 26:10; Acts 9:13; 1 Cor. 6:11; 1 Cor. 1:2; Matt. 22:14; 1 Pet. 1:2; 1 Pet. 14–16; 2 Pet. 3:11; Matt. 18:17–18; Heb. 10:25; 1 Cor. 11:23; Eph. 4:13; Eph. 5:6–7; Eph. 6:18; Phil. 2:4; Rom. 16:16–17; 1 John 3:18; 1 Pet. 1:22.

51. Rom. 3:28; Acts 2:28; Acts 13:38; 1 John 2:1–2; Gal. 6:1; John 20:23; Mark 16:16; 2 Pet. 1:5ff.; Eph. 1:13; 1 Pet. 1:15–18; James 2:17; 1 John 3:21; Heb. 12:4.

52. 1 Cor. 15:29ff.; Matt. 22:31; Rom. 8:11; John 6:39; Phil. 3:10; 2 Cor. 4:14.

FAITH AND REPENTANCE

AND THE LIFE EVERLASTING.

I believe that they who have their part in this resurrection, shall meet the Lord in the air, and when the blessed sentence is pronounced upon them, they shall for ever be with the Lord in joys unspeakable and full of glory: God shall wipe all tears from their eyes; there shall be no fear or sorrow, no mourning or death, a friend shall never go away from thence, and an enemy shall never enter; there shall be fulness without want, light eternal brighter than the sun; day, and no night; joy, and no weeping; difference in degree, and yet all full; there is love without dissimulation, excellency without envy, multitudes without confusion, music without discord; there the understandings are rich, the will is satisfied, the affections are all love, and all joy, and they shall reign with God and Christ for ever and ever.[53]

AMEN.

This is the catholic faith, which except a man believe faithfully, he cannot be saved.

---

53. 1 Thess. 4:17; Rev. 21:4; Rev. 22:5; Matt. 25:34.

Discourse IX[54] of Repentance

1. The whole doctrine of the gospel is comprehended by the holy Ghost in these two summaries, faith and repentance;[55] that those two potent and imperious faculties, which command our lower powers, which are the fountain of actions, the occasion and capacity of laws, and the title to reward or punishment, the Will and the Understanding, that is, the whole man considered in his superior faculties, may become subjects of the kingdom, servants of Jesus, and heirs of glory. Faith supplies our imperfect conceptions, and corrects our ignorance, making us to distinguish good from evil, not only by the proportions of reason, and custom, and old laws, but by the new standard of the gospel; it teaches us all those duties which were enjoined us in order to a participation of mighty glories; it brings our understanding into subjection, making us apt to receive the Spirit for our guide, Christ for our master, the gospel for our rule, the laws of Christianity for our measure of good and evil: and it supposes us naturally ignorant, and comes to supply those defects which in our understandings were left after the spoils of innocence and wisdom made in paradise upon Adam's prevarication, and continued and increased by our neglect, evil customs, voluntary deceptions, and infinite prejudices. And as faith presupposes our ignorance, so repentance presupposes our malice and iniquity. The whole design of Christ's coming, and the doctrines of the gospel, being to recover us from a miserable condition, from ignorance to spiritual wisdom, by the conduct of faith; and from a vicious, habitually depraved life, and ungodly manners, to the purity of the sons of God, by the instrument of repentance.

2. And this is a loud publication of the excellency and glories of the gospel, and the felicities of man over all the other instances of

---

54. *Works* 2:351ff.
55. Acts 20:21.

creation. The angels, who were more excellent spirits than human souls, were not comprehended and made safe within a covenant and provisions of repentance. Their first act of volition was their whole capacity of a blissful or a miserable eternity: they made their own sentence when they made their first election; and having such excellent knowledge, and no weaknesses to prejudge and trouble their choice, what they first did was not capable of repentance; because they had at first, in their intuition and sight, all which could afterward bring them to repentance. But weak man, who knows first by elements, and after long study learns a syllable, and in good time gets a word, could not at first know all those things which were sufficient or apt to determine his choice, but as he grew to understand more, saw more reasons to rescind his first elections. The angels had a full peremptory will, and a satisfied understanding, at first, and therefore were not to mend their first act by a second contradictory; but poor man hath a will always strongest when his understanding is weakest, and chooseth most when he is least able to determine; and therefore is most passionate in his desires, and follows his object with greatest earnestness, when he is blindest, and hath the least reason so to do. And therefore God, pitying man, begins to reckon his choices to be criminal just in the same degree as He gives him understanding; the violences and unreasonable actions of childhood are no more remembered by God, than they are understood by the child: the levities and passions of youth are not aggravated by the imputation of malice, but are sins of a lighter dye, because reason is not yet impressed and marked upon them with characters and tincture in grain: but he who, when he may choose because he understands, shall choose the evil and reject the good, stands marked with a deep guilt, and hath no excuse left to him but as his degrees of ignorance left his choice the more imperfect. And because every sinner, in the style of scripture, is a fool, and hath an election as imperfect as is the action, that is, as great a declension from prudence as it is from piety, and the man understands as imperfectly as he practices; therefore God sent His Son to "take upon Him, not the nature of angels, but the seed of Abraham,[56] and to propound salvation upon such terms as were possible, that is, upon such a piety which relies upon experience and trial of good and evil; and hath given us leave, if we choose amiss at first, to choose again, and choose

---

56. Heb. 2:16.

better; Christ having undertaken to pay for the issues of their first follies, to make up the breach made by our first weaknesses and abused understandings.

3. But as God gave us this mercy by Christ, so He also revealed it by Him. He first used the authority of a Lord, and a creator, and a lawgiver: He required obedience indeed upon reasonable terms, upon the instance of but a few commandments at first, which when He afterwards multiplied, He also appointed ways to expiate the smaller irregularities; but left them eternally bound without remedy who should do any great violence or a crime: but then He bound them but to a temporal death. Only this; as an eternal death was also tacitly implied, so also a remedy was secretly ministered, and repentance particularly preached by homilies distinct from the covenant of Moses' law. The law allowed no repentance for greater crimes; "he that was convicted of adultery was to die without mercy":[57] but God pitied the miseries of man, and the inconveniences of the law, and sent Christ to suffer for the one, and remedy the other; "for so it behoved Christ to suffer, and to rise from the dead, and that repentance and remission of sins should be preached in His name among all nations."[58] And now this is the last and only hope of man, who in his natural condition is imperfect, in his customs vicious, in his habits impotent and criminal. Because man did not remain innocent, it became necessary he should be penitent, and that this penitence should by some means be made acceptable, that is, become the instrument of his pardon and restitution of his hope. Which because it is an act of favour, and depends wholly upon the divine dignation, and was revealed to us by Jesus Christ, who was made not only the Prophet and preacher, but the Mediator of this new covenant and mercy; it was necessary we should become disciples of the holy Jesus, and servants of His institution: that is, run to Him to be made partakers of the mercies of this new covenant, and accept of Him such conditions as He should require of us.

4. This covenant is then consigned to us when we first come to Christ, that is, when we first profess ourselves His disciples and His servants, disciples of His doctrine and servants of His institution; that is, in baptism, in which Christ, who died for our sins, makes us partakers of His death. "For we are buried by baptism into His death,"[59]

57. Lev. 20:10.
58. Luke 24:46.
59. Rom. 6:4.

saith St. Paul; which was also represented in ceremony by the immersion appointed to be the rite of that sacrament. And then it is that God pours forth, together with the sacramental waters, a salutary and holy fountain of grace, to wash the soul from all its stains and impure adherences; and therefore this first access to Christ is in the style of scripture called "regeneration," "the new birth," "redemption," "renovation," "expiation," or "atonement with God," and "justification."[60] And these words in the New testament relate principally and properly to the abolition of sins committed before baptism. For we are "justified freely by His grace, through the redemption that is in Jesus Christ; whom God hath set forth to be a propitiation, to declare His righteousness for the remission of sins that are past; to declare, I say, at this time, His righteousness." And this is that which St. Paul calls "justification by faith," that "boasting might be excluded," and the grace of God by Jesus made exceeding glorious:[61] for this being the proper work of Christ, the first entertainment of a disciple, and manifestation of that state which is first given him as a favour and next intended as a duty, is a total abolition of the precedent guilt of sin, and leaves nothing remaining that can condemn; we then freely receive the entire and perfect effect of that atonement which Christ made for us, we are put into a condition of innocence and favour. And this, I say, is done regularly in baptism, and St. Paul expresses it to this sense; after he had enumerated a series of vices subjected in many, he adds, "and such were some of you; but ye are washed, but ye are sanctified."[62] There is nothing of the old guilt remanent: when "ye were washed, ye were sanctified," or, as the scripture calls it in another place, "ye were redeemed from your vain conversation."[63]

5. For this grace was the formality of the covenant: "Repent and believe the gospel,"[64] "repent and be converted" (so it is in St. Peter's sermon), "and your sins shall be done away,"[65] that was the covenant. But that Christ chose baptism for its signature, appears in the parallel: "Repent, and be baptized, and wash away your sins"; "for Christ loved His church, and gave Himself for it, that He might sanctify and cleanse

---

60. 1 Pet. 3:21; Rom. 5:1; Titus 3:5–7; Rom. 3:26; Gal. 2:16.
61. Rom. 2:24–28.
62. 1 Cor. 6:11.
63. 1 Pet. 1:18.
64. Mark 1:15.
65. Acts 3:19.

it with the washing of water by the word; that He might present it to Himself a glorious church, not having spot, or wrinkle, or any such thing, but that it should be holy, and without blemish."[66] The sanctification is integral, the pardon is universal and immediate.

6. But here the process is short: no more at first but this, "Repent, and be baptized, and wash away your sins";[67] which baptism because it was speedily administered, and yet not without the preparatives of faith and repentance, it is certain those predispositions were but instruments of reception, actions of great facility, of small employment, and such as, supposing the person not unapt, did confess the infiniteness of the divine mercy and fulness of the redemption, and is called by the apostle "a being justified freely."[68]

7. Upon this ground it is that by the doctrine of the church heathen persons, "strangers from the covenant of grace," were invited to a confession of faith and dereliction of false religions, with a promise that at the very first resignation of their persons to the service of Jesus they should obtain full pardon. It was St. Cyprian's counsel to old Demetrianus, "Now in the evening of thy days, when thy soul is almost expiring, repent of thy sins, believe in Jesus, and turn Christian; and although thou art almost in the embraces of death, yet thou shalt be comprehended of immortality." *Baptizatus ad horam securus hinc exit,* saith St. Austin;[69] a baptized person dying immediately shall live eternally and gloriously. And this was the case of the thief upon the cross; he confessed Christ, and repented of his sins, and begged pardon, and did acts enough to facilitate his first access to Christ, and but to remove the hindrances of God's favour; then he was redeemed and reconciled to God by the death of Jesus, that is, he was pardoned with a full, instantaneous, integral, and clear pardon; with such a pardon which declared the glory of God's mercies and the infiniteness of Christ's merits, and such as required a mere reception and entertainment on man's part.

8. But then we, having received so great a favour, enter into covenant to correspond with a proportionable endeavour; the benefit of absolute pardon, that is, salvation of our souls, being not to be received till "the times of refreshing shall come from the presence of the

66. Acts 2:38; Mark 16:16; Eph. 5:25–27.
67. Ignatius of Antioch, *To the Thrallians,* PG 5.678.
68. Rom. 3:24.
69. Augustine, *Sermon to Catechumens,* PG 40.693.

308

Lord":[70] all the interval we have promised to live a holy life, in obedience to the whole discipline of Jesus. That is the condition on our part: and if we prevaricate that, the mercy shewn to the blessed thief is no argument of hope to us, because he was saved by the mercies of the first access, which corresponds to the remission of sins we receive in baptism; and we shall perish, by breaking our own promises and obligations, which Christ passed upon us when He made with us the covenant of an entire and gracious pardon.

9. For in the precise covenant there is nothing else described but pardon so given, and ascertained upon an obedience persevering to the end. And this is clear in all those places of scripture which express a holy and innocent life to have been the purpose and design of Christ's death for us, and redemption of us from the former estate; "Christ bare our sins in His own body on the tree, that we, being dead unto sins, should live unto righteousness: by whose stripes ye are healed."[71] *Exinde;* from our being "healed," from our "dying unto sin," from our being "buried with Christ," from our being "baptized into His death"; the end of Christ's dying for us is "that we should live unto righteousness." Which was also highly and prophetically expressed by St. Zachary in his divine exstasy: this was "the oath which He sware to our forefather Abraham, that He would grant unto us that we, being delivered out of the hands of our enemies, might serve Him without fear, in holiness and righteousness before Him, all the days of our life." And St. Paul[72] discourses to this purpose pertinently and largely; "for the grace of God that bringeth salvation hath appeared to all men, teaching us that denying ungodliness and worldly lusts"—*hi sunt angeli quibus in lavacro renunciavimus,* saith Tertullian;[73] "those are the evil angels, the devil and his works, which we deny or renounce in baptism"—"we should live soberly, righteously, and godly, in this present world," that is, lead a whole life in the pursuit of universal holiness; sobriety, justice, and godliness, being the proper language to signify our religion and respects to God, to our neighbours, and to ourselves. And that this was the very end of our dying in baptism, and the design of Christ's manifestation of our redemption, he adds,[74] "looking for that blessed hope, and the glor-

---

70. Acts 3:19.
71. 1 Pet. 2:24.
72. Titus 2:11–12.
73. Tertullian, *On the Dress of Women,* PL 1.1306.
74. Titus 2:13–14.

ious appearing of the great God and our Saviour Jesus, who gave Himself for us," to this very purpose, "that He might redeem us from all iniquity, and purify unto Himself a peculiar people, zealous of good works." Purifying a people peculiar to Himself, is cleansing it in the laver of regeneration, and appropriating it to Himself in the rites of admission and profession. Which plainly designs the first consignation of our redemption to be in baptism, and that Christ, there cleansing His church "from every spot or wrinkle," made a covenant with us, that we should renounce all our sins, and He should cleanse them all, and then that we should abide in that state. Which is also very explicitly set down by the same apostle in that divine and mysterious epistle to the Romans,[75] "How shall we that are dead to sin live any longer therein? know ye not that so many of us as were baptized into Jesus Christ were baptized into His death?" well, what then? "therefore we are buried with Him by baptism into His death, that like as Christ was raised up from the dead by the glory of the Father, even so we also should walk in newness of life." That's the end and mysteriousness of baptism; it is a consignation into the death of Christ, and we die with Him that once; that is, die to sin, that we may for ever after live the life of righteousness: "knowing this, that our old man is crucified with Him, that the body of sin might be destroyed, that henceforth we should not serve sin";[76] that is, from the day of our baptism to the day of our death. And therefore God, who knows the weaknesses on our part, and yet the strictness and necessity of conserving baptismal grace by the covenant evangelical, hath appointed the auxiliaries of the holy Spirit to be ministered to all baptized people in the holy rite of confirmation, that it might be made possible to be done by divine aids which is necessary to be done by the divine commandments.

10. And this might not be improperly said to be the meaning of those words of our blessed Saviour, "He that speaks a word against the Son of man, it shall be forgiven him; but he that speaks a word against the holy Ghost, it shall not be forgiven him": that is, those sins which were committed in infidelity, before we became disciples of the holy Jesus, are to be remitted in baptism and our first profession of the religion; but the sins committed after baptism and confirmation in which we receive the holy Ghost, and by which the holy Spirit is

75. Rom. 6:2–4.
76. Rom. 6:6.

310

grieved, are to be accounted for with more severity. And therefore the primitive church, understanding our obligations according to this discourse, admitted not any to holy orders who had lapsed and fallen into any sin of which she could take cognizance, that is, such who had not kept the integrity of their baptism;[77] but sins committed before baptism were no impediments to the susception of orders, because they were absolutely extinguished in baptism. This is the nature of the covenant we made in baptism, that's the grace of the gospel, and the effect of faith and repentance: and it is expected we should so remain; for it is no where expressed to be the mercy and intention of the covenant evangelical that this redemption should be any more than once, or that repentance, which is in order to it, can be renewed to the same or so great purposes and present effects.

11. But after we are once reconciled in baptism and put entirely into God's favour, when we have once been redeemed, if we then fall away into sin, we must expect God's dealing with us in another manner and to other purposes. Never must we expect to be so again justified, and upon such terms as formerly; the best days of our repentance are interrupted: not that God will never forgive them that sin after baptism, and recover by repentance; but that restitution by repentance after baptism is another thing than the first redemption. No such entire, clear, and integral, determinate and presential effects of repentance; but an imperfect, little, growing, uncertain, and hazardous reconciliation: a repentance that is always in production, a renovation by parts, a pardon that is revocable, a "salvation" to be "wrought by fear and trembling"; all our remanent life must be in bitterness, our hopes allayed with fears, our meat attempered with coloquintida, and "death is in the pot": as our best actions are imperfect, so our greatest graces are but possibilities and aptnesses to a reconcilement, and all our life we are working ourselves into that condition we had in baptism, and lost by our relapse. As the habit lessens, so does the guilt; as our virtues are imperfect, so is the pardon; and because our piety may be interrupted, our state is uncertain, till our possibilities of sin are ceased, till our "fight is finished," and the victory therefore made sure because there is no more fight. And it is remarkable that St. Peter gives counsel to live holily, in pursuance of our redemption, of our calling, and of our "escaping from that corruption that is in the world through lust," lest we lose the benefit of our

---

77. Augustine, *The Good Spouse*, PL 40.387.

purgation: to which, by way of antithesis, he opposes this, "wherefore the rather give diligence to make your calling and election sure"; and, "if ye do these things, ye shall never fall," meaning, by the perpetuating our state of baptism and first repentance we shall never fall, but be in a sure estate, our "calling and election" shall be "sure"; but not, if we fall; if we "forget we were purged from our old sins";[78] if we forfeit our "calling," we have also made our "election" unsure, moveable, and disputable.

12. So that now the hopes of lapsed sinners rely upon another bottom: and as in Moses' law there was no revelation of repentance, but yet the Jews had hopes in God, and were taught the succours of repentance by the homilies of the prophets and other accessory notices: so in the gospel the covenant was established upon faith and repentance, but it was consigned in baptism, and was verifiable only in the integrity of a following holy life according to the measures of a man; not perfect, but sincere; not faultless, but heartily endeavoured. But yet the mercies of God, in pardoning sinners lapsed after baptism, was declared to us by collateral and indirect occasions; by the sermons of the apostles, and the commentaries of apostolical persons who understood the meaning of the Spirit and the purposes of the divine mercy, and those other significations of His will which the blessed Jesus left upon record in other parts of His testament, as in codicils annexed, besides the precise testament itself. And it is certain, if in the covenant of grace there be the same involution of an after-repentance, as there is of present pardon upon past repentance and future sanctity, it is impossible to justify that a holy life and a persevering sanctity is enjoined by the covenant of the gospel: if, I say, in its first intention it be declared that we may as well, and upon the same terms, hope for pardon upon a recovery hereafter, as upon the perseverance in the present condition.

13. From these premises we may soon understand what is the duty of a Christian in all his life, even to pursue his own undertaking made in baptism, or his first access to Christ and redemption of his person from the guilt and punishment of sins. The state of a Christian is called in scripture "regeneration," "spiritual life," "walking after the Spirit," "walking in newness of life," that is, "a bringing forth fruits meet for repentance." That repentance which, tied up in the same ligament with faith, was the disposition of a Christian to his regeneration and atone-

---

78. 2 Pet. 1:9.

ment, must have a holy life in perpetual succession; for that is the apt and proper fruit of the first repentance which John the baptist preached as an introduction to Christianity, and as an entertaining the redemption by the blood of the covenant. And all that is spoken in the New testament is nothing but a calling upon us to do what we promised in our regeneration, to perform that which was the design of Christ, who therefore redeemed us and "bare our sins in His own body, that we might die unto sin and live unto righteousness."

14. This is that saying of St. Paul,[79] "Follow peace with all men, and holiness, without which no man shall see the Lord; looking diligently lest any man fail of the grace of God, lest any root of bitterness springing up trouble you": plainly saying that unless we pursue the state of holiness and Christian communion into which we were baptized when we received the grace of God, we shall fail of the state of grace, and never come to see the glories of the Lord: and a little before, "Let us draw near with a true heart, in full assurance of faith, having our hearts sprinkled from an evil conscience, and our bodies washed with pure water."[80] That's the first state of our redemption, that's "the covenant God made with us, to remember our sins no more, and to put His laws in our hearts and minds";[81] and this was done when "our bodies" were "washed with water, and our hearts sprinkled from an evil conscience," that is, in baptism. It remains then that we persist in the condition, that we may continue our title to the covenant; for so it follows, "Let us hold fast the profession of our faith without wavering; for if we sin wilfully after the profession, there remains no more sacrifice";[82] that is, if we hold not fast the profession of our faith, and continue not the condition of the covenant, but fall into a contrary state, we have forfeited the mercies of the covenant. So that all our hopes of blessedness, relying upon the covenant made with God in Jesus Christ, are ascertained upon us by "holding fast that profession," by retaining "our hearts" still "sprinkled from an evil conscience," by "following peace with all men, and holiness"; for by not "failing of the grace of God," we shall not fail of our hopes, "the mighty prize of our high calling"; but without all this, we shall never see the face of God.

15. To the same purpose are all those places of scripture, which

---

79. Heb. 12:15.
80. Heb. 10:22.
81. Heb. 10:16–17.
82. Heb. 10:23–26.

entitle us to Christ and the Spirit upon no other condition but a holy life, and a prevailing, habitual, victorious grace. "Know you not your ownselves," brethren, "how that Jesus Christ is in you, except ye be reprobates?"[83] There are but two states of being in order to eternity, either a state of the inhabitation of Christ, or the state of reprobation; either "Christ is in us," or we "are reprobates." But what does that signify, to have "Christ dwelling in us?" That also we learn at the feet of the same doctor; "if Christ be in you, the body is dead by reason of sin, but the spirit is life because of righteousness";[84] the body of sin is mortified, and the life of grace is active, busy, and spiritual, in all them who are not in the state of reprobation: the parallel with that other expression of his, "they that are Christ's have crucified the flesh with the affections and lusts."[85] If sin be vigorous, if it be habitual, if it be beloved, if it be not dead or dying in us, we are not of Christ's portion, we belong not to Him, nor He to us: for "whoever is born of God doth not commit sin, for His seed remaineth in him; and he cannot sin, because he is born of God":[86] that is, every regenerate person is in a condition whose very being is a contradiction and an opposite design to sin; when he was regenerate, and born anew "of water and the Spirit," "the seed of God," the original of piety, was put into him, and bidden to "increase and multiply." "The seed of God," in St. John, is the same with "the word" of God, in St. James, "by which He begat us";[87] and as long as this remains, a regenerate person cannot be given up to sin; for when he is, he quits his baptism, he renounces the covenant, he alters his relation to God in the same degree as he enters into a state of sin.

16. And yet this discourse is no otherwise to be understood than according to the design of the thing itself and the purpose of God; that is, that it be a deep engagement and an effectual consideration for the necessity of a holy life; but at no hand let it be made an instrument of despair, nor an argument to lessen the influences of the divine mercy. For although the nicety and limits of the covenant, being consigned in baptism, are fixed upon the condition of a holy and persevering uninterrupted sanctity; and our redemption is wrought but once, completed but once, we are but once absolutely, entirely, and presentially forgiven,

---

83. 2 Cor. 13:5.
84. Rom. 8:10.
85. Gal. 5:24.
86. 1 John 3:9.
87. James 1:18.

and reconciled to God, this reconciliation being in virtue of the sacrifice, and this sacrifice applied in baptism is one, as "baptism is one," and as the sacrifice is one: yet the mercy of God, besides this great feast, hath fragments, which the apostles and ministers spiritual are to gather up in baskets, and minister to the after-needs of indigent and necessitous disciples.

17. And this we gather, as fragments are gathered, by respersed sayings, instances and examples of the divine mercy recorded in holy scripture. The holy Jesus commands us to "forgive our brother seventy times seven times," when he asks our pardon and implores our mercy; and since the divine mercy is the pattern of ours, and is also procured by ours, the one being made the measure of the other by way of precedent and by way of reward, God will certainly forgive us as we forgive our brother: and it cannot be imagined God should oblige us to give pardon oftener than He will give it Himself, especially since He hath expressed ours to be a title of a proportionable reception of His; and hath also commanded us to ask pardon all days of our life, even in our daily offices, and to beg it in the measure and rule of our own charity and forgiveness to our brother. And therefore God, in His infinite wisdom, foreseeing our frequent relapses and considering our infinite infirmities, appointed in His church an ordinary ministry of pardon: designing the minister to pray for sinners, and promising to accept him in that his advocation, or that He would open or shut heaven respectively to his act on earth; that is, He would hear his prayers, and verify his ministry, to whom He hath "committed the word of reconciliation." This became a duty to Christian ministers, spiritual persons, that they should "restore a person overtaken in a fault,"[88] that is, reduce him to the condition he begins to lose; that they should "pray over sick persons,"[89] who are also commanded to "confess their sins"; and God hath promised that "the sins they have committed shall be forgiven them." Thus St. Paul absolved the incestuous, excommunicate Corinthian; in the person of Christ he forgave him. And this also is the confidence St. John taught the Christian church, upon the stock of the excellent mercy of God, and propitiation of Jesus; "if we confess our sins, He is faithful and just to forgive us our sins, and to cleanse us from all unrighteousness":[90] which

---

88. Gal. 6:1.
89. James 5:14.
90. 1 John 1:9.

discourse he directs to them who were Christians, already initiated into the institution of Jesus; and the epistles which the Spirit sent to the seven Asian churches, and were particularly addressed to the bishops, the angels of those churches, are exhortations, some to perseverance, some to repentance, that they may "return from whence they are fallen."[91] And the case is so with us, that it is impossible we should be actually and perpetually free from sin, in the long succession of a busy, and impotent, and a tempted conversation: and without these reserves of the divine grace and after-emanations from the mercy-seat, no man could be saved; and the death of Christ would become inconsiderable to most of His greatest purposes, for none should have received advantages but newly-baptized persons, whose albs of baptism served them also for a winding-sheet. And therefore our baptism, although it does consign the work of God presently to the baptized person in great, certain, and entire effect, in order to the remission of what is past, in case the catechumen be rightly disposed, or hinders not; yet it hath also influence upon the following periods of our life, and hath admitted us into a lasting state of pardon, to be renewed and actually applied by the sacrament of the Lord's supper, and all other ministries evangelical, and so long as our repentance is timely, active, and effective.

18. But now although it is infinitely certain that the gates of mercy stand open to sinners after baptism, yet it is with some variety, and greater difficulty. He that renounces Christianity, and becomes apostate from his religion, not by a seeming abjuration under a storm, but by a voluntary and hearty dereliction, he seems to have quitted all that grace which he had received when he was illuminated, and to have lost the benefits of his redemption and former expiation. And I conceive this is the full meaning of those words of St. Paul, which are of highest difficulty and latent sense, "for it is impossible for those who were once enlightened," etc., "if they shall fall away, to renew them again unto repentance."[92] The reason is there subjoined, and more clearly explicated a little after; "for if we sin wilfully, after we have received the knowledge of the truth, there remains no more sacrifice for sins . . . for he hath counted the blood of the covenant wherewith he was sanctified, an unholy thing, and hath done despite to the Spirit of grace." The meaning is diverse, according to the degrees of apostasy or relapse.

---

91. Rev. 2:5.
92. Heb. 6:4–6.

They who fall away after they were once enlightened in baptism, and felt all those blessed effects of the sanctification and the emanations of the Spirit, if it be into a contradictory state of sin and mancipation, and obstinate purposes to serve Christ's enemies, then "there remains nothing but a fearful expectation of judgment": but if the backsliding be but the interruption of the first sanctity by a single act, or an unconformed, unresolved, unmalicious habit; then also, "it is impossible to renew them unto repentance," viz. as formerly; that is, they can never be reconciled as before, integrally, fully, and at once, during this life.[93] For that redemption and expiation was by baptism, into Christ's death; and there are no more deaths of Christ, nor any more such sacramental consignations of the benefit of it; "there is no more sacrifice for sins," but the redemption is one, as the sacrifice is one in whose virtue the redemption does operate. And therefore the Novatians, who were zealous men, denied to the first sort of persons the peace of the church, and remitted them to the divine judgment. The church herself was sometimes almost as zealous against the second sort of persons lapsed into capital crimes, granting to them repentance but once;[94] by such disciplines consigning this truth, That every recession from the state of grace in which by baptism we were established and consigned, is a farther step from the possibilities of heaven, and so near a ruin, that the church thought them persons fit to be transmitted to a judicature immediately divine; as supposing either her power to be too little, or the other's malice too great, or else the danger too violent, or the scandal insupportable. For concerning such persons who once were pious, holy, and forgiven (for so is every man and woman worthily and aptly baptized) and afterwards fell into dissolution of manners, "extinguishing the holy Ghost, doing despite to the Spirit of grace, crucifying again the Lord of life"; that is, returning to such a condition from which they were once recovered, and could not otherwise be so but by the death of our dearest Lord; I say, concerning such persons the scripture speaks very suspiciously, and to the sense and signification of an infinite danger. For if the "speaking a word against the holy Ghost" be "not to be pardoned here nor hereafter," what can we imagine to be the end of such an impiety which "crucifies the Lord of life, and puts Him to an open shame"; which "quenches the Spirit, doing despite to the Spirit of

---

93. Chrysostom, *On Heavens*, PG 63.75.
94. Tertullian, *On Penance*, PL 1.1240.

grace"? Certainly that is worse than speaking against Him; and such is every person who falls into wilful apostasy from the faith, or does that violence to holiness which the other does to faith, that is, extinguishes the sparks of illumination, "quenches the Spirit," and is habitually and obstinately criminal in any kind. For the same thing that atheism was in the first period of the world, and idolatry in the second, the same is apostasy in the last; it is a state wholly contradictory to all our religious relation to God, according to the nature and manner of the present communication: only this last, because it is more malicious, and a declension from a greater grace, is something like the fall of angels; and of this the emperor Julian was a sad example.

19. But as these are degrees immediately next, and a little less, so the hopes of pardon are the more visible. Simon Magus spake a word, or at least thought, against the holy Ghost; he "thought He was to be bought with money." Concerning him St. Peter pronounced, "Thou art in the gall of bitterness, and in the bond of iniquity; yet repent, and pray God, if perhaps the thought of thine heart may be forgiven thee";[95] here the matter was of great difficulty, but yet there was a possibility left, at least no impossibility of recovery declared; and therefore St. Jude bids us "of some to have compassion, making a difference; and others save with fear, pulling them out of the fire": meaning, that their condition is only not desperate. And still in descent, retaining the same proportion, every lesser sin is easier pardoned, as better consisting with the state of grace: the whole Spirit is not destroyed, and the body of sin is not introduced: Christ is not quite ejected out of possession, but, like an oppressed prince, still continues His claim; and such is His mercy that He will still do so, till all be lost, or that He is provoked by too much violence, or that antichrist is put in substitution, and "sin reigns in our mortal body." So that I may use the words of St. John, "These things I write unto you, that you sin not; but if any man sin, we have an advocate with the Father, Jesus Christ the righteous: and He is a propitiation for our sins; and not for ours only, but for the sins of the whole world."[96] That is plainly, Although the design of the gospel be that we should erect a throne for Christ to reign in our spirits, and this doctrine of innocence be therefore preached, that ye sin not; yet if one be overtaken in a fault, despair not; Christ is our advocate, and He is the propitiation:

---

95. Acts 8:22–23.
96. 1 John 2:1–2.

He did propitiate the Father by His death, and the benefit of that we receive at our first access to Him; but then He is our advocate too, and prays perpetually for our perseverance or restitution respectively; but His purpose is, and He is able so to do, "to keep you from falling, and to present you faultless before the presence of His glory."

20. This consideration I intend should relate to all Christians of the world: and although by the present custom of the church we are baptized in our infancy, and do not actually reap that fruit of present pardon which persons of a mature age in the primitive church did (for we yet need it not, as we shall when we have past the calentures of youth, which was the time in which the wisest of our fathers in Christ chose for their baptism, as appears in the instance of St. Ambrose, St. Austin, and divers others; yet we must remember that there is a baptism of the Spirit as well as of water: and whenever this happens, whether it be together with that baptism of water, as usually it was when only men and women of years of discretion were baptized; or whether it be ministered in the rite of confirmation, which is an admirable suppletory of an early baptism, and intended by the holy Ghost for a corroborative of baptismal grace, and a defensative against danger; or that, lastly, it be performed by an internal and merely spiritual ministry, when we by acts of our own election verify the promise made in baptism, and so bring back the rite by receiving the effect of baptism; that is, whenever the "filth of our flesh is washed away," and that we have "the answer of a pure conscience towards God," which St. Peter affirms to be the true baptism, and which by the purpose and design of God it is expected we should not defer longer than a great reason or a great necessity enforces; when our sins are first expiated, and the sacrifice and death of Christ is made ours, and we made God's by a more immediate title, which at some time or other happens to all Christians that pretend to any hopes of heaven: then let us look to our standing, and "take heed lest we fall." When we once have "tasted of the heavenly gift, and are made partakers of the holy Ghost, and have tasted the good word of God, and the powers of the world to come," that is, when we are redeemed by an actual mercy and presential application, which every Christian that belongs to God is at some time or other of his life; then a fall into a deadly crime is highly dangerous, but a relapse into a contrary estate is next to desperate.

21. I represent this sad but most true doctrine in the words of St. Peter; "if after they have escaped the pollutions of the world through the knowledge of the Lord and Saviour Jesus Christ, they are again

319

entangled therein and overcome, the latter end is worse with them than the beginning; for it had been better for them not to have known the way of righteousness, than after they have known it to turn from the holy commandment delivered unto them";[97] so that a relapse, after a state of grace, into a state of sin, into confirmed habits, is to us a great sign, and possibly in itself it is more than a sign, even a state, of reprobation and final abscission.

22. The sum of all is this. There are two states of like opposite terms. First, "Christ redeems us from our vain conversation," and reconciles us to God, putting us into an entire condition of pardon, favour, innocence, and acceptance; and becomes our Lord and King, His Spirit dwelling and reigning in us. The opposite state to this is that which in scripture is called a "crucifying the Lord of life," a "doing despite to the Spirit of grace," a "being entangled in the pollutions of the world"; the apostasy, or falling away; an impotency, or disability to do good, viz. of such who "cannot cease from sin";[98] who are slaves of sin, and in whom "sin reigns in their bodies." This condition is a full and integral deletery of the first; it is such a condition which, as it hath no holiness or remanent affections to virtue, so it hath no hope or revelation of a mercy, because all that benefit is lost which they received by the death of Christ: and the first being lost, "there remains no more sacrifice for sins, but a certain fearful expectation of judgment." But between these two states stand all those imperfections and single delinquencies, those slips and falls, those parts of recession and apostasy, those grievings of the Spirit: and so long as any thing of the first state is left, so long we are within the covenant of grace, so long we are within the ordinary limits of mercy and the divine compassion; we are in possibilities of recovery, and the same sacrifice of Christ hath its power over us; Christ is in His possession, though He be disturbed: but then our restitution consists upon the only condition of a renovation of our integrity: as are the degrees of our innocence, so are our degrees of confidence.

23. Now because the intermedial state is divisible, various, successive, and alterable; so also is our condition of pardon. Our flesh shall no more return as that of a little child; our wounds shall never be perfectly cured; but a scar, and pain, and danger of a relapse, shall for ever afflict

---

97. 2 Pet. 2:20–21.
98. 2 Pet. 2:14.

us; our sins shall be pardoned by parts and degrees, to uncertain purposes, but with certain danger of being recalled again; and the pardon shall never be consummate, till that day in which all things have their consummation.

24. And this is evident to have been God's usual dealing with all those upon whom His name is called. God pardoned David's sins of adultery and murder; but the pardon was but to a certain degree, and in a limited expression, "God hath taken away thy sin; thou shalt not die": but this pardon was as imperfect as his condition was, "nevertheless the child that is born unto thee, that shall die."[99] Thus God pardoned the Israelites at the importunity of Moses, and yet threatened to visit that sin upon them in the day of visitation. And so it is in Christianity: when once we have broken and discomposed the golden chain of vocation, election, and justification, which are entire links and methodical periods of our happiness when we first give up our names to Christ, for ever after our condition is imperfect; we have broken our covenant, and we must be saved by the excrescencies and overflowings of mercy. Our whole endeavour must be to be reduced to the state of our baptismal innocence and integrity, because in that the covenant was established. And since our life is full of defailances, and all our endeavours can never make us such as Christ made us, and yet upon that condition our hopes of happiness were established; I mean, of remaining such as He had made us: as are the degrees of our restitution and access to the first federal condition, so also are the degrees of our pardon. But as it is always in imperfection during this life, and subject to change and defailance, so also are the hopes of our felicity; never certain till we are taken from all danger, never perfect till all that is imperfect in us is done away.

25. And therefore in the present condition of things our pardon was properly expressed by David, and St. Paul, by a "covering,"[100] and a "not imputing." For because the body of sin dies divisibly, and fights perpetually, and disputes with hopes of victory, and may also prevail, all this life is a condition of suspense; our sin is rather covered than properly pardoned; God's wrath is suspended, not satisfied; the sin is not to all purposes of anger imputed, but yet is in some sense remanent, or at least lies ready at the door. Our condition is a state of imperfec-

99. 2 Sam. 12:13–14.
100. Rom 4:7; Ps. 32:1–2.

321

tion; and every degree of imperfection brings a degree of recession from the state Christ put us in; and every recession from our innocence is also an abatement of our confidence; the anger of God hovers over our head, and breaks out into temporal judgments; and He retracts them again, and threatens worse, according as we approach to or retire from that first innocence which was the first entertainment of a Christian, and the crown of the evangelical covenant. Upon that we entertained the mercies of redemption; and God established it upon such an obedience, which is a constant, perpetual, and universal sincerity and endeavour: and as we perform our part, so God verifies His, and not only gives a great assistance by the perpetual influences of His holy Spirit, by which we are consigned to the day of redemption, but also takes an account of obedience, not according to the standard of the law and an exact scrutiny, but by an evangelical proportion; in which we are on one side looked upon as persons already redeemed and assisted, and therefore highly engaged; and on the other side, as compassed about with infirmities and enemies, and therefore much pitied. So that, as at first, our "calling and election" is presently good, and shall remain so, if we make it sure; so if we once prevaricate it, we are rendered then full of hazard, difficulty, and uncertainty, and we must, with pains and sedulity, "work out our salvation with fear and trembling"; first, by preventing a fall; or afterwards, by returning to that excellent condition from whence we have departed.

26. But although the pardon of sins after baptism be during this life difficult, imperfect, and revocable; yet because it is to great effects for the present, and in order to a complete pardon in the day of judgment, we are next to enquire what are the parts of duty to which we are obliged, after such prevarications which usually interrupt the state of baptismal innocence, and the life of the Spirit. St. John gives this account: "If we say we have fellowship with God, and walk in darkness, we lie, and do not the truth; but if we walk in the light, as He is in the light, we have communion one with another, and the blood of Jesus cleanseth us from all sin."[101] This state of duty St. Paul calls a "casting off the works of darkness," a "putting on the armour of light," a "walking honestly," a "putting on the Lord Jesus Christ";[102] and to it he confronts, "making provision for the flesh, to fulfil the lusts thereof."

---

101. 1 John 1:6–7.
102. Rom. 13:12–14.

322

St. Peter, describing the duty of a Christian, relates the proportion of it as high as the first precedent, even God himself; "as He which hath called you is holy, so be ye holy in all manner of conversation; not fashioning yourselves according to the former lusts":[103] and again, "seeing then that all these things shall be dissolved, what manner of persons ought we to be in all holy conversation and godliness?"[104] And St. John with the same severity and perfection, "every one that hath this hope," that is, every one who either does not or hath no reason to despair, "purifieth himself, even as God is pure";[105] meaning that he is pure by a divine purity, which God hath prescribed as an imitation of His holiness according to our capacities and possibilities. That purity must needs be a "laying aside all malice, and guile, and hypocrisies, and envies, and evil speaking";[106] so St. Peter expresses it: "a laying aside every weight, and the sin that does so easily beset us";[107] so St. Paul. This is to "walk in the light, as He is in the light," for "in Him is no darkness at all";[108] which we have then imitated, when we have "escaped the corruption that is in the world through lusts";[109] that is, so as we are "not held by them," that we take them for our enemies, for the object and party of our contestation and spiritual fight, when we "contend earnestly" against them, "and resist them unto blood," if need be; that's being "pure as He is pure." But besides this positive rejection of all evil and perpetually contesting against sin, we must pursue the interests of virtue and an active religion;

27. "And besides this," saith St. Peter, "giving all diligence, add to your faith virtue, to your virtue knowledge, and to knowledge temperance, and to temperance patience, and to patience godliness, and to godliness brotherly kindness, and to brotherly kindness charity."[110] All this is an evident prosecution of the first design, the holiness and righteousness of a whole life; the being clear from all spots and blemishes, a being pure, and so presented unto Christ; for upon this the covenant being founded, to this all industries must endeavour, and

---

103. 2 Pet. 1:14–15.
104. 2 Pet. 3:11.
105. 1 John 3:3.
106. 1 Pet. 2:1.
107. Heb. 12:1.
108. 1 John 1:5–7.
109. 2 Pet. 1:4.
110. 2 Pet. 1:5ff.

arrive in their proportions. "For if these things be in you and abound, they shall make that you be neither barren nor unfruitful in the knowledge of our Lord Jesus Christ: but he that lacketh these things is blind, and hath forgotten he was purged from his old sins";[111] that is, he hath lost his baptismal grace, and is put from the first state of his redemption towards that state which is contradictory and destructive of it.

28. Now because all these things are in latitude, distance, and divisibility, and only enjoin a sedulity and great endeavour, all that we can dwell upon is this, That he who endeavours most is most secure, and every degree of negligence is a degree of danger; and although in the intermedial condition between the two states of Christianity and a full impiety there is a state of recovery and possibility, yet there is danger in every part of it; and it increases according as the deflexion and irregularity comes to its height, position, state and finality. So that we must "give all diligence" to "work out our salvation," and it would ever be "with fear and trembling": with fear, that we do not lose our innocence; and with trembling, if we have lost it, for fear we never recover or never be accepted. But holiness of life and uninterrupted sanctity being the condition of our salvation, the ingredient of the covenant, we must proportion our degrees of hope and confidence of heaven according as we have obtained degrees of innocence, or perseverance, or restitution. Only this; as it is certain he is in a state of reprobation who lives unto sin, that is whose actions are habitually criminal, who gives more of his consent to wickedness than to virtue: so it is also certain he is not in the state of God's favour and sanctification, unless he lives unto righteousness; that is, whose desires, and purposes, and endeavours, and actions, and customs, are spiritual, holy, sanctified, and obedient. When sin is dead, and the Spirit is life; when the lusts of the flesh are mortified, and the heart is purged from an evil conscience, and we abound in a whole system of Christian virtues; when our hearts are right to God, and with our affections and our wills we love God, and keep His commandments; when we do not only "cry Lord, Lord," but also "do His will"; then "Christ dwells in us, and we in Christ." Now let all this be taken in the lowest sense that can be imagined, all, I say, which out of scripture I have transcribed; "casting away every weight, laying aside all malice, mortifying the deeds of the flesh, crucifying the old man with all

---

111. 2 Pet. 1:8–9.

his affections and lusts, and then having escaped the corruption that is in the world through lust," besides this, "adding virtue to virtue till all righteousness be fulfilled in us, walking in the light, putting on the Lord Jesus, purifying ourselves as God is pure, following peace with all men, and holiness, resisting unto blood, living in the Spirit, being holy in all manner of conversation as He is holy, being careful and excellent in all conversation and godliness," all this, being a pursuit of the first design of Christ's death, and our reconcilement, can mean no less but that, first, We should have in us no affection to a sin; of which we can best judge, when we never choose it, and never fall under it but by surprise, and never lie under it at all, but instantly recover, judging ourselves severely: and, secondly, That we should choose virtue with great freedom of spirit and alacrity, and pursue it earnestly, integrally, and make it the business of our lives: and that, thirdly, The effect of this be, that sin be crucified in us, and the desires to it dead, flat, and useless; and that our desires of serving Christ be quick-spirited, active, and effective, inquisitive for opportunities, apprehensive of the offer, cheerful in the action, and persevering in the employment.

29. Now let a prudent person imagine what infirmities and oversights can consist with a state thus described, and all that does no violence to the covenant; God pities us, and calls us not to an account for what morally cannot, or certainly will not with great industry be prevented. But whatsoever is inconsistent with this condition is an abatement from our hopes, as it is a retiring from our duty, and is with greater or less difficulty cured, as are the degrees of its distance from that condition which Christ stipulated with us when we became His disciples. For we are just so restored to our state of grace and favour, as we are restored to our state of purity and holiness. Now this redintegration or renewing of us into the first condition, is also called repentance, and is permitted to all persons who still remain within the powers and possibilities of the covenant, that is, who are not in a state contradictory to the state and portion of grace, but with a difficulty increased by all circumstances, and incidences of the crime and person. And this I shall best represent in repeating these considerations;

First, Some sins are past hopes of pardon in this life;

Secondly, All that are pardoned are pardoned by parts, revocably and imperfectly during this life, not quickly nor yet manifestly;

Thirdly, Repentance contains in it many operations, parts, and employments, its terms and purpose being to redintegrate our lost condition; that is, in a second and less perfect sense, but as much as in such

325

circumstances we can, to verify our first obligations of innocence and holiness in all manner of conversation and godliness.

30. Concerning the first, it is too sad a consideration to be too dogmatical and conclusive in it, and therefore I shall only recall those expresses of scripture which may without envy decree the article; such as are those of St. Paul, that there is a certain sort of men, whom he twice describes, whom "it is impossible to renew again unto repentance"; or those of St. Peter, such whose "latter end is worse than the beginning," because "after they once had escaped the pollutions of the world, they are entangled therein"; such who, as our blessed Saviour threatens, "shall never be forgiven in this world nor in the world to come." For there is an unpardonable estate, by reason of its malice and opposition to the covenant of grace; and there is a state unpardonable, because the time of repentance is past. There are days and periods of grace; "If thou hadst known, at least in this thy day," said the weeping Saviour of the world to foreknown and determined Jerusalem. When God's decrees are gone out, they are not always revocable; and therefore it was a great caution of the apostle that we should "follow peace and holiness . . . and look diligently that we fall not from the grace of God, lest any of us become like Esau, to whose repentance there was no place left, though he sought it carefully with tears";[112] meaning, that we also may put ourselves into a condition when it shall be impossible we should be renewed unto repentance; and those are they who "sin a sin unto death, for whom" we have from the apostle no encouragement "to pray."[113] And these are in so general and conclusive terms described in scripture, that every persevering sinner hath great reason to suspect himself to be in the number: if he endeavours as soon as he thinks of it to recover, it is the best sign he was not arrived so far; but he that liveth long in a violent and habitual course of sin, is at the margin and brim of that state of final reprobation; and some men are in it before they be aware, and to some God reckons their days swifter, and their periods shorter. The use I make of this consideration is, that if any man hath reason to suspect, or to be certain, that his time of repentance is past, it is most likely to be a death-bed penitent, after a vicious life, a life contrary to the mercies and grace of the evangelical covenant; for he

---

112. Heb. 12:14–17.
113. 1 John 5:16.

hath provoked God as long as he could, and rejected the offers of grace as long as he lived, and refused virtue till he could not entertain her, and hath done all those things which a person rejected from hopes of repentance can easily be imagined to have done. And if there be any time of rejection, although it may be earlier, yet it is also certainly the last.

31. Concerning the second, I shall add this to the former discourse of it, that perfect pardon of sins is not in this world at all after the first emission and great efflux of it in our first regeneration. During this life we are in imperfection, minority, and under conditions which we have prevaricated; and our recovery is in perpetual flux, in heightenings and declensions, and we are highly uncertain of our acceptation, because we are not certain of our restitution and innocence; we know not whether we have done all that is sufficient to repair the breach made in the first state of favour and baptismal grace. But "he that is dead," saith St. Paul, "is justified from sin";[114] not till then. And therefore in the doctrine of the most learned Jews it is affirmed, "He that is guilty of the profanation of the name of God, he shall not interrupt the apparent malignity of it by his present repentance, nor make atonement in the day of expiation, nor wash the stains away by chastising of himself; but during his life it remains wholly in suspense, and before death is not extinguished"; according to the saying of the prophet Isaiah, "this iniquity shall not be blotted out till ye die, saith the Lord of hosts."[115] And some wise persons have affirmed that Jacob related to this in his expression and appellatives of God, whom he called "the God of Abraham, and the fear of his father Isaac";[116] because, as the doctors of the Jews tell us, Abraham, being dead, was ascribed into the final condition of God's family; but Isaac, being living, had apprehensions of God, not only of a pious, but also of a tremulous fear: he was not sure of his own condition, much less of the degrees of his reconciliation, how far God had forgiven his sins, and how far He had retained them. And it is certain that if every degree of the divine favour be not assured by a holy life, those sins of whose pardon we were most hopeful return in as full vigour and clamorous importunity as ever, and are made more vocal by the appendant ingratitude and other accidental degrees. And this Christ taught us by a parable; for as the lord made his uncharitable servant pay all that

---

114. Rom. 6:7.
115. Isa. 22:14.
116. Gen. 31:42.

debt which he had formerly forgiven him, even "so will God do to us, if we from our hearts forgive not one another their trespasses."[117] "Behold the goodness and severity of God," saith St. Paul: "on them which fell, severity; but on thee goodness, if thou continue in that goodness; otherwise thou shalt be cut off. For this is My covenant which I shall make with them when I shall take away their sins."[118] And if this be true in those sins which God certainly hath forgotten, such as were all those which were committed before our illumination; much rather is it true in those which we committed after, concerning whose actual and full pardon we cannot be certain without a revelation. So that our pardon of sins, when it is granted after the breach of our covenant, is just so secure as our perseverance is: concerning which, because we must ascertain it as well as we can, but ever with fear and trembling, so also is the estate of our pardon hazardous, conditional, revocable, and uncertain; and therefore the best of men do all their lives ask pardon even of those sins for which they have wept bitterly, and done the sharpest and severest penance. And if it be necessary we pray that we may not enter into temptation, because temptation is full of danger, and the danger may bring a sin, and the sin may ruin us; it is also necessary that we understand the condition of our pardon to be, as is the condition of our person, variable as will, sudden as affections, alterable as our purposes, revocable as our own good intentions, and then made as ineffective as our inclinations to good actions. And there is no way to secure our confidence and our hope but by being perfect, and holy, and pure, as our heavenly Father is; that is, in the sense of human capacity, free from the habits of all sin, and active, and industrious, and continuing in the ways of godliness. For upon this only the promise is built, and by our proportion to this state we must proportion our confidence; we have no other revelation. Christ reconciled us to His Father upon no other conditions, and made the covenant upon no other articles, but of a holy life, in obedience universal and perpetual: and the abatements of the rigorous sense of the words, as they are such as may infinitely testify and prove His mercy, so they are such as must secure our duty and habitual graces; an industry manly, constant, and Christian: and because these have so great latitude (and to what degrees God will accept our

---

117. Matt. 18:35.
118. Rom. 11:22–27.

returns, He hath nowhere punctually described) he that is most severe in his determination does best secure himself, and by exacting the strictest account of himself shall obtain the easier scrutiny at the hands of God. The use I make of this consideration is to the same purpose with the former: for if every day of sin, and every criminal act, is a degree of recess from the possibilities of heaven, it would be considered at how great distance a death-bed penitent, after a vicious life, may apprehend himself to stand for mercy and pardon: and since the terms of restitution must, in labour, and in extension of time, or intension of degrees, be of value great enough to restore him to some proportion or equivalence with that state of grace from whence he is fallen, and upon which the covenant was made with him; how impossible, or how near to impossible, it will appear to him to go so far and do so much, in that state, and in those circumstances of disability.

32. Concerning the third particular, I consider that repentance, as it is described in scripture, is a system of holy duties, not of one kind, nor properly consisting of parts as if it were a single grace; but it is the reparation of that estate into which Christ first put us, "a renewing us in the spirit of our mind," so the apostle calls it; and the holy Ghost hath taught this truth to us by the implication of many appellatives, and also by express discourses. For there is in scripture a "repentance to be repented of," and a "repentance never to be repented of." The first is mere sorrow for what is past, an ineffective trouble, producing nothing good; such as was the repentance of Judas, "he repented, and hanged himself"; and such was that of Esau, when it was too late; and so was the repentance of the five foolish virgins: which examples tell us also when ours is an impertinent and ineffectual repentance. To this repentance pardon is nowhere promised in scripture. But there is a repentance which is called "conversion," or "amendment of life," a repentance productive of holy fruits, such as the Baptist and our blessed Saviour preached such as Himself also propounded in the example of the Ninevites;[119] they "repented at the preaching of Jonah," that is, "they fasted, they covered them in sackcloth, they cried mightily unto God, yea, they turned every one from his evil way, and from the violence that was in their hands":[120] and this was it that appeased God in that instance; "God

---

119. Matt. 12:41.
120. Jonah 3:8–10.

saw their works, that they turned from their evil way; and God repented of the evil, and did it not."

33. The same character of repentance we find in the prophet Ezekiel; "when the wicked man turneth away from his wickedness that he hath committed, and doeth that which is lawful and right; if the wicked restore the pledge, give again that he had robbed, walk in the statutes of life without committing iniquity, he hath done that which is lawful and right, he shall surely live, he shall not die."[121] And in the gospel repentance is described with as full and entire comprehensions as in the old prophets. For faith and repentance are the whole duty of the gospel: faith, when it is in conjunction with a practical grace, signifies an intellectual; faith signifies the submission of the understanding to the institution: and repentance includes all that whole practice which is the entire duty of a Christian after he hath been overtaken in a fault. And therefore repentance first includes a renunciation and abolition of all evil, and then also enjoins a pursuit of every virtue, and that till they arrive at an habitual confirmation.[122]

34. Of the first sense are all those expressions of scripture which imply repentance to be the deletery of sins. "Repentance from dead works" St. Paul affirms to be the prime fundamental of the religion; that is, conversion, or returning from dead works: for unless repentance be so construed, it is not good sense. And this is therefore highly verified, because repentance is intended to set us into the condition of our first undertaking, and articles covenanted with God. And therefore it is "a redemption of the time," that is, a recovering what we lost, and making it up by our doubled industry. "Remember whence thou art fallen, repent," that is, return, "and do thy first works," said the Spirit to the angel of the church of Ephesus, or else "I will remove thy candlestick, except thou repent."[123] It is a restitution; "if a man be overtaken in a fault, restore such a one,"[124] that is, put him where he was. And then, that repentance also implies a doing all good, is certain by the sermon of the Baptist, "bring forth fruits meet for repentance":[125] "Do thy first works," was the sermon of the Spirit; "laying aside every weight, and the sin that easily encircles us, let us run with patience the race that is

---

121. Ezek. 18:27; Ezek. 33:15.
122. Clement of Alexandria, *Stromata*, PG 8.990.
123. Rev. 2:5.
124. Gal. 6:1.
125. Matt. 3:8.

set before us"; so St. Paul taught. And St. Peter gives charge that when we "have escaped the corruptions of the world, and of lusts,"[126] besides this, we "give all diligence" to acquire the rosary and conjugation of Christian virtues. And they are proper effects, or rather constituent parts, of a holy repentance: "for godly sorrow worketh repentance," saith St. Paul, "not to be repented of":[127] and that ye may know what is signified by repentance, behold the product was "carefulness, clearing of themselves, indignation, fear, vehement desires, zeal, and revenge"; to which if we add the epithet of holy (for these were the results of a godly sorrow, and the members of a repentance not to be repented of) we are taught that repentance, besides the purging out the malice of iniquity, is also a sanctification of the whole man, a turning nature into grace, passions into reason, and the flesh into spirit.

35. To this purpose I reckon those phrases of scripture calling it a "renewing of our minds";[128] a "renewing of the holy Ghost";[129] a "cleansing of our hands, and purifying our hearts,"[130] that is, a becoming holy in our affections and righteous in our actions; a "transformation,"[131] or utter change; a "crucifying the flesh, with the affections and lusts";[132] a "mortified state";[133] a "purging out the old leaven, and becoming a new conspersion";[134] a "waking out of sleep,[135] and walking honestly, as in the day";[136] a "being born again," and being "born from above";[137] a "new life." And I consider that these preparative actions of repentance, such as are sorrow, and confession of sins, and fasting, and exterior mortifications, and severities, are but forerunners of repentance, some of the retinue, and they are of the family, but they no more complete the duty of repentance than the harbingers are the whole court, or than the fingers are all the body. There "is more joy in heaven," said our blessed Saviour, "over one sinner that repenteth, than

---

126. 2 Pet. 1:4–5.
127. 2 Cor. 8:10.
128. Rom. 12:2.
129. Titus 3:5.
130. James 4:8.
131. Rom. 12:2.
132. Gal. 5:24.
133. Col. 3:5.
134. 1 Cor. 5:7.
135. Eph. 5:14; Rom. 13:11.
136. Rom. 13:13.
137. John 3:5.

over ninety-nine just persons who need no repentance." There is no man but needs a tear and a sorrow, even for his daily weaknesses, and possibly they are the instrumental expiations of our sudden, and frequent, and lesser surprizes of imperfection; but the "just persons need no repentance," that is, need no inversion of state, no transformation from condition to condition, but from the less to the more perfect the best man hath. And therefore those are vain persons who, when they "owe God a hundred," will "write fourscore," or "a thousand," will "write fifty." It was the saying of an excellent person that "repentance is the beginning of philosophy, a flight and renunciation of evil works and words, and the first preparation and entrance into a life which is never to be repented of: and therefore a penitent is not taken with umbrages and appearances, nor quits a real good for an imaginary, or chooses evil for fear of enemies and adverse accidents; but peremptorily conforms his sentence to the divine laws, and submits his whole life in a conformity with them." He that said those excellent words had not been taught the Christian institution, but it was admirable reason and deep philosophy, and most consonant to the reasonableness of virtue, and the proportions and designs of repentance, and no other than the doctrine of Christian philosophy.

36. And it is considerable, since in scripture there is a repentance mentioned which is impertinent and ineffectual as to the obtaining pardon, a repentance implied which is to be repented of, and another expressed which is "never to be repented of," and this is described to be a new state of life, a whole conversion and transformation of the man; it follows that whatsoever in any sense can be called repentance, and yet is less than this new life, must be that ineffective repentance. A sorrow is a repentance, and all the acts of dolorous expression are but the same sorrow in other characters, and they are good when they are parts or instruments of the true repentance: but when they are the whole repentance, that repentance is no better than that of Judas, nor more prosperous than that of Esau. Every sorrow is not a "godly sorrow," and that which is, is but instrumental, and in order to repentance. "Godly sorrow worketh repentance," saith St. Paul; that is, it does its share towards it, as every grace does toward the pardon, as every degree of pardon does towards heaven. By "godly sorrow," it is probable St. Paul means the same thing which the school hath since called contrition; a grief proceeding from a holy principle, from our love of God, and anger that we have offended Him: and yet this is a great way off from that repentance without the performance of which we shall certainly

perish: but no contrition alone is remissive of sins, but as it co-operates towards the integrity of our duty. *Cum conversus ingemuerit,* is the prophet's expression; when a man "mourns, and turns from all his evil way," that's a "godly sorrow," and that's repentance too,[138] but the tears of a dolorous person, though running over with great effusions, and shed in great bitterness, and expressed in actions of punitive justice, all being but the same sense in louder language, being nothing but the expressions of sorrow, are good only as they tend farther; and if they do, they may by degrees bring us to repentance, and that repentance will bring us to heaven; but of themselves they may as well make the sea swell beyond its margin, or water and refresh the sunburnt earth, as move God to mercy, and pierce the heavens. But then to the consideration we may add, that a sorrow upon a death-bed, after a vicious life, is such as cannot easily be understood to be ordinarily so much as the beginning of virtue, or the first instance towards a holy life. For he that till then retained his sins, and now when he is certain and believes he shall die, or is fearful lest he should, is sorrowful that he hath sinned, is only sorrowful because he is like to perish: and such a sorrow may perfectly consist with as great an affection to sin as ever the man had in the highest caresses and invitation of his lust. For even then in certain circumstances he would have refused to have acted his greatest temptation: the boldest and most pungent lust would refuse to be satisfied in the market-place, or with a dagger at his heart; and the greatest intemperance would refuse a pleasant meal if he believed the meat to be mixed with poison: and yet this restraint of appetite is no abatement of the affection, any more than the violent fears which, by being incumbent upon the death-bed penitent, make him grieve for the evil consequents more than to hate the malice and irregularity. He that does not grieve till his greatest fear presses him hard and damnation treads upon his heels, feels indeed the effects of fear, but can have no present benefit of his sorrow, because it had no natural principle, but a violent, unnatural, and intolerable cause, inconsistent with a free, placid, and moral election. But this I speak only by way of caution: for God's mercy is infinite, and can, if He please, make it otherwise; but it is not good to venture unless you have a promise.

37. The same also I consider concerning the purpose of a new life, which that any man should judge to be repentance, that duty which

---

138. Acts 3:19.

restores us, is more unreasonable than to think sorrow will do it. For as a man may sorrow, and yet never be restored (and he may sorrow so much the more because he shall never be restored, as Esau did, as the five foolish virgins did, and as many more do); so he that purposes to lead a new life hath convinced himself that the duty is undone, and therefore his pardon not granted, nor his condition restored. As a letter is not a word, nor a word an action; as an embryo is not a man, nor the seed the fruit: so is a purpose of obedience but the element of repentance, the first imaginations of it differing from the grace itself as a disposition from a habit, or (because itself will best express itself) as the purpose does from the act. For either a holy life is necessary, or it is not necessary. If it be not, why does any man hope to "escape the wrath to come" by resolving to do an unnecessary thing? or if he does not purpose it when he pretends he does, that is a mocking of God, and that is a great way from being an instrument of his restitution. But if a holy life be necessary, as it is certain by infinite testimonies of scriptures it is the *unum necessarium,* "the one great necessary," it cannot reasonably be thought that any thing less than doing it shall serve our turns; that which is only in purpose is not yet done, and yet it is necessary it should be done because it is necessary we should purpose it. And in this we are sufficiently concluded by that ingeminate expression used by St. Paul, "in Jesus Christ nothing can avail but a new creature": nothing but "faith working by charity," nothing but a "keeping the commandments of God,"[139] "and as many as walk according to this rule, peace be on them, and mercy: they are the Israel of God."[140]

---

139. Gal. 6:15; Gal. 5:6; 1 Cor. 7:19.
140. Gal. 6:16.

Of Ecclesiastical Penance
and Confession[141]
[*from* Unum Necessarium]

104. Let no man think it a shame to confess his sin; or if he does, yet let not that shame deter him from it. There is indeed a shame in confession, because nakedness is discovered; but there is also a glory in it, because there is a cure too: there is repentance and amendment. This advice is like that which is given to persons giving their lives in a good cause, requiring them not to be afraid; that is, not to suffer such a fear as to be hindered from dying. For if they suffer a great natural fear, and yet in despite of that fear die constantly and patiently, that fear as it increases their suffering, may also accidentally increase their glory, provided that the fear be not criminal in its cause, nor effective of any unworthy comportment. So is the shame in confession; a great mortification of the man, and highly punitive of the sin; and such that unless it hinders the duty, is not to be directly reproved: but it must be taken care of that it be a shame only for the sin, which by how much greater it is, by so much the more earnestly the man ought to fly to all the means of remedy and instruments of expiation: and then the greater the shame is which the sinner suffers, the more excellent is the repentance which suffers so much for the extinction of his sin. But at no hand let the shame affright the duty; but let it be remembered that this confession is but the memory of the shame, which began when the sin was acted, and abode but as a handmaid of the guilt, and goes away with it. Confession of sins opens them to man, but draws a veil before them that God will the less behold them. And it is a material consideration, that if a man be impatient of the shame here, when it is revealed but to one man, who is also by all the ties of religion and by common honesty obliged to conceal them; or if he account it intolerable that a sin public in the scandal and the infamy, should be made public by solemnity to punish and to extin-

---

141. *Works* 7:481ff.

guish it, the man will be no gainer by refusing to confess, when he shall remember that sins unconfessed are most commonly unpardoned; and unpardoned sins will be made public before all angels, and all the wise and good men of the world, when their shame shall have nothing to make it tolerable.

105. When a penitent confesses his sin, the holy man that ministers to his repentance and hears his confession, must not without great cause lessen the shame of the repenting man; he must directly encourage the duty, but not add confidence to the sinner. For whatsoever directly lessens the shame, lessens also the hatred of sin, and his future caution, and the reward of his repentance; and takes off that which was an excellent defensative against the sin. But with the shame, the minister of religion is to do as he is to do with the man's sorrow: so long as it is a good instrument of repentance, so long it is to be permitted and assisted, but when it becomes irregular, or disposed to evil events, it is to be taken off; and so must the shame of the penitent man, when there is danger lest the man be swallowed up by too much sorrow and shame, or when it is perceived that the shame alone is a hindrance to the duty. In these cases, if the penitent man can be persuaded directly and by choice, for ends of piety and religion to suffer the shame, then let his spirit be supported by other means; but if he cannot, let there be such a confidence wrought in him, which is derived from the circumstances of the person, or the universal calamity and iniquity of man, or the example of great sinners like himself, that have willingly undergone the yoke of the Lord, or from consideration of the divine mercies, or from the easiness and advantages of the duty; but let nothing be offered to lessen the hatred, or the greatness of the sin, lest a temptation to sin hereafter be sowed in the furrows of the present repentance.

106. He that confesseth his sins to the minister of religion, must be sure to express all the great lines of his folly and calamity; that is, all that by which he may make a competent judgment of the state of his soul. Now if the man be of a good life, and yet in his tendency to perfection is willing to pass under the method and discipline of greater sinners, there is no advice to be given to him, but that he do not curiously tell those lesser irregularities which vex his peace rather than discompose his conscience: but what is most remarkable in his infirmities, or the whole state, and the greatest marks and instances and returns of them, he ought to signify, for else he can serve no prudent end in his confession.

107. But secondly, if the man have committed a great sin, it is a

high prudence, and an excellent instance of his repentance, that he confess it, declaring the kind of it, if it be of that nature that the spiritual man may conceal it. But if upon any other account he be bound to reveal every notice of the fact, let him transact that affair wholly between God and his own soul. And this of declaring a single action as it is of great use in the repentance of every man, so it puts on some degrees of necessity, if the man be of a sad, amazed, and an afflicted conscience. For there are some unfortunate persons who have committed some secret facts of shame and horror, at the remembrance of which they are amazed, of the pardon of which they have no sign, for the expiation of which they use no instrument, and they walk up and down like distracted persons, to whom reason is useless, and company is unpleasant, and their sorrow is not holy, but very great, and they know not what to do because they will not ask. I have observed some such; and the only remedy that was fit to be prescribed to such persons, was to reveal their sin to a spiritual man, and by him to be put into such a state of remedy and comfort as is proper for their condition. It is certain that many persons have perished for want of counsel and comfort, which were ready for them if they would have confessed their sin; for he that concealeth his sin, *non dirigetur,* saith Solomon, "he shall not be counselled or directed."

108. And it is a very great fault amongst a very great part of Christians, that in their enquiries of religion, even the best of them ordinarily ask but these two questions, "Is it lawful? Is it necessary?" If they find it lawful, they will do it without scruple or restraint; and then they suffer imperfection, or receive the reward of folly: for it may be lawful, and yet not fit to be done; it may be it is not expedient; and he that will do all that he can do lawfully, would, if he durst, do something that is not lawful. And as great an error is on the other hand in the other question. He that too strictly enquires of an action whether it be necessary or no, would do well to ask also whether it be good? whether it be of advantage to the interest of his soul? For if a christian man or woman; that is, a redeemed, blessed, obliged person, a great beneficiary, endeared to God beyond all the comprehensions of a man's imagination, one that is less than the least of all God's mercies, and yet hath received many great ones and hopes for more, if he should do nothing but what is necessary, that is, nothing but what he is compelled to; then he hath the obligations of a son, and the affections of a slave, which is the greatest undecency of the world in the accounts of christianity. If a Christian will do no more than what is necessary, he will quickly be tempted to

337

omit something of that also. And it is highly considerable that in the matter of souls, "necessity" is a divisible word, and that which in disputation is not necessary, may be necessary in practice: it may be but charity to one and duty to another, that is, when it is not a necessary duty, it may be a necessary charity. And therefore it were much the better if every man without further enquiry would in the accounts of his soul consult a spiritual guide, and whether it be necessary or no, yet let him do it because it is good; and even they who will not for God's sake do that which is simply the best, yet for their own sakes they will or ought to do that which is profitable and of great advantage. Let men do that which is best to themselves; for it is all one to God, save only that He is pleased to take such instances of duty and forwardness of obedience, as the best significations of the best love. And of this nature is confession of sins to a minister of religion, it is one of the most charitable works in the world to ourselves; and in this sense we may use the words of David, "If thou doest well unto thyself, men," (and God) "will speak good of thee," and do good to thee. He that will do every thing that is lawful, and nothing but what is necessary, will be an enemy when he dares, and a friend when he cannot help it.

109. But if the penitent person hath been an habitual sinner, in his confessions he is to take care that the minister of religion understand the degrees of his wickedness, the time of his abode in sin, the greatness of his desires, the frequency of his acting them, not told by numbers, but by general significations of the time, and particular significations of the earnestness of his choice. For this transaction being wholly in order to the benefit and conduct of his soul, the good man that ministers must have as perfect moral accounts as he can, but he is not to be reckoned withal by natural numbers and measures, save only so far as they may declare the violence of desires, and the pleasures and choice of the sin. The purpose of this advice is this; that since the transaction of this affair is for counsel and comfort, in order to pardon and the perfections of repentance, there should be no scruple in the particular circumstances of it, but that it be done heartily and wisely, that is, so as may best serve the ends to which it is designed; and that no man do it in despite of himself, or against his will, for the thing itself is not a direct service of God immediately enjoined, but is a service to ourselves to enable us to do our duty to God, and to receive a more ready and easy and certain pardon from Him. They indeed who pretend it as a necessary duty, have by affixing rules and measures to it of their own, made that which they call necessary to be intolerable and impossible. Indeed it is certain that

when God hath appointed a duty, He also will describe the measures, or else leave us to the conduct of our own choice and reason in it. But where God hath not described the measures, we are to do that which is most agreeable to the analogy of the commandment, or the principal duty, in case it be under a command: but if it be not, then we are only to choose the particulars so as may best minister to the end which is designed in the whole ministration.

110. It is a very pious preparation to the holy sacrament, that we confess our sins to the minister of religion: for since it is necessary that a man be examined, and a self-examination was prescribed to the Corinthians in the time of their lapsed discipline, that though there were divisions amongst them, and no established governors, yet from this duty they were not to be excused, and they must in destitution of a public minister do it themselves, but this is in case only of such necessity: the other is better; that is, it is of better order and more advantage that this part of repentance and holy preparation be performed under the conduct of a spiritual guide. And the reason is pressing. For since it is life or death that is there administered, and the great dispensation of the keys is in that ministry, it were very well if he that ministers did know whether the person presented were fit to communicate or no; and if he be not, it is charity to reject him, and charity to assist him that he may be fitted. There are many sad contingencies in the constitution of ecclesiastical affairs, in which every man that needs this help, and would fain make use of it, cannot; but when he can meet with the blessing, it were well it were more frequently used, and more readily entertained. I end these advices with the words of Origen: "He shall have no pardon who knows his sin and confesses it not; but we must confess always, not that the sin always remains, but that of an old sin an unwearied confession is useful and profitable."[142] But this is to be understood of a general accusation, or of a confession to God; for in confessions to men, there is no other usefulness of repeating our confessions, excepting where such repetition does aggravate the fault of relapsing, and ingratitude, in case the man returns to those sins for which he hoped that before he did receive a pardon.

But because in all repentances there is something penal, it is not amiss that there be some enquiries after the measures and rules of acting

---

142. Origen, *On the Psalms*, PG 17.118.

that part of repentance which consists in corporal austerities, and are commonly called penances.

111. He that hath a great sorrow, need neither be invited nor instructed in the matter of his austerities. For a great sorrow and its own natural expressions and significations, such as are fastings, and abstinence, and tears, and indignation, and restlessness of mind, and prayers for pardon, and mortification of the sin, are all that which will perfect this part of repentance. Only sometimes they need caution for the degrees. Therefore

112. Let the penitent be careful that he do not injure his health, or oppress his spirit, by the zeal of this part of repentance. . . . For all such fierce proceedings are either superstitious—or desperate—or indiscreet—or the effect of a false persuasion concerning them, that they are a direct service of God, that they are simply necessary, and severely enjoined. All which are to be rescinded, or else the penances will be of more hurt than usefulness. Those actions are to minister to repentance; and therefore if they contradict any duty, they destroy what they pretend to serve. For penances as they relate to the sin that is committed, is just to be measured as penitential sorrow is, of which it is a signification and expression. When the sorrow is natural, sensitive, pungent, and material, the penances will be so too. A great sorrow refuses to eat, to sleep, to be cheerful, to be in company, according as the degree is, and as the circumstances of the persons are. But sometimes sorrow is to be chosen, and invited by arts, and ministered to by external instruments, and arguments of invitation; and just so are the penances, they are then to be chosen, so as may make the person a sorrowful mourner, to make him take no delight in sin, but to conceive, and to feel a just displeasure: for if men feel no smart, no real sorrow or pain for their sins, they will be too much in love with it: impunity is "the occasion and opportunity of sin," as the apostle intimates: and they use to proceed in finishing the methods of sin and death, who . . . reckon their pleasures, but never put any smart, or danger, or fears, or sorrows into the balance. But the injunction or susception of penances is a good instrument of repentance, because a little evil takes off the pleasure of the biggest sin in many instances, and we are too apprehensive of the present, that this also becomes a great advantage to this ministry. We refuse great and infinite pleasures hereafter, so we may enjoy little, and few, and inconsiderable ones at present; and we fear not the horrible pains of hell, so we may avoid a little trouble in our persons or our interest. Therefore it

is to be supposed that this way of undertaking a present punishment and smart for our sins (unless every thing when it becomes religious is despoiled of all its powers which it had in nature, and what is reason here is not reason there) will be of great effect and power against sin, and be an excellent instrument of repentance. But it must be so much, and it must be no more; for penances are like fire and water, good so long as they are made to serve our needs, but when they go beyond that, they are not to be endured. For since God in the severest of His anger does not punish one sin with another, let not us do worse to ourselves than the greatest wrath of God in this world will inflict upon us. A sin cannot be a punishment from God. For then it would be that God should be the author of sin, for He is of punishment. If then any punishment be a sin, that sin was unavoidable, derived from God; and indeed it would be a contradiction to the nature of things to say that the same thing can in the same formality be a punishment and a sin, that is, an action, and a passion, voluntary as every sin is, and involuntary as every punishment is; that it should be done by us, and yet against us, by us and by another, and by both entirely: and since punishment is the compensation or the expiation of sin, not the aggravation of the divine anger; it were very strange if God by punishing us should more provoke Himself, and instead of satisfying His justice, or curing the man, make His own anger infinite, and the patient much the worse. Indeed it may happen that one sin may cause or procure another, not by the efficiency of God, or any direct action of His: but first, withdrawing those assistances which would have restrained a sinful progression; secondly, by suffering him to fall into evil temptation, which is too hard for him consisting in his present voluntary indisposition; thirdly, by the nature of sin itself, which may either effect a sin by accident, as a great anger may by the withdrawing God's restraining grace be permitted to pass to an act of murder; or it may dispose to others of like nature, as one degree of lust brings in another; or it may minister matter of fuel to another sin, as intemperance to uncleanness: or one sin may be the end of another, as covetousness may be the servant of luxury. In all these ways, one sin may be effected by another; but in all these, God is only conniving, or at most, takes off some of those helps which the man hath forfeited, and God was not obliged to continue. Thus God hardened Pharaoh's heart, even by way of object and occasion; God hardened him by shewing him a mercy, by taking off his fears when He removed the judgment; and God ministered to him some hope that it be so still. But

God does not inflict the sin: the man's own impious hands do that, not because he cannot help it, but because he chooses and delights in it. Now if God in justice to us will not punish one sin directly by another: let not us in our penitential inflictions commit a sin in indignation against our sin; for that is just as if a man out of impatience of pain in his side, should dash his head against a wall.

113. But if God pleases to inflict a punishment, let us be careful to exchange it into a penance by kissing the rod, and entertaining the issues of the divine justice by approbation of God's proceeding, and confession of our demerit and justification of God. It was a pretty accident and mixture of providence and penance, that happened to the three accusers of Narcissus, bishop of Jerusalem;[143] they accused him falsely of some horrid crimes, but in verification of their indictment bound themselves by a curse: the first, that if his accusation were false, he might be burned to death; the second, that he might die of the king's evil; the third, that he might be blind. God in His anger found out the two first, and their curse happened to them that "delighted in cursing and lies." The first was burnt alive in his own house: and the second perished by the loathsome disease: which when the third espied, and found God's anger so hasty and so heavy, so pressing and so certain, he ran out to meet the rod of God; and repented of his sin so deeply, and wept so bitterly, so continually, that he became blind with weeping: and the anger of God became an instance of repentance; the judgment was sanctified, and so passed into mercy and a pardon: he did indeed meet with his curse, but by the arts of repentance the curse became a blessing. And so it may be to us, *Præveniamus faciem ejus in confessione* let us prevent His anger by sentencing ourselves: or if we do not, let us follow the sad accents of the angry voice of God, and imitate His justice by condemning that which God condemns, and suffering willingly what He imposes; and turning His judgments into voluntary executions, by applying the suffering to our sins, and praying it may be sanctified. For since God smites us that we may repent, if we repent then, we serve the end of the divine judgment: and when we perceive God smites our sin, if we submit to it, and are pleased that our sin is smitten, we are enemies to it after the example of God; and that is a good act of repentance.

114. For the quality or kind of penances, this is the best measure:

---

143. Eusebius, *Ecclesiastical History*, PG 20.554.

those are the best which serve most ends; not those which most vex us, but such which will most please God. If they be only actions punitive and vindictive, they do indeed punish the man, and help so far as they can to destroy the sin; but of these alone S. Paul[144] said well, "Bodily exercise profiteth but little"; but of the latter sort, he added, "but godliness is profitable to all things, having the promise of the life that now is, and of that which is to come": and this indeed is our exactest measure. Fastings alone, lyings upon the ground, disciplines and direct chastisements of the body, which have nothing in them but toleration and revenge, are of some use; they vex the body, and crucify the sinner, but the sin lives for all them: but if we add prayer, or any action symbolical, as meditation, reading, solitariness, silence, there is much more done towards the extinction of the sin. But he that adds alms, or something that not only is an act contrary to a former state of sin, but such which is apt to deprecate the fault, to obey God, and to do good to men, "he hath chosen the better part, which will not easily be taken from him." Fasting, prayer, and alms together, are the best penances, or acts of exterior repentance in the world. If they be single, fasting is of the least force, and alms done in obedience and the love of God is the best.

115. For the quantity of penances, the old rule is the best that I know, but that it is too general and indefinite. It is S. Cyprian's *Quam magna deliquimus, tam granditer defleamus*, "if our sins were great, so must our sorrow or penances be; as one is, so must be the other." For sorrow and penances I reckon as the same thing in this question; save only that in some instances of corporal inflictions, the sin is opposed in its proper matter; as intemperance is by fasting; effeminacy by suffering hardships; whereas sorrow opposes it only in general: and in some other instances of penances, there is a duty distinctly and directly served, as in prayer and alms. But although this rule be indefinite and unlimited, we find it made more minute by Hugo de S. Victore, *Si in correctione minor est afflictio quam in culpa fuit delectalio, non est dignus pœnitentia tuæ fructus*. Our sorrow, either in the direct passion, or in its voluntary expressions, distinctly or conjunctly, must at least equal the pleasure we took in the committing of a sin. And this rule is indeed very good, if we use it with these cautions. First, that this be understood principally in

---

144. 1 Tim. 4:8.

our repentances for single sins; for in these only the rule can be properly and without scruple applied, where the measures can be best observed. For in habitual and long courses of sin there is no other measures but to do very much, and very long, and until we die, and never think ourselves safe but while we are doing our repentances. Secondly, that this measure be not thought equal commutation for the sin, but be only used as an act of deprecation and repentance, of the hatred of sin and opposition to it; for he that sets a value upon his punitive actions of repentance, and rests in them, will be hasty in finishing the repentance, and leaving it off even while the sin is alive. For in these cases it is to be regarded, that penances, or the punitive actions of repentance, are not for the extinction of the punishment immediately, but for the guilt. That is, there is no remains of punishment after the whole guilt is taken off: but the guilt itself goes away by parts, and these external actions of repentance have the same effect in their proportion which is wrought by the internal. Therefore as no man can say that he hath sufficiently repented of his sins by an inward sorrow and hatred: so neither can he be secure that he hath made compensation by the suffering penances; for if one sin deserves an eternal hell, it is well if upon the account of any actions, and any sufferings, we be at last accepted and acquitted.

116. In the performing the punitive parts of external repentance, it is prudent that we rather extend them than intend them: that is, let us rather do many single acts of several instances, than dwell upon one with such intension of spirit as may be apt to produce any violent effects upon the body or the spirit. In all these cases, prudence and proportion to the end is our best measures. For these outward significations of repentance are not in any kind or instance necessary to the constitution of repentance; but apt and excellent expressions and significations, exercises and ministries of repentance. Prayer and alms are of themselves distinct duties, and therefore come not in their whole nature to this reckoning: but the precise acts of corporal punishment are here intended. And that these were not necessary parts of repentance, the primitive church believed, and declared, by absolving dying persons, though they did not survive the beginnings of their public repentance. But that she enjoined them to suffer such severities in case they did recover, she declared that these were useful and proper exercises and ministries of the grace itself. And although inward repentance did expiate all sins, even in the mosaical covenant, yet they had also a time and manner of its solemnity, their day of expiation, and so must we have many. But if any man will refuse this way of repentance, I shall only say

to him the words of S. Paul[145] to them who rejected the ecclesiastical customs and usages, "We have no such custom, neither the churches of God." But let him be sure that he perform his internal repentance with the more exactness; as he had need look to his own strengths that refuses the assistance of auxiliaries. But it is not good to be too nice and inquisitive, when the whole article is matter of practice. For what doth God demand of us but inward sincerity of a returning, penitent, obedient heart, and that this be exercised and ministered unto by fit and convenient offices to that purpose? This is all, and from this we are to make no abatements.

THE PRAYER

O eternal God, gracious and merciful, the fountain of pardon and holiness, hear the cries and regard the supplications of Thy servant. I have gone astray all my days, and I will for ever pray unto Thee and cry mightily for pardon. Work in Thy servant such a sorrow that may be deadly unto the whole body of sin, but the parent of an excellent repentance. O suffer me not any more to do an act of shame; nor to undergo the shame and confusion of face, which is the portion of the impenitent and persevering sinners at the day of sad accounts. I humbly confess my sins to Thee, do Thou hide them from all the world; and while I mourn for them, let the angels rejoice; and while I am killing them by the aids of Thy spirit, let me be written in the book of life, and my sins be blotted out of the black registers of death; that my sins being covered and cured, dead and buried in the grave of Jesus, I may live to Thee my God a life of righteousness, and grow in it till I shall arrive at a state of glory.

---

145. 1 Cor. 11:16.

CHAPTER FOUR

Sermon, Discourse and Prayer

INTRODUCTION

The writings of Jeremy Taylor are those of a priest who preached the eternal Word in the words of time and pronounced among men what is ineffable in itself. Divine mystery is therefore the presence the priest celebrates in those *appealing discourses* (cf. Luke 4:20), which the Greek Fathers called *homilies* and the Latin Fathers called *sermons.* In England this unique form of rhetoric was commonly called the *power of the pulpit,* and it found new life with John Fisher, the bishop of Rochester, at the century's beginning, and new heights with John Donne, the dean of St. Paul's, at its conclusion. Almost all great preachers, from Fisher to Donne, preached without a written text; William Perkins in *Art of Prophesying,* first published in 1592, speaks of "the received custom for preachers to speak by heart (*memoriter*) before the people." Afterward these free and easy discourses, good talking rather than set speeches, were written down, usually by other hands and probably without revision by the preacher. Taylor was later, and things were different. Bacon, in drawing a picture for James I of the happiness of England under his reign, described as an element of that good fortune "his Church enlightened with good preachers, a heaven with stars."

Taylor was certainly the brightest star to shine among the Carolines. His major collection of sermons is entitled *Eniautos,* or a *Course of Sermons for all the Sundays of the year, fitted to the great necessities and for supplying the wants of preaching in many parts of this nation.* The *Eniautos,* or *one year* collection of fifty-two sermons has no reference to the liturgical year or life of Christ, which was already covered in the

347

Great Exemplar. It gives us, rather, a general survey of human life and the mortal condition, the vanity of our desires, the folly and emptiness of our ambitions, and the misery of our lives. We are made of dust, Taylor says, for "man is a lump of folly and unavoidable necessities; and our hearts, so intricate and various and trifling, so full of wantonness and foolish thoughts, come in for many a well deserved if not altogether novel castigation."[1]

Taylor's view of the world, its vanities and temptations, was derived from what Coleridge called "his oceanic reading of the ancients," and was more classical than Christian.[2] But that Platonic philosophy, which the early Greek Fathers absorbed from the Neoplatonism of their day, and which was so potent an influence in the Anglican theology of Taylor's times, opened for him another world of which the existing world is but an evanescent shadow and which we apprehend not with the senses but with the mind. The recognition of this unseen eternal world behind the flux of phenomena is the vision that inspires Taylor's preaching as he lifts man out of the darkness of time and up to the brightness of eternity.

To pass from shadow to substance, from the pleasures of the senses to the contemplations of heavenly realities, from dwelling on the transitory earth to residence amid intellectual and eternal essences, was for Jeremy Taylor the progress from earth to heaven and the purpose of his preaching. "Children and fools," he wrote, "choose to please their senses rather than their reason, because they still dwell within the regions of sense, and have little residence amongst intellectual essences."[3] The growth in grace was for him the growth in this life of the spirit; for it was possible, he said, "to taste of this perfection while in our mortal state on earth; a man's heart and eye may be in the state of perfection, that is, heaven, before he sets his feet upon that golden threshold; and God, "the eternal essence," would now and then grant his worshippers "little antepasts of heaven," opening for him "little loopholes of eternity"; "God sometimes draws aside the curtains of peace, and shews man his throne, and visits him with irradiations of glory, and sends him a little star to stand over his dwelling, and then covers it with a cloud."[4] Here indeed the preacher is priest and shares in

---

1. *Works* 3:266.
2. Smith, p. lv.
3. Ibid.
4. Smith, p. lv.

those divine communications; Taylor's *appealing discourse* brings forth the only-begotten Word, which is the source in man of eternal life.

Taylor was distinguished from those English preachers who had most prominently preceded him in that he was in no sense an improvisator. He exercises every legitimate art of finished literary oratory, from the abrupt beginning to the solemn and stately close. In a sermon *The House of Feasting* he cites the proverb, "Let us eat, drink, and be merry, for tomorrow we die," and abruptly comments, "this is the epicure's proverb, begun upon a weak mistake, started by chance from the discourses of drink, and thought witty by the undiscerning company."[5] By contrast with this abrupt beginning he almost invariably ends in a studied verbal harmony that promotes its own peculiar peace. As he developed his text, which took about an hour, but never more to deliver, metaphor and simile become his language of communication with man, and images from light and color, and living creatures on the wing fly him to God; he is always at the service of grace, and his words present the Word:

> Jesus was like the rainbow, which God set in the clouds as a sacrament to confirm a promise and establish a grace. He was half made of the glories of the light, and half of the moisture of a cloud. In His best days, He was but half triumph and half sorrow.[6]

At Trinity College in Dublin, while he was bishop of Down and Connor in the north of Ireland, Taylor preached a sermon entitled *Via Intelligentiae* or *On the Way of Understanding*, the complete text of which is printed in this fourth chapter. Here he is at his very best. The poet, or rather the prophet, or perhaps the priest, emerges in the preacher. He reaches mystical heights and brings his readers with him into the world of his faith, which is the world of God's spirit and essence. Vision and style, or faith and language, are here made one, like a painter's coloring and the world of his unique perception, and that peace, which Augustine called *tranquilitas ordinis* or the harmony of good order is the reward.

There have been authors of eminence, it is true, who have made

---

5. *Works* 4:180.
6. *Works* 4:436.

but a sparing use of metaphors, yet the power of thinking in images, *le don des images*, has always been a habit of mind essential for the preacher, as he conveys the wisdom of another land. Thomas Fuller, a contemporary of Taylor's, wrote that "while reasons are the pillars of the fabric of a sermon, similitudes are the windows which give the best light, and the sermons of all ages abound in windows of this kind."[7] Taylor's sermons, like some late Gothic church, are full of light, and have a unique quality, seldom found in other preachers:

> The figures of other preachers, rich and abundant as they often are, partake of the nature of rhetorical figures; to produce their effect, to persuade the will, or satisfy the understanding, they must be familiar to their audience, and the sense of this appeal to an audience always accompanies them. But the images of Jeremy Taylor, although he too was an orator, are a poet's images; they surprise us by their novelty of expression, and his aim seems to be to express his own emotions rather than to excite those of others, to delight the imagination rather than to move the will, to enrich and feed the mind with lyric tenderness and beauty, rather than to furnish it with motives for action.

> In his Oxford lectures on Poetry, Keble illustrates this distinction between rhetorical and poetic use of images by comparing Burke's description of Marie Antoinette, "decorating and cheering the elevated sphere she just began to move in; glittering like the morning star," with what Jeremy Taylor says, in his funeral sermon of Lady Carbery: "In all her Religion, in all her actions of relation towards God, she had a strange evenness and untroubled passage, sliding towards her ocean of God and infinity, with a certain and silent motion." Both illustrations, Keble says, are models of splendid style, "but while Burke speaks as an accomplished orator, Taylor touches the heights of poetry."[8]

Taylor's sermons were preached to Lady Carbery and her household, who persuaded Taylor, against his wishes, to publish them, "for

---

7. Smith, p. xxxv.
8. Ibid. p. xxxvi.

the appetites of the hunger and thirst after righteousness of that dear Lady, that rare soul would brook no objections," and when she died *Eniautos* was being prepared for press. *The Funeral Sermon, at the obsequies of the Countess of Carbery* was a model of its kind, and marked an advance upon the conventional type of elegy in prose and verse: it offers no preposterous panegyric of the deceased, but a reasonable and thoughtful enumeration of her qualities, what Taylor himself called "a drawing in water colours":

> She was . . . of a temperate, plain and natural diet, without curiosity or an intemperate palate, She spent less time in dressing than many servants. Her recreations were little and seldom, her prayers often, her reading much. She was of a most noble and charitable soul; a great lover of honourable actions, and as great a dispiser of base things. Hugely loving to oblige others, she was very unwilling to be in arrear to any upon the stock of courtesies and liberality. So free in all acts of favour, that she would not stay to hear herself thanked. . . . She was an excellent friend, and hugely dear to very many, especially to the best and most discerning persons; to all that conversed with her, and could understand her great worth and sweetness. She was of an honourable, nice and tender reputation; and of the pleasures of the world, which were laid before her in heaps, she took a very small and inconsiderable share.[9]

The twenty *Discourses* Taylor packed into the *Great Exemplar,* and which with numerous *prayers* and prolonged *considerations* broke the sequence of the narrative and enlarged the volume, were originally sermons Taylor preached at Uppingham, when he was for the first and only time a parish priest and enjoyed the care of souls. There the Earl of Northampton was his patron and inspiration, and he weaned Taylor away from "problems and inactive discourses . . . and disputings, which begin commonly in mistakes, proceed with zeal and fancy, and end not at all, but in schisms and uncharitable names, and too often dip their feet in blood."[10] Thus did the revolutionary die and the preacher come to life! The *Discourses* lack the color of the sermons, but the vision is the

---

9. *Works* 8:449.
10. Gosse, p. 56.

same divine awareness. The *Discourses* on *Meditation* and *Prayer* are included in this chapter with shorter excerpts from some others.

Sermon, discourse and *prayer* are essentially the same in Taylor; indeed his sermons are extended prayers, and his prayers are sermons in miniature. To feast as often as one can upon "these glorious communications of eternity," and to live as much as possible "in heaven, while still on earth,"[11] was for Jeremy Taylor, in his more mystical moments, the essence of religion, and the mystery to be preached and prayed. This divine presence is man's only consolation in a world of sorrow, and his "only redemption from its vanity and nothingness and dust."

> But so have I seen a Rose newly springing from the clefts of its hood, and at first it was fair as the Morning, and full with the dew of Heaven, as a Lamb's fleece; but when a ruder breath had forced open its virgin modesty, and dismantled its too youthful and unripe retirements, it began to put on darknesse, and to decline to softnesse, and the symptomes of a sickly age; it bowed the head, and broke its stalk, and at night having lost some of its leaves, and all its beauty, it fell into the portion of weeds and outworn faces.[12]

Prayer is man's only means of ascent and escape, and it enables us to participate in eternity while we are still prisoners in time. When Taylor writes of prayer he does so with the sincerest unction and floats heavenward on the wings of his fairest images, like that symbol of prayer, the ascending lark, whose attempt he so beautifully describes "to get to heaven, and climb above the clouds." Prayer, he says, "is the peace of our spirit . . . the stillness of our thoughts . . . the evennesse of recollection . . . the seat of meditation . . . the rest of our cares . . . and the calm of our tempest: prayer is the issue of a quiet minde . . . of untroubled thoughts: it is the daughter of charity, and the sister of meekness."[13]

> For so have I seen a lark rising from his bed of grasse and soaring upwards sings as he rises, and hopes to get to heaven,

---

11. Smith, p. lv.
12. *Works* 3:270.
13. Smith, p. lv.

and climbe above the clouds; but the poor bird was beaten back with the loud sighings of an eastern winde, and his motion made irregular and unconstant, descending more at every breath of the tempest, then it could recover by the liberation and frequent weighing of his wings; till the little creature was forc'd to sit down and pant, and stay till the storm was over, and then it made a prosperous flight, and did rise and sing as if it had learned musick and motion from an Angell as he passed sometimes through the aire about his ministries here below.[14]

Such is the nature of prayer and man's flight to God. We must learn music and motion from an angel, for Christianity is not so much a divine institution as "a divine flame and temper of spirit," for in heaven we shall first see and then love, but on earth we must first love and then the divine knowledge will be bestowed upon us. His ideal, therefore, of Christianity was such a religion "as leads us to huge felicity through pleasant ways";[15] and since of these ways, prayers were to him of supreme importance, some of Jeremy Taylor's loveliest writing is in the numerous prayers with which he fills his every work. Some of these conclude this chapter. Each of these prayers, as Sir Edmund Gosse has said, "is like a gush of music; they are among the most exquisite of their kind in the English language, and display the delicate wholesomeness of his conscience, and the inimitable distinction of his style."[16]

---

14. *Works* 4:310.
15. Smith, p. xxv.
16. Gosse, p. 59.

Sermon VI[1]

VIA INTELLIGENTIÆ

John vii. 17
If Any Man Will Do His Will, He Shall Know
of the Doctrine, Whether It Be of God,
Or Whether I Speak of Myself.

The ancients in their mythological learning tell us, that when Jupiter espied the men of the world striving for truth, and pulling her in pieces to secure her to themselves, he sent Mercury down amongst them, and he with his usual arts dressed error up in the imagery of truth, and thrust her into the crowd, and so left them to contend still: and though then by contention men were sure to get but little truth, yet they were as earnest as ever, and lost peace too, in their importune contentions for the very image of truth. And this indeed is no wonder: but when truth and peace are brought into the world together, and bound up in the same bundle of life; when we are taught a religion by the Prince of peace, who is the truth itself, to see men contending for this truth to the breach of that peace; and when men fall out, to see that they should make christianity their theme: that is one of the greatest wonders in the world. For christianity is "a soft and gentle institution"; it was brought into the world to soften the asperities of human nature, and to cure the barbarities of evil men, and the contentions of the passionate. The eagle seeing her breast wounded, and espying the arrow that hurt her to be feathered, cried out "the feathered nation is destroyed by their own feathers"; that is, a Christian fighting and wrangling with a Christian; and indeed that's very sad: but wrangling about peace too; that peace itself should be the argument of a war, that's unnatural; and if it were not that there are many who are *homines multæ religionis, nullius pæne pietatis,* "men of much religion and little godliness," it would not be that there should be so many quarrels in and concerning that religion which is wholly made up of truth and peace, and was sent amongst us to

---

1. *Works* 8:363ff.

reconcile the hearts of men when they were tempted to uncharitableness by any other unhappy argument. Disputation cures no vice, but kindles a great many, and makes passion evaporate into sin: and though men esteem it learning, yet it is the most useless learning in the world. When Eudamidas[2] the son of Archidamus heard old Xenocrates disputing about wisdom, he asked very soberly, "If the old man be yet disputing and enquiring concerning wisdom, what time will he have to make use of it?" Christianity is all for practice, and so much time as is spent in quarrels about it is a diminution to its interest: men enquire so much what it is, that they have but little time left to be Christians. I remember a saying of Erasmus, that when he first read the New testament with fear and a good mind, with a purpose to understand it and obey it, he found it very useful and very pleasant: but when afterwards he fell on reading the vast differences of commentaries, then he understood it less than he did before, then he began not to understand it. For indeed the truths of God are best dressed in the plain culture and simplicity of the Spirit; but the truths that men commonly teach are like the reflections of a multiplying glass: for one piece of good money you shall have forty that are fantastical; and it is forty to one if your finger hit upon the right. Men have wearied themselves in the dark, having been amused with false fires: and instead of going home, have wandered all night "in untrodden, unsafe, uneasy ways"; but have not found out what their soul desires. But therefore since we are so miserable, and are in error, and have wandered very far, we must do as wandering travellers use to do, go back just to that place from whence they wandered, and begin upon a new account. Let us go to the truth itself, to Christ, and He will tell us an easy way of ending all our quarrels: for we shall find christianity to be the easiest and the hardest thing in the world: it is like a secret in arithmetic, infinitely hard till it be found out by a right operation, and then it is so plain, we wonder we did not understand it earlier.

Christ's way of finding out of truth is by "doing the will of God."[3] We will try that by and by, if possible we may find that easy and certain: in the mean time let us consider what ways men have propounded to find out truth, and upon the foundation of that to establish peace in christendom.

1. That there is but one true way is agreed upon; and therefore

---

2. Plutarch, *Moralia*, LCL, vol. 3, p. 319.
3. John 7:17.

almost every church of one denomination that lives under government propounds to you a system or collective body of articles, and tells you, that's the true religion, and they are the church, and the peculiar people of God: like Brutus and Cassius, of whom one says, *ubicunque ipsi essent, prætexebantesse rempublicam,* "they supposed themselves were the commonwealth"; and these are the church, and out of this church they will hardly allow salvation. But of this there can be no end; for divide the church into twenty parts, and in what part soever your lot falls, you and your party are damned by the other nineteen; and men on all hands almost keep their own proselytes by affrighting them with the fearful sermons of damnation: but in the mean time here is no security to them that are not able to judge for themselves, and no peace for them that are.

2. Others cast about to cure this, and conclude that it must be done by submission to an infallible guide; this must do it or nothing: and this is the way of the church of Rome; follow but the pope and his clergy, and you are safe, at least as safe as their warrant can make you. Indeed this were a very good way, if it were a way at all; but it is none; for this can never end our controversies: not only because the greatest controversies are about this infallible guide; but also because, 1) We cannot find that there is upon earth any such guide at all. 2) We do not find it necessary that there should. 3) We find that they who pretend to be this infallible guide are themselves infinitely deceived. 4) That they do not believe themselves to be infallible, whatever they say to us; because they do not put an end to all their own questions that trouble them. 5) Because they have no peace but what is constrained by force and government. 6) And lastly, because if there were such a guide, we should fail of truth by many other causes: for it may be that guide would not do his duty; or we are fallible followers of this infallible leader; or we should not understand his meaning at all times, or we should be perverse at some times, or something as bad: because we all confess that God is an infallible guide, and that some way or other He does teach us sufficiently, and yet it does come to pass by our faults that we are as far to seek for peace and truth as ever.

3. Some very wise men finding this to fail, have undertaken to reconcile the differences of christendom by a way of moderation. Thus they have projected to reconcile the papists and the Lutherans, the Lutherans and the Calvinists, the remonstrants and contra-remonstrants, and project that each side should abate of their asperities, and pare away something of their propositions, and join in common terms

357

and phrases of accommodation, each of them sparing something, and promising they shall have a great deal of peace or the exchange of a little of their opinion. This was the way of Cassander, Modrevius, Andreas Frisius, Erasmus, Spalato, Grotius, and indeed of Charles the fifth in part, but something more heartily of Ferdinand the second. This device produced the conferences at Poissy, at Montpellier, at Ratisbon, at the Hague, at many places more: and what was the event of these? Their parties when their delegates returned, either disclaimed their moderation, or their respective princes had some other ends to serve, or they permitted the meetings upon uncertain hopes, and a trial if any good might come; or it may be they were both in the wrong, and their mutual abatement was nothing but a mutual quitting of what they could not get, and the shaking hands of false friends; or it may be it was all of it nothing but hypocrisy and arts of craftiness, and, like Lucian's[4] man, every one could be a man and a pestle when he pleased. And the council of Trent, though under another cover, made use of the artifice, but made the secret manifest and common: for at this day the jesuits in the questions *De auxiliis divinæ gratiæ* have prevailed with the Dominicans to use their expressions, and yet they think they still keep the sentence of their own order. From hence can succeed nothing but folly and a fantastic peace: this is but the skinning of an old sore, it will break out upon all occasions.

4. Others who understand things beyond the common rate, observing that many of our controversies and peevish wranglings are kept up by the ill stating of the question, endeavour to declare things wisely, and make the matter intelligible, and the words clear; hoping by this means to cut off all disputes. Indeed this is a very good way, so far as it can go: and would prevail very much, if all men were wise, and would consent to those statings, and would not fall out upon the main enquiry when it were well stated: but we find by a sad experience that few questions are well stated; and when they are, they are not consented to; and when they are agreed on by both sides that they are well stated, it is nothing else but a drawing up the armies in *battalia* with great skill and discipline; the next thing they do is, they thrust their swords into one another's sides.

5. What remedy after all this? Some other good men have propounded one way yet: but that is a way of peace rather than truth; and

---

4. Lucian, *The Lover of Lies*, LCL, vol. 3, p. 372.

that is, that all opinions should be tolerated and none persecuted, and then all the world will be at peace. Indeed this relies upon a great reasonableness; not only because opinions cannot be forced, but because if men receive no hurt it is to be hoped they will do none: but we find that this alone will not do it: for besides that all men are not so just as not to do any injury (for some men begin the evil) besides this (I say) there are very many men amongst us who are not content that you permit them; for they will not permit you, but "rule over your faith,"[5] and say that their way is not only true, but necessary; and therefore the truth of God is at stake, and all indifference and moderation is carnal wisdom, and want of zeal for God: nay more than so, they preach for toleration when themselves are under the rod, who when they got the rod into their own hands thought toleration itself to be intolerable. Thus do the papists, and thus the Calvinists: and for their cruelty they pretend charity: they will indeed force you to come in, but it is in true zeal for your soul: and if they do you violence, it is no more than if they pull your arm out of joint, when to save you from drowning they draw you out of a river; and if you complain, it is no more to be regarded than the outcries of children against their rulers, or sick men against physicians. But as to the thing itself, the truth is, it is better in contemplation than practice: for reckon all that is got by it when you come to handle it, and it can never satisfy for the infinite disorders happening in the government; the scandal to religion, the secret dangers to public societies, the growth of heresy, the nursing up of parties to a grandeur so considerable as to be able in their own time to change the laws and the government. So that if the question be whether mere opinions are to be persecuted, it is certainly true, they ought not. But if it be considered how by opinions men rifle the affairs of kingdoms, it is also as certain, they ought not to be made public and permitted. And what is now to be done? must truth be for ever in the dark, and the world for ever be divided, and societies disturbed, and governments weakened, and our spirits debauched with error, and the uncertain opinions, and the pedantry of talking men? Certainly there is a way to cure all this evil; and the wise Governor of all the world hath not been wanting in so necessary a matter as to lead us into all truth. But the way hath not yet been hit upon, and yet I have told you all the ways of man and his imaginations in order to truth and peace: and you see these will not do; we can find no

5. 2 Cor. 1:24.

rest for the soles of our feet amidst all the waters of contention and disputations, and little artifices of divided schools. "Every man is a liar," and his understanding is weak, and his propositions uncertain, and his opinions trifling, and his contrivances imperfect, and neither truth nor peace does come from man. I know I am in an auditory of inquisitive persons, whose business is to study for truth, that they may find it for themselves and teach it unto others: I am in a school of prophets and prophets' sons, who all ask Pilate's question, "What is truth?" You look for it in your books, and you tug hard for it in your disputations, and you derive it from the cisterns of the fathers, and you enquire after the old ways, and sometimes are taken with new appearances, and you rejoice in false lights, or are delighted with little umbrages and peep of day. But where is there a man, or a society of men, that can be at rest in his enquiry, and is sure he understands all the truths of God? where is there a man but the more he studies and enquires, still he discovers nothing so clearly as his own ignorance? This is a demonstration that we are not in the right way, that we do not enquire wisely, that our method is not artificial. If men did fall upon the right way, it were impossible so many learned men should be engaged in contrary parties and opinions. We have examined all ways but one, all but God's way. Let us (having missed in all the other) try this: let us go to God for truth; for truth comes from God only, and His ways are plain, and His sayings are true, and His promises Yea and Amen: and if we miss the truth it is because we will not find it: for certain it is, that all that truth which God hath made necessary, He hath also made legible and plain, and if we will open our eyes we shall see the sun, and if "we will walk in the light," we shall "rejoice in the light": only let us withdraw the curtains, let us remove the impediments and the sin that doth so easily beset us: that's God's way. Every man must in his station do that portion of duty which God requires of him, and then he shall be taught of God all that is fit for him to learn: there is no other way for him but this. "The fear of the Lord is the beginning of wisdom, and a good understanding have all they that do thereafter."[6] And so said David of himself,[7] "I have more understanding than my teachers, because I keep Thy commandments." And this is the only way which Christ hath taught us: if you ask, "What is truth?" you must not do as Pilate did, ask the question, and then go

---

6. Ps. 111:10.
7. Ps. 119:10.

away from Him that only can give you an answer: for as God is the author of truth, so He is the teacher of it; and the way to learn it is this of my text: for so saith our blessed Lord, "If any man will do His will, he shall know of the doctrine whether it be of God or no."

My text is simple as truth itself, but greatly comprehensive, and contains a truth that alone will enable you to understand all mysteries, and to expound all prophecies, and to interpret all scriptures, and to search into all secrets, all (I mean) which concern our happiness and our duty: and it being an affirmative hypothetical, is plainly to be resolved into this proposition: The way to judge of religion is by doing of our duty; and theology is rather a divine life than a divine knowledge. In heaven indeed we shall first see, and then love; but here on earth we must first love, and love will open our eyes as well as our hearts, and we shall then see and perceive and understand.

In the handling of which proposition I shall first represent to you that the certain causes of our errors are nothing but direct sins, nothing makes us fools and ignorants but living vicious lives; and then I shall proceed to the direct demonstration of the article in question, that holiness is the only way of truth and understanding.

1. No man understands the word of God as it ought to be understood, unless he lays aside all affections to sin; of which because we have taken very little care, the product hath been that we have had very little wisdom, and very little knowledge in the ways of God. *KAKIA ESTI PHTHARTIKĒ TĒS ARCHĒS*, saith Aristotle,[8] wickedness does corrupt a man's reasoning, it gives him false principles and evil measures of things: the sweet wine that Ulysses gave to the Cyclops put his eye out; and a man that hath contracted evil affections, and made a league with sin, sees only by those measures. A covetous man understands nothing to be good that is not profitable; and a voluptuous man likes your reasoning well enough if you discourse of *bonum jucundum*, the pleasures of the sense, the ravishments of lust, the noises and inadvertencies, the mirth and songs of merry company; but if you talk to him of the melancholy lectures of the cross, the content of resignation, the peace of meekness, and the joys of the holy Ghost, and of rest in God, after your long discourse and his great silence he cries out, "What's the matter?" He knows not what you mean: either you must fit his humour, or change your discourse.

---

8. Aristotle, *Nicomachean Ethics*, LCL, p. 420.

I remember that Arrianus tells of a gentleman that was banished from Rome, and in his sorrow visited the philosopher, and he heard him talk wisely, and believed him, and promised him to leave all the thoughts of Rome and splendours of the court, and retire to the course of a severe philosophy; but before the good man's lectures were done, there came "letters from Cæsar," to recall him home, to give him pardon, and promise him great employment. He presently grew weary of the good man's sermon, and wished he would make an end, thought his discourse was dull and flat; for his head and heart were full of another story and new principles; and by these measures he could hear only and he could understand.

Every man understands by his affections more than by his reason: and when the wolf in the fable went to school to learn to spell, whatever letters were told him, he could never make any thing of them but *agnus;* he thought of nothing but his belly; and if a man be very hungry, you must give him meat before you give him counsel. A man's mind must be like your proposition before it can be entertained: for whatever you put into a man it will smell of the vessel: it is a man's mind that gives the emphasis, and makes your argument to prevail.

And upon this account it is that there are so many false doctrines in the only article of repentance. Men know they must repent, but the definition of repentance they take from the convenience of their own affairs: what they will not part with, that is not necessary to be parted with, and they will repent, but not restore: they will say *Nollem factum,* they "wish they had never done it":[9] but since it is done, you must give them leave to rejoice in their purchase: they will ask forgiveness of God; but they sooner forgive themselves, and suppose that God is of their mind: if you tie them to hard terms, your doctrine is not to be understood, or it is but one doctor's opinion, and therefore they will fairly take their leave, and get them another teacher.

What makes these evil, these dangerous and desperate doctrines? Not the obscurity of the thing, but the cloud upon the heart; for say you what you will, he that hears must be the expounder, and we can never suppose but a man will give sentence in behalf of what he passionately loves. And so it comes to pass that, as Rabbi Moses observed, as God for the greatest sin imposed the least oblation, as a she-goat for the sin of idolatry; for a woman accused of adultery, a barley-cake; so do most

---

9. Lactantius, *The Divine Institutes*, PL 6.722.

men; they think to expiate the worst of their sins with a trifling, with a pretended little insignificant repentance. God indeed did so, that the cheapness of the oblation might teach them to hope for pardon, not from the ceremony, but from a severe internal repentance: but men take any argument to lessen their repentance, that they may not lessen their pleasures or their estates, and that repentance may be nothing but a word, and mortification signify nothing against their pleasures, but be a term of art only, fitted for the schools or for the pulpit, but nothing relative to practice, or the extermination of their sin. So that it is no wonder we understand so little of religion: it is because we are in love with that which destroys it; and as a man does not care to hear what does not please him, so neither does he believe it; he cannot, he will not understand it.

And the same is the case in the matter of pride; the church hath extremely suffered by it in many ages. Arius missed a bishopric, and therefore turned heretic: *ETARASSE TĒN EKKLĒSIAN*, saith the story,[10] "he disturbed and shaked the church"; for he did not understand this truth, that the peace of the church was better than the satisfaction of his person, or the promoting his foolish opinion. And do not we see and feel that at this very day the pride of men makes it seem impossible for many persons to obey their superiors, and they do not see (what they can read[11] every day) that it is a sin "to speak evil of dignities"?

A man would think it a very easy thing to understand the thirteenth chapter to the Romans,[12] "Whosoever resisteth the power, resisteth the ordinance of God"; and yet we know a generation of men to whom these words were so obscure, that they thought it lawful to fight against their king. A man would think it easy to believe that those who were "in the gainsaying of Corah,"[13] who rose up against the high-priest, were in a very sad condition: and yet there are too many amongst us who are in the gainsaying of Corah, and think they do very well; that they are the "godly party," and the good people of God. Why? what's the matter? In the world there can be nothing plainer than these words, "Let every soul be subject to the higher powers,"[14] and that you need not make a scruple who are these higher powers, it is as plainly said, "there is no

---

10. Epiphanius, *Heresies*, PG 42.202.
11. Jude 8:1.
12. Jude 8:2.
13. Jude 11:1ff.
14. Rom. 13:1.

power but of God"; all that are set over you by the laws of your nation, these "are over you in the Lord":[15] and yet men will not understand these plain things; they deny to do their notorious duty, and yet believe they are in the right, and if they sometimes obey "for wrath," they oftener disobey "for conscience sake." Where is the fault? The words are plain, the duty is certain, the book lies open; but alas, it is "sealed within,"[16] that is, "men have eyes and will not see, ears and will not hear."[17] But the wonder is the less; for we know when God said to Jonas,[18] "Doest thou well to be angry?" he answered God to His face, "I do well to be angry even unto the death." Let God declare His mind never so plainly, if men will not lay aside the evil principle that is within, their open love to their secret sin, they may kill an apostle, and yet be so ignorant as to "think they do God good service";[19] they may disturb kingdoms, and break the peace of a well-ordered church, and rise up against their fathers, and be cruel to their brethren, and stir up the people to sedition; and all this with a cold stomach and a hot liver, with a hard heart and a tender conscience, with humble carriage and a proud spirit. For thus men hate repentance, because they scorn to confess an error; they will not return to peace and truth, because they fear to lose the good opinion of the people whom themselves have cozened; they are afraid to be good, lest they should confess they had formerly done amiss: and he that observes how much evil is done, and how many heresies are risen, and how much obstinacy and unreasonable perseverance in folly dwells in the world upon the stock of pride, may easily conclude that no learning is sufficient to make a proud man understand the truth of God, unless he first learn to be humble. But *obedite et intelligetis* (saith the prophet), "obey" and be humble, leave the foolish affections of sin, and then "ye shall understand." That's the first particular: all remaining affections to sin hinder the learning and understanding of the things of God.

2. He that means to understand the will of God and the truth of religion must lay aside all inordinate affections to the world (2 Cor. iii. 14). S. Paul complained that there was "at that day a veil upon the hearts of the Jews in the reading of the Old testament": they looked for a

---

15. 1 Thess. 5:12.
16. Rev. 5:1.
17. Jer. 5:21; Ezek. 12:2.
18. Jon. 4:9.
19. John 16:2.

temporal prince to be their Messias, and their affections and hopes dwelt in secular advantages; and so long as that veil was there, they could not see, and they would not accept the poor despised Jesus.

For the things of the world, besides that they entangle one another, and make much business, and spend much time, they also take up the attentions of a man's mind, and spend his faculties, and make them trifling and secular with the very handling and conversation. And therefore the Pythagoreans taught their disciples "a separation from the things of the body, if they would purely find out truth and the excellencies of wisdom."[20] Had not he lost his labour that would have discoursed wisely to Apicius, and told him of the books of fate and the secrets of the other world, the abstractions of the soul and its brisker immortality, that saints and angels eat not, and that the spirit of a man lives for ever upon wisdom, and holiness and contemplation? The fat glutton would have stared a while upon the preacher, and then have fallen asleep. But if you had discoursed well and knowingly of a lamprey, a large mullet, or a boar,

animal propter convivia natum,[21]

and have sent him a cook from Asia to make new sauces, he would have attended carefully, and taken in your discourses greedily. And so it is in the questions and secrets of christianity: which made S. Paul,[22] when he intended to convert Felix, discourse first with him about "temperance, righteousness and judgment to come." He began in the right point; he knew it was to no purpose to preach Jesus Christ crucified to an intemperate person, to an usurper of other men's rights, to one whose soul dwelt in the world, and cared not for the sentence of the last day. The philosophers began their wisdom with the meditation of death, and S. Paul his with the discourse of the day of judgment: to take the heart off from this world and the amabilities of it, which dishonour and baffle the understanding, and made Solomon himself become a child, and fooled into idolatry, by the prettiness of a talking woman. Men now-a-days love not a religion that will cost them dear: if your doctrine calls upon men to part with any considerable part of their estates, you must

---

20. Plotinus, *Enneads*, LCL, vol. 1, p. 204.
21. Juvenal, *Satires*, LCL, p. 14.
22. Acts 24:25.

pardon them if they cannot believe you; they understand it not. I shall give you one great instance of it.

When we consider the infinite unreasonableness that is in the popish religion, how against common sense their doctrine of transubstantiation is, how against the common experience of human nature is the doctrine of the pope's infallibility, how against scripture is the doctrine of indulgences and purgatory; we may well think it a wonder that no more men are persuaded to leave such unlearned follies. But then on the other side the wonder will cease if we mark how many temporal ends are served by these doctrines. If you destroy the doctrine of purgatory and indulgences, you take away the priest's income, and make the "see apostolic" to be poor; if you deny the pope's infallibility, you will despise his authority, and examine his propositions, and discover his failings, and put him to answer hard arguments, and lessen his power: and indeed when we run through all the propositions of difference between them and us, and see that in every one of them they serve an end of money or of power, it will be very visible that the way to confute them is not by learned disputations (for we see they have been too long without effect, and without prosperity); the men must be cured of their affections to the world, *ut nudi nudum sequantur crucifixum,* "that with naked and devested affections they might follow the naked crucified Jesus," and they they would soon learn the truths of God, which till then will be impossible to be apprehended. "Men," as S. Basil[23] says, "when they expound scripture, always bring in something of themselves": but till there be, as one said, "a rising out from their own seats, until they go out from their dark dungeons," they can never see the light of heaven.[24] And how many men are there amongst us who are therefore enemies to the religion, because it seems to be against their profit? The argument of Demetrius[25] is unanswerable, "By this craft they get their livings": leave them in their livings, and they will let your religion alone; if not, they think they have reason to speak against it. When men's souls are possessed with the world, their souls cannot be invested with holy truths. As S. Isidore said: the soul must be informed, "insouled," or animated with the propositions that you put in, or you shall never do any good, or get disciples to Christ. Now because

---

23. Basil, *The Hexaemeron*, PG 29.189.
24. Plotinus, *Enneads* 2.9.6, p. 242.
25. Acts 19:25.

a man cannot serve two masters; because he cannot vigorously attend two objects; because there can be but one living soul in any living creature; if the world have got possession, talk no more of your questions, shut your bibles, and read no more of the words of God to them, for they cannot "tell of the doctrine whether it be of God," or of the world. That is the second particular: worldly affections hinder true understandings in religion.

3. No man, how learned soever, can understand the word of God, or be at peace in the questions of religion, unless he be a master over his passions;

> If you wish to see
> The truth in a clear light,
> Forsake joys and fears . . .
> Where these reign the mind
> Is clouded and bound in chains.

said the wise Boethius,[26] "a man must first learn himself before he can learn God." *Tua te fallit imago*[27] nothing deceives a man so soon as a man's self; when a man is (that I may use Plato's[28] expression) SYMPE-PHYRMENOS TĒ GENESEI, "mingled with his nature and his congenial" infirmities of anger and desire, he can never have any thing but a knowledge partly moral and partly natural: his whole life is but imagination; his knowledge is inclination and opinion; he judges of heavenly things by the measures of his fears and his desires, and his reason is half of it sense, and determinable by the principles of sense . . . "then a man learns well when he is a philosopher in his passions."[29] Passionate men are to be taught the first elements of religion: and let men pretend to as much learning as they please, they must begin again at Christ's cross; they must learn true mortification and crucifixion of their anger and desires, before they can be good scholars in Christ's school, or be admitted into the more secret enquiries of religion, or profit in spiritual understanding. It was an excellent proverb of the Jews, *In passionibus Spiritus sanctus non habitat*, "the holy Ghost never dwells in the house of passion." Truth enters into the heart of man when it is empty and

---

26. Boethius, *Consolation of Philosophy*, I, m. 7, LCL, pp. 168–70.
27. Ovid, *Metamorphoses*, LCL, vol. 1, p. 156.
28. Plato is not the correct source here; cfr. Simplicius on Epictetus.
29. Gregory Nazianzen, *Letters*, PG 37.70.

clean and still; but when the mind is shaken with passion as with a storm, you can never "hear the voice of the charmer though he charm very wisely": and you will very hardly sheath a sword when it is held by a loose and a paralytic arm. He that means to learn the secrets of God's wisdom must be, as Plato[30] says, *KATA TĒN LOGIKĒN ZŌĒN OYSIŌMENOS* "his soul must be consubstantiated with reason," not invested with passion: to him that is otherwise, things are but in the dark, his notion is obscure and his sight troubled; and therefore though we often meet with passionate fools, yet we seldom or never hear of a very passionate wise man.

I have now done with the first part of my undertaking, and proved to you that our evil life is the cause of our controversies and ignorances in religion and of the things of God. You see what hinders us from becoming good divines. But all this while we are but in the preparation to the mysteries of godliness: when we have thrown off all affections to sin, when we have stripped ourselves from all fond adherences to the things of the world, and have broken the chains and dominion of our passions; then we may say with David,[31] *Ecce paratum est cor meum, Deus,* "my heart is ready, O God, my heart is ready": then we may say, "Speak, Lord, for Thy servant heareth":[32] but we are not yet instructed. It remains therefore that we enquire what is that immediate principle or means by which we shall certainly and infallibly be led into all truth, and be taught the mind of God, and understand all His secrets; and this is worth our knowledge. I cannot say that this will end your labours, and put a period to your studies, and make your learning easy; it may possibly increase your labour, but it will make it profitable; it will not end your studies, but it will direct them; it will not make human learning easy, but it will make it wise unto salvation, and conduct it into true notices and ways of wisdom.

I am now to describe to you the right way of knowledge: *Qui facit voluntatem Patris mei,* saith Christ,[33] that's the way; "do God's will, and you shall understand God's word." And it was an excellent saying of S. Peter,[34] "Add to your faith virtue," etc. "If these things be in you and

---

30. Plato is again quoted instead of Simplicius as above.
31. Ps. 57:7.
32. 1 Sam. 3:9.
33. John 7:17.
34. 2 Pet. 1:5.

abound, ye shall not be unfruitful in the knowledge of our Lord Jesus Christ." For in this case 'tis not enough that our hindrances of knowledge are removed; for that is but the opening of the covering of the book of God; but when it is opened, it is written with a hand that every eye cannot read. Though the windows of the east be open, yet every eye cannot behold the glories of the sun; *OPHTHALMOS MĒ ĒLIOEIDĒS GINOMENOS ĒLION OY BLEPEI*, saith Plotinus,[35] "the eye that is not made solar cannot see the sun"; the eye must be fitted to the splendour: and it is not the wit of the man, but the spirit of the man; not so much his head as his heart, that learns the divine philosophy.

1. Now in this enquiry I must take one thing for a *præcognitum*, that every good man is "taught of God":[36] and indeed unless He teach us, we shall make but ill scholars ourselves, and worse guides to others. *Nemo potest Deum scire nisi a Deo doceatur*, said S. Irenæus.[37] If God teaches us, then all is well; but if we do not learn wisdom at His feet, from whence should we have it? it can come from no other spring. And therefore it naturally follows, that by how much nearer we are to God, by so much better we are like to be instructed.

But this being supposed, as being most evident, we can easily proceed by wonderful degrees and steps of progression in the economy of this divine philosophy; for,

2. There is in every righteous man a new vital principle; the Spirit of grace is the Spirit of wisdom, and teaches us by secret inspirations, by proper arguments, by actual persuasions, by personal applications, by effects and energies: and as the soul of a man is the cause of all his vital operations, so is the Spirit of God the life of that life, and the cause of all actions and productions spiritual: and the consequence of this is what S. John[38] tells us of, "Ye have received the unction from above, and that anointing teacheth you all things": all things of some one kind; that is, certainly, "all things that pertain to life and godliness";[39] all that by which a man is wise and happy. We see this by common experience. Unless the soul have a new life put into it, unless there be a vital principle within, unless the Spirit of life be the informer of the spirit of

---

35. Plotinus, *Enneads* 1.6.9, p. 258.
36. Isa. 54:13; John 6:45, 1 Thess. 4:9.
37. Irenaeus, *Against Heresies*, PG 7.989.
38. 1 John 2:27.
39. 2 Pet. 1:3.

the man, the word of God will be as dead in the operation as the body in its powers and possibilities. *Sol et homo generant hominem,*[40] saith our philosophy, "a man alone does not beget a man, but a man and the sun"; for without the influence of the celestial bodies all natural actions are ineffective: and so it is in the operations of the soul.

Which principle divers fanaticks, both among us and in the church of Rome, misunderstanding, look for new revelations, and expect to be conducted by ecstasy, and will not pray but in a transfiguration, and live upon raptures and extravagant expectations, and separate themselves from the conversation of men by affectations, by new measures and singularities, and destroy order, and despise government, and live upon illiterate phantasms and ignorant discourses. These men do *PSEY-DESTHAI TO HAGION PNEYMA,*[41] "they belie the holy Ghost": for the Spirit of God makes men wise; it is an evil spirit that makes them fools. The Spirit of God makes us "wise unto salvation"; it does not spend its holy influences in disguises and convulsions of the understanding: God's spirit does not destroy reason, but heightens it; He never disorders the beauties of government, but is a God of order; it is the Spirit of humility, and teaches no pride; He is to be found in churches and pulpits, upon altars and in the doctors' chairs; not in conventicles and mutinous corners of a house: He goes in company with His own ordinances, and makes progressions by the measures of life; His infusions are just as our acquisitions, and His graces pursue the methods of nature; that which was imperfect He leads on to perfection, and that which was weak He makes strong: He opens the heart, not to receive murmurs, or to attend to secret whispers, but to hear the word of God; and then He opens the heart, and creates a new one; and without this new creation, this new principle of life, we may hear the word of God, but we can never understand it; we hear the sound, but are never the better; unless there be in our hearts a secret conviction by the Spirit of God, the gospel in itself is a dead letter, and worketh not in us the light and righteousness of God.

Do not we see this by daily experience? Even those things which a good man and an evil man know, they do not know them both alike. A wicked man does know that good is lovely, and sin is of an evil and

---

40. Reference to Claudius Coelestinus, the medieval philosopher, *On the Marvels of the World.*

41. Acts 5:3.

destructive nature; and when he is reproved, he is convinced; and when he is observed, he is ashamed; and when he has done, he is unsatisfied; and when he pursues his sin, he does it in the dark. Tell him he shall die, and he sighs deeply, but he knows it as well as you. Proceed, and say that after death comes judgment, and the poor man believes and trembles; he knows that God is angry with him; and if you tell him that for aught he knows he may be in hell to-morrow, he knows that it is an intolerable truth, but it is also undeniable. And yet after all this, he runs to commit his sin with as certain an event and resolution as if he knew no argument against it: these notices of things terrible and true pass through his understanding as an eagle through the air; as long as her flight lasted the air was shaken, but there remains no path behind her.

Now since at the same time we see other persons, not so learned it may be, not so much versed in scriptures, yet they say a thing is good and lay hold of it; they believe glorious things of heaven, and they live accordingly, as men that believe themselves; half a word is enough to make them understand; a nod is a sufficient reproof; the crowing of a cock, the singing of a lark, the dawning of the day, and the washing their hands, are to them competent memorials of religion, and warnings of their duty. What is the reason of this difference? They both read the scriptures, they read and hear the same sermons, they have capable understandings, they both believe what they hear and what they read, and yet the event is vastly different. The reason is that which I am now speaking of; the one understands by one principle, the other by another; the one understands by nature, and the other by grace; the one by human learning, and the other by divine; the one reads the scriptures without, and the other within; the one understands as a son of man, the other as a son of God; the one perceives by the proportions of the world, and the other by the measures of the Spirit; the one understands by reason, and the other by love; and therefore he does not only understand the sermons of the Spirit, and perceives their meaning: but he pierces deeper, and knows the meaning of that meaning; that is, the secret of the Spirit, that which is spiritually discerned, that which gives life to the proposition, and activity to the soul. And the reason is, because he hath a divine principle within him, and a new understanding; that is, plainly, he hath love, and that's more than knowledge; as was rarely well observed by S. Paul,[42] "Knowledge puffeth up, but charity edifieth"; that is, charity

---

42. 1 Cor. 8:1.

makes the best scholars. No sermons can edify you, no scriptures can build you up a holy building to God, unless the love of God be in your hearts, and "purify your souls from all filthiness of the flesh and spirit."[43]

But so it is in the regions of stars, where a vast body of fire is so divided by eccentric motions, that it looks as if nature had parted them into orbs and round shells of plain and purest materials: but where the cause is simple, and the matter without variety, the motions must be uniform; and in heaven we should either espy no motion, or no variety. But God, who designed the heavens to be the causes of all changes and motions here below, hath placed His angels in their houses of light, and given to every one of His appointed officers a portion of the fiery matter to circumagitate and roll: and now the wonder ceases; for if it be enquired why this part of the fire runs eastward, and the other to the south, they being both indifferent to either, it is because an angel of God sits in the centre, and makes the same matter turn, not by the bent of its own mobility and inclination, but in order to the needs of man, and the great purposes of God. And so it is in the understandings of men; when they all receive the same notions, and are taught by the same master, and give full consent to all the propositions, and can of themselves have nothing to distinguish them in the events, it is because God has sent His divine spirit, and kindles a new fire, and creates a braver capacity, and applies the actives to the passives, and blesses their operation. For there is in the heart of man such a dead sea, and an indisposition to holy flames, like as in the cold rivers in the north, so as the fires will not burn them, and the sun itself will never warm them, till God's holy spirit does from the temple of the New Jerusalem bring a holy flame, and make it shine and burn.

"The natural man," saith the holy apostle,[44] "cannot perceive the things of the Spirit; they are foolishness unto him; for they are spiritually discerned": for he that discourses of things by the measures of sense, thinks nothing good but that which is delicious to the palate, or pleases the brutish part of man; and therefore while he estimates the secrets of religion by such measures, they must needs seem as insipid as cork, or the uncondited mushroom; for they have nothing at all of that in their constitution. A voluptuous person is like the dogs of Sicily, so

---

43. 2 Cor. 7:1.
44. 1 Cor. 2:14.

filled with the deliciousness of plants that grow in every furrow and hedge, that they can never keep the scent of their game. *ADYNATON ANAMIXAI HYDATI PYR' HOYTŌS OIMAI TRYPHĒN KAI KATANYXIN,* said S. Chrysostom,[45] "the fire and water can never mingle; so neither can sensuality, and the watchfulness and wise discerning of the spirit." *Pilato interroganti de veritate Christus non respondit,* "when the wicked governor asked of Christ concerning truth, Christ gave him no answer"; he was not fit to hear it.

He therefore who so understands the words of God that he not only believes but loves the proposition; he who consents with all his heart, and being convinced of the truth does also apprehend the necessity, and obeys the precept, and delights in the discovery, and lays his hand upon his heart, and reduces the notices of things to the practice of duty; he who dares trust his proposition, and drives it on to the utmost issue, resolving to go after it whithersoever it can invite him; this man walks in the Spirit; at least thus far he is gone towards it; his understanding is brought *in obsequium Christi,*[46] "into the obedience of Christ." This is a "loving God with all our mind";[47] and whatever goes less than this, is but memory, and not understanding; or else such notice of things by which a man is neither the wiser nor the better.

3. Sometimes God gives to His choicest, His most elect and precious servants, a knowledge even of secret things, which He communicates not to others. We find it greatly remarked in the case of Abraham (Gen. xviii. 17), "And the Lord said, Shall I hide from Abraham that thing that I do?" Why not from Abraham? God tells us, ver. 19, "For I know him, that he will command his children and his household after him, and they shall keep the way of the Lord, to do justice and judgment." And though this be irregular and infrequent, yet it is a reward of their piety, and the proper increase also of the spiritual man. We find this spoken by God to Daniel, and promised to be the lot of the righteous man in the days of the Messias; Dan. xii. 10, "Many shall be purified, and made white, and tried; but the wicked shall do wickedly": and what then? "None of the wicked shall understand, but the wise shall understand." Where besides that the wise man and the wicked are opposed, plainly signifying that the wicked man is a fool and an igno-

---

45. Chrysostom, *On Compunction,* PG 47.404, 414.
46. 2 Cor. 10:5.
47. Matt. 22:37.

rant; it is plainly said that "none of the wicked shall understand" the wisdom and mysteriousness of the kingdom of the Messias.

4. A good life is the best way to understand wisdom and religion, because by the experiences and relishes of religion there is conveyed to them such a sweetness, to which all wicked men are strangers: there is in the things of God to them which practise them a deliciousness that makes us love them, and that love admits us into God's cabinet, and strangely clarifies the understanding by the purification of the heart. For when our reason is raised up by the Spirit of Christ, it is turned quickly into experience; when our faith relies upon the principles of Christ, it is changed into vision; and so long as we know God only in the ways of man, by contentious learning, by arguing and dispute, we see nothing but the shadow of Him, and in that shadow we meet with many dark appearances, little certainty, and much conjecture: but when we know Him with the eyes of holiness, and the intuition of gracious experiences, with a quiet spirit and the peace of enjoyment; then we shall hear what we never heard, and see what our eyes never saw; then the mysteries of godliness shall be opened unto us, and clear as the windows of the morning: and this is rarely well expressed by the apostle, "If we stand up from the dead and awake from sleep, then Christ shall give us light."[48]

For although the scriptures themselves are written by the Spirit of God, yet they are written within and without: and besides the light that shines upon the face of them, unless there be a light shining within our hearts, unfolding the leaves, and interpreting the mysterious sense of the Spirit, convincing our consciences and preaching to our hearts; to look for Christ in the leaves of the gospel, is to look for the living amongst the dead. There is a life in them, but that life is, according to S. Paul's expression, "hid with Christ in God": and unless the Spirit of God be the *promo-condus*, we shall never draw it forth.

Human learning brings excellent ministries towards this: it is admirably useful for the reproof of heresies, for the detection of fallacies, for the letter of the scripture, for collateral testimonies, for exterior advantages; but there is something beyond this, that human learning without the addition of divine can never reach. Moses was learned in all the learning of the Egyptians; and the holy men of God contemplated

---

48. Eph. 5:14.

the glories of God in the admirable order, motion, and influences, of the heaven: but besides all this, they were taught of God something far beyond these prettinesses. Pythagoras read Moses's books, and so did Plato; and yet they became not proselytes of the religion, though they were learned scholars of such a master. The reason is, because that which they drew forth from thence was not the life and secret of it.

Tradidit arcano quodcunque volumine Moses.[49]

There is a secret in these books, which few men, none but the godly, did understand: and though much of this secret is made manifest in the gospel, yet even here also there is a letter and there is a spirit: still there is a reserve for God's secret ones, even all those deep mysteries which the Old testament covered in figures, and stories, and names, and prophecies, and which Christ hath, and by His spirit will yet reveal more plainly to all that will understand them by their proper measures. For although the gospel is infinitely more legible and plain than the obscurer leaves of the law, yet there is a seal upon them also; "which seal no man shall open but he that is worthy."[50] We may understand something of it by the three children of the captivity; they were all skilled in all the wisdom of the Chaldees, and so was Daniel: but there was something beyond that in him; "the wisdom of the most high God was in him,"[51] and that taught him a learning beyond his learning.

In all scripture there is a spiritual sense, a spiritual *cabala*, which as it tends directly to holiness, so it is best and truest understood by the sons of the Spirit, who love God, and therefore know Him. *GNOSIS HEKASTON DI HOMOIOTĒTA GINETAI,*[52] "every thing is best known by its own similitudes and analogies."

But I must take some other time to speak fully of these things. I have but one thing more to say, and then I shall make my applications of this doctrine, and so conclude.

5. Lastly, there is a sort of God's dear servants who walk in perfectness, who "perfect holiness in the fear of God"; and they have a degree of clarity and divine knowledge more than we can discourse of,

---

49. Juvenal, p. 272.
50. Rev. 5:2ff.
51. Dan. 4:8–18, 5:11.
52. Aristotle, *Nicomachean Ethics*, p. 324.

and more certain than the demonstrations of geometry, brighter than the sun, and indeficient as the light of heaven. This is called by the apostle the *APAYGASMA TOY THEOY*. Christ is this "brightness of God," manifested in the hearts of His dearest servants.

But I shall say no more of this at this time, for this is to be felt and not to be talked of; and they that never touched it with their finger, may secretly perhaps laugh at it in their heart, and be never the wiser. All that I shall now say of it is, that a good man is united unto God as a flame touches a flame, and combines into splendour and to glory: so is the spirit of a man united unto Christ by the Spirit of God. These are the friends of God, and they best know God's mind, and they only that are so know how much such men do know. They have a special "unction from above";[53] so that now you are come to the top of all; this is the highest round of the ladder, and the angels stand upon it: they dwell in love and contemplation, they worship and obey, but dispute not: and our quarrels and impertinent wranglings about religion are nothing else but the want of the measures of this state. Our light is like a candle, every wind of vain doctrine blows it out, or spends the wax, and makes the light tremulous; but the lights of heaven are fixed and bright, and shine for ever.

But that we may speak not only things mysterious, but things intelligible; how does it come to pass, by what means and what economy is it effected, that a holy life is the best determination of all questions, and the surest way of knowledge? Is it to be supposed that a godly man is better enabled to determine the questions of purgatory or transubstantiation? is the gift of chastity the best way to reconcile Thomas and Scotus? and is a temperate man always a better scholar than a drunkard? To this I answer, that in all things in which true wisdom consists, holiness, which is the best wisdom, is the surest way of understanding them. And this,

1. Is effected by holiness as a proper and natural instrument: for naturally every thing is best discerned by its proper light and congenial instrument. For as the eye sees visible objects, and the understanding perceives the intellectual; so does the spirit the things of the Spirit. "The natural man," saith S. Paul,[54] "knows not the things of God, for they are spiritually discerned": that is, they are discovered by a proper

---

53. 1 John 2:20.
54. 1 Cor. 2:14.

376

light, and concerning these things an unsanctified man discourses piti-
fully, with an imperfect idea, as a blind man does of light and colours
which he never saw.

A good man though unlearned in secular notices, is like the windows of the temple, narrow without and broad within: he sees not so
much of what profits not abroad, but whatsoever is within, and concerns religion and the glorifications of God, that he sees with a broad
inspection: but all human learning without God is but blindness and
ignorant folly.

But when it is "righteousness dipped in the wells of truth," it is
like an eye of gold in a rich garment, or like the light of heaven, it shews
itself by its own splendour. What learning is it to discourse of the
philosophy of the sacrament, if you do not feel the virtue of it? And the
man that can with eloquence and subtilty discourse of the instrumental
efficacy of baptismal waters, talks ignorantly in respect of him who hath
"the answer of a good conscience"[55] within, and is cleansed by the
purifications of the Spirit. If the question concern any thing that can
perfect a man and make him happy, all that is the proper knowledge and
notice of the good man. How can a wicked man understand the purities
of the heart? and how can an evil and unworthy communicant tell what
it is to have received Christ by faith, to dwell with Him, to be united to
Him, to receive Him in his heart? The good man only understands that:
the one sees the colour, and the other feels the substance; the one
discourses of the sacrament, and the other receives Christ; the one
discourses for or against transubstantiation, but the good man feels
himself to be changed, and so joined to Christ, that he only understands
the true sense of transubstantiation, while He becomes to Christ bone
of His bone, flesh of His flesh, and of the same Spirit with his Lord.

We talk much of reformation, and (blessed be God) once we have
felt the good of it: but of late we have smarted under the name and
pretension. The woman that lost her groat, *everrit domum*, not *evertit*;[56]
she "swept the house," she did not "turn the house out of doors." That
was but an ill reformation that untiled the roof and broke the walls, and
was digging down the foundation.

Now among all the pretensions of reformation, who can tell better
what is, and what is not, true reformation, than he that is truly reformed

55. 1 Pet. 3:21.
56. Luke 15:8.

himself? he knows what pleases God, and can best tell by what instruments He is reconciled. "The mouth of the just bringeth forth wisdom; and the lips of the righteous know what is acceptable," saith Solomon.[57] He cannot be couzened by names of things, and feels that reformation to be imposture that is sacrilegious: himself is humble and obedient, and therefore knows that is not truth that persuades to schism and disobedience; and most of the questions of christendom are such which either are good for nothing, and therefore to be laid aside; or if they be complicated with action, and are ministries of practice, no man can judge them so well as the spiritual man. That which best pleases God, that which does good to our neighbour, that which teaches sobriety, that which combines with government, that which speaks honour of God and does Him honour, that only is truth. Holiness therefore is a proper and natural instrument of divine knowledge, and must needs be the best way of instruction in the questions of christendom, because in the most of them a duty is complicated with a proposition.

No man that intends to live holily can ever suffer any pretences of religion to be made, to teach him to fight against his king. And when the men of Geneva turned their bishop out of doors, they might easily have considered that the same person was their prince too, and that must needs be a strange religion that rose up against Moses and Aaron at the same time: but that hath been the method ever since. There was no church till then was ever governed without an apostle or a bishop: and since then, they who go from their bishop have said very often to their king too, *nolumus hunc regnare:*[58] and when we see men pretending religion, and yet refuse to own the king's supremacy, they may upon the stock of holiness easily reprove their own folly, by considering that such recusancy does introduce into our churches the very worst, the most intolerable parts of popery: for perfect submission to kings is the glory of the protestant cause: and really the reprovable doctrines of the church of Rome are by nothing so much confuted, as that they destroy good life by consequent and evident deduction; as by an induction of particulars were easy to make apparent, if this were the proper season for it.

2. Holiness is not only an advantage to the learning all wisdom and holiness, but for the discerning that which is wise and holy from what is

---

57. Prov. 10:31–32.
58. Luke 19:14.

378

trifling and useless and contentious; and to one of these heads all questions will return: and therefore in all, from holiness we have the best instructions. And this brings me to the next particle of the general consideration. For that which we are taught by the holy Spirit of God, this new nature, this vital principle within us, it is that which is worth our learning; not vain and empty, idle and insignificant notions, in which when you have laboured till your eyes are fixed in their orbs, and your flesh unfixed from its bones, you are no better and no wiser. If the Spirit of God be your teacher, He will teach you such truths as will make you know and love God, and become like to Him, and enjoy Him for ever, by passing from similitude to union and eternal fruition. But what are you the better if any man should pretend to teach you whether every angel makes a species, and what is the individuation of the soul in the state of separation? what are you the wiser if you should study and find out what place Adam should for ever have lived in if he had not fallen? and what is any man the more learned if he hears the disputes, whether Adam should have multiplied children in the state of innocence, and what would have been the event of things if one child had been born before his father's sin?

Too many scholars have lived upon air and empty notions for many ages past, and troubled themselves with tying and untying knots, like hypochondriacs in a fit of melancholy, thinking of nothing, and troubling themselves with nothing, and falling out about nothings, and being very wise and very learned in things that are not and work not, and were never planted in paradise by the finger of God. Men's notions are too often like the mules, begotten by equivocal and unnatural generations; but they make no species: they are begotten, but they can beget nothing; they are the effects of long study, but they can do no good when they are produced: they are not that which Solomon calls *via intelligentiæ*,[59] "the way of understanding." If the Spirit of God be our teacher, we shall learn to avoid evil, and to do good, to be wise and to be holy, to be profitable and careful: and they that walk in this way shall find more peace in their consciences, more skill in the scriptures, more satisfaction in their doubts, than can be obtained by all the polemical and impertinent disputations of the world. And if the holy Spirit can teach us how vain a thing it is to do foolish things, He also will teach us how vain a thing it is to trouble the world with foolish questions, to disturb

---

59. Prov. 9:6, 21:16.

the church for interest or pride, to resist government in things indifferent, to spend the people's zeal in things unprofitable, to make religion to
consist in outsides, and opposition to circumstances and trifling regards. No, no; the man that is wise, he that is conducted by the Spirit of
God, knows better in what Christ's kingdom does consist, than to
throw away his time and interest, and peace and safety—for what? for
religion? no: for the body of religion? not so much: for the garment of
the body of religion? no, not for so much; but for the fringes of the
garment of the body of religion; for such and no better are the disputes
that trouble our discontented brethren; they are things, or rather circumstances and manners of things, in which the soul and spirit is not at
all concerned.

3. Holiness of life is the best way of finding out truth and understanding, not only as a natural medium, nor only as a prudent medium,
but as a means by way of divine blessing. "He that hath My commandments and keepeth them, he it is that loveth Me; and he that loveth Me
shall be loved of My Father, and I will love him, and will manifest
Myself to him."[60] Here we have a promise for it; and upon that we
may rely.

The old man that confuted the Arian priest by a plain recital of his
creed, found a mighty power of God effecting His own work by a
strange manner, and by a very plain instrument: it wrought a divine
blessing just as sacraments use to do: and this lightning sometimes
comes in a strange manner as a peculiar blessing to good men. For God
kept the secrets of His kingdom from the wise heathens and the learned
Jews, revealing them to babes, not because they had less learning, but
because they had more love; they were children and babes in malice,
they loved Christ, and so He became to them a light and a glory. S. Paul
had more learning than they all; and Moses was instructed in all the
learning of the Egyptians: yet because he was the meekest man upon
earth, he was also the wisest, and to his human learning in which he was
excellent, he had a divine light and excellent wisdom superadded to him
by way of spiritual blessings. And S. Paul, though he went very far to
the knowledge of many great and excellent truths by the force of human
learning, yet he was far short of perfective truth and true wisdom till he
learned a new lesson in a new school, at the feet of one greater than his
Gamaliel; his learning grew much greater, his notions brighter, his skill

---

60. John 14:21.

deeper, by the love of Christ, and his desires, his passionate desires after Jesus.

The force and use of human learning, and of this divine learning I am now speaking of, are both well expressed by the prophet Isaiah (xxix. 11, 12), "And the vision of all is become unto you as the words of a book that is sealed, which men deliver to one that is learned, saying, Read this, I pray thee: and he saith, I cannot, for it is sealed. And the book is delivered to him that is not learned, saying, Read this, I pray thee: and he saith, I am not learned." He that is no learned man, who is not bred up in the schools of the prophets, cannot read God's book for want of learning. For human learning is the gate and first entrance of divine vision; not the only one indeed, but the common gate. But beyond this, there must be another learning; for he that is learned, bring the book to him, and you are not much the better as to the secret part of it, if the book be sealed, if his eyes be closed, if his heart be not opened, if God does not speak to him in the secret way of discipline. Human learning is an excellent foundation; but the top-stone is laid by love and conformity to the will of God. For we may further observe, that blindness, error and ignorance are the punishments which God sends upon wicked and ungodly men. *Etiamsi propter nostræ intelligentiæ tarditatem et vitæ demeritum veritas nondum se apertissime ostenderit*, was S. Austin's expression, "the truth hath not yet been manifested fully to us by reason of our demerits": our sins have hindered the brightness of the truth from shining upon us. And S. Paul[61] observes, that when the heathens gave themselves over to lusts, "God gave them over to strong delusions, and to believe a lie." But "God giveth to a man that is good in His sight, wisdom and knowledge and joy," said the wise preacher.[62] But this is most expressly promised in the New testament, and particularly in that admirable sermon which our blessed Saviour[63] preached a little before His death. "The Comforter, which is the holy Ghost, whom the Father will send in My name, He shall teach you all things." Well; there's our teacher told of plainly: but how shall we obtain this teacher, and how shall we be taught? ver. 15, 16, 17, Christ will pray for us that we may have this Spirit. That's well; but shall all Christians have the Spirit? Yes, all that will live like Christians; for so said Christ, "If ye

---

61. Rom. 1:25–26.
62. Eccles. 2:26.
63. John 14:26.

381

love Me, keep My commandments; and I will pray the Father and He will give you another Comforter, that may abide with you for ever; even the Spirit of truth, whom the world cannot receive, because it seeth Him not, neither knoweth Him." Mark these things: the Spirit of God is our teacher; He will abide with us for ever to be our teacher; He will teach us all things: but how? "If ye love Christ," if ye keep His commandments, but not else: if ye be of the world, that is of worldly affections, ye cannot see Him, ye cannot know Him. And this is the particular I am now to speak to, the way by which the Spirit of God teaches us in all the ways and secrets of God, is love and holiness.

Secreta Dei Deo nostro et filiis domus ejus, "God's secrets are to Himself and the sons of His house," saith the Jewish proverb.[64] Love is the great instrument of divine knowledge, "the height of all that is to be taught or learned." Love is obedience, and we learn His words best when we practise them: *A GAR DEI MANTHANONTAS POIEIN TAYTA POIOYNTES MANTHANOMEN,* said Aristotle;[65] "those things which they that learn ought to practise, even while they practise they will best learn." S. Austin, "Unless we come to Christ, we shall never learn: for so our blessed Lord teaches us by the grace of His spirit, that what any one learns, he not only sees it by knowledge, but desires it by choice, and perfects it by practice."[66]

4. When this is reduced to practice and experience, we find not only in things of practice, but even in deepest mysteries, not only the choicest and most eminent saints, but even every good man can best tell what is true, and best reprove an error.

He that goes about to speak of and to understand the mysterious Trinity, and does it by words and names of man's invention, or by such which signify contingently, if he reckons this mystery by the mythology of numbers, by the *cabala* of letters, by the distinctions of the school, and by the weak inventions of disputing people; if he only talks of essences and existences, *hypostases* and personalities, distinctions without difference, and priority in co-equalities, and unity in pluralities, and of superior predicates of no larger extent than the inferior subjects, he may amuse himself, and find his understanding will be like S. Peter's upon the mount of Tabor at the transfiguration: he may build three

---

64. Clement of Alexandria, *Stromata*, PG 9.9.
65. Aristotle, p. 70.
66. Augustine, *The Grace of Christ*, PL 44.568.

tabernacles in his head, and talk something, but he knows not what. But the good man that feels the "power of the Father," and he to whom the Son is become "wisdom, righteousness, sanctification, and redemption"; he "in whose heart the love of the Spirit of God is spread," to whom God hath communicated the "holy Ghost, the Comforter"; this man, though he understands nothing of that which is unintelligible, yet he only understands the mysteriousness of the holy Trinity. No man can be convinced well and wisely of the article of the holy, blessed, and undivided Trinity, but he that feels the mightiness of the Father begetting him to a new life, the wisdom of the Son building him up in a most holy faith, and the love of the Spirit of God making him to become like unto God.

He that hath passed from his childhood in grace under the spiritual generation of the Father, and is gone forward to be a "young man" in Christ, strong and vigorous in holy actions and holy undertakings, and from thence is become an old disciple, and strong and grown old in religion, and the conversation of the Spirit; this man best understands the secret and undiscernible economy, he feels this unintelligible mystery, and sees with his heart what his tongue can never express, and his metaphysics can never prove. In these cases faith and love are the best knowledge, and Jesus Christ is best known by "the grace of our Lord Jesus Christ"; and if the kingdom of God be in us, then we know God, and are known of Him; and when we communicate of the Spirit of God, when we pray for Him, and have received Him, and entertained Him, and dwelt with Him, and warmed ourselves by His holy fires, then we know Him too. But there is no other satisfactory knowledge of the blessed Trinity but this; and therefore whatever thing is spoken of God metaphysically, there is no knowing of God theologically, and as He ought to be known, but by the measures of holiness, and the proper light of the Spirit of God.

But in this case experience is the best learning, and christianity is the best institution, and the Spirit of God is the best teacher, and holiness is the greatest wisdom; and he that sins most is the most ignorant, and the humble and obedient man is the best scholar: "for the Spirit of God is a loving Spirit," and "will not enter into a polluted soul";[67] but "he that keepeth the law . . . getteth the understanding

---

67. Wisd. 1:6.

thereof, and the perfection of the fear of the Lord is wisdom," said the wise Ben-Sirach.[68] And now give me leave to apply the doctrine to you, and so I shall dismiss you from this attention.

Many ways have been attempted to reconcile the differences of the church in matters of religion, and all the counsels of man have yet proved ineffective: let us now try God's method, let us betake ourselves to live holily, and then the Spirit of God will lead us into all truth. And indeed it matters not what religion any man is of, if he be a villain; the opinion of his sect, as it will not save his soul, so neither will it do good to the public: but this is a sure rule; if the holy man best understands wisdom and religion, then by the proportions of holiness we shall best measure the doctrines that are obtruded to the disturbance of our peace, and the dishonour of the gospel. And therefore,

1. That is no good religion whose principles destroy any duty of religion. He that shall maintain it to be lawful to make a war for the defence of his opinion, be it what it will, his doctrine is against godliness. Any thing that is proud, any thing that is peevish and scornful, any thing that is uncharitable, is against the *HYGIAINOYSA DIDASCALIA*, that "form of sound doctrine" which the apostle[69] speaks of. And I remember that Ammianus Marcellinus[70] telling of George a proud and factious minister, that he was an informer against his brethren, he says, he did it *oblitus professionis suæ, quæ nil nisi justum suadet et lene*, "he forgot his profession, which teaches nothing but justice and meekness, kindnesses and charity." And however Bellarmine and others are pleased to take but indirect and imperfect notice of it, yet "goodness" is the best note of the true church.

2. It is but an ill sign of holiness when a man is busy in troubling himself and his superior in little scruples and fantastic opinions, about things not concerning the life of religion, or the pleasure of God, or the excellencies of the Spirit. A good man knows how to please God, how to converse with Him, how to advance the kingdom of the Lord Jesus, to set forward holiness, and the love of God and of his brother; and he knows also that there is no godliness in spending our time and our talk, our heart and our spirits, about the garments and outsides of religion:

---

68. Eccles. 21:11.
69. 1 Tim. 1:10; 2 Tim. 4:3; Titus 2:1.
70. Ammianus Marcellinus, *Roman History*, LCL, vol. 2, p. 258.

and they can ill teach others, that do not know that religion does not consist in these things; but obedience may, and reductively that is religion: and he that for that which is no part of religion, destroys religion directly by neglecting that duty that is adopted into religion, is a man of fancy and of the world; but he gives but an ill account that he is a man of God, and a son of the Spirit.

Spend not your time in that which profits not; for your labour and your health, your time and your studies are very valuable; and it is a thousand pities to see a diligent and a hopeful person spend himself in gathering cockle-shells and little pebbles, in telling sands upon the shores, and making garlands of useless daisies. Study that which is profitable, that which will make you useful to churches and commonwealths, that which will make you desirable and wise. Only I shall add this to you, that in learning there are variety of things as well as in religion: there is mint and cummin, and there are the weighty things of the law; so there are studies more and less useful, and every thing that is useful will be required in its time: and I may in this also use the words of our blessed Saviour, "these things ought you to look after, and not to leave the other unregarded." But your great care is to be in the things of God and of religion, in holiness and true wisdom, remembering the saying of Origen,[71] that the knowledge that arises from goodness is "something that is more certain and more divine than all demonstration" than all other learnings of the world.

3. That's no good religion that disturbs government, or shakes a foundation of public peace. Kings and bishops are the foundations and the great principles of unity, of peace, and government; like Rachel and Leah they build up the house of Israel: and those blind Samsons that shake these pillars, intend to pull the house down. "My son, fear God and the king," saith Solomon,[72] "and meddle not with them that are given to change." That is not truth that loves changes; and the new-nothings of heretical and schismatical preachers are infinitely far from the blessings of truth.

In the holy language "truth" hath a mysterious name, *emet*; it consists of three letters, the first, and the last, and the middlemost of the Hebrew letters; implying to us that truth is first, and will be last, and it

---

71. Origen, *Against Celsus*, PG 11.655.
72. Prov. 24:21.

is the same all the way, and combines and unites all extremes: it ties all ends together. Truth is lasting, and ever full of blessing: for the Jews observe that those letters which signify truth, are both in the figure and the number quadrate, firm and cubical; these signify a foundation, and an abode for ever. Whereas on the other side, the word which in Hebrew signifies "a lie," *secher*, is made of letters whose numbers are imperfect, and their figure pointed and voluble; to signify that a lie hath no foundation.

And this very observation will give good light in our questions and disputes: and I give my instance in episcopal government, which hath been of so lasting an abode, of so long a blessing, hath its firmament by the principles of christianity, hath been blessed by the issues of that stabiliment; it hath for sixteen hundred years combined with monarchy, and hath been taught by the Spirit which hath so long dwelt in God's church, and hath now (according to the promise of Jesus, that says "the gates of hell shall never prevail against the church") been restored amongst us by a heap of miracles; and as it went away, so now it is returned again in the hand of monarchy, and in the bosom of our fundamental laws. Now that doctrine must needs be suspected of error, and an intolerable lie, that speaks against this truth, which hath had so long a testimony from God, and from the wisdom and experience of so many ages, of all our ancestors, and all our laws.

When the Spirit of God wrote in Greek, Christ is called A and Ω; if He had spoken Hebrew, He had been called *emet*, He is truth, the same yesterday and to-day and for ever: and whoever opposes this holy sanction which Christ's spirit hath sanctified, His word hath warranted, His blessings have endeared, His promises have ratified, and His church hath always kept; he fights against this *emet*, and *secher* is his portion; his lot is a lie, his portion is there where holiness can never dwell.

And now to conclude, to you fathers and brethren, you who are or intend to be of the clergy; you see here the best *compendium* of your studies, the best abbreviature of your labours, the truest method of wisdom, and the infallible, the only way of judging concerning the disputes and questions in christendom. It is not by reading multitudes of books, but by studying the truth of God: it is not by laborious commentaries of the doctors that you can finish your work, but by the expositions of the Spirit of God: it is not by the rules of metaphysics, but by the proportions of holiness: and when all books are read, and all arguments examined, and all authorities alleged, nothing can be found to be true that is unholy. "Give yourselves to reading, to exhortation, and to doctrine," saith S. Paul.[73] "Read" all good books you can; but "exhortation" unto good life is the best instrument, and the best teacher of true "doctrine," of that which is "according to godliness."

And let me tell you this; the great learning of the fathers was more owing to their piety than to their skill; more to God than to themselves: and to this purpose is that excellent ejaculation of S. Chrysostom,[74] with which I will conclude, "O blessed and happy men, whose names are in the book of life, from whom the devils fled, and heretics did fear them, who (by holiness) have stopped the mouths of them that spake perverse things!" But I, like David, will cry out, Where are Thy loving-kindnesses which have been ever of old? where is the blessed quire of bishops and doctors, who shined like lights in the world, and contained the word of life? *Dulce est meminisse,* their very memory is pleasant. Where is that Evodius, the sweet savour of the church, the successor and imitator of the holy apostles? where is Ignatius, in whom God dwelt? where is S. Dionysius the areopagite, that bird of paradise, that celestial eagle? where is Hippolytus, that good man, ANĒR CHRĒSTOS, that gentle sweet person? where is great S. Basil, a man almost equal to the apostles? where is Athanasius, rich in virtue? where is Gregory Nyssen, that great divine? and Ephrem the great Syrian, that stirred up the sluggish, and awakened the sleepers, and comforted the afflicted, and brought the young men to discipline; the looking-glass of the religious, the captain of the penitents, the destruction of heresies, the receptacle of graces, the habitation of the holy Ghost? These were the men that prevailed against error, because they lived according to truth: and whoever shall oppose you and the truth you walk by, may better be confuted by your lives than by your disputations. Let "your adversaries have no evil thing to say of you," and then you will best silence them. For all heresies and false doctrines are but like Myron's counterfeit cow, it deceived none but beasts; and these can cozen none but the wicked and the negligent, them that love a lie, and live according to it. But if ye become "burning and shining lights"; if ye "do not detain the truth in unrighteousness"; if ye "walk in light" and "live in the spirit"; your doctrines will be true, and that truth will prevail. But if ye live wickedly and scandalously, every little schismatic shall put you to

---

73. 1 Tim. 4:13.
74. Chrysostom, *The End of the Ages*, PG 63.938.

shame, and draw disciples after him, and abuse your flocks, and feed them with colocynths and hemlock, and place heresy in the chairs appointed for your religion.

I pray God give you all grace to follow this wisdom, to study this learning, to labour for the understanding of godliness; so your time and your studies, your persons and your labours, will be holy and useful, sanctified and blessed, beneficial to men and pleasing to God, through Him who is the "Wisdom of the Father," "who is made" to all that love Him "wisdom, and righteousness, and sanctification, and redemption": to whom with the Father, etc.

Discourse XII[75]
[*from the* Great Exemplar]

Of the Second Additional Precept of Christ; viz., of Prayer

1. The soul of a Christian is the house of God; "ye are God's building,"[76] saith St. Paul: but the house of God is the house of prayer; and therefore prayer is the work of the soul, whose organs are intended for instruments of the divine praises; and when every stop and pause of those instruments is but the conclusion of a collect, and every breathing is a prayer, then the body becomes a temple, and the soul is the sanctuary and more private recess and place of intercourse. Prayer is the great duty, and the greatest privilege of a Christian; it is his intercourse with God, his sanctuary in troubles, his remedy for sins, his cure of griefs, and, as St. Gregory[77] calls it, "it is the principal instrument whereby we minister to God in execution of the decrees of eternal predestination"; and those things which God intends for us, we bring to ourselves by the mediation of holy prayers. Prayer is the "ascent of the mind to God, and a petitioning for such things as we need for our support and duty."[78] It is an abstract and summary of Christian religion. Prayer is an act of religion and divine worship, confessing His power and His mercy; it celebrates His attributes, and confesses His glories, and reveres His person, and implores His aid, and gives thanks for His blessings: it is an act of humility, condescension, and dependence, expressed in the prostration of our bodies, and humiliation of our spirits: it is an act of charity, when we pray for others; it is an act of repentance, when it confesses and begs pardon for our sins, and exercises every grace according to the design of the man, and the matter of the prayer. So that there will be less need to amass arguments to invite us to this duty; every part is an excellence, and every end of it is a blessing, and

---

75. *Works* 2:464ff.
76. 1 Cor. 3:9.
77. Gregory (Pope), *Dialogues*, PL 77.185.
78. John Damascene, *Orthodox Faith*, PG 94.1089.

every design is a motive, and every need is an impulsive to this holy office. Let us but remember how many needs we have, at how cheap a rate we may obtain their remedies, and yet how honourable the employment is, to go to God with confidence, and to fetch our supplies with easiness and joy; and then without farther preface we may address ourselves to the understanding of that duty by which we imitate the employment of angels and beatified spirits, by which we ascend to God in spirit while we remain on earth, and God descends on earth while He yet resides in heaven, sitting there on the throne of His kingdom.

2. Our first enquiry must be concerning the matter of our prayers; for our desires are not to be the rule of our prayers, unless reason and religion be the rule of our desires. The old heathens prayed to their gods for such things which they were ashamed to name publicly before men; and these were their private prayers, which they durst not for their undecency or iniquity make public. And indeed sometimes the best men ask of God things not unlawful in themselves, yet very hurtful to them: and therefore as by the Spirit of God and right reason we are taught in general what is lawful to be asked; so it is still to be submitted to God, when we have asked lawful things, to grant to us in kindness, or to deny us in mercy: after all the rules that can be given us, we not being able in many instances to judge for ourselves, unless also we could certainly pronounce concerning future contingencies. But the holy Ghost being now sent upon the church, and the rule of Christ being left to His church, together with His form of prayer taught and prescribed to His disciples, we have sufficient instruction for the matter of our prayers, so far as concerns the lawfulness or unlawfulness. And the rule is easy and of no variety. For first, we are bound to pray for all things that concern our duty, all that we are bound to labour for; such as are glory and grace, necessary assistances of the Spirit, and rewards spiritual, heaven and heavenly things. Secondly, concerning those things which we may with safety hope for, but are not matter of duty to us, we may lawfully testify our hope and express our desires by petition: but if in their particulars they are under no express promise, but only conveniences of our life and person, it is only lawful to pray for them under condition that they may conform to God's will and our duty, as they are good, and placed in the best order of eternity. Therefore, first, for spiritual blessings let our prayers be particularly importunate, perpetual, and persevering; secondly, for temporal blessings let them be generally short, conditional, and modest; and thirdly, whatsoever things are of mixed nature, more spiritual than riches, and less necessary than graces, such as are gifts and

exterior aids, we may pray for them as we may desire them, and as we may expect them; that is, with more confidence and less restraint than in the matter of temporal requests, but with more reservedness, and less boldness of petition, than when we pray for the graces of sanctification. In the first case we are bound to pray; in the second, it is only lawful under certain conditions; in the third, it becomes to us an act of zeal, nobleness, and Christian prudence. But the matter of our prayers is best taught us in the form our Lord taught His disciples; which because it is short, mysterious, and, like the treasures of the Spirit, full of wisdom and latent senses, it is not improper to draw forth those excellencies which are intended and signified by every petition; that by so excellent an authority we may know what it is lawful to beg of God.[79]

3. "Our Father, which art in heaven." The address reminds us of many parts of our duty; "if God be our Father, where is" His fear, and reverence, and obedience? "If ye were Abraham's children, ye would do the works of Abraham"; and, "Ye are of your father the devil, for his works ye do." Let us not dare to call Him Father, if we be rebels and enemies; but if we be obedient, then we know He is our Father, and will give us a child's portion, and the inheritance of sons. But it is observable that Christ, here speaking concerning private prayer, does describe it in a form of plural signification; to tell us that we are to draw into the communication of our prayers all those who are confederated in the common relation of sons to the same Father. "Which art in heaven,"[80] tells us, where our hopes and our hearts must be fixed, whither our desires and our prayers must tend: *sursum corda;* "where our treasure is, there must our hearts be also."

4. "Hallowed be Thy name"; that is, Let Thy name, Thy essence and glorious attributes, be honoured and adored in all the world, believed by faith, loved by charity, celebrated with praises, thanked with eucharist; and let Thy name be hallowed in us, as it is in itself. Thy name being called upon us, let us walk worthy of that calling, that "our light may shine before men, that they, seeing our good works, may glorify Thee, our Father which art in heaven." In order also to the sanctification of Thy name, grant that all our praises, hymns, eucharistical remembrances, and representments of Thy glories, may be useful, blessed, and effectual, for the dispersing Thy fame, and advancing Thy

---

79. Tertullian, *On Prayer*, PL 1.1150.
80. Leo, *Sermon on Ascension*, PL 54.499.

honour over all the world. This is a direct and formal act of worshipping and adoration: the name of God is representative of God himself, and it signifies, Be Thou worshipped and adored, be Thou thanked and celebrated with honour and eucharist.

5. "Thy kingdom come"; that is, As Thou hast caused to be preached and published the coming of Thy kingdom, the peace and truth, the revelation and glories of the gospel: so let it come verily and effectually to us and all the world; that Thou mayest truly reign in our spirits, exercising absolute dominion, subduing all Thine enemies, ruling in our faculties, in the understanding by faith, in the will by charity, in the passions by mortification, in the members by a chaste and right use of the parts. And as it was more particularly, and in the letter, proper at the beginning of Christ's preaching, when He also taught the prayer that God would hasten the coming of the gospel to all the world; so now also and ever it will be in its proportion necessary and pious, to pray that it may come still; making greater progress in the world, extending itself where yet it is not, and intending it where it is already; that the kingdom of Christ may not only be in us in name and form and honourable appellatives, but in effect and power. This petition in the first ages of Christianity was not expounded to signify a prayer for Christ's second coming; because, the gospel not being preached to all the world, they prayed for the delay of the day of judgment, that Christ's kingdom upon earth might have its proper increment; but since then, every age, as it is more forward in time, so it is more earnest in desire to accomplish the intermedial prophecies, that the kingdom of God the Father might come in glories infinite. And indeed the kingdom of grace being in order to the kingdom of glory, this, as it is principally to be desired, so may possibly be intended chiefly: which also is the more probable, because the address of this prayer being to God the Father, it is proper to observe that the kingdom of grace, or of the gospel, is called the kingdom of the Son;[81] and that of glory, in the style of the Scripture, is the kingdom of the Father. St. German, patriarch of Constantinople, expounds it with some little difference, but not ill: "Thy kingdom come," that is, let Thy holy Spirit come into us; for "the kingdom of heaven is within us," saith the holy scripture: and so it intimates our desires that the promise of the Father, and the prophecies of old, and the holy Ghost the Comforter, may come upon us. Let that "anointing from

---

81. Col. 1:13; Rev. 1:9; Matt. 13:41; Luke 6:20.

above" descend upon us, whereby we may be anointed kings and priests, in a spiritual kingdom and priesthood, by a holy chrism.

6. "Thy will be done in earth, as it is in heaven"; that is, the whole economy and dispensation of Thy providence be the guide of the world and the measure of our desire; that we be patient in all accidents, conformable to God's will both in doing and in suffering; submitting to changes, and even to persecutions, and doing all God's will: which because without God's aid we cannot do, therefore we beg it of Him by prayer; but by His aid we are confident we may do it in the manner of angelical obedience; that is, promptly, readily, cheerfully, and with all our faculties. Or thus; As the angels in heaven serve Thee with harmony, concord, and peace; so let us all join in the service of Thy majesty, with peace and purity, and love unfeigned; that as all the angels are in peace, and amongst them there is no persecutor, and none persecuted, there is none afflicting or afflicted, none assaulting or assaulted, but all in sweetness and peaceable serenity glorifying Thee; so let Thy will be done on earth, by all the world, in peace and unity, in charity and tranquillity; that with one heart and one voice we may glorify Thee, our universal Father; having in us nothing that may displease Thee, having quitted all our own desires and pretensions, living in angelic conformity, our souls subject to Thee, and our passions to our souls; that in earth also Thy will may be done, as in the spirit and soul, which is a portion of the heavenly substance. These three petitions are addressed to God, by way of adoration. In the first, the soul puts on the affections of a child, and divests itself of its own interest, offering itself up wholly to the designs and glorifications of God. In the second, it puts on the relation and duty of a subject to her legitimate prince, seeking the promotion of his regal interest. In the third, she puts on the affection of a spouse, loving the same love, and choosing the same object, and delighting in unions and conformities.

The next part descends lower, and makes addresses to God in relation to our own necessities.

7. "Give us this day our daily bread"; that is, give unto us all that is necessary for the support of our lives, the bread of our necessity; so the Syriac interpreter reads it, "This day give us the portion of bread which is day by day necessary"; give us the bread or support which we shall need all our lives, only this day minister our present part. For we pray for the necessary bread or maintenance which God knows we shall need all our days; but, that we "be not careful for to-morrow," we are taught to pray, not that it be all at once represented or deposited, but that God

would minister it as we need it, how He pleases: but our needs are to be the measure of our desires, our desires must not make our needs; that we may be confident of the divine providence, and not at all covetous: for therefore God feeds His people with extemporary provisions, that by needing always, they may learn to pray to Him; and by being still supplied, may learn to trust Him for the future, and thank Him for that is past, and rejoice in the present. So God rained down *manna*, giving them their daily portion; and so all fathers and masters minister to their children and servants, giving them their proportion as they eat it, not the meat of a year at once; and yet no child or servant fears want, if his parent or lord were good, and wise, and rich. And it is necessary for all to pray this prayer: the poor, because they want the bread, and have it not deposited but in the hands of God: "mercy ploughing the fields of heaven" (as Job's expression is) brings them corn; and "the cattle upon a thousand hills are God's," and they find the poor man meat. The rich also need this prayer; because although they have the bread, yet they need the blessing; and what they have now may perish, or be taken from them; and as preservation is a perpetual creation, so the continuing to rich men what God hath already bestowed is a continual giving it. Young men must pray, because their needs are like to be the longer; and old men, because they are present. But all these are to pray but for the present that which in estimation of law is to be reckoned as imminent upon the present, and part of this state and condition; but it is great improvidence, and an unchristian spirit, for old men to heap up provisions, and load their sumpters still the more by how much their way is shorter. But there is also a Bread which came down from heaven, a diviner nutriment of our souls, the food and wine of angels, Christ himself, as He communicates Himself in the expresses of His word and sacraments; and if we be destitute of this bread, we are miserable and perishing people. We must pray that our souls also may feed upon those celestial viands prepared for us in the antepasts of the gospel, till the great and fuller meal of the supper of the Lamb shall answer all our prayers, and satisfy every desire.

8. "Forgive us our trespasses, as we forgive them that trespass against us"; not only those sins of infirmity, invasion, and sudden surprise, which, like excrescencies of luxuriant trees, adhere to many actions by inadvertency, and either natural weakness or accidental prejudice; but also all those great sins which were washed off from our souls, and the stain taken away, in baptism, or when by choice, and after the use of reason, we gave up our names to Christ, when we first

received the adoption of sons: for even those things were so pardoned that we must for ever confess and glory in the divine mercy, and still ascertain it by performing what we then promised, and which were the conditions of our covenant. For although Christ hath taken off the guilt, yet still there remains the disreputation; and St. Paul calls himself "the chiefest of sinners," not referring to his present condition, but to his former persecuting the church of God, which is one of the greatest crimes in the world; and for ever he asked pardon for it: and so must we, knowing that they may return; if we shake off the yoke of Christ, and break His cords from us, the bands of the covenant evangelical, the sins will return so as to undo us. And this we pray, with a tacit obligation to forgive: for so only, and upon that condition, we beg pardon to be given or continued respectively; that is, as we from our hearts forgive them that did us injury in any kind, never entertaining so much as a thought of revenge, but contrariwise loving them that did us wrong; for so we beg that God should do to us. And therefore it is but a lesser revenge to say, I will forgive, but I will never have to do with him; for if he become an object of charity, we must have to do with him, to relieve him; because he needs prayers, we must have to do with him, and pray for him: and to refuse his society when it is reasonably and innocently offered, is to deny that to him which Christians have only been taught to deny to persons excommunicate, to persons under punishment, i.e. to persons not yet forgiven: and we shall have but an evil portion if God should forgive our sins, and should not also love us, and do us grace, and bestow benefits upon us. So we must forgive others; so God forgives us.

9. "And lead us not into temptation." St. Cyprian,[82] out of an old Latin copy, reads it, "Suffer us not to be led into temptation": that is, suffer us not to be overcome by temptation. And therefore we are bound to prevent our access to such temptation whose very approximation is dangerous, and the contact is irregular and evil; such as are temptations of the flesh: yet in other temptations the assault sometimes makes confident, and hardens a resolution; for some spirits who are softened by fair usages, are steeled and emboldened by a persecution. But of what nature soever the temptations be, whether they be such whose approach a Christian is bound to fear, or such which are the certain lot of Christians, (such are troubles and persecutions, into which "when we enter" we must "count it joy"), yet we are to pray that

---

82. Cyprian, *The Lord's Prayer*, PL 4.556.

we enter not into the possession of the temptation, that we be not overcome by it.

10. "But deliver us from evil"; from the assaults or violence of evil, from "the wicked one," who not only presents us with objects, but heightens our concupiscence, and makes us imaginative, fantastical and passionate; setting on the temptation, making the lust active, and the man full of appetite, and the appetite full of energy and power: therefore deliver us from the evil one, who is interested as an enemy in every hostility and in every danger.[83] Let not Satan have any power or advantage over us; and let not evil men prevail upon us in our danger, much less to our ruin. Make us "safe under the covering of Thy wings" against all fraud and every violence; that no temptation destroy our hopes, or break our strength, or alter our state, or overthrow our glories. In these last petitions which concern ourselves, the soul hath affections proper to her own needs; as in the former, proportion to God's glory. In the first of these, the affection of a poor, indigent, and necessitous beggar; in the second, of a delinquent and penitent servant; in the last, of a person in affliction or danger. And after all this, the reason of our confidence is derived from God;

11. "For Thine is the kingdom, the power, and the glory, for ever." That is, these which we beg are for the honour of Thy kingdom, for the manifestation of Thy power, and the glory of Thy name and mercies: and it is an express doxology or adoration, which is apt and fit to conclude all our prayers and addresses to God.

12. These are the generals and great treasures of matter to which all our present or sudden needs are reducible; and when we make our prayers more minute and particular, if the instance be in matter of duty and merely spiritual, there is no danger; but when our needs are temporal, or we are transported with secular desires, all descending to particulars is a confining the divine providence, a judging for ourselves, a begging a temptation oftentimes, sometimes a mischief: and to beg beyond the necessities of our life, is a mutiny against that providence, which assigns to Christians no more but "food and raiment" for their own use: all other excrescencies of possessions being entrusted to the rich man's dispensation, only as to a steward; and he shall be accountable for the coat that lies by him as the portion of moths, and for the

---

83. Ibid. p. 557.

shoes which are the spoils of mouldiness and the contumely of plenty. "Grant me, O Lord, not what I desire, but what is profitable for me"; for sometimes we desire that which in the succeeding event of things will undo us. This rule is in all things that concern ourselves. There is some little difference in the affairs and necessities of other men: for provided we submit to the divine providence, and pray for good things for others only with a tacit condition, so far as they are good and profitable in order to the best ends; yet if we be particular, there is no covetousness in it; there may be indiscretion in the particular, but in the general no fault, because it is a prayer and a design of charity. "For kings, and all that are in authority," we may yet enlarge, and pray for a peaceable reign, true lieges, strong armies, victories and fair success in their just wars, health, long life, and riches; because they have a capacity which private persons have not: and whatsoever is good for single persons, and whatsoever is apt for their uses as public persons, all that we may and we must pray for, either particularly, for so we may; or in general significations, for so we must at least: "that we may lead a godly, peaceable, and quiet life, in all godliness and honesty"; that is St. Paul's rule, and the prescribed measure and purpose of such prayers. And in this instance of kings, we may pray for defeating all the king's enemies, such as are truly such; and we have no other restraint upon us in this, but that we keep our desires confined within the limits of the end we are commanded; that is, so far to confound the king's enemies, that he may do his duty, and we do ours, and receive the blessing: ever, as much as we can, to distinguish the malice from the person. But if the enemies themselves will not also separate what our intentions distinguish, that is, if they will not return to their duty; then, let the prayers operate as God pleases, we must be zealous for the end of the king's authority and peaceable government. By enemies, I mean rebels or invaders, tyrants and usurpers; for in other wars there are many other considerations, not proper for this place.

13. The next consideration will be concerning the manner; I mean both the manner of our persons, and the manner of our prayers: that is, with what conditions we ought to approach to God, and with what circumstances the prayers may, or ought to be performed. The conditions to make our prayers holy and certain to prevail, are,

First, that we live good lives, endeavouring to conform by holy obedience to all the divine commandments. This condition is expressly recorded by St. John; "Beloved, if our hearts condemn us not, then have we confidence towards God, and whatsoever we ask of Him we shall obtain."[84] and St. James affirms that "the effectual fervent prayer of a righteous man availeth much";[85] and our blessed Saviour, limiting the confidence of our prayers for forgiveness to our charity and forgiving others, plainly tells us, that the uncharitable and unrighteous person shall not be heard. And the blind man in the gospel understood well what he said, "Now we know that God heareth not sinners; but if any man be a worshipper, and doeth His will, him He heareth."[86] And it was so decreed and resolved a point in the doctrine of their religion, that it was a proverbial saying. And although this discourse of the blind man was of a restrained occasion, and signified, if Christ had been a false prophet, God would not have attested His sermons with the power of miracles; yet in general also He had been taught by David, "If I regard iniquity in my heart[87] the Lord will not hear my prayer." And therefore when men "pray in every place," (for so they are commanded) "let them lift up pure hands, without anger and contention."[88] And indeed although every sin entertained with a free choice and a full understanding is an obstruction to our prayers, yet the special sin of uncharitableness makes the biggest cloud, and is in the proper matter of it an indisposition for us to receive mercy: for he who is softened with apprehension of his own needs of mercy, will be tenderhearted towards his brother; and therefore he that hath no bowels here, can have no aptness there to receive, or heartily to hope for mercy. But this rule is to be understood of persons who persevere in the habit and remanent affections of sin; so long as they entertain sin with love, complacency, and joy, they are in a state of enmity with God, and therefore in no fit disposition to receive pardon and the entertainment of friends: but penitent sinners and returning souls, loaden and grieved with their heavy pressures, are, next to holy innocents, the aptest persons in the world to be heard in their prayers for pardon. But they are in no farther disposition to large favours, and more eminent charities: a sinner, in the beginning of his penance, will be heard for himself, and yet also he needs the prayers of holy persons more signally than others; for he hath but some very few degrees of dispositions to reconciliation: but in prayers of intercession

---

84. 1 John 3:21.
85. James 5:16.
86. John 9:31.
87. Ps. 71:18.
88. 1 Tim. 2:8.

or mediation for others, only holy and very pious persons are fit to be interested. All men, as matter of duty, must pray for all men: but in the great necessities of a prince, of a church, or kingdom, or of a family, or of a great danger and calamity to a single person, only a Noah, a David, a Daniel, a Jeremy, an Enoch, or Job, are fit and proportioned advocates. God so requires holiness in us that our prayers may be accepted, that He entertains them in several degrees, according to the degrees of our sanctity; to fewer or more purposes, according as we are little or great in the kingdom of heaven. As for those irregular donations of good things which wicked persons ask for and have, they are either no mercies, but instruments of cursing and crime, or else they are designs of grace, intended to convince them of their unworthiness; and so, if they become not instruments of their conversion, they are aggravations of their ruin.

14. Secondly: The second condition I have already explained in the description of the matter of our prayers. For although we may lawfully ask for whatsoever we need, and this leave is consigned to us in those words of our blessed Saviour, "Your heavenly Father knoweth what you have need of": yet because God's providence walks in the great deep, that is, His footsteps are in the water, and leave no impression; no former act of grace becomes a precedent that He will give us that in kind which then He saw convenient, and therefore gave us, and now He sees to be inconvenient, and therefore does deny. Therefore in all things but what are matter of necessary and unmingled duty, we must send up our prayers; but humility, mortification, and conformity to the divine will, must attend for an answer, and bring back, not what the public embassy pretends, but what they have in private instructions to desire; accounting that for the best satisfaction which God pleases, not what I have either unnecessarily, or vainly, or sinfully desired.

15. Thirdly: When our persons are disposed by sanctity, and the matter of our prayers is hallowed by prudence and religious intendments, then we are bound to entertain a full persuasion and confident hope that God will hear us. "What things soever ye desire, when ye pray, believe that ye receive them, and ye shall obtain them,"[89] said our blessed Saviour: and St. James taught from that oracle, "If any of you lack wisdom, let him ask it of God: but let him ask in faith, nothing wavering; for he that wavereth is like a wave of the sea, driven with the

---

89. Mark 11:24.

wind, and tossed to and fro":[90] meaning, that when there is no fault in the matter of our prayers, but that we ask things pleasing to God, and there is no indisposition and hostility in our persons and manners between God and us, then to doubt were to distrust God; for all being right on our parts, if we doubt the issue, the defailance must be on that part which to suspect were infinite impiety. But after we have done all we can, if, out of humility, and fear that we are not truly disposed, we doubt of the issue, it is a modesty which will not at all discommend our persons, nor impede the event; provided we at no hand suspect either God's power or veracity. Putting trust in God is an excellent advantage to our prayers; "I will deliver him," saith God, "because he hath put his trust in Me." And yet distrusting ourselves, and suspecting our own dispositions, as it pulls us back in our actual confidence of the event, so, because it abates nothing of our confidence in God, it prepares us to receive the reward of humility, and not to lose the praise of a holy trusting in the Almighty.

16. These conditions are essential: some other there are which are incidents and accessories, but at no hand to be neglected. And the first is, actual or habitual attention to our prayers, which we are to procure with moral and severe endeavours, that we desire not God to hear us when we do not hear ourselves. To which purpose we must avoid, as much as our duty will permit us, multiplicity of cares and exterior employments: for a river cut into many rivulets divides also its strength, and grows contemptible, and apt to be forded by a lamb, and drunk up by a summer sun: so is the spirit of man busied in variety, and divided in itself: it abates its fervour, cools into indifferency, and becomes trifling by its dispersion and inadvertency. Aquinas was once asked, with what compendium a man might best become learned? he answered, By reading of one book: meaning, that an understanding entertained with several objects is intent upon neither, and profits not. And so it is when we pray to God: if the cares of the world intervene, they choke our desire into an indifferency, and suppress the flame into a smoke, and strangle the spirit; but this, being an habitual carelessness and intemperance of spirit, is an enemy to an habitual attention, and therefore is highly criminal, and makes our prayers to be but the labour of the lips, because our desires are lessened by the remanent affections of the world. But besides an habitual attention in our prayers, that is, a desire in general of

---

90. James 1:5–6.

all that our prayers pretend to in particular, there is also for the accommodation, and to facilitate the access of our prayers, required, that we attend actually to the words or sense of every collect or petition. To this we must contend with prayer, with actual dereliction and seposition of all our other affairs, though innocent and good in other kinds, by a present spirit. And the use of it is, that such attention is an actual conversing with God; it occasions the exercise of many acts of virtue, it increases zeal and fervency, and by reflection enkindles love and holy desires. And although there is no rule to determine the degree of our actual attention, and it is ordinarily impossible never to wander with a thought, or to be interrupted with a sudden immission into our spirit in the midst of prayers; yet our duty is, by mortification of our secular desires, by suppression of all our irregular passions, by reducing them to indifferency, by severity of spirit, by enkindling our holy appetites and desires of holy things, by silence, and meditation, and repose, to get as forward in this excellency as we can; to which also we may be very much helped by ejaculatory prayers and short breathings; in which as by reason of their short abode upon the spirit there is less fear of diversion, so also they may so often be renewed that nothing of the devotion may be unspent, or expire for want of oil to feed and entertain the flame. But the determination of the case of conscience is this: Habitual attention is absolutely necessary in our prayers; that is, it is altogether our duty to desire of God all that we pray for, though our mind be not actually attending to the form of words; and therefore all worldly desires that are inordinate must be rescinded, that we more earnestly attend on God than on the world. He that prays to God to give him the gift of chastity, and yet secretly wishes rather for an opportunity of lust, and desires God would not hear him (as St. Austin[91] confesses of himself in his youth), that man sins for want of holy and habitual desires; he prays only with his lips what he in no sense attests in his heart. Secondly, actual attention to our prayers is also necessary, not ever to avoid a sin, but that the present prayer become effectual. He that means to feast, and to get thanks of God, must invite the poor; and yet he that invites the rich, in that he sins not, though he hath no reward of God for that. So that prayer perishes to which the man gives no degree of actual attention, for the prayer is as if it were not; it is no more than a dream, or an act of custom and order, nothing of devotion; and so accidentally becomes a

---

91. Augustine, *Confessions*, PL 32.757.

sin (I mean there where, and in what degrees, it is avoidable) by taking God's name in vain. Thirdly, it is not necessary to the prevalency of the prayer that the spirit actually accompany every clause or word; if it says a hearty Amen, or in any part of it attests the whole, it is such an attention which the present condition of most men will sometimes permit. Fourthly, a wandering of the spirit through carelessness, or any vice or inordinate passion, is in that degree criminal as is the cause, and it is heightened by the greatness of the interruption. Fifthly, it is only excused by our endeavours to cure it, and by our after-acts, either of sorrow, or repetition of the prayer, and reinforcing the intention. And certainly if we repeat our prayer in which we have observed our spirits too much to wander, and resolve still to repeat it as our opportunities permit, it may in a good degree defeat the purpose of the enemy, when his own arts shall return upon his head, and the wandering of our spirits be made the occasion of a prayer, and the parent of a new devotion. Lastly, according to the degrees of our actual attention, so our prayers are more or less perfect: a present spirit being a great instrument and testimony of wisdom, and apt to many great purposes; and our continual abode with God being a great endearment of our persons, by increasing the affections.

17. Secondly: The second accessory is intension of spirit, or fervency; such as was that of our blessed Saviour, who prayed to His Father with strong cries and loud petitions, not clamorous in language, but strong in spirit. St. Paul also, when he was pressed with a strong temptation, prayed thrice, that is, earnestly; and St. James affirms this to be of great value and efficacy to the obtaining blessings, "The effectual fervent prayer of a just person avails much"; and Elias, though "a man of like passions," yet by earnest prayer he obtained rain, or drought, according as he desired. Now this is properly produced by the greatness of our desire of heavenly things, our true value and estimate of religion, our sense of present pressures, our fears: and it hath some accidental increases by the disposition of our body, the strength of fancy, and the tenderness of spirit, and assiduity of the dropping of religious discourses; and in all men is necessary to be so great, as that we prefer heaven and religion before the world, and desire them rather, with the choice of our wills and understanding: though there cannot always be that degree of sensual, pungent, or delectable affections towards religion, as towards the desires of nature and sense: yet ever we must prefer celestial objects, restraining the appetites of the world, lest they be immoderate, and heightening the desires of grace and glory, lest they

become indifferent, and the fire upon the altar of incense be extinct. But the greater zeal and fervour of desire we have in our prayers, the sooner and the greater will the return of the prayer be, if the prayer be for spiritual objects. For other things our desires must be according to our needs, not by a value derived from the nature of the thing, but the usefulness it is of to us, in order to our greater and better purposes.

18. Thirdly: Of the same consideration it is, that we "persevere and be importunate"[92] in our prayers, by repetition of our desires, and not remitting either our affections or our offices, till God, overcome by our importunity, give a gracious answer. Jacob wrestled with the angel all night, and would not dismiss him till he had given him a blessing; "Let Me alone," saith God, as if He felt a pressure and burden lying upon Him by our prayers, or could not quit Himself nor depart unless we give Him leave. And since God is detained by our prayers, and we may keep Him as long as we please, and that He will not go away till we leave speaking to Him; he that will dismiss Him till he hath His blessing, knows not the value of His benediction, or understands not the energy and power of a persevering prayer. And to this purpose Christ "spake a parable, that men ought always to pray, and not to faint."[93] "Praying without ceasing,"[94] St. Paul calls it; that is, with continual addresses, frequent interpellations, never ceasing renewing the request till I obtain my desire. For it is not enough to recommend our desires to God with one hearty prayer, and then forget to ask Him any more; but so long as our needs continue, so long, in all times, and upon all occasions, to renew and repeat our desires: and this is "praying continually." Just as the widow did to the unjust judge; she never left going to him, she troubled him every day with her clamorous suit; so must we "pray always," that is, every day, and many times every day, according to our occasions and necessities, or our devotion and zeal, or as we are determined by the customs and laws of a church; never giving over through weariness or distrust, often renewing our desires by a continual succession of devotions, returning at certain and determinate periods. For God's blessings, though they come infallibly, yet not always speedily; saving only that it is a blessing to be delayed, that we may increase our desire, and renew our prayers, and do acts of confidence and patience,

---

92. Rom. 12:12.
93. Luke 18:1.
94. 1 Thess. 5:17.

and ascertain and increase the blessing when it comes. For we do not more desire to be blessed than God does to hear us importunate for blessing; and He weighs every sigh, and bottles up every tear, and records every prayer, and looks through the cloud with delight to see us upon our knees, and when He sees His time, His light breaks through it, and shines upon us. Only we must not make our accounts for God according to the course of the sun, but the measures of eternity. He measures us by our needs, and we must not measure Him by our impatience. "God is not slack, as some men count slackness," saith the Apostle;[95] and we find it so, when we have waited long. All the elapsed time is no part of the tediousness; the trouble of it is past with itself: and for the future, we know not how little it may be; for aught we know, we are already entered into the cloud that brings the blessing. However, pray till it comes: for we shall never miss to receive our desire, if it be holy, or innocent, and safe; or else we are sure of a great reward of our prayers.

19. And in this, so determined, there is no danger of blasphemy, or vain repetitions: for those repetitions are vain which repeat the words, not the devotion, which renew the expression and not the desire; and he that may pray the same prayer to-morrow which he said to-day, may pray the same at night which he said in the morning, and the same at noon which he said at night, and so in all the hours of prayer, and in all the opportunities of devotion. Christ in His agony "went thrice, and said the same words,"[96] but He had intervals for repetition; and His need and His devotion pressed Him forward: and whenever our needs do so, it is all one if we say the same words or others, so we express our desire, and tell our needs, and beg the remedy. In the same office, and the same hour of prayer, to repeat the same things often hath but few excuses to make it reasonable, and fewer to make it pious: but to think that the prayer is better for such repetition, is the fault which the holy Jesus condemned in the gentiles, who in their hymns would say a name over a hundred times. But in this we have no rule to determine us in numbers and proportion, but right reason. God loves not any words the more for being said often; and those repetitions which are unreasonable in prudent estimation, cannot in any account be esteemed pious. But

---

95. 2 Pet. 3:9.
96. Matt. 26:44.

where a reasonable cause allows the repetition, the same cause that makes it reasonable makes it also proper for devotion. He that speaks his needs, and expresses nothing but his fervour and greatness of desire, cannot be vain or long in his prayers; he that speaks impertinently, that is, unreasonably and without desires, is long, though he speak but two syllables; he that thinks for speaking much to be heard the sooner, thinks God is delighted in the labour of the lips: but when reason is the guide, and piety is the rule, and necessity is the measure, and desire gives the proportion, let the prayer be very long; he that shall blame it for its length, must proclaim his disrelish both of reason and religion, his despite of necessity, and contempt of zeal.

20. As a part and instance of our importunity in prayer, it is usually reckoned and advised, that in cases of great, sudden, and violent need, we corroborate our prayers with a vow of doing something holy and religious in an uncommanded instance, something to which God had not formerly bound our duty, though fairly invited our will; or else, if we choose a duty in which we were obliged, then to vow the doing of it in a more excellent manner, with a greater inclination of the will, with a more fervent repetition of the act, with some more noble circumstance, with a fuller assent of the understanding, or else adding a new promise to our old duty, to make it become more necessary to us, and to secure our duty. In this case, as it requires great prudence and caution in the susception, lest what we piously intend obtain a present blessing, and lay a lasting snare; so if it be prudent in the manner, holy in the matter, useful in the consequence, and safe in all the circumstances of the person, it is an endearing us and our prayer to God by the increase of duty and charity, and therefore a more probable way of making our prayers gracious and acceptable. And the religion of vows was not only hallowed by the example of Jacob at Bethel, of Hannah praying for a child and God hearing her, of David vowing a temple to God; and made regular and safe by the rules and cautions in Moses' law: but left by our blessed Saviour in the same constitution He found it, He having innovated nothing in the matter of vows: and it was practised accordingly in the instance of St. Paul at Cenchrea; of Ananias and Sapphira,[97] who vowed their possessions to the use of the church; and of the widows in the apostolical age, who therefore vowed to remain in the state of

---

97. Jerome, *Letters*, PL 22.1107.

widowhood, because concerning them who married after the entry into religion, St. Paul[98] says, "they have broken their first faith": and such were they of whom our blessed Saviour affirms, that "some make themselves eunuchs for the kingdom of heaven," that is, such who promise to God a life of chastity. And concerning the success of prayer, so seconded with a prudent and religious vow, besides the instances of scripture,[99] we have the perpetual experience and witness of all Christendom; and in particular our Saxon kings have been remarked for this part of importunity in their own chronicles. Oswy[100] got a great victory with unlikely forces against Penda the Dane after his earnest prayer, and an appendent vow: and Ceadwalla obtained of God power to recover the Isle of Wight from the hands of infidels, after he had prayed and promised to return the fourth part of it to be employed in the proper services of God and of religion. This can have no objection or suspicion in it among wise and disabused persons; for it can be nothing but an increasing and a renewed act of duty, or devotion, or zeal, or charity, and the importunity of prayer, acted in a more vital and real expression.

21. First: All else that is to be considered concerning prayer is extrinsecal and accidental to it. Prayer is public, or private: in the communion or society of saints, or in our closets: these prayers have less temptation to vanity; the other have more advantages of charity, example, fervour, and energy. In public offices we avoid singularity, in the private we avoid hypocrisy: those are of more edification, these of greater retiredness and silence of spirit: those serve the needs of all the world in the first intention, and our own by consequence; these serve our own needs first, and the public only by a secondary intention: these have more pleasure, they more duty: these are the best instruments of repentance, where our confessions may be more particular, and our shame less scandalous; the other are better for eucharist and instruction, for edification of the church, and glorification of God.

22. Secondly: The posture of our bodies in prayer had as great variety as the ceremonies and civilities of several nations came to. The Jews most commonly prayed standing: so did the pharisee and the publican in the temple.[101] So did the primitive Christians, in all their greater festivals and intervals of jubilee; in their penances they kneeled.

---

98. 1 Tim. 5:12.
99. Eccles. 5:4; Ps. 132:1–2; Deut. 23:21; Acts 18:18.
100. Bede, *Ecclesiastical History*, PL 95.212.
101. Neh. 9:5; Mark 11:25; Luke 18:11.

The monks in Cassian[102] sate when they sung the psalter. And in every country, whatsoever by the custom of the nation was a symbol of reverence and humility, of silence and attention, of gravity and modesty, that posture they translated to their prayers. But in all nations bowing the head, that is, a laying down our glory at the feet of God, was the manner of worshippers; and this was always the more humble and the lower, as their devotion was higher; and was very often expressed by prostration, or lying flat upon the ground; and this all nations did, and all religions. Our deportment ought to be grave, decent, humble, apt for adoration, apt to edify; and when we address ourselves to prayer, not instantly to leap into the office, as the judges of the Areopage into their sentence, "without preface or preparatory affections"; but considering in what presence we speak, and to what purposes, let us balance our fervour with reverential fear: and when we have done, not rise from the ground as if we vaulted, or were glad we had done; but as we begin with desires of assistance, so end with desires of pardon and acceptance, concluding our longer offices with a shorter mental prayer, of more private reflection and reverence, designing to mend what we have done amiss, or to give thanks and proceed if we did well and according to our powers.

23. Thirdly: In private prayers it is permitted to every man to speak his prayers, or only to think them, which is a speaking to God. Vocal or mental prayer is all one to God, but in order to us they have their several advantages. The sacrifice of the heart, and the calves of the lips, make up a holocaust to God: but words are the arrest of the desires, and keep the spirit fixed, and in less permissions to wander from fancy to fancy. And mental prayer is apt to make the greater fervour, if it wander not; our office is more determined by words, but we then actually think of God when our spirits only speak. Mental prayer, when our spirits wander, is like a watch standing still because the spring is down; wind it up again, and it goes on regularly: but in vocal prayer, if the words run on, and the spirit wanders, the clock strikes false, the hand points not to the right hour, because something is in disorder, and the striking is nothing but noise. In mental prayer, we confess God's omniscience; in vocal prayer, we call the angels to witness. In the first, our spirits rejoice in God; in the second, the angels rejoice in us. Mental prayer is the best remedy against lightness and indifference of affec-

---

102. Cassian, *Monastic Institutions*, PL 49.85.

tions; but vocal prayer is the aptest instrument of communion. That is more angelical, but yet fittest for the state of separation and glory; this is but human, but it is apter for our present constitution. They have their distinct proprieties, and may be used according to several accidents, occasions, or dispositions.

THE PRAYER

O holy and eternal God, who hast commanded us to pray unto Thee in all our necessities, and to give thanks unto Thee for all our instances of joy and blessing, and to adore Thee in all Thy attributes and communications, Thy own glories and Thy eternal mercies; give unto me Thy servant the spirit of prayer and supplication, that I may understand what is good for me, that I may desire regularly, and choose the best things, that I may conform to Thy will, and submit to Thy disposing, relinquishing my own affections and imperfect choice. Sanctify my heart and spirit, that I may sanctify Thy name, and that I may be gracious and accepted in Thine eyes. Give me the humility and obedience of a servant, that I may also have the hope and confidence of a son, making humble and confident addresses to the throne of grace; that in all my necessities I may come to Thee for aids, and may trust in Thee for a gracious answer, and may receive satisfaction and supply.

Via Pacis[103]

A SHORT METHOD OF PEACE AND HOLINESS
WITH A MANUAL OF DAILY PRAYERS FITTED
TO THE DAYS OF THE WEEK

Sunday
Decad the First

1. It is the highest wisdom by despising the world to arrive at heaven; for they are blessed whose daily exercise it is to converse with God by prayer and obedience, by love and patience.

2. It is the extremest folly to labour for that which will bring torment in the end, and no satisfaction in the little enjoyment of it; to be unwearied in the pursuit of the world, and to be soon tired in whatsoever we begin to do for Christ.

3. Watch over thyself, counsel thyself, reprove thyself, censure thyself, and judge thyself impartially; whatever thou dost to others, do not neglect thyself: for every man profits so much as he does violence to himself.

4. They that follow their own sensuality, stain their consciences, and lose the grace of God; but he that endeavours to please God, whatever he suffers, is beloved of God: for it is not a question whether we shall or shall not suffer, but whether we shall suffer for God or for the world; whether we shall take pains in religion or in sin, to get heaven or to get riches.

5. What availeth knowledge without the fear of God? A humble ignorant man is better than a proud scholar, who studies natural things, and knows not himself. The more thou knowest, the more grievously thou shalt be judged: many get no profit by their labour, because they contend for knowledge rather than for holy life; and the time shall come

---

103. *Works* 7:618ff.

when it shall more avail thee to have subdued one lust than to have known all mysteries.

6. No man truly knows himself but he groweth daily more contemptible in his own eyes; desire not to be known, and to be little esteemed of by men.

7. If all be well within, nothing can hurt us from without; for from inordinate love and vain fear comes all unquietness of spirit and distraction of our senses.

8. He to whom all things are one, who draweth all things to one, and seeth all things in one, may enjoy true peace and rest of spirit.

9. It is not much business that distracts any man, but the want of purity, constancy, and tendency towards God. Who hinders thee more than the unmortified desires of thine own heart? As soon as ever a man desires any thing inordinately, he is presently disquieted in himself. He that hath not wholly subdued himself is quickly tempted and overcome in small and trifling things. The weak in spirit is he that is in a manner subject to his appetite, and he quickly falls into indignation, and contention, and envy.

10. He is truly great that is great in charity and little in himself.

Monday
The Second Decad
11. We rather often believe and speak evil of others than good. But they that are truly virtuous do not easily credit evil that is told them of their neighbours: for if others may do amiss, then may these also speak amiss; man is frail and prone to evil, and therefore may soon fail in words.

12. Be not rash in thy proceedings, nor confident and pertinacious in thy conceits; but consult with him that is wise, and seek to be instructed by a better than thyself.

13. The more humble and resigned we are to God, the more prudent we are in our affairs to men, and peaceable in ourselves.

14. The proud and the covetous can never rest.

15. Be not ashamed to be or to be esteemed poor in this world: for he that hears God teaching him will find that it is the best wisdom to withdraw all our affections from secular honour and troublesome riches, and to place them upon eternal treasures, and by patience, by humility, by suffering scorn and contempt, and all the will of God, to get the true riches.

16. Be not proud of well-doing, for the judgment of God is far differing from the judgment of men.

17. Lay not thine heart open to every one, but with the wise and them that fear God: converse not much with young people and strangers: flatter not the rich, neither do thou willingly or lightly appear before great personages: never be partaker with the persecutors.

18. It is easier, and safer, and more pleasant to live in obedience, than to be at our own disposing.

19. Always yield to others when there is cause; for that is no shame, but honour: but it is shame to stand stiff in a foolish or weak argument or resolution.

20. The talk of worldly affairs hindereth much, although re-counted with a fair intention: we speak willingly, but seldom return to silence.

Tuesday
The Third Decad

21. Watch and pray, lest your time pass without profit or fruit; but devout discourses do greatly further our spiritual progress, if persons of one mind and spirit be gathered together in God.

22. We should enjoy more peace if we did not busy ourselves with the words and deeds of other men, which appertain not to our charge.

23. He that esteems his progress in religion to consist in exterior observances, his devotion will quickly be at an end; but to free ourselves of passions, is to lay the axe at the root of the tree, and the true way of peace.

24. It is good that we sometimes be contradicted and ill thought of, and that we always bear it well, even when we deserve to be well spoken of; perfect peace and security cannot be had in this world.

25. All the saints have profited by tribulations; and they that could not bear temptations, became reprobates, and fell from God.

26. Think not all is well within when all is well without, or that thy being pleased is a sign that God is pleased; but suspect every thing that is prosperous, unless it promotes piety, and charity, and humility.

27. Do no evil, for no interest, and to please no man, for no friendship, and for no fear.

28. God regards not how much we do, but from how much it proceeds; he does much that loves much.

29. Patiently suffer that from others, which thou canst not mend

in them, until God please to do it for thee; and remember that thou mend thyself, since thou art so willing others should not offend in any thing.

30. Every man's virtue is best seen in adversity and temptation.

Wednesday
The Fourth Decad

31. Begin every day to repent, not that thou shouldst at all defer it, or stand at the door, but because all that is past ought to seem little to thee, because it is so in itself; begin the next day with the same zeal, and the same fear, and the same humility, as if thou hadst never begun before.

32. A little omission of any usual exercise of piety cannot happen to thee without some loss and considerable detriment, even though it be upon a considerable cause.

33. Be not slow in common and usual acts of piety and devotion, and quick and prompt at singularities; but having first done what thou art bound to, proceed to counsels and perfections, and the extraordinaries of religion, as you see cause.

34. He that desires much to hear news, is never void of passions, and secular desires, and adherencies to the world.

35. Complain not too much of hindrances of devotion; if thou let men alone, they will let you alone; and if you desire not to converse with them, let them know it, and they will not desire to converse with thee.

36. Draw not to thyself the affairs of others, neither involve thyself in the suits and parties of great personages.

37. Know that if any trouble happen to thee, it is what thou hast deserved, and therefore brought upon thyself; but if any comfort come to thee, it is a gift of God, and what thou didst not deserve: and remember that oftentimes when thy body complains of trouble, it is not so much the greatness of trouble, as littleness of thy spirit, that makes thee to complain.

38. He that knows how to suffer any thing for God; that desires heartily the will of God may be done in him; that studies to please others rather than himself, to do the will of his superior, not his own; that chooseth the least portion, and is not greedy for the biggest; that takes the lowest place, and does not murmur secretly: he is in the best condition and state of things.

39. Let no man despair of mercy or success, so long as he hath life and health.

40. Every man must pass through fire and water, before he can come to refreshment.

Thursday
The Fifth Decad

41. Soon may a man lose that by negligence, which hath by much labour, and a long time, and a mighty grace scarcely been obtained. And what shall become of us before night, who are weary so early in the morning? Woe be to that man who would be at rest, even when he hath scarcely a footstep of holiness appearing in his conversation.

42. So think, and so do, as if thou wert to die to-day, and at night to give an account of thy whole life.

43. Beg not a long life, but a good one; for length of days oftentimes prolongs the evil, and augments the guilt: it were well if that little time we live, we would live well.

44. Entertain the same opinions and thoughts of thy sin and of thy present state, as thou wilt in the days of sorrow. Thou wilt then think thyself very miserable and very foolish, for neglecting one hour, and one day of thy salvation: think so now, and thou wilt be more provident of thy time and of thy talent. For there will a time come, when every careless man shall desire the respite of one hour for prayer and repentance, and I know not who will grant it. Happy is he that so lives, that in the day of death he rejoices, and is not amazed.

45. He that would die comfortably, may serve his ends by first procuring to himself a contempt of the world, a fervent desire of growing in grace, love of discipline, a laborious repentance, a prompt obedience, self-denial, and toleration of every cross accident for the love of Christ, and a tender charity.

46. While thou art well, thou mayest do much good if thou wilt; but when thou art sick, neither thou nor I can tell what thou shalt be able to do: it is not very much, nor very good; few men mend with sickness, as they are but few who by travel and a wandering life become devout.

47. Be not troubled nor faint in the labours of mortification, and the austerities of repentance; for in hell one hour is more intolerable than a hundred years in the house of repentance: and try, for if thou canst not endure God punishing thy follies gently, for a while, to amend thee, how wilt thou endure His vengeance for ever to undo thee?

413

48. In thy prayers wait for God, and think not every hearty prayer can procure every thing thou askest. These things which the saints did not obtain without many prayers, and much labour, and a shower of tears, and a long protracted watchfulness, and industry, do thou expect also in its own time, and by its usual measures. Do thou valiantly, and hope confidently, and wait patiently, and thou shalt find thou wilt not be deceived.

49. Be careful thou dost not speak a lie in thy prayers, which though not observed, is frequently practised by careless persons, especially in the forms of confession, affirming things which they have not thought, professing sorrow which is not, making a vow they mean not.

50. If thou meanest to be devout, and to enlarge thy religion, do it rather by increasing thy ordinary devotions than thy extraordinary: for if they be not regular, but come by chance, they will not last long; but if they be added to your ordinary offices, or made to be daily, thy spirit will by use and custom be made tender, and not willing to go less.

Friday
The Sixth Decad

51. He is a truly charitable and good man, who when he receives injuries, grieves rather for the malice of him that injures him, than for his own suffering; who willingly prays for him that wrongs him, and from his heart forgives all his faults; who stays not, but quickly asks pardon of others for his errors or mistakes; who sooner shews mercy than anger; who thinks better of others than himself; who offers violence to his appetite, and in all things endeavours to subdue the flesh to the spirit. This is an excellent abbreviature of the whole duty of a Christian.

52. No man can have felicity in two states of things; if he takes it in God here, in Him he shall have it hereafter, for God will last for ever. But if he takes felicity in things of this world, where will his felicity be when this world is done? Either here alone, or hereafter, must be thy portion.

53. Avoid those things in thyself, which in others do most displease thee; and remember that as thine eye observes others, so art thou observed by God, by angels, and by men.

54. He that puts his confidence in God only, is neither overjoyed in any great good thing of this life, nor sorrowful for a little thing: let God be thy love and thy fear, and He also will be thy salvation and thy refuge.

55. Do not omit thy prayers for want of a good oratory or place to pray in, nor thy duty for want of temporal encouragements. For he that does both upon God's account, cares not how or what he suffers, so he suffer well, and be the friend of Christ; nor where nor when he prays, so he may do it frequently, fervently, and acceptably.

56. Very often remember and meditate upon the wounds and stripes, the shame and the pain, the death and the burial of our Lord Jesus; for nothing will more enable us to bear our cross patiently, injuries charitably, the labour of religion comfortably, and censuring words and detractions with meekness and quietness.

57. Esteem not thyself to have profited in religion, unless thou thinkest well of others, and meanly of thyself: therefore never accuse any but thyself, and he that diligently watches himself, will be willing enough to be silent concerning others.

58. It is no great matter to live lovingly with good-natured, with humble and meek persons: but he that can do so with the froward, with the wilful, and the ignorant, with the peevish and perverse, he only hath true charity: always remembering that our true solid peace, the peace of God, consists rather in compliance with others than in being complied with, in suffering and forbearing rather than in contention and victory.

59. Simplicity in our intentions, and purity of affections, are the two wings of a soul, investing it with the robes and resemblances of a seraphim. Intend the honour of God principally and sincerely, and mingle not thy affections with any creature, but in just subordination to God, and to religion, and thou shalt have joy, if there be any such thing in this world. For there is no joy but in God, and no sorrow but in an evil conscience.

60. Take not much care what, or who is for thee, or against thee. The judgment of none is to be regarded, if God's judgment be otherwise. Thou art neither better nor worse in thyself for any account that is made of thee by any but by God alone: secure that to thee, and He will secure all the rest.

Saturday
The Seventh Decad

61. Blessed is he that understands what it is to love Jesus, and contends earnestly to be like Him; nothing else can satisfy, or make us perfect. But be thou a bearer of His cross, as well as a lover of His kingdom: suffer tribulation for Him, or from Him, with the same spirit thou receivest consolation: follow Him as well for the bitter cup of His

passion as for the loaves; and remember, that if it be a hard saying, Take up My cross and follow Me, it is a harder saying, Go ye cursed into everlasting fire.

62. No man can always have the same spiritual pleasure in his prayers, for the greatest saints have sometimes suffered the banishment of the heart; sometimes are fervent, sometimes they feel a barrenness of devotion: for this Spirit comes and goes. Rest therefore only in God, and in doing thy duty: and know, that if thou beest overjoyed to day, this hour will pass away, and temptation and sadness will succeed.

63. In all afflictions, seek rather for patience than for comfort: if thou preservest that, this will return. Any man would serve God, if he felt pleasure in it always; but the virtuous does it when his soul is full of heaviness, and regards not himself but God, and hates that consolation that lessens his compunction, but loves any thing whereby he is made more humble.

64. That which thou dost not understand when thou readest, thou shalt understand in the day of thy visitation: for there are many secrets of religion which are not perceived till they be felt, and are not felt but in the day of a great calamity.

65. He that prays, despairs not: but sad is the condition of him that cannot pray; happy are they that can and do, and love to do it.

66. He that will be pleased in his prayers, must make his prayers his rule: all our duty is there set down, because in all our duty we beg the divine assistance; and remember, that you are bound to do all those duties, for the doing of which you have prayed for the divine assistance.

67. Be doing actions of religion as often as thou canst, and thy worldly pleasures as seldom, that if thou beest surprised by sudden death, it may be odds but thou mayest be taken at thy prayers.

68. Watch, and resist the devil in all his temptations and snares: his chief designs are these; to hinder thy desire in good; to put thee by from any spiritual employment, from prayers especially, from the meditation of the passion, from the remembrance of thy sins, from humble confession of them, from speedy repentance, from the custody of thy senses and of thy heart, from firm purposes of growing in grace, from reading good books, and frequent receiving the holy sacrament. It is all one to him if he deceives thee by a lie or by truth; whether he amaze or trouble thee, by love of the present or fear of the future. Watch him but in these things, and there will be no part left unarmed in which he can wound thee.

69. Remember how the proud have fallen, and they who have

presumed upon their own strength have been disgraced; and that the boldest and greatest talkers in the days of peace have been the most dejected and pusillanimous in the day of temptation.

70. No man ought to think he hath found peace when nothing troubles him; or that God loves him because he hath no enemy; nor that all is well because every thing is according to his mind; nor that he is a holy person because he prays with great sweetness and comfort. But he is at peace who is reconciled to God; and God loves him when he hath overcome himself; and all is well when nothing pleases him but God, being thankful in the midst of his afflictions; and he is holy who when he hath lost his comfort loses nothing of his duty, but is still the same when God changes His face towards him.

Agenda,
or
Things To Be Done[104]

THE DIARY, OR A RULE TO SPEND EACH DAY RELIGIOUSLY

1. Suppose every day to be a day of business: for your whole life is a race, and a battle; a merchandise, and a journey. Every day propound to yourself a rosary or a chaplet of good works, to present to God at night.

2. Rise as soon as your health and other occasions shall permit; but it is good to be as regular as you can, and as early. Remember, he that rises first to prayer, hath a more early title to a blessing. But he that changes night into day, labour into idleness, watchfulness to sleep, changes his hopes of blessing into a dream.

3. Never let any one think it an excuse to lie in bed, because he hath nothing to do when he is up: for whoever hath a soul, and hopes to save that soul, hath work enough to do to "make his calling and election sure," to serve God and to pray, to read and to meditate, to repent and to amend, to do good to others and to keep evil from themselves. And if thou hast little to do, thou oughtest to employ the more time in laying up for a greater crown of glory.

4. At your opening your eyes, enter upon the day with some act of piety.

a) of thanksgiving for the preservation of you the night past,
b) of the glorification of God for the works of the creation, or any thing for the honour of God.

5. When you first go off from your bed, solemnly and devoutly

---

104. Ibid. pp. 611ff.

bow your head, and worship the holy Trinity, the Father, Son, and holy Ghost.

6. When you are making ready, be as silent as you can, and spend that time in holy thoughts; there being no way left to redeem that time from loss, but by meditation and short mental prayers. If you choose to speak, speak something of God's praises, of His goodness, His mercies, or His greatness: ever resolving that the first-fruits of thy reason, and of all thy faculties, shall be presented to God, to sanctify the whole harvest of thy conversation.

7. Be not curious, nor careless in your habit, but always keep these measures.

a) Be not troublesome to thyself, or to others, by unhandsomeness or uncleanness.
b) Let it be according to your state and quality.
c) Make religion to be the difference of your habit, so as to be best attired upon holy or festival days.

8. In your dressing, let there be ejaculations fitted to the several actions of dressing: as at washing your hands and face, pray God to cleanse your soul from sin: in putting on your clothes, pray Him to clothe your soul with the righteousness of your Saviour; and so in all the rest. For religion must not only be the garment of your soul, to invest it all over; but it must be also as the fringes to every of your actions, that something of religion appear in every one of them besides the innocence of all of them.

9. As soon as you are dressed with the first preparation of your clothes, that you can decently do it, kneel and say the Lord's prayer; then rise from your knees and do what is necessary for you in order to your further dressing, or affairs of the house, which is speedily to be done; and then finish your dressing according to the foregoing rules.

10. When you are dressed, retire yourself to your closet; and go to your usual devotions, which it is good that at the first prayers they were divided into seven actions of piety.

a) an act of adoration.
b) of thanksgiving.
c) of oblation.
d) of confession.
e) of petition.

419

f) of intercession.

g) of meditation, or serious, deliberate, useful reading[105] of the holy scriptures.

11. I advise that your reading should be governed by these measures.

a) Let it be not of the whole Bible in order, but for your devotion use the New testament, and such portions of the Old as contain the precepts of holy life.

b) The historical and less useful part, let it be read at such other times which you have of leisure from your domestic employments.

c) Those portions of scripture which you use in your prayers, let them not be long; a chapter at once, no more: but then what time you can afford, spend it in thinking and meditating upon the holy precepts which you read.

d) Be sure to meditate so long till you make some act of piety upon the occasion of what you meditate; either that you get some new arguments against a sin, or some new encouragements to virtue; some spiritual strength and advantage, or else some act of prayer to God or glorification of Him.

e) I advise that you would read your chapter in the midst of your prayers in the morning, if they be divided according to the number of the former actions; because little interruptions will be apt to make your prayers less tedious, and yourself more attent upon them: but if you find any other way more agreeing to your spirit and disposition, use your liberty without scruple.

12. Before you go forth of your closet, after your prayers are done, set yourself down a little while and consider what you are to do that day, what matter of business is like to employ you or to tempt you; and take particular resolution against that, whether it be matter of wrangling, or anger, or covetousness, or vain courtship, or feasting: and when you enter upon it, remember upon what you resolved in your closet. If you are likely to have nothing extraordinary that day, a general recommendation of the affairs of that day to God in your prayers will be sufficient; but if there be any thing foreseen that is not usual, be

---

105. Chrysostom, *Sermon on Lazarus*, PG 48.991.

sure to be armed for it by a hearty, though a short prayer, and an earnest prudent resolution beforehand, and then watch when the thing comes.

13. Whosoever hath children or servants, let him or her take care that all the children and servants of the family say their prayers before they begin their work. The Lord's prayer, and the ten commandments, with the short verse at the end of every commandment which the church uses, and the creed, is a very good office for them if they be not fitted for more regular offices. And to these also it were good that some proper prayer were apportioned, and they taught it. It were well if they would serve themselves of this form set down at the end of this diary.

14. Then go about the affairs of your house and proper employment, ever avoiding idleness, or too much earnestness of affection upon the things of the world: do your business prudently, temperately, diligently, humbly, charitably.

15. Let there be no idle person in or about your family, of beggars, or unemployed servants, but find them all work and meat; call upon them carefully; reprove them without reproaches or fierce railings. Be a master or a mistress and a friend to them, and exact of them to be faithful and diligent.

16. In your servants suffer any offence against yourself rather than against God; endure not that they should swear, or lie, or steal, or be wanton, or curse each other, or be railers, or slanderers, or tell-tales, or sowers of dissension in the family or amongst neighbours.

17. In all your entercourse with your neighbours in the day let your affairs be wholly matter of business or civility, and always managed with justice and charity; never let it be matter of curiosity or enquiry into the actions of others; always without censuring or rash judgment, without backbiting, slandering, or detraction: do it not yourself, neither converse with them that do. He or she that loves tale-bearers shall never be beloved or be innocent.

18. Before dinner and supper, as often as it is convenient or can be had, let the public prayers of the church, or some parts of them, be said publicly in the family, and let as many be present as you can. The same rule is also to be observed for Sundays and holy-days for their going to church. Let no servant be always detained, but relieved and provided for by changes.

19. Let your meal be temperate and wholesome, according to your quality and the season; begun and ended with prayer: and be sure that in

the course of your meal, and before you rise, you recollect yourself, and send your heart up to God with some holy and short ejaculation; remembering your duty, fearing to offend, or desiring and sighing after the eternal supper of the Lamb.

20. After meal, use what innocent refreshment you please to refresh your mind or body with these measures:

a) Let it not be too expensive of time.
b) Let it not hinder your devotion nor your business.
c) Let it be always without violence or passion.
d) Let it not then wholly take you up when you are at it; but let your heart retire with some holy thoughts and sober recollections, lest your mind be seized upon by it, and your affections carried off from better things: secure your affections for God, and sober and severe employment. Here you may be refreshed, but take heed you neither dwell here nor sin here; it is better never to use recreation than at any time to sin by it. But you may use recreation and avoid sin, and that's the best temper; but if you cannot do both, be more careful of your soul than of your refreshment, and that's the best security. But then in what you use to sin, carefully avoid it, and change your refreshment for some other instance in which you can be more innocent.

21. Entertain no long discourses with any, but if you can bring in something to season it with religion: as God must be in all your thoughts, so if it be possible let Him be in all your discourses, at least let Him be at one end of it; and when you cannot speak of Him, be sure you forget not to think of Him.

22. Toward the declining of the day be sure to retire to your private devotions. Read, meditate, and pray; in which I propound to you this method.

On the Lord's day meditate of the glories of the creation, the works of God, and all His benefits to mankind, and to you in particular. Then let your devotion be humbly upon your knees, to say over the viii. and xix. psalms, and sometimes the civ., with proper collects which you shall find or get: adding the form of thanksgiving which is in the Rule of Holy Living, in the manner as is there directed; or some other of your own choosing.

Meditate on
$\left\{\begin{array}{l}\text{Monday}\\\text{Tuesday}\\\text{Wednesday}\\\text{Thursday}\end{array}\right\}$
on
$\left\{\begin{array}{l}\text{a) Death.}\\\text{b) Judgment.}\\\text{c) Heaven.}\\\text{d) Hell.}\end{array}\right.$

Saying your usual prayers, and adding some ejaculations or short sayings of your own, according to the matter of your devotion.

On Friday, recollect your sins that you have done that week, and all your life-time; and let your devotion be to recite humbly and devoutly some penitential litanies, whereof you may serve yourself in the Rule of Holy Living.

On Saturday at the same time, meditate on the passion of our blessed Saviour and all the mysteries of our redemption, which you may do and pray together, by using the forms made to that purpose in the Rule of Holy Living. In all your devotions begin and end with the Lord's prayer.

Upon these two days and Sunday, you may choose some portions out of the Life of Christ, to read and help your meditation, proper to the mysteries you are appointed to meditate, or any other devout books.

23. Read not much at a time; but meditate as much as your time and capacity and disposition will give you leave: ever remembering, that little reading, and much thinking; little speaking, and much hearing; frequent and short prayers, and great devotion, is the best way to be wise, to be holy, to be devout.

24. Before you go to bed, bethink yourself of the day past; if nothing extraordinary hath happened, your conscience is the sooner examined; but if you have had any difference or disagreement with any one, or a great feast, or great company, or a great joy, or a great sorrow, then recollect yourself with the more diligence: ask pardon for what is amiss; give God thanks for what was good: if you have omitted any duty, make amends next day; and yet if nothing be found that was amiss, be humbled still and thankful, and pray God for pardon if any thing be amiss that you know not of. If all these things be in your offices, for your last prayers, be sure to apply them according to what you find in your examination: but if they be not, supply them with short ejaculations before you begin your last prayers, or at the end of them. Remember also, and be sure to take notice of all the mercies and deliverances of yourself and your relatives that day.

25. As you are going to bed, as often as you can conveniently, or that you are not hindered by company, meditate of death, and the preparations to your grave. When you lie down, close your eyes with a short prayer, commit yourself into the hands of your faithful Creator; and when you have done, trust Him with yourself, as you must do when you are dying.

26. If you awake in the night, fill up the intervals or spaces of your not sleeping by holy thoughts and aspirations, and remember the sins of your youth: and sometimes remember your dead, and that you shall die; and pray to God to send to you and all mankind a mercy in the day of judgment.

27. Upon the holy-days observe the same rules; only let the matter of your meditations be according to the mystery of the day. As upon Christmas day meditate on the birth of our blessed Saviour, and read that story and considerations which are in the Life of Christ: and to your ordinary devotions of every day add the prayer which is fitted to the mystery which you shall find in the Life of Christ, or in the Rule of Holy Living. Upon the day of the annunciation of our Lady-day, meditate on the incarnation of our blessed Saviour; and so upon all the festivals of the year.

28. Set apart one day for fasting once a week, or once a fortnight, or once a month at least, but let it be with these cautions and measures:

a) Do not choose a festival of the church for your fasting day.
b) Eat nothing till your afternoon devotions be done, if the health of your body will permit it: if not, take something, though it be the less.
c) When you eat your meal, let it be no more than ordinary, lest your fasting day end in an intemperate evening.
d) Let the actions of all the day be proportionable to it, abstain from your usual recreations on that day, and from greater mirth.
e) Be sure to design beforehand the purposes of your fast, either for repentance, or for mortification, or for the advantages of prayer; and let your devotions be accordingly. But be sure not to think fasting or eating fish, or eating nothing, of itself to be pleasing to God, but as it serves to one of these purposes.
f) Let some part of that day extraordinary be set apart for prayer, for the actions of repentance, for confession of sins, and for begging of those graces for whose sake you set apart that day.
g) Be sure that on that day you set apart something for the poor; for fasting and alms are the wings of prayer.

h) It is best to choose that day for your fast, which is used generally by all Christians, as Friday and Saturday; but do not call it a fasting day, unless also it be a day of extraordinary devotion and of alms.

29. From observation of all the days of your life, gather out the four extraordinaries:

a) All the great and shameful sins you have committed.
b) All the excellent or greater acts of piety which by God's grace you have performed.
c) All the great blessings you have received.
d) All the dangers and great sicknesses you have escaped.

And upon all the days of your extraordinary devotions, let them be brought forth, and produce their acts of virtue:

a) Repentance and prayers for pardon.
b) Resolutions to proceed and increase in good works.
c) Thanksgiving to God.
d) Fear and watchfulness, lest we fall into worse, as a punishment for our sin.

30. Keep a little catalogue of these, and at the foot of them set down what promises and vows you have made, and kept or broken, and do according as you are obliged.

31. Receive the blessed sacrament as often as you can: endeavour to have it once a month, besides the solemn and great festivals of the year.

32. Confess your sins often, hear the word of God, make religion the business of your life, your study and chiefest care, and be sure that in all things a spiritual guide take you by the hand.

THOU SHALT ALWAYS REJOICE IN THE EVENING, IF THOU DOST SPEND THE DAY VIRTUOUSLY.[106]

---

106. Thomas Kempis, *Imitation of Christ*, bk. 1.25.

425

CHAPTER FIVE

Holy Living and
Holy Dying

INTRODUCTION

A common interest in Jeremy Taylor, "that master of verbal magic," occasioned in a London bookshop the chance meeting of Logan Pearsall Smith with Robert Gathorne-Hardy. Smith was then preparing his anthology, and Gathorne-Hardy was compiling a bibliography of Taylor's writings; soon afterward, in the spring of 1929, *The Golden Grove* was published, combining the labors of each, and a friendship began that aroused new interest in Jeremy Taylor, at least among the bibliophiles. In early summer of that year they visited Golden Grove, "where Taylor had collected, like rare flowers, the images which glitter and tremble and blossom in his writings . . . and brought forth, as easily, it seems, as a thrush sings, the loveliest prose in all our lovely language."[1] Smith later wrote of the mystery, and holiness and beauty of this place and pilgrimage:

> Strange, as another sentimental pilgrim, Henry James, has expressed it, strange and special the effect of the empty places we stand and wonder in today for the sake of these vanished people; "the irresistible reconstruction, to the all but baffled vision, of irrevocable presences and aspects, the conscious, shining, mocking void, sad somehow with excess of serenity." Something of the effect he describes I have experienced at the Golden Grove in Wales, in which Jeremy Taylor preached

---

1. Gathorne-Hardy p. 2.

his golden sermons; in the rectory garden at Bemerton, where George Herbert butterfly-netted his butterfly conceits, and in the nearby soil of Sidney's Arcadia out of which, like a blue flower, the word *romantic* grew.[2]

Taylor left no verbal image of Golden Grove for posterity; his thoughts were elsewhere, for "He who stilleth the raging of the sea, and the noise of the waves, and the madness of the people, had provided a plank,"[3] and life and death became here Taylor's experience and his theme. As a poem *Spring and Fall* came two hundred years later, but Hopkins caught the Taylor mood of every Golden Grove:

> Margaret, are you grieving
> Over Goldengrove unleaving?
> Leaves like the things of man, you
> With your fresh thoughts care for, can you?
> Ah! as the heart grows older
> It will come to such sights colder
> By and by, nor spare a sigh
> Though worlds of wanwood leafmeal lie;
> And yet you will weep and know why.
> Now no matter, child, the name:
> Sorrow's springs are the same.
> Nor mouth had, no nor mind, expressed
> What heart heard of, ghost guessed:
> It is the blight man was born for,
> It is Margaret you mourn for.[4]

The mystery of spring and fall was clearly and sadly felt in lovely Golden Grove for in October 1650 Taylor lost, first, his "Margaret"—Frances, the Countess of Carbery, "the tender providence that shrouded him under her wings"—and, then, in April 1651, Phoebe, "the affectionate wife, who chose to beg with him than to feast without him." *Holy Living* (1650) and *Holy Dying* (1651) lead us into the very heart of these times, and this place, and their mystery of life and death:

---

2. Ibid. p. 3.
3. *Works* 5:341.
4. G. M. Hopkins, *Poems and Prose* (Middlesex: Penguin, 1953), p. 50.

Since we stay not here, being people but of a day's abode, and our age is like that of a fly and contemporary with a gourd, we must look somewhere else for an abiding city, a place in another country to fix our house in, whose walls and foundation is God, where we must find rest, or else be restless for ever. For whatever ease we can have or fancy here is shortly to be changed into sadness or tediousness, it goes away too soon, like the periods of our life; or stays too long, like the sorrows of a sinner. Its own weariness, or a contrary disturbance, is its load, or it is eased by its revolution into vanity and forgetfulness. And where either there is sorrow or an end of joy there can be no true felicity, which must be had by some instrument and in some period of our duration. We must carry up our affections to the mansions prepared for us above, where eternity is the measure, felicity is the state, angels are the company, the Lamb is the light, and God is the portion and inheritance.[5]

One year after the execution of the King in 1649 Taylor published the *Rule of Exercises of Holy Living,* and its lengthy subtitle neatly summarizes its contents: *The means and instruments of obtaining every virtue, and the remedies against every vice, and considerations serving to the resisting all temptations, together with prayers containing the Whole Duty of a Christian.* Biographers and critics do not regard this *Rule and Exercise* as Taylor's finest contribution to literature. Nor did Taylor. He discussed (1) holiness, (2) sobriety, (3) justice, and (4) the duties of religion in this new age of darkness in which men had lost their way. "I had reasons enough inviting me to draw into one body those advices which the several necessities of many men most use at some time or another and many of them daily: that by a collection of holy precepts they might less feel the want of personal and attending guides, and that the rules for conduct of souls might be committed to a book which they might always have; since they could not always have a prophet at their needs, nor be suffered to go up to the house of the Lord to inquire of the appointed oracle."[6] At Golden Grove Taylor remained and wrote his *Holy Living,* "regulations for behaviour after the flood, for men who

5. *Works* 3:276.
6. *Works* 3:2.

crowd back to the village only to find priest and altar, bell and prayer-book swept away"; and the prophet made loud his lamentation. One cannot appreciate the appeal *Holy Living* made to Anglican minds if one does not recognize the fierce and ironical resignation of its despairing, royalist preface:

> I have lived to see religion painted on banners, and thrust out of churches, and the temple turned into a tabernacle, and that tabernacle made an ambulatory, and covered with skins of beasts and torn curtains, and God to be worshipped, not as He is, the Father of our Lord Jesus, an afflicted Prince, the King of sufferings; nor as the God of peace; which two appellatives God newly took upon Him in the New Testament, and glories in for ever: but He is owned now rather as the Lord of hosts, which title He was pleased to lay aside when the kingdom of the gospel was preached by the Prince of peace. But when religion puts on armour, and God is not acknowledged by His New testament titles, religion may have in it the power of the sword, but not the power of godliness; and we may complain of this to God, and amongst them that are afflicted, but we have no remedy but what we must expect from the fellowship of Christ's sufferings, and the returns of the God of peace.[7]

Although *Holy Living* was written for those in the troubled waters of the times, and consequently impersonal and objective, nevertheless, there are at times glimpses, biographical and autobiographical, of life at Golden Grove and the spiritual habits of the holy man. He speaks, for example, of slipping aside several times during the day "to make frequent colloquies or short discoursings between God and his own soul"; again, "he rises early to see the preparation which the sun makes when he is coming forth from his chambers in the east"; furthermore, he sets apart "some solemn time every year, in which, for the time, quitting all worldly business, he may attend wholly to fasting and prayer, and the dressing of his soul by confessions, meditations and attendances upon God."

Jeremy Taylor's masterpiece, *The Rule and Exercises of Holy Dying*, was published on October 1651, on the first anniversary of Lady Car-

---

7. *Works* 3:1.

bery's death, and only six months after the death of his own wife; "in the coldness of his own hearthstone, in the like coldness at Golden Grove, he sat down and wrote one of the most beautiful prose compositions of the seventeenth century, a threnody palpitating with enthusiasm and emotion."[8]

> My Lord, it is your dear lady's anniversary, and she deserved the biggest honour, and the longest memory, and the fairest monument, and the most solemn mourning; and in order to it, give me leave, my lord, to cover her hearse with these following sheets. This book was intended first to minister to her piety, and she desired all good people should partake of the advantages which are here recorded; she knew how to live rarely well, and she desired to know how to die; and God taught her by an experiment. But since her work is done, and God supplied her with provisions of His own, before I could minister to her and perfect what she desired, it is necessary to present to your lordship those bundles of cypress which were intended to dress her closet, but come now to dress her hearse. My lord, both your lordship and myself have lately seen and felt such sorrows of death, and such sad departure of dearest friends, that it is more than high time we should think ourselves nearly concerned in the accidents. Death hath come so near to you as to fetch a portion from your very heart; and now you cannot choose but dig your own grave, and place your coffin in your eye, when the angel hath dressed your scene of sorrow and meditation with so particular and so near an object: and therefore, as it is my duty, I am come to minister to your pious thoughts, and to direct your sorrows, that they may turn into virtues and advantages.[9]

Holy Dying was the earliest work of its kind in English, and was in many ways remarkably new. The conception of death, for example, which prevailed in the poetry, philosophy and sermons of his day was anthropomorphic and positive—the skeleton that hides to surprise his victims, or "the unsparing pursuivant with eagles wings." By compari-

---

8. Gosse, p. 89.
9. *Works* 3:257.

son, Taylor is forceful and fresh, and shows death to be easy and simple, if it be shorn of "its pomp and solemn bugbears":

> It is the same harmless thing that a poor shepherd suffered yesterday, as a maid-servant to-day; and at the same time in which you die, in that very night a thousand creatures die with you, some wise men, and many fools; and the wisdom of the first will not quit him, and the folly of the last does not make him unable to die.[10]

The fifth chapter of *Holy Dying* is a lengthy discourse on the nature of the rite, which the Romans called *Extreme Unction*, and which he called *The Visitation of the Sick* or *the assistance that is to be done to dying persons by the ministry of their clergy guides*. This chapter, like the chapter on ecclesiastical penance in *Unum Necessarium*, situates the rite within the broader context of the subject matter, and prayers and care, pleading and healing surround the rite that is one of "those five commonly called sacraments":

> God who hath made no new covenant with dying persons distinct from the covenant of the living, hath also appointed no distinct sacraments for them . . . but the Holy Ghost, that anointing from above, descends upon us in several effluxes, but ever by the ministry of the Church. Our heads are anointed with that sacred unction in baptism; our foreheads in confirmation; our hands in ordination; all our senses in the visitation of the sick; and all by the ministry of especially deputed and instructed persons . . . and, therefore, it established as an apostlical rule; is any man sick among you? let him send for the elders of the church, and let them pray over him.[11]

In the more passionate parts of *Holy Dying* images bud and branch in a marvellous profusion, and Taylor, steeped in the loftiest poetry of antiquity, is eloquent; nowhere are the references so frequent to Lucretius, Horace and Lucian, to Persius, Ovid and Petronius Arbiter. It had

---

10. *Works* 3:339.
11. *Works* 3:401.

an instant effect in humanizing the piety of English readers, which controversy had bitterly enraged, and it soon became one with *Holy Living* in popular piety; together they inspired the Methodism of Wesley and the Tractarianism of Keble, whose sermon on "National Apostasy" at St. Mary's Church marks the beginning of the Oxford Movement.

Taylor's object in writing his books of devotion was to provide Anglicanism with those manuals of prayer and piety that were so popular in Romanism. Nowhere does he mention the *Introduction à la vie Dévote* of St. Francis de Sales, which clearly influenced him. Like de Sales, and other spiritual writers of his times, Taylor was a director of souls and a spiritual guide, especially for holy women; and just as de Sales wrote his *Introduction* for the edification of Madame de Clarmoisy, Taylor wrote his *Holy Living* and *Holy Dying* for Lady Carbery. These and his other devotional works became the favorite reading for generations of pious English men and women. John Keats, "whose name is writ in water," in the English cemetery in Rome, is not the least among the disciples:

> On Christmas Eve, as he [Keats] lay in bed staring glassily at the ceiling, he suddenly turned to Severn [his companion] and said: "I think a malignant being must have power over us— over whom the Almighty has little or no influence." He could not accept the bible completely. But was there not some other book? He had always trusted books. "I feel the horrible want of some faith—some hope—something to rest on now—there must be such a book." . . . [Keats in January asks Severn to find him a copy of Jeremy Taylor.] . . . "Finally, as the days passed and Keats became worse, Severn turned to Dr. Clark, who himself looked around Rome and found a volume of Jeremy Taylor, containing both *Holy Living* and *Holy Dying*, and Severn began to read from it to Keats every evening." . . . It was within another few days (January 25–26) that he could no longer "bear any books." But generally, from now until the end, he would turn to Severn and ask him to read for a while from Jeremy Taylor.[12]

---

12. W. J. Bate, *John Keats* (Cambridge: Harvard University Press, 1963), p. 691.

To The Right Honourable
and Truly Noble
Richard Lord Vaughan
Earl of Carbery, Knight of the Honourable
Order of the Bath[1]

My Lord,

I have lived to see religion painted upon banners, and thrust out of churches, and the temple turned into a tabernacle, and that tabernacle made ambulatory, and covered with skins of beasts and torn curtains, and God to be worshipped, not as He is, the Father of our Lord Jesus, an afflicted Prince, the King of sufferings; nor as the God of peace; which two appellatives God newly took upon Him in the New testament, and glories in for ever: but He is owned now rather as the Lord of hosts, which title He was pleased to lay aside when the kingdom of the gospel was preached by the Prince of peace. But when religion puts on armour, and God is not acknowledged by His New testament titles, religion may have in it the power of the sword, but not the power of godliness; and we may complain of this to God, and amongst them that are afflicted, but we have no remedy but what we must expect from the fellowship of Christ's sufferings, and the returns of the God of peace. In the mean time, and now that religion pretends to stranger actions upon new principles, and men are apt to prefer a prosperous error before an afflicted truth, and some will think they are religious enough if their worshippings have in them the prevailing ingredient; and the ministers of religion are so scattered, that they cannot unite to stop the inundation, and from chairs or pulpits, from their synods or tribunals, chastise the iniquity of the error, and the ambition of evil guides, and

---

1. *Works* 3:1–3.

435

the infidelity of the willingly seduced multitude, and that those few good people who have no other plot in their religion but to serve God and save their souls, do want such assistances of ghostly counsel as may serve their emergent needs, and assist their endeavours in the acquist of virtues, and relieve their dangers when they are tempted to sin and death; I thought I had reasons enough inviting me to draw into one body those advices, which the several necessities of many men must use at some time or other, and many of them daily: that by a collection of holy precepts they might less feel the want of personal and attending guides, and that the rules for conduct of souls might be committed to a book, which they might always have; since they could not always have a prophet at their needs, nor be suffered to go up to the house of the Lord to enquire of the appointed oracles.

I know, my lord, that there are some interested persons who add scorn to the afflictions of the church of England, and because she is afflicted by men, call her "forsaken of the Lord"; and because her solemn assemblies are scattered, think that the religion is lost, and the church divorced from God, supposing Christ, who was a man of sorrows, to be angry with His spouse when she is like Him, for that's the true state of the error; and that He, who promised His Spirit to assist His servants in their troubles, will, because they are in trouble, take away the Comforter from them; who cannot be a comforter, but while He cures our sadnesses, and relieves our sorrows, and turns our persecutions into joys, and crowns, and sceptres. But concerning the present state of the church of England, I consider that because we now want the blessings of external communion in many degrees, and the circumstances of a prosperous and unafflicted people, we are to take estimate of ourselves with single judgments, and every man is to give sentence concerning the state of his own soul by the precepts and rules of our Law-giver, not by the after-decrees and usages of the church; that is, by the essential parts of religion rather than by the uncertain significations of any exterior adherencies; for though it be uncertain, when a man is the member of a church, whether he be a member of Christ or no, because in the church's net there are fishes good and bad; yet we may be sure that if we be members of Christ, we are of a church to all purposes of spiritual religion and salvation; and in order to this, give me leave to speak this great truth:

That man does certainly belong to God who believes and is baptized into all the articles of the christian faith, and studies to improve his knowledge in the matters of God, so as may best make him to live a holy life; he that, in obedience to Christ, worships God diligently, frequently, and constantly, with natural religion, that is of prayer, praises, and thanksgiving; he that takes all opportunities to remember Christ's death by a frequent sacrament, as it can be had, or else by inward acts of understanding, will, and memory (which is the spiritual communion) supplies the want of the external rite; he that lives chastely, and is merciful; and despises the world, using it as a man, but never suffering it to rifle a duty; and is just in his dealing, and diligent in his calling; he that is humble in his spirit; and obedient to government; and content in his fortune and employment; he that does his duty because he loves God; and especially if after all this he be afflicted, and patient, or prepared to suffer affliction for the cause of God: the man that hath these twelve signs of grace and predestination does as certainly belong to God, and is His son as surely, as he is His creature.

And if my brethren in persecution, and in the bonds of the Lord Jesus, can truly shew these marks, they shall not need be troubled that others can shew a prosperous outside, great revenues, public assemblies, uninterrupted successions of bishops, prevailing armies, or any arm of flesh, or less certain circumstance. These are the marks of the Lord Jesus, and the characters of a Christian: this is a good religion; and these things God's grace hath put into our powers, and God's laws have made to be our duty, and the nature of men, and the needs of commonwealths, have made to be necessary. The other accidents and pomps of a church are things without our power, and are not in our choice: they are good to be used when they may be had, and they help to illustrate or advantage it: but if any of them constitute a church in the being of a society and a government, yet they are not of its constitution as it is christian, and hopes to be saved.

And now the case is so with us that we are reduced to that religion which no man can forbid; which we can keep in the midst of a persecution; by which the martyrs in the days of our fathers went to heaven; that by which we can be servants of God, and receive the spirit of Christ, and make use of His comforts, and live in His love and in charity with all men: and they that do so, cannot perish.

My lord, I have now described some general lines and features of that religion which I have more particularly set down in the following pages: in which I have neither served nor disserved the interest of any party of Christians, as they are divided by uncharitable names from the rest of their brethren; and no man will have reason to be angry with me for refusing to mingle in his unnecessary or vicious quarrels; especially while I study to do him good by conducting him in the narrow way to heaven, without intricating him in the labyrinths and wild turnings of questions and uncertain talkings. I have told what men ought to do, and by what means they may be assisted; and in most cases I have also told them why: and yet with as much quickness as I could think necessary to establish a rule, and not to engage in homily or discourse. . . .

The Rule and Exercises of Holy Living, etc.[2]

CHAPTER I
CONSIDERATION OF THE GENERAL INSTRUMENTS AND MEANS SERVING TO A HOLY LIFE, BY WAY OF INTRODUCTION

It is necessary that every man should consider, that since God hath given him an excellent nature, wisdom and choice, an understanding soul and an immortal spirit, having made him lord over the beasts, and but a little lower than the angels; He hath also appointed for him a work and a service great enough to employ those abilities, and hath also designed him to a state of life after this, to which he can only arrive by that service and obedience: and therefore as every man is wholly God's own portion by the title of creation, so all our labours and care, all our powers and faculties, must be wholly employed in the service of God, even all the days of our life; that this life being ended, we may live with Him for ever.

Neither is it sufficient that we think of the service of God as a work of the least necessity, or of small employment, but that it be done by us as God intended it; that it be done with great earnestness and passion, with much zeal and desire; that we refuse no labour, that we bestow upon it much time; that we use the best guides, and arrive at the end of glory by all the ways of grace, of prudence, and religion.

And indeed if we consider, how much of our lives is taken up by the needs of nature; how many years are wholly spent before we come to any use of reason; how many years more before that reason is useful to us to any great purposes; how imperfect our discourse is made by our evil education, false principles, ill company, bad examples, and want of experience; how many parts of our wisest and best years are spent in

---

2. *Works* 3:4ff.

eating and sleeping, in necessary businesses and unnecessary vanities, in worldly civilities and less useful circumstances, in the learning arts and sciences, languages or trades: that little portion of hours that is left for the practices of piety and religious walking with God is so short and trifling, that were not the goodness of God infinitely great, it might seem unreasonable or impossible for us to expect of Him eternal joys in heaven, even after the well spending those few minutes which are left for God and God's service after we have served ourselves and our own occasions.

And yet it is considerable that the fruit which comes from the many days of recreation and vanity, is very little; and although we scatter much, yet we gather but little profit: but from the few hours we spend in prayer and the exercises of a pious life the return is great and profitable; and what we sow in the minutes and spare portions of a few years, grows up to crowns and sceptres in a happy and a glorious eternity.

Therefore, first, although it cannot be enjoined that the greatest part of our time be spent in the direct actions of devotion and religion, yet it will become not only a duty but also a great providence, to lay aside for the services of God and the businesses of the Spirit as much as we can; because God rewards our minutes with long and eternal happiness; and the greater portion of our time we give to God, the more we treasure up for ourselves; and "no man is a better merchant than he that lays out his time upon God, and his money upon the poor."

Only, secondly, it becomes us to remember, and to adore God's goodness for it, that God hath not only permitted us to serve the necessities of our nature, but hath made them to become parts of our duty; that if we, by directing these actions to the glory of God, intend them as instruments to continue our persons in His service, He, by adopting them into religion, may turn our nature into grace, and accept our natural actions as actions of religion. God is pleased to esteem it for a part of His service, if we eat or drink, so it be done temperately, and as may best preserve our health, that our health may enable our services towards Him: and there is no one minute of our lives, after we are come to the use of reason, but we are or may be doing the work of God, even then when we most of all serve ourselves.

To which if we add, thirdly, that in these and all other actions of our lives we always stand before God, acting and speaking, and thinking in His presence, and that it matters not that our conscience is sealed with secrecy, since it lies open to God; it will concern us to behave ourselves carefully, as in the presence of our judge.

These three considerations rightly managed, and applied to the several parts and instances of our lives, will be like Elisha stretched upon the child, apt to put life and quickness into every part of it, and to make us live the life of grace and do the work of God.

I shall therefore by way of introduction reduce these three to practice, and shew how every Christian may improve all and each of these to the advantage of piety in the whole course of his life: that if he please to bear but one of them upon his spirit, he may feel the benefit, like an universal instrument, helpful in all spiritual and temporal actions.

Section I
The First General Instrument of Holy Living, Care of Our Time

He that is choice of his time will also be choice of his company, and choice of his actions: lest the first engage him in vanity and loss; and the latter, by being criminal, be a throwing his time and himself away, and a going back in the accounts of eternity.

God hath given to man a short time here upon earth, and yet upon this short time eternity depends; but so that for every hour of our life, after we are persons capable of laws and know good from evil, we must give account to the great Judge of men and angels. And this is it which our blessed Saviour told us, that we must account for every idle word: not meaning that every word which is not designed to edification, or is less prudent, shall be reckoned for a sin; but that the time which we spend in our idle talking and unprofitable discoursings, that time which might and ought to have been employed to spiritual and useful purposes, that is to be accounted for.

For we must remember that we have a great work to do, many enemies to conquer, many evils to prevent, much danger to run through, many difficulties to be mastered, many necessities to serve, and much good to do, many children to provide for, or many friends to support, or many poor to relieve, or many diseases to cure, besides the needs of nature and of relation, our private and our public cares, and duties of the world which necessity and the providence of God hath adopted into the family of Religion.

And that we need not fear this instrument to be a snare to us, or that the duty must end in scruple, vexation, and eternal fears, we must remember that the life of every man may be so ordered, and indeed must, that it may be a perpetual serving of God: the greatest trouble and most busy trade and worldly incumbrances, when they are necessary, or

441

charitable, or profitable in order to any of those ends which we are bound to serve, whether public or private, being a doing God's work. For God provides the good things of the world to serve the needs of nature by the labours of the ploughman, the skill and pains of the artisan, and the dangers and traffic of the merchant: these men are in their calling the ministers of the divine providence, and the stewards of the creation, and servants of a great family of God, the world, in the employment of procuring necessaries for food and clothing, ornament and physic. In their proportions also a king and a priest and a prophet, a judge and an advocate, doing the works of their employment according to their proper rules, are doing the work of God, because they serve those necessities, which God hath made, and yet made no provisions for them but by their ministry. So that no man can complain that his calling takes him off from religion: his calling itself and his very worldly employment in honest trades and offices is a serving of God; and if it be moderately pursued, and according to the rules of christian prudence, will leave void spaces enough for prayers and retirements of a more spiritual religion.

God hath given every man work enough to do, that there shall be no room for idleness; and yet hath so ordered the world that there shall be space for devotion: he that hath the fewest businesses of the world, is called upon to spend more time in the dressing of his soul; and he that hath the most affairs, may so order them that they shall be a service of God; whilst at certain periods they are blessed with prayers and actions of religion, and all day long are hallowed by a holy intention.

However, so long as idleness is quite shut out from our lives, all the sins of wantonness, softness, and effeminacy, are prevented, and there is but little room left for temptation; and therefore to a busy man temptation is fain to climb up together with his businesses, and sins creep upon him only by accidents and occasions: whereas to an idle person they come in a full body, and with open violence, and the impudence of a restless importunity.

Idleness is called the sin of Sodom and her daughters,[3] and indeed is "the burial of a living man";[4] an idle person being so useless to any purposes of God and man that he is like one that is dead, unconcerned in the changes and necessities of the world; and he only lives to spend his

---

3. Ezek. 16:49.
4. Seneca, *Letters* (82), LCL, vol. 2, p. 242.

time, and eat the fruits of the earth: like a vermin or a wolf; when their time comes they die and perish, and in the mean time do no good; they neither plough nor carry burdens; all that they do either is unprofitable or mischievous.

Idleness is the greatest prodigality in the world: it throws away that which is invaluable in respect of its present use, and irreparable when it is past, being to be recovered by no power of art or nature. . . .

Section II
The Second General Instrument of Holy Living, Purity of Intention

That we should intend and design God's glory in every action we do, whether it be natural or chosen, is expressed by St. Paul,[5] "whether ye eat or drink, do all to the glory of God." Which rule when we observe, every action of nature becomes religious, and every meal is an act of worship and shall have its reward in its proportion, as well as an act of prayer. Blessed be that goodness and grace of God which, out of infinite desire to glorify and save mankind, would make the very works of nature capable of becoming acts of virtue, that all our life-time we may do Him service.

This grace is so excellent that it sanctifies the most common action of our life; and yet so necessary, that without it the very best actions of our devotions are imperfect and vicious. For he that prays out of custom, or gives alms for praise, or fasts to be accounted religious, is but a pharisee in his devotion, and a beggar in his alms, and a hypocrite in his fast. But a holy end sanctifies all these and all other actions which can be made holy, and gives distinction to them, and procures acceptance.

For as to know the end distinguishes a man from a beast, so to choose a good end distinguishes him from an evil man. Hezekiah repeated his good deeds upon his sick-bed, and obtained favour of God; but the pharisee was accounted insolent for doing[6] the same thing: because this man did it to upbraid his brother, the other to obtain a mercy of God. Zacharias questioned with the angel about his message, and was made speechless for his incredulity; but the blessed Virgin Mary questioned too, and was blameless; for she did it to enquire after the manner of the thing, but he did not believe the thing itself: he doubted of God's power, or the truth of the messenger; but she only of

---

5. 1 Cor. 10:31.
6. Luke 6:42.

her own incapacity. This was it which distinguished the mourning of David from the exclamation of Saul; the confession of Pharaoh from that of Manasses; the tears of Peter from the repentance of Judas: for the praise is not in the deed done, but in the manner of its doing.[7] If a man visits his sick friend, and watches at his pillow for charity's sake, and because of his old affection, we approve it: but if he does it in hope of legacy, he is a vulture, and only watches for the carcase. The same things are honest and dishonest: the manner of doing them, and the end of the design, makes the separation.

Holy intention is to the actions of a man that which the soul is to the body, or form to its matter, or the root to the tree, or the sun to the world, or the fountain to a river, or the base to a pillar: for without these the body is a dead trunk, the matter is sluggish, the tree is a block, the world is darkness, the river is quickly dry, the pillar rushes into flatness and a ruin; and the action is sinful, or unprofitable and vain. The poor farmer that gave a dish of cold water to Artaxerxes[8] was rewarded with a golden goblet; and he that gives the same to a disciple in the name of a disciple, shall have a crown: but if he gives water in despite when the disciple needs wine or a cordial, his reward shall be to want that water to cool his tongue.

But this duty must be reduced to rules:

Rules for Our Intentions

1. In every action reflect upon the end; and in your undertaking it, consider why you do it, and what you propound to yourself for a reward, and to your action as its end.

2. Begin every action in the name of the Father, of the Son, and of the Holy Ghost: the meaning of which is, first, that we be careful that we do not the action without the permission or warrant of God: secondly, that we design it to the glory of God, if not in the direct action, yet at least in its consequence; if not in the particular, yet at least in the whole order of things and accidents: thirdly, that it may be so blessed, that what you intend for innocent and holy purposes, may not by any chance, or abuse, or misunderstanding of men, be turned into evil, or made the occasion of sin.

---

7. Seneca, *Moral Essays* (Benefits), LCL, vol. 3, p. 22.
8. Plutarch, *Lives*, LCL, vol. 2, p. 134.

Section III
The Third General Instrument of Holy Living:
or the Practice of the Presence of God

That God is present in all places, that He sees every action, hears all discourses, and understands every thought, is no strange thing to a christian ear, who hath been taught this doctrine, not only by right reason, and the consent of all the wise men in the world, but also by God himself in holy scripture. "Am I a God at hand, saith the Lord, and not a God afar off? can any hide himself in secret places, that I shall not see him? saith the Lord; do not I fill heaven and earth?"[9] "neither is there any creature that is not manifest in His sight, but all things are naked and open to the eyes of Him with whom we have to do";[10] "for in Him we live, and move, and have our being."[11] God is wholly in every place, included in no place; not bound with cords except those of love; not divided into parts, not changeable into several shapes; filling heaven and earth with His present power, and with His never absent nature: so St. Augustine[12] expresses this article. So that we may imagine God to be as the air and the sea, and we all enclosed in His circle, wrapped up in the lap of His infinite nature; or as infants in the wombs of their pregnant mothers: and we can no more be removed from the presence of God than from our own being.

Several Manners of the Divine Presence

The presence of God is understood by us in several manners, and to several purposes.

1. God is present by His essence; which, because it is infinite, cannot be contained within the limits of any place; and because He is of an essential purity and spiritual nature, He cannot be undervalued by being supposed present in the places of unnatural uncleanness: because as the sun, reflecting upon the mud of strands and shores, is unpolluted in its beams, so is God not dishonoured when we suppose Him in every of His creatures, and in every part of every one of them; and is still as unmixt with any unhandsome adherence as is the soul in the bowels of the body.

---

9. Jer. 23:23–24.
10. Heb. 4:13.
11. Acts 17:28.
12. Augustine, *City of God*, PL 41–219.

2. God is every where present by His power. He rolls the orbs of heaven with His hand; He fixes the earth with His foot; He guides all the creatures with His eye, and refreshes them with His influence: He makes the powers of hell to shake with His terrors, and binds the devils with His word, and throws them out with His command; and sends the angels on embassies with His decrees: He hardens the joints of infants, and confirms the bones, when they are fashioned beneath secretly in the earth. He it is that assists at the numerous productions of fishes; and there is not one hollowness in the bottom of the sea but He shews Himself to be Lord of it, by sustaining there the creatures that come to dwell in it: and in the wilderness, the bittern and the stork, the dragon and the satyr, the unicorn and the elk, live upon His provisions, and revere His power, and feel the force of His almightiness.

3. God is more specially present in some places by the several and more special manifestations of Himself to extraordinary purposes. First, by glory. Thus His seat is in heaven; because there He sits encircled with all the outward demonstrations of His glory, which He is pleased to shew to all the inhabitants of those His inward and secret courts. And thus they that "die in the Lord," may be properly said to be "gone to God"; with whom although they were before, yet now they enter into His courts, into the secret of His tabernacle, into the retinue and splendour of His glory. That is called walking with God; but this is dwelling, or being, with Him. "I desire to be dissolved and to be with Christ"; so said St. Paul. But this manner of the divine presence is reserved for the elect people of God, and for their portion in their country.

4. God is by grace and benediction specially present in holy places,[13] and in the solemn assemblies of His servants. If holy people meet in grots and dens of the earth, when persecution or a public necessity disturbs the public order, circumstance and convenience, God fails not to come thither to them: but God is also, by the same or a greater reason, present there where they meet ordinarily by order, and public authority: there God is present ordinarily, that is, at every such meeting. God will go out of His way to meet His saints, when themselves are forced out of their way of order by a sad necessity: but else God's usual way is to be present in those places where His servants are

---

13. Matt. 18:20; Heb. 10:25.

appointed ordinarily[14] to meet. But His presence there signifies nothing but a readiness to hear their prayers, to bless their persons, to accept their offices, and to like even the circumstance of orderly and public meeting. For thither the prayers of consecration, the public authority separating it, and God's love of order, and the reasonable customs of religion, have, in ordinary, and in a certain degree, fixed this manner of His presence; and He loves to have it so.

5. God is especially present in the hearts of His people, by His Holy Spirit: and indeed the hearts of holy men are temples in the truth of things, and in type and shadow they are heaven itself. For God reigns in the hearts of His servants: there is His kingdom. The power of grace hath subdued all His enemies: there is His power. They serve Him night and day, and give Him thanks and praise: that is His glory. This is the religion and worship of God in the temple. The temple itself is the heart of man; Christ is the high priest, who from thence sends up the incense of prayers, and joins them to His own intercession, and presents all together to His Father; and the Holy Ghost, by His dwelling there, hath also consecrated it into a temple,[15] and God dwells in our hearts by faith, and Christ by His spirit, and the Spirit by His purities: so that we are also cabinets of the mysterious Trinity; and what is this short of heaven itself, but as infancy is short of manhood, and letters of words? The same state of life it is, but not the same age. It is heaven in a looking-glass, dark but yet true, representing the beauties of the soul, and the graces of God, and the images of His eternal glory, by the reality of a special presence.

6. God is specially present in the consciences of all persons, good and bad, by way of testimony and judgment; that is, He is there a remembrancer to call our actions to mind, a witness to bring them to judgment, and a judge to acquit or to condemn. And although this manner of presence is in this life after the manner of this life, that is, imperfect, and we forget many actions of our lives; yet the greatest changes of our state of grace or sin, our most considerable actions, are always present, like capital letters to an aged and dim eye; and at the day of judgment God shall draw aside the cloud, and manifest this manner of His presence more notoriously, and make it appear that He was an

---

14. 1 Kings 5:9; Ps. 138:1–2.
15. 1 Cor. 3:16; 2 Cor. 6:16.

observer of our very thoughts; and that He only laid those things by, which, because we covered with dust and negligence, were not then discerned. But when we are risen from our dust and imperfection, they all appear plain and legible.

Now the consideration of this great truth is of a very universal use in the whole course of the life of a Christian. All the consequents and effects of it are universal. He that remembers that God stands a witness and a judge beholding every secrecy, besides his impiety must have put on impudence, if he be not much restrained in his temptation to sin. "For the greatest part of sin is taken away[16] if a man have a witness of his conversation": and he is a great despiser of God, who sends a boy away when he is going to commit fornication, and yet will dare to do it though he knows God is present, and cannot be sent off: as if the eye of a little boy were more awful than the all-seeing eye of God. He is to be feared in public, He is to be feared in private: if you go forth, He spies you; if you go in, He sees you: when you light the candle, He observes you; when you put it out, then also God marks you. Be sure that while you are in His sight, you behave yourself as becomes so holy a presence. But if you will sin, retire yourself wisely, and go where God cannot see: for no where else can you be safe. And certainly if men would always actually consider and really esteem this truth, that God is the great eye of the world, always watching over our actions, and an ever-open ear to hear all our words, and an unwearied arm ever lifted up to crush a sinner into ruin, it would be the readiest way in the world to make sin to cease from amongst the children of men, and for men to approach to the blessed estate of the saints in heaven, who cannot sin, for they always walk in the presence and behold the face of God. . . .

A Prayer for Preacher and Guide

Lord, sanctify and forgive all that I have tempted to evil by my discourse or my example; instruct them in the right way whom I have led to error, and let me never run further on the score of sin: but do Thou blot out all the evils I have done, by the spunge of Thy passion, and the blood of Thy cross: and give me a deep and excellent repentance, and a free and a gracious pardon, that Thou mayest answer for me, O Lord, and enable me to stand upright in judgment. For in Thee, O Lord, have I trusted; let me never be confounded: pity me and

---

16. Seneca, *Letters* (11), LCL, vol. 1, p. 64.

instruct me, guide me and support me, pardon me and save me, for my sweet Saviour Jesus Christ his sake. Amen.

A Prayer for Patron and Benefactors

O almighty God, Thou fountain of all good, of all excellency both to men and angels, extend Thine abundant favour and loving kindness to my patron, to all my friends and benefactors. Reward them and make them plentiful recompense for all the good which from Thy merciful providence they have conveyed unto me; let the light of Thy countenance shine upon them, and let them never come into any affliction or sadness but such as may be an instrument of Thy glory and their eternal comfort; forgive them all their sins; let Thy divinest spirit preserve them from all deeds of darkness; let Thy ministering angels guard their persons from the violence of the spirits of darkness; and Thou who knowest every degree of their necessity by Thy infinite wisdom, give supply to all their needs by Thy glorious mercy, preserving their persons, sanctifying their hearts, and leading them in the ways of righteousness, by the waters of comfort, to the land of eternal rest and glory, through Jesus Christ our Lord. Amen.

CHAPTER IV

Of Christian Religion

Religion in a large sense doth signify the whole duty of man, comprehending in it justice, charity, and sobriety; because all these being commanded by God, they become a part of that honour and worship which we are bound to pay to Him: and thus the word is used in St. James, "Pure religion and undefiled before God and the Father is this, to visit the fatherless and widows in their affliction, and to keep himself unspotted from the world."[17] But in a more restrained sense, it is taken for that part of duty which particularly relates to God in our worshippings and adoration of Him, in confessing His excellencies, loving His person, admiring His goodness, believing His word, and doing all that which may in a proper and direct manner do Him honour: it contains the duties of the first table only; and so it is called godli-

---

17. James 1:27.

ness,[18] and is by St. Paul distinguished from justice and sobriety. In this sense I am now to explicate the parts of it.

Of the Internal Actions of Religion

Those I call the internal actions of religion, in which the soul only is employed, and ministers to God in the special actions of faith, hope, and charity. Faith believes the revelations of God, hope expects His promises, and charity loves His excellencies and mercies. Faith gives our understanding to God, hope gives up all the passions and affections to heaven and heavenly things, and charity gives the will to the service of God. Faith is opposed to infidelity, hope to despair, charity to enmity and hostility: and these three sanctify the whole man, and make our duty to God and obedience to His commandments to be chosen, reasonable, and delightful, and therefore to be entire, persevering, and universal.

Section I
Of Faith
The Acts and Offices of Faith Are,

1. To believe every thing which God hath revealed to us; and when once we are convinced that God hath spoken it, to make no further enquiry, but humbly to submit; ever remembering that there are some things which our understanding cannot fathom, nor search out their depth.

2. To believe nothing concerning God but what is honourable and excellent, as knowing that belief to be no honouring of God, which entertains of Him any dishonourable thoughts. Faith is the parent of charity, and whatsoever faith entertains must be apt to produce love to God; but he that believes God to be cruel or unmerciful, or a rejoicer in the unavoidable damnation of the greatest part of mankind, or that He speaks one thing and privately means another, thinks evil thoughts concerning God, and such as for which we should hate a man, and therefore are great enemies of faith, being apt to destroy charity. Our faith concerning God must be as Himself hath revealed and described His own excellencies, and in our discourses we must remove from Him all imperfection, and attribute to Him all excellency.

3. To give ourselves wholly up to Christ in heart and desire, to become disciples of His doctrine with choice (besides conviction), being

---

18. Titus 2:12.

in the presence of God but as idiots, that is, without any principles of our own to hinder the truth of God; but sucking in greedily all that God hath taught us, believing it infinitely, and loving to believe it. For this is an act of love, reflected upon faith; or an act of faith, leaning upon love.

4. To believe all God's promises, and that whatsoever is promised in scripture shall on God's part be as surely performed as if we had it in possession; this act makes us to rely upon God with the same confidence as we did on our parents when we were children, when we made no doubt but whatsoever we needed we should have it if it were in their power.

5. To believe also the conditions of the promise, or that part of the revelation which concerns our duty. Many are apt to believe the article of remission of sins, but they believe it without the condition of repentance, or the fruits of holy life; and that is to believe the article otherwise than God intended it. For the covenant of the gospel is the great object of faith, and that supposes our duty to answer His grace; that God will be our God so long as we are His people: the other is not faith, but flattery.

6. To profess publicly the doctrine of Jesus Christ, openly owning whatsoever He hath revealed and commanded, not being ashamed of the word of God, or of any practices enjoined by it; and this, without complying with any man's interest, not regarding favour, nor being moved with good words, not fearing disgrace, or loss, or inconvenience, or death itself.

7. To pray without doubting, without weariness, without faintness, entertaining no jealousies or suspicions of God, but being confident of God's hearing us, and of His returns to us, whatsoever the manner or the instance be, that if we do our duty it will be gracious and merciful.

These acts of faith are in several degrees in the servants of Jesus; some have it but as a grain of mustard seed, some grow up to a plant, some have the fulness of faith; but the least faith that is, must be a persuasion so strong as to make us undertake the doing of all that duty which Christ built upon the foundation of believing.

Section II
Of the Hope of a Christian
Faith differs from hope, in the extension of its object, and in the intension of degree. St. Austin thus accounts their differences:[19] faith is

---

19. Augustine, *Enchiridion*, PL 40.231.

of all things revealed, good and bad, rewards and punishments, of things past, present, and to come, of things that concern us, and of things that concern us not; but hope hath for its object things only that are good, and fit to be hoped for, future, and concerning ourselves: and because these things are offered to us upon conditions of which we may so fail, as we may change our will, therefore our certainty is less than the adherences of faith; which (because faith relies only upon one proposition, that is, the truth of the word of God) cannot be made uncertain in themselves, though the object of our hope may become uncertain to us and to our possession. For it is infallibly certain that there is heaven for all the godly, and for me amongst them all, if I do my duty: but that I shall enter into heaven is the object of my hope, not of my faith; and is so sure, as it is certain I shall persevere in the ways of God.

The Acts of Hope Are,

1. To rely upon God with a confident expectation of His promises, ever esteeming that every promise of God is a magazine of all that grace and relief which we can need in that instance for which the promise is made; every degree of hope is a degree of confidence.

2. To esteem all the danger of an action, and the possibilities of miscarriage, and every cross accident that can intervene, to be no defect on God's part, but either a mercy on His part, or a fault on ours: for then we shall be sure to trust in God, when we see Him to be our confidence, and ourselves the cause of all mischances; the hope of a Christian is prudent and religious.

3. To rejoice in the midst of a misfortune or seeming sadness, knowing that this may work for good, and will, if we be not wanting to our souls. This is a direct act of hope, to look through the cloud, and look for a beam of the light from God; and this is called in scripture, "rejoicing in tribulation," when "the God of hope fills us with all joy in believing": every degree of hope brings a degree of joy.

4. To desire, to pray, and to long for, the great object of our hope, the mighty price of our high calling; and to desire the other things of this life as they are promised, that is, so far as they are made necessary and useful to us in order to God's glory and the great end of souls. . . .

Section III
Of Charity, or the Love of God
Love is the greatest thing that God can give us, for Himself is love; and it is the greatest thing we can give to God, for it will also give

ourselves, and carry with it all that is ours. The apostle calls it the band of perfection; it is the old, and it is the new, and it is the great commandment, and it is all the commandments; for it is the fulfilling of the law. It does the work of all other graces, without any instrument but its own immediate virtue. For as the love to sin makes a man sin against all his own reason, and all the discourses of wisdom, and all the advices of his friends, and without temptation, and without opportunity; so does the love of God; it makes a man chaste without the laborious arts of fasting and exterior disciplines, temperate in the midst of feasts, and is active enough to choose it without any intermedial appetites, and reaches at glory through the very heart of grace, without any other arms but those of love. It is a grace that loves God for Himself, and our neighbours for God. The consideration of God's goodness and bounty, the experience of those profitable and excellent emanations from Him, may be, and most commonly are, the first motive of our love; but when we are once entered, and have tasted the goodness of God, we love the spring for its own excellency, passing from passion to reason, from thanking to adoring, from sense to spirit, from considering ourselves to an union with God: and this is the image and little representation of heaven; it is beatitude in picture, or rather the infancy and beginnings of glory.

We need no incentives by way of special enumeration to move us to the love of God; for we cannot love any thing for any reason real or imaginary, but that excellence is infinitely more eminent in God. There can but two things create love, perfection and usefulness; to which answer on our part, first, admiration, and secondly, desire; and both these are centred in love. For the entertainment of the first, there is in God an infinite nature, immensity or vastness without extension or limit, immutability, eternity, omnipotence, omniscience, holiness, dominion, providence, bounty, mercy, justice, perfection in Himself, and the end to which all things and all actions must be directed, and will at last arrive. The consideration of which may be heightened, if we consider our distance from all these glories; our smallness and limited nature, our nothing, our inconstancy, our age like a span, our weakness and ignorance, our poverty, our inadvertency and inconsideration, our disabilities and disaffections to do good, our harsh natures and unmerciful inclinations, our universal iniquity, and our necessities and dependencies, not only on God originally and essentially, but even our need of the meanest of God's creatures, and our being obnoxious to the weakest and most contemptible. But for the entertainment of the second, we may consider that in Him is a torrent of pleasure for the voluptuous; He is the fountain of honour for the ambitious, an inexhaustible treasure for the covetous. Our vices are in love with fantastic pleasures and images of perfection, which are truly and really to be found no where but in God.[20] And therefore our virtues have such proper objects, that it is but reasonable they should all turn into love; for certain it is that this love will turn all into virtue. For in the scrutinies for righteousness and judgment, when it is enquired whether such a person be a good man or no, the meaning is not, what does he believe, or what does he hope, but what he loves.[21]

The Acts of Love to God Are,

1. Love does all things which may please the beloved person, it performs all his commandments; and this is one of the greatest instances and arguments of our love that God requires of us, "this is love, that we keep His commandments": love is obedient.

2. It does all the intimations and secret significations of his pleasure whom we love; and this is an argument of a great degree of it. The first instance is it that makes the love accepted: but this gives a greatness and singularity to it. The first is the least, and less than it cannot do our duty; but without this second we cannot come to perfection. Great love is also pliant and inquisitive in the instances of its expression.

3. Love gives away all things that so he may advance the interest of the beloved person: it relieves all that he would have relieved, and spends itself in such real significations as it is enabled withal. He never loved God that will quit any thing of his religion to save his money: love is always liberal and communicative.

4. It suffers all things that are imposed by its beloved, or that can happen for his sake, or that intervene in his service, cheerfully, sweetly, willingly; expecting that God should turn them into good, and instruments of felicity. "Charity hopeth all things, endureth all things": love is patient and content with any thing, so it be together with its beloved.

5. Love is also impatient of any thing that may displease the beloved person, hating all sin as the enemy of its friend; for love contracts all the same relations, and marries the same friendships and the same hatreds; and all affection to a sin is perfectly inconsistent with the love

---

20. Augustine, *Confessions*, PL 32.116.
21. Augustine, *Enchiridion*, PL 40.231.

of God. Love is not divided between God and God's enemy: we must love God with all our heart; that is, give Him a whole and undivided affection, having love for nothing else but such things which He allows and which He commands or loves Himself.

Section IV
Of Reading or Hearing the Word of God

Reading and hearing the word of God are but the several circumstances of the same duty; instrumental especially to faith, but consequently to all other graces of the Spirit. It is all one to us whether by the eye or by the ear the Spirit conveys His precepts to us. If we hear St. Paul saying to us, that "whoremongers and adulterers God will judge," or read it in one of his epistles, in either of them we are equally and sufficiently instructed. The scriptures read are the same thing to us which the same doctrine was when it was preached by the disciples of our blessed Lord, and we are to learn of either with the same dispositions. There are many that cannot read the word, and they must take it in by the ear; and they that can read find the same word of God by the eye. It is necessary that all men learn it in some way or other, and it is sufficient in order to their practice that they learn it any way. The word of God is all those commandments and revelations, those promises and threatenings, the stories and sermons recorded in the Bible; nothing else is the word of God that we know of by any certain instrument. The good books and spiritual discourses, the sermons or homilies written or spoken by men, are but the word of men, or rather explications of, and exhortations according to, the word of God; but of themselves they are not the word of God. In a sermon, the text only is in a proper sense to be called God's word: and yet good sermons are of great use and convenience for the advantages of religion. He that preaches an hour together against drunkenness with the tongue of men or angels, hath spoke no other word of God but this, "be not drunk with wine, wherein there is excess"; and he that writes that sermon in a book, and publishes that book, hath preached to all that read it a louder sermon than could be spoken in a church. This I say to this purpose, that we may separate truth from error, popular opinions from substantial truths. For God preaches to us in the scripture, and by His secret assistances and spiritual thoughts and holy motions; good men preach to us when they, by popular arguments, and human arts and compliances, expound and press any of those doctrines which God hath preached unto us in His holy word. But,

First, the Holy Ghost is certainly the best preacher in the world, and the words of scripture the best sermons.

Secondly, all the doctrine of salvation is plainly set down there, that the most unlearned person by hearing it read may understand all his duty. What can be plainer spoken than this, "thou shalt not kill"; "be not drunk with wine"; "husbands, love your wives"; "whatsoever ye would that men should do to you, do ye so to them": the wit of man cannot more plainly tell us our duty, or more fully, than the Holy Ghost hath done already.

Thirdly, good sermons and good books are of excellent use, but yet they can serve no other end but that we practise the plain doctrines of scripture.

Fourthly, what Abraham in the parable said concerning the brethren of the rich man is here very proper, "they have Moses and the prophets, let them hear them; but if they refuse to hear these, neither will they believe though one should arise from the dead to preach unto them."[22]

Fifthly, reading the holy scriptures is a duty expressly commanded us,[23] and is called in scripture "preaching": all other preaching is the effect of human skill and industry, and although of great benefit, yet it is but an ecclesiastical ordinance; the law of God concerning preaching being expressed in the matter of reading the scriptures, and hearing that word of God which is, and as it is, there described.

But this duty is reduced to practice in the following rules:

Rules for Hearing or Reading the Word of God

1. Set apart some portion of thy time, according to the opportunities of thy calling and necessary employment, for the reading of holy scripture; and if it be possible, every day read or hear some of it read; you are sure that book teaches all truth, commands all holiness, and promises all happiness.

2. When it is in your power to choose, accustom yourself to such portions which are most plain and certain duty, and which contain the story of the life and death of our blessed Saviour. Read the gospels, the psalms of David; and especially those portions of scripture which by the wisdom of the church are appointed to be publicly read upon Sundays

---

22. Luke 16:29–31.
23. Deut. 31:11; Luke 24:45; Matt. 22:29; Acts 15:21; 2 Tim. 3:16; Rev. 1:3.

and holidays, viz., the epistles and gospels. In the choice of any other portions you may advise with a spiritual guide, that you may spend your time with most profit.

3. Fail not diligently to attend to the reading of holy scriptures upon those days wherein it is most publicly and solemnly read in churches; for at such times, besides the learning our duty, we obtain a blessing along with it; it becoming to us upon those days a part of the solemn divine worship.

4. When the word of God is read or preached to you, be sure you be of a ready heart and mind, free from worldly cares and thoughts, diligent to hear, careful to mark, studious to remember, and desirous to practise all that is commanded, and to live according to it: do not hear for any other end but to become better in your life, and to be instructed in every good work, and to increase in the love and service of God.

5. Beg of God by prayer that He would give you the spirit of obedience and profit, and that He would by His spirit write the word in your heart, and that you describe it in your life. To which purpose serve yourself of some affectionate ejaculations to that purpose, before and after this duty.

Concerning spiritual books and ordinary sermons, take in these advices also:

6. Let not a prejudice to any man's person hinder thee from receiving good by his doctrine, if it be according to godliness; but, if occasion offer it, or especially if duty present it to thee, that is, if it be preached in that assembly where thou art bound to be present, accept the word preached as a message from God, and the minister as His angel in that ministration.

7. Consider and remark the doctrine that is represented to thee in any discourse; and if the preacher adds accidental advantages, any thing to comply with thy weakness, or to put thy spirit into action or holy resolution, remember it, and make use of it. But if the preacher be a weak person; yet the text is the doctrine thou art to remember; that contains all thy duty; it is worth thy attendance to hear that spoken often, and renewed upon thy thoughts; and though thou beest a learned man, yet the same thing which thou knowest already, if spoken by another, may be made active by that application. I can better be comforted by my own considerations if another hand applies them, than if I do it myself; because the word of God does not work as a natural agent, but as a divine instrument: it does not prevail by the force of deduction and artificial discoursings only, but chiefly by way of blessing in the

ordinance, and in the ministry of an appointed person. At least obey the public order, and reverence the constitution, and give good example of humility, charity, and obedience.

8. When scriptures are read, you are only to enquire with diligence and modesty into the meaning of the spirit; but if homilies or sermons be made upon the words of scripture, you are to consider whether all that be spoken be conformable to the scriptures. For although you may practise for human reasons and human arguments, ministered from the preacher's art; yet you must practise nothing but the command of God, nothing but the doctrine of scripture, that is, the text.

9. Use the advice of some spiritual or other prudent man for the choice of such spiritual books which may be of use and benefit for the edification of thy spirit in the ways of holy living; and esteem that time well accounted for, that is prudently and affectionately employed in hearing or reading good books and pious discourses; ever remembering that God, by hearing us speak to Him in prayer, obliges us to hear Him speak to us in His word, by what instrument soever it be conveyed.

Section V
Of Fasting

Fasting, if it be considered in itself, without relation to spiritual ends, is a duty no where enjoined or counselled; but christianity hath to do with it as it may be made an instrument of the spirit, by subduing the lusts of the flesh, or removing any hindrances of religion. And it hath been practised by all ages of the church, and advised in order to three ministries; to prayer; to mortification of bodily lusts; and to repentance: and it is to be practised according to the following measures:

Rules for Christian Fasting

1. Fasting in order to prayer is to be measured by the proportions of the times of prayer; that is, it ought to be a total fast from all things during the solemnity, unless a probable necessity intervene. Thus the Jews ate nothing upon the sabbath days, till their great offices were performed, that is, about the sixth hour; and St. Peter used it as an argument that the apostles in Pentecost were not drunk, because it was but the third hour of the day, of such a day in which it was not lawful to eat or drink till the sixth hour; and the Jews were offended at the disciples for plucking the ears of corn on the sabbath early in the morning, because it was before the time in which by their customs they

esteemed it lawful to break their fast. In imitation of this custom, and in prosecution of the reason of it, the christian church hath religiously observed fasting before the holy communion; and the more devout persons, though without any obligation at all, refused to eat or drink till they had finished their morning devotions; and further yet, upon days of public humiliation, which are designed to be spent wholly in devotion, and for the averting God's judgments, if they were imminent, fasting is commanded together with prayer—commanded, I say, by the church— to this end, that the spirit might be clearer and more angelical when it is quitted in some proportions from the loads of flesh.

2. Fasting, when it is in order to prayer, must be a total abstinence from all meat, or else an abatement of the quantity: for the help which fasting does to prayer cannot be served by changing flesh into fish, or milk-meats into dry diet, but by turning much into little, or little into none at all, during the time of solemn or extraordinary prayer.

3. Fasting, as it is instrumental to prayer, must be attended with other aids of the like virtue and efficacy; such as are, removing for the time all worldly cares and secular businesses: and therefore our blessed Saviour enfolds these parts within the same caution; "take heed lest your hearts be overcharged with surfeiting and drunkenness, and the cares of this world, and that day overtake you unawares." To which add alms; for upon the wings of fasting and alms holy prayer infallibly mounts up to heaven.[24]

4. When fasting is intended to serve the duty of repentance, it is then best chosen when it is short, sharp, and afflictive; that is, either a total abstinence from all nourishment, according as we shall appoint or be appointed, during such a time as is separate for the solemnity and attendance upon the employment: or, if we shall extend our severity beyond the solemn days, and keep our anger against our sin as we are to keep our sorrow, that is, always in a readiness, and often to be called upon; then to refuse a pleasant morsel, to abstain from the bread of our desires, and only to take wholesome and less pleasing nourishment, vexing our appetite by the refusing a lawful satisfaction, since in its petulancy and luxury it preyed upon an unlawful.

5. Fasting designed for repentance, must be ever joined with an extreme care that we fast from sin: for there is no greater folly or undecency in the world, than to commit that for which I am now

24. Augustine, *Sermon on Lent*, PL 39.2022.

judging and condemning myself. This is the best fast, and the other may serve to promote the interest of this, by increasing the disaffection to it, and multiplying arguments against it.

6. He that fasts for repentance must during that solemnity abstain from all bodily delights, and the sensuality of all his senses and his appetites: for a man must not, when he mourns in his fast, be merry in his sport; weep at dinner and laugh all day after, have a silence in his kitchen and music in his chamber, judge the stomach and feast the other senses. . . .

The Benefits of Fasting

He that undertakes to enumerate the benefits of fasting, may in the next page also reckon all the benefits of physic: for fasting is not to be commended as a duty, but as an instrument; and in that sense no man can reprove it, or undervalue it, but he that knows neither spiritual arts nor spiritual necessities. But by the doctors of the church it is called the nourishment of prayer, the restraint of lust, the wings of the soul, the diet of angels, the instrument of humility and self-denial, the purification of the spirit; and the paleness and meagreness of visage which is consequent to the daily fast of great mortifiers, is by St. Basil[25] said to be the mark in the forehead which the angel observed, when he signed the saints in the forehead to escape the wrath of God: "the soul that is greatly vexed, which goeth stooping and feeble, and the eyes that fail, and the hungry soul, shall give Thee praise and righteousness, O Lord."[26]

Section VI
Of Keeping Festivals, and Days Holy to the Lord; Particularly the Lord's Day

True natural religion, that which was common to all nations and ages, did principally rely upon four great propositions: That there is one God; that God is nothing of those things which we see; that God takes care of all things below, and governs all the world; that He is the great Creator of all things without Himself: and according to these were framed the four first precepts of the decalogue. In the first, the unity of the Godhead is expressly affirmed: in the second, His invisibility and

---

25. Basil, *On Fasting*, PG 31.186.
26. Bar. 2:18.

immateriality: in the third, is affirmed God's government and providence, by avenging them that swear falsely by His name; by which also His omniscience is declared: in the fourth commandment, He proclaims Himself the Maker of heaven and earth; for in memory of God's rest from the work of six days, the seventh was hallowed into a sabbath, and the keeping it was a confessing God to be the great maker of heaven and earth; and consequently to this, it also was a confession of His goodness, His omnipotence, and His wisdom; all which were written with a sunbeam in the great book of the creature.

So long as the law of the sabbath was bound upon God's people, so long God would have that to be the solemn manner of confessing these attributes; but when, the priesthood being changed, there was a change also of the law, the great duty remained unalterable in changed circumstances. We are eternally bound to confess God almighty to be the maker of heaven and earth; but the manner of confessing it is changed from a rest, or a doing nothing, to a speaking something; from a day to a symbol; from a ceremony to a substance; from a Jewish rite to a christian duty; we profess it in our creed, we confess it in our lives; we describe it by every line of our life, by every action of duty, by faith, and trust, and obedience: and we do also upon great reason comply with the Jewish manner of confessing the creation, so far as it is instrumental to a real duty. We keep one day in seven, and so confess the manner and circumstance of the creation; and we rest also, that we may tend holy duties: so imitating God's rest better than the Jew in Synesius, who lay upon his face from evening to evening, and could not by stripes or wounds be raised up to steer the ship in a great storm. God's rest was not a natural cessation; He who could not labour could not be said to rest: but God's rest is to be understood to be a beholding and a rejoicing in His work finished: and therefore we truly represent God's rest, when we confess and rejoice in God's works and God's glory.

This the christian church does upon every day, but especially upon the Lord's day, which she hath set apart for this and all other offices of religion, being determined to this day by the resurrection of her dearest Lord, it being the first day of joy the church ever had. And now upon the Lord's day we are not tied to the rest of the sabbath, but to all the work of the sabbath; and we are to abstain from bodily labour, not because it is a direct duty to us as it was to the Jews, but because it is necessary in order to our duty, that we attend to the offices of religion.

The observation of the Lord's day differs nothing from the observation of the sabbath in the matter of religion, but in the manner. They differ in the ceremony and external rite: rest with them was the principal, with us it is the accessory. They differ in the office or forms of worship: for they were then to worship God as a Creator and a gentle Father; we are to add to that, our Redeemer, and all His other excellencies and mercies. And though we have more natural and proper reason to keep the Lord's day than the sabbath, yet the Jews had a divine commandment for their day, which we have not for ours: but we have many commandments to do all that honour to God which was intended in the fourth commandment; and the apostles appointed the first day of the week for doing it in solemn assemblies. And the manner of worshipping God, and doing Him solemn honour and service upon this day, we may best observe in the following measures.

Rules for Keeping the Lord's Day and Other Christian Festivals

1. When you go about to distinguish festival days from common, do it not by lessening the devotions of ordinary days, that the common devotion may seem bigger upon festivals; but on every day keep your ordinary devotions entire, and enlarge upon the holy day.

2. Upon the Lord's day, we must abstain from all servile and laborious works, except such which are matters of necessity, of common life, or of great charity; for these are permitted by that authority which hath separated the day for holy uses. The sabbath of the Jews, though consisting principally in rest, and established by God, did yield to these; the labour of love and the labours of religion were not against the reason and the spirit of the commandment, for which the letter was decreed, and to which it ought to minister; and therefore much more is it so on the Lord's day, where the letter is wholly turned into spirit, and there is no commandment of God but of spiritual and holy actions. The priests might kill their beasts, and dress them for sacrifice; and Christ, though born under the law, might heal a sick man; and the sick man might carry his bed to witness his recovery, and confess the mercy, and leap and dance to God for joy; and an ox might be led to water, and an ass be haled out of a ditch; and a man may take physic, and he may eat meat, and therefore there were of necessity some to prepare and minister it: and the performing these labours did not consist in minutes and just determining stages; but they had even then a reasonable latitude; so only as to exclude unnecessary labour, or such as did not minister to charity or religion. And therefore this is to be enlarged in the gospel, whose sabbath or rest is but a circumstance, and accessory to the prin-

cipal and spiritual duties. Upon the christian sabbath necessity is to be
served first, then charity, and then religion; for this is to give place to
charity in great instances, and the second to the first in all; and in all
cases God is to be worshipped in spirit and in truth.

3. The Lord's day, being the remembrance of a great blessing,
must be a day of joy, festivity, spiritual rejoicing, and thanksgiving; and
therefore it is a proper work of the day to let your devotions spend
themselves in singing or reading psalms, in recounting the great works
of God, in remembering His mercies, in worshipping His excellencies,
in celebrating His attributes, in admiring His person, in sending portions of pleasant meat to them for whom nothing is provided,[27] and in
all the arts and instruments of advancing God's glory and the reputation
of religion; in which it were a great decency that a memorial of the
resurrection should be inserted, that the particular religion of the day be
not swallowed up in the general. And of this we may the more easily
serve ourselves, by rising seasonably in the morning to private devotion,
and by retiring at the leisures and spaces of the day not employed in
public offices.

4. Fail not to be present at the public hours and places of prayer,
entering early and cheerfully, attending reverently and devoutly, abiding patiently during the whole office, piously assisting at the prayers,
and gladly also hearing the sermon; and at no hand omitting to receive
the holy communion, when it is offered, unless some great reason
excuse it; this being the great solemnity of thanksgiving, and a proper
work of the day.

5. After the solemnities are past, and in the intervals between the
morning and evening devotion, as you shall find opportunity, visit sick
persons, reconcile differences, do offices of neighbourhood, enquire
into the needs of the poor, especially housekeepers, relieve them as they
shall need and as you are able: for then we truly rejoice in God, when
we make our neighbours, the poor members of Christ, rejoice together
with us.

6. Whatsoever you are to do yourself as necessary, you are to take
care that others also who are under your charge do in their station and
manner. Let your servants be called to church, and all your family that
can be spared from necessary and great household ministries; those that

---

27. Neh. 8:10.

cannot, let them go by turns, and be supplied otherwise as well as they may; and provide on these days especially that they be instructed in the articles of faith and necessary parts of their duty.

7. Those who labour hard in the week must be eased upon the Lord's day, such ease being a great charity and alms; but at no hand must they be permitted to use any unlawful games, any thing forbidden by the laws, any thing that is scandalous, or any thing that is dangerous and apt to mingle sin with it; no games prompting to wantonness, to drunkenness, to quarrelling, to ridiculous and superstitious customs; but let their refreshments be innocent, and charitable, and of good report, and not exclusive of the duties of religion.

8. Beyond these bounds because neither God nor man hath passed any obligation upon us, we must preserve our christian liberty, and not suffer ourselves to be entangled with a yoke of bondage; for even a good action may become a snare to us if we make it an occasion of scruple by a pretence of necessity, binding loads upon the conscience not with the bands of God, but of men, and of fancy, or of opinion, or of tyranny. Whatsoever is laid upon us by the hands of man must be acted and accounted of by the measures of a man: but our best measure is this; he keeps the Lord's day best, that keeps it with most religion and with most charity.

9. What the church hath done in the article of the resurrection, she hath in some measure done in the other articles of the nativity, of the ascension, and of the descent of the Holy Ghost at Pentecost: and so great blessings deserve an anniversary solemnity; since he is a very unthankful person that does not often record them in the whole year, and esteem them the ground of his hopes, the object of his faith, the comfort of his troubles, and the great effluxes of the divine mercy, greater than all the victories over our temporal enemies, for which all glad persons usually give thanks; and if with great reason the memory of the resurrection does return solemnly every week, it is but reason the other should return once a year. To which I add that the commemoration of the articles of our Creed in solemn days and offices is a very excellent instrument to convey and imprint the sense and memory of it upon the spirits of the most ignorant persons: for as a picture may with more fancy convey a story to a man than a plain narrative either in word or writing; so a real representment, and an office of remembrance, and a day to declare it, is far more impressive than a picture, or any other art of making and fixing imagery.

10. The memories of the saints are precious to God, and therefore

they ought also to be so to us; and such persons who serve God by holy living, industrious preaching, and religious dying, ought to have their names preserved in honour, and God be glorified in them, and their holy doctrines and lives published and imitated; and we by so doing give testimony to the article of the communion of saints. But in these cases as every church is to be sparing in the number of days, so also should she be temperate in her injunctions, not imposing them but upon voluntary and unbusied persons, without snare or burden. But the holy day is best kept by giving God thanks for the excellent persons, apostles or martyrs, we then remember, and by imitating their lives; this all may do: and they that can also keep the solemnity, must do that too when it is publicly enjoined.

The Rule and Exercises
of Holy Dying[28]

DEDICATION

... Both your lordship and myself have lately seen and felt such sorrows of death, and such sad departure of dearest friends, that it is more than high time we should think ourselves nearly concerned in the accidents. Death hath come so near to you as to fetch a portion from your very heart; and now you cannot choose but dig your own grave, and place your coffin in your eye, when the angel hath dressed your scene of sorrow and meditation with so particular and so near an object: and therefore, as it is my duty, I am come to minister to your pious thoughts, and to direct your sorrows, that they may turn into virtues and advantages.

And since I know your lordship to be so constant and regular in your devotions, and so tender in the matter of justice, so ready in the expressions of charity, and so apprehensive of religion; and that you are a person whose work of grace is apt, and must every day grow towards those degrees where when you arrive you shall triumph over imperfection, and choose nothing but what may please God; I could not by any compendium conduct and assist your pious purposes so well as by that which is the great argument and the great instrument of Holy Living, the consideration and exercises of Death.

My lord, it is a great art to die well, and to be learnt by men in health, by them that can discourse and consider, by those whose understanding and acts of reason are not abated with fear or pains: and as the greatest part of death is passed by the preceding years of our life, so also in those years are the greatest preparations to it; and he that prepares not for death before his last sickness, is like him that begins to study philosophy when he is going to dispute publicly in the faculty. All that a

---

28. *Works* 3:258ff.

sick and dying man can do is but to exercise those virtues which he before acquired, and to perfect that repentance which was begun more early. And of this, my lord, my book, I think, is a good testimony; not only because it represents the vanity of a late and sick-bed repentance, but because it contains in it so many precepts and meditations, so many propositions and various duties, such forms of exercise, and the degrees and difficulties of so many graces which are necessary preparatives to a holy death, that the very learning the duties requires study and skill, time, and understanding in the ways of godliness: and it were very vain to say so much is necessary, and not to suppose more time to learn them, more skill to practise them, more opportunities to desire them, more abilities both of body and mind, than can be supposed in a sick, amazed, timorous, and weak person; whose natural acts are disabled, whose senses are weak, whose discerning faculties are lessened, whose principles are made intricate and entangled, upon whose eye sits a cloud, and the heart is broken with sickness, and the liver pierced through with sorrows and the strokes of death. And therefore, my lord, it is intended by the necessity of affairs, that the precepts of dying well be part of the studies of them that live in health, and the days of discourse and understanding. . . .

CHAPTER I

A GENERAL PREPARATION TOWARDS A HOLY AND BLESSED DEATH, BY WAY OF CONSIDERATION

Section I
Consideration of the Vanity and Shortness of Man's Life

A man is a bubble, said the Greek proverb; which Lucian represents with advantages and its proper circumstances, to this purpose; saying, that all the world is a storm, and men rise up in their several generations, like bubbles descending *a Jove pluvio*, from God and the dew of heaven, from a tear and drop of man, from nature and Providence: and some of these instantly sink into the deluge of their first parent, and are hidden in a sheet of water, having had no other business in the world but to be born that they might be able to die: others float up and down two or three turns, and suddenly disappear, and give their place to others: and they that live longest upon the face of the waters, are in perpetual motion, restless and uneasy; and being crushed with the great drop of a cloud sink into flatness and a froth; the change not being great, it being hardly possible it should be more a nothing than it was before. So is every man: he is born in vanity and sin; he comes into the world like morning mushrooms, soon thrusting up their heads into the air, and conversing with their kindred of the same production, and as soon they turn into dust and forgetfulness: some of them without any other interest in the affairs of the world but that they made their parents a little glad, and very sorrowful: others ride longer in the storm; it may be until seven years of vanity be expired, and then peradventure the sun shines hot upon their heads, and they fall into the shades below, into the cover of death and darkness of the grave to hide them. But if the bubble stands the shock of a bigger drop, and outlives the chances of a child, of a careless nurse, of drowning in a pail of water, of being overlaid by a sleepy servant, or such little accidents, then the young man dances like a bubble, empty and gay, and shines like a dove's neck, or the image of a rainbow, which hath no substance, and whose very imagery and colours are fantastical; and so he dances out the gaiety of his youth, and is all the while in a storm, and endures only because he is not knocked on the head by a drop of bigger rain, or crushed by the pressure of a load of indigested meat, or quenched by the disorder of an ill-placed humour: and to preserve a man alive in the midst of so many chances and hostilities, is as great a miracle as to create him; to preserve him from rushing into nothing, and at first to draw him up from nothing, were equally the issues of an almighty power. And therefore the wise men of the world have contended who shall best fit man's condition with words signifying his vanity and short abode. Homer calls a man "a leaf," the smallest, the weakest piece of a short-lived, unsteady plant: Pindar calls him "the dream of a shadow": another, "the dream of the shadow of smoke": but St. James spake by a more excellent spirit, saying, "our life is but a vapour," viz., drawn from the earth by a celestial influence; made of smoke, or the lighter parts of water, tossed with every wind, moved by the motion of a superior body, without virtue in itself, lifted up on high or left below, according as it pleases the sun its foster-father. But it is lighter yet; it is but "appearing"; a fantastic vapour, an apparition, nothing real: it is not so much as a mist, not the matter of a shower, nor substantial enough to make a cloud; but it is like Cassiopeia's chair, or Pelops' shoulder, or the circles of heaven, PHAINOMENA, than which *you* cannot have a word that can signify a verier nothing. And yet the expression is one degree more made diminutive: a "vapour," and "fantastical," or a "mere appearance," and this but for a little while neither;

the very dream, the phantasm disappears in a small time, "like the shadow that departeth"; or "like a tale that is told"; or "as a dream, when one awaketh." A man is so vain, so unfixed, so perishing a creature, that he cannot long last in the scene of fancy: a man goes off, and is forgotten, like the dream of a distracted person. The sum of all is this: that *thou* art a man, than whom there is not in the world any greater instance of heights and declensions, of lights and shadows, of misery and folly, of laughter and tears, of groans and death.

And because this consideration is of great usefulness and great necessity to many purposes of wisdom and the spirit; all the succession of time, all the changes in nature, all the varieties of light and darkness, the thousand thousands of accidents in the world, and every contingency to every man, and to every creature, doth preach our funeral sermon, and calls *us* to look and see how the old sexton Time throws up the earth, and digs a grave where we must lay our sins or our sorrows, and sow our bodies, till they rise again in a fair or in an intolerable eternity. Every revolution which the sun makes about the world, divides between life and death; and death possesses both those portions by the next morrow; and we are dead to all those months which we have already lived, and we shall never live them over again: and still God makes little periods of our age. First we change our world, when we come from the womb to feel the warmth of the sun. Then we sleep and enter into the image of death, in which state we are unconcerned in all the changes of the world: and if our mothers or our nurses die, or a wild boar destroy our vineyards, or our king be sick, we regard it not, but during that state are as disinterest as if our eyes were closed with the clay that weeps in the bowels of the earth. At the end of seven years our teeth fall and die before us, representing a formal prologue to the tragedy; and still every seven years it is odds but we shall finish the last scene: and when nature, or chance, or vice, takes our body in pieces, weakening some parts and loosing others, we taste the grave and the solemnities of our own funerals, first in those parts that ministered to vice, and next in them that served for ornament, and in a short time even they that served for necessity become useless, and entangled like the wheels of a broken clock. Baldness is but a dressing to our funerals, the proper ornament of mourning, and of a person entered very far into the regions and possession of death: and we have many more of the same signification; gray hairs, rotten teeth, dim eyes, trembling joints, short breath, stiff limbs, wrinkled skin, short memory, decayed appetite. Every day's necessity calls for a reparation of that portion which death fed on all night, when we lay in his lap, and slept in his outer chambers. The very spirits of a man prey upon the daily portion of bread and flesh, and every meal is a rescue from one death, and lays up for another; and while we think a thought, we die; and the clock strikes, and reckons on our portion of eternity: we form our words with the breath of our nostrils, we have the less to live upon for every word we speak.

Thus nature calls us to meditate of death by those things which are the instruments of acting it: and God by all the variety of His providence makes us see death every where, in all variety of circumstances, and dressed up for all the fancies and the expectation of every single person. Nature hath given us one harvest every year, but death hath two, and the spring and the autumn send throngs of men and women to charnel-houses; and all the summer long men are recovering from their evils of the spring, till the dog days come, and then the Sirian star makes the summer deadly; and the fruits of autumn are laid up for all the year's provision, and the man that gathers them eats and surfeits, and dies and needs them not, and himself is laid up for eternity; and he that escapes till winter only stays for another opportunity which the distempers of that quarter minister to him with great variety. Thus death reigns in all the portions of our time; the autumn with its fruits provides disorders for us, and the winter's cold turns them into sharp diseases, and the spring brings flowers to strew our hearse, and the summer gives green turf and brambles to bind upon our graves. Calentures and surfeit, cold and agues, are the four quarters of the year, and all minister to death; and you can go no whither but you tread upon a dead man's bones.

The wild fellow in Petronius that escaped upon a broken table from the furies of a shipwreck, as he was sunning himself upon the rocky shore espied a man rolled upon his floating bed of waves, ballasted with sand in the folds of his garment, and carried by his civil enemy, the sea, towards the shore to find a grave: and it cast him into some sad thoughts: that "peradventure this man's wife in some part of the continent, safe and warm, looks next month for the good man's return; or, it may be, his son knows nothing of the tempest; or his father thinks of that affectionate kiss, which still is warm upon the good old man's cheek, ever since he took a kind farewell; and he weeps with joy to think how blessed he shall be when his beloved boy returns into the circle of his father's arms. These are the thoughts of mortals, this is the end and sum of all their designs"; a dark night and an ill guide, a boisterous sea and a broken cable, a hard rock and a rough wind, dashed in pieces the fortune of a whole family, and they that shall weep loudest

470

for the accident are not yet entered into the storm, and yet have suffered shipwreck. Then looking upon the carcass, he knew it, and found it to be the master of the ship, who "the day before cast up the accounts of his patrimony and his trade, and named the day when he thought to be at home": "see how the man swims who was so angry two days since"; his passions are becalmed with the storm, his accounts cast up, his cares at an end, his voyage done, and his gains are the strange events of death, which whether they be good or evil, the men that are alive seldom trouble themselves concerning the interest of the dead.

But seas alone do not break our vessel in pieces: every where we may be shipwrecked. A valiant general, when he is to reap the harvest of his crowns and triumphs, fights unprosperously; or falls into a fever with joy and wine, and changes his laurel into cypress, his triumphal chariot to a hearse, dying the night before he was appointed to perish in the drunkenness of his festival joys. It was a sad arrest of the loose-nesses and wilder feasts of the French court, when their king Henry the second was killed really by the sportive image of a fight. And many brides have died under the hands of paranymphs and maidens, dressing them for uneasy joy, the new and undiscerned chains of marriage, according to the saying of Bensirah, the wise Jew, "the bride went into her chamber, and knew not what should befal her there." Some have been paying their vows, and giving thanks for a prosperous return to their own house, and the roof hath descended upon their heads, and turned their loud religion into the deeper silence of a grave. And how many teeming mothers have rejoiced over their swelling wombs, and pleased themselves in becoming the channels of blessing to a family, and the midwife hath quickly bound their heads and feet, and carried them forth to burial? Or else the birth-day of an heir hath seen the coffin of the father brought into the house, and the divided mother hath been forced to travail twice, with a painful birth, and a sadder death.[29]

There is no state, no accident, no circumstance of our life, but it hath been soured by some sad instance of a dying friend: a friendly meeting often ends in some sad mischance, and makes an eternal part-ing: and when the poet Aeschylus was sitting under the walls of his house, an eagle hovering over his bald head, mistook it for a stone, and let fall his oyster, hoping there to break the shell, but pierced the poor man's skull.

---

29. Prudentius, PL 59.881.

Death meets us everywhere, and is procured by every instrument and in all chances, and enters in at many doors; by violence and secret influence, by the aspect of a star and the stink of a mist, by the emissions of a cloud and the meeting of a vapour, by the fall of a chariot and the stumbling at a stone, by a full meal or an empty stomach, by watching at the wine or by watching at prayers, by the sun or the moon, by a heat or a cold, by sleepless nights or sleeping days, by water frozen into the hardness and sharpness of a dagger, or water thawed into the floods of a river, by a hair or a raisin, by violent motion or sitting still, by severity or dissolution, by God's mercy or God's anger; by every thing in providence and every thing in manners, by every thing in nature and every thing in chance;

eripitur persona, manet res;[30]

we take pains to heap up things useful to our life, and get our death in the purchase; and the person is snatched away, and the goods remain. And all this is the law and constitution of nature; it is a punishment to our sins, the unalterable event of providence, and the decree of heaven: the chains that confine us to this condition are strong as destiny, and immutable as the eternal laws of God.

I have conversed with some men who rejoiced in the death or calamity of others, and accounted it as a judgment upon them for being on the other side, and against them in the contention: but within the revolution of a few months, the same man met with a more uneasy and unhandsome death: which when I saw, I wept, and was afraid; for I knew that it must be so with all men; for we also shall die, and end our quarrels and contentions by passing to a final sentence.

Section II
The Consideration Reduced to Practice

It will be very material to our best and noblest purposes if we represent this scene of change and sorrow a little more dressed up in circumstances, for so we shall be more apt to practise those rules the doctrine of which is consequent to this consideration. It is a mighty change that is made by the death of every person, and it is visible to us who are alive. Reckon but from the sprightfulness of youth, and the fair

---

30. Lucretius, *On the Nature of Things*, LCL, vol. 1, p. 192.

cheeks and full eyes of childhood, from the vigorousness and strong flexure of the joints of five-and-twenty, to the hollowness and dead paleness, to the loathsomeness and horror of a three days' burial, and we shall perceive the distance to be very great and very strange. But so have I seen a rose newly springing from the clefts of its hood, and at first it was fair as the morning, and full with the dew of heaven as a lamb's fleece; but when a ruder breath had forced open its virgin modesty, and dismantled its too youthful and unripe retirements, it began to put on darkness, and to decline to softness and the symptoms of a sickly age; it bowed the head, and broke its stalk, and at night having lost some of its leaves and all its beauty, it fell into the portion of weeds and outworn faces. The same is the portion of every man and every woman, the heritage of worms and serpents, rottenness and cold dishonour, and our beauty so changed, that our acquaintance quickly knew us not; and that change mingled with so much horror, or else meets so with our fears and weak discoursings, that they who six hours ago tended upon us either with charitable or ambitious services, cannot without some regret stay in the room alone where the body lies stripped of its life and honour. I have read of a fair young German gentleman who living often refused to be pictured, but put off the importunity of his friends' desire by giving way that after a few days' burial they might send a painter to his vault, and if they saw cause for it draw the image of his death unto the life: they did so, and found his face half eaten, and his midriff and backbone full of serpents; and so he stands pictured among his armed ancestors. So does the fairest beauty change, and it will be as bad with you and me; and then what servants shall we have to wait upon us in the grave? what friends to visit us? what officious people to cleanse away the moist and unwholesome cloud reflected upon our faces from the sides of the weeping vaults, which are the longest weepers for our funeral?

This discourse will be useful if we consider and practise by the following rules and considerations respectively:

1. All the rich and all the covetous men in the world will perceive, and all the world will perceive for them, that it is but an ill recompence for all their cares, that by this time all that shall be left will be this, that the neighbours shall say, "he died a rich man"; and yet his wealth will not profit him in the grave, but hugely swell the sad accounts of doomsday. And he that kills the Lord's people with unjust or ambitious wars for an unrewarding interest, shall have this character, that he threw away all the days of his life, that one year might be reckoned with

473

his name, and computed by his reign or consulship; and many men by great labours and affronts, many indignities and crimes, labour only for a pompous epitaph and a loud title upon their marble; whilst those into whose possessions their heirs or kindred are entered, are forgotten, and lie unregarded as their ashes, and without concernment or relation, as the turf upon the face of their grave. A man may read a sermon, the best and most passionate that every man preached, if he shall but enter into the sepulchres of kings. In the same Escurial where the Spanish princes live in greatness and power, and decree war or peace, they have wisely placed a cemetery where their ashes and their glory shall sleep till time shall be no more; and where our kings have been crowned, their ancestors lay interred, and they must walk over their grandsire's head to take his crown. There is an acre sown with royal seed, the copy of the greatest change, from rich to naked, from ceiled roofs to arched coffins, from living like gods to die like men. There is enough to cool the flames of lust, to abate the heights of pride, to appease the itch of covetous desires, to sully and dash out the dissembling colours of a lustful, artificial, and imaginary beauty. There the warlike and the peaceful, the fortunate and the miserable, the beloved and the despised princes mingle their dust, and pay down their symbol of mortality, and tell all the world, that when we die our ashes shall be equal to kings, and our accounts easier, and our pains or our crowns shall be less. To my apprehension it is a sad record, which is left by Athenæus concerning Ninus, the great Assyrian monarch, whose life and death is summed up in these words: "Ninus the Assyrian had an ocean of gold, and other riches more than the sand in the Caspian sea; he never saw the stars, and perhaps he never desired it; he never stirred up the holy fire among the Magi, nor touched his god with the sacred rod according to the laws; he never offered sacrifice, nor worshipped the deity, nor administered justice, nor spake to his people, nor numbered them; but he was most valiant to eat and drink, and having mingled his wines he threw the rest upon the stones. This man is dead: behold his sepulchre; and now hear where Ninus is. Sometimes I was Ninus, and drew the breath of a living man; but now am nothing but clay. I have nothing, but what I did eat, and what I served to myself in lust, that was and is all my portion. The wealth with which I was esteemed blessed, my enemies meeting together shall bear away, as the mad Thyades carry a raw goat. I am gone to hell; and when I went thither, I neither carried gold, nor horse, nor silver chariot. I that wore a mitre, am now a little heap of dust." I know not any thing that can better represent the evil condition of a wicked man, or a changing greatness. From the greatest secular dignity to dust and ashes his nature bears him, and from thence to hell his sins carry him, and there he shall be for ever under the dominion of chains and devils, wrath and an intolerable calamity. This is the reward of an unsanctified condition, and a greatness ill gotten or ill administered.

2. Let no man extend his thoughts or let his hopes wander towards future and far-distant events and accidental contingencies. This day is mine and yours, but ye know not what shall be on the morrow; and every morning creeps out of a dark cloud, leaving behind it an ignorance and silence deep as midnight, and undiscerned as are the phantasms that make a chrisom-child to smile: so that we cannot discern what comes hereafter, unless we had a light from heaven brighter than the vision of an angel, even the spirit of prophecy. Without revelation we cannot tell whether we shall eat tomorrow, or whether a squinzy shall choke us: and it is written in the unrevealed folds of divine predestination that many who are this day alive shall to-morrow be laid upon the cold earth, and the women shall weep over their shroud, and dress them for their funeral. St. James in his epistle notes the folly of some men his contemporaries, who were so impatient of the event of to-morrow, or the accidents of next year, or the good or evils of old age, that they would consult astrologers and witches, oracles and devils, what should befal them the next calends: what should be the event of such a voyage, what God had written in His book concerning the success of battles, the election of emperors, the heir of families, the price of merchandise, the return of the Tyrian fleet, the rate of Sidonian carpets; and as they were taught by the crafty and lying demons, so they would expect the issue; and oftentimes by disposing their affairs in order towards such events, really did produce some little accidents according to their expectation; and that made them trust the oracles in greater things, and in all. Against this he opposes his counsel, that we should not search after forbidden records, much less by uncertain significations; for whatsoever is disposed to happen by the order of natural causes or civil counsels, may be rescinded by a peculiar decree of providence, or be prevented by the death of the interested persons; who, while their hopes are full, and their causes conjoined, and the work brought forward, and the sickle put into the harvest, and the first-fruits offered and ready to be eaten, even then if they put forth their hand to an event that stands but at the door, at that door their body may be carried forth to burial, before the expectation shall enter into fruition. When Richilda the widow of Albert earl of Ebersberg, had feasted the emperor Henry the third and

petitioned in behalf of her nephew Welpho for some lands formerly possessed by the earl her husband; just as the emperor held out his hand to signify his consent, the chamber floor suddenly fell under them, and Richilda falling upon the edge of a bathing vessel was bruised to death, and stayed not to see her nephew sleep in those lands which the emperor was reaching forth to her, and placed at the door of restitution.

3. As our hopes must be confined, so must our designs: let us not project long designs, crafty plots, and diggings so deep that the intrigues of a design shall never be unfolded till our grand-children have forgotten our virtues or our vices. The work of our soul is cut short, facile, sweet, and plain, and fitted to the small portions of our shorter life; and as we must not trouble our enquiry, so neither must we intricate our labour and purposes with what we shall never enjoy. This rule does not forbid us to plant orchards which shall feed our nephews with their fruit; for by such provisions they do something towards an imaginary immortality, and do charity to their relatives: but such projects are reproved, which discompose our present duty by long and future designs; such which by casting our labours to events at distance make us less to remember our death standing at the door. It is fit for a man to work for his day's wages, or to contrive for the hire of a week, or to lay a train to make provisions for such a time as is within our eye, and in our duty, and within the usual periods of man's life; for whatsoever is made necessary, is also made prudent: but while we plot and busy ourselves in the toils of an ambitious war, or the levies of a great estate, night enters in upon us, and tells all the world how like fools we lived, and how deceived and miserably we died. Seneca[31] tells of Senecio Cornelius, a man crafty in getting, and tenacious in holding a great estate, and one who was as diligent in the care of his body as of his money, curious of his health, as of his possessions, that he all day long attended upon his sick and dying friend; but when he went away, was quickly comforted, supped merrily, went to bed cheerfully, and on a sudden being surprised by a squinzy, scarce drew his breath until the morning, but by that time died, being snatched from the torrent of his fortune, and the swelling tide of wealth, and a likely hope bigger than the necessities of ten men. This accident was much noted then in Rome, because it happened in so great a fortune, and in the midst of wealthy designs; and presently it

---

31. Seneca, *Letters* (101), LCL, vol. 3, p. 158.

made wise men to consider, how imprudent a person he is who disposes of ten years to come, when he is not lord of to-morrow.

4. Though we must not look so far off and pry abroad, yet we must be busy near at hand; we must with all arts of the spirit seize upon the present, because it passes from us while we speak, and because in it all our certainty does consist. We must take our waters as out of a torrent and sudden shower, which will quickly cease dropping from above, and quickly cease running in our channels here below; this instant will never return again, and yet it may be this instant will declare or secure the fortune of a whole eternity. The old Greeks and Romans taught us the prudence of this rule, but christianity teaches us the religion of it. They so seized upon the present that they would lose nothing of the day's pleasure: "let us eat and drink, for to-morrow we shall die"; that was their philosophy; and at their solemn feasts they would talk of death to heighten the present drinking, and that they might warm their veins with a fuller chalice, as knowing the drink that was poured upon their graves would be cold and without relish. "Break the beds, drink your wine, crown your heads with roses, and besmear your curled locks with nard; for God bids you to remember death": so the epigrammatist speaks the sense of their drunken principles. Something towards this signification is that of Solomon, "there is nothing better for a man than that he should eat and drink, and that he should make his soul enjoy good in his labour; for that is his portion; for who shall bring him to see that which shall be after him?"[32] But although he concludes all this to be vanity, yet because it was the best thing that was then commonly known that they should seize upon the present with a temperate use of permitted pleasures. I had reason to say, that christianity taught us to turn this into religion. For he that by a present and a constant holiness secures the present, and makes it useful to his noblest purposes, he turns his condition into his best advantage, by making his unavoidable fate become his necessary religion.

To the purpose of this rule is that collect of Tuscan hieroglyphics: "our life is very short, beauty is a cozenage, money is false and fugitive; empire is odious, and hated by them that have it not, and uneasy to them that have; victory is always uncertain, and peace most commonly is but a fraudulent bargain; old age is miserable, death is the period, and is a

---

32. Eccles. 2:24, 3:22.

happy one if it be not soured by the sins of our life: but nothing continues but the effects of that wisdom which employs the present time in the acts of a holy religion and a peaceable conscience":[33] they make us to live even beyond our funerals, embalmed in the spices and odours of a good name, and entombed in the grave of the holy Jesus, where we shall be dressed for a blessed resurrection to the state of angels and beatified spirits.

5. Since we stay not here, being people but of a day's abode, and our age is like that of a fly and contemporary with a gourd, we must look somewhere else for an abiding city, a place in another country to fix our house in, whose walls and foundation is God, where we must find rest, or else be restless for ever. For whatsoever ease we can have or fancy here is shortly to be changed into sadness or tediousness: it goes away too soon, like the periods of our life: or stays too long, like the sorrows of a sinner: its own weariness, or a contrary disturbance, is its load; or it is eased by its revolution into vanity and forgetfulness; and where either there is sorrow or an end of joy, there can be no true felicity: which because it must be had by some instrument and in some period of our duration, we must carry up our affections to the mansions prepared for us above, where eternity is the measure, felicity is the state, angels are the company, the Lamb is the light, and God is the portion and inheritance.

Section III
Rules and Spiritual Arts of Lengthening Our Days, and to Take Off the Objection of a Short Life

1. In the accounts of a man's life, we do not reckon that portion of days in which we are shut up in the prison of the womb; we tell our years from the day of our birth: and the same reason that makes our reckoning to stay so long, says also that then it begins too soon. For then we are beholden to others to make the account for us; for we know not of a long time whether we be alive or no, having but some little approaches and symptoms of a life. To feed, and sleep, and move a little, and imperfectly, is the state of an unborn child; and when he is born, he does no more for a good while; and what is it that shall make him to be esteemed to live the life of a man? and when shall that account begin? For we should be loth to have the accounts of our age taken by the

---

33. Found in Camerarius, 16th-century German classical scholar and Taylor source.

measures of a beast: and fools and distracted persons are reckoned as civilly dead; they are no parts of the commonwealth, not subject to laws, but secured by them in charity, and kept from violence as a man keeps his ox: and a third part of our life is spent, before we enter into a higher order, into the state of a man.

2. Neither must we think that the life of a man begins when he can feed himself, or walk alone, when he can fight, or beget his like; for so he is contemporary with a camel or a cow; but he is first a man when he comes to a certain, steady use of reason, according to his proportion: and when that is, all the world of men cannot tell precisely. Some are called at age at fourteen; some at one-and-twenty; some, never; but all men, late enough; for the life of a man comes upon him slowly and insensibly. But as when the sun approaches towards the gates of the morning, he first opens a little eye of heaven, and sends away the spirits of darkness, and gives light to a cock, and calls up the lark to matins, and by and by gilds the fringes of a cloud, and peeps over the eastern hills, thrusting out his golden horns, like those which decked the brows of Moses when he was forced to wear a veil because himself had seen the face of God; and still while a man tells the story, the sun gets up higher, till he shews a fair face and a full light, and then he shines one whole day, under a cloud often, and sometimes weeping great and little showers, and sets quickly: so is a man's reason and his life. He first begins to perceive himself to see or taste, making little reflections upon his actions of sense, and can discourse of flies and dogs, shells and play, horses and liberty: but when he is strong enough to enter into arts and little institutions, he is at first entertained with trifles and impertinent things, not because he needs them, but because his understanding is no bigger, and little images of things are laid before him, like a cock-boat to a whale, only to play withal: but before a man comes to be wise, he is half dead with gouts and consumptions, with catarrhs and aches, with sore eyes and a worn-out body. So that if we must not reckon the life of a man but by the accounts of his reason, he is long before his soul be dressed; and he is not to be called a man without a wise and an adorned soul, a soul at least furnished with what is necessary towards his well-being: but by that time his soul is thus furnished, his body is decayed; and then you can hardly reckon him to be alive, when his body is possessed by so many degrees of death.

3. But there is yet another arrest. At first he wants strength of body, and then he wants the use of reason: and when that is come, it is ten to one but he stops by the impediments of vice, and wants the

strengths of the spirit; and we know that body and soul and spirit are the constituent parts of every christian man. And now let us consider, what that thing is, which we call years of discretion. The young man is past his tutors, and arrived at the bondage of a caitive spirit; he is run from discipline, and is let loose to passion; the man by this time hath wit enough to choose his vice, to act his lust, to court his mistress, to talk confidently, and ignorantly, and perpetually, to despise his betters, to deny nothing to his appetite, to do things that when he is indeed a man he must for ever be ashamed of: for this is all the discretion that most men shew in the first stage of their manhood; they can discern good from evil; and they prove their skill by leaving all that is good, and wallowing in the evils of folly and an unbridled appetite. And by this time the young man hath contracted vicious habits, and is a beast in manners, and therefore it will not be fitting to reckon the beginning of his life; he is a fool in his understanding, and that is a sad death; and he is dead in trespasses and sins, and that is a sadder: so that he hath no life but a natural, the life of a beast or a tree; in all other capacities he is dead; he neither hath the intellectual nor the spiritual life, neither the life of a man nor of a Christian; and this sad truth lasts too long. For old age seizes upon most men while they still retain the minds of boys and vicious youth, doing actions from principles of great folly, and a mighty ignorance, admiring things useless and hurtful, and filling up all the dimensions of their abode with businesses of empty affairs, being at leisure to attend no virtue: they cannot pray, because they are busy, and because they are passionate; they cannot communicate, because they have quarrels and intrigues of perplexed causes, complicated hostilities, and things of the world, and therefore they cannot attend to the things of God: little considering that they must find a time to die in; when death comes, they must be at leisure for that. Such men are like sailors loosing from a port, and tossed immediately with a perpetual tempest lasting till their cordage crack, and either they sink, or return back again to the same place: they did not make a voyage, though they were long at sea. The business and impertinent affairs of most men steal all their time, and they are restless in a foolish motion: but this is not the progress of a man; he is no farther advanced in the course of a life, though he reckon many years; for still his soul is childish, and trifling like an untaught boy.

If the parts of this sad complaint find their remedy, we have by the same instruments also cured the evils and the vanity of a short life. Therefore,

1. *Be* infinitely curious *you* do not set back your life in the accounts of God by the intermingling of criminal actions, or the contracting vicious habits. There are some vices which carry a sword in their hand, and cut a man off before his time. There is a sword of the Lord, and there is a sword of a man, and there is a sword of the devil. Every vice of our own managing in the matter of carnality, of lust or rage, ambition or revenge, is a sword of Satan put into the hands of a man: these are the destroying angels; sin is the Apollyon, the destroyer that is gone out, not from the Lord, but from the tempter; and we hug the poison, and twist willingly with the vipers, till they bring us into the regions of an irrecoverable sorrow. We use to reckon persons as good as dead if they have lost their limbs and their teeth, and are confined to a hospital, and converse with none but surgeons and physicians, mourners and divines, those *pollinctores,* the dressers of bodies and souls to funeral: but it is worse when the soul, the principle of life, is employed wholly in the offices of death: and that man was worse than dead of whom Seneca[34] tells, that, being a rich fool, when he was lifted up from the baths and set into a soft couch, asked his slaves, *An ego jam sedeo,* "do I now sit?" The beast was so drowned in sensuality and the death of his soul, that whether he did sit or no, he was to believe another. Idleness and every vice is as much of death as a long disease is, or the expense of ten years; and "she that lives in pleasures is dead while she liveth," saith the apostle;[35] and it is the style of the Spirit concerning wicked persons, "they are dead in trespasses and sins."[36] For as every sensual pleasure and every day of idleness and useless living lops off a little branch from our short life, so every deadly sin and every habitual vice does quite destroy us; but innocence leaves us in our natural portions and perfect period; we lose nothing of our life if we lose nothing of our soul's health; and therefore he that would live a full age, must avoid a sin, as he would decline the regions of death and the dishonours of the grave.

2. If we would have our life lengthened, let us begin betimes to live in the accounts of reason and sober counsels, of religion and the spirit, and then we shall have no reason to complain that our abode on earth is so short: many men find it long enough, and indeed it is so to all

---

34. Seneca, *Moral Essays* (Brevity of Life), LCL, vol. 2, p. 324.
35. 1 Tim. 5:6.
36. Eph. 2:1.

senses. But when we spend in waste what God hath given us in plenty, when we sacrifice our youth to folly, our manhood to lust and rage, our old age to covetousness and irreligion, not beginning to live till we are to die, designing that time to virtue which indeed is infirm to every thing and profitable to nothing; then we make our lives short, and lust runs away with all the vigorous and healthful part of it, and pride and animosity steal the manly portion, and craftiness and interest possess old age: *velut ex pleno et abundanti perdimus,* we spend as if we had too much time, and knew not what to do with it: we fear every thing, like weak and silly mortals; and desire strangely and greedily, as if we were immortal: we complain our life is short, and yet we throw away much of it, and are weary of many of its parts; we complain the day is long, and the night is long, and we want company, and seek out arts to drive the time away, and then weep because it is gone too soon. But so the treasure of the capitol is but a small estate, when Cæsar comes to finger it, and to pay with it all his legions: and the revenue of all Egypt and the eastern provinces was but a little sum, when they were to support the luxury of Mark Antony, and feed the riot of Cleopatra; but a thousand crowns is a vast proportion to be spent in the cottage of a frugal person, or to feed a hermit. Just so is our life: it is too short to serve the ambition of a haughty prince or an usurping rebel; too little time to purchase great wealth, to satisfy the pride of a vain-glorious fool, to trample upon all the enemies of our just or unjust interest; but for the obtaining virtue, for the purchase of sobriety and modesty, for the actions of religion, God gave us time sufficient, if we make the "outgoings of the morning and evening," that is, our infancy and old age, to be taken into the computations of a man. Which we may see in the following particulars.

1. If, our childhood being first consecrated by a forward baptism, it be seconded by a holy education and a complying obedience; if our youth be chaste and temperate, modest and industrious, proceeding through a prudent and sober manhood to a religious old age; then we have lived our whole duration, and shall never die, but be changed, in a just time, to the preparations of a better and an immortal life.

2. If, besides the ordinary returns of our prayers and periodical and festival solemnities, and our seldom communions, we would allow to religion and the studies of wisdom those great shares that are trifled away upon vain sorrow, foolish mirth, troublesome ambition, busy covetousness, watchful lust, and impertinent amours, and balls and re-vellings and banquets, all that which was spent viciously, and all that

time that lay fallow and without employment, our life would quickly amount to a great sum. Tostatus Abulensis was a very painful person, and a great clerk, and in the days of his manhood he wrote so many books, and they not ill ones, that the world computed a sheet for every day of his life; I suppose they meant, after he came to the use of reason and the state of a man; and John Scotus died about the two-and-thirtieth year of his age; and yet besides his public disputations, his daily lectures of divinity in public and private, the books that he wrote, being lately collected and printed at Lyons, do equal the number of volumes of any two the most voluminous fathers of the Latin church. Every man is not enabled to such employments, but every man is called and enabled to the works of a sober and a religious life; and there are many saints of God that can reckon as many volumes of religion and mountains of piety, as those others did of good books. St. Ambrose (and I think, from his example, St. Augustine) divided every day into three "tertias" of employment: eight hours he spent in the necessities of nature and recreation; eight hours in charity and doing assistance to others, despatching their businesses, reconciling their enmities, reproving their vices, correcting their errors, instructing their ignorances, transacting the affairs of his diocese; and the other eight hours he spent in study and prayer. If we were thus minute and curious in the spending our time, it is impossible but our life would seem very long. For so have I seen an amorous person tell the minutes of his absence from his fancied joy, and while he told the sands of his hour-glass, or the throbs and little beatings of his watch, by dividing an hour into so many members, he spun out its length by number, and so translated a day into the tediousness of a month. And if we tell our days by canonical hours of prayer, our weeks by a constant revolution of fasting days or days of special devotion, and over all these draw a black cypress, a veil of penitential sorrow and severe mortification, we shall soon answer the calumny and objection of a short life. He that governs the day and divides the hours, hastens from the eyes and observation of a merry sinner; but loves to stand still, and behold and tell the sighs, and number the groans and sadly delicious accents of a grieved penitent. It is a vast work that any man may do if he never be idle: and it is a huge way that a man may go in virtue, if he never goes out of his way by a vicious habit or a great crime: and he that perpetually reads good books, if his parts be answerable, will have a huge stock of knowledge. It is so in all things else. Strive not to forget your time, and suffer none of it to pass undiscerned; and then measure your life, and tell me how you find the measure of its abode. However, the time we live is worth the money we pay for it, and therefore it is not to be thrown away.

3. When vicious men are dying, and scared with the affrighting truths of an evil conscience, they would give all the world for a year, for a month: nay, we read of some that called out with amazement, *inducias usque ad mane*, "truce but till the morning": and if that year or some few months were given, those men think they could do miracles in it. And let us awhile suppose what Dives would have done, if he had been loosed from the pains of hell, and permitted to live on earth one year. Would all the pleasures of the world have kept him one hour from the temple? would he not perpetually have been under the hands of priests, or at the feet of the doctors, or by Moses' chair, or attending as near the altar as he could get, or relieving poor Lazarus, or praying to God, and crucifying all his sin? I have read of a melancholic person who saw hell but in a dream or vision, and the amazement was such that he would have chosen ten times to die rather than feel again so much of that horror; and such a person cannot be fancied but that he would spend a year in such holiness, that the religion of a few months would equal the devotion of many years even of a good man. Let us but compute the proportions. If we should spend all our years of reason so as such a person would spend that one, can it be thought that life would be short and trifling, in which he had performed such a religion, served God with so much holiness, mortified sin with so great a labour, purchased virtue at such a rate and so rare an industry? It must needs be that such a man must die when he ought to die, and be like ripe and pleasant fruit falling from a fair tree, and gathered into baskets for the planter's use. He that hath done all his business, and is begotten to a glorious hope by the seed of an immortal spirit, can never die too soon, nor live too long.

Xerxes wept sadly, when he saw his army of two million three hundred thousand men, because he considered that within a hundred years all the youth of that army should be dust and ashes: and yet as Seneca[37] well observes of him, he was the man that should bring them to their graves; and he consumed all that army in two years, for whom he feared and wept the death after a hundred. Just so we do all. We complain that within thirty or forty years, a little more, or a great deal less, we shall descend again into the bowels of our mother, and that our life is too short for any great employment; and yet we throw away five

---

37. Seneca, *Moral Essays*, LCL, vol. 2, p. 342.

and thirty years of our forty, and the remaining five we divide between art and nature, civility and customs, necessity and convenience, prudent counsels and religion: but the portion of the last is little and contemptible, and yet that little is all that we can prudently account of our lives. We bring that fate and that death near us, of whose approach we are so sadly apprehensive.

4. In taking the accounts of your life, do not reckon by great distances, and by the periods of pleasure, or the satisfaction of your hopes, or the stating your desires; but *let* every intermedial day and hour pass with observation. He that reckons he hath lived but so many harvests, thinks they come not often enough, and that they go away too soon: some lose the day with longing for the night, and the night in waiting for the day. Hope and fantastic expectations spend much of our lives: and while with passion we look for a coronation, or the death of an enemy, or a day of joy, passing from fancy to possession without any intermedial notices, we throw away a precious year, and use it but as the burden of our time, fit to be pared off and thrown away, that we may come at those little pleasures which first steal our hearts, and then steal our life.

5. A strict course of piety is the way to prolong our lives in the natural sense, and to add good portions to the number of our years: and sin is sometimes by natural causality, very often by the anger of God and the divine judgment, a cause of sudden and untimely death. Concerning which I shall add nothing to what I have somewhere else said of this article, but only the observation of Epiphanius;[38] that for three thousand three hundred and thirty-two years, even to the twentieth age, there was not one example of a son that died before his father; but the course of nature was kept, that he who was first born in the descending line did first die (I speak of natural death, and therefore Abel cannot be opposed to this observation), till that Terah the father of Abraham taught the people a new religion, to make images of clay and worship them; and concerning him it was first remarked that "Haran died before his father Terah in the land of his nativity"; God by an unheard-of judgment and a rare accident punishing his newly invented crime by the untimely death of his son.

6. But if I shall describe a living man, a man that hath that life that distinguishes him from a fool or a bird, that which gives him a capacity

---

38. Epiphanius, *Heresies*, PG 41.186.

next to angels, we shall find that even a good man lives not long, because it is long before he is born to this life, and longer yet before he hath a man's growth. "He that can look upon death, and see its face with the same countenance with which he hears its story;[39] that can endure all the labours of his life with his soul supporting his body; that can equally despise riches when he hath them and when he hath them not; that is not sadder if they lie in his neighbour's trunks, nor more brag if they shine round about his own walls; he that is neither moved with good fortune coming to him nor going from him; that can look upon another man's lands evenly and pleasedly as if they were his own, and yet look upon his own, and use them too, just as if they were another man's; that neither spends his goods prodigally and like a fool, nor yet keeps them avariciously and like a wretch; that weighs not benefits by weight and number, but by the mind and circumstances of him that gives them; that never thinks his charity expensive if a worthy person be the receiver; he that does nothing for opinion sake, but every thing for conscience, being as curious of his thoughts as of his actings in markets and theatres, and is as much in awe of himself as of a whole assembly; he that knows God looks on, and contrives his secret affairs as in the presence of God and His holy angels; that eats and drinks because he needs it, not that he may serve a lust or load his belly; he that is bountiful and cheerful to his friends, and charitable and apt to forgive his enemies; that loves his country, and obeys his prince, and desires and endeavours nothing more than that he may do honour to God"; this person may reckon his life to be the life of a man, and compute his months, not by the course of the sun, but the zodiac and circle of his virtues; because these are such things which fools and children and birds and beasts cannot have; these are therefore the actions of life, because they are the seeds of immortality. That day in which we have done some excellent thing we may as truly reckon to be added to our life as were the fifteen years to the days of Hezekiah.

Section IV
Consideration of the Miseries of Man's Life

As our life is very short, so it is very miserable; and therefore it is well it is short. God in pity to mankind, lest his burden should be insupportable and his nature an intolerable load, hath reduced our state

---

39. Seneca, *The Happy Life*, vol. 2, p. 146.

of misery to an abbreviature; and the greater our misery is, the less while it is like to last; the sorrows of a man's spirit being like ponderous weights, which by the greatness of their burden make a swifter motion, and descend into the grave to rest and ease our wearied limbs; for then only we shall sleep quietly, when those fetters are knocked off, which not only bound our souls in prison, but also ate the flesh till the very bones opened the secret garments of their cartilages, discovering their nakedness and sorrow.

1. Here is no place to sit down in, but you must rise as soon as you are set, for we have gnats in our chambers, and worms in our gardens, and spiders and flies in the palaces of the greatest kings. How few men in the world are prosperous! What an infinite number of slaves and beggars, of persecuted and oppressed people, fill all corners of the earth with groans, and heaven itself with weeping prayers and sad remembrances! How many provinces and kingdoms are afflicted by a violent war, or made desolate by popular diseases! Some whole countries are remarked with fatal evils, or periodical sicknesses. Grand Cairo in Egypt feels the plague every three years returning like a quartan ague, and destroying many thousands of persons. All the inhabitants of Arabia the desert are in continual fear of being buried in huge heaps of sand, and therefore dwell in tents and ambulatory houses, or retire to unfruitful mountains, to prolong an uneasy and wilder life. And all the countries round about the Adriatic sea feel such violent convulsions by tempests and intolerable earthquakes, that sometimes whole cities find a tomb, and every man sinks with his own house made ready to become his monument, and his bed is crushed into the disorders of a grave. Was not all the world drowned at one deluge and breach of the divine anger; and shall not all the world again be destroyed by fire? Are there not many thousands that die every night, and that groan and weep sadly every day? But what shall we think of that great evil which for the sins of men God hath suffered to possess the greatest part of mankind? Most of the men that are now alive, or that have been living for many ages, are Jews, Heathens, or Turks; and God was pleased to suffer a base epileptic person, a villain and a vicious, to set up a religion which hath filled all the nearer parts of Asia, and much of Africa, and some part of Europe; so that the greatest number of men and women born in so many kingdoms and provinces are infallibly made Mahometans, strangers and enemies to Christ by whom alone we can be saved: this consideration is extremely sad, when we remember how universal and how great an evil it is, that so many millions of sons and daughters are born to enter into

the possession of devils to eternal ages. These evils are the miseries of great parts of mankind, and we cannot easily consider more particularly the evils which happen to us, being the inseparable affections or incidents to the whole nature of man.

2. We find that all the women in the world are either born for barrenness, or the pains of childbirth, and yet this is one of our greatest blessings; but such indeed are the blessings of this world, we cannot be well with nor without many things. Perfumes make our heads ache, roses prick our fingers, and in our very blood, where our life dwells, is the scene under which nature acts many sharp fevers and heavy sicknesses. It were too sad if I should tell how many persons are afflicted with evil spirits, with spectres and illusions of the night; and that huge multitudes of men and women live upon man's flesh; nay, worse yet, upon the sins of men, upon the sins of their sons and of their daughters, and they pay their souls down for the bread they eat, buying this day's meal with the price of the last night's sin.

3. Or if you please in charity to visit a hospital, which is indeed a map of the whole world, there you shall see the effects of Adam's sin, and the ruins of human nature; bodies laid up in heaps like the bones of a destroyed town, *homines precarii spiritus et male harentis,* men whose souls seem to be borrowed, and are kept there by art and the force of medicine, whose miseries are so great that few people have charity or humanity enough to visit them, fewer have the heart to dress them, and we pity them in civility or with a transient prayer, but we do not feel their sorrows by the mercies of a religious pity; and therefore as we leave their sorrows in many degrees unrelieved and uneased, so we contract by our unmercifulness a guilt by which ourselves become liable to the same calamities. Those many that need pity, and those infinites of people that refuse to pity, are miserable upon a several charge, but yet they almost make up all mankind.

4. All wicked men are in love with that which entangles them in huge varieties of troubles; they are slaves to the worst of masters, to sin and to the devil, to a passion, and to an imperious woman. Good men are for ever persecuted, and God chastises every son whom He receives, and whatsoever is easy is trifling and worth nothing, and whatsoever is excellent is not to be obtained without labour and sorrow; and the conditions and states of men that are free from great cares are such as have in them nothing rich and orderly, and those that have are stuck full of thorns and trouble. Kings are full of care; and learned men in all

ages have been observed to be very poor, *et honestas miserias accusant*, "they complain of their honest miseries."

5. But these evils are notorious and confessed; even they also whose felicity men stare at and admire, besides their splendour and the sharpness of their light, will with their appendent sorrows wring a tear from the most resolved eye; for not only the winter quarter is full of storms and cold and darkness, but the beauteous spring hath blasts and sharp frosts, the fruitful teeming summer is melted with heat, and burnt with the kisses of the sun her friend, and choked with dust, and the rich autumn is full of sickness; and we are weary of that which we enjoy, because sorrow is its biggest portion: and when we remember that upon the fairest face is placed one of the worst sinks of the body, the nose, we may use it not only as a mortification to the pride of beauty, but as an allay to the fairest outside of condition which any of the sons and daughters of Adam do possess. For *look* upon kings and conquerors: I will not tell, that many of them fall into the condition of servants, and their subjects rule over them, and stand upon the ruins of their families, and that to such persons the sorrow is bigger than usually happens in smaller fortunes; but let us suppose them still conquerors, and see what a goodly purchase they get by all their pains, and amazing fears, and continual dangers. They carry their arms beyond Ister, and pass the Euphrates, and bind the Germans with the bounds of the river Rhine: I speak in the style of the Roman greatness; for now-a-days the biggest fortune swells not beyond the limits of a petty province or two, and a hill confines the progress of their prosperity, or a river checks it: but whatsoever tempts the pride and vanity of ambitious persons, is not so big as the smallest star which we see scattered in disorder and unregarded upon the pavement and floor of heaven. And if we would suppose the pismires had but our understandings, they also would have the method of a man's greatness, and divide their little mole-hills into provinces and exarchates: and if they also grew as vicious and as miserable, one of their princes would lead an army out and kill his neighbour ants, that he might reign over the next handful of a turf. But then if we consider at what price and with what felicity all this is purchased, the sting of the painted snake will quickly appear, and the fairest of their fortunes will properly enter into this account of human infelicities.

We may guess at it by the constitution of Augustus's fortune, who struggled for his power first with the Roman citizens, then with Brutus and Cassius and all the fortune of the republic; then with his colleague

Mark Antony; then with his kindred and nearest relatives; and after he was wearied with slaughter of the Romans, before he could sit down and rest in his imperial chair, he was forced to carry armies into Macedonia, Galatia, beyond Euphrates, Rhine, and Danubius; and when he dwelt at home in greatness and within the circles of a mighty power, he hardly escaped the sword of the Egnatii, of Lepidus, Cæpio, and Murena; and after he had entirely reduced the felicity and grandeur into his own family, his daughter, his only child, conspired with many of the young nobility, and being joined with adulterous complications, as with an impious sacrament, they affrighted and destroyed the fortune of the old man, and wrought him more sorrow than all the troubles that were hatched in the baths and beds of Egypt between Antony and Cleopatra. This was the greatest fortune that the world had then or ever since, and therefore we cannot expect it to be better in a less prosperity.

6. The prosperity of this world is so infinitely soured with the overflowing of evils, that he is counted the most happy who hath the fewest; all conditions being evil and miserable, they are only distinguished by the number of calamities. The collector of the Roman and foreign examples, when he had reckoned two and twenty instances of great fortunes, every one of which had been allayed with great variety of evils; in all his reading or experience, he could tell but of two who had been famed for an entire prosperity, Quintus Metellus, and Gyges the king of Lydia: and yet concerning the one of them he tells that his felicity was so inconsiderable (and yet it was the bigger of the two) that the oracle said that Aglaus Sophidius the poor Arcadian shepherd was more happy than he, that is, he had fewer troubles; for so indeed we are to reckon the pleasures of this life; the limit of our joy is the absence of some degrees of sorrow, and he that hath the least of this, is the most prosperous person. But then we must look for prosperity not in palaces or courts of princes, not in the tents of conquerors, or in the gaieties of fortunate and prevailing sinners; but something rather in the cottages of honest, innocent, and contented persons, whose mind is no bigger than their fortune, nor their virtue less than their security. As for others, whose fortune looks bigger, and allures fools to follow it like the wandering fires of the night, till they run into rivers or are broken upon rocks with staring and running after them, they are all in the condition of Marius, than whose condition nothing was more constant, and nothing more mutable; if we reckon them amongst the happy, they are the most happy men; if we reckon them amongst the miserable, they are the most miserable. For just as is a man's condition, great or little, so is the

490

state of his misery; all have their share; but kings and princes, great generals and consuls, rich men and mighty, as they have the biggest business and the biggest charge, and are answerable to God for the greatest accounts, so they have the biggest trouble; that the uneasiness of their appendage may divide the good and evil of the world, making the poor man's fortune as eligible as the greatest; and also restraining the vanity of man's spirit, which a great fortune is apt to swell from a vapour to a bubble; but God in mercy hath mingled wormwood with their wine, and so restrained the drunkenness and follies of prosperity.

7. Man never hath one day to himself of entire peace from the things of this world, but either something troubles him, or nothing satisfies him, or his very fulness swells him and makes him breathe short upon his bed. Men's joys are troublesome, and besides that the fear of losing them takes away the present pleasure, and a man hath need of another felicity to preserve this, they are also wavering and full of trepidation, not only from their inconstant nature, but from their weak foundation: they arise from vanity, and they dwell upon ice, and they converse with the wind, and they have the wings of a bird, and are serious but as the resolutions of a child, commenced by chance, and managed by folly, and proceed by inadvertency, and end in vanity and forgetfulness. So that as Livius Drusus said of himself, he never had any play days or days of quiet when he was a boy, for he was troublesome and busy, a restless and unquiet man; the same may every man observe to be true of himself; he is always restless and uneasy, he dwells upon the waters, and leans upon thorns, and lays his head upon a sharp stone.[40]

Section V
This Consideration Reduced to Practice

1. The effect of this consideration is this, that the sadnesses of this life help to sweeten the bitter cup of death. For let our life be never so long, if our strength were great as that of oxen and camels, if our sinews were strong as the cordage at the foot of an oak, if we were as fighting and prosperous people as Siccius Dentatus, who was on the prevailing side in a hundred and twenty battles, who had three hundred and twelve public rewards assigned him by his generals and princes for his valour and conduct in sieges and sharp encounters, and, besides all this, had his share in nine triumphs; yet still the period shall be that all this shall end

---

40. Ibid.

in death, and the people shall talk of us awhile, good or bad, according as we deserve, or as they please, and once it shall come to pass that concerning every one of us it shall be told in the neighbourhood, that we are dead. This we are apt to think a sad story; but therefore let us help it with a sadder: for we therefore need not be much troubled that we shall die, because we are not here in ease, nor do we dwell in a fair condition; but our days are full of sorrow and anguish, dishonoured, and made unhappy with many sins, with a frail and a foolish spirit, entangled with difficult cases of conscience, insnared with passions, amazed with fears, full of cares, divided with curiosities and contradictory interests, made airy and impertinent with vanities, abused with ignorance and prodigious errors, made ridiculous with a thousand weaknesses, worn away with labours, loaden with diseases, daily vexed with dangers and temptations, and in love with misery; we are weakened with delights, afflicted with want, with the evils of myself and of all my family, and with the sadnesses of all my friends, and of all good men, even of the whole church; and therefore methinks we need not be troubled that God is pleased to put an end to all these troubles, and to let them sit down in a natural period, which, if we please, may be to us the beginning of a better life. When the prince of Persia wept because his army should all die in the revolution of an age, Artabanus told him that they should all meet with evils so many and so great that every man of them should wish himself dead long before that. Indeed it were a sad thing to be cut of the stone, and we that are in health tremble to think of it; but the man that is wearied with the disease looks upon that sharpness as upon his cure and remedy; and as none need to have a tooth drawn, so none could well endure it, but he that felt the pain of it in his head: so is our life so full of evils, that therefore death is no evil to them that have felt the smart of this, or hope for the joys of a better.

2. But as it helps to ease a certain sorrow, as a fire draws out fire, and a nail drives forth a nail, so it instructs us in a present duty, that is, that we should not be so fond of a perpetual storm, nor doat upon the transient gauds and gilded thorns of this world. They are not worth a passion, nor worth a sigh or a groan, not of the price of one night's watching; and therefore they are mistaken and miserable persons, who, since Adam planted thorns round about paradise, are more in love with that hedge than all the fruits of the garden, sottish admirers of things that hurt them, of sweet poisons, gilded daggers, and silken halters. Tell them they have lost a bounteous friend, a rich purchase, a fair farm, a wealthy donative, and you dissolve their patience; it is an evil bigger

than their spirit can bear; it brings sickness and death; they can neither eat nor sleep with such a sorrow. But if you represent to them the evils of a vicious habit, and the dangers of a state of sin; if you tell them they have displeased God, and interrupted their hopes of heaven; it may be they will be so civil as to hear it patiently, and to treat you kindly, and first to commend, and then forget your story, because they prefer this world with all its sorrows before the pure unmingled felicities of heaven. But it is strange that any man should be so passionately in love with the thorns which grow on his own ground, that he should wear them for armlets, and knit them in his shirt, and prefer them before a kingdom and immortality. No man loves this world the better for his being poor; but men that love it because they have great possessions, love it because it is troublesome and chargeable, full of noise and temptation, because it is unsafe and ungoverned, flattered and abused; and he that considers the troubles of an overlong garment and of a crammed stomach, a trailing gown and a loaden table, may justly understand that all that for which men are so passionate, is their hurt and their objection, that which a temperate man would avoid, and a wise man cannot love.

He that is no fool, but can consider wisely, if he be in love with this world, we need not despair but that a witty man might reconcile him with tortures, and make him think charitably of the rack, and be brought to dwell with vipers and dragons, and entertain his guests with the shrieks of mandrakes, cats, and screech-owls, with the filing of iron, and the harshness of rending of silk, or to admire the harmony that is made by a herd of evening wolves when they miss their draught of blood in their midnight revels. The groans of a man in a fit of the stone are worse than all these; and the distractions of a troubled conscience are worse than those groans; and yet a careless merry sinner is worse than all that. But if we could from one of the battlements of heaven espy how many men and women at this time lie fainting and dying for want of bread, how many young men are hewn down by the sword of war, how many poor orphans are now weeping over the graves of their father by whose life they were enabled to eat: if we could but hear how many mariners and passengers are at this present in a storm, and shriek out because their keel dashes against a rock, or bulges under them, how many people there are that weep with want, and are mad with oppression, or are desperate by too quick a sense of a constant infelicity; in all reason we should be glad to be out of the noise and participation of so many evils. This is a place of sorrows and tears, of great evils and a constant calamity: let us remove from hence, at least in affections and preparation of mind.

CHAPTER III
OF THE STATE OF SICKNESS, AND THE TEMPTATIONS INCIDENT TO IT, WITH THEIR PROPER REMEDIES

Section I
Of the State of Sickness

Adam's sin brought death into the world, and man did die the same day in which he sinned, according as God had threatened. He did not die, as death is taken for a separation of soul and body; that is not death properly, but the ending of the last act of death; just as a man is said to be born, when he ceases any longer to be borne in his mother's womb; but whereas to man was intended a life long and happy, without sickness, sorrow, or infelicity, and this life should be lived here or in a better place, and the passage from one to the other should have been easy, safe, and pleasant, now that man sinned, he fell from that state to a contrary.

If Adam had stood, he should not always have lived in this world; for this world was not a place capable of giving a dwelling to all those myriads of men and women, which should have been born in all the generations of infinite and eternal ages; for so it must have been, if man had not died at all, nor yet have removed hence at all. Neither is it likely that man's innocence should have lost to him all possibility of going thither, where the duration is better, measured by a better time, subject to fewer changes, and which is now the reward of a returning virtue, which in all natural senses is less than innocence, save that it is heightened by Christ to an equality of acceptation with the state of innocence: but so it must have been, that his innocence should have been punished with an eternal confinement to this state, which in all reason is the less perfect, the state of a traveller, not of one possessed of his inheritance. It is therefore certain, man should have changed his abode: for so did Enoch, and so did Elias, and so shall all the world that shall be alive at the day of judgment; they shall not die, but they shall change their place and their abode, their duration and their state, and all this without death.

That death therefore which God threatened to Adam, and which passed upon his posterity, is not the going out of this world, but the manner of going. If he had stayed in innocence, he should have gone from hence placidly and fairly, without vexatious and afflictive circumstances; he should not have died by sickness, misfortune, defect, or unwillingness: but when he fell, then he began to die; the "same day," so said God, and that must needs be true: and therefore it must mean that upon that very day he fell into an evil and dangerous condition, a state of change and affliction; then death began, that is, the man began to die by a natural diminution, and aptness to disease and misery. His first state was, and should have been so long as it lasted, a happy duration; his second was a daily and miserable change, and this was the dying properly.

This appears in the great instance of damnation, which, in the style of scripture, is called eternal death: not because it kills or ends the duration; it hath not so much good in it; but because it is a perpetual infelicity. Change or separation of soul and body is but accidental to death; death may be with or without either: but the formality, the curse and the sting of death, that is, misery, sorrow, fear, diminution, defect, anguish, dishonour, and whatsoever is miserable and afflictive in nature, that is death. Death is not an action, but a whole state and condition; and this was first brought in upon us by the offence of one man.

But this went no farther than thus to subject us to temporal infelicity. If it had proceeded so as was supposed, man had been much more miserable; for man had more than one original sin, in this sense: and though this death entered first upon us by Adam's fault, yet it came nearer unto us and increased upon us by the sins of more of our forefathers. For Adam's sin left us in strength enough to contend with human calamities for almost a thousand years together: but the sins of his children, our forefathers, took off from us half the strength about the time of the flood; and then from five hundred to two hundred and fifty, and from thence to one hundred and twenty, and from thence to threescore and ten; so often halving it, till it is almost come to nothing. But by the sins of men in the several generations of the world, death, that is, misery and disease, is hastened so upon us, that we are of a contemptible age: and because we are to die by suffering evils, and by the daily lessening of our strength and health; this death is so long a doing, that it makes so great a part of our short life useless and unserviceable, that we have not time enough to get the perfection of a single manufacture, but ten or twelve generations of the world must go to the making up of one wise man, or one excellent art: and in the succession of those ages there happen so many changes and interruptions, so many wars and violences, that seven years' fighting sets a whole kingdom back in learning and virtue, to which they were creeping, it may be, a whole age.

And thus also we do evil to our posterity, as Adam did to his, and Cham did to his, and Eli to his, and all they to theirs who by sins caused God to shorten the life and multiply the evils of mankind: and for this reason it is the world grows worse and worse, because so many original sins are multiplied, and so many evils from parents descend upon the succeeding generations of men, that they derive nothing from us but original misery.

But He who restored the law of nature, did also restore us to the condition of nature; which, being violated by the introduction of death, Christ then repaired when He suffered and overcame death for us; that is, He hath taken away the unhappiness of sickness, and the sting of death, and the dishonours of the grave, of dissolution and weakness, of decay and change, and hath turned them into acts of favour, into instances of comfort, into opportunities of virtue; Christ hath now knit them into rosaries and coronets, He hath put them into promises and rewards, He hath made them part of the portion of His elect; they are instruments, and earnests, and securities, and passages, to the greatest perfection of human nature, and the divine promises. So that it is possible for us now to be reconciled to sickness; it came in by sin, and therefore is cured when it is turned into virtue; and although it may have in it the uneasiness of labour, yet it will not be uneasy as sin, or the restlessness of a discomposed conscience: if therefore we can well manage our state of sickness, that we may not fall by pain, as we usually do by pleasure, we need not fear; for no evil shall happen to us.

Section X
Acts of Charity, by Way of Prayer and Ejaculation; Which May Also Be Used for Thanksgiving, in Case of Recovery

O my soul, thou hast said unto the Lord, Thou art my Lord; my goodness extendeth not to Thee, but to the saints that are in the earth, and to the excellent, in whom is all my delight: the Lord is the portion of my inheritance and of my cup; Thou maintainest my lot.[41]

As for God, His way is perfect; the word of the Lord is tried, He is a buckler to all those that trust in Him. For who is God except the

---

41. Ps. 16:2–5.

Lord? or who is a rock save our God? It is God that girdeth me with strength, and maketh my way perfect.[42]

Be not Thou far from me, O Lord; O my strength, haste Thee to help me. Deliver my soul from the sword, my darling from the power of the dog. Save me from the lion's mouth; and Thou hast heard me also from among the horns of the unicorns. I will declare Thy name unto my brethren; in the midst of the congregation will I praise Thee. Ye that fear the Lord, praise the Lord; ye sons of God, glorify Him, and fear before Him all ye sons of men. For He hath not despised nor abhorred the affliction of the afflicted, neither hath He hid His face from him, but when he cried unto Him, He heard.[43]

As the hart panteth after the water-brooks, so longeth my soul after Thee, O God. My soul thirsteth for God, for the living God: when shall I come and appear before the Lord? O my God, my soul is cast down within me; all Thy waves and billows are gone over me: as with a sword in my bones I am reproached. Yet the Lord will command His loving-kindness in the daytime; and in the night His song shall be with me, and my prayer unto the God of my life.[44]

Bless ye the Lord in the congregations, even the Lord from the fountains of Israel.[45]

My mouth shall shew forth Thy righteousness and Thy salvation all the day, for I know not the numbers thereof; I will go in the strength of the Lord God, I will make mention of Thy righteousness, even of Thine only. O God, Thou hast taught me from my youth, and hitherto have I declared Thy wondrous works; but I will hope continually, and will yet praise Thee more and more. Thy righteousness, O God, is very high, who hast done great things; O God, who is like unto Thee? Thou which hast shewed me great and sore troubles shalt quicken me again, and shalt bring me up again from the depths of the earth: Thou shalt increase Thy goodness towards me, and comfort me on every side. My lips shall greatly rejoice when I sing unto Thee, and my soul which Thou hast redeemed.[46]

Blessed be the Lord God, the God of Israel, who only doth won-

---

42. Ps. 18:30–32.
43. Ps. 22:19–24.
44. Ps. 42:1ff.
45. Ps. 68:26.
46. Ps. 71:15ff.

drous things: and blessed be His glorious name for ever; and let the whole earth be filled with His glory. Amen, Amen.[47]

I love the Lord, because He hath heard my voice and my supplication. The sorrows of death compassed me; I found trouble and sorrow; then called I upon the name of the Lord: O Lord, I beseech Thee, deliver my soul. Gracious is the Lord and righteous; yea, our God is merciful. The Lord preserveth the simple: I was brought low, and He helped me. Return to Thy rest, O my soul, the Lord hath dealt bountifully with me: for Thou hast delivered my soul from death, mine eyes from tears, and my feet from falling. Precious in the sight of the Lord is the death of His saints. O Lord, truly I am Thy servant; I am Thy servant, and the son of Thine handmaid: Thou shalt loose my bonds.[48]

He that loveth not the Lord Jesus, let him be accursed.[49]

O that I might love Thee as well as ever any creature loved Thee! He that dwelleth in love, dwelleth in God. There is no fear in love.[50]

The Prayer

O most gracious and eternal God and loving Father, who hast poured out Thy bowels upon us, and sent the Son of Thy love unto us to die for love, and to make us dwell in love, and the eternal comprehensions of Thy divine mercies, O be pleased to inflame my heart with a holy charity towards Thee and all the world. Lord, I forgive all that ever have offended me, and beg, that both they and I may enter into the possession of Thy mercies, and feel a gracious pardon from the same fountain of grace: and do Thou forgive me all the acts of scandal whereby I have provoked, or tempted, or lessened, or disturbed any person. Lord, let me never have my portion amongst those that divide the union, and disturb the peace, and break the charities of the church and christian communion. And though I am fallen into evil times, in which christendom is divided by the names of an evil division; yet I am in charity with all Christians, with all that love the Lord Jesus, and long for His coming, and I would give my life to save the soul of any of my brethren; and I humbly beg of Thee, that the public calamity of the several societies of the church may not be imputed to my soul, to any evil purposes.

---

47. Ps. 72:18–19.
48. Ps. 116:1ff.
49. 1 Cor. 16:22.
50. 1 John 4:16–18.

II.

Lord, preserve me in the unity of Thy holy church, in the love of God and of my neighbours. Let Thy grace enlarge my heart to remember, deeply to resent, faithfully to use, wisely to improve, and humbly to give thanks to Thee for all Thy favours, with which Thou hast enriched my soul, and supported my estate, and preserved my person, and rescued me from danger, and invited me to goodness in all the days and periods of my life. Thou hast led me through it with an excellent conduct; and I have gone astray after the manner of men: but my heart is towards Thee. O do unto Thy servant as Thou usest to do unto those that love Thy name; let Thy truth comfort me, Thy mercy deliver me, Thy staff support me, Thy grace sanctify my sorrow, and Thy goodness pardon all my sins, Thy angels guide me with safety in this shadow of death, and Thy most holy spirit lead me into the land of righteousness, for Thy name's sake, which is so comfortable, and for Jesus Christ his sake, our dearest Lord and most gracious Saviour. Amen.

CHAPTER V

OF THE VISITATION OF THE SICK: OR THE ASSISTANCE
THAT IS TO BE DONE TO DYING PERSONS BY
THE MINISTRY OF THEIR CLERGY GUIDES

Section I

God, who hath made no new covenant with dying persons distinct from the covenant of the living, hath also appointed no distinct sacraments for them, no other manner of usages but such as are common to all the spiritual necessities of living and healthful persons. In all the days of our religion, from our baptism to the resignation and delivery of our soul, God hath appointed His servants to minister to the necessities, and eternally to bless, and prudently to guide, and wisely to judge concerning souls; and the Holy Ghost, that anointing from above, descends upon us in several effluxes, but ever by the ministries of the church. Our heads are anointed with that sacred unction, baptism, not in ceremony, but in real and proper effect; our foreheads in confirmation, our hands in ordinations, all our senses in the visitation of the sick; and all by the ministry of especially deputed and instructed persons: and we, who all our lifetime derive blessings from the fountains of grace by the channels of ecclesiastical ministries, must do it then especially when our needs are most pungent and actual.

1. We cannot give up our names to Christ, but the holy man that ministers in religion must enrol them, and present the persons, and consign the grace; when we beg for God's spirit, the minister can best present our prayers, and by his advocation hallow our private desires, and turn them into public and potent offices.

2. If we desire to be established and confirmed in the grace and religion of our baptism, the holy man whose hands were anointed by a special ordination to that and its symbolical purposes, lays his hands upon the catechumen, and the anointing from above descends by that ministry.

3. If we would eat the body and drink the blood of our Lord, we must address ourselves to the Lord's table, and he that stands there to bless and to minister can reach it forth, and feed thy soul; and without his ministry thou canst not be nourished with that heavenly feast, nor thy body consigned to immortality, nor thy soul refreshed with the sacramental bread from heaven; except by spiritual suppletories, in cases of necessity and an impossible communion.

4. If we have committed sins, the spiritual man is appointed to restore us, and to pray for us, and to receive our confessions, and to enquire into our wounds, and to infuse oil and remedy, and to pronounce pardon.

5. If we be cut off from the communion of the faithful by our own demerits, their holy hands must reconcile us and give us peace; they are our appointed comforters, our instructors, our ordinary judges; and in the whole, what the children of Israel begged of Moses,[51] that God would no more speak to them alone, but by His servant Moses, lest they should be consumed; God, in compliance with our infirmities, hath of His own goodness established as a perpetual law in all ages of christianity, that God will speak to us by His ministers, and our solemn prayers shall be made to Him by their advocation, and His blessings descend from heaven by their hands, and our offices return thither by their presidencies, and our repentance shall be managed by them, and our pardon in many degrees ministered by them: God comforts us by their sermons, and reproves us by their discipline, and cuts off some by

---

51. Exod. 20:19.

their severity, and reconciles others by their gentleness, and relieves us by their prayers, and instructs us by their discourses, and heals our sicknesses by their intercession presented to God, and united to Christ's advocation: and in all this they are no causes, but servants, of the will of God, instruments of the divine grace and order, stewards and dispensers of the mysteries, and appointed to our souls to serve and lead, and to help in all accidents, dangers, and necessities.

And they who received us in our baptism, are also to carry us to our grave, and to take care that our end be as our life was, or should have been: and therefore it is established as an apostolical rule, "Is any man sick among you? let him send for the elders of the church, and let them pray over him, etc."[52]

The sum of the duties and offices respectively implied in these words, is in the following rules;

Section II
Rules for the Manner of Visitation of Sick Persons

1. Let the minister of religion be sent to not only against the agony of death, but be advised with in the whole conduct of the sickness; for in sickness indefinitely, and therefore in every sickness, and therefore in such which are not mortal, which end in health, which have no agony or final temptations, St. James gives the advice; and the sick man, being bound to require them, is also tied to do it, when he can know them, and his own necessity. It is a very great evil, both in the matter of prudence and piety, that they fear the priest as they fear the embalmer or the sexton's spade, and love not to converse with him unless they can converse with no man else, and think his office so much to relate to the other world that he is not to be treated with while we hope to live in this, and indeed that our religion be taken care of only when we die: and the event is this (of which I have seen some sad experience), that the man is deadly sick, and his reason is useless, and he is laid to sleep, and his life is in the confines of the grave, so that he can do nothing towards the trimming of his lamp; and the curate shall say a few prayers by him, and talk to a dead man, and the man is not in a condition to be helped, but in a condition to need it hugely. He cannot be called upon to confess his sins, and he is not able to remember them, and he cannot understand

---

52. James 5:14.

501

an advice, nor hear a free discourse, nor be altered from a passion, nor cured of his fear, nor comforted upon any grounds of reason or religion, and no man can tell what is likely to be his fate; or if he does, he cannot prophesy good things concerning him, but evil. Let the spiritual man come when the sick man can be conversed withal and instructed, when he can take medicine and amend, when he understands, or can be taught to understand, the case of his soul, and the rules of his conscience; and then his advice may turn into advantage: it cannot otherwise be useful.

2. The entercourses of the minister with the sick man have so much variety in them that they are not to be transacted at once; and therefore they do not well that send once to see the good man with sorrow, and hear him pray, and thank him, and dismiss him civilly, and desire to see his face no more. To dress a soul for funeral is not a work to be despatched at one meeting; at first he needs a comfort, and anon something to make him willing to die; and by and by he is tempted to impatience, and that needs a special cure; and it is a great work to make his confessions well and with advantages; and it may be the man is careless and indifferent, and then he needs to understand the evil of his sin, and the danger of his person; and his cases of conscience may be so many and so intricate that he is not quickly to be reduced to peace, and one time the holy man must pray, and another time he must exhort, a third time administer the holy sacrament; and he that ought to watch all the periods and little portions of his life, lest he should be surprised and overcome, had need be watched when he is sick, and assisted and called upon, and reminded of the several parts of his duty in every instant of his temptation. This article was well provided for among the easter-lings, for the priests in their visitations of a sick person did abide in their attendance and ministry for seven days together. The want of this makes the visitations fruitless, and the calling of the clergy contempti-ble, while it is not suffered to imprint its proper effects upon them that need it in a lasting ministry.

3. St. James advises that when a man is sick he should send for the elders,[53] one sick man for many presbyters; and so did the eastern churches, they sent for seven: and, like a college of physicians, they ministered spiritual remedies, and sent up prayers like a choir of singing clerks. In cities they might do so, while the Christians were few and the

---

53. Ibid.

priests many: but when they that dwelt in the *pagi* or villages ceased to be pagans, and were baptized, it grew to be an impossible felicity, unless in few cases, and to some more eminent persons; but because they need it most, God hath taken care that they may best have it; and they that can are not very prudent if they neglect it.

4. Whether they be many or few that are sent to the sick person, let the curate of his parish, or his own confessor, be amongst them; that is, let him not be wholly advised by strangers, who know not his particular necessities; but he that is the ordinary judge cannot safely be passed by in his extraordinary necessity, which in so great portions depends upon his whole life past; and it is a matter of suspicion when we decline his judgment that knows us best, and with whom we formerly did converse, either by choice or by law, by private election or public constitution. It concerns us then to make severe and profitable judgments, and not to conspire against ourselves, or procure such assistances which may handle us softly, or comply with our weaknesses more than relieve our necessities.

5. When the ministers of religion are come, first let them do their ordinary offices, that is, pray for grace to the sick man, for patience, for resignation; for health, if it seems good to God in order to His great ends. For that is one of the ends of the advice of the apostle: and therefore the minister is to be sent for, not while the case is desperate, but before the sickness is come to its crisis or period. Let him discourse concerning the causes of sickness, and by a general instrument move him to consider concerning his condition. Let him call upon him to set his soul in order; to trim his lamp; to dress his soul; to renew acts of grace by way of prayer; to make amends in all the evils he hath done; and to supply all the defects of duty, as much as his past condition requires, and his present can admit.

6. According as the condition of the sickness or the weakness of the man is observed, so the exhortation is to be less, and the prayers more, because the life of the man was his main preparatory; and therefore if his condition be full of pain and infirmity, the shortness and small number of his own acts is to be supplied by the act of the ministers and standers by, who are in such case to speak more to God for him than to talk to him. For the prayer of the righteous,[54] when it is fervent, hath

---

54. James 5:16.

a promise to prevail much in behalf of the sick person; but exhortations must prevail with their own proper weight, not by the passion of the speaker. But yet this assistance by way of prayers is not to be done by long offices, but by frequent, and fervent, and holy; in which offices if the sick man joins, let them be short and apt to comply with his little strength and great infirmities; if they be said in his behalf without his conjunction, they that pray may prudently use their own liberty, and take no measures but their own devotions and opportunities, and the sick man's necessities. . . .

Bibliography

1. PRIMARY SOURCES

Heber, Reginald and Charles Page Eden, eds. *The Whole Works of the Right Reverend Jeremy Taylor, D.D. with a Life of the Author, 10 volumes.* London: Longman, Green, Longmans, Roberts and Green, 1847–52.

Rust, Bishop George. *A Funeral Sermon Preached at the Obsequies of the Right Reverend Father in God, Jeremy, Lord Bishop of Down,* printed in the Heber-Eden edition of *The Whole Works of the Right Reverend Jeremy Taylor, D.D.*

APPENDIX
A LIST OF TAYLOR'S WORKS AND THEIR
FIRST EDITION DATES*

1.	A Sermon preached in Saint Marie's Church in Oxford, upon the Anniversary of the Gunpowder Treason	1638
2.	Episcopacy asserted against the Acephali and Aërians, new and old	1642
3.	A Discourse concerning Prayer Extempore	1646
4.	A Discourse of the Liberty of Prophesying	1646

---

* From William Brown's *Jeremy Taylor* (London: Macmillan, 1925), pp. 211–13.

BIBLIOGRAPHY

5.	A New and Easy Institution of Grammar. (With Wyat)	1647
6.	Apology for Authorized and Set Forms of Liturgy	1647
7.	The Great Exemplar	1649
8.	Funeral Sermon at the Obsequies of the Lady Frances, Countess of Carbery	1650
9.	The Rule and Exercises of Holy Living	1650
10.	The Rule and Exercises of Holy Dying	1651
11.	Clerus Domini	1651
12.	A Discourse of Baptism	1652
13.	A Short Catechism	1652
14.	Two Discourses: (1) Of Baptism; (2) Of Prayer	1653
15.	Sermons for all the Sundays in the Year	1653–5
16.	The Real Presence and Spiritual of Christ in the Blessed Sacrament	1654
17.	Unum Necessarium	1655
18.	The Golden Grove	1655
19.	A Discourse of Auxiliary Beauty	1656
20.	A Discourse of Friendship	1657
21.	Polemical and Moral Discourses	1657
22.	Collection of Offices	1658
23.	"Letter" in John Stearne's Thanatologia, Dublin	1659
24.	The Worthy Communicant	1660
25.	Ductor Dubitantium	1660
26.	Letters on Original Sin in "A Second Part of the Mixture of Scholastical Divinity" by Henry Jeanes	1660
27.	Letter on Prayer, prefixed to Henry Leslie's "Discourse"	1660
28.	A Sermon preached at the Consecration of two Archbishops and ten Bishops, in St. Patrick's Cathedral, in Dublin, January 27, 1660	1661
29.	The Whole Duty of the Clergy	1661
30.	A Sermon preached at the Opening of the Parliament of Ireland, May 8, 1661	1661
31.	Via Intelligentiae: A Sermon to the Dublin University	1662
32.	Defence and Introduction to the Rite of Confirmation	1663

BIBLIOGRAPHY

33. A Sermon preached in Christ's Church, Dublin, at
    the Funeral of the Archbishop of Armagh   1663
34. A Dissuasive from Popery, Pt. 1, 1664, Pt. 2   1667

POSTHUMOUS

35. Christ's Yoke an Easy Yoke (two sermons)   1675
36. Contemplations of the State of Man   1684
37. On the Reverence due to the Altar. Now first
    printed from the original manuscript, Oxford.
    (Edited by John Barrow, and also in 1899 by
    Vernon Staley)   1848

2. DISSERTATIONS ON JEREMY TAYLOR

Antoine, Sister Mary Salome. "The Rhetoric of Jeremy Taylor's Prose: Ornament of the Sunday Sermons." Ph.D. diss., The Catholic University of America, Washington, D.C. 1946.

Carroll, Thomas Kilian. "Jeremy Taylor, Liturgist and Ecumenist: A Study of Taylor's Sacramental Theology and Its Ecumenical Implications After Vatican II." Doctor of Divinity (D.D.) diss., Angelicum University, Rome, 1970.

————. "Jeremy Taylor and the Anglican-Puritan Crisis in Worship 1640–1660: A Theological, Ecumenical and Pastoral Critique of Taylor's Liturgical Compositions and the Puritan *Westminster Directory* in the Light of the Contemporary Liturgical Renewal." Doctor of Sacred Liturgy (D.S. Lit) diss., Pontifical Liturgical Institute, San Anselmo, Rome, 1973.

de Ricci Albrecht, Sister Mary Catherine. "The Exemplum in the Sermons of Jeremy Taylor." Master of Arts (M.A.) diss., The Catholic University of America, Washington, D.C., 1947.

Herndon, S. "Jeremy Taylor's Use of the Bible." Ph.D. diss., New York University, New York, 1949.

Jackson, Robert S. "The Meditative Life of Christ: A Study of the Background and Structure of Jeremy Taylor's *The Great Exemplar*." Ph.D. diss., University of Michigan, Ann Arbor, 1959.

Peterson, Raymond A. "The Theology of Jeremy Taylor: An Investigation of the Temper of Caroline Anglicanism." Ph.D. diss., Union Theological Seminary, New York, 1961.

BIBLIOGRAPHY

3. SELECTED BIBLIOGRAPHY

Addleshaw, George. *The High Church Tradition: A Study in the Liturgical Thought of the Seventeenth Century.* London: Faber and Faber, 1941.

Armstrong, Martin. *Jeremy Taylor: A Selection from His Works.* London: Waltham St. Lawrence, 1923.

Bolton, Frederick R. *The Caroline Tradition of the Church of Ireland with Particular Reference to Bishop Jeremy Taylor.* London: S.P.C.K., 1958.

Boone-Porter, Harry. *Jeremy Taylor, Liturgist.* London: S.P.C.K., 1979.

Brinkley, Roberta F., ed. *Coleridge on the Seventeenth Century.* Durham, NC: University of North Carolina Press, 1955.

Brown, William. *Jeremy Taylor.* London: Macmillan, 1925.

Bryant, Arthur. *The England of Charles the Second.* London: Longmans, Green and Co., 1934.

Buchan, John. *Oliver Cromwell.* London: Hodder and Stoughton, 1934.

Bush, Douglas. *English Literature in the Earlier Seventeenth Century.* Oxford: Clarendon Press, 1945.

Coats, Robert H. *Types of English Piety.* Edinburgh: T. and T. Clark, 1912.

Cropper, Margaret. *Flame Touches Flame, Six Anglican Saints of the Seventeenth Century.* London: Longmans, Green and Co., 1949.

Cross, Frank. *Anglicanism.* Milwaukee, WI: Morehouse Publishing, 1935.

———. *The Oxford Movement and the Seventeenth Century.* London: Oxford University Press, 1933.

Cuming, Geoffrey. *A History of Anglican Liturgy.* London: Macmillan, 1969.

Davies, Horton. *The Worship of the English Puritan.* London: Westminster Press, 1948.

———. *Worship and Theology in England, Vol. 2.* Princeton, NJ: Princeton University Press, 1970.

Dugmore, Clifford W. *Eucharistic Doctrine in England from Hooker to Waterland.* London: Macmillan, 1942.

Frere, Walter H., ed. *A Devotionarie Book of John Evelyn of Wotton.* London: Macmillan, 1936.

Gathorne-Hardy, Robert. *A Bibliography of the Writings of Jeremy Taylor to 1700.* Dekalb, IL: Northern Illinois University, 1971.

BIBLIOGRAPHY

Gest, Margaret. *The House of Understanding*. Philadelphia: University of Pennsylvania, 1954.

Gosse, Edmond. *Jeremy Taylor*. London: Macmillan, 1904.

Grisbrooke, W. Jardine. *Anglican Liturgies of the Seventeenth and Eighteenth Centuries*. London: S.P.C.K., 1958.

Hughes, H. Trevor. *The Piety of Jeremy Taylor*. London: Macmillan, 1960.

Huntley, Frank L. *Jeremy Taylor and the Great Rebellion: A Study of His Mind and Temper in Controversy*. Ann Arbor, MI: University of Michigan Press, 1970.

Janelle, Pierre. *English Devotional Literature in the 16th and 17th Centuries*. London: S.P.C.K., 1956.

McAdoo, Henry R. *The Structure of Caroline Moral Theology*. London: Longmans, Green and Co., 1949.

―――. *The Spirit of Anglicanism*. London: Adam and Charles Black, 1965.

―――. *The Eucharistic Theology of Jeremy Taylor Today*. Norwich: Canterbury Press, 1988.

Miller, Perry. *The New England Mind: The Seventeenth Century*. New York: Macmillan, 1939.

Milosh, Joseph E. *The Scale of Perfection and the English Mystical Tradition*. Madison, WI: University of Wisconsin Press, 1966.

Mitchell, W. F. *English Pulpit Oratory from Andrew's to Tillotson*. London: S.P.C.K., 1932.

Morgan, Edmond S. *Visible Saints, the History of a Puritan Idea*. New York: New York University Press, 1963.

Morton, Arthur L. *The World of the Ranters*. New York: International Publishers, 1970.

Mueller, William R. *John Donne: Preacher*. Princeton, NJ: Princeton University Press, 1962.

Nicolson, Marjorie. H., ed. *The Conway Letters*. New Haven, CT: Yale University Press, 1930.

New, John F. *Anglican and Puritan, the Basis of Their Opposition, 1558–1640*. Stanford, CA: Stanford University Press, 1964.

Richardson, Caroline F. *English Preachers and Preaching 1640–1670*. London: Macmillan, 1928.

Shaw, William A. *History of the English Church During the Civil Wars and the Commonwealth*. London: Royal Historical Society, 1900.

Skipton, H. P. *The Life and Times of Nicholas Ferrar*. London: A. R. Mowbray and Co., 1907.

BIBLIOGRAPHY

Smith, Logan P. *The Golden Grove, Selections from Jeremy Taylor*. Oxford: Clarendon Press, 1930.

———. *Donne's Sermons: Selected Passages*. Oxford: Clarendon Press, 1919.

Smyth, Charles H. *The Art of Preaching*. London: Macmillan, 1940.

Stanwood, Paul. *Jeremy Taylor, Holy Living and Holy Dying*. Oxford: Clarendon Press, 1989.

Stone, Darwell. *A History of the Doctrine of the Holy Eucharist*. London: Longman, Green and Co., 1909.

Stranks, Charles J. *The Life and Writings of Jeremy Taylor*. London: S.P.C.K., 1952.

———. *Anglican Devotion*. London: S.P.C.K., 1961.

Summers, Joseph H. *George Herbert: His Religion and Art*. London: Chatto and Windus, 1954.

Sykes, Norman. *The Church of England and the Non-Episcopal Churches in the Sixteenth and Seventeenth Centuries*. Cambridge: University Press, 1948.

———. *Old Priest and New Presbyter*. Cambridge: University Press, 1956.

———. *Man as Churchman*. Cambridge: University Press, 1961.

———. *The English Religious Tradition*. Westport, CT: Hyperion Press, 1979.

Trevelyan, George M. *England under the Stuarts*. New York: Barnes and Noble, 1960.

Trevor-Roper, Hugh. *Archbishop Laud, 1573–1645*. London: Macmillan and Co., 1940.

Tulloch, John. *Rational Theology and Christian Philosophy in England in the Seventeenth Century*. Edinburgh: W. Blackwood and Sons, 1874.

Tuve, Rosemund. *Elizabethan and Metaphysical Imagery*. Chicago: University of Chicago Press, 1961.

Wakefield, Gordon. *Puritan Devotion*. London: Epworth Press, 1957.

Wakeman, Henry O. *The Church and the Puritans 1570–1660*. London: Rivington's, 1897.

Walker, Daniel P. *The Decline of Hell: Seventeenth Century Discussion of Eternal Torment*. Chicago: University of Chicago Press, 1964.

Walton, Isaak. *The Lives of John Donne, Sir Henry Wotton, Richard Hooker, George Herbert and Robert Sanderson*. London: Oxford University Press, 1927.

Wand, John. *The High Church Schism*. London: Faith Press, 1951.

BIBLIOGRAPHY

Watkin, Edward. *Poets and Mystics*. London: Sheed and Ward, 1953.

Watkins, Owen. *The Puritan Experience: Studies in Spiritual Autobiography*. London: Routledge and Keegan Paul, 1972.

Wedgwood, Cicely. *The King's Peace, 1637–1641*. London: Collins, 1955.

———. *Seventeenth Century English Literature*. London: Oxford University Press, 1961.

———. *Poetry and Politics under the Stuarts*. Cambridge: Cambridge University Press, 1960.

Westfall, R. *Science and Religion in Seventeenth Century England*. New Haven, CT: Yale University, 1958.

White, Helen. *English Devotional Literature, 1600–1640*. Madison, WI: University of Wisconsin Press, 1931.

Wiley, Margaret. *The Subtle Knot: Creative Skepticism in Seventeenth Century England*. London: Allen and Unwin, 1952.

Willey, Basil. *The Seventeenth Century Background*. London: Chatto and Windas, 1934.

Williamson, George. *Seventeenth Century Contexts*. London: Faber and Faber, 1960.

Williamson, Ross. *Jeremy Taylor*. London: Dobson, 1952.

Willmott, R. *Bishop Jeremy Taylor*. London: John W. Parker, 1848.

Wood, Thomas. *English Casuistical Divinity During the Seventeenth Century*. London: S.P.C.K., 1952.

Index to Preface
and Introduction

INDEXES

INDEXES

Index to Texts

Other Volumes in this Series

Menahem Nahum of Chernobyl • THE LIGHT OF THE EYES
Early Dominicans • SELECTED WRITINGS
John Climacus • THE LADDER OF DIVINE ASCENT
Francis and Clare • THE COMPLETE WORKS
Gregory Palamas • THE TRIADS
Pietists • SELECTED WRITINGS
The Shakers • TWO CENTURIES OF SPIRITUAL REFLECTION
Zohar • THE BOOK OF ENLIGHTENMENT
Luis de León • THE NAMES OF CHRIST
Quaker Spirituality • SELECTED WRITINGS
Emanuel Swedenborg • THE UNIVERSAL HUMAN AND SOUL-BODY
INTERACTION
Augustine of Hippo • SELECTED WRITINGS
Safed Spirituality • RULES OF MYSTICAL PIETY, THE BEGINNING OF WISDOM
Maximus Confessor • SELECTED WRITINGS
John Cassian • CONFERENCES
Johannes Tauler • SERMONS
John Ruusbroec • THE SPIRITUAL ESPOUSALS AND OTHER WORKS
Ibn 'Abbād of Ronda • LETTERS ON THE SŪFĪ PATH
Angelus Silesius • THE CHERUBINIC WANDERER
The Early Kabbalah •
Meister Eckhart • TEACHER AND PREACHER
John of the Cross • SELECTED WRITINGS
Pseudo-Dionysius • THE COMPLETE WORKS
Bernard of Clairvaux • SELECTED WORKS
Devotio Moderna • BASIC WRITINGS
The Pursuit of Wisdom • AND OTHER WORKS BY THE AUTHOR OF THE
CLOUD OF UNKNOWING
Richard Rolle • THE ENGLISH WRITINGS
Francis de Sales, Jane de Chantal • LETTERS OF SPIRITUAL DIRECTION
Albert and Thomas • SELECTED WRITINGS
Robert Bellarmine • SPIRITUAL WRITINGS
Nicodemos of the Holy Mountain • A HANDBOOK OF SPIRITUAL COUNSEL
Henry Suso • THE EXEMPLAR, WITH TWO GERMAN SERMONS
Bérulle and the French School • SELECTED WRITINGS
The Talmud • SELECTED WRITINGS
Ephrem the Syrian • SELECTED HYMNS
Hildegard of Bingen • SCIVIAS
Birgitta of Sweden • LIFE AND SELECTED REVELATIONS
John Donne • SELECTIONS FROM *DIVINE POEMS*, SERMONS, *DEVOTIONS* AND
PRAYERS